Here's what people say about Paul Yao's training:

D1286721

FOUNDATIONS *of*

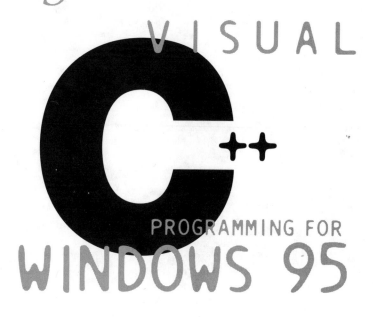

VISUAL

C++

PROGRAMMING FOR

WINDOWS 95

FOUNDATIONS *of*

VISUAL

C
++

PROGRAMMING FOR

WINDOWS 95

PAUL YAO & JOSEPH YAO

Foundations of Visual C++ Programming for Windows 95

Published by
IDG Books Worldwide, Inc.
An International Data Group Company
919 East Hillsdale Boulevard, Suite 400
Foster City, CA 94404

Library of Congress Catalog Card No.: 97-75061

ISBN 1-56884-321-6

Printed in the United States of America

First Printing, June, 1995

10 9 8 7 6 5 4 3 2 1

Distributed in the United States by IDG Books Worldwide, Inc.

Published in the United States of America

FROM THE PUBLISHER

Foundations of Visual C++ 2.0 Programming for Windows 95 is a book designed, written, and edited *by* working programmers *for* working programmers. We asked you what you wanted from a book when your goal was to become productive with a new programming tool. You told us to publish a book that:

- Is written from the perspective of a professional programmer
- Provides great coding examples that can be readily applied to your programs
- Serves as a tutorial that facilitates mastery of complex techniques, features, and concepts
- Serves as a comprehensive reference, achieving "dog-eared" status on your short-shelf of must-have books
- Provides a comprehensive index (since programmers always go to the index first!)
- Includes a fully indexed and linked electronic reference for quick and portable reference

Our goal is to deliver all of this and more. We offer no gimmicks; no promise of instant proficiency through repetition or over simplification. Sure, it's okay to learn the basics of driving a car doing 20 MPH with your dad in an empty parking lot. But if you're competing the next day in the Indy 500 (the metaphorical equivalent of trying to code for Windows 95!), you need entirely different preparation. You need to know the capabilities of your machine, the idiosyncrasies of the course, and how to translate that knowledge into a competitive advantage.

Like all Programmers Press books, this book is written by real programmers (Paul Yao is a world renowned trainer and programmer who has taught Visual C++ in several Fortune 500 companies). It is meticulously edited for technical accuracy, completeness, and readability. It is a book you will come to trust and rely on.

Thank you for choosing our product.

Christopher J. Williams
Group Publisher and Vice President
IDG Books Worldwide, Inc.

ABOUT IDG BOOKS WORLDWIDE

Welcome to the world of IDG Books Worldwide.

IDG Books Worldwide, Inc. is a subsidiary of International Data Group, the world's largest publisher of computer-related information and the leading global provider of information services o information technology. IDG was founded more than 25 years ago and now employs more than 7,500 people worldwide. IDG publishes more than 235 computer publications in 67 countries (see listing below). More than fifty million people read one or more IDG publications each mon

Launched in 1990, IDG Books Worldwide is today the #1 publisher of best-selling computer book in the United States. We are proud to have received 3 awards from the Computer Press Association in recognition of editorial excellence, and our best-selling ...For Dummies™ series has more than 1 million copies in print with translations in 24 languages. IDG Books, through a recent joint ventu with IDG's Hi-Tech Beijing, became the first U.S. publisher to publish a computer book in the Peo ple's Republic of China. In record time, IDG Books has become the first choice for millions of read around the world who want to learn how to better manage their businesses.

Our mission is simple: Every IDG book is designed to bring extra value and skill-building instruc tions to the reader. Our books are written by experts who understand and care about our readers. The knowledge base of our editorial staff comes from years of experience in publishing, education and journalism — experience which we use to produce books for the '90s. In short, we care abou books, so we attract the best people. We devote special attention to details such as audience, inter design, use of icons, and illustrations. And because we use an efficient process of authoring, editir and desktop publishing our books electronically, we can spend more time ensuring superior cont and spend less time on the technicalities of making books.

You can count on our commitment to deliver high-quality books at competitive prices on topic consumers want to read about. At IDG, we value quality, and we have been delivering quality f more than 25 years. You'll find no better book on a subject than an IDG book.

John J. Kilcullen

John Kilcullen
President and CEO
IDG Books Worldwide, Inc.

WINNER
Eighth Annual
Computer Press
Awards 1992

WINNER
Ninth Annual
Computer Press
Awards 1993

IDG Books Worldwide, Inc. is a subsidiary of International Data Group, the world's largest publisher of computer-related information and the leading global prov information services on information technology. International Data Group publishes over 235 computer publications in 67 countries. More than fifty million peop one or more International Data Group publications each month. The officers are Patrick J. McGovern, Founder and Board Chairman; Kelly Conlin, President; Jim Chief Operating Officer. International Data Group's publications include: **ARGENTINA'S** Computerworld Argentina, Infoworld Argentina; **AUSTRALIA'S** Comput Australia, Computer Living, Australian PC World, Australian Macworld, Network World, Mobile Business Australia, Publish!, Reseller, IDG Sources; **AUSTRIA'S** C erwelt Oesterreich, PC Test; **BELGIUM'S** Data News (CW); **BOLIVIA'S** Computerworld; **BRAZIL'S** Computerworld, Connections, Game Power, Mundo Unix, PC Publish, Super Game; **BULGARIA'S** Computerworld Bulgaria, PC & Mac World Bulgaria, Network World Bulgaria; **CANADA'S** CIO Canada, Computerworld Canad Canada, Network World Canada, Reseller; **CHILE'S** Computerworld Chile, Informatica; **COLOMBIA'S** Computerworld Colombia, PC World; **COSTA RICA'S** PC **CZECH REPUBLIC'S** Computerworld, Elektronika, PC World; **DENMARK'S** Communications World, Computerworld Danmark, Computerworld Focus, Macintc duktkatalog, Macworld Danmark, PC World Danmark, PC Produktguide, Tech World, Windows World; **ECUADOR'S** PC World Ecuador; **EGYPT'S** Computerworl Middle East, PC World Middle East; **FINLAND'S** MikroPC, Tietoviikko, Tietoverkko; **FRANCE'S** Distributique, GOLDEN MAC, InfoPC, Le Guide du Monde Inform Le Monde Informatique, Telecoms & Reseaux; **GERMANY'S** Computerwoche, Computerwoche Focus, Computerwoche Extra, Electronic Entertainment, Gamepro mation Management, Macwelt, Netzwelt, PC Welt, Publish, Publish; **GREECE'S** Publish & Macworld; **HONG KONG'S** Computerworld Hong Kong, PC World Hon HUNGARY'S Computerworld SZT, PC World; **INDIA'S** Computers & Communications; **INDONESIA'S** Info Komputer; **IRELAND'S** ComputerScope; **ISRAEL'S** Windows, Computerworld Israel, Multimedia, PC World Israel; **ITALY'S** Computerworld Italia, Lotus Magazine, Macworld Italia, Networking Italia, PC Shopping World Italia; **JAPAN'S** Computerworld Today, Information Systems World, Macworld Japan, Nikkei Personal Computing, SunWorld Japan, Windows World; **KENY** African Computer News; **KOREA'S** Computerworld Korea, Macworld Korea, PC World Korea; **LATIN AMERICA'S** GamePro; **MALAYSIA'S** Computerworld Mala World Malaysia; **MEXICO'S** Compu Edicion, Compu Manufactura, Computacion/Punto de Venta, Computerworld Mexico, MacWorld, Mundo Unix, PC World, W THE NETHERLANDS' Computer! Totaal, Computable (CW), LAN Magazine, Lotus Magazine, MacWorld; **NEW ZEALAND'S** Computer Buyer, Computerwo Zealand, Network World, New Zealand PC World; **NIGERIA'S** PC World Africa; **NORWAY'S** Computerworld Norge, Lotusworld Norge, Macworld Norge, Maxi Da world, PC World Ekspress, PC World Nettverk, PC World Norge, PC World's Produktguide, Publish& Multimedia World, Student Data, Unix World, Windowsworl ISTAN'S PC World Pakistan; **PANAMA'S** PC World Panama; **PERU'S** Computerworld Peru, PC World; **PEOPLE'S REPUBLIC OF CHINA'S** China Computerworl Infoworld, China PC Info Magazine, Computer Fan, PC World China, Electronics International, Electronics Today/Multimedia World, Electronic Product World, Chi work World, Software World Magazine, Telecom Product World; **PHILIPPINES'** Computerworld Philippines, PC Digest (PCW); **POLAND'S** Computerworld Polan puterworld Special Report, Networld, PC World/Komputer, Sunworld; **PORTUGAL'S** Cerebro/PC World, Correio Informatico/Computerworld, MacIn; **ROMANIA** puterworld, PC World, Telecom Romania; **RUSSIA'S** Computerworld-Moscow, Mir - PK (PCW), Sety (Networks); **SINGAPORE'S** Computerworld Southeast Asia, P Singapore; **SLOVENIA'S** Monitor Magazine; **SOUTH AFRICA'S** Computer Mail (CIO),Computing S.A.,Network World S.A., Software World; **SPAIN'S** Advanced Amiga World, Computerworld Espana, Communicaciones World, Macworld Espana, NeXTWORLD, Super Juegos Magazine (GamePro), PC World Espana, Publis DEN'S Attack, ComputerSweden, Corporate Computing, Macworld, Mikrodatorn, Natverk & Kommunikation, PC World, CAP & Design, DataIngenjoren, Maxi Da dows World; **SWITZERLAND'S** Computerworld Schweiz, Macworld Schweiz, PC Tip; **TAIWAN'S** Computerworld Taiwan, PC World Taiwan; **THAILAND'S** Th puterworld; **TURKEY'S** Computerworld Monitor, Macworld Turkiye, PC World Turkiye; **UKRAINE'S** Computerworld, Comput:rs+Software Magazine; **UNITED** DOM'S Computing /Computerworld, Connexion/Network World, Lotus Magazine, Macworld, Open Computing/Sunworld; **UNITED STATES'** Advanced Systems World, Cable in the Classroom, CD Review, CIO, Computerworld, Computerworld Client/Server Journal, Digital Video, DOS World, Electronic Entertainment M (E2), Federal Computer Week, Game Hits, GamePro, IDG Books, Infoworld, Laser Event, Macworld, Maximize, Multimedia World, Network World, PC Letter, PC Publish, SWATPro, Video Event; **URUGUAY'S** PC World Uruguay; **VENEZUELA'S** Computerworld Venezuela, PC World; **VIETNAM'S** PC World Vietnam.

ABOUT THE AUTHORS

Paul L. Yao has been a tireless champion of Windows software development efforts by bringing high-quality technical data to the light of day in his numerous articles, books, lectures, and workshops.

President of The Paul Yao Company, his involvement with Windows dates back to 1986, when he co-authored the very first book ever published on Windows programming. It quickly became the primary guide for developers working to create software for Windows 1.x. Since then, he has written several books and numerous articles. Paul is a contributing editor to *Microsoft Systems Journal*, where he published the first public article on Windows NT programming. Currently, Paul writes on topics critical to Windows programmers for The Paul Yao Series (IDG Books Worldwide Professional Publishing Group).

While he was researching his first book, Paul also worked on a team that created the first publicly available training course on Windows programming. In 1990, Paul created The Power Programming Workshops. Over the past six years, Paul has maintained a full-time training schedule of on-site workshops to groups of 10 or more C and C++ programmers. There are currently six workshops developed by Paul available exclusively from The Paul Yao Company.

A Windows programming whiz himself, Paul developed several commercially available Windows products and add-ons, including one of the first alternative shells to Windows. Some of his other programming projects include writing graphic device drivers, and developing a multimedia extension for a commercially available programmer tool. He was a technical advisor for a new printer language technology.

A member of Windows World/COMDEX Advisory Board, Paul has been a judge at the Windows Open, a contest for mission-critical Windows custom applications. He regularly speaks at industry forums and internal corporate events.

Joseph S. D. Yao has been a UNIX guru since the introduction of the UNIX operating system outside of Bell Labs in the early 1970s. He was the head teaching assistant and, later, head teaching fellow for Harvard College's introductory computer course, Nat. Sci. 110 — "Programming for Poets." During the 1980s, Joseph was answering C questions on the Usenet newsgroup comp.lang.c. Currently, he is a principal software engineer for EISI, a subsidiary of Hadron, Inc., in Fairfax, VA. He brings, to this his first book, experience with several different C++ programming systems under the UNIX operating system with MIT's X11 Windows System, and under Microsoft Windows. Joseph, his wife, and their two daughters live in Silver Spring, MD.

For More Information...

For general information on IDG Books in the U.S., including information on discounts and premiums, contact IDG Books at 800-434-3422.

For information on where to purchase IDG's books outside the U.S., contact Christina Turner at 415-655-3022.

For information on translations, contact Marc Jeffrey Mikulich, Foreign Rights Manager, at IDG Books Worldwide; fax number: 415-655-3295.

For sales inquiries and special prices for bulk quantities, contact Tony Real at 800-434-3422 or 415-655-3048.

For information on using IDG's books in the classroom and ordering examination copies, contact Jim Kelly at 800-434-2086.

Foundations of Visual C++ Programming for Windows 95 is distributed in Canada by Macmillan of Canada, a Division of Canada Publishing Corporation; by Computer and Technical Books in Miami, Florida, for South America and the Caribbean; by Longman Singapore in Singapore, Malaysia, Thailand, and Korea; by Toppan Co. Ltd. in Japan; by Asia Computerworld in Hong Kong; by Woodslane Pty. Ltd. in Australia and New Zealand; and by Transword Publishers Ltd. in the U.K. and Europe.

Dedication

To our Dad, the late Dr. Kenneth Tsoong-Sieu Yao

Credits

Group Publisher and Vice President
Christopher J. Williams

Associate Publisher
Amorette Pedersen

Editorial Director
Anne Marie Walker

Director of Production
Beth A. Roberts

Project Editor
Susan Pink

Manuscript Editor
John Pont

Technical Editor
Dan Daly

Composition and Layout
Ronnie K. Bucci

Proofreader
Mildred Rosenzweig

Indexer
Liz Cunningham

CD-ROM Production
Bruce Boyle

Cover Design
Draper and Liew, Inc.

Cover Photo
John Harquail/Masterfile

Acknowledgments

Paul Yao would like to thank, first and foremost, the customers of The Paul Yao Company who have provided support materially and morally for the past ten years. I look forward to many more years of working together. Thank you also to the many software developers who have asked probing questions during on-site workshops, via e-mail, and at industry conferences. I look forward to meeting more software engineers on-line and in person.

The authors also want to thank the two dozen technical reviewers, who gave so much energy and contributed so many valuable insights into ways this book could be made better, including Pat Bierne at Corel Systems; Sandra Capri and Duane Schwartzwald at Hewlett-Packard; David Durant, an independent consultant; Dan Jeffrey, another independent consultant; Lon Fisher, Tom Jebo, Dan Kirby, and Paul Klemond at Microsoft; and Patty Gilbert at Symantec. A special word of thanks is due to John Thorson at Microsoft, for his painstaking efforts and very thorough technical reviews. Thanks also to Todd Jones of Wilder Technologies for helping us understand some of the subtleties of internationalizing Windows application software.

At Microsoft, thanks are due Denis Gilbert, the General Manager of the Visual C++ development group, for support of this book project. Thanks also to Dean McCrory, the development lead for MFC, for help in understanding architectural issues of MFC. Others at Microsoft who we also thank are Mike Blaszczak, Robert Hess, George Moore, Ed Mills, Lou Perazzoli, Brian Smith, Jon Thomason, and Tandy Trower. Thanks to Kathy Gill at Microsoft's public relations firm, Waggener Edstrom, for supplying the Windows 95 Resource Kits.

At IDG, the authors thank Chris Williams for his trust in our vision of the book. For editorial support and guidance, thanks are due to Trudy Neuhaus and Denise Peters. For her painstaking editorial efforts and project management support, thanks to Susan Pink. Thanks are also due to Amorette Pedersen for marketing and moral support, Dan Daly for a thorough technical review, and John Pont for a very thorough copy edit of the original manuscript.

The authors also wish to thank the staff of The Paul Yao Company for help with every phase of this book. Thanks are due to Rebecca Brocard for project management and marketing direction. Thanks are also due to Piper Strick for all her work in coordinating the review.

Joe Yao wishes to thank his loving wife, Mary Ruth, and their children, Teresa Grace and Christina Marie, for their support during his project. He also would like to thank his mother, Mary Grace Yao, and Mary Ruth's parents, John and Nancy Venditti, for help taking care of the children while Joe was working. Last but not least, Joe would like to thank Don Jewell and Kurt Reisler of Hadron, Inc., as well as our clients, and also the Kensington Volunteer Fire Department, for time off to work on this project.

The publisher would like to give special thanks to Patrick McGovern, without whom this book would not have been possible.

Contents Overview

When first starting to program for any operating system, it's hard to know where to begin. Part I introduces the basics of programming for Microsoft Windows.

The starting point for learning the Microsoft Foundation Class (MFC) library is the Windows Application Programming Interface (API). This chapter introduces the Win16 and Win32 APIs, the native programming interfaces for Microsoft's Windows family of operating systems.

The key components of every implementation of Microsoft Windows are KERNEL, USER, and GDI. This chapter describes the role each plays, and introduces some of the ways that the MFC classes wrap around key operating system data structures.

One of the basic challenges that programmers face when first starting to write code for an operating system is learning to use the programming tools. This chapter provides a quick introduction to Microsoft's Visual C++ development tools.

Windows are the most important user-interface object in Microsoft Windows. This chapter introduces the windowing classes, and describes "rules of the road" for properly creating and maintaining windows.

This chapter introduces the user-interface objects that allow for command input, including menus, keyboard accelerators, and toolbars.

This chapter shows you how to create dialog boxes. A five-step approach helps simplify what is otherwise the most complex user-interface object in Windows.

Applications create output on both display screens and printers by calling Windows' Graphics Device Interface (GDI) library. This chapter introduces you to the basic concepts of creating text output, with a focus on sending output to a window using MFC's CDC-derived classes.

Programs retrieve mouse and keyboard input by responding to various messages. This chapter discusses the context in which user input occurs, and describes what an MFC program must do to properly handle application input state.

Part IV covers advanced topics in MFC/Windows programming.

One feature of MFC is that it simplifies the creation of data-centric applications via its Document/View architecture classes. This chapter introduces these classes, and lays out the basics you need for putting Document/View to work for you.

Memory is the currency of software. This chapter introduces the fundamental memory management choices available to a programmer building MFC programs to run on Windows 95 and Windows NT.

Table of Contents

Introduction

*T*his book combines three topics together to help C programmers develop software for Microsoft Windows using the Microsoft Foundation Class (MFC) library. The first topic is an introduction to C++ programming for C programmers, with a focus on the same "sane subset" that Microsoft chose for MFC itself. The second topic is the Windows Win32 API. The third topic is the MFC class library itself, which organizes the Win16 and Win32 APIs of Microsoft Windows.

The aim of this book is to help programmers create MFC programs for Windows 95 that run as 32-bit, Win32 programs. The ideal audience for this book consists of C programmers with no Windows programming experience. But we've included material of sufficient depth that there's something here for those with experience in all of the book's three topics: C++, MFC, and Win32. Because all three subjects are crucial for success in building robust MFC programs for Windows 95, we've integrated these subjects into a coherent, focused discussion.

Programmers building Win16 programs with MFC will also find help in these pages, because Microsoft made MFC portable with much common code between the 16-bit and 32-bit versions.

What You Need

To take advantage of the material in this book, at a minimum you need a compiler that comes bundled with the MFC class library. The examples in this book were built with Microsoft's Visual C++, version 2.0, but that's not the only compiler that comes bundled in MFC. Microsoft's Languages

Group has licensed MFC to other compiler vendors, including Symantec, MetaWare, and Watcom. In addition, using products like Bristol Technologies' Wind/u, you can compile most Win32/MFC programs to run under X Windows on Unix systems.

To run Win32/MFC programs, you'll need one of the following operating systems: Windows 3.1 with Win32s extensions, Windows 95, or Windows NT. These may be running "native" on your system, or under an emulator such as Insignia Solutions' SoftWindows or Linux WINE.

About the Paul Yao Series

This is the first book in The Paul Yao Series, published by IDG Books Worldwide Professional Publishing Group. This series aims to help professional programmers develop software for the Microsoft Windows family of operating systems. Writing in the clear style that has made his other books so popular, Paul Yao and IDG created this series to help explain the core technologies required to build successful Windows application software. Co-authors in this series are expert software engineers, chosen for their depth of knowledge in critical development areas. Look for other books in this series at your local bookstore.

I

System Architecture

*T*he Microsoft Foundation Class (MFC) library builds on the native programming interface of Microsoft Windows. For this reason, an understanding of the Windows programming interface will help you understand and use the MFC library. In this part, we introduce terms, concepts, and some product history from a "Microsoft-centric" point of view. Because you are reading this book, we presume that you are interested in using the MFC library to develop software that runs in Windows. Although you might be tempted to jump ahead to other, more "relevant" chapters, patient reading of the information in Part I will give you a broader perspective on the Windows family of operating systems.

Be careful not to confuse an operating system with an *Application Programming Interface (API)*. Whereas the former is a packaged product, the latter is a protocol — that is, function calls and data structures — for accessing some set of services. With the release of Windows 95, Microsoft has begun to close the door on its older, 16-bit API, which it calls Win16. At the same time, Microsoft is promoting a newer, 32-bit interface, the Win32 API, as the primary Windows API. The MFC library hides many of the differences between Win16 and Win32. As such, a Win16 application that's built with MFC will more easily port to Win32 than a comparable Win16 application in C.

Most of the function calls that an application makes are dispatched into one of three core, system components: KERNEL, GDI, and USER. In Part I, you'll learn about the functional differences between these three parts. We'll also discuss the internal data structures that each part creates, and we'll describe how MFC manages to encapsulate (or ignore) key data structures.

This part provides background reading for programmers who are just getting started with programming for Microsoft Windows. If you already have much experience programming in C or C++ for Windows 3.1 or Windows NT, you might decide to skip this part entirely.

The Windows Programming Interface

*A*t one time, software developers who wanted to build applications to run in Microsoft Windows had to write in C. Such programs connected directly to the Windows Application Programming Interface (API), a bare-bones set of functions provided by the operating system. In those days, besides a Windows-compatible compiler, the only available developer tools were packaged by Microsoft into the *Software Development Kit*, or SDK.

Learning to use the SDK to develop Windows programs has always been a difficult and tedious task. Part of the reason is because it requires a new way of thinking. Graphical output is quite different from character-based output. Event-driven, interactive programs can crash in ways that sequence-oriented, "batch" programs won't. It takes additional time and effort to figure out that you need to anticipate all of the different types of input that a user will send to a program.

Then, you must get used to working with all the quirks in the user-interface objects — windows, menus, dialogs, cursors, icons, and so on — that Windows provides. These built-in objects let you be productive once you learn how to use them, but the learning can be quite time-consuming.

Even after a programmer has mastered the new mindset, there is little organization in the function calls. The large number of function calls — several thousand — makes it hard to find all of the ones you might need to use. Once you do find them, you'll spend more time figuring out their many quirks and inconsistencies. It's no wonder that a development manager at Lotus compared debugging Windows software to "trying to staple Jello."

Windows application developers now have a wider range of choices. SDK programming, as it's sometimes called, is still an option for C programmers. But with the availability of Windows-compatible Pascal, FORTRAN, and COBOL compilers, C is no longer a requirement for building Windows applications. Developers can choose from languages such as Smalltalk, which is a favorite among object-oriented purists. BASIC, long considered a beginners' language, has been souped-up and reincarnated as Microsoft's Visual Basic, a product that has been used for small- to medium-size projects.

Programmers can also use C++ for building Windows applications. With its built-in C compatibility, C++ *can* be used for SDK-style programming. However, such use doesn't take advantage of the object-oriented features of the language. Realizing the benefits of those features requires a class library that's written to simplify the tedious housekeeping chores and frequent quirks that make SDK programming such a challenge. Several such libraries are commercially available, including Borland's Object Windows Library (OWL) and the Microsoft Foundation Class (MFC) library. The MFC library is, of course, the subject of this book.

All the languages and development tools that you can use to build Windows applications have one thing in common: each ultimately relies on the native Windows API. Although the native API may be quirky and difficult to code for, it is still the ultimate connection to the operating system's capabilities and features. As such, the better you understand the API, the more you'll know about choices that are available to you.

For example, you'll occasionally find that even the best language or tool hides a capability of the native API. In such cases, you can almost always get what you want by calling native functions directly, whether you're writing in C++, Visual Basic, or Smalltalk. You can even call native API functions from programs such as spreadsheets and word processors, a capability that never ceases to amaze us.

An understanding of the native API is helpful no matter which Windows development tool you use. However, it's essential when you're coding for the MFC library, because the structure of MFC mirrors the structure of the native API. In particular, MFC encapsulates key Windows data structures. Many MFC classes have member functions with names that are identical to those of native API functions. In most cases, you'll find that the MFC class member function is implemented as a call to the native API.

Operating Systems and APIs

It's important that you have a clear understanding of the distinction between an *operating system* and an *application programming interface (API)*. To most programmers, the two are synonymous because other operating systems have only a single programming interface. For example, the MS-DOS operating system has a programming interface, as do the various versions of the UNIX operating system. From its very first version, however, Windows has always supported multiple programming interfaces. For example, Windows 1.01 ran both Win16 and MS-DOS programs.

An operating system is a product. It might come packaged on floppy disks or on a CD-ROM, or preinstalled on the hard disk of a computer system. A single operating system can support multiple programming interfaces. For example, Windows NT supports five programming interfaces: MS-DOS, Win16, Win32, POSIX (Portable Operating System Interface), and the OS/2 console API (only on Intel x86 implementations). Windows 95, on the other hand, supports three programming interfaces: MS-DOS, Win16, and Win32.

With the various implementations of Windows, a given executable file generally can call only one programming interface. For example, the program file CALC.EXE cannot call both Win16 and Win32 API functions. Even under Windows NT, with its POSIX and OS/2 interface support, an executable file can be loyal to only one API. At program load time, the operating system loader connects an executable file to the proper API.

Win16 is a 16-bit API that was created for 16-bit processors, and it relies on 16-bit values. Win32 is a 32-bit API created for the current generation of 32-bit CPUs, and it relies on 32-bit values (with an occasional 64-bit value). In general, Microsoft is trying to provide some support for both interfaces in all of their current operating systems. And even though Win16 has received all the glory in the past, Microsoft is trying to entice developers to make Win32 their API of choice.

Although we've been referring to "the" native API, the various Windows operating systems support two different programming interfaces: a 16-bit interface known as the *Win16 API*, and a 32-bit interface known as the *Win32 API*. The two APIs are so similar that the MFC library manages to be compatible with both of them — that is, it's not only possible but quite easy to write a single MFC program that you can compile and link into either a Win16 executable or a Win32 executable. (Although it's easy to do, you need a Win16-compatible compiler and linker to build Win16 programs, and a Win32-compatible compiler and linker to build

Win32 programs.) Although MFC manages to hide many differences between Win16 and Win32, understanding both of these APIs will help you take greater advantage of each.

We'll start by taking a look at the older, 16-bit Windows interface, Win16. Next, we'll study key features of Win32, the 32-bit Windows interface. (If the presence of two Windows APIs confuses you, see the sidebar, "Operating Systems and APIs.") Both APIs are implemented using three libraries: KERNEL, USER, and GDI. As we'll detail in Chapter 2, each of these libraries provides system objects that are encapsulated in MFC classes.

The 16-Bit Windows Programming Interface

The Win16 API became available in 1985 with the first version of Windows, and it was the primary programming interface for Windows 1.x, 2.x, and 3.x. The Win16 API was built for the 16-bit CPUs that were popular in the mid-1980s, the Intel 8088 and 80286. Because Intel's newer 32-bit processors are backward compatible, 80386, 80486, and Pentium-based systems can run Win16 programs.

Perhaps the most important characteristic of the Win16 API is that it was the primary programming interface for Windows 3.0, which became a huge hit shortly after its introduction in May of 1990. Win16 is far from perfect, which is why Microsoft introduced Win32. But the success of Windows 3.0 required Microsoft to make Win32 as compatible as possible with Win16, without tying Win32 to the less portable, more archaic features of Windows 3.x.

Two distinguishing characteristics of Win16 programs are the file format and the memory architecture that they support. A Win16 executable file holds code and data in *segments*. On 16-bit Intel processors, segments are the unit of memory addressing, and they can be as small as 1 byte or as large as 64K. The segmentation of processor memory was first introduced to support the porting of code from older, 8-bit processors. Although workable as a memory scheme, segmentation is an annoying feature when you're working with blocks of data larger than 64K, the maximum size of a segment. Such objects must be divided into 64K chunks and handled chunk by chunk.

Another characteristic of the Win16 API is its preference for 16-bit (short) integers. Such values fit easily into the 16-bit registers used by early Intel processors. In a few cases, 32-bit values are used by various Win16 function calls, but the overall preference is for 16-bit values. For example, the Win16 version of the Graphics Device Interface (GDI) library uses 16-bit signed integers as its drawing coordinates, providing a range from −32,768 to +32,767. (And Windows 95 still relies on a 16-bit GDI, which is why even Win32 programs running in Windows 95 can count on only 16-bit graphics.)

The creators of the Win16 API knew the value of writing a portable API, but they had to compromise that goal in a number of ways. For one thing, the Win16 API never had built-in support for file I/O. Instead, Win16 programs rely on MS-DOS to read and write file data. Many programmers use C-runtime library routines to enhance the portability of their Win16 programs. Because certain file system features are available only by calling MS-DOS interrupts, however, even the best-written Win16 programs can contain MS-DOS-dependent code. For example, you must call an MS-DOS interrupt to find a disk volume name.

The platform-dependent nature of Win16 is also evident in functions created to control Intel-specific memory features (examples have curious names such as AllocSelector, AllocCStoDSAlias, SetSelectorBase, Global-DosAlloc, and GlobalPageLock). Although they were not part of the original API, such functions were added to help solve specific problems that arose during the evolution of Windows. Whatever the cause for such functions, their presence in a Win16 application represents processor-specific baggage that is difficult to port to other processors.

Another feature that ties some — but not all — Win16 programs to MS-DOS involves an MS-DOS feature called terminate-and-stay-resident programs, or TSRs. As a single-tasking environment, MS-DOS usually allows only one program to run at a time. However, a TSR can be loaded and left in memory to provide services to other programs. This feature makes TSRs ideal for providing device driver support, which is exactly how they're used by many vendors of hardware adapters. A surprisingly large number of MS-DOS programs rely on MS-DOS TSRs as device drivers that control application-specific hardware adapters.

A Win16 program can also access MS-DOS TSRs. This feature has enabled developers of MS-DOS software to port their applications to Windows. Microsoft allowed Win16 programs to access TSRs as a short-term fix, with the hope that developers of TSRs would eventually write drivers that were more Windows-compatible. Programs that rely on such drivers won't run in Win32 until new Windows NT- or Windows 95-specific device drivers are written to replace MS-DOS-specific drivers.

Despite its segmented memory architecture, 16-bit orientation, and MS-DOS-specific features, the Win16 API running on Windows 3.x has been a major success in the market. As of this writing, Microsoft has shipped more than 70 million copies of Windows. This success has prompted support for Win16 programs on numerous platforms, including non-Intel-based systems. Table 1-1 summarizes available support for Win16 programs.

Table 1-1
Platforms That Support the Win16 API

Processor	Operating System
Intel x86 (80386 and greater)	Native binary support on Windows 3.x, Windows 95, and Windows NT.
Silicon Graphics MIPS R4000	Emulation of Win16 and Intel x86 on Windows NT 3.1 and 3.5.
Digital Alpha	Emulation of Win16 and Intel x86 on Windows NT 3.1 and 3.5.
Motorola PowerPC 601	Emulation of Win16 and Intel x86 on Windows NT 3.1 and 3.5.
HP Workstation and Sun SPARC	Binary emulation on HP-UX and SunOS with WABI (Windows Application Binary Interface) emulation.
(various)	Source compatible on UNIX with Bristol Technology's Wind/U.
Intel x86 (80386 and greater)	Native machine instructions and emulation of Win16 API on OS/2 2.x.
(various)	Emulation of Win16 and Intel x86 by Insignia SoftWindows on Macintosh System 7 and on UNIX implementations on IRIS, NextStep, HP, DEC, SUN, and SGI.
Intel x86	Linux Operating System with WINE (WINdows Emulator); only available on Intel versions of Linux.

Even with platform-specific function calls, a Win16 program is quite portable to different platforms. On the surface, this API seems to have everything necessary for being a portable API. Unlike the Win32 API, which requires the recompiling of source code for different processors, Win16 has the added bonus of being *binary-compatible* between the different platforms. As indicated in Table 1-1, Win16 programs can even run on non-Intel processors, through emulation of the Intel x86 instruction set.

Although such emulation layers make Win16 programs extremely portable, there is a high performance cost. For example, although Win16 programs can run on UNIX workstations, in most cases they run much slower than they would on a system equipped with an Intel x86 processor. And they are certainly much slower than similar programs running the native instruction set. Although such portability is useful as a short-term fix, few users want to pay RISC workstation prices to get Intel 80386 performance.

Microsoft seems to have a strategy of making its products obsolete before someone else does. Developers can choose from many graphical APIs — including Macintosh, Motif, and OS/2 Presentation Manager — and Microsoft has been particularly aggressive in developing and promoting Win32 as a replacement for the Win16 API. Although it is quite compatible with Win16, Win32 sheds platform-specific features that tie Win16 to Intel x86 processors and to the MS-DOS operating system. Microsoft has designated Win32 as the successor to its currently reigning Win16 API.

The Win32 Programming Interface

Microsoft started work on the Win32 API in 1991. A primary design goal for Win32 was compatibility with the Win16 API. The success of Windows 3.x (and therefore of the Win16 API) was due in large part to the breadth and depth of available Win16 applications. It only makes sense, then, that Microsoft would do what it could to coax software developers to port their Win16 code to the newer API and to make porting as easy as possible.

A second design goal was for Win32 to exploit the power of 32-bit processors. Hardware advances have made both memory and CPU power relatively inexpensive. Win32 was built not only for the current generation of 32-bit (and 64-bit) processors but also for new processors that are still being developed.

To move its operating systems away from their reliance on Intel microprocessors, Microsoft added a third design goal for Win32, portability. Previous Microsoft operating systems had been built for Intel processors, but Microsoft decided to broaden the range of supported processors by making Win32 as portable as possible. Although one operating system from Microsoft — Windows 95 — runs only on Intel platforms, another — Windows NT — has been ported to several non-Intel processors. Microsoft's third design goal was to make Win32 a portable API, capable of running on a wide range of processors and platforms.

WIN16 COMPATIBILITY

The Win32 API was created as the cornerstone for a new generation of operating systems from Microsoft. However, operating systems can't succeed without application software. Because Windows 3.x — and its Win16 API — has been such a success, Microsoft established Win16 compatibility as the most important design goal for Win32.

It's easy to create lofty design goals such as upward compatibility, but those goals are not always easy to achieve. And yet, Microsoft has done an outstanding job of making it easy to port code from Win16 to Win32. Our assertion that Microsoft has successfully met this design goal is supported by our own development efforts as well as our unscientific survey of developers who have ported code.

It's interesting to note that Win32 represents Microsoft's second attempt to create a successor API to Win16. The first attempt, which produced a terribly *incompatible* API, was the OS/2 Presentation Manager. Although compatibility was among the stated goals for Presentation Manager, the OS/2 developers got caught up in trying to "fix" the warts and blemishes in Win16. When they were finished, the resulting Presentation Manager API was architecturally the same as Win16, but it was quite different at the detail level. In particular, a large number of function names, data structures, and symbolic constant names were different in OS/2. As a result, too much effort was required for porting Win16 code to the Presentation Manager API, and most developers avoided it entirely.

The high cost of porting from Win16 to the OS/2 Presentation Manager is one of the main reasons why Microsoft abandoned OS/2 in 1991. At that time, IBM, which had been a partner with Microsoft in the development of OS/2, became the operating system's sole owner. From the grand mistake of this experience came Microsoft's iron-clad resolution to make Win32 *truly* compatible with Win16.

A liberal use of typedefs hides many differences between Win16 and Win32. For example, the Win16 POINT is defined with 16-bit integers, as in:

```
typedef struct tagPOINT
{
    int x;
    int y;
} POINT;
```

The corresponding Win32 structure is made up of 32-bit integers:

```
typedef struct tagPOINT
{
    LONG x;
    LONG y;
} POINT;
```

This example demonstrates the single most important difference between Win16 and Win32: Win32 integers are exclusively 32 bits wide. Like an old country road that has been upgraded to handle more traffic, the conversion from Win16 to Win32 doubled the data bit capacity. Win16 programmers who have relied on the rich set of typedef data types instead of using native C types have already paved the way for an easy port to Win32. MFC source code gains the benefit of Win16-to-Win32 portability almost for free.

It's worth noting that some glitches can occur in even the best planned porting efforts. In particular, the high degree of portability between the two APIs doesn't automatically accommodate changes in a program's data file format. To support the file format of a Win16 program that writes 16-bit integer values, a compatible Win32 program must read 16-bit values. For example, a Win16 program might write a POINT to a file like this:

```
POINT pt;
write (hf, &pt, sizeof(POINT));
```

At first glance, there would seem to be no problem when a Win32 program tried to read the same values with the following:

```
POINT pt;
read (hf, &pt, sizeof(POINT));
```

However, the Win32 program won't get the expected results. The reason is as simple as it is sinister; the Win16 program's POINT is only 4 bytes, while the Win32 POINT is 8 bytes.

Setting aside this minor glitch, Win16-to-Win32 ports are surprisingly easy. Andrew Schulman, a well-known columnist and skeptic of Microsoft hype, ported his WINIO library, "2,500 lines of grungy [Win16] code," to Win32. He described the experience in the article, "At Last: Write Bona Fide 32-Bit Programs that Run on Windows 3.1 Using Win32s," which appeared in the April 1993 issue of *Microsoft Systems Journal*:

> **The port turned out to be absurdly easy, and even though WINIO is now happily running under Win32[s] along with many of my programs that rely on WINIO, I keep thinking that I must have missed something.**

The MFC developers took advantage of the high level of Win16-to-Win32 compatibility by building a class library that can support *both* APIs. From a single set of source code, you can use the 16-bit tools to build a Win16 executable and the 32-bit tools to build a Win32 executable. In some cases, MFC further refines cross-API compatibility by hiding minor and unavoidable incompatibilities between Win16 and Win32.

Microsoft wanted to ensure that the port from Win16 to Win32 is as easy as possible. But this wasn't the only design goal they pursued when building Win32. Another goal was to ensure that the new API could take advantage of the faster, more capable 32-bit processors that have become widely available. Let's take a moment to consider some of what this design goal required.

32-BIT OPERATION

Perhaps the most important improvement that Win32 provides over Win16 programming is access to a flat address space. A Win16 program must address memory using the quirky segmented addressing scheme of 16-bit Intel x86 processors. Although the Intel documentation for the 8088 and 80286 processors sings the praises of segmented addressing (it helps organize a program, it enforces memory boundaries leading to more robust programs, and so on), programmers who have worked with segmented addressing disagree. At the machine-code level and in higher-level languages, segmented addressing is a difficult, clumsy way to access memory. For example, segmented addressing requires you to worry about *two* different pointer sizes: 16-bit NEAR pointers and 32-bit FAR pointers. With Win32, segmented addressing is gone. There is only one pointer size — 32 bits — for accessing anything you want to put into a 4-gigabyte address space.

On Windows 95 and Windows NT, flat memory addressing is provided in a private, per-process address space. By contrast, Win16 programs running on Windows 1.x, 2.x, and 3.x run in a common, shared address space. Many developers took advantage of this by writing Win16 programs that shared memory simply by sharing addresses. Aside from this minor benefit, however, the lack of address space boundaries compromises system stability and security. It also forces applications to compete with each other for address space. By contrast, Win32 programs on Windows 95 and Windows NT have exclusive use of a private address space. (Win32 programs running in Win32s — which is hosted on Windows 3.1 — share a single address space with currently running Win16 programs.)

With 32-bit operation, a Win32 program also has access to a wider range of values than a Win16 program. Most Win16 parameters are short, 16-bit integers. For example, the x- and y-coordinates passed to the GDI drawing library must be in the range −32,766 to +32,767. You pass 32-bit-wide parameters to Win32 GDI when you draw, which gives you a drawing space in the range −2,147,483,647 to +2,147,483,648.

Although the Win32 GDI defines 32-bit parameters, not all current versions of Windows recognize the full range of values. At present, only Windows NT provides a 32-bit GDI. Both Win32s and Windows 95 provide a 16-bit GDI that uses only the lower 16 bits of the 32-bit parameters.

Another benefit that Win32 programs enjoy over Win16 programs is improved performance when working with 32-bit integer values. For example, when a Win16 program is compiled, the resulting machine code uses Intel's 16-bit instruction set to allow the program to run on Intel 80286 processors. With the 16-bit registers in that processor, operations on 32-bit values require at least two processor instructions (and usually more) to handle overflows and extensions of sign bits. On the other hand, when Win32 programs are compiled, they can operate on 32-bit values with a single machine instruction.

Better operation with 32-bit values points to another key benefit of Win32 over Win16: portability. The 16-bit operation of Intel x86 processors is handled in a unique way. On the other hand, 32-bit Intel processors (80386 and later) handle 32-bit operations in ways that are similar to non-Intel processors. After all, many processors today either are 32-bit processors or can support a 32-bit operating mode. For example, the DEC Alpha is a 64-bit chip that also supports a 32-bit operating mode when running Windows NT.

On the downside, a Win32 program will probably consume slightly more disk space and RAM than a comparable Win16 program. This happens because all values are supposed to be 32 bits wide, even if a smaller range of values will actually be stored. As the slide in hardware prices continues, this will become less of a factor.

PORTABILITY

A third design goal in the creation of Win32 was portability. Processors have become faster and faster, but it has always taken many years to develop new operating systems with APIs that can exploit the capabilities of new processors. With its highly portable Win32 API, Microsoft plans to be among the first companies to provide system software for the coming generations of processors. What's more important, though, is that Win32 applications will help launch future generations of faster, more capable CPUs.

A portable Win32 API benefits both software developers and end users. Portability helps developers by reducing the effort required to support multiple platforms. Instead of wrestling with the tedious task of porting to various platforms, developers can focus their efforts on adding features. End users benefit from having a wider range of applications available on hardware platforms that span a wider price-performance range.

Although Win16 programs also run on multiple platforms, this capability is achieved through emulation of the Intel x86 instruction set, which carries a high performance cost. Win16 has numerous "Intel-isms" — for example, segmented addressing — that are cumbersome to emulate. And the reliance of Win16 programs on MS-DOS makes it difficult to provide complete support. For example, some Win16 programs rely on undocumented MS-DOS features and quirks that are difficult to implement reliably on non-Intel processors.

While creating the Win32 API, Microsoft dropped 31 platform-specific Win16 functions: 20 of these functions manipulated Intel-specific data structures, 3 accessed MS-DOS-specific capabilities, and 8 reflected a Win16-centric model for processes or device drivers. The removal of these functions frees Win32 from the burden of Win16 baggage, thereby enhancing its portability. Although dropping these functions might slightly hamper the porting of some code from Win16 to Win32, the improvement in overall portability was deemed worth the cost.

Microsoft provides a table of all Win16 and Win32 functions in \msvc20\lib\win32api.csv, a file that ships with the Microsoft Visual C++ 2.0 (and later) compiler. This text file has one line per function call (or symbolic constant), and can be read from a spreadsheet program that understands CSV-formatted files. Items marked "dropped" exist in Win16 but are not included in Win32. Although this table indicates that 137 functions have been dropped, most have simply been replaced, so the functional capability is still available. By our reckoning, only 31 of the 1,855 functions in the two APIs — less than 2% — have truly been dropped.

Another way that Win32 cuts the ties to MS-DOS is by providing a complete set of file I/O functions. Win16 programs must rely on MS-DOS itself to access the file system. MS-DOS-style software interrupt system calls, which some Win16 programs depend on, are not available to Win32 programs.

For the sake of portability, Win32 programs cannot access MS-DOS device drivers, as is possible in Win16. Win32 programs with special hardware needs require an operating-system-specific device driver. Platform-specific code will continue to exist where it belongs — within device drivers — but MS-DOS-specific drivers are not supported in Win32.

Software portability is enhanced by good design, but nothing proves portability better than actually getting software to run on more than one platform. To ensure that nonportable features were excluded from Win32, Microsoft simultaneously developed Win32 implementations on two hardware platforms. These implementations were incorporated into a new, portable operating system that was also being developed: Windows NT.

The first two implementations of Win32 (and of Windows NT) were for 32-bit, Intel x86 processors and for the MIPS R4000 RISC processors. Both versions shipped in July of 1992. The portable design of Win32 — and of Windows NT — was validated two months later, when Microsoft shipped an implementation for the DEC Alpha. This is not meant to imply that the port to the Alpha platform took only two months. The team at DEC had been working on the port for at least a year. But that port, along with others such as the one to the PowerPC, validate the portability claims that Microsoft has made about both Windows NT and the Win32 API. Table 1-2 lists Win32 implementations that are available (or are soon to be available) as of this writing.

Table 1-2

Platforms That Support the Win32 API

Processor	Operating System
Intel x86 (80386 and greater)	Windows 3.1 running Win32s, which is a subset of the Win32 API.
Intel x86 (80386 and greater)	Windows 95 runs most GUI portions of Win32. Windows NT provides complete implementation.
Silicon Graphics MIPS R4000	Windows NT
Digital Alpha	Windows NT
Motorola PowerPC 601	Windows NT
Motorola 68xxx	WINGS on Macintosh System 7
(various)	UNIX with Bristol Wind/U

Of all Win32 implementations, the one that is expected to have the biggest impact on the world of computer software is Windows 95 — known during its development as "Chicago." Built as the replacement for the popular Windows 3.x operating system, Windows 95 supports both the Win16 API and the Win32 API. Users who upgrade to Windows 95 will still be able to run their existing Win16 applications, but they will also be able to run new applications that take advantage of the additional features of Win32.

Although as many as 20% of the more than 70 million users of Windows 3.x are expected to upgrade in the first year after Microsoft ships Windows 95, that still leaves millions of Windows 3.1 users who won't be able to run Win32 applications. To help those users get *some* (but not all) of the benefits of Win32, and to encourage developers to consider writing to the Win32 API, Microsoft created Win32s.

WIN32S: WINDOWS 3.1 SUPPORT FOR THE WIN32 API

When Microsoft shipped Windows NT in 1992, its native API was the Win32 API. To support Win16 applications, this new operating system was equipped with the *WOW* (Windows-on-Windows NT) layer, which converts Win16 calls to their Win32 equivalents. At the same time, Microsoft made available an add-on to Windows 3.1, called Win32s, which converts Win32 calls to their Win16 equivalents. Win32s enables the Windows 3.1 loader to recognize, load, and begin execution of Win32 executable files.

Although WOW enables Windows NT to support all of Win16, Win32s supports only part of the entire Win32 API (as suggested by the letter *s* in its name, which stands for *subset*). The entire Win32 API is present, but functions without Win16 equivalents are stubbed out and simply return an error code. Therefore, it's possible to write a single Win32 executable file that runs on Windows 3.1, Windows 95, and Windows NT. On Windows 3.1, such a program might disable access to Win32 features that are unavailable in Win32s.

We believe that the subset provided by Win32s makes support on all three platforms reasonable for all but the most demanding applications. After all, the Win16 API — which does all the "real work" to support Win32s — supports the diverse collection of Win16 applications currently on the market. You should probably target the Win32s API if your user base includes a large number of casual users who aren't likely to upgrade to Windows 95 or Windows NT any time soon. For applications written for leading-edge, power users, however, you'll want to target the broader Win32 support of Windows 95 and Windows NT. And, of course, if your application absolutely requires Win32 features that are not supported by Win32s, you'll choose Windows 95 and Windows NT as your target platforms.

A Win32 program can query whether it's being run on Win32s by calling GetVersion( ). Under Win32s, code such as the following example tests for Win32s by examining whether the high-order sign bit is set:

```
#define WIN31_OR_WIN95   0x80000000
#define WIN95            0x00000004

int nVer = GetVersion();
// high bit of high word 0 for NT, 1 for 32s and 95
if( nVer & WIN31_OR_WIN95)
{
    if( nVer & WIN95)
    {
        //Win95
    }
    else
    {
        //Win32s
    }
}
else
{
    // NT
}
```

As mentioned earlier in this chapter, Microsoft provides a table of all Win16 and Win32 functions in the file \msvc20\lib\win32api.csv, which ships with the Microsoft Visual C++ 2.0 (and later) compiler. The fourth column in the table indicates whether Win32s supports a particular function. (*Y* indicates that Win32s supports the function, and *N* means that Win32s does not support the function.) Table 1-3 summarizes the Win32 features that are not provided by Win32s.

Win32s provides a *subset* of the Win32 API — that is, it doesn't support every feature and function. On the other hand, it provides a *superset* of Win16. In addition to providing access to the entire Win16 API, it provides new capabilities. Although a Win32 program running in Win32s has access to fewer features than it would on Windows 95 or Windows NT, such a program has access to more features than are provided by Windows 3.1 alone. Table 1-4 summarizes the ways in which Win32s enhances Windows 3.1.

Table 1-3

Win32 Features Not Provided by Win32s

Feature	Description
GDI enhancements	The 32-bit GDI has such drawing capabilities as paths, bezier curves, and bitmap rotation.
Multithread support	Because Windows 3.1 is a single-threaded environment, the thread and process APIs of Win32 are not supportable by Win32s.
Network APIs	Named pipes and mail slots are not supported, although the Socket API is.
Security	The Win32 security enhancements support discretionary access of Windows NT, which is not available under Windows 3.1 and, therefore, is not supported by either Win32s or Windows 95.
Tape backup	Win32 tape backup support is not provided.
Remote Procedure Call (RPC)	Support for control of a process on a different computer via network communication is not provided (although client-side RPC is supported).
Console API	Support for building character-based applications is not provided. In Windows 3.1, this is provided by the MS-DOS API.

Table 1-4

Win32s Enhancements to Windows 3.1

Feature	Description
32-bit addressing	Win32 processes access a flat, 32-bit address space instead of the segmented address space of Win16.
32-bit heap	Win32 heap allocation routines such as HeapAlloc and HeapFree are supported.
Structured exception handling	This Win32 API feature is also provided under Win32s. Structured exception handling helps you build more robust software by simplifying the process of catching exceptions — that is, abnormal hardware or software errors.
Shared memory	Win32s provides some of the interprocess memory sharing support of Win32.
Virtual memory	To allow greater control over a program's address space, certain Win32 virtual memory functions and features are provided in Win32s.
File I/O	Win32s provides file I/O functions to replace the MS-DOS functions that Win16 programs rely on, but that Win32 programs can't use.
Universal thunks	Win32s allows a Win32 program to call Win16 DLLs.

In creating the Win32 API, Microsoft hopes to ride the momentum of its past success with Windows while creating a new wave of operating systems and applications that take advantage of the power of 32-bit processors. Clearly, there are two different APIs: one built for 16-bit operation, and one for 32-bit operation. But a high level of compatibility makes it easy to port code between the two.

Continuing our journey through the native Windows APIs, Chapter 2 discusses the key data structures and common elements that make up the two APIs. Although these might seem like hidden details that MFC developers won't need to deal with, they form the foundation on which MFC is built. As such, they are essential for understanding the structure and capabilities of MFC itself.

Operating System Components and Data Structures

We can gain insight into the structure of MFC by examining the operating system on which the MFC classes are based. We'll examine the key data structures of the Windows API, because several MFC classes encapsulate these data structures. Because API data structures are best understood in the context of the system components that create and maintain them, the discussion in this chapter is organized in terms of the core components of Windows.

Without doubt, Win16's most important parts are KERNEL, USER, and GDI. The Win16 KERNEL has three separate implementations, one for each memory mode of Windows 3.x. The three implementations of the Win16 KERNEL are KERNEL.EXE (Real mode), KRNL286.EXE (Standard mode), and KRNL386.EXE (386-Enhanced mode). The other two libraries are named USER.EXE and GDI.EXE. Although they are all dynamic link libraries, which usually have a default extension of .DLL, this extension wasn't introduced until Windows 3.x. For backward compatibility, the various implementations of Windows use the older names. Under Win16, KERNEL, USER, and GDI contain the core of the programming interface.

Win32 has similarly named pieces, with minor name changes to distinguish them from their 16-bit cousins: KERNEL32, USER32, and GDI32. On Windows 95 and Windows NT, these components reside in the following files: KERNEL32.DLL, USER32.DLL, and GDI32.DLL. Under Win32, the core of the programming interface is found in KERNEL32, USER32, and GDI32.

Each core component is implemented as a *dynamic link library* (*DLL*). Dynamic link libraries allow efficient sharing of code and data between processes. They play a key role in the various Windows implementations, not only because the core components are implemented as DLLs, but because developers can package and distribute their own components as DLLs.

Native System Objects and Object Handles

In the various implementations of the Win16 and Win32 APIs, the three major components create and maintain a private set of objects. This may sound promising to C++ programmers hoping to apply object-oriented programming (OOP) principles to Windows. By themselves, however, native system objects lack object-oriented features. You don't define them using anything analogous to C++ classes, and the Windows API makes no use of inheritance. (Part II provides a more complete introduction to object-oriented programming and C++ features such as classes and inheritance.)

In his book, *Object Oriented Design with Applications* (Redwood City, CA: The Benjamin/Cummings Publishing Company, Inc. 1991), noted OOP expert Grady Booch says that "...programming without inheritance is distinctly not object-oriented; we call it *programming with abstract data types.*" Whether you agree that inheritance is necessary for a program to be considered object-oriented, most Windows programs that we have encountered are decidedly *not* object-oriented.

The Windows API *does* realize another feature that some consider essential to be "object-oriented," namely *encapsulation.* The system never hands out pointers to its internal data objects; instead, it identifies them using *handles.* A handle is an identifier that has meaning only to the system component that created the object. By itself, it's just a number (16 bits in the Win16 API and 32 bits in the Win32 API). As a parameter to native API functions, it provides complete control over the life and death of system objects. MFC programs rarely use handles directly, but the handle values are present in the MFC objects for those occasions when you need to call native API functions.

KERNEL: The Core Operating System

The Win16 KERNEL of Windows 3.1 supports capabilities that are typically associated with operating systems: process loading, context switching, file I/O (which is actually performed by MS-DOS but managed by the KERNEL), and memory management. Additional operating system capabilities are provided by the Win32 API and implemented in Windows 95 and Windows NT. Table 2-1 describes the low-level operating system features provided in Windows 95 and Windows NT.

Table 2-1
New KERNEL Capabilities Provided in Win32

Feature	Description
Threads	The unit of scheduling in Windows 95 and Windows NT. At start-up, a process is granted a single thread. A process can add threads by calling Win32 (or C-runtime) functions. To keep from running into each other, two or more threads operating on the same data need traffic signals. Win32 provides four synchronization objects for this task: critical section objects, mutexes, events, and semaphores.
Critical section objects	High-performance synchronization objects used to coordinate the activities of two or more threads in the same process. Only one thread is allowed to access the protected data object. Typical use is to protect a critical section of code.
Mutexes	Interprocess synchronization objects used to prevent more than one thread at a time from accessing a protected data object.
Events	Interprocess synchronization objects used to start waiting threads. Events are like a starter's gun at a race. Two types are supported: manual-reset and auto-reset.
Semaphores	Interprocess synchronization objects used to limit the maximum number of threads that simultaneously access a particular resource.
Memory mapped files	The memory mapped file facility supports two types of operations. First, it provides automatic mapping of a file's contents to a range of memory addresses. This simplifies the task of moving data between disk and memory buffers. Second, it provides the mechanism for sharing data between multiple processes.

Perhaps the most important enhancement in the Win32 API is support for *threads*. Threads are defined as "the unit of scheduling," but this dry definition is like telling those who have always ridden a bus that their new car is a "unit of transportation." The remarkable freedom that the new automobile gives former bus passengers is analogous to the relationship between threads and the processes in your program. Threads give you tremendous freedom to control the scheduling of the different tasks within your program. But with the increased freedom comes increased responsibility — and increased effort — for ensuring that the activities of different threads are properly coordinated.

When a program starts running, the operating system provides a single thread. A thread has its own stack, but it shares the address space — and other process resources — with all the other threads owned by the process. Additional threads can be started by calling a Win32 function, CreateThread. In the following code fragment, main is called from the first thread created by the operating system. The CreateThread function allocates a stack, creates a thread, and then passes control to our ThreadMain function:

```
// First thread entry point.
main()
{

    // Create a second thread.
    DWORD dwThreadID;
    CreateThread (lpsa, 0, ThreadMain, 0, 0, &dwThreadID);

    //
    // Here, two threads are running in this process.
    //
}
// Second thread entry point.
DWORD ThreadMain(DWORD dwInput)
{
    ...
}
```

Programmers who have never used threads may be tempted to overuse them because of the ease with which they are created, and the promise they hold for increased access to the CPU. But the challenge of working with more than one thread is like the challenge of having more than one car on the road at the same time: without a clear set of rules, you're bound to have a collision. To avoid introducing bugs into your program, all resources — memory, files, data objects, or hardware devices — that two threads share must be protected. Because they are usually timing dependent and therefore difficult to reproduce, bugs created by the interaction of two threads are the hardest to find. We suggest that you approach multithreaded programming with caution.

Aside from some enhancements to make version 3.0 safe for multithread use, in general, MFC only minimally supports KERNEL capabilities. Support includes a class for threads (CWinThread) and another for file I/O (CFile). To access most KERNEL capabilities, you must call Win32 functions directly.

GDI: The Graphics Library

Windows' second major system component is the *Graphics Device Interface (GDI)*, the system's primary graphic output library. (We say "primary" because with the introduction of the OpenGL 3D package and the WinG graphic support, GDI is not alone.) When you see a pixel illuminated on a display screen, or a line of text on printed output, you can be sure that GDI made it possible. Windows itself uses GDI to draw the user interface, including windows, menus, and dialog boxes.

GDI provides two basic types of service: creation of graphic output and storage of graphic images. Graphic output is created by making calls to a rich set of drawing functions. GDI receives drawing requests, massages the data, and calls a device driver to create device-specific drawing instructions. There are three types of drawing functions: text, vector (line-drawing) graphics, and raster (bitmap) graphics.

GDI supports two types of graphic image storage: *bitmaps* and *metafiles*. Bitmaps are arrays of pixels. A common way to create a bitmap is with dedicated scanner hardware that converts an image on paper into a digital bitmap. A bitmap can also be created with a drawing program such as Windows Paintbrush. When you write your Windows program, you can either take a bitmap from one of these two sources or create your own bitmap to store graphic data that you want to display in a window or on a printed page.

A drawback to the use of bitmaps is the space they consume, both on disk and in RAM. Previous versions of Windows used bitmaps to draw the tiny, but complex, ornaments of a window frame: the system menu, the minimize box, the maximize box, and the scroll bar arrows. The cost in terms of memory consumed was easily justified by the greater speed — compared to drawing the complex images with native GDI calls — with which these window components are drawn.

Metafiles are the other mechanism that GDI provides for storing pictures. A metafile is made up of a set of records, each of which represents a call to a GDI function plus all the call's parameters. This quality of storing only function call parameters makes metafiles quite compact, and metafiles generally consume less space than bitmaps. They also tend to be more easily scalable than bitmaps. But because they are native to GDI, you can't create a metafile using a device such as a scanner. Instead, a Windows program must make GDI calls to create a metafile. The other major disadvantage to using metafiles is that they tend to draw more slowly than a comparable bitmap.

GDI provides a rich set of primitives for creating graphic output on displays, printers, bitmaps, and metafiles. GDI also supports a broad range of devices, from very smart Postscript printers to very dumb dot-matrix printers. This broad support is easy on smart devices: GDI lets the device do most or all of the drawing work. For dumb devices, GDI provides *software simulations* that convert high-level graphic calls into a set of simpler, low-level drawing calls.

Consider the case in which an application calls GDI's Rectangle function to draw a rectangle. When drawing to a Postscript printer, GDI passes the rectangle data directly through to the driver. It's up to the driver to create the Postscript commands that produce a properly positioned, properly drawn rectangle. On a dot-matrix printer that presumably doesn't have built-in support for rectangle drawing, GDI converts the single rectangle into several, simpler instructions. First are details about filling individual scan lines for the interior; next come the coordinates for drawing the rectangle's border.

If the simplest drawing instructions are still too hard to implement by a printer, GDI provides help by rendering graphic data to a bitmap. The printer driver can request that GDI draw to a bitmap. Once the drawing is complete, the printer driver is supplied with the raw bitmap bits. The printer driver can then convert the bits into the commands needed to produce graphic images on its own hardware. These commands are sent through the spooler to the printer.

MFC supports 80% of GDI's 300 functions, which is considerably more support than MFC provides for KERNEL capabilities. Table 2-2 lists the GDI functions that are *not* supported by MFC. As with KERNEL functions, access to functions that are not supported by MFC is as simple as calling the native functions directly. We suspect you won't need this capability too often, because MFC manages to pack GDI's core graphics capabilities into its various drawing classes.

Table 2-2
Win32 Functions That Are Not Supported in MFC Classes

Function Group	Functions
Coordinates	CombineTransform, GetDCOrgEx, GetGraphicsMode, GetWorldTransform, LineDDA, ModifyWorldTransform, SetGraphicsMode, SetWorldTransform
Device-independent bitmaps (DIBs)	CreateDIBitmap, CreateDIBSection, GetDIBColorTable, GetDIBits, SetDIBColorTable, SetDIBits, SetDIBitsToDevice, StretchDIBits
Drawing	PolyTextOut
Fonts	AddFontResource, CreateScalableFontResource, EnumFontFamilies, EnumFonts, GetRasterizerCaps, RemoveFontResource
Metafiles	CopyEnhMetaFile, CopyMetaFile, EnumEnhMetafile, EnumMetaFile, GetEnhMetaFile, GetEnhMetaFileBits, GetEnhMetaFileDescription, GetEnhMetaFileHeader, GetEnhMetaFilePaletteEntries, GetMetaFile, GetMetaFileBits, GetMetaRgn, GetWinMetaFileBits, PlayEnhMetaFileRecord, PlayMetaFileRecord, SetEnhMetaFileBits, SetMetaFileBitsEx
Multithreaded drawing	CancelDC
Regions	GetClipRgn, SetMetaRgn
Palettes	GetSystemPaletteEntries, GetSystemPaletteUse, SetSystemPaletteUse
Windows NT batching of GDI calls	GdiFlush, GdiGetBatchLimit, GdiSetBatchLimit
Unknown	ChoosePixelFormat, SetPixelFormat, SwapBuffers

Although MFC doesn't add graphics capabilities to native GDI functions, it *does* organize GDI's 300-odd functions in a way that makes them easier to comprehend. GDI has always created its own internal objects, but nothing in the API itself helps distinguish one object from another. MFC's set of classes, listed in Table 2-3, make it clear which objects GDI creates. Perhaps more important, MFC's assignment of GDI functions to one class or another identifies which functions affect which objects.

Table 2-3
MFC's Classes Wrap Native GDI Objects

Class Name	Description
CDC	Wraps the GDI *device context* (DC) object. We refer to DCs as device *connections* because they connect a program to a graphic device. This is the base class for the other four DC classes in this table.
CClientDC	A DC for drawing in a window's *client area*, which is the portion of a window in which applications can draw. The client area excludes the caption bar, the menu bar, the scroll bar, and the borders, which are collectively known as the *nonclient area*.
CWindowDC	A DC for drawing anywhere in a window, including the client area and the nonclient area.
CPaintDC	A DC for drawing in the client area of a window in response to a WM_PAINT message. The system sends this important message to a window to let it know that its client area has been damaged and must be repaired.
CMetaFileDC	A DC used to store graphic calls in a GDI metafile.
CGdiObject	The base class for the six GDI attribute objects: CPen, CBrush, CFont, CBitmap, CPalette, and CRgn.
CPen	A drawing attribute that describes the color, width, and style (solid or dotted) of lines.
CBrush	A drawing attribute that describes the color and pattern for filled areas.
CFont	A drawing attribute that describes the font name, size, and other characteristics of text characters.
CBitmap	A mechanism for storing graphic images as an array of pixels.
CPalette	A table of colors. This is used both for drawing and as a way to describe the proper colors to use for a device-independent bitmap (DIB).
CRgn	A region is made up of one or more rectangles. Windows uses regions to define where a program may draw and where it may not draw, behavior that's known as *clipping*. The windowing software makes extensive use of regions to enforce the boundaries between different windows.

USER: The User Interface

The USER.EXE library in Win16 and the USER32.DLL library in Win32 provide support for all user-interface objects, including windows, menus, dialog boxes, dialog box controls, cursors, and icons. Of these, the most important is undoubtedly the window. Other user-interface objects either *are* windows — such as dialog boxes and dialog box controls — or appear only when connected to a window — for example, menus, cursors, and icons.

Underscoring the importance of a window is the simple fact that without a window, an application can't interact with a user. User input, whether it is from the mouse or the keyboard, always goes to one window or another. Users see menus that are connected to a window, and after a user selects a menu command, notification is sent to a window for processing. Similarly, when an application wants to get a user's attention, a window provides the stage and the application's data serves as actors that perform within a window.

In addition to their role in the user interface, windows play another important role: the operating system makes application scheduling decisions based on how a user interacts with windows. In response to mouse or keyboard activity, the system delivers *messages* to a particular window. At the level of the user interface, messages are like a processor time slice — that is, the receipt of a message means access to the processor. In non-preemptive Windows (version 3.1 and earlier), messages were the *only* means for getting access to the processor. Although Windows 95 and Windows NT both have preemptive schedulers and support background processing via threads, the schedulers give way to the urgency of delivering messages to windows. When a message is waiting to be delivered to a window, the thread associated with that window gets a slight priority boost.

In the user interface, all input arrives in the form of messages, and it's up to you — the application programmer — to respond to this input in a reasonable fashion. What's reasonable? For a word-processing program, it's reasonable to accept keyboard input and echo the characters as formatted text. A crossword puzzle program might take keyboard input and place letters in a series of game cells. In other words, as the application programmer for a Windows application, it's up to you to decide. A large part of the work you do in designing an application involves deciding which messages to respond to, and then writing code to respond to those messages in a meaningful way.

When you are writing code that responds to messages, Windows requires you to adopt an *event-driven* programming style. It's quite different from the *sequence-driven* programming familiar to most programmers, and for that reason, it can seem awkward at first. Event-driven programs don't rely on users following a specific sequence in their actions. Event-driven programming has more in common with interrupt-driven device drivers or video game software than with the sequence-oriented approach familiar to many programmers.

Event-driven programming will be comfortable to a programmer who has been using object-oriented programming techniques or tools. Experienced C++ programmers will tell you that the member functions of a C++ class must also be written in a way that is sequence independent. It's our opinion that the nonsequential nature of C++ class methods is a natural solution to the event-driven needs of a Windows program.

MFC wraps native system windows in its CWnd class, which serves as the base class for dozens of specialized window classes, including frame windows, dialog windows, and MDI (Multiple Document Interface) windows. Although CWnd provides an object-oriented wrapper, it does not diminish the importance of the native system object in an MFC program. Like a Windows program in C, the structure of an MFC program's user-interface code will be built around the windows that the program uses. And just like Windows programs in C, MFC programs are triggered to respond to messages sent by the system.

The system sends all messages for a particular window to a special function called a *window procedure*. A window procedure in C has a large switch statement. MFC implements a window procedure for MFC programs, complete with a hidden switch statement. An MFC window processes messages using member functions of a CWnd-derived class that has one member function per Windows system message. Table 2-4 provides a brief sampling of the 200 different messages in the native Windows API. By convention, all system message names start with the WM_ prefix, which stands for window message.

Table 2-4

A Sampling of the Messages Generated by Windows

Message	Description
WM_CREATE	A window has been created. Like a C++ constructor, it means that the window has been created and that it's time to initialize window data. Unlike a CWnd constructor, however, the receipt of this message tells you that the system window has been created and is ready for initialization.
WM_DESTROY	A window has been destroyed. As with a C++ destructor, now is a good time to clean up after a window. When you receive this message, the window itself still exists.
WM_MOVE	A window has moved.
WM_SIZE	A window's client area has changed size.
WM_PAINT	A window has been damaged, and it's time to redraw the contents of the window.
WM_LBUTTONDOWN	The user has clicked the left mouse button while the cursor is in the window's client area.
WM_MOUSEMOVE	The user has moved the mouse while the cursor is in the window's client area.
WM_KEYDOWN	The user has pressed a key on the keyboard.
WM_CHAR	The user has pressed a key on the keyboard that corresponds to a printable character.

Several compiler vendors ship tools that let you tap into system message traffic. In older versions of their compiler, Microsoft shipped SPY. Current versions provide an enhancement called SPY++. We think of SPY++ as a doctor's stethoscope; you use both tools to listen to some of the rumblings that occur below the surface. You can use SPY++ to gain familiarity with the types of messages that a window receives. We think you'll use SPY++ quite often to decide which messages you should pay attention to in your program's windowing code.

Developers who have worked with other graphical user interface (GUI) systems — for example, Macintosh, X-Windows, or OS/2 Presentation Manager — will find much that is familiar in the Windows messaging system. In most cases, the messages in the OS/2 Presentation Manager have the same names as the messages used by Windows. Other GUIs have messages with different names, but the fundamental concepts are the same in all these systems.

Peering into System Operations with SPY++

The Windows system delivers messages to individual windows, notifying them of user activity. As such, understanding the available types of messages is clearly important to your success in Windows programming. But with more than 200 messages in the system, it's sometimes hard to figure out which messages you should pay attention to. Microsoft's SPY++ utility, which is bundled with Visual C++ versions 2.0 and later, shows you every message that gets sent to a window. It is also a handy utility for sleuthing through the system to figure out which windows, threads, and processes are present in a particular application. To start SPY++, you click the SPYXX.EXE icon, which is shown in Figure 2-1.

Figure 2-1
Clicking this icon starts the window-thread-process spying operation.

When SPY++ first comes up, it displays a list of windows running in the system. You can open up other windows in SPY++ to learn about the processes and threads currently running in the system. Each of these lists are tightly interconnected, because processes own threads, and threads own windows. And starting in the window list, you can get a more precise idea of the parent-child relationships that exist between various windows.

To give you an idea of typical use, Figure 2-2 shows SPY++ displaying three lists: a process list, a thread list, and a window list. Although SPY++ can tell you about any Windows program that's running in the system, in our example SPY++ is actually spying on itself. In Figure 2-2, the window list shows that the main window has four child windows. Some of these windows also have their own child windows. In other words, one of the things that SPY++ helps you learn is how an application might organize its windows in the creation of a user interface.

In general, you'll find that applications typically prefer to create fewer rather than more windows. Consider a spreadsheet program: should individual cells each be a window, or should a group of cells be a window? If you run SPY++ with any commercially available spreadsheet program, you learn that groups of cells are windows. This design decision was made because of the relatively high overhead of a window. You'll want to follow this strategy in designing the windowing for your own applications.

During the development of a Windows program, you might have a bug that prevents your program from terminating properly. Although all of the windows in your program might be hidden, the process itself is still running in the system. Using the details that you can see in the Process window in SPY++, you could quickly ascertain whether or not your program has

Continued

Continued from previous page

shut down properly. You open the Process window in SPY++ by selecting the Spy|Processes menu item. The Process window shows all of the processes that are currently running in the system. Nested in the hierarchy under each process is a list of the threads that are owned by that process. (Remember that threads are the unit of scheduling in Windows 95 and in Windows NT.) Any windows that are owned by a thread are listed in the hierarchy under that thread.

Similarly, when you are adding new threads to a program, you aren't always sure that secondary threads are created and destroyed at the proper time. The Threads window in SPY++ lets you know exactly how many threads are currently running in your program. To open the Threads window in SPY++, you choose the Spy|Threads menu item. This window lists all of the threads in the system, sorted by thread ID. The items in the Threads window also serve as the top of a hierarchy, this time for the windows that are connected to threads. A quick glance at this listing shows that more threads are windowless than have windows. Such threads have no user interface; instead, they provide services to the threads that do have windows.

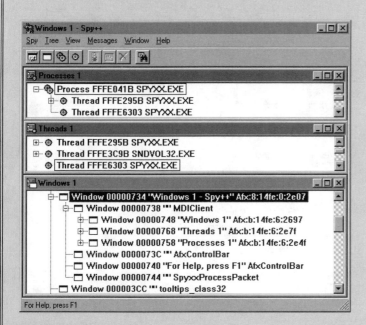

Figure 2-2
To get more details about individual processes, threads, or windows, click an item in any SPY++ window.

Continued

Continued from previous page

The hierarchies shown by SPY++ suggest the hierarchy of system objects: processes own threads, and threads own windows. You can't have a process without a thread, because it wouldn't be able to accomplish any work. But you *can* have a thread that has no windows. Threads that have windows get a priority boost when one of their windows receives a message. This mechanism allows the user interfaces of both Windows 95 and Windows NT to be highly responsive to user input.

To see the messages that are being sent to a window, you open a Messages window in SPY++. There are several ways to select a window for spying, but we prefer to use the Finder Tool. Select the SpyIFind Windows... menu item, which opens a dialog box containing the Finder Tool. After clicking the Show Messages button, click and drag the Finder Tool onto the window that interests you.

As shown in Figure 2-3, the Messages window shows all the messages being delivered to a window, with either one or two lines per message. The leftmost column lists the handle — or ID — of the window that is receiving a message. For each message, the second column contains either P, S, or R. We'll tell you more about that column in a moment. The third column lists the message received, and the decoded values of two 4-byte parameters that were passed along with the message.

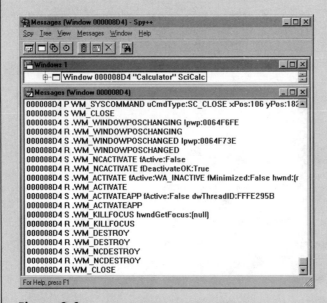

Figure 2-3
SPY++ showing messages received by CALC.

Continued

Continued from previous page

Even without understanding the meaning of individual messages, you can see with SPY++ that a lot of message traffic is associated with even the smallest user-interface actions. When viewing the Messages window, you can learn more about a particular message by selecting the message (click the message with the right mouse button), and then selecting the Help item from the menu that is displayed.

The second column in SPY++ indicates whether a message was Posted (P) to a message queue, or was Sent (S) directly to the window. The difference between posting and sending has to do with whether the sender of the message wanted to wait for a reply. Posted messages wait in a message queue until the recipient asks for a new message. Such messages notify the recipient that something has occurred, but no reply is necessary.

Sent messages don't wait in a message queue; instead, the sender of a message waits for a reply. A sent message behaves like a function call; the message sender waits until the recipient processes the message and provides a return value. SPY++ flags the reply to a sent message with an R in the second column of the Messages window.

Figure 2-3 shows the messages that are generated when the user closes a window. The first message displayed in the window, WM_SYSCOMMAND, starts the window-closing process. It's the only queued message in the entire data stream. The other messages each indicate an additional step in the window shutdown and closing process. The process continues until the window has been completely destroyed, which is represented in Figure 2-3 by the WM_DESTROY and WM_NCDESTROY messages.

For all the great things SPY++ shows you about the system, we strongly urge you to spend some time learning how to use it. You'll find this program quite useful as you begin building your Windows application software.

Given the importance of the window, it's not surprising that one of the most important classes in the MFC library is CWnd, the class that encapsulates the native system window. CWnd is a base class for almost 25% (30 of 126 total classes) of the classes in the MFC library. CWnd has member functions that correspond to each of the windowing functions in the native API. Of course, these are implemented as inline functions to minimize the overhead of accessing the underlying system function calls.

For example, the ShowWindow function in the native API, which can make a window minimized or maximized, is declared as follows:

```
BOOL ShowWindow (HWND hwnd, int nCmdShow)
```

MFC has a CWnd::ShowWindow function, which is declared as follows:

```
BOOL Cwnd::ShowWindow(int nCmdShow)
```

The CWnd implementation for this function provides a window handle (m_hWnd) value, and then calls the native API function:

```
inline BOOL CWnd::ShowWindow (int nCmdShow)
    { return ::ShowWindow(m_hWnd, nCmdShow); }
```

The MFC development team has wrapped Windows API functions in the MFC classes. A minimal amount of KERNEL functional capability is wrapped in MFC classes, along with most GDI functions and almost every USER function. For KERNEL and GDI functions, MFC provides a bit of organization to help you wade through the thousands of available functions. For USER functions, MFC hides some of the grungy details of window creation and maintenance. It also adds support for some new user-interface objects, such as dockable tool bars and other types of control bars, including status bar windows.

From time to time, you may find yourself perusing the documentation (and help files) of the native API. We encourage you to do this because the Win16 and Win32 APIs are the engine for all Windows applications. The MFC library tames the raw horsepower of the native API for you by organizing it and handling mundane administrative work. From time to time, however, you'll want to — or need to — bypass the MFC framework and tap directly into the power source for all Windows software, the native API.

Although the native Win16 and Win32 APIs are the source of power for MFC, they are extremely quirky programming interfaces. Because MFC does such a nice job of taming some of the wilder aspects of Win32, you'll want to use MFC instead of Win32 whenever possible. MFC hides some of the tedious housekeeping chores of Win32, while making full use of the paradigms on which Win32 was built.

3 Understanding the Visual C++ Tools

While you're reading about the capabilities and features of C++ that make it different from C, as well as later when we're describing some of the features of the MFC library, you'll probably want to start Microsoft Visual C++ and try out these features. If you've worked through the tutorial on using Visual C++ 2.0 in the distribution, you're probably already familiar with the tools we describe in the following sections. If not, this information will help you easily start, use, and exit a Visual C++ session.

Starting a New Project

When you first open Visual C++, you see a blank workspace, a menu bar, and a toolbar. Very few tools or menu items are enabled. Before you can do anything else, you need to start a *project*. Once you start a project, the appropriate tools are enabled, and you can start working with Visual C++. When you start a project using a helper called the *AppWizard*, Visual C++ also automatically records how to compile and load your source code files. Here's how you start a new project:

1. From the Start button on the Windows 95 task bar, select Programs | Microsoft Visual C++ 2.0 | Visual C++. This brings up the Visual C++ Integrated Development Environment (IDE), which is shown in Figure 3-1.

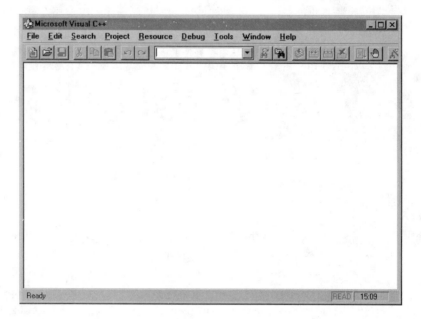

Figure 3-1
*The Microsoft Visual C++ workspace, also known as the Integrated
Development Environment (IDE).*

2. Select File|New. As shown in Figure 3-2, the IDE displays a list of
   different types of programming files and other constructs that you
   could be creating. Select Project and click the OK button, or simply
   double-click Project. The IDE will display a series of dialog boxes
   that will help you set up your programming project.

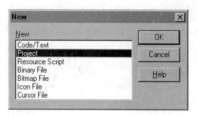

Figure 3-2
Visual C++ offers these choices for new file types.

3. The first dialog box to be displayed is shown in Figure 3-3. In the Project Name field, enter the name of the new project. The name you enter will be the default name of the project subdirectory, the target executable file, and the default makefile. (We'll explain the term *makefile* and the concept of a *target* file in the next section.) In Figure 3-4, the project name "pegasus" has been entered in the Project Name box. This name is automatically copied into the New Subdirectory box and the Project Path. If you want to change the New Subdirectory entry, you can do so, and this is also reflected in the Project Path.

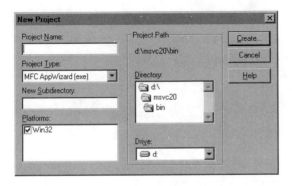

Figure 3-3
You use the New Project dialog box to enter a project name and a path for storing the files for your new project.

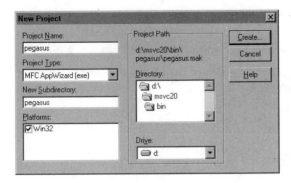

Figure 3-4
The Project Name "pegasus" is entered, and reflected in the New Subdirectory and the Project Path.

4. If the drive and directory listed under the Project Path aren't the ones in which you want your new project directory to appear, use the Drive and Directory boxes to change drives and open or close folder icons until you have the path you want. If the New Subdirectory box isn't empty, it's added to the drive and directory you've selected, and the project name is added to get the Project Path. In Figure 3-5, the drive and directory have been set to d:\programs.

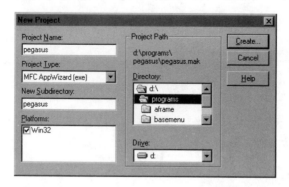

Figure 3-5
The drive and directory are set to d:\programs.

5. Under Project Type, press the arrow next to the box, and select a type of project from the drop-down list. The default is MFC AppWizard (exe), which is what you'll choose when we get to MFC programs. For the types of examples we'll be showing you in the chapters introducing C++, choose Console Application, as shown in Figure 3-6. A Console Application will run in an MS-DOS window. When it's done, the window will disappear instantly. For test applications, you should put a sleep or a request for input as the last action, so that you have time to see the program's output!

6. Click the Create button to accept the contents of this dialog box. If you've selected the Console Application Project Type, the AppWizard won't run (we'll describe AppWizard a bit later in this chapter), and the project will be created at this time.

7. As shown in Figure 3-7, a dialog window is displayed asking for files to be added to the project. Unless you have existing files that you

want to add to this project, you can safely close this dialog box by clicking the Close button.

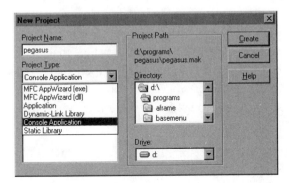

Figure 3-6
Choosing the Console Application Project Type.

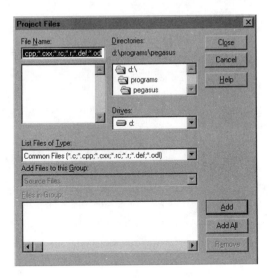

Figure 3-7
The Project Files dialog.

8. The *project window* is left on the workspace. This window provides a graphical display of the dependencies in the makefile. Figure 3-8

shows our pegasus.mak makefile. The makefile represents the entire project, in Visual C++. All of the project files and resources (of which there aren't yet any, in this example) are displayed graphically in the project window, and can be opened by double-clicking their names in this window. Later, when you open the makefile to resume work on the project, you'll notice that all of the other files that were open in your last project session are automatically reopened. The Visual C++ File menu stores the names of the last four makefiles opened, as well as the names of the last four files of any other type opened.

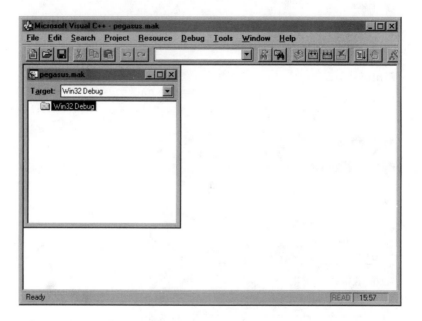

Figure 3-8
The project window, representing the makefile.

What's a Makefile?

The window that's left in your workspace is the *project window*. It shows a graphical representation of a makefile. The *makefile* is a text file that shows how to compile your entire application. It does this by listing the *dependencies* among the source, object, executable, and data files for your new application. Each file that is to be made is a *target* that depends on one or more other files that are *sources* for the final product.

To understand how dependencies work, imagine that we want to make a program file named sort.exe. This program file is loaded from the object files main.obj, sort.obj, and file.obj. These files are, in turn, compiled from main.cpp, sort.cpp, and file.cpp. These files each include several header files. In other words, sort.exe is a target file that depends on the three object files. In turn, each of the three object files is a target file that depends on its own source file and header files. If you change any of the files on which file.obj depends, you need to recompile file.obj. As a result of this recompiling, sort.exe will be out of date with respect to file.obj, and will need to be reloaded. The same sort of calculation is done for each target file and its dependencies.

Makefiles are read by a *make* program. The original make program was part of the UNIX Programmers' Workbench (PWB) system, and later became part of the base release of the UNIX system. This program's functional capabilities were soon copied to many other platforms. The version used for Visual C++ is Microsoft's *nmake*, which includes many powerful features that are not available with other make programs.

You won't need to know any details about the makefiles or nmake. The Visual Workbench keeps track of dependencies, and it can create and run your programs for you. If you are curious, nmake is documented in Books Online.

Creating C++ Source and Header Files in Your Project

To create C++ source files or header files:

1. Select File|New. This opens a dialog box that lets you choose the type of file you would like to create. We've already seen this dialog box in Figure 3-2.

2. Select Code/Text, and click the OK button. A text window is displayed, and you can enter and edit your file. As shown in Figure 3-9, this window doesn't really have a name of its own. You name this file when you save it, either explicitly (with Ctrl-S or File|Save) or on closing the file.

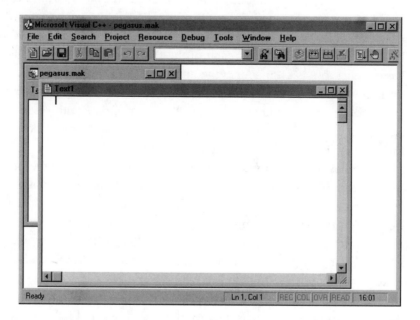

Figure 3-9
A code/text window immediately after creation.

Updating Dependencies in the Makefile

When you create new source files, they don't have any dependency relationships defined. As you write code, some dependencies are created: the executable depends on the object files, and an object file depends on its source file and its header files. You can tell the Visual Workbench to update these dependencies in your makefile at any time, in any one of several ways.

Before updating dependencies, you need to make sure that you've saved each source file that you've edited, either individually or by selecting File|Save All. You can then safely update any new dependencies.

If you've added one new file, and the window in which you edited it is still selected, you can choose Project|Update Dependencies, and the IDE will ask whether you want to add that file to the project. When you choose Yes, the file will be added, and the dependencies from that file will become part of the project. You can choose the Project|Update Dependencies menu item at any time, and the dependencies for the currently selected file will be updated.

If you've added several new files, or have closed the window with a new file, you should choose Project|Files to bring up the dialog box shown in Figure 3-7, which allows you to add the files to the project. You can then choose Project|Update All Dependencies. You can choose this menu item at any time, to update all the makefile dependencies for files that are already part of the project. Otherwise, dependencies are updated immediately before compiling.

Compiling, Building, and Executing

The Project menu has options that allow you to compile each source file individually, or to build and run the executable on which you're working. The Visual C++ IDE is really much more helpful here than you probably would have imagined. The menu changes slightly, depending on which source file you have selected. For example, if you're working on main.cpp, which is part of sort.exe, you have the following choices:

- To compile only main.cpp into main.obj, select main.cpp in the project window or select a window in which main.cpp appears. Choose the Project menu. You'll find that one of the menu items is Compile main.cpp. Select that menu item.

- To build the executable sort.exe, compiling any C++ source files if they or their included header files are out of date, choose the Project menu. You'll find that one of the menu items is Build sort.exe. Select that menu item.

- To rebuild all of the files in the makefile, whether or not they are out of date with respect to any of their dependent files, choose Project|Rebuild All. Avoid selecting this build option except when you really want to rebuild each and every part of your program. In most cases, Project|Build is the better choice because it only rebuilds files that have changed.

■ To execute sort.exe, rebuilding it first if it doesn't exist yet or is out of date with respect to some dependent file, choose the Project menu. You'll find that one of the menu items is Execute sort.exe. Select that menu item. If the executable sort.exe needs to be rebuilt, the IDE will ask whether you want to rebuild it. If you choose Yes (as you usually should), you'll then have to wait for the rebuild to finish, and select Project|Execute sort.exe again.

Note that all of these commands also have keyboard shortcuts that help you speed up the process when you're in the thick of the debug-edit-compile-run cycle.

Using Wizards

Two Wizards can help you build your MFC programs: the AppWizard and the ClassWizard. We'll mention them briefly here, and return to them later in the book, when we build MFC programs.

In our previous example of creating a project, we set the Project Type to Console Application, and after we clicked the Create button, the project was created with no further information needed. However, if you are creating a new project and — as shown in Figure 3-10 — the Project Type is either MFC AppWizard (exe) or MFC AppWizard (dll), the AppWizard is called immediately after you click the Create button. AppWizard gathers more information to help you create the type of application you've chosen.

Using the AppWizard involves six steps, each of which is shown in a dialog box on a separate wizard property sheet page. You can step forward and backward through these pages, using the Next and Back buttons; and at any time, you can choose to use the default settings for the remaining pages by clicking the Finish button. On each page, the results of your choices are shown graphically next to your choices.

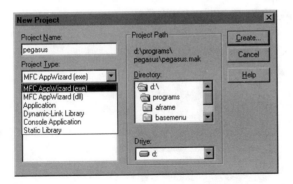

Figure 3-10

Choosing the MFC AppWizard (exe) Project Type.

The six steps of the AppWizard are:

1. Choosing the type of application, as shown in Figure 3-11. A single-document interface (SDI) application has menus, but displays only one document at one time. A multiple-document interface (MDI) application can display more than one document at a time. A dialog-based interface application has a relatively simple user interface, typically with only a few choices that the user can make in response to a request for information. These application types are discussed more fully in the chapters on Document/View Architecture and on Dialog Boxes. At this step, you also choose the language: English, French, or German.

2. Deciding whether you want any database support, as shown in Figure 3-12. If you choose to include a database view, you're asked for a data source. This topic is beyond the scope of this book.

3. Choosing the type of OLE (Object Linking and Embedding) support you would like, as shown in Figure 3-13. OLE is Microsoft's architecture for compound documents — that is, files that contain objects of various types, such as word-processing document sections, picture sections, and spreadsheet sections. Each part of a compound document can be updated separately, by the tool that is needed to manipulate that part. This topic is also beyond the scope of this book.

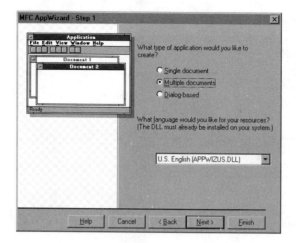

Figure 3-11
MFC AppWizard, Step 1: Choosing the application type.

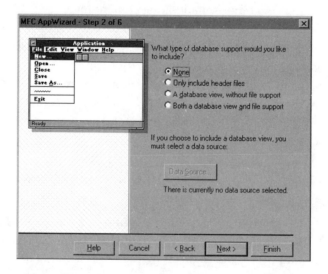

Figure 3-12
MFC AppWizard, Step 2: Choosing the database support.

4. Choosing various features that you'd like to have in your application, as shown in Figure 3-14. This is sort of a miscellaneous features dialog box. It includes several features of the overall framing window,

including whether to include printing support and the number of most-recently-used (MRU) files to list in the File menu. Several of the features offered at this point are covered later in this book. If you click the Advanced button in this dialog, the AppWizard displays a property sheet with two pages, which are shown in Figures 3-15 and 3-16. One page allows you to change several names associated with the project; the other allows you to change some details of the frame window in which the application will be displayed. You will not often change the values on this Advanced property sheet.

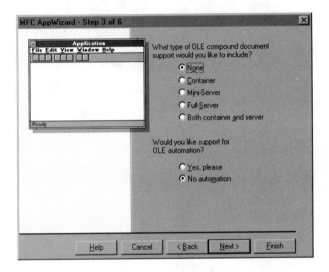

Figure 3-13
MFC AppWizard, Step 3: Choosing the OLE support.

5. Specifying the form you want for the makefile and the source code files that AppWizard helps you create. As shown in Figure 3-17, AppWizard asks you the following questions:

Would you like source file comments to be generated? (Yes or No.)

What type of makefile would you like for your project? (Visual C++ makefile, or external makefile.)

How would you like to link to the MFC library? (Static library or shared DLL.)

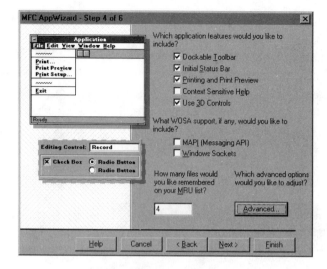

Figure 3-14

MFC AppWizard, Step 4: Choosing application features.

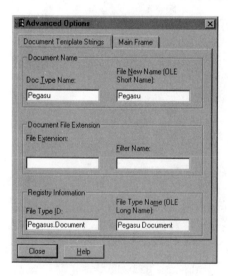

Figure 3-15

MFC AppWizard, Step 4: Choosing advanced options from the Document Template Strings property page.

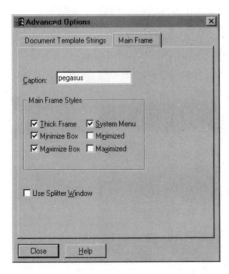

Figure 3-16
MFC AppWizard, Step 4: Choosing advanced options from the Main
Frame property page.

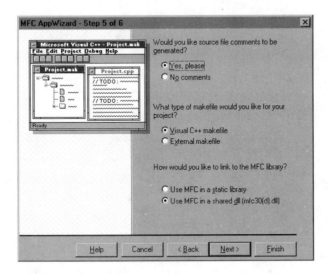

Figure 3-17
MFC AppWizard, Step 5: Choosing the desired form for the makefile and
the source code files.

6. Reviewing the information that the AppWizard displays indicating which applications classes will be generated for this application, in which header and source files they are to be found, and what their base classes are. Figure 3-18 shows the dialog box in which the AppWizard displays this information. This information will be more understandable once we've discussed how your application classes are inherited from the MFC base classes.

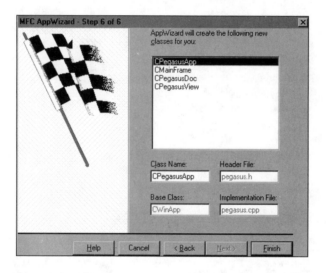

Figure 3-18

MFC AppWizard, Step 6: Reviewing the names of the applications classes, the header and source files, and the base classes for your application.

When you click the Finish button, a dialog box is displayed that summarizes all of the information that the AppWizard has just gathered. Figure 3-19 shows an example of this dialog box. This dialog gives you one last chance to cancel the project, which you can do by clicking the Cancel button. If you accept the information displayed in this dialog by clicking the OK button, the AppWizard creates for your application not only a makefile, but your first source files that form the frame and some of the support for the type of application that you've chosen. Figure 3-20 shows the top-level source code and resource files created for your project (as well as a readme.txt file to help keep them straight!). Figure 3-21 shows the deeper-level header, image, and resource files placed in the Dependencies subdirectory.

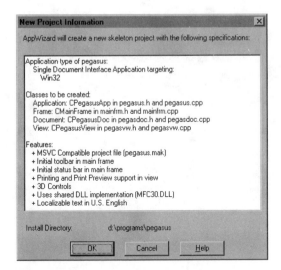

Figure 3-19
Confirming the new project information.

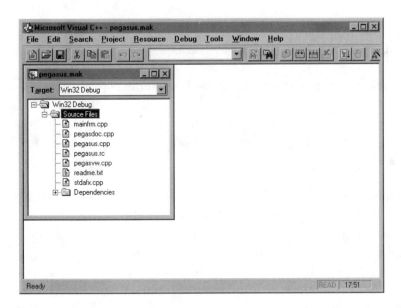

Figure 3-20
The project window displaying the top-level source code and resource files
for the project.

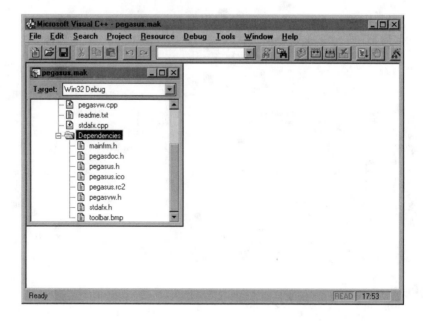

Figure 3-21

The project window displaying the header, image, and resource files that are placed in the Dependencies subdirectory.

Once your application framework is created, you can use the Class-Wizard to generate new classes that inherit from the MFC library classes, and to modify existing classes. You can then use these classes in your application. Chapter 6 provides an in-depth introduction to the C++ concepts of classes and inheritance, and Chapters 9 and 10 describe using the ClassWizard to apply this to the MFC library.

Now that you understand the Visual C++ tools and the architecture of the Windows API, you're ready to start tackling some of the other issues in building MFC-based software. If you need to brush up on your C++ programming skills, you'll want to read all of the chapters in Part II, "OOP and C++ Basics." We don't claim that you'll find complete coverage of the language here; just the features you'll need for writing code using MFC.

On the other hand, if you're already comfortable with object-oriented C++ programming, you're ready to jump ahead to Part III, "MFC Programming Fundamentals." The chapters in Part III are a tutorial introduction to building Windows programs using the MFC library. The emphasis is on providing the essentials that you'll need in any Windows programming project, including the creation of user-interface objects such as windows, menus, and dialogs, handling mouse and keyboard input, and creating and controlling dialog boxes.

The remainder of the book presents specific topics in using the MFC library to create MS-Windows applications. Welcome to the world of Windows programming — and best wishes on your MFC programming projects!

II OOP and C++ Basics

*T*he chapters in Part II are intended to help experienced C programmers understand the MFC library by
introducing the basic concepts and structures of object-
oriented programming and the C++ language. This is not
a complete course in C++. For that, we would direct you
to one of the references listed at the end of this introduction or in the Recommended Reading list, which you'll
find at the end of this book.

If you don't already know C, you shouldn't start with
this book. Before reading this book, you should work
through a tutorial or some instruction in object-oriented
program design in the C++ programming language. To
some degree, programming in C++ may be easier for you if
you don't have to overlay it on procedural program design
and the C language constructs, or object-oriented programming (OOP) concepts from other programming languages.

If you already know C++, you may read as much or as
little of Part II as you want. If you do read this part,
though, you may find some concepts or points of view that
are new to you.

That leaves the person who knows C but hasn't yet learned C++. The chapters in this part of the book are meant for you. This is not a complete introduction to C++, but we'll cover everything you need in order to understand the MFC library. Some concepts are fully explained here; we just touch on others, but they are discussed more fully later in the book when they are illustrated in a program.

Chapter 4 introduces you to the basic concepts of object-oriented programming. In Chapter 5, we cover the little differences from C that might trip you up when you are reading or writing a C++ program. In Chapter 6, we cover the concept of *classes*, which is the most significant difference between C and C++. Then, in Chapter 7, we cover other major language differences between C and C++.

You could make an argument for stopping there and using these new C++ language elements to write programs in "a better C." In our humble opinion (IOHO), this is somewhat akin to buying a pipe wrench because, being heavier than your hammer, it makes a better hammer. Sure, it works, and it works better. But hammering is not what a pipe wrench is made for, and you can't beat a pipe wrench at the job for which it *is* made. Similarly, C++ is made for writing programs in an object-oriented style. In one way or another, all of the features that make it "a better C" are aimed at better supporting data objects.

In Chapter 8, we tackle the subject of object-oriented C++ program design. Even if you skip the rest of the chapters in this part because you are familiar with the differences between the language elements of C and C++, this is a good place to review their proper use.

C++ is still an evolving language. Bjarne Stroustrup, the original author, and the other members of the ANSI/ISO Standards Committees are still hammering out the last little details of what the "standard" version will do. The following chapters describe parts of the language that are stable and usable, and that are available in Microsoft Visual C++ 2.0 (except for "unexpected exceptions" and certain keywords that are clearly labeled). To get a good feel for the entire C++ language, you should have some good references, and possibly take a professional course in C++. For the elements of C++, our authorities are the following works. They should be yours, too. When we refer to them throughout this book, we'll use the abbreviations that follow the titles.

- *The C++ Programming Language*, second edition (C++/PL). Bjarne Stroustrup. Reading, MA: Addison-Wesley, 1991 (1993 edition).

- *The Design and Evolution of C++* (C++/D&E). Bjarne Stroustrup. Reading, MA: Addison-Wesley, 1994.

- *The Annotated C++ Reference Manual* (ARM). Margaret A. Ellis and Bjarne Stroustrup. Reading, MA: Addison-Wesley, 1990 (1992 edition).

- *Working Paper for Draft Proposed International Standard for Information Systems — Programming Language C++* (Draft Standard). Washington, DC: ANSI X3J16 / ISO WG21 Joint Technical Committee. CBEMA, January 1994 (approved March 1994).

On the Internet, you can access information on C++ and Microsoft Visual C++ in the following Usenet newsgroups:

- comp.lang.c++ (See particularly the FAQ and the recurring article Learn C/C++ Today, by Vinit S. Carpenter.)
- comp.std.c++
- comp.object
- comp.os.ms-windows.programmer.tools
- comp.os.ms-windows.programmer.win32
- comp.os.ms-windows.programmer.misc
- comp.os.ms-windows.programmer.controls
- comp.os.ms-windows.programmer.drivers
- comp.os.ms-windows.programmer.graphics
- comp.os.ms-windows.programmer.ole

Because the list of active newsgroups is constantly changing, this is not a complete list; however, it suggests several places you can start. As with all Usenet newsgroups, you should first read the netiquette articles in news.announce.newusers, and then read the FAQs (answers to Frequently Asked Questions, or "Just the FAQs, Ma'am") before posting your own questions.

CHAPTER

4

What Is Object-Oriented Programming?

*A*ny discussion of C++ must start by noting that C++ has its origins in the C language, with some additions to support object-oriented programming (OOP). But most people would be hard-pressed to explain the term *object-oriented programming*. Before we get into the nuts and bolts of C++, we'll describe the concepts of object-oriented programming. We won't try to explain all aspects of OOP in one chapter — literally shelves full of books already try to do that (several of which are mentioned in the Recommended Reading list). We just want you to be comfortable enough with the basic concepts of OOP, so that you can see how and why they're used in C++.

Paradigms Past, Present, and Future

Object-oriented programming is often described as a "new paradigm for programming." A paradigm is nothing more than a way of looking at things. Software development paradigms have been changing ever since people started programming. As we find new techniques and new tools that make programming (and more important, programming *correctly*) easier and better, we change our ideas about how things should be done. In other words, we change our *model* or *paradigm* of our programming process. Let's take a quick look at some of the changes we've seen over the past several decades of programming.

Although the following discussion might give you the impression that the process of changing paradigms over the years has been: (a) linear,

(b) carefully planned, and (c) accepted by everyone, this certainly isn't the case. Most of the changes, especially early on, were simply a result of adding new ideas to existing programming languages or procedures to make programming easier or safer (that is, easier to do *correctly*). As with all history, we tend to remember the changes that became popular, even though many of the evolutionary side trails are still in use. And many of the steps we describe in the following sections as "past" are still in use by some programmers — either because of the programmers' resistance to change, or because a particular approach better suits their needs.

MACHINE LANGUAGE

The first computers in which instructions and data were stored in the same memory had relatively simple sets of instructions. Part of an instruction word typically specified which operation was being performed (the *op code*), and the rest of the instruction either identified the data's numeric address in memory, or somehow modified the basic operation. (For an example of these op codes, see the sidebar accompanying this section.) To put a program into a computer, a programmer had to figure out which numbers corresponded to the desired instructions in the computer, at what numeric addresses the data was to be stored, and where in the computer's memory the program should be loaded. After gathering all of this information, machine language programmers would sit down with their lists of numbers and manually load them into their computers.

The paradigm of the day (even though it wasn't yet called a "paradigm") was that the machines were expensive and the people were not. All of the work involved in getting a program working and running on a computer fell to the programmer. This person did all of the required translation, because it was believed that precious computation cycles should not be wasted on such tasks. Designing a program was essentially a process of writing down the algorithm, verifying it, attempting to translate it into the machine's language, and then simply hacking the code until it produced (more or less) the desired results.

As you can imagine, this process was extremely error-prone. Although program size was limited to the size of the computer's memory — often only 4K-8K, as opposed to the megabytes you now have on your desktop — the programmer still had to write thousands of instructions, and then enter them correctly. In addition, the first programmers usually had to write *all* of the code themselves. They had no libraries for such tasks as printf( ) or even writing a character to a printer (assuming that the computer had a printer, and didn't just leave its data in a memory area for the programmer to read using the console lights and switches!). A programmer might spend weeks writing a program, an hour or more entering the program via switches, and several hours waiting while the program ran. If the program crashed the system, or the results showed that the program contained an error, the programmer had to repeat the entire process in order to debug and fix the program.

Some of the early programmers decided that they would be more productive if they could enter their instructions in a *symbolic* form — that is, in word-like symbols that represented both instructions and data. Rather than use their computers solely for calculations, they would then have the computer do the mechanical work of translating these symbols into the numbers that represented the instructions and data inside the computer. From these ideas for easier and better programming came the *assembler* and *macro assembler* languages.

ASSEMBLER AND MACRO ASSEMBLER LANGUAGES

When people started writing programs to translate easily remembered (*mnemonic*) symbols into computer instructions and data, which could then be loaded and run, the first *assemblers* were born. These programs helped speed up coding and fixing programs, because programmers could now look at the listings and remember the instructions, without performing a tedious number-to-instruction translation. Soon after the first assemblers were developed, it became possible to use names as symbolic labels for data, rather than using the numeric addresses of the data. Life was wonderful!

Some programmers noticed that they often used the same groups of instructions together, perhaps with only minor changes to data addresses. For example, there would be groups of instructions that involved entering or exiting subroutines, or performing common procedures. This observation led to two developments. One was the development of *libraries* of code that contained frequently used routines. This in turn required the development of *linking loaders*, or *link editors*, which allowed programmers to combine code they had written with code from a common library. The other development was the concept of a programming *macro*, which is a set of instructions that can be added to a program simply by using a symbolic name in the code. The symbol might look like a single machine instruction, but the *macro assembler* would expand it into zero, one, or more actual instructions before *assembling* the program into a machine-executable file. For example, to read a character from the terminal, a programmer might simply enter $getch r0, and let the macro processor expand that symbolic name into the correct instructions.

An Example of Op Codes

In most present-day computers, both the instructions and the data for running programs are stored as numbers in the computer's main memory. An op code is the part of a word in memory that specifies which operation the instruction should perform. The rest of the word (or words, in a multiword instruction) contains information that modifies the operation: a data address in memory, an I/O address, or other information that modifies the operation and specifies how it should be performed.

Much like today's RISC computer systems, many of the earliest computers had extremely simple instruction sets. In those days, however, the simplicity arose less from a theory of what makes a good instruction set than from the fact that instruction sets were wired into the computer using vacuum tubes or transistors, diodes, resistors, and other electronic components. It was less expensive and easier to get things right if you used a simple instruction set.

Table 4-1 provides an example of the instruction set for the DEC PDP-8, an early

microcomputer (or minicomputer, depending on who is doing the classification). As shown in Figure 4-1, the PDP-8 has 12 bits in its word. The first three bits are the op code, and the remaining nine bits are either data addresses or some other modifier to the basic instruction.

With the last two op codes in Table 4-1, the remaining nine bits are not filled with an address. Instead, some of those bits are used to modify the meanings of these op codes. With the I/O instructions, for example, different bit patterns might tell you which device you are addressing, and what you want it to do. With the *Operate Microinstructions* op code, different patterns indicate various operations and tests on the accumulator, or (with special-purpose hardware) additional integer and floating-point arithmetic operations.

Happily, today's programmers don't have to worry about this kind of detail. For most applications, compilers for higher-level languages handle all of this work.

Continued

Continued from previous page

Table 4-1
An Example of Op Codes (from the DEC PDP-8)

Op Code	Mnemonic	Description
0	AND	Logical AND, from data at the given address to data in the accumulator
1	TAD	Two's Complement Add, from data at the given address to data in the accumulator
2	ISZ	Increment [add one to] the data at the given address, and Skip one instruction if the new value is Zero
3	DCA	Deposit the data in the accumulator to the given address, and Clear the Accumulator
4	JMS	JuMp to Subroutine at the given address
5	JMP	JuMP (unconditionally) to the given address
6	(varies)	Programmed Data Transfer (I/O) instructions
7	(varies)	Operate Microinstructions

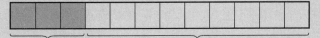

Bits 0-2:
Op Code

Bits 3-11:
Data Address or Modifier

Figure 4-1
The PDP-8 instruction word format.

The paradigm still emphasized the programmer's need to understand the machine; but now the machine was also being used to support the programmer, as well as the application. The responsibility for performing the more tedious, error-prone parts of the programming process was being shifted from the programmer to the machine! It was less likely that a number that didn't represent a real instruction would be entered as an instruction, because the assembler wasn't supposed to allow that. Because programs were becoming easier to read, people could better study how programs were written. People who wrote systems programs began making it easy to write large sections of machine code in just a few lines, and code that handled frequently performed tasks was saved in libraries and macros, so that it could be reused.

Of course, there were still problems:

- In an assembly-language program, which translates directly into machine instructions, you can write sequences of instructions that wouldn't make much sense from the point of view of higher-level programming constructs. In fact, you can very easily write sequences of instructions that make no sense at all! The computer doesn't check, and it doesn't care; it will do whatever you tell it to until something is directly impossible, and then it will crash.

- When you translate a program into its executable form, all of the data is simply numbers in a large address space. So are the instructions! Why is this a problem? When a programmer writes assembly-language programs, the instructions in those programs translate simply and directly into their counterpart machine instructions. The machine instructions on almost all types of processors don't check whether the bits on which they operate are integers, floating-point data, addresses, or even other instructions! Some assembler-language programs not only used this fact, but relied on it. On the whole, however, this is a field in which bugs could propagate.

- Because computers execute their instructions linearly, one after the other, this is the way the programmers thought about their programs. Programs were designed linearly, from the beginning to the end, with occasional unconditional and conditional jumps to other parts of the code. Beginning programmers still do this, in their first attempts at program design.

- Translating the original formulas for calculations to assembler language was still a manual task, as was translating the algorithms for using those formulas. This was another ripe field for errors. If you used the wrong mnemonic (for example, JMP instead of JMS), your program could be assembled, but it would still be wrong.

Some modularization was being employed, with chunks of frequently used code being put in one place so that a program could store a return address, jump to the subroutine code, and then use the return address to jump back. Many computers eventually put this capability into a hardware instruction.

Some programmers had an interesting thought. If they could write assembler programs to get computers to translate mnemonic op codes into machine-executable form, why couldn't they write programs to translate formulas, written in a form that humans could understand, into executable programs? In this way, the first of the human-readable programming languages were written: the formula translators.

HIGHER-LEVEL LANGUAGES AND STRUCTURED PROGRAMMING

Because its modern-day descendant keeps the same name, FORTRAN is probably the best-known of the formula translator languages. However, many such languages were once used. For example, although ALGOL is not as popular as it once was, its children and grandchildren — C and C++, ADA, and Pascal and its many offshoots — are still much in evidence.

The primary purpose of the formula translators was to make the language of the program more closely resemble the language of the problem — that is, mathematical formulas. For some programmers, another goal was the capability of running the same program on more than one type of computer, without learning an entirely new language! However, many of the statements in the different versions of these languages were still quite machine-dependent, because developers continued to think in terms of the machines' individual architectures.

In addition to making arithmetic more readable, the new languages added another new wrinkle: *control structures*, such as DO loops, and multiway branches — similar to, but not the same as, C switch statements. At first, the control structures simply mirrored control structures that were provided by the machine and assembly languages. Later, to make programming even easier, more control structures and data structures were added, such as subroutines, value-returning functions, multiple data types, and structures that allowed modules to be compiled separately and linked together. In the quest for more productive programming approaches, more and better control structures seemed to be one answer. The new structures included nested blocks and nested variable scopes, programmer-defined data types, and other structures that enhanced readability, modularity, and decomposability.

Macro Assembler Languages

Rather than code in the binary language of computers, assembler programmers could use mnemonics, which the computer could then translate into its own language. This wasn't a big step in language terms, but it did reflect an acceptance of the idea that the computer could perform steps in its own programming. Until people accepted the fact that the computer could not only solve mathematical problems, but also serve as a tool for its own programming, modern programming languages could never evolve.

Figure 4-2 shows some sample macro assembler language code for the DEC PDP-11. The example shows some practices we would consider odd, such as putting data inline with instructions.

```
; This defines the "print" macro.  It prints a string that
; immediately follows it.  This was a common practice.
.macro print
      mov    #$1,r0     ; Put the address of a local label
                        ; in register 0.
      jsr    outstr     ; Call the subroutine.
      beq    $2         ; Skip if no error.
      jmp    error      ; Go to an error routine.
$2:
      mov    #$1,r0     ; Look at the following string.
$3:
      tstb   (r0)+      ; Test a byte and increment.
      bne    $3         ; Is it NUL?  If so, end the loop.
      bit    $1,r0      ; Test whether the address is odd.
      beq    $4         ; If not, skip an instruction.
      inc    r0         ; If so, make it even.
$4:
      mov    r0,pc      ; Skip the string!
$1:                     ; Label for the string.
.endmacro

; Here is some code that uses the macro.  Note how compact it is,
; because of the macro use.

      print             ; The macro is called simply.
      .asciz <The answer is ... >    ; Macro to enter a string.
      mov    #47,r0     ; Do some answer checking.
      jsr    check_answer
      print
      ; We can also enter a string as octal bytes, and often did.
      .byte  114, 151, 156, 165, 170, 041, 015, 012, 0
.end
```

Figure 4-2
Sample macro assembler language code.

More and more, programmers recognized the importance of controlling the flow of their programs. At one time, flowcharts seemed to be the mark of the professional programmer. Eventually, the paradigm of *structured programming* techniques was consciously introduced to the programming world. Over the past couple of decades, the understanding of these techniques has evolved from the simple catchphrase, top-down design and bottom-up programming — signifying functional decomposition and modular programming — to numerous complete sets of techniques for structured problem analysis, system design, and computer programming. By addressing both functional and data structure and design, most of these newer sets of techniques recognize that data design is at least as important as functional design, if not more so. They also stress the necessity of analysis and design for getting programming *right*.

As they developed increasingly larger systems, programmers began to realize that the procedure-oriented languages didn't provide the tools they needed for such concepts as *data abstraction*, *data hiding* (also called *encapsulation*), *modularity*, and strong association not only of data types to functions (as with strong typing of arguments and return values), but of functions to data types.

Meanwhile, parallel to the evolution of procedure-oriented languages, a concept of *object-oriented* languages had evolved. During the mid-1960s, several event simulation languages introduced the concepts of *objects* and *classes*. Over the next few decades, these concepts evolved and eventually reached the point at which they could be used to solve the programming and design problems facing today's programmers.

OBJECT-ORIENTED LANGUAGES

As we understand them now, the concepts of *objects* and *classes* are complementary. An *object* is an instantiation of a class, or a member of that class. A *class* is a description of the objects it contains. In object-oriented programming, the design focuses on the class as the unit of modularization, and the object as the unit of programming.

When we talk about *classes* in this chapter, we'll almost always be talking about the object-oriented concept of classes. In Chapter 6, we'll introduce C++'s *class* construct, which is an implementation of this concept.

A class provides the capsule into which you put all the elements of your abstraction, or model, of the part of your program that the class describes. Like a C *struct*, the class contains data members. Also associated with the class are procedures, which are called *methods* in classical object-oriented terminology, or *member functions* in C++. These methods define the relationships between classes. When a method is called to cause an action between two objects (or, in C++, one object's member function is called on another object), this is classically called a *message* between the two objects. Because the class has its own scope, names defined inside the class are local to the class, and must be accessed through the class name or through objects in the class. In C++, names of members in the class can also be hidden inside the class, or they can be made visible to the outside world.

In addition to features for data abstraction, data hiding, and modularity, which are also available (in different ways) in procedure-oriented languages, object-oriented languages offer another concept that isn't found anywhere else. Classes can be defined that *inherit* all of the data and functions that are members of an existing class, and then redefine them or add to them. As a result, we can use a library class that does almost everything we need, and we can add the required functional capabilities without having the original source code or rewriting the library! You'll use this feature extensively when you write code with the Microsoft Foundation Class (MFC) library; you'll base the classes for your code on library classes, inheriting all of their capabilities, and adding those that you need for your particular project.

Our programming paradigm now includes its predecessors, and it goes further. Where previous paradigms based programming modules on procedures, now the "module" is the class, which includes not only data, but the functions that show how the data is to be manipulated. The class hides the details of how an abstracted data type is implemented, and it makes public only the interface between itself and the other modules (classes). In effect, the class *is* an abstraction, or representation, of part of the real world with which the program is dealing. A class also lets the abstraction be extended to handle new situations, because new classes can be created by inheriting all of the attributes and actions of the existing class. Our new analysis and design methods need to reflect these new ways of looking at the program.

Is this the "silver bullet," the ultimate programming tool that solves all of our problems and makes programming as easy as a walk on the beach? Of course not. Already, various problems and disagreements are being discussed in committees and on the pages of the programming journals. From them will come extensions and offshoots that will once again change our programming paradigms. Or perhaps new ideas will come from a startling new direction. For now, however, object-oriented programming takes the older programming paradigms and reworks them into a model of programming that is — once learned — easier and safer than what we've had before.

Object-Oriented Programming, Design, and Analysis

As with any form of programming, and perhaps more so than most, object-oriented programming requires proper analysis of the problem that is to be solved, and proper design of a programming solution. The following sections cover some highlights of the analysis and design process, from an object-oriented viewpoint. You'll find various tools for effective analysis and design described in books by Booch, Coad and Yourdon, Rumbaugh et al., Shlaer and Mellor, Yourdon, and others (see the Recommended Reading list at the end of this book). These sources introduce several notation styles that can be helpful in the analysis and design of your programs. It's as true in programming as in any other discipline: "If you don't write it down, you didn't do it." Having a way to write down your analysis and design results keeps them useful long after you might have forgotten them, and lets you pass them on to others. The notations can also help you better understand and express the concepts we describe in the following sections, and they may help you uncover design flaws in your programs.

TERMINOLOGY

The following sections define several terms that are often used in discussions about object-oriented techniques. Several of these terms are also used in other programming methodologies.

Data abstraction

Abstraction is something we do every day. Looking at an object, we see those things about it that have meaning to us. We *abstract* the properties of the object, and keep only what we need.

In data abstraction, we need to do consciously what we do unconsciously all the time. We need to look at the problem we're trying to model in our program, and at the physical or conceptual entities and actions that make up the problem. We need to find the properties that will help us solve our problem, and then use only that *abstraction* of the problem and its elements in our problem-solving efforts and our program design.

Abstraction usually occurs at several different levels, which is helpful in object-oriented design and programming. At a higher level of abstraction, a problem might seem to consist of the interaction of certain objects. At a finer level of abstraction, some of those objects might be decomposed into other objects with their own interactions. For example, if we are designing an office-wide project management system, at one level we're looking at interactions among different components of the company: different divisions and different senior managers. Within the various components, though, there may be different ideas about how their part of the project should be managed. As a result, you must deal with a finer level of abstraction, and you must work with different models of the same concept simultaneously.

Data abstraction is a basic feature of object-oriented programming. Classes are abstractions of things or ideas. Objects are instances of those classes.

Data hiding

Anyone who has designed library routines for use by other programmers has faced the problem of anticipating how the routines might be misused or abused. This problem is typically solved by creating an interface that's publicly known, and then trying to ensure that the interface is the only part of the implementation to which programmers have access.

This concept is known as *data hiding*, or *encapsulation*. The programming language that is used contributes greatly to the programmer's ability to hide information. If variables are global, none of that information can be hidden. If routines are global, a clever programmer can access and use routines that are supposed to be internal to the implementation. If data types (such as C structs) are freely available, the clever programmer could also access and use data elements that aren't part of the published interface to do things in a "clever" way. This is done more often than we care to think about with C stdio, which is why so many "clever" programs break when compiled with a version of stdio that is fundamentally different from the original version.

Data hiding is also a basic feature of object-oriented programming. As much as possible, the basic data, functions, and even structures are hidden within the class definitions. They can be accessed only by the objects that are in those classes. (In C++, you can also define *friend*s of those classes, which are not in the class but still have access to its members. Although this isn't part of classical OOP, it's a very useful compromise.)

Modularity

You can think of a modular program as a collection of little black boxes. Each black box deals with its own part of the problem. It takes its input, gives its output, and helps support the program in just that one, small way. Each box does one thing, but does it well. If you remove one little black box and replace it with another one that is completely different internally but behaves exactly the same externally, nothing in the program is affected.

In a modular program, anything in the program having to do with the module is right there in the module. As a result, you can predict what will happen for any given action, which is always helpful for proper programming. You won't encounter cases in which an action in another module — for example, changing the values of shared data — affects what happens in the current module.

Modularity is also considered a basic feature of object-oriented programming. Effective modularization supports effective data hiding, and vice versa. Classes are the modules of object-oriented programming.

Inheritance

Inheritance is a unique and essential quality of object-oriented programming. In other forms of programming, data types don't have hierarchical parent-child relationships with each other. In object-oriented programming, one class can *inherit* all of the data and functions that are members of another class. In addition, the inheriting class can define its own data and functions, and in the process change the meanings it gives to some of the inherited data and functions. In this way, a program can use objects in a class of its own that performs tasks unique to that program, while still being able to use all of the capabilities associated with the library class that provides a basis for the new class.

Many names have been used to describe the relationship between a parent class and its children. *Parent* and *child* are often used. They are also called a *base* class and its *derived* or *inherited* classes. The child class is a more specialized, restrictive class than the parent — everything that "is a" child-class member also "is a" parent-class member, but not vice versa. As such, some developers also use the terms *subclass* for the child and *superclass* for the parent. These different terms all mean the same thing; they just highlight different facets of the same relationship. These terms used in discussing general object-oriented programming are also used to describe their implementation in the C++ version of classes.

One good test for an inheritance relationship was referred to in the preceding paragraph. This is the "is-a" test. If everything that "is a" member of the child class also "is a" member of the parent class (but not necessarily vice versa), then that's a good indication for an inheritance relationship. For example, if we have a class of trees (the biological kind), a class of maples, and a class of pines, then we know that a pine "is a" tree, and a maple "is a" tree. But it's not true that a pine "is a" maple. In other words, the classes of pines and maples are good child classes for the tree class, but not for each other.

Multiple inheritance occurs when a class inherits from more than one parent class. This isn't allowed in all object-oriented programming languages, but it is possible in C++. Multiple inheritance causes some problems in ambiguity, and is usually not necessary. However, for the few cases in which objects in a class really do belong to two independent classes, multiple inheritance can be very helpful.

Polymorphism is another term related to inheritance. This term requires some explanation.

When writing programs, we typically expect that the type of an object is known at compile time. If a routine deals with objects in a particular class, we can pass to it objects of that class or objects of any derived class. Once inside the routine, all objects are treated as being objects of the base class. This is usually appropriate, because only the common data and functional elements inherited from the base class are being used. However, there may be circumstances in which it's more appropriate for some part of the routine to act differently for different derived classes.

Polymorphic People

Polymorphism means having different forms, or different roles. We'll illustrate this concept by describing how a person can be polymorphic, and then bring this analogy back to classes. Because people are such complex entities, we'll limit our observations to just a couple of qualities.

We're all human beings; we can think of this as our base class. As members of this class, we share certain common attributes such as sleeping, eating, and drinking. For our example, we'll also classify people by their training in first aid and emergency medicine. Separating them out by their specialized training is much the same thing that we do in C++ when we define multiple *subclasses* for more specialized objects, that are still also members of their base classes. We declare them to show their most complete set of capabilities: Dr. Rick and Nurse Kyle; Paramedic Cindy and EMT Joe; First-Aider Chris and Citizen Kurt. During their work day (or night!), we can readily see which is in class by their uniforms and actions.

But these people are still also humans, and have all of the attributes and actions of humans. When they go out to eat at a restaurant, they're not normally distinguishable. At the restaurant, they're all dressed in regular clothes, and they all eat in more or less the same way. At the restaurant, they're just acting as humans. In the same way, a C++ object that's using one of the base class's member functions is indistinguishable from any other object that shares the same base class and is using that function.

If a medical emergency arose in the restaurant, though, the people with specialized training would act differently from other people who might be present. The EMT would exhibit the attributes and actions that are unique to the subclass of humans known as EMTs. Members of the other subclasses would act according to the specific training given at those levels. When the situation is over, they can resume the more general role played by a member of the class of humans. The quality of *polymorphism* is what allows the more specialized, subclass role to be called on, even though the object is acting in its role as a member of its superclass, or base class. While it's acting solely as a member of its base class, you can't superficially tell it from any other member of the base class, But, for specific situations, you can have it act in its special role as a member of its subclass. The object has to change its role — to "morph" to its more specialized self — to be able to use its own routines. This is polymorphism.

If a language is *polymorphic*, it allows certain elements to be defined on a per-class basis. For those elements, the program automatically determines the object's "real" type, and decides which version of the element should be used. Using these elements, a routine can then do the appropriate thing for each derived class. C++ implements polymorphism through the use of virtual functions, which are discussed in Chapter 6.

Persistence

Persistence is the life of a data object. It's sometimes confused with *scope*, which is the part of a program within which the name of the object is recognized. Sometimes the two can be different. An object within a program may have a shorter life than its name. It may outlast its name, but be unusable; or it may last longer than the program, but still be usable in a future instance of the same or different programs.

If a variable is local to a functional block, and that variable names an object, it seems reasonably clear that the lifetime of the object and its name are much the same. Even if an object is global to a program, the scope and the lifetime of the object would seem to be the same as the life of the program. The object *persists* for exactly the lifetime of the variable, and then disappears.

But if we have a pointer, ptr, to an object, the name of the object — that is, the de-referenced pointer (*ptr) — exists before the object is allocated, and it exists after the object is destroyed. The object's persistence is less than the life of its name. As many novice programmers have found, if the program tries to de-reference the pointer before the object is allocated or after it's de-allocated, the program will behave incorrectly and often crash.

On the other hand, if the object to which a pointer refers isn't destroyed before leaving the scope of the pointer, the object may well persist, but we have no way of referencing it, because its name is gone. The object will continue to persist uselessly until the program ends, unless some type of garbage collection can find it and destroy it before then.

An object can also persist between invocations of a program. Of course, such data must be stored somewhere between invocations of the program. When used in this way, a persistent object can be referenced each time a program is invoked, and the object can consistently have the same data, or it can retain any changes that have been made. This capability, which requires special support, is often used to store such state information as the locations of windows and icons, and user prefer-ences. (Because the term *persistent object* is used to refer to objects that persist between uses in programs, some books only refer to this part of an object's life when talking about persistence, rather than the object's entire life. This is usually done when talking about some particular implementation of persistence, when that part of the object's life is the only part that causes a persistence-related problem! Realizing that persis-tence does refer to an object's entire life can sometimes help lead to innovative ideas on how to handle persistence problems.)

OBJECT-ORIENTED ANALYSIS AND DESIGN

In object-oriented programming, analysis of the problem proceeds in somewhat the same way that it does in other types of programming. We still break down the problem into more manageable components, or sub-problems. However, where we used to look for *procedures* (which are actions), and then determined which procedures called each other and what data they used, we now break down the problem into classes of *objects* (which are things), and look for the relationships and interactions among the classes of objects.

A *class* defines a group of objects, so we are looking for common characteristics of things in the problem domain. Do we have a group of machines with common characteristics? Do we have a group of geomet-ric patterns with common traits that can be handled similarly under cer-tain circumstances? Do we have a group of people with some common characteristics (for example, all have names, ages, and social security numbers)? If so, we have a class.

The first important point to remember, when doing this level of abstraction, is that the characteristics we want to consider are those that are important to the problem. For example, if we are designing a pay-roll system, it is completely unimportant whether any of the people have red hair. (It might even be cause for a discrimination lawsuit!) On the other hand, hair color might be quite relevant if we are designing a dating service program or emulating a Sherlock Holmes mystery story.

Next, we need to consider class relationships. Do any members of a class require special treatment or have special properties besides what we would normally have for members of that class? If so, we might need to define a *subclass*. In the payroll example, we might have one special subclass for employees who are managers, another for salespeople (who work on commission), and yet another for nonexempt employees (who are paid hourly wages plus overtime).

On the other hand, we may design some classes that have similarities and can be treated the same way in some instances. In such cases, we may want to group these classes into *superclasses* that share common code for handling these similar circumstances, rather than rewriting essentially the same code for each class. For a drawing program, we might design classes of shapes, including circles, squares, arcs, and lines. Having written down these separate classes, we might find that they share several characteristics, such as being shown on a specific display, being placed at a specific point on the display, being visible or not, containing other shapes, being contained by other shapes, or being attached to other shapes.

Throughout this chapter, we've been discussing *inheritance* relationships. One way to characterize these relationships is by asking whether a member of one class is a member of another class. Is a manager also an employee? Is a salesperson an employee? If so, we should probably handle those classes as subclasses of the employee class. Is a square a displayable shape? Is an arc a displayable shape? If so, shape is a good superclass for those shapes.

It's important to define a useful inheritance hierarchy, and to know where in your hierarchy certain operations belong. If certain operations belong in a superclass, it doesn't make sense to repeat them in slightly different form in a subclass. If the language supports *polymorphism* (as we'll find C++ does, through *virtual member functions*), a general routine can be written for the superclass that performs slightly different and appropriate actions for each subclass. On the other hand, if an operation must determine which "real" class an object belongs to, and support different actions for objects of different types, these actions should probably move down the hierarchy to a subclass.

Figure 4-3 shows a class diagram for a possible payroll program. The Employee class contains general information that's important for paying all employees. The Manager and Salesperson classes are subclasses of the Employee class. They inherit all of the data and functions of the Employee class, while adding new ones that are appropriate for those more specialized subclasses.

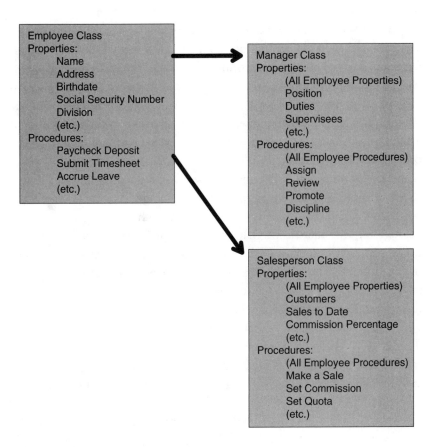

Figure 4-3
A simple example of class inheritance.

Another type of relationship is characterized by whether a member of one class contains a member of another class. For example, an auto dealership has a stock of tires of different types, as well as a stock of cars. If there's some reason to break down the components of the car, then one class that will be contained in the auto class is the tire class. For this example, we'll be specific about the fact that a car has a right-front tire (as well as a left-front, right-rear, left-rear, and spare tire), because it's physically possible that some misguided but enthusiastic mechanic might put a different type of tire in each location. As a result, the auto class will have at least five instances of the tire class (after all, we want to count the spare). This type of "containing" relationship, in which one class is part of another class, is called *aggregation*.

The other relationship between classes that we need to consider involves their actions on one another. In the payroll example, we might have an employee payroll account — account being a financial class that we haven't mentioned — and this class may "pay" the employees. The employee might arrange for the "pay" to occur as a direct deposit, as a mailed check, as a hand-delivered check, as a check going in a batch to a remote location, or in some other form — perhaps as benefits, goods, or services. For each of these cases, we have to decide which properties (data) of each class will change, and who (which objects of which class) should have the authority to make those changes.

As much as possible, we want to make each class responsible for maintaining the data inside that class and inside objects of that class. By doing so, our program is more reliable and consistent. Classical object-oriented terminology calls an action of one class on another a *message* between the two classes. Rather than allowing an outside procedure to reach in, take money from the account object, and put the money into the employee object, the account object takes a certain amount of money from *itself* (!), and sends a message to the employee object, which then accepts the message (and the money!) and deposits the money appropriately. When we get into the design of a program, we will be trying to give each class as much authority and control over its inner workings as possible. By doing so, we encapsulate and modularize the abstraction of whatever thing or concept the class is supposed to represent.

It's difficult to get very far in the analysis phase without considering some element of the program design. The design is likely to be influenced by the programming language used, because different languages have different properties. This isn't necessarily a problem. After all, you want to take advantage of a language's capabilities. Problems arise when you start doing analysis, design, and programming all at the same time. Although you can consider the final program during analysis and design, programming language constructs and phrases really don't have a place in analysis and design. Some programmers like to use C-like pseudocode during design; but without strict personal discipline, this is likely to degenerate into simultaneous design and programming.

When translating your object-oriented analysis into a design for a C++ program, you should consider the features that C++ offers. For example, C++ allows the class to have control — via *constructor* functions — over the initialization of its objects, whether they're created by entering a function or a block or by allocating an object using the *new* operator. With its *destructor* functions, C++ also allows the class to have control over what happens when the object goes away by the program exiting its block or, if it's an allocated object, by having the *delete* operator called on it. C++ also supports *multiple inheritance*, which allows classes to inherit from more than one class. However, this capability is not to be taken lightly. It should be used only if a class absolutely must inherit from two unrelated inheritance hierarchies.

We'll go into more detail about these and other topics in C++ design and programming later in this part of the book. First, we'll describe some of the features of C++ that will not be familiar to the C programmer. We'll start with some small differences that you might find in a C++ program.

5 Small Differences between C and C++

*A*t some time in your programming career, you might have read a C++ program and been lulled into thinking it was a familiar C program. This isn't at all surprising; C++ is rooted in C, and the descendants of the original language processor still translate C++ into C before compiling a program. However, you can get tripped up by some small differences between C and C++. This chapter will help you understand and recognize those small differences.

The chapters in this part of the book focus on C++, the language, and only rarely mention Microsoft Visual C++, the software product. Before we start in on C++, though, you may want to read Chapter 3, "Understanding the Visual C++ Tools." This chapter describes how to use the tools provided by the Visual C++ IDE, so you can try out some of the features we describe here.

To help you understand the relationship between C and C++, we'll start with a brief history of the two languages. We'll then dive into the differences between C and C++.

A Brief History of C and C++

The C programming language was originally written by Dennis Ritchie at AT&T Bell Labs in 1972 for the 16-bit DEC PDP-11 minicomputer. It was written as part of the effort to modularize the fledgling UNIX operating system and to write most of the OS and the system applications in a higher-level language. The C language is thus designed from the start as both a systems programming language and an applications language. Within a year, C was ported to a variety of other machine architectures. In 1978, Ritchie and Steve Johnson wrote the Portable C Compiler (pcc), which — along with the UNIX operating system — has since been ported to almost every computer architecture imaginable.

The C language evolved somewhat between 1972 and 1978, when Brian Kernighan and Dennis Ritchie published their book, *The C Programming Language*. Since that time, their book has defined the version of C known as "K&R C." Of course, vendors all added their own extra features — also known as incompatibilities — to their respective versions. In 1983, an ANSI standards committee was convened to define a standard version of C. The committee took input from numerous sources, including another new offshoot of C called C++. In 1989, the ANSI committee published its standard; and in 1990, the joint ANSI/ISO committee published the international standard that we use today.

Meanwhile, in 1979, Bjarne Stroustrup had the idea of adding object-oriented classes to C. His first language, C with Classes, was reported on within Bell Labs in 1980, and outside Bell Labs in 1982. In 1984, this language matured into C++. The original version, called *Cfront*, was implemented as a front-end preprocessor that translated C++ into C for compilation by a native C compiler. Starting in 1987, numerous different compilers implemented the language both as front ends to C and as native compilers, and several programming support environments were built.

In the years 1985 to 1991, between the first and second editions of Stroustrup's book *The C++ Programming Language* (C++/PL), the C++ language evolved greatly, partly due to the USENIX C++ conferences held in those years. In 1990, the ANSI C++ standards committee first met, and Stroustrup submitted his new *Annotated C++ Reference Manual* (ARM) to start the standardization work. In 1991, the ISO and ANSI committees started meeting together, to make the resulting standard a truly international standard.

As of 1995, the Draft Standard has been submitted for recognition as a standard. This isn't an automatic process, but it's likely that the first ANSI/ISO C++ Standard will be dated 1995. Then the Committee will go back to consider what should be put in the next C++ Standard.

Stronger Data Typing

We'll start looking at the differences between C and C++ by examining the strong typing done in C++. Strong typing means that the language strongly enforces a matching of data types in such things as function arguments and returns, and assignments of values to variables. Strong typing in C++ is not a separate, specific feature. It is a basic design criterion underlying a number of different features. Strong typing helps the person who is trying to write correct programs.

For C programmers, what does stronger typing mean? It means that a C++ program must explicitly specify a host of things that a C programmer might assume to be defaults. For example, a C++ program must explicitly declare integer arguments and return values to functions; it must define routines that return no value as void; and it must declare all routines (or #include their declarations) before using them. In C++, you cannot assume that all pointers are interchangeable, nor can you assume that they are all really integer-type objects.

On the other hand, when programming in C++, you are assured that you are not accidentally calling a routine with the wrong argument type — you literally can't! What's more, because C++ is so strict about requiring arguments to a function to be of the types declared for that function, C++ can have function and operator *overloading*, which allows you to define the same function or operator in several different ways, depending on what types of data are passed to them!

The following sections describe differences between C and C++ that specifically have to do with data types. Later in this chapter, we'll describe more differences that relate to stronger data typing.

CHAR IS A REAL DATA TYPE

In C, char is sort of a second-class data type. You can define objects as type char; but to do any work with them, including passing them to functions and returning them from functions, the compiler promotes them to int type values.

With the stronger typing in C++, char is a full data type in its own right. It does not have to become an int of any sort before it can be useful.

A char literal is not an int, as it is in C; it has the type and size of a char. This is similar to the strengthening of float and the separation of float from double that occurred in ANSI/ISO C.

The important point to remember here is that you should not assume that a char looks, acts, or has the size of an int. This point also becomes significant when we talk about function and operator overloading, as well as in general for well-structured, object-oriented design.

Char Arrays Are No Bigger Than You Make Them

In C, it is perfectly legal, although not good practice, to declare a character array whose size is determined solely by its initializer. In some C compilers — although not in ANSI/ISO C — you can declare an array that has an initializer that is larger than the array itself, and the compiler will either expand the array to fit the initializer or truncate the initializer:

```
char hi[10]   = "Hello, world"; /* Actually 13 */
```

C++ has a much stricter view of data type definitions. An array must have a declared size, and an array of N characters must contain no more than N characters, including any terminating NUL character. The preceding example is not legal in C++. You must avoid anything like it; instead, make sure that your array is at least as large as its initializer:

```
char hi2[16]  = "Hello, world";
```

wchar_t Is a Data Type, Not a Typedef

In C, the wide character data type, wchar_t, is defined in a header file as a typedefed data type. If the particular header file in which it's defined (which should be <stddef.h>) isn't included, the data type doesn't get defined.

In C++, wchar_t is a basic, built-in type. It provides a wider type for holding as large a character as is needed by the largest character set a given C++ compiler supports. The wchar_t data type has one of the integer data types as its *underlying type*, and wide character objects behave like the underlying type. Other than that, wide character strings follow the same rules as regular character strings. Just as in C, wide character literals and strings are written as follows:

```
wchar_t x_wide          = L'X';
wchar_t hi_and_wide[16]  = L"Hello, world";
```

Regular character objects and strings should never be mixed with wide character objects and strings.

The actual underlying type used in a given implementation depends on the largest character size the implementors feel they'll need to handle. Unicode is a 16-bit character set that's now widely used (pun accidental). Unicode has been merged with the new 32-bit ISO 10646 character set standard, and is now a subset of it.

ENUMS ARE REAL, DISTINCT DATA TYPES

In C, enumeration type objects (enums) are basically syntactic sugar sprinkled over integer type objects (ints). In other words, in C, any enum or int value can be assigned to any enum variable, whether or not the value is an enum of the variable's type, and even whether or not it's within the enum variable's range! In C++, each enum is a type of its own. This means that you may not freely assign an int or an enum to another enum type. It also means that the size of any given enum will be whatever the compiler wants to give it, which may be different from the size of an int, as it was in C.

For example, two enum types are defined in Figure 5-1, with one object of each type. As shown in this example, it is *only* legal to assign a value of the same enum type to each of the enum objects. It is *not* legal to assign an integer value to an enum object.

However, it is legal to assign an enum to an int. The enum is promoted to its underlying integer representation.

You probably noticed that our declarations of the two data objects are also different from those in C. This is another small difference between C and C++. This difference is discussed in the section, "Type Specifications Also Define Type Names," later in this chapter.

```
enum color {red, orange, yellow, green, blue, violet};
enum menu {File, Edit, View, Insert, Format, Help};

color my_color;
menu my_menu;

my_color = red;          /* valid */
my_menu = File;          /* valid */
my_color = File;         /* invalid in C++ */
my_color = 1;            /* invalid in C++ */

if (sizeof(int) == sizeof(color)) {
        /* implementation dependent in C++ */
}
```

Figure 5-1
Enums are distinct data types.

Data Structure Enhancements

Data structures in C++ are defined with the type specifiers *struct*, *union*, and *class*. The C++ implementation of a class is a new and essential concept in C++, and we will discuss it in detail in the next chapter. For now, you should just be aware that its syntax is an extension of that of the C-language struct. In C++, a struct is defined as a special kind of class. A union is also a special kind of class: one that has only one member, with different ways of looking at that member.

Because classes are special to C++, and need to represent the object-oriented concept of class, their syntax includes a number of changes from that of C structs. Some of these changes simply make classes easier to use. Other changes tighten up the concepts of classes, structs, and unions, and clarify the differences among them. These changes are discussed in the following sections.

Enumeration types are defined with the type specifier enum. Although enumerations are not the same as data structures, their declarations are syntactically similar, and some of the following sections also apply to enums.

TYPE SPECIFICATIONS ALSO DEFINE TYPE NAMES

If we construct a data type using the type specifiers struct, union, enum, or class, the construct name defines a data type name. For example, in Figure 5-1, we defined an enum color, and subsequently used color as a data type name, just as though we had defined it using typedef. This is done so that user-defined types can be used as naturally as predefined types. If you want, however, you can still use the type specifier before the name:

```
enum color foreground;
```

In fact, there are cases in which you still *must* use the type specifier. This is necessary to distinguish the type name from a different use of the same name in the same scope.

Obviously, you can't construct two types with the same construct name. Similarly, you can't use typedef to define a type name that's the same as a construct name.

TYPES MAY NOT BE DEFINED IN PASSING

In C, types may be defined wherever they are used. For example, they may be defined in expressions such as type casts and calls to sizeof( ), in declarations of function arguments, and in declarations of function return values.

In C++, every defined data type is unique, whether or not it resembles another data type. (We discuss this further in the next section, "Identical Structures Are Not Interchangeable.") Consequently, definitions "in passing" are not allowed in C++. Types should be defined at a global scope, typically in header files. If a data type must be local to a source file or a function, it may be defined within the file. To ensure that we always know where to find them, we define ours at the beginning of their scopes.

Figure 5-2 shows examples of several miscreant data type definitions. If you've never done anything like this, so much the better; these represent fairly bad programming practices. However, we have seen these things done before, and C code that uses these constructs and isn't changed will fail in C++.

```
struct { int x; } *p;          /* This code is legal. */
p = (struct { int x; } *) NULL;      /* This is not. */

struct mach_reg { int x; } *getreg(int addr)
{
        /*
        ** Not legal C++.
        */
}

int reg_value(struct mr { int x; } *reg)
{
        /*
        ** Also not legal.
        */
}
```

Figure 5-2
Types illegally defined in passing.

Note that the untagged type declaration in the first line then leaves you with an object whose type you can never again reference, because the type doesn't have a name! Not the best of ideas. In the getreg( ) and reg_value( ) functions, even though the defined types do have name tags, the types are only defined within the scope of their respective functions. That leaves the returned or passed data objects also unnamed outside of the functions! This is not good, usable code.

IDENTICAL STRUCTURES ARE NOT INTERCHANGEABLE

In C, it's possible to have two "compatible" structure types specified whose members all have the same names and types, and to have objects of these two different types used interchangeably. In C++, each type specification defines a new and distinct type. In Figure 5-3, the three different structs are in fact different, non-interchangeable data types, which is different from what is allowed in C.

```
struct complex { double real, imaginary; };
struct cplx { double real, imaginary; };

complex c1;
cplx c2;
struct { double real, imaginary } c3;
```

```
complex result;

complex inverse(complex x);

result = inverse(c1);      /* valid */
result = inverse(c2);      /* not valid in C++ */
result = inverse(c3);      /* not valid in C++ */
```

Figure 5-3
Similarly constructed data types can no longer be used in place of each other.

A STRUCTURE HAS A SCOPE

The ANSI/ISO C standard describes four types of scope for identifiers. Two of these are used for most types of identifiers in the many different ways that identifiers can be used. These are *file* scope, which is used for identifiers that are seen throughout a source code file; and *block* scope, which is used for identifiers that are seen only within a block, such as a function definition block or a control structure block. The other two types of scope are *function* scope, which is used only for labels, and *function prototype* scope, which is used only for the variables in a function prototype.

Appropriately, C++ introduces a new type of scope which is associated with data structures. *Class* scope refers to all structures, such as structs, classes, and unions. Anything declared within the definition of one of these data structures is local to that structure.

This concept should be familiar to you, because structure member names have been "local" to structs for the past few versions of C. This concept has been extended so that all declarations within a structure are local to that structure. As shown in Figure 5-4, this means that a substructure defined within a structure (a nested structure) is local to that structure. As we'll see in the next chapter, this concept is also very important when we are dealing with structures' *member functions* (a concept we'll also define in that chapter).

In this example, the internal structure can't be used outside the scope of the external structure. However, the example also shows that a scope can be extended outside, when necessary, using the *scope resolution* operator. Details on how and when this can be used are discussed in the next chapter.

```
struct box {
        int type;
        struct size {
                int height;
                int width;
        };
};

box my_box;        /* This is fine, of course. */
size my_size;      /* This is not legal C++. */

/*
** The "::" operator can be used to make something
** defined within a structure visible outside of that structure.
** This operator will be discussed at length in the next
** chapter.
*/
box::size my_size;   /* This is now legal. */
```

Figure 5-4
The internal structure's scope is the external structure.

Objects that are local to a structure can always be accessed by objects and functions that are within the scope of the structure. If the programmer has granted certain privileges, those objects can also be accessed outside the class scope, either through an object of that type or through the data type itself. We'll discuss this in greater detail in the next chapter.

NAMELESS UNIONS INSIDE AND OUTSIDE STRUCTURES

In C, every substructure within a structure must have a name. As shown in Figure 5-5, when structures are nested, the result may be complex terms, such as:

```
procp->p_uid.pu_integer
```

As shown in Figure 5-6, the particular case of a union inside a struct or class is easier to handle in C++. You can leave the union nameless and simply use the name of the union member as though it were a member of the struct or class. This union is called an *anonymous* union. This isn't a union with a hidden name, as the term might imply. It's an unnamed union that doesn't declare any members in the scope of the class in which it's defined.

```
/*
** A C-language structure with a union inside must have a
** name for the union.
*/

struct proc {
        ...
        union {
                long int pu_long;
                int pu_integer;
                char *pu_name;
        } p_uid;
        ...
};

struct proc *procp;

/*
** Note that the union name is required to address a
** member of the union.
*/
...
int n = procp->p_uid.pu_integer;
```

Figure 5-5

A union inside a C-language structure.

```
/*
** A C++ structure with a union inside does not need a
** name for the union. The members of that union are
** addressed as though they were members of the structure.
*/

struct proc {
        ...
        union {
                long int p_long;
                int p_integer;
                char *p_name;
        };
        ...
};

proc *procp;

/*
** Note that the union name is not required to address a
** member of the union.
*/
...
int n = procp->p_integer;
```

Figure 5-6

A union inside a C++ structure.

Anonymous unions may also be used outside of other structures. If the anonymous union is defined in a function, or outside any function or class, the members can be used as though they were variables in the scope in which they were defined. In this case, there can't be any variables declared with the anonymous union as their type. If the union is defined at file scope, it must also be declared static. There are further restrictions on anonymous unions described in C++/PL or the Draft Standard.

Rules for Data Objects

Because we are working in an object-oriented language, we must be very clear about where data objects are defined, and what their scopes are. This section presents some of the rules for defining data objects and their scopes in C++. Other rules are either identical to those for C or useful only in arcane situations that are beyond the scope of this book.

DATA OBJECTS MUST BE INITIALIZED EXACTLY ONCE

Some C compilers and linkers allow an object to be initialized in several different source files, as long as it is initialized in the same way. C++ has an explicit rule that objects may be initialized in only one location. This rule removes any possibility of an object appearing to be initialized to different values in different locations. More important, it removes any possibility that code will be broken because a person who is maintaining the code has changed an object's initialization in only one place when the object is initialized in more than one place.

CONST DATA OBJECTS MUST BE INITIALIZED

As you probably know from ANSI/ISO C, data objects may be declared const to inform the compiler that they will not change while the program is running. The C++ compiler may then do to them whatever else it might choose, such as putting them into read-only memory segments, or even using inline constants instead! (Obviously, it can't use inline constants when the program does things like taking the address of the constant data object.)

Because you can't modify a const data object, it *must* be initialized when it is declared. If the const data object has also been declared extern, this may be done in exactly one place in all the modules that are linked together in any one program.

This seems fairly obvious. In C, it is possible, although perhaps not always meaningful, to declare an uninitialized const object. This is forbidden in C++.

CONST DATA OBJECTS ARE STATIC BY DEFAULT

If you define a data object as const, it will be static unless you explicitly declare it extern. Because of this, you can (and should!) use const objects in your programs to refer to constant values. This is preferable to using constant values defined by the #define preprocessor directive. Const data objects can be handled the same way any other data objects are handled, while constants that you #define can't.

If you declare a const data object as extern, it must be declared as extern in all of your source files. It's probably best to declare it in a header file. However, it still must be defined and initialized in only one location.

CONST DATA OBJECTS MAY BE USED IN PLACE OF CONSTANTS

You can use const data objects anywhere that a constant can be used. In particular, integer const objects (or floating const objects that are cast to integers) may be used as array sizes in declarations, in case expressions, as bit-field lengths in data structures, and as initializers in enumerations.

CONST AND VOLATILE POINTER USE

The rules for using the *const* and *volatile* type specifiers in C are slightly different from the rules for using them in C++. The differences are primarily in pointer assignments, and sometimes cause misunderstandings.

Throughout the discussion of assignments in this chapter, you should remember that the same rules hold for the implicit assignment to an argument in a function call.

The const keyword should be familiar to ANSI/ISO C programmers, but it originated in C++. Programmers who are more familiar with K&R C may not be as familiar with const. We'll describe its use first. We'll introduce volatile, which has very similar syntax but a totally different meaning, later in this section.

The const keyword is simply a signal to the compiler that it is not allowed to do anything that might change the value of the object that it modifies. This may include a number of restrictions that aren't immediately obvious.

If you declare a simple object as const, it's fairly obvious that that object becomes unchangeable:

```
const long int liLength     = 65536L;
```

In C++, this can even be used in places where C only allows defined constants to be used. The keyword const may be used either before or after the data type name. If a data structure is declared const, all members of that structure are unchangeable, with one exception. If you want to make sure that specific members of a data structure remain changeable, you can declare them *mutable* (this is not yet implemented in Microsoft's Visual C++ 2.0).

If you use the const keyword in the declaration of a pointer object, there are three places you can put it, with two different possible meanings. If you put the const either immediately before or after the type of the object at which the pointer is pointing, you're declaring a pointer to a const object:

```
const char *hi1     = "Hello, world!";
char const *hi2     = "Hello, world!";
```

This declaration says that the pointer points to something that's a char or an array of char, and will treat it as const — that is, unchangeable. The object to which either of these pointers is pointing may not be changed. However, you can change the pointer itself. You can assign to it any pointer to either a const char or a char (that is, the address of any const char or char). Assigning it a pointer to char is called "increasing the const-ness," which is perfectly allowable. It just means that a non-const char or array of char won't be changed through that pointer.

However, in C++ you may *not* assign the value of a pointer to a const char or the address of a const char to a pointer to char (without performing a cast). The reason is simple: if you could do that, the program could change the const char through the char * variable! A cast, of course, is your last-ditch tool to break all strong typing promises and make the program do what you think it should:

```
char *cp    = hi1;           /* Illegal. */
char *cp    = (char *) hi1;  /* Legal, but dangerous! */
```

Anytime you do a cast like this, you should stop and think whether this is actually breaking your program design in some way.

The third place to put the const is directly in front of the pointer variable name:

```
char * const hi3    = "Hello, world!";
```

In this declaration, the pointer itself is const. You may not change its value. You may, however, change the value of the object at which it's pointing! The following is accepted by the compiler:

```
*hi3 = 'J';
printf("%s\n", hi3);
```

This produces:

```
Jello, world!
```

If you want to keep both the pointer and the object to which it points unchangeable, you must use const twice:

```
const char * const hi4    = "Hello, world!";
```

So far, so good. When we start getting to pointers to pointers to objects, though, people start having problems. Let's go through some scenarios:

```
const char **cpp;     /* pointer to pointer to const char */
char const **cpp;     /* same */
char * const *cpp;    /* pointer to const pointer to char */
char ** const cpp;    /* const pointer to pointer to char */

/* pointer to const pointer to const char */
const char * const *cpp;
```

By now, you may be a little dizzy trying to parse these declarations! Remember that you need to start at a variable, and parse outward. If it helps, you can write things out as follows:

```
const char * const *cpp;
                    cpp is a ...
                    pointer to a ...
           const ...
         pointer to a ...
     char ...
const
"Cpp is a pointer to a const pointer to a char const."
```

When we get to this depth in an actual program, it helps to use typedef to create intermediate names, to keep track of the types.

So, what's the problem with pointer pointers? The problem comes when you want to have a pointer to a char * variable, and you want to assign it to a const char ** variable. This seems like such a reasonable thing to do, because it's just increasing const-ness. C lets you do it. But C++ doesn't.

The problem is that C++ won't allow anything to happen that would allow something it's promised to hold const to be changed. This can allow it! How can that be?

Suppose we take two pointers, one to const char, and one just to char. Let's see what might happen if we allow assignment of the address of the char pointer to a const char ** variable, on the principle of "increasing const-ness":

```
const char **cpp;
const char *hi       = "Hello, world!"
char *cp;

cpp = &cp;      /* Illegal, but let's assume it's not. */
...      /* Stuff happens. */
*cpp = hi;      /* Perfectly legal ... but what has happened? */
```

It's always perfectly legal to assign a const char * value to the pointer pointed to by a const char ** variable (that is, *cpp). But, in the first assignment in this example, we allowed that pointer to be a regular char * pointer. We're now in the very sticky situation of having assigned a const char pointer to a char pointer. This is illegal, because the const char value or array can now be modified through the char pointer!

In C++, to preserve const-ness, you can only add const-ness if the const keyword is added in every place between the first added const and the variable, except at the variable itself. In other words, adding a const must propagate to the right. So, the following two scenarios are valid:

```
char **cpp;
const char * const *CocCopp      = cpp;

char * const *****cCopppppp;
char * const ** const * const * const *cCoppCopCopCopp  = cCopppppp;
                    /* ^ First added "const" must propagate right. */
```

The volatile keyword has a similar syntax, but the meaning is quite different. It tells the compiler that the value of an object might change without the program changing it. This is *not* the opposite of const, but something quite different. It usually means that the volatile object is a memory-mapped I/O address, or a machine register, or shared memory, or something else that can change independently of the actions of the program. As such, it's primarily a suggestion to the compiler, that usually means that references to this value should *not* be heavily optimized. In other words, if the compiler moves the value somewhere else to work on it, it can't assume that the value in the object will stay the same as the value that was stored.

Because the two concepts aren't opposites, there's nothing wrong with declaring an object to be const volatile (or volatile const — the order really doesn't matter). What you are saying with const volatile is that the *program* promises not to change the value, but something else might. You can substitute volatile or const volatile for const in any of the legal statements shown previously in this section, and they would still be legal.

When assigning a value to a variable, you also need to preserve volatile-ness. But, because it means something quite different from const, there isn't a problem in the language with an assignment such as:

```
short int *sp;
volatile short int **vspp    = &sp;
```

Just as with const, the data type of the receiving variable has to have volatile everywhere the original value did. But you can add a volatile at any other place in the new data type! This now allows a back door to assign a volatile {Type} * value to a {Type} * variable; that was prevented with const. We can only guess that the ANSI/ISO committee wasn't as concerned about this, because volatile isn't as strong a promise to the programmer as const. To be safe, you should probably apply the same rules to volatile and const volatile assignments with type conversions as are enforced for const assignments with type conversions.

Nonlocal Data Objects May Be Initialized by Expressions

In C, global external data objects and static data objects can only be initialized using compile-time constants. In C++, you may initialize them using any functions, variables, and other values that are defined at that point.

However, you must be careful when doing this. There is no defined order in which objects will be initialized. If you call a routine that uses other global or static data objects that are initialized in this way, or data objects initialized within main( ), the results will be unpredictable. You could corrupt the data area, crash the program, or initialize your data to something randomly different from what you had intended.

Declarations Are Valid Statements Anywhere

You may need to initialize a data object in a block scope (including in a function) using values that aren't available when you enter its scope. Unlike C, in which all variables must be declared at the beginning of a block scope, C++ allows you to declare variables anywhere that a statement is valid.

You're allowed to do this in order to localize an object's declaration and initialization. As shown in Figure 5-7, the primary reason we use this feature is to initialize an object that has its value calculated from other values not available on scope entry, especially if that object is declared const. We may also use this feature if there's a high cost in program overhead (because of constructor functions) or clarity to initialize a structure separately from its declaration. For all other purposes, we declare our variables at the beginning of a scope. This ensures that we always know where to find declarations.

```
/*
** The draw_screen_box() function draws a character-cell
** box exactly the size of the window. To find the size
** of the window, though, we first need to calculate
** several parameters.
*/
draw_screen_box()
{
        /*
        ** Most declarations are made at the start of the
        ** block, so that we know where to find them.
        */
        register char *cp;
        int i;

        /*
        ** Get the window information in a system-
        ** independent manner, whether it be an MS
        ** Window, an X11 Window, a Mac Window, or even a
        ** physical MS DOS video screen.
        */
        my_window win =
                get_system_independent_window_info();

        ...      / Do something with the window. */

        /*
        ** Get the height and width of the window. These
        ** constants can be computed only after we have
        ** gotten the my_window structure.
        */

        const unsigned int height = get_height(win);
        const unsigned int width = get_width(win);

        /*
        ** The following value can only be created
        ** after the preceding code. Because it's a
        ** more complex object, we declare it where
        ** it's initialized. The reasons for this
        ** are given in the next chapter.
        */
        my_window subwin =
                sub_window(win, 0, 0, width, height/2);

        ...

}
```

Figure 5-7

A case in which declarations must follow other executable statements.

Rules for Functions and Operations

Just as they do in C, C++ functions and operations define actions that may be performed on or with data objects. As detailed in the following sections, the changes that have been made in C++ strengthen the relationships between the functions and their data, and extend the usability of functions and operators.

FUNCTIONS USE PROTOTYPE FORMAT

When defining or declaring functions in C++, you must use the prototype-format parameter syntax, with identifiers declared inside the parameter list. You may not use the older syntax that omits arguments in a function declaration, and in the function definition places function argument types immediately after the function parameter list.

Before using them, you must declare all functions, either in the same source file or (preferably) by including a header file or files that contain the declarations. This gives the compiler the information it needs to verify that arguments of the proper types are being passed. You may no longer use an undeclared function.

A function prototype with empty parentheses, as in the following example, now declares a function with no arguments:

```
int random();
```

It is possible to defeat function prototyping. You can declare a function to have undetermined arguments by using ellipses instead of argument type declarations:

```
int strlen(...);
```

Or, you can use type casts to conceal data objects' real types. However, this is not a good idea; it often highlights a problem with the program design.

FUNCTION RETURN VALUES ARE ENFORCED

In C, you may get warnings if a routine doesn't always return values, but the program will still compile and run. You may also get a compile-time warning if a return value doesn't match the type of the function. This is frequently seen in missing or bad return values from main( ).

In C++, functions that return values must have the returned data type properly declared in the definition and all declarations. Further, all returns must be of the appropriate type. A function that returns no value must be declared void, and it may not return a value in any case.

Interestingly, to support decades of code written without a proper return value from main( ), the sole exception is that main( ) is allowed to just fall through at the end of the routine. This is interpreted as a return(0).

FUNCTION OVERLOADING

When we think about strongly typed functions, we expect that any given function will only accept arguments with a specified set of data types, and will return only one data type. We might also expect to find various functions with different names that each do the same thing on data objects of various types. For example, as in C, there might be different functions to return the absolute values of different numeric data types, such as abs( ) (for integers), labs( ) (for long integers), and fabs( ) (for floating-point numbers).

However, this is not the case in C++! Instead, you can *overload* functions. That is, you can define multiple functions with the same name but different argument types. In C, it would have been possible to define a function with an int argument in one module, and in another module pass that function an object that has a pointer type. C++'s strong typing guarantees that an argument of one type won't be accidentally passed as if it were another type; the correct function will always be called for a given set of arguments. For example, you could define the absolute-value function as shown in Figure 5-8 (capitalized so as not to conflict with the C-library abs( ) function).

Notice that if no function is defined with exactly the argument types used, the C++ compiler does some promotion of integral and floating-point types. It knows exactly which overloads are available, because all functions are prototyped before use, either in the same source file or in an include file.

Overloaded functions are often used in defining functions that are members of classes. This is discussed in the next chapter.

```
struct complex {double real, imag; };

/* For use with char, int, and long int types. */
long int Abs(long int x)
{
        return(x < 0 ? -x : x);
}

/* For use with float and double types. */
double Abs(double x)
{
        return(x < 0.0 ? -x : x);
}

/* For use with complex types. */
complex Abs(complex x)
{
        return(sqrt(x.real * x.real + x.imag * x.imag));
}
```

Figure 5-8
Overloaded absolute value functions.

FUNCTIONS MAY HAVE DEFAULT ARGUMENTS

When you design a function, you may have in mind certain ways in which it will normally be used. In C++, you can design these uses into the function by assigning default values to some or all of the arguments.

When you declare a function prototype with default argument values, all arguments following the first argument with a default value must also have default values. In other words, if one argument has a default value, each of the following arguments *must* have a default value. However, you don't have to declare all defaults in a single prototype. This is shown in Figure 5-9. This allows you to declare some default values for arguments in an include file, and others in the individual source files.

As shown in this example, when calling a function with default values for some of its arguments, you must explicitly specify all of the arguments up to and including the last one that you want to specify. There can be no blank arguments, as allowed in some other languages.

Figure 5-9

A function with default arguments.

```
/*
** The following is a simple example of arguments with
** default values. The draw_circle() routine requires
** the radius argument. However, the x and y arguments
** may be omitted, or just the y argument may be omitted.
*/

int draw_circle(int radius, int x = 0, int y = 0);

/*
** The following are legal calls to this function.
*/

n = draw_circle(5);         /* Circle at 0,0 radius 5 */
n = draw_circle(5, 3);      /* Circle at 3,0 radius 5 */
n = draw_circle(5, 3, 3);   /* Circle at 3,3 radius 5 */

/*
** The following are not legal calls to this
** function.
*/

n = draw_circle();          /* Requires radius. */
n = draw_circle(, 3);       /* Also requires radius. */
n = draw_circle(5, , 3);    /* Can't skip an argument. */

/*
** The following function declaration might appear in a
** header file. Note that the final argument does not
** have a default value. This declaration must be
** supplemented by another one before it is called, to
** give that final argument a default value.
*/

int draw_box(int flag, int x = 0, int y = 0,
             int height = 10, int width = 10,
             enum color hue);

/*
** The following declaration supplements the previous
** example. As in C, the argument names in different
** function prototypes do not have to be identical.
*/

int draw_box(int f, int x, int y, int h, int w, enum
             color h = red);
/*
** Now we have completed the example: there are no "holes"
```

```
** without default values between the first argument with
** a default value and the end of the function prototype.
*/

/*
** The following is not legal C++: the first argument has
** no default value.
*/
i = draw_box();

/* This is fine: it uses all of the defaults. */
i = draw_box(0);

/* Likewise fine: this replaces two defaults. */
i = draw_box(0, 248, 120);

/*
** The following is not legal C++: arguments may not be
** missing.
*/
i = draw_box(0, , , 20, 35);
```

Functions May Be Declared Inline

When writing a function, you might sometimes wonder how efficient it will be for the program to call the function each time it is needed. By declaring a function, you can check argument types and have all the advantages of a function. However, in some cases — the Abs( ) function in Figure 5-8, for example — it might be more efficient if the function were compiled inline. But, how do you know which is more efficient when you are writing the code? More important, because the answer might be different for different machine architectures, how do you do this portably?

For this purpose, C++ has introduced the *inline* function specifier. If you declare your function to be inline, you give the compiler permission to compile the function inline. However, you should note that, depending on the guidelines built into the compiler, it also might not compile the function inline. Like the register storage class specifier, the inline function specifier only gives a suggestion to the compiler.

If the compiler does, in fact, make the function inline, there may be no function address for debuggers. (Think about it.) It is also conceivable that the function might be inlined in some places but not in others. In such cases, there will be an actual function with an address. It's also important that you define an inline function to be inline in every source file in which it appears, and it must be defined the same way in each file. In other words, put it in a header file!

What's the difference between a macro definition in a header file, and an inline function definition in a header file? A macro can't have the full complexity of a function, although (as we'll describe in a moment) you probably don't want to declare very complex functions to be inline. Even more important, an inline function definition gives you strong type checking for arguments and return values, the ability to use default arguments, and all the other advantages of a real function, without necessarily all of the overhead.

There are a few other problems with inline code. Of course, a recursive function could not be inlined even if you specified it as such; there is no general method for automatically turning recursion into iteration (although some computer scientists are still working on it). If long functions are inlined (in C++, if they're marked inline and the compiler goes along with it), there will be a correspondingly large increase in memory space used, and possibly even a decrease in efficiency due to decreased localization of code. In general, it's best to specify as inline only simple, preferably one-line functions. For example, the Abs( ) function that we defined in the discussion of function overloading would be a good candidate for being declared inline.

OPERATOR OVERLOADING

Operators can also be overloaded. This gives you the ability to write programs in a more natural-looking style, treating defined types in the same way as built-in types.

Both unary and binary operators may be overloaded. However, only those operators that are already in C++ may be overloaded, and they must keep the same precedence and associativity as the original operators. In other words, no matter how the operators in the following expression are defined, the * operator must be performed before the + operator:

```
x * y + z
```

Similarly, the following expression must always be performed from right to left:

```
x = y = z
```

And, the following expression must always be performed from left to right:

```
x << y << z
```

You will see an example of this when we briefly discuss C++ iostreams I/O, a bit later in this chapter.

Which C++ operators may be overloaded?

The C++ unary prefix operators are:

```
!
~
+
-
*
&
++
--
new
delete
sizeof
```

Of these operators, sizeof may not be overloaded.

The C++ unary postfix operators are:

```
++
--
```

When overloading them, we can distinguish them from their prefix cousins by pretending that they are binary operators with a second argument that we can always ignore because it is always 0. Although this may seem a bit odd, it solves the problem of differentiating the prefix operators from the postfix operators when overloading.

The C++ binary operators are:

+	-	*	/	%	^
&	|	=	<	>	<=
>=	==	!=	,	+=	-=
*=	/=	%=	^=	&=	|=
<<	>>	<<=	>>=	&&	||
->	.	.*	->*	::	[]
new[]	delete[]				

The following binary operators cannot be overloaded:

```
    .
    .*
    ::
```

The only C++ ternary operator is ?:, as in:

```
(condition) ? (value1) : (value2)
```

This operator may not be overloaded.

The C++ function call is considered an *n*-ary operator, ( ). It may be overloaded.

In the Draft Standard, the typeid function is sometimes considered a unary prefix operator, and sometimes it is not. You can think of the typeid function and the various types of casts as meta-operators, because they deal with types rather than values. They may not be overloaded.

How to overload an operator

An operator may be overloaded by defining a function whose name is the keyword *operator* followed by the operator that is being redefined. The function must have an appropriate return type and arguments: one argument for a prefix unary operator, and two arguments for a binary operator or a postfix unary operator. The function body is just a normal function body; it returns the value that the operation is to return. For example, using the *complex* structure that we defined in Figure 5-3, we could define a + operator as shown in Figure 5-10.

```
struct complex { double real, imaginary };

/*
** This function defines complex addition.
*/
complex operator + (complex a, complex b)
{
        struct complex result;

        result.real = a.real + b.real;
        result.imaginary = a.imaginary + b.imaginary;

        return(result);
}

/* Once we have complex addition, we can do this. */

complex a, b, c;

...     /* (set values for a and b) */

c = a + b;
```

Figure 5-10
A function overloading an operator.

Once the operator overloading is defined for a particular new data type, we can use the overloaded operator for objects of that type anywhere that the declaration of the overload is in scope.

Operator overloading is discussed further in the next chapter. We will describe a more efficient way of defining overloaded operations, as *member functions* of classes. We will find that there is an implicit first argument to a function that is a member of a class; this will modify the number of arguments needed for an *operator* function. In addition, the operators =, ( ), [ ], and -> have special rules for overloading, and may be overloaded only in the context of a class. These special cases are all covered in the next chapter.

STDIO IS NO LONGER THE STANDARD I/O

The C standard I/O package has been replaced by a C++ iostreams class library. Without going into it in detail, if the left operand of the operator << is an iostream, such as cout (which replaces stdout), then output will go to that iostream. If the left operand of the operator >> is an iostream, such as cin (which replaces stdin), then input will be read from that iostream. Here are two iostream equivalents to common C stdio usages:

```
printf("Hello, world #%d\n", 1);    /* becomes: */
cout << "Hello, world #" << 1 << endl;

scanf("%s %d %d\n", str, &i, &j);    /* becomes */
cin >> str >> i >> j;
```

Notice that these have to operate from left to right. Each >> or << operator in turn acts on its right argument, and then returns the iostream to be the left argument for the next operator. For each different data type used as a right argument, a different overloaded operator function is actually called to do the I/O.

This demonstrates a common use of operator overloading in which the overloaded functionality has nothing to do with the original meaning of the operators. The operators retain only their original precedence and associativity — which can't be changed — but those are part of what made these operators ideal for their job. We mention this here because it's confusing to those who see it without recognizing it for what it is, and because it is commonly used outside of Windows programs. Within Windows programs, a different technique is used to display text (see Chapter 13), and this method is used only for file I/O that isn't done through the MFC library.

New C++ Keywords and Operators

The special symbols in this section are new to C++. They are introduced here so that you will recognize them when reading C++ code, so that you won't use them in C code that might someday be ported to C++, and so that you won't accidentally misuse them when writing C++ code.

NEW C++ KEYWORDS

Almost everyone has used some of the following C++ keywords as variable, function, label, or type names in C code. Do not use the following in C++ code except as the keywords that they have become:

catch
class
delete
friend
inline
new
operator
private
protected
public
template
this
throw
try
virtual

The following keywords are defined in the Draft Standard but aren't yet implemented in Microsoft Visual C++ 2.0. You should try to avoid using these keywords as names in your C++ code; or if you do, you should try to define or declare them in a module that can be easily removed (for example, an include file such as bool.h):

asm
bool
const_cast
dynamic_cast
explicit
false
mutable
namespace
reinterpret_cast
static_cast
true
typeid
using
wchar_t

In ANSI/ISO C, the keyword wchar_t, or wide character type, is a defined type, but it is not a keyword. If you don't #include <stddef.h> in a C program, the word is not reserved. In Visual C++ 2.0 (and 2.1), this is conditionally defined in <stddef.h> and a dozen other header files that use it. Microsoft will probably make it a proper keyword in due time.

The following are proposed equivalents for the operators they name. They will be reserved words, but are not yet implemented in Visual C++ 2.0:

```
and
and_eq
bitand
bitor
compl
not
not_eq
or
or_eq
xor
xor_eq
```

You should already be familiar with the following C++ keywords because they are also ANSI/ISO C keywords:

```
const
enum
signed
void
volatile
```

They were not part of the original K&R C. This may surprise you, because most of them are also recognized by many recent C compilers that are not fully ANSI/ISO-compatible.

NEW C++ OPERATORS

The following operators are defined in C++, but not in ANSI/ISO C:

```
->*
.*
::
new
delete
new[]
delete[]
```

Note that, technically, the keywords that are included in the preceding list are actually operators. This is important for operator overloading. As we've mentioned, only symbols that are already defined as C++ operators can be overloaded. Because new and delete (and their array forms) are operators, they can also be overloaded.

The .*, ->*, and :: operators are discussed in Chapter 6, "Understanding C++ Classes." The new and delete operators are discussed in Chapter 7, "Other Differences between C and C++."

// THIS IS ALSO A COMMENT

In all of the examples in this chapter, we have used the C-style /* ... */ comments. This is still acceptable in C++. However, another style of comment is allowed in C++.

Two slashes together on a line (//) indicate that everything from that point on is a comment. Many people use only this style of commenting in their C++ code, so that it is visually distinguishable from C code at a glance. This is purely a matter of preference.

The most important point about a style of commenting is that you should have one, and you should adhere to it. The second most important point is that your commenting style should easily convey all of the information that would be needed by someone who is unfamiliar with the code. All the rest is a matter of preference.

Commenting Style

Commenting style is largely a matter of preference. After trying several styles, we came up with these guidelines:

- You should usually place single-line comments on lines by themselves. About the only exceptions are commenting short declarations at the beginning of a function, and making short comments in Figures in this book.

- On a single-line comment, make sure that the end of the comment is distinguishable. If the comment is not preceded or followed by other lines of the program, this should suffice:

  ```
  // Comment comment comment comment.
  ```

  Otherwise, it's a good idea to explicitly terminate the comment:

  ```
  /* Comment. */
  // Comment. //
  ```

- There should be a block comment at the head of a file and before each function. Block comments are also used before multiline data objects or control structures, or for any multiline comments. Each line of a block comment should start with something that makes it clear that the entire block is a comment; there should be no "naked" comment lines:

  ```
  //
  // This is a short block comment
  // with C++-style comment delimiters.
  //

  /*
  ** This is a short block comment.
  ** with C-style comment delimiters.
  ** Each line starts with "**".
  */
  ```

The following example illustrates the aesthetically less-pleasing "naked" comment lines:

```
/* This is also a short block comment
   using a commenting style that is,
   unfortunately, not uncommon. The
   comment lines have nothing at the
   beginning to distinguish them, and
   the comment block ends in a manner
   that does not set it apart well. */
```

Continued

Continued from previous page

- Except at the beginning of a file, comment blocks should start with a comment delimiter. They should also end with a comment delimiter immediately below the starting delimiter. This helps make them stand out:

```
//
// This is one way to do it.
//

/*
** This works, too.
*/
```

- At the beginning of a file, the comment block should be delimited at the top and bottom by a fixed-length line that naturally starts or ends the comment:

```
/////////////////////////////////////////
//
// (Name of file, description, history,
//      and other information)
//
/////////////////////////////////////////
Here's an alternative:
/**************************************\
**
** (Name of file, description, history,
**      and other information)
**
\**************************************/
```

Summary

This chapter has described various small differences between C and C++. All of the changes from C to C++ contribute to making C++ a stronger language. All of them make C++ a language in which simple programming mistakes are more easily caught and fixed early in the software production process.

To really use this tool, we need to explore some more significant changes in the language, as well as the concepts behind the language. In the next chapter, we will discuss the heart of C++: the concept of classes. Then, after going over more language additions in C++, we will discuss object-oriented design and programming in C++. We will use the tools and concepts gathered in these chapters as a springboard for jumping into the use of the Microsoft Foundation Class library.

CHAPTER

6

Understanding C++ Classes

*I*n our introduction to object-oriented programming in Chapter 4, we described *classes* as a means for defining groups of objects or ideas. When we design a program, we create these definitions by abstracting the elements of interest as data elements and procedural elements of the class. Classes form the modules with which we can build object-oriented programs.

Classes are also one of the major differences between C and C++. In fact, the first version of C++ was called C with Classes. The syntax of C++ classes is an extension of the syntax for the C-language structures. The meaning has been expanded greatly, though, to include object-oriented programming constructs and capabilities such as:

- *Member functions* — functions associated with a class, that define how to use objects in that class.

- *Constructor and destructor functions* — member functions that give the programmer control over the actions at the creation and deletion of all objects of that class.

- *Inheritance* — the capability to define a new class that has all of the properties and procedures of an existing class, but with added elements.

- *Virtual functions* — the capability to declare special member functions in such a way that each inherited type has its own version, and so that the version of the member function defined for an object's declared type will be used, even if it's being used in an inherited procedure (and so is cast to its base type).

- *Access protections* — the capability to designate members, both data and functions, as private to a class, as available only to the class and inherited classes, or as available to all parts of the program.

- *Scope resolution* — the capability to resolve ambiguities in scope caused by inheritance problems, or by the natural protection that keeps a name from having a meaning outside of its scope.

Like a C *struct*, a C++ *class* defines the data members of a particular type. Unlike the C struct, however, a C++ class also establishes a context in which these objects may be used. It does this by allowing the programmer to restrict access to the data within an object, and to define the actions which may be performed on that object. The *class* also allows the programmer to define relationships between one data type and another. For example, one data type may extend or include another type. A data type may also be declared a *friend* of another, which means that it is granted limited access to the hidden parts of the other data type.

One of the goals of C++ was for user-defined types to behave as much as possible like native C++ types. Some of the C++ features discussed in Chapter 5, as well as many of the features discussed in this chapter, exist just for that reason. To increase the similarity, some of the new features of classes that are available in C++ can also be used for the built-in types. The intention is to make the phrases *data types* (or *types*) and *classes* interchangeable in C++ to as great a degree as is possible.

The following section describes some of the basic features of the C++ implementation of classes. It presents a simple example to help illustrate how the concept of classes is expressed in C++.

A Simple Class Example

We'll start our exploration of classes with a simple example involving a class of complex numbers. We chose this class because it's fairly small, but still rich enough that we can demonstrate many of the properties of C++ classes.

Although our example class resembles the double_complex class in the Standard C++ library described in the Draft Standard (and not to be confused with Microsoft's proprietary MFC library), the two classes are not identical. For the sake of simplicity, we've taken some liberties with the design of this class. If you're not comfortable with complex numbers, or you want to review them, you can refer to the accompanying sidebar. However, the important points in our example have nothing to do with the math that's involved. Trust us to get the arithmetic right, and concentrate on the class concepts that are illustrated by this example.

The data in a complex number is fairly well-defined: it consists of two real numbers, the *real* component and the *imaginary* component. To give us as wide a range of values as possible, let's make both components have *double* as their data type.

Complex Numbers

Complex numbers aren't really all that complex. They are simply a pair of numbers, *x* and *y*, that are usually written as though they are a simple algebraic sum with a variable *i*, as in:

$$x + yi$$

The trick is that the "variable" *i* is actually the square root of -1! "What's that?," you say. "Negative numbers don't have real square roots!" You're right, and that's why *i* is called an *imaginary* number. The sum of a *real* number *x* and an *imaginary* number *yi* (which is the real number *y* times *i*) is called a *complex* number, *x + yi*.

What good is a complex number? In the real world, engineers have found all sorts of complicated natural phenomena that can be easily described using complex-number formulas! Complex numbers are used in many of the more in-depth calculations regarding electrical circuits, radio and light waves, and the motion of fluids such as water or air.

When doing simple arithmetic with complex numbers, you can treat the complex number just like an algebraic *binomial* (the sum of two *terms*, or parts that can't be simplified by merging them together). Here's the only trick: if you multiply two complex numbers together and the result contains a term with i^2 in it, remember to turn that expression into −1, and then simplify!

If you're not used to working with complex numbers, this may seem odd. In that case, as we mentioned, you can leave the arithmetic to us, and concentrate on the C++ class concepts.

For one of the more arcane formulas in our example, we didn't trust our memory, because we haven't used it (the formula!) for years. We verified the math with Ruel V. Churchill's *Complex Variables and Applications*, second edition (McGraw-Hill, 1960).

We need to list what we want to do with these numbers. Because they are numbers, the first things that come to mind are that we'll want to add them, subtract them, multiply them, and divide them. We may even want to perform more complicated mathematics with them. In a computer program, we also want to create variables that can contain the values of these numbers; we want to be able to assign values to the variables; and we need to be able to print them out. To introduce the concept of *member functions*, let's start with this last, simple task, printing the values that are assigned to variables.

MEMBER FUNCTIONS IN A C++ CLASS

Figure 6-1 shows our first cut at the *Complex* class. You can see that the form of the class definition looks a bit like a C-language struct. In addition to the data members, however, the class definition also includes a function header. This is our first *member function*.

```
//
// This example shows part of a complete class of complex
// numbers.
//
class Complex {
    double Real;
    double Imag;

public:
    void print();
};

void Complex::print()
{
    cout << "(" << Real << " + " << Imag << "i)";
}
```

Figure 6-1
Our first cut at the Complex class.

In C structs, only data can be members. You can define functions for which those structs are supposed to be the arguments or return values, but there is no way of enforcing this. For example, if you have a hammer structure and a wrench structure, you might write a pound( ) function that is supposed to take a pointer to a hammer as its argument. However, there is no way you can absolutely prevent yourself or others from accidentally calling pound( ) with an argument that is a pointer to a wrench.

In C++, you select the member function pound( ) from the hammer data object on which you want to call it. No matter how much you want to pound with the wrench, if your data object is a wrench, there is just no way that you can select the hammer object's member function, pound( ).

In our Complex class example, you'll notice that the declaration is in the form of a normal function prototype. A member function is called as a member of a data object in its class. As a result, the member function can have the same name as a nonmember function or member functions of other classes, without risk of confusion. For example, if we have a Complex object cNum, we call the print( ) function as follows:

```
cNum.print()
```

Because the only way to get at that particular print( ) function is through a data object of that class, there is no confusion.

In our example, the member function is defined outside the class definition. As a result, we need to do something to show that it's being defined within the context of its class. We do this by using the *scope resolution* operator, ::, in the function header to join the class name to the function name. In this case, the member function is short enough that we could have defined it inside the class definition. By default, a function that is defined inside the class definition is an *inline* function unless you explicitly make it external. (Inline functions are described in Chapter 5.)

When you call a member function, you want it to operate on the data object through which it is called. However, the member function in our example doesn't have any arguments, so you might wonder how it can refer to that object. Because a member function is in the same class scope as the object's other members, it has direct access to all of the members defined for that class. Within the member function, you can refer directly to the members of your data object. Thus, in Complex::print( ), you can use the names of members of cNum — that is, Real and Imag — as simple variable names.

You can also use the keyword *this* to refer to the data object through which the function has been called. Because *this* is treated as a pointer to the original data object, the following terms would have the same meaning in Complex::print( ):

```
this->Real
Real
```

The primary uses for the term *this* are as an argument passed from the member function to other functions, or as a value assigned to other pointers.

In our simple example, we could have included the modifier *const* after the function header in both the class definition and the member function definition, as follows:

```
void Complex::print() const
{
    cout << "(" << Real << " + " << Imag << "i)";
}
```

Doing so would declare that the object pointed to by *this* wouldn't be changed in the body of the function. In effect, the declaration of *this* would change from *Complex ** (pointer-to-*Complex*) to *const Complex ** (pointer-to-*const-Complex*). This is a good programming practice if you aren't going to change the argument. We'll add it to subsequent versions of the Complex class in this chapter.

A similar change would occur if *volatile* appeared after the function header. The declaration would change from pointer-to-*Complex* to pointer-to-*volatile-Complex*. This usage isn't seen as often as the *const* usage, though.

Finally, you'll notice that in the class definition, we labeled the print( ) function as *public*. This label defines the level of access outside functions have to the different members. There are three levels of access: *public*, *protected*, and *private*. By default, all names defined inside a class definition are *private* — that is, only class member functions and other functions or objects with privileges inside that class can use those names. By declaring this function as *public*, we make it available from any function. This is typical of class definitions: we make the data *private*, and we make *public* those functions that define the way the object will be used. The third access restriction, *protected*, will be covered later in this chapter.

Classes, Structs, and Unions

The concept of access restrictions is the only difference between C++ structs and classes. As mentioned, all members of a class are considered *private* unless they are explicitly labeled otherwise. A struct can have all the same constructs as a class, but its members are considered *public* unless explicitly labeled otherwise.

You might be surprised to find that a *union* is also considered a special type of class. It can also have all the same constructs as a class, but all of its data members are assumed to refer to the same piece of data (after all, this is still a *union*). Its members are considered *public* unless explicitly labeled otherwise.

In the following section, we'll explicitly define as *private* all of the members that we want to be private to the class. This is another good programming practice; we make sure that small changes to the class won't accidentally change the access controls to these members.

ACCESSING AN OBJECT'S VALUE

So far, we've seen that a class can have both data members and function members, and that we normally protect the data members from public access. But if we can't access the data members of an object in a class, how do we assign a value to that object? And, once it's assigned, how do we use that value?

In the following sections, we'll look at several different ways to accomplish these tasks. First, let's look at how we can assign a value to an object when the object is first created.

Initializing objects with constructor functions

One way we can create an object is by entering the scope of an *automatic* or *static* variable of that type. For example, we can enter a function or a control block in which we define a local variable of the desired type.

The other way we can create an object is by dynamically allocating it with the *new* operator. The *new* operator takes a data type name as its operand, and it returns a pointer to a new object of that type. It's like a version of malloc( ) that knows about data types and their sizes. However, the malloc( ) function can't check the size that's passed to it, and it returns a pointer to an untyped extent of memory.

Regardless of how an object is created, its creation is accompanied by a call to a *constructor function* of the class in which the object is defined. A constructor function gives a class control over the creation of objects from that class by defining what should be done to initialize those objects. The constructor function always has the same name as the class. As with other functions, whether members of a class or not, you can *overload* the function name so that different functions are called, depending on which arguments are passed.

The *default* constructor function is the function that's called if you simply declare a variable or use the *new* operator, and you don't specify any initializing values:

```
Complex cNum;           // A declaration without initializers
Complex *pcPtr;

pcPtr = new Complex;  // Operator 'new' called with no initializers
```

In the absence of any other initializing values, the default constructor function defines the values that we want stored in the object. There are no arguments (remember, the object itself is named by *this*). For our example, let's just set the values to 0. With this addition, our class definition looks like Figure 6-2.

```
//
// This example shows part of a complete class of complex
// numbers.
//
class Complex {
private:
    double Real;
    double Imag;

public:
    // This is our "default" constructor function.
    Complex()
        { Real = 0; Imag = 0; };

    // The "print" function has been moved inside the class
    // definition. This makes it inline.
    void print() const
        { cout << "(" << Real << " + " << Imag << "i)"; };
};
```

Figure 6-2

Adding a constructor function to the Complex class.

The constructor function is declared much like any other member function, except that there's never a return value. As a result, we don't declare a return type — not even *void*. Because our example is so simple, we have defined the function inside the class definition, which makes it an inline function, and, therefore, a static function.

Another useful constructor function that we can declare is the *copy* constructor function. The copy constructor function takes one argument, which is an object of the same type as the object being constructed. It copies the old object to the new object, making any needed changes — such as allocating and copying new strings and other sub-objects, rather than just copying pointers to them. This function is called when you declare a variable with a value in any of the following ways:

```
Complex cNum1    = cOldNum;  // cOldNum already had a Complex value.
Complex cNum2(cOldNum);      // Same here; new syntax!
Complex *cpPtr;              // A pointer, needs to be initialized!

pcPtr = new Complex(cOldNum);   // A "new" object with an old value
                                // Sometimes old values are best!
```

Other constructors can be used for such tasks as converting a double to a Complex, or converting a pair of doubles to a Complex. In fact, we can combine these two ideas by using a default value for the second argument of this constructor function. Figure 6-3 shows our class definition with these additions.

In the *copy* constructor function, all we do is copy each field, one by one, from the old object to the new object. In fact, we really don't need to define a copy constructor function for a class that is this simple. If we don't define one, C++ defines one for us that does exactly the same thing, a field-by-field copy! Defining our own copy constructor function becomes important if the class has pointer members. If we just copy a pointer member, the pointer in the new object will be pointing to the same data as the pointer in the old object. We are more likely to want to make a new copy of this data for the new object, for each pointer member in the class.

You might be wondering whether we need to define more constructor functions for the cases in which we want to convert two integers or an integer and a floating-point number to a Complex value. After all, the strong typing in C++ would suggest that it wouldn't want to treat these different numeric types as the same. In fact, C++ does convert numeric-type arguments, if there aren't other overloaded functions for them. In other words, if we had a Complex::Complex(int, int) constructor function, it would be called if we tried to construct a Complex out of two ints; but because we don't have that function, C++ uses the existing Complex::Complex(double, double) constructor function. As shown in the following examples, we can initialize new objects with any numeric values:

```
Complex cNum1(1.2, 3);    // Becomes 1.2 + (3.0 * i)
Complex cNum2(7);         // Becomes 7.0 + (0.0 * i)
```

```
//
// This example shows part of a complete class of complex
// numbers, with constructor functions.
//
class Complex {
private:
    double Real;
    double Imag;

public:
    // This was our "default" constructor function.
    Complex()
        { Real = 0; Imag = 0; };

    // This is our "copy" constructor function.
    Complex(const Complex cx)
        { Real = cx.Real; Imag = cx.Imag; };

    // This is a constructor function for "real" numbers.
    Complex(const double x, const double y = 0)
        { Real = x; Imag = y; };

    void print() const
        { cout << "(" << Real << " + " << Imag << "i)"; };
};
```

Figure 6-3
More constructor functions for the Complex class.

Accessing objects' values with member functions

If an object already exists and its data members are private, how can we change its values? Similarly, once those values are set, how do we use them?

The immediate response to those questions might be to use member functions. In fact, if the data members can be accessed only by member functions, this might seem to be the only right solution. Such a solution is shown for our Complex class in Figure 6-4.

```
class Complex {
private:
    double Real;
    double Imag;

public:
    ...
    double setReal(double x) { Real = x; return(Real); };
    double setImag(double x) { Imag = x; return(Imag); };
    double getReal() { return(Real); };
    double getImag() { return(Imag); };
};
```

Figure 6-4
Using member functions to get and set values.

For certain members of some classes, this might be the right solution. But consider what you're doing. You're giving away complete access to members that had been private. The only remaining advantage is that you're still hiding the internal representation of the data. If you change the members' names or internal types later, you can still use these member functions, with some modification to the function bodies. Otherwise, the data members are now completely exposed to the manipulations of the rest of the program, as though they were never hidden.

Although this might be the solution for some classes, we're going to take another approach with this class: using overloaded operators.

Accessing objects' values with overloaded operators

In our example, a class of complex numbers, the most natural way to assign a value to an existing object is by using the assignment operator. In fact, we can define new, class-specific functions for most of the C++ operators. This is called *operator overloading*. We discussed this same concept in Chapter 5, but we didn't mention classes.

As we mentioned earlier, one goal in the development of C++ was to make all of the data types — both user-defined and built-in — appear as much alike as possible. One way this is accomplished is by extending the normal C++ operators so that they also work with user-defined types, via operator overloading. Operator overloading functions for a class are best defined as member functions in that class, or as *friend* functions (which we'll discuss later in this chapter). Like top-level overloaded operators, only those operators already present in C++ may be overloaded, and they must keep the same precedence and associativity as the built-in versions.

As we mentioned in Chapter 5, operator overloading functions must have the same number of arguments as the original operators. Because member functions have one implicit argument — *this* — member functions for unary operators require no arguments, and member functions for binary operators require one argument. Figure 5-10 in Chapter 5 provided an example of a function overloading operators at the global level. Figure 6-5 shows some unary and binary operator overloading functions for our Complex class. We don't yet show an assignment operator overloading, because there are some special rules that we need to mention first.

```
class Complex {
private:
    double Real;
    double Imag;

public:
    ...
    // This function overloads unary minus.
    Complex operator - () const
        { return(Complex(-Real, -Imag)); };

    // This function overloads binary plus (add).
    Complex operator + (const Complex a) const
        { return(Complex(Real + a.Real, Imag + b.Imag)); };
    ...
};
```

Figure 6-5
Member functions overloading operators.

Because these are member functions, they can be called with member function syntax. They can also be called with the operator syntax. For example, we can express the addition of two Complex numbers in either of the following ways:

```
Complex a(0.,0.), b(1.,1.), c;

c = a.operator+(b);
c = a + b;
```

In the operator function definitions in Figure 6-5, *this* is declared
const by adding the keyword after the function headers. For the binary
operator example in Figure 6-5, the second operand is also declared
const. Unless you plan to change an operand, it's generally a good idea
to declare it as const.

Functions overloading the operators =, ( ), [], and -> must be member functions of some class. There are special rules for each of these
operators. In this section, we'll focus on the special rules for the assignment operator. The other operators are more rarely used, and their
restrictions aren't described in this book. They are described in the ARM,
in C++/PL, and in the Draft Standard.

The assignment operator, =, should be overloaded to do the same
thing as the copy constructor function. There is always a default = operator overloaded, which does a member-by-member copy of the class
objects, but this may not be what you want. The return value of an
overloaded = operator should always be *this.

To fully understand the assignment operator function, you need to
understand the concept of *references*. The argument and the return values to the assignment operator overloading function are references. In a
reference declaration, an ampersand (&) appears after the type in the
declaration, and before the variable or function that is being declared. A
reference variable doesn't declare a new variable as we know it — that
is, it doesn't declare a new area of storage in which we can store a copy
of an object. Instead, a reference variable refers back to the original
object. The two uses here of the concept of references are a *reference
argument* and a *reference return value*.

As shown in the following example, we can declare an argument to
have a reference type:

```
void foo(Complex & cNum)
```

Without the reference, the argument is copied when the function is
called, and anything done inside the function is done only to the copy.
With the reference, the argument inside the function refers to the same

object that was passed to the function. This saves the overhead involved in copying the object, and makes it possible to make changes directly to the original object. On the other hand, you may not want to allow changes to the original object. A reference argument is something that should be used only after you've carefully considered its pros and cons.

We can also declare a return value to have a reference type:

```
double & getReal() { return(Real); }
```

In this example, the Complex::getReal( ) member function is declared to return the Real data member by reference. If our only action is to make a copy, this declaration has no effect. But we can treat a reference-type return value as an lvalue, and try to change its value:

```
cNum.getReal() = 21.0;
```

With the reference, this is now perfectly legitimate! It changes the value of the Real data member to 21.0. With this understanding of references, let's return to the assignment operator overloading function.

The default assignment operator overloading function for a class takes an argument of type *const*-reference-to-the class, and it returns a type of reference-to-the class. Again, the reference argument means that the argument is not a copy; it's the same as the object that is passed as the right operand. The reference return value means that the value returned is also not a copy; it is, in fact, the argument that's returned, which should be *this for the assignment operator.

You should also follow these conventions when defining your own version of the default assignment function. So, an assignment operator overloading function will take as its right argument an object of that class. When the function is called with this argument, it will neither copy the object nor change it. It will return the object to which the assignment was made — not a copy, but the real thing.

Once you've defined your version of the default assignment function, or decided to use the language's default, you may want to overload other assignment functions that take different arguments. You should still use a reference argument and a reference return value.

We can now add the first assignment operator overloading function shown in Figure 6-6 to the Complex class. While we're at it, let's overload another assignment operator that allows us to assign Real numbers to Complex objects.

```
//
// This example shows part of a complete class of complex numbers,
// with overloaded operators.
//
class Complex {
private:
    double Real;
    double Imag;

public:
    ...
    // This function overloads assignment.
    Complex & operator = (const Complex & a)
        { Real = a.Real; Imag = a.Imag; return(*this); };

    // This function overloads assignment, for "real" numbers.
    Complex & operator = (const double & d)
        { Real = d; Imag = 0.0; return(*this); };
    ...
};
```

Figure 6-6
The Complex class, with overloaded assignment operators.

Two words of caution are necessary regarding operator overloading. First, make sure that your operator overloads make sense. An overloaded function should do roughly the same thing as the original. For example, the + operator should add, concatenate, or do something similar. It should not compare, reduce, walk the dog, or anything else that is similarly remote from what you expect of +. Part of the confusion with the use of << and >> in the iostream package is because the operators' use there is totally unrelated to their use with numbers.

Second, use moderation in your use of operators. One of the authors wrote his very first programming term project in PPL, a language that allows you to define any arbitrary symbol string as a unary or binary operator, with its own associativity and precedence. Mistaking permission for license, the programming neophyte went hog-wild, turned all the functions into randomly-chosen operator strings, and handed in a program that more closely resembled dense, unreadable APL code than PPL. His teaching fellow handed it back and told him to take the time to make it readable and to add comments: good advice then and now.

A LITTLE HELP FROM YOUR FRIENDS

Member functions of a class are called through a specific object in that class, and they refer to that object as an implied first argument, *this*. In some cases, however, you will need to write functions that need access to the scope of the class, but that cannot or should not be member functions. For example, operator overloading functions providing iostream output to a class such as the Complex class must have an ostream object as their first, explicit argument. As another example, a project design might require functions that belong in the scope of one class, but need access to the members in another class.

Friend functions are functions that aren't member functions of a class, but still have the same access privileges to members of the class as its member functions do. Friend functions may be functions defined in the top-level scope, or they may be member functions of a class that has already been declared. One reason you might declare a function to be a friend of a class is so that it has access to multiple classes. Another reason you might declare it a friend of a class is so that it can overload another function or operator in the same scope, to handle the new class.

To generalize the Complex::print( ) function that we defined earlier so that we can use it with any output stream, we need to overload the operator <<. Figure 6-7 shows how we can do this.

```
//
// This example shows part of a complete class of complex numbers,
// with a "friend" function overloading the "<<" operator.
//
class Complex {
    double Real;
    double Imag;

public:
    ...

    // The "friend" function that overloads "<<" for this class.
    friend ostream & operator << (ostream & o, const Complex & c);
};

//
// This function needs to be a "friend" to the Complex class,
// because it requires access to the private data members of that
// class.
//
```

```
ostream & operator << (ostream & osOut, const Complex & cNum)
{
    osOut << "(" << cNum.Real << " + " << cNum.Imag << "i)";
    return(osOut);
}
```

Figure 6-7
Adding a friend function to the Complex class for iostream output.

An entire class may be declared to be a friend of another class. For example, if class B declares, within its braces, that class A is a friend, all member functions in class A have access to the members of class B:

```
class A {
    ...
};
class B {
    ...
    friend A;
};
```

LAYING AN OBJECT TO REST

If an object is created on entry to the scope of the variable that describes it, the object is destroyed on exit from that scope. In some cases, that exit is unexpected. For example, it might occur as a result of some error-handling code. An object that's created with the *new* operator is also eventually destroyed by a matching *delete* operator (in the absence of any memory leaks). Again, we might not know in advance which use of *delete* in the program will destroy the object. And it might not always be obvious which class of object is being destroyed at a given point in the program. (When we discuss inherited classes, we'll see that an object can sometimes be referenced by a pointer to a subclass or a superclass of the object's class.)

A class will sometimes have resources which, when an object in that class is destroyed, should be taken care of in a class-specific way. These resources might include other objects to which the deleted object points — if it has the only pointer to them — or some sort of registry showing how many and what objects of that type exist.

When an object is destroyed, its *destructor* function is called. The destructor function is almost, but not quite, anti-parallel to the constructor function. Where the constructor function makes sure that an object comes into the world with enough resources to start its work, the destructor function makes sure that any resources still with the object on its destruction are saved and recycled.

A destructor function is a member function that handles any cleanup for a newly deleted object of its class. A destructor function has the same name as its class, preceded by a tilde (~). It is declared and defined with no arguments and no return type (not even *void*!), and it cannot return a value.

We don't show a Complex::~Complex( ) destructor function here, because a simple class such as our Complex class almost never needs to have a destructor function. However, many other classes will need this capability.

A Class Example with Inheritance

In Chapter 4, we introduced *inheritance* as a new and essential feature of object-oriented programming. With this feature, one class can inherit the data members and the member functions of another class. The inheriting class is called a *subclass*, a *child* class, or a *derived* class. The class from which the derived class inherits is called a *superclass*, a *parent* class, or a *base* class.

A derived class can in turn have its own children, which inherit its properties, and so on, forming a hierarchy of classes. This hierarchy of classes usually adds little or no overhead to a program, while making the program easier to read and understand. Although some languages require that all classes must be in a single hierarchy with a single common root class, C++ has no such requirement. C++ easily supports multiple class hierarchies. The MFC library classes almost all have a single root class (CObject) only because all of the CObject-derived classes share certain properties that are used by some of the MFC library functions.

As mentioned in Chapter 4, you'll typically set up an inheritance hierarchy of classes for one of two reasons. First, you might need to create a class for certain objects that require special treatment. In such cases, you can put those objects in a subclass with member functions that meet their special needs. On the other hand, you might have several classes with similar needs or properties. In this case, it might make sense to put the similar functions in a more general class, where they can be inherited by the more specific subclasses. This approach has the advantage of placing similar code in one place, so it's more easily maintained. It has the (minor) disadvantage that you must keep track of more class relationships. However, you can easily keep track of these relationships by using any of the design notations from the books mentioned in Chapter 4.

For our example of class inheritance, we'll use a simple binary tree class. The class shown in Listing 6-1 is so simple it doesn't even have any data! This class exists solely to give us access to the binary-tree methods of insertion and searching that it provides. The classes that inherit from this base class will provide their own ways of storing and getting the data, and of testing for equality and ordering between data elements. For now, let's just look at the base class.

Listing 6-1
The Tree Base Class

```
/////////////////////////////////////////////////////////////////////
//
// Tree.h - contains definitions of the base "Tree" structure.
//
// @(#)$Header:$
//
// Description:
//      This file contains the base type and information for the bare
//      sorting and searching routines in the Tree module.  It needs
//      to be augmented to do anything that is actually useful.
//
/////////////////////////////////////////////////////////////////////

//
// This forward declaration of the Tree class is needed because
// the Node class is defined before it and refers to it.
// Re-ordering the class definitions wouldn't help: the Tree class
// also refers to the Node class.
//
class Tree;

class Node {
    protected:
        // The data members need to be seen by the children, too.
        Node *left;
        Node *right;
```

```
    private:
        // These functions are part of the private implementation.
        void balance();         // Not implemented, here.  //
        void list(int depth);   // Called by Tree::list(). //

    public:
        // These functions are part of the public interface.
        Node();
        virtual int is_greater(Node *t)   = 0;
        virtual int is_equal(Node *t)     = 0;
        virtual void print()              = 0;

        // Let the Tree class have access to Node members.
        friend Tree;
};

class Tree {
    protected:
        // The data members need to be seen by the children, too.
        Node *root;

    public:
        // These functions are part of the public interface.
        Tree();
        Node *insert(Node *x);
        Node *search(Node *x);
        void list();
};
```

THE *PROTECTED* ACCESS RESTRICTION

Looking at the listing, you'll notice a new access restriction label: *protected*. As mentioned previously, all members of a class are considered *private* unless they are explicitly labeled otherwise. However, if members are completely *private* to one class, the classes that inherit from that class won't be able to access their own members because the names of those members are inherited! The *protected* restriction is a middle ground; members that are *protected* are accessible to subclasses, but not to the general public.

VIRTUAL MEMBER FUNCTIONS

Listing 6-1 introduces another new concept: the *virtual* member function. The virtual member function provides a means for allowing a base class and various derived classes to behave in different ways.

A nonvirtual member function of a base class should do something useful and interesting for the base class and for all derived classes — for example, Node::list( ) in Listing 6-1. Within the function, however, you can only declare and use objects of the base class; in this case, type Node. You have no way of knowing ahead of time what classes might be derived from this class, and what their behaviors might be. Any data members or member functions used inside the function will normally refer to the base class version of those members.

If you define a second member function as *virtual*, however, you can define a different version of this second function (with the same argument types) for each derived type. It then doesn't matter that you call the object in the first, inherited member function a Node. If the first function was actually called for an object of a derived type, when you call the second function from within the first it will use the correct version of the function for the object's declared type! The virtual functions in our example are Node::is_greater( ), Node::is_equal( ), and Node::print( ). The behavior of these functions will differ in our derived classes.

If you define a member function in a base class as *virtual*, that function will be virtual in all derived classes, as well. If you declare a function with the same name and argument types in a derived class, even if you don't explicitly label it *virtual*, it will override the inherited function as a virtual member function.

It looks like we're setting the values of these functions to the number 0 in the class definition. This is just a convention to show that a default value isn't expected for this class. This notation makes the virtual member function a *pure virtual member function*, which, in turn, makes the entire class an *abstract class*. As a result, we are not allowed to declare any objects of this class! This class exists solely to provide its properties to derived classes.

In general, if you're going to define different versions of a member function for different derived classes, you should make that function virtual. It's not illegal to define a nonvirtual function, and then redefine it in a derived class, with the same name and argument list. The problem that will arise is that, if you try to call the redefined member function from inside an inherited function, the base-class version of the function will be called instead! This is almost always not what you wanted.

If you define a virtual member function, and you don't want the base member function ever called, you can leave the base-class version of it undefined. The compiler will point out to you, at compile time, any places where you've accidentally used the base member function. If you actually don't want to ever have an object that's an instance of the base class, you should define one or more of the virtual member functions as pure. That will make the class an abstract base class, and no objects can be declared in that class.

INTERCHANGING THE BASE CLASS AND DERIVED CLASSES

From our description of virtual member functions, you might have the impression that you could easily pass an object of a derived class to a function that's expecting an object of its base class. On the contrary, this would violate some of the strong typing rules that help us ensure that our C++ programs are correct. However, a pointer to a member of a base class can be cast as a pointer to a member of one of its derived classes, and vice-versa.

If a pointer to a member of a derived class is cast as a pointer to a member of the base class, you can pass the pointer to a function inherited from the base class. As a result, the functions in the base class can reference objects of the derived class (which have all of the properties and procedures of the base class *plus* their own) as though they were objects of the base class.

Although it's risky, you can also cast a pointer to an object that's declared to be of the base class, and reference it as an object of the derived class. You should be sure that the object to which you're pointing was initially a member of the derived class. Otherwise, you might be trying to access members of the derived class that aren't really there! To help us verify that this type of cast is correct, a new set of *dynamic cast* operators is defined for C++. However, they aren't yet available in Microsoft Visual C++. Instead, the MFC library provides a completely different means for getting RunTime Type Information (RTTI), which we will cover in Chapter 9.

THE C++ INHERITANCE MECHANISM

Listing 6-2 presents the Mytree class, which is derived from the Tree class via C++ class inheritance.

Listing 6-2

The Mytree Derived Class

```
///////////////////////////////////////////////////////////////
//
// Mytree.h - Header file defining the classes that actually do the
//            work.
//
// @(#)$Header:$
//
// Description:
//    The classes described herein are based on the Tree classes,
//    but extend them so that we can do actual work.
//
///////////////////////////////////////////////////////////////


//
// This forward declaration of the Mytree class is needed because
// the Mynode class is defined before it and refers to it.
// Re-ordering the class definitions wouldn't help: the Mytree class
// also refers to the Mynode class.
//
class Mytree;

class Mynode : public Node
{
    private:
        // These are part of the private implementation.
        char *key;
        char *data;

    public:
        // These functions are part of the public interface.
        Mynode()
            { key = NULL; data = NULL; };
        Mynode(Mynode & t);
        Mynode(char *inkey, char *indata);
        ~Mynode();

        int is_greater(Node *t)
            { return(strcmp(key, ((Mynode *)t)->key) > 0); };
        int is_equal(Node *t)
            { return(strcmp(key, ((Mynode *)t)->key) == 0); };
        void print();

        // Let the Tree class have access to Node members.
        friend Mytree;
};

class Mytree : public Tree
{
    private:
```

```
        // These functions are part of the private implementation.
        Mynode *insert(Mynode *mnPtr);
        Mynode *search(Mynode *mnPtr);

    public:
        // These functions are part of the public interface.
        Mynode *insert(char *key, char *data);
        Mynode *search(char *key);
};
```

Listing 6-2 shows you how the class inheritance relationships are defined. After the name of the new, derived class is declared, you'll find a colon (:), another access restriction keyword, and the name of the parent class. The body of the new class contains only those members that are new in the derived class. Of course, these members must have their own access restriction labels. Even though they aren't explicitly referenced here, all members of the base class are incorporated into the derived class.

You might be wondering why there is another access restriction keyword before the base class name. We'll look at that in the following section. In subsequent sections, we'll examine several other concepts that require a second look in the light of C++ inheritance.

MORE ON ACCESS RESTRICTIONS

When the derived classes in our example are declared, there's an access restriction keyword before the base class name. How does this affect the declaration of the new class?

Just to review, we've already seen that there are three levels of access to the data members and member functions of a class. Members may be *private*, which means they are accessible only within the scope of that class — that is, within member functions and friend functions of that class. Members may be *public*, which means they are accessible in all scopes in which the class is defined. Finally, members may be *protected*, which means the members are accessible only within the scope of that class *and* within the scopes of all derived classes.

When we define a derived class, these access permissions are modified by the access specifier that precedes the name of the base class.

The access permissions are logically added. The more restrictive permission is applied to the base class's members when they are accessed through an object of the derived class:

- If the access specifier is *public*, the access permissions of the base class's members are the same in the derived class.

- If the access specifier is *protected*, all *public* members of the base class are *protected* in the derived class. All other access permissions remain the same.

- If the access specifier is *private*, all of the base class's members are *private* in the derived class.

These access restrictions are summarized in Table 6-1.

Table 6-1

Access Restrictions for Members of the Base Class

Declaration of the base class in the derived class's header	Declarations of the members in the base class		
	private	protected	public
private	private	private	private
protected	private	protected	protected
public	private	protected	public

If no access specifier is explicitly used and the new class is defined as a struct, the default specifier is *public*; otherwise, it's *private*. This is similar to the rule we mentioned earlier about default access specifiers inside the class or struct: *public* for structs, and *private* for classes.

VIRTUAL MEMBER FUNCTIONS IN THE DERIVED CLASS

Notice that the arguments to the virtual member functions, as declared in the derived class in Listing 6-2, are identical to the arguments in the base class in Listing 6-1. They have to be identical. Remember, if the argument types are different, the function becomes a separate, overloaded function. The declarations of a virtual function in each of the derived classes must have the same argument types as in the base class. They should also have the same return type. As you can see, though, the virtual function in the derived class doesn't need the keyword virtual; that's inherited from the base type. These definitions of the virtual member functions override the definitions of the same virtual member functions in the base class, for all objects of class Mytree.

In our Mytree class, the member functions insert( ) and search( ) are also redefined. Because their argument types differ from those used in the Tree::insert( ) and Tree::search( ) functions, in the base class, they are overloaded functions. This is true even though the Mynode class, which is the argument type for one set of functions, is derived from the Node class, which is the argument type in the base class. Because the argument types are different, we can't use virtual member functions here.

CONSTRUCTOR AND DESTRUCTOR FUNCTIONS, REVISITED

If an object belongs to a class that has a hierarchy of base classes, when the object is declared or allocated, the constructors for the base classes are called. The constructor for the top class in the hierarchy is called first, then the constructor for its child, and so on in line until the constructor for the object's class is called. This depth-first process is reversed when an object is destroyed by leaving scope or being deleted. In this case, the destructor function for the object's class is called first, followed in order by the destructor functions for its parent class, and then its parent, and so on to the deepest class, at the top of the class hierarchy.

A constructor member function can't be declared virtual. This is reasonable; when you declare or allocate something, you want to build a specific type of a specific object. As such, a constructor function for that specific class is called. On the other hand, a destructor member function can be declared virtual. If you are destroying an object out of scope, you want to be sure that the correct destructor function for the object's real scope is called.

MULTIPLE INHERITANCE

It's perfectly legal for a class to be defined with more than one immediate base class. Base classes are each declared with their own access specifier, or they can use the default for the type of class that's being defined. The order in which base classes are listed determines the order in which constructors and destructors are called. A class can be defined as a base class only once for any derived class, but it can be a base class for more than one of the new class's immediate base classes. In other words, a class can be a grandparent (or great–grandparent) through more than one of the new class's parent classes. This usually causes one copy of an object of the multiply inherited grandparent class for each parent class of which it is a base class. Although this can cause some ambiguities, C++ has several ways of letting you resolve them. This is beyond the scope of this book.

Multiple inheritance is sometimes considered to be problematic because of the possible ambiguities, and because it's easy to use it where it's not needed in your program design. The Microsoft Foundation Class library deliberately did not use it. In fact, CObject is a base type for most MFC library classes, but isn't prepared to resolve any ambiguities that arise from multiple inheritance; so it can be risky to try using multiple inheritance with MFC library classes.

Choosing Contexts with the :: Operator

We've already mentioned how you use the *scope resolution* operator, ::, when defining a class member function outside of its scope. More generally, this operator selects a class scope when there's a possibility of ambiguity, or when the name being used is hidden deep in another scope. The left operand is the name of the class being selected. The right operand is the name being resolved. In the following sections, we'll describe some specific examples that demonstrate how you can use the scope resolution operator.

SELECTING A LOWER-LEVEL SCOPE

In a few cases, it's reasonable to select a lower-level scope. You might select a lower-level scope when defining a member function. You also might do this if you are defining classes inside the class whose scope is your current context, and then referencing names that are parts of the inner class. You can see examples of these situations in Figure 6-8 and Figure 6-9.

```
//
// The Node class, besides all its other members, has a
// member function named print().
//
class Node {
    ...

    public:
        void print();
        ...
};


//
// We must go into the Node class's scope to define the
// member function print().
//
void Node::print()
{
    ...
}
```

Figure 6-8
Selecting the class scope in which the member function is defined.

In Figure 6-8, the example is fairly simple. We are defining a *void*-returning function in the Node class scope, so the function name needs to be declared as in that scope, Node::print( ). In Figure 6-9, the situation is just a little more complicated. The function is in the *outer* class scope; so, as before, the function name needs to be declared as in that scope, outer::get_value( ). The return type name is *also* in the outer class scope. The inner class is defined only inside the outer class; so the type name also needs to be declared as in that scope: outer::inner. Those are the ins and outs of Figure 6-9.

In some cases, selecting a lower-level scope is inappropriate. From the top-level scope, you can't arbitrarily select any member from any class scope. (For an exception to this, see the section on *static* class members, later in this chapter.) From within a class scope, the only other class scopes that you can select are those that are defined within that class, and, if the class is a derived class, any parent classes.

```
//
// This class has another class defined within it. From
// outside the outer class's scope, we must select the
// outer class's scope to access the inner class.
//
class outer {
    private:
        class inner {
                ...
            public:
                void print_2();
        };
        inner inner_one;
        ...

    public:
        void print();
        inner get_value();
        ...
};

//
// The type of this function is a name inside the "outer"
// scope. We need to select the "outer" to be able to
// reference the type named "inner". We also still need
// to select the "outer" scope to get the name of the
// function so that we can define it.
//
outer::inner outer::get_value()
{
    ...
}
```

Figure 6-9
Selecting the class scope in which a type name is defined.

SELECTING A NESTED SCOPE

To go into a nested class definition, you can use the :: operator as many times as is necessary. For example, in Figure 6-9, an inner class is defined within the outer class. Member functions of the inner class can be defined as shown in Figure 6-10.

```
//
// The inner class in Figure 6-9 has a member function.
// That class can be thought of as type "outer::inner".
// To select that nested scope and define the member
// function, we need to use the class resolution operator
// twice.
//
void outer::inner::print_2()
{
    ...
}
```

Figure 6-10
Selecting a nested-class scope.

SELECTING A HIDDEN SCOPE

A name is *hidden* if the same name is found in a closer scope. This can happen if the same name is found in nested scopes, or in a derived class and its base class. The compiler normally selects the instance of the name that is closest in scope to the place where it is being used. By using the :: operator, you can specify a different instance of the name.

Figure 6-11 provides a simple example illustrating this use of the :: operator. The base class, Base, has a member function called output( ), which takes an argument of type int. Its derived class, Child, also has a member function named output( ), but this function takes an argument of type double. If we're dealing with an object from the Child class, what happens when we call the output( ) member function with an integer argument? If we don't explicitly ask for the Base class version of output( ), the C++ compiler will convert the integer to a double and pass it to Child's output( ) function. To get the version that correctly deals with integers, we need to specify the scope.

For this simple example, we've sketched out just enough of the classes to demonstrate the need for the scope resolution operator. In some cases, this usage is helpful for resolving ambiguity. However, if you find yourself resorting to this in a real design, first check that this isn't the result of a bad design!

```
//
// The following base class and its derived class both have member
// functions named output(). They have different type arguments,
// though, so they are different (overloaded) functions.
//
class Base {
        ...

    public:
        void output(int i);
        ...
};

class Child: public Base {
        ...

    public:
        void output(double d);
        ...
};

main()
{
    ...
    Child *chPtr    = ...;

    //
    // This converts the integer to a double, and calls Child's
    // output function.
    //
    chPtr->output(1);

    //
    // This keeps the integer, and calls Base's output function.
    //
    chPtr->Base::output(1);
    ...
}
```

Figure 6-11

The name of an object in a base class might be hidden by an object of the same name that's used differently in the derived class.

SELECTING THE TOP-LEVEL SCOPE

If a name declared inside a class is the same as a name in a file or a global scope outside any class, the name inside the class hides the other name as long as you remain in that class's scope. This is a special case of a hidden name. To reference the external name, you need to specify the top-level scope by using the scope resolution operator with no left operand and the name as the right operand.

Figure 6-12 provides an example in which we define our Complex class's sin( ) and cos( ) member functions in terms of the top-level sin( ) and cos( ) functions in the Standard C++ math library. Because both functions are renamed in the scope of the class, we need to specify the scope of the top-level functions each time we use them.

```
#include <math.h>

//
// This example shows part of a complete class of complex
// numbers, including trigonometric functions. The
// complex trigonometric functions are defined using the
// real-number trigonometric functions.
//
class Complex {
    private:
        double Real, Imag;

    public:
        Complex()
            { Real = 0; Imag = 0; };
        Complex(double re, double im)
            { Real = re; Imag = im; };
        ...
        Complex sin() const
            {
                return(Complex(cosh(Imag) * ::sin(Real),
                               sinh(Imag) * ::cos(Real)));
            };
        Complex cos() const
            {
                return(Complex(cosh(Imag) * ::cos(Real),
                               sinh(Imag) * ::sin(Real)));
            };
};
```

Figure 6-12
Selecting a top-level scope from within a class scope.

In this example, the function names that are used in the definitions of the Complex sin( ) and cos( ) member functions must refer back to the top-level versions of those functions. The syntax shown in this example lets them do just that.

Incidentally, defining a name inside a control block also hides any instances of that name in the file or global scopes. In this situation, you can use the :: operator to reference a name in the top-level scope! Because control blocks don't have names, you can only select instances of the name in the current scope or the top-level scope. The example in Figure 6-13 shows how this is done.

```
static int count     = 0;        // Top-level version.
void do_it()
{
    int count        = 0;        // First-level scope.

    // Increment the local instance.
    ++count;
    // Increment the top-level instance.
    ++::count;

    // Nested control block.
    {
        int count    = 0;        // Second-level scope.

        // Increment the local instance.
        ++count;
        // Increment the top-level instance.
        ++::count;
        //
        // There is no way to select the version of
        // 'count' from the first-level scope.
        //
    }
}
```

Figure 6-13
Selecting the top-level scope from an inner control block.

Static Class Members

Members in a class may be declared *static*. A *static* data member is shared among all objects in that class. In other words, if a data member is declared static, it is stored as a single data object, separate from any objects of that class, even though it's accessed as part of each of those objects. The static data member also must be defined separately. As shown in Figure 6-14, even if access to this data member is *private* or *protected*, it still must be defined at file scope.

```
class Mytree {
        ...
        static int MytreeCount;
        ...
};

int Mytree::MytreeCount    = 0;
```

Figure 6-14

An example of a static member of a class.

Member functions may also be declared static. If they are, they can be accessed independent of any object of that class. Consequently, they don't have the pointer *this* as an implicit first argument. Without *this*, they also can't access members simply by name. Instead, a particular object must be specified. For example, a static member function of our Complex class couldn't use the members Real and Imag in expressions, because there is no way to determine the object of which they are members! Instead, there must be some object *X* for which the static member function can say *X*.Real and *X*.Imag.

A static member function can still directly use the names of static data members, enumerators, and types declared inside the scope of the class. Outside the class, static member functions may be called directly by using the class name, the :: operator, and the function member name. They may also be called in the usual way, by being selected through an object in that class. Figure 6-15 shows an example of a static member function.

Static member functions were a very useful addition to C++. They provide functions which are members of a class, but can be called without requiring an object of the class to be made available or invented. They can be used for such things as introducing external, asynchronous control signals to a class, or for getting status information from a class. All of these things could also be done by global friend functions; but it's better to localize the functionality inside the class, and it also keeps the number of symbols defined in the global namespace low. In fact, some programmers had the habit of inventing classes that were only populated by static functions, to keep the function names from being global. (C++ now has the *namespace* feature to do this, although it's not yet implemented by Microsoft.)

Because they don't have the implicit first argument, *this*, static member functions can't be used for overloading operators.

```
class Example {
    private:
        static int count;
        int value;
        enum { no, yes } answer;
        struct inner {
            int in1;
            double in2;
        };
        struct inner inny;
        ...

    public:
        ...
        static int show(int, int);
        ...
};

// The definition of the static member function.
int Example::show(int a, int b)
{
    //
    // Within the body of the function, we can refer
    // to count and the values yes and no, and we can
    // declare a struct inner. We cannot refer to a
    // value, an answer, or an inny directly: they
    // have to be part of an Example object.
    //
    ...
}

void another_function()
{
    int v;
    Example a, *b = &a;

    //
    // The following are all valid calls of the static
    // member function show().
    //

    v = a.show(0, 0);
    v = b->show(1, 2);
    v = Example::show(-1, -1);
}
```

Figure 6-15

This example shows a static member function, what it can do, and how it may be called.

Class Libraries

We can't leave this chapter without mentioning *class libraries* and, in particular, the MFC library. Libraries include both the compiled (or source) C++ routines, and the header files that source files must include. The header files are important because they define the interface to the library. Without them, we would have to put the definitions of classes and function prototypes in our C++ source files. One mistype, or one implementation change between versions of a library, could cause us grief while we try to figure out what's wrong in our code. As a result, the header files provide the form of the class library, while the body of the library — included on your command line in the system-dependent manner for your system and compiler — provides the substance.

Although C++ tries to hide information within classes, programmers still need to know what's really in there before they can use the library. One way around this is to have a hidden set of classes in the library that implement the library functions, and an open set that shows only the interface that the programmer needs to understand. In the MFC library, everything is out in the open; the interface *is* the implementation. Whether this is preferable depends on your priorities in using the library.

Class libraries can be used simply by creating objects of the classes provided in the library, and manipulating them using their member functions. The libraries can also be used by deriving classes that more accurately model your problem domain from the library classes. This is a more object-oriented approach, and this is the approach used by Microsoft Visual C++ when constructing a program using the MFC library. We'll discuss this further in Chapter 9.

Summary

We've seen in this chapter that C++ classes form the conceptual models for objects and their behavior. You can control how objects are created and destroyed, and — with member functions — how they act and interact. You can expand a class definition by using the powerful concept of class inheritance. In fact, class inheritance is said by many to be the distinction between a true object-oriented language and one that simply offers good data-oriented facilities.

In the next chapter, we'll examine a few more features in C++ that require in-depth explanation. We'll go on to discuss object-oriented design, before plunging into the uses of the MFC library.

CHAPTER 7

Other Differences between C and C++

*I*n Chapter 5, you learned about several small differences between C and C++. Chapter 6 covers perhaps the most important difference between the two languages, the C++ implementation of the concept of classes. This chapter introduces several other C++ features that you should understand to help you build programs with the MFC library, and to help you not only build safer, more error-free programs, but build them more easily. Specifically, this chapter discusses the *new* and *delete* operators, reference types, linkage to non-C++ routines and data, templates, and exceptions.

Dynamic Object Allocation

In C, you allocate raw space using malloc( ), calloc( ), or realloc( ), and you release it with free( ). This raw space is untyped. If you call calloc( ), the space is filled entirely with zero bits, which isn't necessarily the right thing to do for some data types! If you call realloc( ), the space is filled with the contents of a previously allocated (and now de-allocated) space. When you call free( ), the space becomes technically unusable, and is in an undefined state — you don't know whether it still has its previous contents. Other than that, these routines do nothing to the raw space.

This approach is unacceptable in C++, because C++ has no concept of untyped space. Everything in C++ is an object of some type or another. As we saw in the preceding chapter, when an object is created, C++ wants to be able to run the associated constructor function or functions.

This can't be done if the allocated space has no type while it's being allocated. Similarly, when an object is destroyed, C++ wants to run the destructor function or functions that are associated with that object. This can't be done if the function that destroys the object and frees up the space can't determine the object's type.

To avoid these problems in the allocation and returning of space, C++ introduces four new operators: *new, new[], delete,* and *delete[]*. These operators may or may not be compatible with the space allocation done by malloc( ). At start-up, they appear to be compatible in Microsoft Visual C++ 2.0. However, the new and delete operators can be redefined by operator overloading at any time, for a single class or for all classes. For your most portable code, you should avoid using malloc( ), free( ), and the related functions we've mentioned in the same program as the new and delete operators.

THE NEW OPERATOR

The *new* operator provides a means for dynamically creating a new object in C++. When the new operator is called with the name of a data type as its argument, a pointer to a new object of that type is returned. From the C++ point of view, this is much better than a call to malloc( ), which returns untyped, uninitialized, raw space.

After the new operator is called and finishes its job, the default constructor function for the object is usually called, if it exists. By providing the new operator with the appropriate initializer arguments after the type name, you can instead specify a call to the copy constructor function or any other constructor function. You specify the copy constructor by using an object of the same type as the one you are creating. Other constructors are specified by using the arguments for those functions. Figure 7-1 shows several examples in which the new operator is used with the Complex class we defined in Chapter 6.

If you're using the new operator with a data type that has more than one part in its name, you might want to put the type name in parentheses. Better yet, typedef the type name to a simple name, and use the simple name. For example, if you want an object of type pointer-to-function-returning-int, you might first write:

```
int (**fn)()    = new int (*)();
```

```
//
// The following code declares a pointer to a Complex
// object and defines it as pointing to a newly allocated
// object of that type. This is the simplest way to use
// the new operator. Because there is a "default"
// constructor function, it is called for this object.
//

Complex *cxpPtr1    = new Complex;

//
// The following code does the same thing, but
// initializes the value of the Complex object by passing
// numeric arguments to the appropriate constructor
// function for the object.
//

Complex *cxpPtr2    = new Complex(5, 3.14159);

//
// The following code calls the Complex class's "copy"
// constructor function to pass the value of the already-
// existing Complex object to the new Complex object.
//

Complex *cxpPtr3    = new Complex(*cxpPtr2);
```

Figure 7-1

Using the new operator with the Complex data type that we defined in the previous chapter.

But the C++ compiler will return a compilation error, because it understands the new expression as:

```
(new int) (*)()
```

You need to use:

```
int (**fn)()    = new (int (*)());
```

Or, a better solution is:

```
typedef int (*int_func_p)();
int_func_p *fn    = new int_func_p;
```

Perhaps the best solution to this problem is to always put your argument to new in parentheses, whether the argument is one word or multiple parts.

For any given class, it's possible to overload the new operator for that class. If you do so, you must make sure that space is somehow allocated for the object of that class. C++ doesn't specify whether you should allocate the space in new or in the constructor function. If you allocate space in an unexpected way, however, make sure you document it well.

It's also possible to overload the new operator at the top level, for all classes. Please remember, though, that it's a lot of work to make sure that you're doing this correctly for all types. There are probably other, simpler ways to make your application more efficient.

THE new[] OPERATOR

The new operator allocates only one object at a time. Another operator — new[] — lets you create arrays of objects. The new[] operator, when called with a data type name as its argument, also returns a value of pointer-to-type, but the pointer is to the first element of an array. The following example shows how you use new[]:

```
Complex *cxpPtr    = new Complex[10];
```

In this example, space is allocated for an array of 10 Complex objects. The new[] operator returns a pointer to the first element, which is assigned to cxpPtr.

Interestingly, you can allocate an array of 0 of any object! Each call to new type [0] returns a unique value of a pointer to an array of zero objects.

We discussed several ways to use initializers with the new operator. Unfortunately, you can't use an initializer with the new[] operator. After allocating the array, you need to initialize each element of the array individually.

THE delete OPERATOR

Where the new operator lets us allocate objects using an operator that knows about object types, the delete operator gives us a way to destroy those objects:

```
delete cxpPtr1;
delete cxpPtr2;
delete cxpPtr3;
```

The delete operator acts on a single object that was initially created using the new operator. Its argument is a pointer to that object. When the delete operator is called, if there's a destructor function for that object's class, it is called first, before the space is returned to the system. If there's any chance that the object will be deleted while it's cast to one of its parent classes, the destructor function should be a virtual member function.

Of course, you shouldn't try to access an object after it's deleted, even though the pointer value won't be changed. The result would be, as the Draft Standard says, "undefined." Virtually anything could happen — but usually your data will be corrupted, and your program will crash.

The delete operator works properly only when it is called on a pointer to an object that was created by the new operator. However, it will also accept a NULL pointer as an argument, and gracefully do nothing! The delete operator always has a void return value.

Just as you can with the new operator, you can overload the delete operator at the top level or for specific classes. In fact, if you overload the new operator, you'll almost certainly have to overload the delete operator. If you do so, you need to make sure that all the used space is properly reclaimed. You also need to remember to have your overloaded delete operator gracefully ignore a NULL pointer argument.

THE DELETE[] OPERATOR

Just as the new operator creates only one object at a time, the delete operator destroys only one object at a time. To destroy an array object that was created by the new[] operator, you must use the delete[] operator. To delete the object that was created in our new[] example in a previous section, you would write:

```
delete [] cxpPtr;
```

The delete[] operator works properly only on pointers that are returned from calls to the new[] operator. Like the delete operator, delete[] will accept a NULL pointer as an argument and gracefully ignore it. The delete[] operator also accepts and destroys pointers to zero-length arrays created by the new[] operator.

Reference Types

Reference types are constructed from other types. There aren't any
objects of reference types. A name that's declared with a reference type
is actually an alias, or a *reference*, to another object of the same type
without the reference. This is somewhat confusing to those of us who
started as C programmers, because we were taught repeatedly that each
variable declaration sets aside some new storage space for a new data
object. In fact, a reference type declaration seems more like a FORTRAN
language EQUIVALENCE statement than a variable declaration in C!

As shown in Figure 7-2, reference types are written with an ampersand (&) after the type and before the name of the reference variable or
function that is being declared.

```
const int nBuckets  = 101;
//
// The following is an integer array, followed by a reference to an
// element of that array.
//
int iBuckets[nBuckets];
int & iCenter   = iBuckets[nBuckets/2];
```

Figure 7-2
A sample reference type declaration.

You can create references to almost any data type, except bit fields
and other references. You can't have an array of references, and you
can't have pointers to references. References are commonly used as variables or class data members (as in the preceding example), as parameters to functions, and as function returns. These uses of references are
discussed in the following sections.

REFERENCE VARIABLES

Figure 7-2 shows a typical use of a reference variable. The variable iCenter
is used to refer to the center member of the integer array iBuckets. Anything that's done using the name iCenter is actually done to the array member to which this name refers. Reference variables become more useful as

the expression that names the original object becomes more complex. Who hasn't cringed at expressions like the following?

```
proc_array[selector].p_access->pa_groups[i].mode =
    ((proc_array[selector].p_access->pa_groups[i].mode & O_READ)
        | O_WRITE);
```

Using a reference variable, this can be rewritten as:

```
int & ProcMode  = proc_array[selector].p_access->pa_groups[i].mode;
ProcMode = ((ProcMode & O_READ) | O_WRITE);
```

A reference variable must be initialized when and where it's declared. Once it's initialized, the reference can't be changed. In Figure 7-2, the following expression seems to be assigning the value of iBuckets[nBuckets/2] to iCenter:

```
int & iCenter   = iBuckets[nBuckets/2];
```

In fact, it's actually forming the reference from the array member to the reference variable. Now that this reference is initialized, any assignments to iCenter will actually be assignments to the referenced array member. Any other operations on iCenter will also be operations on the referenced array member, as long as iCenter is in scope.

Class data members can also have reference types. If a class has a reference-type member, the reference member also must be initialized when an object of that class is declared, or when an object of that class is created using the new operator. As shown in Figure 7-3, a special syntax was created for initializing data members during the entrance to a constructor function. Once a reference data member is initialized, it can't be changed. It continues to reference the same object until that object is destroyed, or the object containing the reference member is destroyed.

It's possible to get a reference to something that doesn't exist! For example, after you have created a reference to an object, the object might go away either by leaving its scope or by being destroyed with the delete operator. Obviously, any use of the reference beyond that point has "undefined" results. In Figure 7-3, notice that the argument *outside*, to the second constructor function, must be declared as a reference argument; otherwise, its scope is only the constructor function itself! Reference arguments are described in the next section.

```
//
// This class contains a reference data member. The constructor
// functions use special syntax to initialize the reference data
// member before the function is entered; because, by the time
// you're inside the function, it's too late - the reference already
// exists, and can't be reassigned!
// The syntax allows you to initialize any member, after the colon
// that follows the argument list, by giving its name and its
// initial value.
//
class RefExample {
    private:
        int held;
        int & holder;
        ...
    public:
        RefExample(): holder(held)
            { held = 0; };
        RefExample(int & outside): holder(outside)
            { held = -1; };
        ...
};
```

Figure 7-3
This example shows reference data members being initialized in constructor functions.

REFERENCE ARGUMENTS

An argument to a function can be declared by reference. This use of references will be familiar to anyone who has programmed in languages that allow arguments by reference. In C++, this is just a specific use of the concept of reference types.

As shown in Figure 7-4, an argument declared by reference is declared in the normal way, but with the & after the type declaration and before the name.

```
double Abs(const Complex & cxNum)
{
    return(sqrt(cxNum.Real * cxNum.Real + cxNum.Imag * cxNum.Imag));
}
```

Figure 7-4
An example of a reference argument.

When you call a function, the argument is usually copied, and that copy is passed to the function. Anything taking place inside the function is done only to the copy. With a *reference* argument, the argument inside the function refers to exactly the same object that was passed to the function! Anything done to the object inside the function is actually being done to the original object. Sometimes, but not always, this is what was intended. You need to be aware of this fact when using functions that have reference arguments.

The other advantage of using a reference argument is that no copying has to be done! Although the Complex object used in our example is relatively small, the use of reference arguments can provide more significant benefits when you are working with larger objects — for example, MS-Windows objects based on the MFC library CWnd classes. Even though the object in our example is being passed by reference, we've declared it *const*, which makes it clear that the object is not to be changed. To another person reading our code, this usually indicates that the argument is passed this way simply to save the trouble of copying.

You might recall that we mentioned the use of reference arguments in the preceding chapter, when we discussed overloading operators with class member functions. There, we introduced a trick that uses both reference arguments and reference function returns. We'll see it again in the following section.

REFERENCE FUNCTION RETURNS

If we declare a function with the & after the return type and before the function name, we are declaring that the function returns a reference. In other words, when this function is called, it doesn't return a *copy* of an object, it returns a reference to the object itself. How does this work?

If the function returns a pure value anyway (for example, the values 0 or 1), this reference obviously doesn't have any real meaning. It means something only if the function returns an existing object. The reference also doesn't mean anything if the first thing we do with the returned reference is to make a copy of it in some other memory location. It makes sense only if the returned reference is used directly. Figure 7-5 provides an example showing how reference function returns are used.

```
#include <stdlib.h>

const int nBuckets  = 101;
static int iBuckets[nBuckets];

// This function returns a random element of iBuckets[].
int & getBucket()
{
    register int i  = rand();

    i = (int) ((i * (double) nBuckets) / RAND_MAX);

    // Can't happen, but let's be safe.
    if (i < 0)
        i = 0;
    if (i >= nBuckets)
        i = nBuckets - 1;

    return(iBuckets[i]);
}
```

Figure 7-5
An example of reference function returns.

In this example, the return value is iBuckets[i]. Actually, it would be more correct to say that the return *reference* is iBuckets[i]. The value is *not* returned. Instead, a reference to that array member is returned.

What's the difference? As mentioned previously, there is no difference if the only use of the reference is to copy the value somewhere else, as in:

```
int iTest   = getBucket();
```

The difference arises if the returned reference is used as a variable name, as in the following example:

```
getBucket() = 1001;
```

Here's another example:

```
++getBucket();
```

To a C programmer, this probably looks odd. How can you assign a value to a function call? How can you increment it? In fact, the function call returns a reference to an element of the integer array iBuckets. This array element is the object to which we're assigning a value and which we're incrementing.

Obviously, the reference that is returned must be to something that will persist after the function has returned. In our example, we used an array that was outside the function's scope to provide return references. You could also use a *static* object declared inside the function's scope. You should avoid returning a reference to an automatic variable, which goes away as the function returns. This includes automatic argument variables.

On the other hand, if a reference argument variable is of the same type as the return type, you can certainly return it! This capability can be used for many purposes. Figure 7-6 shows a version of the function from Figure 7-5 that's been generalized to use an array that is passed as an argument. The new Verify( ) function illustrates the feature we're describing.

In this example, the array and its size are passed to the function. Range verification is moved out of the function and into a new function, Verify( ). The selected element and the highest and lowest elements of the array are passed to the function *by reference*. The addresses of the highest and lowest elements are compared to the address of the element itself, and if any errors are detected, the array boundaries are returned instead of the selected element. Remember that there are no pointers to references. When we take the address of these reference arguments, we're taking the address of the original array elements! When we return one of the arguments, we're still returning a reference to one of the original array elements, which in turn is returned — by reference — from getBucket( ). (Note that the use of code such as Verify( ) can be bad programming practice, if you don't always make absolutely sure that the three arguments are all members of the same array. It is a good example for this feature of C++.)

We mentioned the same idea when we discussed overloading the assignment operator within a class. The assignment operator needs to return a reference. The reference is to (*this), because the implicit argument to a class member function is a pointer rather than a reference. You might be wondering why it isn't a reference. When the behavior of classes and member functions was first defined, references weren't a part of C++. By the time references were added, it was too late to go back and change all the existing C++ code.

References were first added to fix some problems with operator overloading; but their use is, obviously, much greater than that. However, there can be the temptation to abuse them. When used locally, for clarity (as in the ProcMode example, earlier in this chapter), they can increase the correctness of a C++ program. When used with careless abandon, they can make it unclear what the program is doing — not only to the original programmer, and therefore to the original program; but also to the other programmers like you who will have to build on this code. Like all other features, use references where they're needed, not just for the sake of using them.

```
#include <stdlib.h>

int & Verify(int &, int &, int &);

//
// This function returns a random element of the passed argument
// iBuckets[].
//
int & getBucket(int * const & iBuckets, const int nBuckets)
{
    register int i  = rand();

    i = (int) ((i * (double) nBuckets) / RAND_MAX);

    return(Verify(iBuckets[i], iBuckets[0], iBuckets[nBuckets-1]));
}

//
// This function verifies that the element isn't out of range.
// The arguments absolutely must always be members of the same
// array.
//
int & Verify(int & elem, int & low, int & high)
{
    if (&elem < &low)
        return(low);
    if (&elem > &high)
        return(high);
    return(elem);
}
```

Figure 7-6

Returning a reference argument as a reference function return.

Linkage to Non-C++ Routines and Data

Sometimes, you might need to call existing routines that are written in a language other than C++. A special syntax is needed to declare these routines. Why is this special syntax necessary?

We've made frequent reference to the fact that you can overload C++ functions by declaring them multiple times with different argument types. The different function *signatures* — that is, the function names plus the argument types — name different functions. As such, you can call these different functions using the same name with different argument types, and the right function is always called.

This is done by *name mangling*. (Yes, really!) As its name implies, name mangling involves mixing up a function name with the names of its argument types in a consistent way, so that when the program is linked, the correct function calls and definitions are automatically put together. If a call is made to the function with a different set of arguments, and that particular overload is not defined, you'll know this at link time rather than waiting until that particular function call is made during testing by you (or during execution by your users!).

Unfortunately, this doesn't provide a means for telling the linker that you simply want the function whose link-time name is, for example, _grow_kudzu, and not a mangled version thereof. If we do have a C function called grow_kudzu( ), and we want to declare it as such, we can simply declare it as follows:

```
extern "C" int grow_kudzu();
```

"C" and "C++" are the only languages currently allowed in this syntax. If you omit the string entirely, this reverts to a C++ extern statement.

You can use the same syntax for either functions or data that are declared externally. Because data names aren't mangled, this may not be necessary for data. However, you should use this syntax anyway because it has the added advantage of documenting the origin of the external data. And if you don't use it, you might someday find yourself using a different C++ compiler that puts out data link-time names differently in C and C++.

If you need to declare more than one thing in this way, you can declare them together in a block:

```
extern "C" {
    int grow_kudzu();
    int grow_kale();
    int grow_korn();
    int fields[];
    int vines[];
}
```

There are several restrictions on the use of this construct. Because you can have only one C function with a particular name, you can't declare more than one such function. (In other words, there is no overloading within C.) On the other hand, if you've declared one particular function signature to be a C function, you can't redefine it in C++. The function arguments and return values must be of types that can be shared in C and C++. In addition, because this construct declares some top-level linkages, it can appear only at the file scope level, and not inside a function.

It is possible that a given implementation of C++ might not be able to provide this capability. This might occur because no implementation of C is sufficiently compatible to be linked with that particular implementation of C++. Considering the relationship between the two languages, however, this is unlikely.

Microsoft Visual C++ supports this capability. Because all of the C library functions have already been declared this way in the C++ header files, all you have to do is #include the appropriate header files, and you can use most of your favorite C library functions. As we've mentioned elsewhere in this book, it's a good idea to avoid using certain C library functions, such as printf( ) and malloc( ). Instead, you should use the appropriate C++ constructs.

Templates

Templates in C++ define families of classes or functions that use exactly the same code, except for changing a data type or other parameter. The parameters that change between uses of the template are defined as arguments to the template.

This sounds like preprocessor #define macros. You might wonder why we need another such capability. It's important that you understand the difference.

Preprocessor macros are used solely for text replacement. That's all. This is one reason why they're used so extensively in the USENIX Obfuscated C Code Contest (OCCC). Macro bodies don't have to make sense — and in the OCCC, they usually don't! Whatever text you put into a macro body, the same text, with argument substitutions, will come spilling out when you invoke the macro.

Templates, on the other hand, are part of the C++ language. A template must define a valid C++ class or function, or a static data member of a template class. Like any other class or function, the parts of a template class or function must be valid either on their own or *at the point of the template's definition*, if the template arguments are properly defined. This is unlike a preprocessor macro. It doesn't matter what's valid or invalid when a macro is defined, only whether the macro's subsequent use produces valid C++ code. Templates also perform type checking of their arguments. Macros obviously can't do this.

The declaration of a template starts with the keyword *template*, followed by a list of one or more arguments. At least one argument is needed for a template; after all, something is needed to distinguish the different classes or functions from each other! The argument list is written between angle braces — that is, < and > — instead of parentheses. Because the compiler takes a fairly simple approach to matching angle braces, you must be careful if you use expressions involving the relationships less-than (<) and greater-than (>) anywhere that the compiler expects to see template arguments. It is usually helpful to put such expressions in parentheses.

Template arguments almost always include one argument that's declared as a *class* argument. The actual type name that's passed as a *class* argument can be any type, because the C++ concept of classes includes all of the built-in types. The *class* argument is needed in the function template — and it is usually used in the class template — to distinguish between different uses, or *instantiations*, of the template.

Template arguments can also be of any data type. When the template is called, however, the non-*class* arguments all must be either constant expressions or the names of data or functions that are extern. This is necessary for preventing illegal leakage of objects that should be local. In particular, a string constant is a data object that is not extern, so it can't be used unless it's in a global array or is pointed to by a global pointer.

When defining a template, you must use the template arguments in the body of the template definition to distinguish one use of the template from another. In other words, each set of arguments must produce a different class or function. Otherwise, we might end up with two different uses of the same template (with different arguments) that create the same function or class.

There are specific ways to invoke the use of a template, either explicitly or implicitly, and to override the normal definition of a template for specific cases. We'll see examples of these in the following sections. As we discuss these, you should remember that even if we name different uses of the template, these are only compiled into actual code if they're used. As such, we should make our template definitions as complete as possible, without worrying about wasting space with unused template instances.

In the following sections, we'll introduce examples of template use. First, we'll describe a simple example of a function template. Then, we'll introduce a class template, and show you how to declare the class member functions and static data members in their own, parallel templates.

A FUNCTION TEMPLATE EXAMPLE

In Chapter 5, we used the Abs( ) absolute-value function to introduce the concept of operator overloads. We defined various overloaded functions that returned the absolute value for different types of data.

At the time, overloading might have seemed like the greatest thing since sliced bread. It is useful. But it has the disadvantage of producing code even when that code isn't used in the program. In the case of Abs( ), this isn't a significant problem because the functions are short enough that they could be declared inline. However, this isn't a good general solution.

Most of the Abs( ) functions have identical code, but are used for different types. This makes Abs( ) a prime candidate for a function template. Figure 7-7 shows a function template for the Abs( ) function that will generate all of these functions, as needed.

```
//
// This template defines a family of functions.  The template has a
// class parameter, NumClass. The functions generated by this
// template differ from each other only in that their argument and
// return value types are of the NumClass type.
//
template <class NumClass>
inline NumClass Abs(const NumClass x)
{
    return(x < 0 ? -x : x);
}


//
// The following is an "explicit specialization" of the template
// function Abs() for the Complex class described in Chapter 6.
//
inline double Abs<Complex>(const Complex cxNum)
{
    return(sqrt(cxNum.Real * cxNum.Real + cxNum.Imag * cxNum.Imag));
}


//
// The following is an "explicit instantiation" of the template
// function Abs() for the "int" class [type].
//
template inline int Abs<int>(const int);
```

Figure 7-7
A function template for the Abs() function.

In this example, notice that the class argument is used in the function declaration to declare an argument to Abs( ). This is essential. If the template didn't vary the function *signature* (that is, its name plus its argument types), all uses of the template would produce a function with the same signature. As mentioned previously in our discussion of overloaded functions, the various overloads must differ in argument type; otherwise, we're talking about the same function. And you can't define a single function more than once! As it is, each different use with a different data type argument gives us a different overloaded Abs( ) function.

Once the template is defined, we can use it as is. For example, to use it on a long integer, you could call:

```
long int liOldNum;
long int liNum  = Abs(liOldNum);
```

In this code, the type of the argument implies that the version of the Abs( ) function that deals with the long int data type should be used; and so that version is generated, if it didn't already exist.

We can also explicitly specify which use, or *instantiation*, of the template we want:

```
long int liOldNum;
long int liNum  = Abs<long int>(liOldNum);  // Same as before
double dNum     = Abs<double>(liOldNum);    // Argument is converted
                                            // before Abs is called
```

An *explicit instantiation* can also be done independently of any use, just to make sure that the function generated by that use of the template is present in the program:

```
template inline int Abs<int>(const int);
```

This creates an instance of the template, based on the class argument *int*.

Some uses of the function being defined in the template might not fit the usual mold, as expressed in the body of the template. For example, even though our version of Abs( ) works with all scalar data types, we might want to generalize it to work with our Complex data type from Chapter 6. To handle this special case, we can write an *explicit specialization* of the function. In Figure 7-6, the Abs( ) function has a specialization for the Complex data type. This specialization declares Abs( ) with a double return type, rather than a Complex, and a different formula for figuring out the return value. Rather than creating a separate, independent function that then takes up unused space if it's not needed, this specialization becomes part of the template definition.

A function template is sometimes necessary when the function is a member function of a class that has been generated by a class template. In the next section, we'll see how this is declared.

A CLASS TEMPLATE EXAMPLE

A *class template* is also called a *parameterized type*. As such, the idea has been around in C++ since the mid-1980s. Although its current implementation is fairly straightforward, you need to consider a few points when using or defining a class template.

As the name implies, a class template defines a family of classes that differ only in regard to the values that are passed as arguments to the template. How do we name a class in that family? We might define a class template whose header is, for example:

```
template <class Type, int Size>
class ArrayList {
    ...
```

In this example, the names of the classes are the template name followed by the arguments. In other words, ArrayList<int,100> could be the name of a class in this family. Another class in this family could be ArrayList<Complex,1>. If a constant is required in the class name, you can use any constant expression that's equal to the original. For example, ArrayList<int,2*2*5*5> is the same as ArrayList<int,100>. Unlike function templates, the plain template name is never used by itself outside the class template definition. Inside the body of the class template definition, you can to refer to the class using either the template name with its arguments, or the plain template name. However, any constructor and destructor function names should use just the template name, without the arguments attached.

A common use for templates is in the creation of *container classes* — that is, classes that have their own capabilities in addition to holding objects of other types. Figure 7-8 provides an example of a container class. It has linked-list properties and procedures, and it holds a fixed-size array of some object. The type of the object and the size of the array are parameters to the class template. This incomplete definition simply highlights the points we want to make about class templates. The MFC library has several more complete templates for container classes (called *collection classes* in the Microsoft documentation): CArray, CList, CMap, CTypedPtrArray, CTypedPtrList, and CTypedPtrMap. These are documented in the MFC Library Reference manual.

The first point we'll make about this example is to remind you that the name of each class is the template name followed by its arguments. In this example template definition, we don't yet have any specific uses of the template, but we do need to use the class name several times within the template definition. The type of the link pointer *next* within the class part of the definition must be the same as the class itself. Because it's still within the template definition, we simply use the template name plus the names of the formal arguments.

```
template <class Type, int Size>
class ArrayList {
    private:
        Type array[Size];
        // The following could be declared "ArrayList *":
        ArrayList<Type,Size> *next;
        static int count;
        ...
    public:
        // default constructor function
        ArrayList();
        // copy constructor function
        ArrayList(ArrayList<Type,Size> arg);
        // destructor function
        ~ArrayList();
        ...
};

// A static data member must be initialized.
template <class Type, int Size>
int ArrayList<Type,Size>::count     = 0;

// The constructor simply increases count.
template <class Type, int Size>
ArrayList<Type,Size>::ArrayList()
{
    ++count;
}

// The destructor simply decreases count.
template <class Type, int Size>
ArrayList<Type,Size>::~ArrayList()
{
    --count;
}
```

Figure 7-8
A (partial) definition of a class template.

We need to do the same thing when we initialize the static data members and define the member functions. If we do this outside the class definition, however, we must make sure that each of these definitions is within its own template declaration. However, they are still very much part of the class for which they're defined. When any particular use of the class template is instantiated, all of the parts of the class are instantiated, including the static data members and all of the defined member functions. On the other hand, you shouldn't try to instantiate parts of the class template without instantiating the class to which they belong.

Like function templates, class templates can be *explicitly instantiated*, independent of any use. If there is some set of arguments for which you don't want to use the normal template, you can also define an *explicit specialization* of the class. You can also define explicit specializations of the member functions.

When designing or using class templates, you need to make sure that any functions or data objects that are made by one of your instantiations will actually exist, at least by the time the program is linked. For our simple example, this isn't a problem. But suppose we have defined a *friend* function in our class template body, such as the following?

```
friend print(Type t);
friend ostream & operator << (ostream & os, Type t);
```

Once a use of the template is declared, new instances of these functions are legally declared and may be used in the program. They need to exist for the program to load and run properly.

Before you define a template, it's a good idea to first build a function or class that's an instance of your template. Once you have that working, you can generalize it by pulling out the values that will differ between different instantiations of the template, and make them the template arguments. That way, you can separate the work of getting the function or class correct from the work of getting the template correct.

Templates are a powerful new addition to C++. With careful use, they can make some programs much easier to write and to understand.

Exceptions

In a well-structured program, the control flow is fairly easy to understand. Blocks typically have one entry and one exit. Nested blocks, including functions, are entered one by one, and then exited in a last-in, first-out manner. We try to avoid the spaghetti code that characterizes those older programs in which the unstructured use of gotos resulted in maintenance nightmares.

Despite our best efforts, however, something might go wrong deep in the middle of a program. Even if we could anticipate everything that might go wrong, it would be tedious to program all of the nested blocks to recognize a particular error return, and then pass that return back to the level at which it can be easily handled.

We find another case in which we might want to jump out of a number of nested blocks when a deeply nested part of a program has come to a natural end. A programmer might want to explicitly declare that the program is returning to a specific, previous level.

In C, the functions setjmp( ) and longjmp( ) were introduced to help programmers solve these types of problems. The setjmp( ) call stores the stack environment, and the longjmp( ) call unwinds the stack until it's the same as the stored environment. The call to longjmp( ) also returns an integer value, which — when the stack is unwound — appears to the return level as a return value from the setjmp( ) call.

For a C++ programmer, the use of setjmp( ) and longjmp( ) presents several problems:

- There are no object semantics in the concept of unwinding a stack. In C++, when we leave a stack frame or other scope, we need to destroy the objects that are local to that scope, calling any destructor functions that are necessary along the way.

- The return value for this mechanism must be an integer. The possible size of an integer, and thus the number of meanings you can encode in it, keeps getting larger. However, it is more in keeping with both object-oriented and structured programming to allow the return of any type of object to the handler, so that the error return information can be better structured.

- The C language has no semantics that prevent the improper use of the setjmp( ) and longjmp( ) functions. As is consistent with C's philosophy, these are just functions, and the compiler makes no effort to distinguish them from other functions. A longjmp( ) can be called from a stack frame outside the call to setjmp( ), or with an improper stack environment argument. These functions can even be replaced by user functions of the same names that perform completely different tasks.

In C++, a special mechanism handles *exceptions* — that is, events that don't usually happen. The mechanism uses the keywords *try*, *catch*, and *throw*. The *try* keyword is placed immediately before a control block within which we want to catch these exceptions. Immediately after this block, we add one or more control blocks containing *exception handler* code. Each of these handlers is preceded by the keyword *catch* and an argument declaration for the handler. When an exception condition occurs inside the *try block*, the keyword *throw* is used, with an argument, to pass control to an appropriate exception handler.

Let's look at several examples of this mechanism.

A SIMPLE EXCEPTION EXAMPLE

Figure 7-9 shows a fairly simple example of exception handling, involving no nesting of exception handlers and only primitive data types.

In addition to including blocks that are written inside it, notice that the try block dynamically includes any function calls inside it. This includes function calls that are side effects of dealing with objects, such as constructor or destructor functions, operator overloading functions, and other member functions.

The handler blocks are written immediately after the try block. Each one starts with the *catch* keyword, and each has an argument of a different type. When an exception is thrown, the handlers are checked in the order in which they appear, until one is found that matches the type of the thrown argument. When this happens, control passes to that control block, and the thrown argument is used as the argument for that block. When the handler block is done, if it doesn't pass control again (for example, via exit( ), abort( ), or another throw), control is passed to the end of all the handler blocks.

The last handler in the example has an ellipsis (...) for its argument. As in a function prototype, this means that no argument type is specified. For the handler, this means that it accepts any argument type. Obviously, a handler like this must be the last one listed. The argument is not available to this handler (with one exception, which is mentioned in the next section).

Because the try block includes all of the blocks in the try block and dynamically includes all of the functions that are called from inside the

try block, a throw can appear anywhere inside those blocks and functions. The throw can take any type as an object to be returned. In fact, a
more realistic example would use exception-specific classes for the
objects being returned, and the arguments to the catch blocks would be
of those types. The uses of throw in our example have parentheses
around the argument. This isn't really necessary, just as it isn't necessary
for a return. However, it does help to group the throw argument, and is
a good programming habit.

```
main()
{
    ...
    //
    // The following block of code may contain several subblocks
    // and function calls, all of which are (dynamically) under the
    // control of the initial "try", for the purposes of exception
    // handling.
    //
    try {
        ...
        f(x);
        ...
    }
    catch (const int & i) {
        cout << "Integer exception " << i << "." << endl;
    }
    catch (const char * & cp) {
        cout << "String exception \"" << cp << "\"." << endl;
    }
    catch (...) {
        cout << "Unknown exception." << endl;
        abort();
    }
    ...
}

void f(int x)
{
    ...
    if (int_problem)
        throw(42);
    ...
    if (string_problem)
        throw("The Answer.");
    ...
}
```

Figure 7-9

A simple exception example.

NESTED EXCEPTION HANDLERS

Try blocks can be nested, either as they are written or dynamically. Try blocks are dynamically nested if a function is called from inside a try block, and that function has a try block which is then entered.

If an exception is thrown from inside a nested try block, the innermost try block is examined first to determine whether a handler there matches the type of the thrown argument. If there is a matching handler, control passes to that handler, and the exception is satisfied. If there isn't a match, the next try block out is similarly checked, and so on, for all nested try blocks.

If a handler decides that it wants to pass the exception on up the chain, it can do one of two things. It can throw another exception itself, which is passed on to be handled by the next enclosing try block (if any). Or, it can use throw with no argument:

```
throw;
```

This code takes the argument to the throw expression that landed us in this handler, and passes it out as the argument to this throw. This use of throw without an argument can be done only from within an exception handler block. This works even from within a handler that has an ellipsis (...) as its argument. This is the only exception to the rule that such a handler doesn't have access to its argument.

UNHANDLED EXCEPTIONS

If all nested try blocks have been searched for a handler to a particular exception (that is, a handler with the same type argument as the argument to throw), and no matching handler is found, the thrown exception isn't caught. This might happen if a function that throws an exception is sometimes called from within a try block, and is sometimes called without being inside a try block. If an exception isn't caught, the terminate( ) function is called. The default action of terminate( ) is to call abort( ).

You can change the function that is called by terminate( ), by calling the set_terminate( ) function. The set_terminate( ) function takes as its argument a pointer to a function declared with a *void* return. The set_terminate( ) function returns the address of the function that was previously to be called by terminate( ). Here are the steps for temporarily setting your own termination function:

1. Call set_terminate( ) with your termination function, and save the function pointer that it returns.

2. Enter your try block.

3. On exit from your try block, call set_terminate( ) with the saved function pointer that it had previously returned, ignoring the new return value.

Of course, if your termination function is ever really called, you shouldn't be returning from your try block. It's an error for your termination function not to terminate.

UNEXPECTED EXCEPTIONS

WARNING: The features described in this section aren't implemented in Microsoft Visual C++ 2.0. We have two reasons for describing them. First, they are in the Draft Standard, and Microsoft is aware of them, and will probably include them in a future release. Second, you might encounter these features in code that you are porting to Visual C++. Rather than leave you puzzled over these features, we'll describe them for you.

A function can declare which exception classes it will allow to be thrown through it. If a function that it calls throws an exception, and the type of the argument to throw is not in the list of allowed exception classes, the exception is considered *unexpected*.

The list of allowed exception classes follows the function header and precedes the function body. It starts with the keyword throw, which is followed by the allowed exception classes in parentheses, separated by commas. In the example shown in Figure 7-10, we assume defined classes Bad_Spelling, Bad_Grammar, and Bad_Punctuation. The parse( ) function is being declared.

In this example, if any exceptions are thrown with arguments whose data types are other than the three named in the list, those exceptions are considered to be *unexpected*. Only three classes of exceptions are expected from inside this function.

```
int parse(char *sentence, RuleBook *rules)
throw(Bad_Spelling, Bad_Grammar, Bad_Punctuation)
{
    ...
}
```

Figure 7-10

An example showing the declaration of a function with a list of allowed exception classes.

If an unexpected exception occurs, the unexpected( ) function is called. The default action of unexpected( ) is to call terminate( ). As with terminate( ), you can change the function that is called by unexpected( ). In this case, you call the set_unexpected( ) function. This function takes as its argument a pointer to a function declared with a *void* return. The set_unexpected( ) function returns the address of the function that was previously to be called by unexpected( ). So, you can temporarily set your own unexpected( ) function using set_unexpected( ), in the same three steps listed previously for temporarily setting your own termi- nate( ) function using set_terminate( ). It's illegal for the function which you set to be called by unexpected( ) to return, but it may throw another exception.

A function can declare that it won't allow any exception classes to be thrown through it. It does this by having an empty throw( ) list after the function header.

The throw( ) list of allowed exception classes after the function header is not a part of the function signature. It does not affect overload matching (or link-time name mangling).

OTHER VERSIONS OF EXCEPTION HANDLERS

There are other versions of exception handlers, both in old versions of Microsoft Visual C++ and in Microsoft Windows NT. We'll mention them here so that you can recognize them, and can replace them with the standard C++ exception handlers.

Microsoft Windows NT introduced the concept of *structured exceptions.* You can recognize them by their use of the keywords _ _try, _ _except, and _ _finally. Their semantics differ somewhat from the standard

C++ excéptions. Microsoft recommends that you use the standard C++ exceptions, and strongly recommends that you avoid mixing the two. If you absolutely must use them, Microsoft's on-line *C/C++ Programming Techniques* manual provides guidelines for their use.

Previous versions of Microsoft Visual C++ have used the MFC library macros TRY, CATCH, AND_CATCH, END_CATCH, THROW, and THROW_LAST. These are now obsolete. There is a technical note on converting these macros to the new form. It can be briefly summarized as follows: END_CATCH disappears, and the others are converted directly to the standard C++ use.

We should also note that in the Microsoft Visual C++ 2.0 runtime library, setjmp( ) and longjmp( ) can be set up to have destructor functions properly called when unwinding the stack. However, this is not a good reason to use these functions. Although they might seem convenient, these functions are definitely not portable. If you need to do something like this, use the standard C++ exceptions.

Summary

This chapter has covered various C++ features that you should understand to help you build programs with the MFC library, and to help you not only build safer, more error-free programs, but to build them more easily. You should now be able to recognize, understand, and use the new and delete operators, reference types, linkage to non-C++ routines and data, templates, and standard C++ exceptions.

In the next chapter, we'll examine the important issues involving object-oriented design and programming in C++, before moving on to a look at the MFC library itself.

8

Object-Oriented Programming in C++

*U*nlike the chapters that provide examples of MFC programming, our discussion of object-oriented programming in C++ can't be presented in a "cookbook" or tutorial style. The process of software design and programming still isn't as codified as we'd like to think it will one day be. What we'll provide in this chapter are some hints, some pitfalls to avoid, and some rules to live by. Or, at least, to program by.

We'll start by providing an overview of the software development process. Then, we'll discuss the essential activities that make up this process. Throughout this discussion, we'll be describing ideal conditions — that is, what the software development process should be. In every case, nontechnical considerations will influence how well we can perform these tasks. This leads us to the last topic we'll discuss in this chapter, management of the software development process.

The Software Development Process

The process that you use for developing software goes a long way toward determining how easy it is to get your software working, and how likely it is that the software will be correct when you're done. In this section, we'll offer some observations on the software development process as a whole.

There's no one *right* way that you should always follow in your software development efforts. However, adopting a standard process is helpful for ensuring that your efforts produce the desired results. This is true whether you're working by yourself or on one of several software engineering teams that are involved in a project.

Analysis and design are integral parts of any programming activity. Even those software engineers who claim that they don't design — that is, they just sit down and program — must have some idea of what they're trying to accomplish when they sit down to start coding. At the other extreme, some organizations insist on full, formal analysis and design documentation for every programming effort, no matter how large or small.

Without external, objective documentation — which may be either formal or informal — a project often becomes so large that its creator can't remember all of its details. The result is usually inconsistencies in actions, objects, and interfaces. Of course, requiring full, formal documentation for even the smallest, one-page programming project might be inefficient. However, any experienced programmer will probably agree that a seemingly small programming project sometimes takes on a life of its own. In such cases, code that you had expected to throw away in a week lives on indefinitely in the form of larger and larger programs. As a result, some form of documentation, at a level appropriate for the scope and importance of the project, is usually a good idea. Although automated documentation tools can be helpful, the analyses and design ideas ultimately must be written down by the person or persons who came up with them.

If you're working by yourself, your documentation procedures might be quite informal. However, if someone else might want to use your software or build on it, you can support their efforts by providing an adequate paper trail. Most programmers like to believe that anyone who sees their code will want to reuse it. Without adequate documentation, however, the person who wants to reuse code won't be able to figure out the original programmer's intentions simply by looking at the code. This holds true even when the person who wants to reuse the code is the person who created it! Proper documentation is helpful whether you are returning to your own code after being away from it for months or years, or even just a few days.

If you're working as a member of a software engineering team, a standard development process is essential. Such a process will help you and the other developers keep track of each other's progress. As you progress from one phase of your work to another, a standard process allows you to keep track of what you're doing as well as make sure that you get it right.

MODELS OF SOFTWARE DEVELOPMENT

Many people have tried to create meaningful models of the software development process. They're still trying, and the models are getting more and more useful.

In almost all of the models, the three important parts of the software development process are analysis, design, and implementation. *Analysis* is the process of defining exactly what the problem is (and, by extension, what isn't part of the problem), along with any constraints on how we obtain a solution. *Design* is the process of working with this problem definition to create a program structure that will handle each part of the problem. *Implementation*, of course, is the stage in which we actually create a working product. Implementation includes coding, review, testing, debugging, release, and support of the product. If the analysis produces a problem statement that accurately describes the problem, and the design produces a program structure that accurately meets the needs of the problem statement, and the implementation accurately reproduces the design in an actual running program, we can be reasonably confident that the program "works."

Figure 8-1 shows an early model of the relationship between these three parts of the software development process. This illustration of the "waterfall model" is based on a similar figure in DeGrace and Stahl's *Wicked Problems, Righteous Solutions* (Prentice-Hall, 1990). In this model, each task is a closed, complete entity, and the separate tasks might even be performed by completely different organizations. When the product of one task is complete, it cascades down to the next step. Each task is self-contained, taking input only from the previous task.

Some managers prefer this model because it identifies separate, well-defined tasks and milestones. You can assemble a strike force to perform one task, and then reassign them to other tasks when their first one is complete. But this model has several problems. First, there's no room for feedback, or for growth of any stage of the work once it's done. If a design problem is identified after the design stage is complete, you have to go back to the beginning and redo your analysis and design. Of course, you could always bypass the system, and either fill in the missing parts after a task is complete, or introduce parts in subsequent steps that don't come from anything in the previous steps. But this defeats the whole purpose of using a standard process in the first place. Rather than bypass the process, we should have a process that allows us to go back and fix errors or fill in missing pieces.

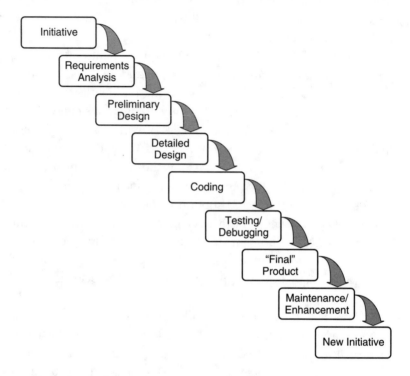

Figure 8-1
The waterfall model of software development.

We view software development as an incremental process, at all levels. We start with a base of analysis, and try to build our design on this foundation. But if we encounter unanswered questions after our analysis is complete, we can always go back and broaden our base. Similarly, if we find during implementation that some needs aren't met by the existing analysis and design, we may need to revisit those steps. This can happen regardless of how completely we believe we've done our analysis and design. With some systems, there are questions that don't become apparent until you're well into the implementation.

This process will be familiar to anyone who has tried to build an earthen embankment for supporting a garden wall. Despite having plenty of experience with this type of project, you might find that your base isn't broad enough to support the wall at the height you've planned. This isn't a problem because you can always add to the base, which can then support the higher levels of the wall. This earthen wall model of software development is illustrated in Figure 8-2.

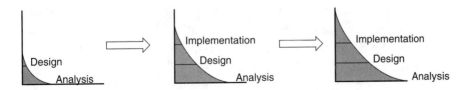

Figure 8-2

An incremental, "earthen wall" model of software development.

We don't intend to encourage incomplete work in the initial analysis or design. You should do your best in all stages of the development effort. But your software development process should also include both the time and the means for making the products of previous stages more robust, as the software development teams gain experience with the problem.

METHODOLOGIES AND NOTATIONS

Joe's first law of software engineering has been, "Say what you mean." This is an important principle during all stages of the software development process. But simply saying something becomes meaningless if you don't write it down. It is either forgotten or, worse yet, is interpreted and misinterpreted. It's as true in software development as in many other fields, "If you don't write it down, you didn't do it."

But, what should we write down? This is an important question, and so is its companion question: How should we write it down?

We need to write down as much as is necessary to communicate the important points of our analysis, design, and implementation. We need to be able to pass these on, not only to others, but also to ourselves, when we come back to the problem after a vacation or even after one night's sleep. We need to capture the important points of the analysis, showing the problem statement and the constraints. We need to describe the design, and especially the interfaces between the various components of the design. We need to describe the implementation, because no implementation is ever truly self-describing, and some are downright arcane. And, perhaps most important, we need to show how the design proceeds from the problem statement, and how the implementation proceeds from the design.

English-language narratives usually don't have the necessary precision or clarity for properly describing all of these points. Such narratives might be acceptable for small projects, but they become unwieldy for larger projects.

For larger projects, you will usually need to adopt an analysis and design methodology, along with the notation style used in that methodology. Numerous methodologies for object-oriented analysis and design are described in the books we've listed as Recommended Reading at the end of this book. These methodologies use various notations to help you keep track of things. The major methodologies are compared in Yourdon's *Object-Oriented Systems Design*. Each of these methodologies provides a concise means for recording your analysis and design results. The more useful methodologies also give you ways to connect features of the analysis, the design, and the implementation. When you're working on a project that's big enough to require some form of technical notation, Yourdon's book is a good place to start.

Your choice of a methodology and a notation style ultimately depend on your project and your needs. For larger projects, however, the bottom line is that you *will* need some type of structured methods for your analysis and design; the methods you choose will influence or direct your choice of notation style.

DIVIDE AND CONQUER — AND REINTEGRATE

Regardless of which methodology you use for analysis and design, one basic idea is common to all of them: If a task is fairly complex, you should somehow divide it into smaller tasks that are simpler and more easily handled.

Every problem has an inherent level of complexity. Part of the analysis task is dividing a problem into its less-complex elements. From each of these elements, we can abstract only those aspects that are relevant to the solution of our problem. It's these essential aspects that find their way into our design. In the design process, we break down the problem along lines that are derived both from the problem statement and from the computer environment in which we'll be programming. We might have to separate the problem into parts that can be handled by different teams — possibly in separate places — and the natural lines of division will be those that we've already defined for solving the problem. In the implementation process, each part of the design is broken down into the programming constructs that the language provides. In this way, we can transform a highly complex problem into a series of simpler problems that each can be easily handled by an individual programmer or a programming team.

This process has been described in many books on software engineering. This technique is classically called *divide and conquer*. But this name is incomplete, just as the picture painted in the preceding paragraph is incomplete. The problem isn't really solved until the parts are reassembled as an integrated whole.

Whenever you make a division during the design and analysis stages of the software development process, it's important that you also describe how you're going to put the parts back together again. When dividing work among several teams, you must identify the interfaces between the separate parts of the software on which the different teams will be working. In fact, you should do this even if only one team or one programmer is involved. If the design divides the problem into parts that can be programmed separately from each other, you must make sure that you define ahead of time the interfaces between these parts, that will bring the program back together again. By doing so, you define the means by which the parts of the program can be reassembled to form a complete, integrated solution to the problem. In other words, a problem isn't solved until you can divide, conquer, and *reintegrate* the parts into a working whole.

Analysis

Analysis is the process of defining exactly what the problem is, along with identifying any constraints on how we can obtain a solution. During the analysis phase of your software development effort, you should also start to divide the problem into its basic units, and start to abstract from those units the parts that you'll need for solving the problem.

Analysis starts with addressing the components of the problem to help us find out what the problem really is. We need to do this even if we've been handed a meticulously composed problem statement. Such a problem statement is always helpful as a starting point and continuing reference; however, unless the problem statement is the result of careful analysis (as we describe it here), we often find that we're missing vital information if we go right from the problem statement to a design. Even more, if our problem statement is less than meticulous — something on the order of, "There's a problem here, somewhere. Fix it!" — then we absolutely need to do this analysis. Of course, the amount of time and other resources we should budget for the analysis depends on the size of the project and how badly it will affect the users if it fails unexpectedly.

In some cases, natural divisions in the problem will be apparent, which will help us divide up the work involved in the analysis itself. For example, one team might consider constraints from existing hardware and software, while another team looks at new hardware or software that needs to be integrated into the system, and still other teams seek input to the problem definition from the people who actually have the problem.

Talking with the people involved is often the most difficult part of the analysis task. You may hear different ideas about what needs to be done, depending on whether you are speaking with the workers who will use the software, their supervisor, or the group whose budget pays for the work. If you immediately encounter significant differences, you might need to request a meeting with all of these people together, so that you can get them to agree on what they want you to do. Better yet, you might request that a higher-level manager in their organization conduct the meeting. That way, you're not placed in the unpleasant position of being the referee for people with whom you'll soon be working.

Another problem you might encounter is that people often try to describe the problem in terms of an imagined solution. For example, they might tell you that they need a program that queries their database, aligns and evaluates the fields, and presents graphic reports. Sounds like they know what they're talking about, doesn't it? However, it may be that their "database" is a flat file; the output they need is a simple table of sums; and the high-powered, graphics-oriented relational database management system they're requesting is a spreadsheet.

You need to have the elements of the problem described to you in the terms used by the people who have the problem. To make sure you have it right, paraphrase what they've told you, and ask them to confirm whether this is what they said. Try to make sure that they haven't left out anything that might be obvious to them, but not to you. Never leave portions of your analysis as unspecified items that you'll agree on later! Remember, you can always come back to your analysis and amend it, as necessary. Open-ended sections of an analysis usually come back to haunt you, and they often require more effort than the core system. For example, you may think that the idea of "system management functions" is an obvious list of functions that is small enough that the time needed to program them is insignificant, while the time needed to describe them is more than you want to spend on them up front. However, the people requesting the system might have a wonderful, grand scheme for an elaborate management function. Specifying earlier what you both mean saves trouble later, when unspecified but different ideas collide. (If it sounds to you as though this is written from sorry experience — unfortunately, you're right.)

When your analysis is complete, it should be signed by both you and the people for whom you are solving the problem. By signing this document, both parties are agreeing that, as far as they know at this time, the document is a complete, precise statement of the problem and the constraints to a solution. This important document establishes the framework for your design and your programming effort. This is not to say that this document is engraved in stone. As we've mentioned, you might subsequently uncover parts of the problem that weren't apparent during your analysis, and you might need to amend the problem statement. Similarly, the people for whom you are solving the problem might realize that they need you to do more than was initially expected. In either case, you'll have to revisit the problem statement. If you have to amend the problem statement, you might also need to negotiate for other things, such as more time or additional compensation.

Compared to all of this, getting the specifications for existing or new hardware and software that are required as part of the problem statement seems almost trivial. (Those of you who have tried to do this know that it's often far from trivial to get good working specifications for hardware and software components — but it is simpler than getting the "people" part of the problem statement done!)

Once you have your problem statement, you can start working on the object-oriented part of the analysis. First, you need to determine which classes of objects are found in the problem. When you have a first cut at this, you can start identifying the relevant properties of these classes.

Just as the problem as a whole has an inherent level of complexity, so does each class. Each class must be analyzed to determine which properties of the class are relevant for solving the problem. For example, if it is a class of people, are we interested in their personal characteristics (for the purposes of the problem)? It seems unlikely, unless we're programming a dating service. Do their financial characteristics matter? They do if we're creating a banking program or a payroll application. What about their behavior? This is probably relevant only if we are building a work performance evaluation program for use by supervisors and managers. You can probably continue with this example as far as you might want.

This process — picking out those characteristics in which we're interested and ignoring the rest — is called *abstraction*. We *abstract* only those properties of each class that we need to use, and we ignore the rest. If we realize that we're ignoring properties that affect our solution, we need to add those properties back into our abstraction.

We can take our abstraction to various levels. In the previous examples, we treated a person at a very high level of abstraction — that is, as a thinking and acting being. We can abstract at a different level, and describe the person as a collection of interacting organ systems. Is this useful? Only if we're developing a medical program (or an organ bank). Is it useful to describe the person at the cellular level? Only if we're describing activity at that level. At the molecular level? You can see that it's possible to abstract so deeply into a class that the results aren't useful. Or, if they are useful, perhaps we need to redefine the classes or add to them.

In addition to the properties of each class, we need to describe how each class acts. Any changes to the properties of an object of a class should be made by an action of that class. Actions also might involve changes to objects of other classes. You need to consider all of these actions and interactions in your analysis.

Throughout this process, we're trying to perform our analysis from an object-oriented perspective. At the same time, we're trying to avoid creating any part of the structure of the program that will solve our problem. That's the province of design. When we have a fairly complete description of the class components of our problem, we can start the design phase. On the other hand, if we seem to be overanalyzing the problem, and we're taking forever to produce an absolutely complete analysis, perhaps we should move ahead to the design phase, lest we suffer from paralysis by analysis.

Design

In the design phase, we want to create a clean, simple structure for a program that will solve our problem. We say *a* program, rather than *the* program, because most problems can be solved by several different but perfectly acceptable program designs and programs.

DERIVING CLASSES FOR YOUR DESIGN

Your analysis provides a statement of the problem that your program is to solve and identifies the constraints on the solution. You have also started to break down the problem into its component classes, and you have considered the properties and actions of these classes. All of this is done exclusively (or mostly exclusively) from the perspective of the problem. In other words, the abstractions are all done in reference to the real-world classes and objects.

During the design phase, you take these concepts and use them to create the structure of a program that provides a solution to the problem. At this point, you might realize that a better solution is possible in another programming language. If so, you might decide to use that language, unless your constraints include the use of C++ or an MS-Windows GUI. Once you have chosen the programming language, your design can take advantage of that language's characteristics. We'll continue to assume that C++ is your language of choice; otherwise, we'd be writing a different book.

Although the classes you described during the analysis phase might very well be the classes you will use in the design, you should take another look at them. Perhaps several classes share common features that should be programmed once and then inherited by those classes? If so, you could define a *superclass* for those classes, from which they can inherit common data and methods. Similarly, you might discover that a class contains several types of elements, which are sometimes treated the same way, and sometimes require special treatment? Perhaps these objects should be in *subclasses* that derive some data and methods from their common ancestor, and have some methods of their own. You might also find that objects in one class are always part of objects in another class. In such cases, the second class has members that are objects of the first class. We mentioned some concrete instances of each of these cases when we discussed these ideas in Chapter 4.

When you're looking at classes, it's important to remember that even though objects might initially appear to belong in a common class, sometimes they really don't. For example, if you're modeling the action in a soccer game, you might initially decide to place referees and players together as a class of human beings, and then separate the two groups as subclasses. However, even though we have to remember that they're all human in a real game, this fact is completely irrelevant for a game simulation. A referee's functions in a game are completely different from a player's. The seemingly obvious grouping turns out actually to be a mistake.

Along with the classes that are derived from the problem statement, you will probably add to the design classes that are internal to the particular system design that you're creating. For example, you might need classes to provide interfaces to system resources. You'll definitely need classes that provide interfaces between the various types of classes that need to interact, but that don't have simple interfaces with each other. You don't want to give each of these classes full access to all parts of the other, because that violates the data encapsulation that classes are used to enforce.

IMPLEMENTATION VERSUS INTERFACE

The preceding section raised an important point. Classes exist, in part, to make sure that their contents aren't available to each other. On the other hand, they have to work together to solve the problem. How do we resolve this conflict?

When two classes need to work with each other, they should have a well-defined interface. To meet this requirement, the designer needs to declare which parts of one class may be affected by another class, and which parts may not. We've already seen that the data members of a class are usually kept private from other classes. These are seen as implementation details, and no other class should know about them. However, if the class's interface contains public functions that give free access to the data members, the implementation is no longer hidden. The interface should be designed to limit access to class members so that they'll always be used correctly. Because the class should be controlling its own data, the class might have member functions that change the data only in specific, tightly controlled ways. If this doesn't give other program components enough access to class members, *friend* functions might do the trick. This approach separates the interface from the implementation. It also allows you to change the implementation internally to the class, without affecting the interface.

The implementation of binary trees in Chapter 6 provides an example of the separation of implementation and interface. When learning about data structures, many programmers are taught that a binary tree is implemented as a set of paired pointer structures, and the root of the tree is just a pointer to the tree's structure. In the binary trees example, however, the *Tree* structure is separate, and it has in it only a pointer to a *Node*. The *Node* is our paired pointer structure. Some of the interface functions for the *Node* are *private*. Why is this?

If we were implementing the tree structure in C, one node would be the same as any other node. We could start an insertion, a search, or a printout halfway down the tree, and there would be no complaint; after all, a node is a node. With a binary tree, however, we want these operations to occur *only* at the root of the tree. The interface to a binary tree is therefore entirely in the *Tree* structure. The internal implementation — which gives us our speed in the general, completely random case — is hidden inside the *Node* class, whose interface is not publicly available.

This concept of keeping the implementation and the interface separate can be seen at several different levels in the design. It's necessary inside the class, and we've seen a couple of ways to accomplish that. At the topmost level of the design is some type of user interface — a GUI, or command lines, or buttons, levers, lights, and whistles — and we need to make this interface a metaphor for the underlying process, while hiding the implementation details. In between the exterior, black-box interface level of the design and the interior, implementation levels, we can usually group classes into software *components* that also have internal implementations and external interfaces.

DERIVING COMPONENTS FOR YOUR DESIGN

The notion of software *components* is introduced by Bjarne Stroustrup in *The C++ Programming Language* (Reading, MA: Addison-Wesley, 1991). Components are groups of classes in your design and implementation. Each component does one thing, and does it well. Each component has a well-defined interface with some of the other components, so that they all come together to solve your problem. In other words, the *component* level falls somewhere between the integrated solution to the problem and the level of individual classes. It's at this component level that you can find a logical breakdown of tasks for different design and programming teams.

There are often several different ways to organize classes into components. One obvious first cut is to separate the user interface, the interfaces for any existing hardware and software, and the interfaces to stored data that the program uses. You'll encounter a similar concept in the MFC library's use of documents, which are the stored data, and views, which are the user interfaces to those documents. The MFC library provides extensive support for creating a Windows-based GUI. We'll provide in-depth coverage of these capabilities in Chapter 9, which presents MFC library concepts, and Chapter 15, which discusses the Document/View architecture.

In addition to the GUI components that are supported by the MFC library, you still need to put together components that will provide the data interface and the interface to any other hardware and software. This will differ for each system that you use, and is beyond the scope of this book. As you gain experience with various types of systems, you'll often recognize patterns in the different types of problems that you face. This leads us to consider the concept of software reuse, both in program design and in the development of software components.

REUSING PROGRAM STRUCTURES AND COMPONENTS

Software reuse is typically viewed in terms of libraries of classes and routines that can be included in one program after another. Although this view is certainly valid, an even more important concept is the reuse of software designs.

As you gain experience in writing new programs and supporting existing code, you'll find that not only routines but entire program structures can be copied from one program to another. During the program design stage, you can actively search for patterns that suggest that a previous program structure can be reused, in whole or in part. A recently published book (*Design Patterns*, by Gamma et al. Addison-Wesley, 1995) identifies several patterns for object-oriented program designs. With help from this type of resource, you can gradually increase the "library" of program structures that you can recognize.

Of course, the same approach is valid for software components and the classes themselves. Books on software design patterns can give you some initial help with recognizing patterns of software components that you can pull from libraries or existing code and reuse. Over time, you will begin to recognize more patterns, which will allow you to reuse more software.

Although the technology isn't quite there yet, software repositories and software databases hold great promise for supporting the reuse of existing code. In the meantime, you can boost your own productivity by continually adding to your personal store of reusable software designs and components.

With experience, you'll also adopt the practice of writing software that can be reused. This is a useful practice, up to a point. You may benefit by writing a routine that can handle a slightly more general case than you had originally intended, because you'll often encounter cases that you didn't anticipate. However, there is a danger here. You might spend an inordinate amount of time making a routine more general, and then never reuse it. Don't hurt your implementation by trying to make your design or implementation too general. Deciding when to generalize requires judgment, which in turn depends on experience. Even with experience, you won't always get it right. Writing reusable software is usually good. At the time you're writing software, there will often be no way to tell whether the investment in time taken to make it more usable will pay off in future reuse. Nonetheless, you do need to be aware of the temptation to generalize more than will ever be useful.

TAKING ADVANTAGE OF LANGUAGE FEATURES

While you're thinking about what you can reuse, make sure you don't also overlook some of the more obvious things you can use. While you are developing your design, be sure to consider the features of the language and the libraries that you plan to use.

In C++, the use of classes and inheritance will come naturally with the general plan of design we've been describing. If you create several classes whose structures are exactly parallel, you can design them as *parameterized types,* and implement them with the new *template* feature described in the previous chapter. If you have classes with identical behavior except for one or two aspects, you should design them as subclasses of a base class that describes the majority of their behavior, and put the varying aspects of their behavior in virtual functions. This lets you minimize the amount of redundant code that you must write, while switching out behavior depending on an object's true, underlying type. If you don't want to have any objects for which the underlying type is your new base type, you can make this part of your design. You can implement this by making the base type *abstract.* To do this, declare at least one virtual function in the base class as a *pure* virtual function — that is, declare it in the class definition as initialized with the value 0.

The MFC library promotes a *Document/View* program architecture for the user interface. The AppWizard helps you put together a proto-type user interface using the MFC library classes. The ClassWizard helps you connect the GUI to your own procedures and classes. These tools and tasks will be discussed in the following chapters. You should also read the article, "MFC: Using the MFC Source Files," in the on-line *MFC Encyclopedia* on your Microsoft Visual C++ CD-ROM. This article describes Microsoft's conventions for grouping class members into con-structors, attributes, operations, overridables, and (untouchable) imple-mentation members.

PROGRAM OPTIMIZATION

Countless sins have been committed in the name of making an otherwise acceptable program design more efficient. Part of the problem is that many people are taught to think of programming at the machine level, even if they're being taught to program in a higher-level language.

Compilers can now optimize code better than any but the most expert machine-language programmers could ever do. Processors are faster than we could have imagined just a few years ago. There's no need for anyone to design clever but hard-to-understand features to improve a program's performance. In particular, there's no need to avoid using any of the features of a higher-level language such as C++ for fear of incurring overhead. Not only are the features well optimized, sometimes they produce no code at all! Some features only produce better compile-time error checking. In addition, the compiler determines program behavior at compile time, and it may leave out massive dynamic runtime code. For example, when we described all of the default constructor and destructor functions for newly defined or derived classes and how and when they are called, we were describing the effect that the running program produces. The same effect can often be produced with one or two inline instructions, rather than a call to a separate routine. Another example is the use of static type checking in a program, rather than the more expensive (and usually unnecessary) dynamic runtime type checking.

The most effective method for building a program is by first making it work right, and then making it work fast. We're told that 80% of the time spent by a running program is typically found in only 20% of the code. We're also told that software engineers do an extremely poor job of guessing ahead of time just where they'll encounter that 20% of the code. The lesson here is that, first and foremost, the program should be designed and written so that it works correctly. You can then instrument the program by inserting code to determine which parts of the code are taking the most time. Once you know which sections are taking the most time, and why, you can optimize those particular sections, if you still believe it to be necessary.

We're not saying that you should start sloppy and then optimize. In fact, the best time to optimize is during the design process. However, this is not done by adding clever and complex optimization routines.

Optimization is a result of choosing the right basic classes, designs, and algorithms for your program. For example, if a given sorting technique is optimal for truly random data, but your program is almost always presented with partially ordered data, you may need to change your underlying algorithm to take advantage of this fact. You need to design for efficiency, not break your design for efficiency.

EVALUATING YOUR DESIGN

As we've mentioned, you can find more than one way to design and implement almost every program. Given that fact, we need to be able to evaluate whether a given design is a good solution for our problem. By knowing ahead of time the criteria for a good design, you can make even better design decisions.

For an object-oriented design, we need to look at our class designs and the designs of the relationships between the classes. If we have well-defined software components, we can apply similar criteria for evaluating those components. The following paragraphs describe some points you should consider.

To what extent are classes (or components) dependent on each other? Classes that are unintentionally closely coupled could indicate a problem with the design. An example of an appropriate use of close coupling is provided by the *Tree* and *Node* classes in Chapter 6. These classes must be closely coupled, because they are the interface and the implementation of a single concept. However, you should reconsider the design of two classes if those classes are closely coupled, with a similar dependency on each other's internal structures, but aren't similarly related — that is, they don't provide two different tools with which to work on the same concept.

To what extent are classes internally cohesive and consistent? To what extent do the members of the class depend on each other? A class is internally cohesive if the members of the class need to work together to provide the activity that you expect of the class. On the other hand, if some parts of the class don't interact or work with the other parts at all, they probably belong in another class. The members are internally consistent if the class is internally cohesive and the member functions keep the data members consistent with each other. What this means depends on the semantics of the class. There may be numeric values that need to track each other, or pointers that need to be consistent with each other, or values that must be valid whenever an object is in a given state.

How well do classes encapsulate their data? Are exceptions handled properly? Do objects in the classes have appropriate persistence, lasting as long as they're needed, but no longer? Are the objects visible only in the contexts in which they're needed?

How deep and broad are the class hierarchies? A class inheritance hierarchy that is too broad, with many independent or sibling classes, might indicate that class inheritance isn't being used properly. If the hierarchy is too deep, with only one child class at many points in the hierarchy, it's possible that inheritance is being overused. Of course, you should temper both of these judgments by asking whether these classes are required by the problem statement and the constraints. Based on the problem, perhaps it is appropriate to have a single base class with numerous subclasses. And, when using a class library such as the MFC library, you'll often find that creating a single inherited class from a library class is necessary for making the class useful in your application.

Does your design expect the unexpected? The typical default action for an exception — terminating the program — is not particularly user friendly. Your design may include specific actions for specific, likely *unexpected* input, and a more general action that is to be taken for the truly bizarre unexpected program behavior.

How clear is your design? If you had to take several weeks' leave from your project, could you come back to your design and immediately understand it? Similarly, how simple are the component parts? Remember that one of the purposes of the design is to divide the problem into parts that can be readily understood and handled by the programming team. Are the classes and objects simple? Are the methods (that is, the member function descriptions) and the protocols for interfaces and messages simple? Is the design as small as possible, and not infected with "creeping featurism"? Will the design remain fairly stable, even when the need eventually arises to extend your design so that it can handle things it wasn't originally intended to handle?

You may be able to answer some of these questions, but not others. The more questions you can answer positively, the more confident you can be that your design is sound.

Implementation

The design phase produces a program structure. This structure should be clean, simple, and straightforward. If the design is sufficiently detailed, the implementation may not require much work at all.

Like the other tasks, you can make implementation easier by dividing it into subtasks. Implement one class or design concept at a time. Test it and make sure that it's working, before you go on to the next part. If you have an interface to an external component or to a section of the program that's being written by another group, test the interface thoroughly on your own program stubs before combining it with the other component. You should also make sure that you account for unexpected behavior. This way, you'll have more confidence in your component's behavior when the other side of the interface starts acting differently from the way it was supposed to. Notice that we say "when," rather than "if." There will always be inconsistencies that you need to iron out. (Please don't send us the few cases in which this wasn't true — such cases are themselves inconsistencies!)

For each class, make sure that you have all of the member functions that you need. If the constructor and destructor functions provided by C++ aren't enough, you will have to make sure that you write your own. This is particularly true if the data members include pointers to objects that need to be duplicated, rather than the pointers being copied. You may find that you've implemented one operator that requires another operator or another constructor function that you haven't provided. You may need to block some default C++ member functions, virtual member functions, or type conversions by declaring your own without defining them. Once you've done this, any accidental unintended use of these functions in your code will cause a compiler error, rather than generating default code that does the wrong thing.

When trying to decide whether a particular approach to implementing the design will work, you should consider different ways of doing the same thing. You might simply think about various possibilities, or you might actually experiment with different ways of doing the same thing. At this stage, you might try a few quick prototypes to determine the best fit. However, prototypes present their own potential pitfalls. They often turn into preliminary implementations; and code that you plugged in for testing and without heed for the final design may become part of the final product. A prototype should be like stage scenery. It gives the desired illusion from the front, but is hastily constructed and causes no grief when it's finally torn down. Prototyping is fine, as long as you remember that a prototype is *always* thrown away when you've completed the testing for which it was built.

When writing code, make sure that you code for the unexpected, as well as for the expected. The design should include plans for handling the most likely of unexpected events, such as the user typing gibberish or clicking the wrong mouse button. You should handle other exception conditions reasonably, or pass them on to a higher-level exception handler that is part of the design.

It's important that you understand and use the features of your target language. We mentioned this in the section on design, but it's even more important during the implementation phase. If you were building a wooden chair and you had a saw, it wouldn't make sense to use a chisel or an axe to make smooth cuts in the wood. It also wouldn't make sense to use a handsaw if a power saw were available. Know your tools, and use them appropriately.

Strong typing is a powerful C++ feature that allows you to rely on the compiler to do a lot of your correctness checking for you. The compiler will catch errors in static typing at compile time, if you don't inhibit it by using too many type casts. To help you catch all sorts of untidy loose ends for which the compiler might not issue warnings, versions of the Unix *lint* program are available for C and C++ under the Microsoft operating systems. Tools such as *lint* and strong compiler warning messages are important for making sure that a program is correct. The earlier you can catch an error, the less expensive it is to fix.

Although review, testing, and debugging are essential parts of the implementation process, organizations often fail to budget enough time for these tasks. In some cases, an organization that is unwilling to pay anything to get it right the first time ends up spending far more to fix problems that should have been caught before they got out the door. Other times, it's the organization's customers who must pay the price for code that isn't properly checked for flaws. Programming is a human process, and even though we should strive for perfection in what we do, we should also acknowledge that we are likely to produce flaws. Enough time and resources must be allocated for thoroughly reviewing, testing, and debugging code under both expected and unexpected conditions, before a product is delivered.

Many people new to the software business assume that the delivery of a product is the end of the implementation phase. Those who have been in the business for a while know that this is just the beginning. Almost inevitably, new features will be needed as soon as the product is out the door. In addition, bugs will need to be fixed. We can hope that any bugs found by the users won't be major errors that should have been caught during your review, test, and debugging stage. This stage of a software product's life is known as *maintenance*, and software developers used to assign it to the least-experienced people they had. Increasingly, the software industry is realizing that this support stage is an inevitable and important part of the implementation stage, and including it in the software development process.

Management

When attending his first software engineering class, one of the authors thought that he would be finding out all sorts of wonderful technical secrets about how to develop good software. Instead, he found himself in a classroom full of business school types, learning about managing the software engineering process. It was a strange, but enlightening experience.

Engineering a successful software project is as much a social process as it is a technical process. Effective management is needed, whether your project involves one person or multiple teams, each with its own team manager, and managed by an overall project manager. Management is a human, social process. It's a mistake to think that solutions to all of the problems in a software engineering project will be technical in nature. Effective management is needed throughout the process.

The managers of a software engineering project must be familiar with all of the software engineering concepts being used in the project. Project managers might not write a line of code or contribute to the design, but they need to be able to understand and track the progress of a project. If part of the project bogs down, the manager needs to be able to spot this and supply help before the delay becomes a crisis. The manager also needs to be able to recognize when some part of the project is going especially well, and reward that person or group, either tangibly or intangibly.

Sometimes, for reasons having to do with an organization's structure, the project manager might not be a technical person. If that's the case, one of the first executive decisions the project manager should make is whom to hire as the technical manager for the project.

If an organization is moving to a new technology, such as object-oriented design and programming or use of the MFC library, management needs to support this change from the top down. The change needs to be staged, as an evolutionary change, rather than a revolutionary change.

Management needs to select a software development process based on a realistic technical appraisal of the organization's needs. It then needs to follow up on its own decisions by basing performance appraisals on the new process. For example, perhaps an organization has historically rewarded managers based on the number of lines of code that their team has produced. If that organization is starting to promote code reuse, the reward system must be revised to place value on the ability to do the same programming task *without* writing thousands of lines of code. Tasks that were historically considered less productive, such as documenting the design process or providing good on-line documentation, now need to be rewarded. Management also needs to recognize that different workers have different skills that might be better used in specific parts of the software development process, and assign them to teams and evaluate them accordingly.

This isn't all going to happen overnight. Change takes time in even the best organizations. In addition, it's unlikely that everyone will change. Just as our description of the software development process assumed ideal conditions, the conditions we've described here are the ideals for software engineering and development.

A more complete discussion of the management of software projects is beyond the scope of this book. There are some excellent books and articles on the topic, such as the works by Brooks and by Weinberg that we've listed as Recommended Reading. Weinberg and the other members of his publishing group, Dorset House, continue to turn out consistently excellent books on the subject.

Summary

At the beginning of this chapter, we promised you some words to program by. Here's a synopsis of the key points we've shared in this chapter:

- "Say what you mean"...and then write it down.

- Find a software development model that you can use. Then, find and use a software development process that supports this model. Finally, find and use analysis and design methodologies and notations that support your software development model and process.

- Do your analysis and design as well as you can, but leave room to come back and fill in what you might have missed.

- Divide and conquer, and then reintegrate.

- In your analysis, define the problem in the language used by those who are most familiar with the problem. Avoid the temptation to define the problem in computer-related terms. As far as you can, divide the components of the problem into classes without leaving the problem context language, and find the appropriate abstractions in the same language.

- In your design, find the appropriate classes and their properties, actions, and relationships. Add any classes that are needed for the final implementation. Divide the classes into components by function, such as GUI, data handling, or device handling. Be sure to separate implementation and interface.

- Design for reuse. Design to allow yourself to reuse existing software components, and design to create components that can be reused. But don't let design for reuse get in the way of design for use.

- Understand and use language and library features in your design and implementation.

- Focus first on making your program work right, and then on making it work fast. The most effective optimization is to use an efficient design in the first place.

- To make sure that you have a good design, you need to evaluate your design against standard design criteria.

- Expect the unexpected. Design and program to handle exceptions.

- Review, testing, debugging, and support are vital parts of a program's implementation.

- If you prototype, get all you can out of your prototypes, then be sure to throw away the prototypes when you're done with them.

- Management is an important part of the software development process.

We've introduced you to enough of the C++ language and related object-oriented design and programming concepts that you should be able to understand our discussion of the Microsoft Foundation Class (MFC) library. In the next part of this book, we'll start by introducing you to the major MFC library concepts. We'll then proceed to give you descriptions and examples of how to use those concepts to create programs that can be used with the Microsoft Windows family of operating systems, starting with Windows 95 and Windows NT. These programs can also be used with some other operating systems that support partial use of the MFC library.

III

MFC Programming Fundamentals

*T*he six chapters in Part III introduce you to the basics of programming with the Microsoft Foundation Class (MFC) library. We'll start in Chapter 9 with a look at the structure and organization of MFC. In Chapter 10, we describe how to create and maintain windows, the main components of a user interface. Windows aren't the only element in the user interface, however, and in Chapter 11 we'll show you how to build menus and toolbars. Chapter 12 shows you how to build and maintain dialog boxes, another important user-interface object.

In addition to covering the basics of managing user-interface objects, this part of the book also describes how an MFC program interacts with the user. On the output side of the user-interface equation, Chapter 13 introduces you to Windows' Graphics Device Interface (GDI). Because all output in a Windows program is graphical, a Windows program must rely on the GDI to put even the simplest line of text on a display screen or on a printed page. Chapter 14 discusses fetching input from the user, which involves retrieving keyboard and mouse input.

9

Understanding the MFC Library

*T*he Microsoft Foundation Class (MFC) library is an attempt by Microsoft to provide C++ programmers with an object-oriented programming interface to Windows. Although the development team originally tried to create an entirely new programming interface, their first attempt was over-engineered and failed to create a truly usable class library. The team scaled back its goals and created the efficient MFC library that Microsoft eventually shipped.

This chapter is your introduction to the MFC library. We'll start with a brief history of a predecessor to MFC, sometimes known internally at Microsoft as "Old AFX." Next, we'll describe design principles and structural elements of MFC — key architectural features that shape what you can do with the classes in this library. And finally, we'll focus on specific MFC features that you'll use when building Windows programs: the library-provided WinMain( ) entry point, and the important CWinApp application object class.

An Overview of the MFC Library

Microsoft created the MFC library with the goal of facilitating and simplifying the process of programming for Microsoft Windows. The development team tempered that basic goal with some design principles they learned along the way. Your development efforts with MFC — and your overall understanding of the library — will be enhanced with an understanding of the history behind its development. For that reason, we'll start by discussing the development team's original plans and the design principles that grew out of their experiences.

As described in Steve Sinofsky's article, "A Tale of AFX," which appeared in the *Microsoft Developers Newsletter*, and as verified in our conversations with members of the development team, Microsoft's *Application Framework* (AFX) team was assembled in 1989 and began work on a portable C++ class library for building graphical applications. (AFX stands for *Application Framework* — the *X* is just a placeholder to make it "sound cool.") Their goal was a single library that would support the development of Windows applications, OS/2 Presentation Manager applications, and applications for the Apple Macintosh (running on Motorola 68xxx CPUs). The team believed that the power of object-oriented technology would allow them to create an easy-to-program, portable GUI.

About one year into the development effort, the team had implemented — in less than a megabyte of source code — a good portion of the desired features. They had "fixed" problems with the Windows API by creating a windowing system distinct from that used by Microsoft Windows. They also fixed problems with the handling of graphical output by creating their own graphics library, which was quite different from GDI. In short, they had created an entirely new programming interface with a new set of programming paradigms. It was time, they decided, to test how well their system worked.

The test involved writing applications that used the class library. The applications they created were quite varied: a word processor, a game, a Smalltalk interpreter, and a drawing program. There were numerous difficulties in writing the code, which was odd considering that the class library developers themselves were having the problems. Their efforts produced large, slow programs. In particular, programs ended up being around *twice* the size of comparable C programs. At that point, the group decided to abandon "Old AFX" and to start building a new class library from scratch.

Although their first attempt didn't produce the class library they wanted, it did provide the AFX group with some important insights into the development of a class library. These lessons formed the basis for the design principles the AFX group used in building the Microsoft Foundation Class library we have today.

A key error of the AFX team was believing too much in the hype surrounding object-oriented programming. For example, the mere fact that you are using classes doesn't guarantee good design. The ability to create classes that represent abstractions doesn't mean you should create arbitrary abstractions without taking into account other factors such as the tradeoffs between size and performance. Bad design is still bad design, even when packaged in a different way. Some of the AFX team members dubbed themselves "recovering OOP-aholics" as the group set out to build a class library that would be small, fast, and functional.

In starting work on the class library that eventually became the MFC library, the AFX team changed their goals dramatically. Instead of targeting multiple platforms, they aimed their efforts squarely at encapsulating the Windows API. Instead of creating abstraction for its own sake, they focused on making *usable* classes. They also avoided complex C++ constructs — for example, multiple inheritance and templates — and focused instead on using a "sane subset" of C++. And finally, instead of hiding the native API under a mountain of abstract classes and new paradigms, they made it easy to access the underlying, native API. This was done for two reasons. First, they wanted to simplify the process of porting existing Win16 code to the MFC library. Second, they wanted to ensure that all the capabilities of the native API would be available to application programs — even if this meant bypassing the class library and calling native API functions directly.

One developer who worked on MFC pointed out that another difference between Old AFX and MFC was the design approach taken. Old AFX used a top-down design, in which arbitrary abstractions were created and imposed on Windows. For the new class library, the decision was made to use a bottom-up design approach. In other words, from the first version of MFC, its classes were built on existing Windows API objects. The resulting classes avoided the overhead and waste that had been part of Old AFX.

As you get started with MFC programming, you'll notice that the letters *AFX* appear in many places in the MFC source files. You'll encounter function names such as AfxGetApp( ), symbolic constants such as AFX_IDS_APP_TITLE, and data structures such as AFX_MSGMAP_ENTRY. Such identifiers are *not* found in the native Windows APIs; instead, they are creations of the AFX team. They make up the scaffolding of the MFC library, and thus are marked with the development team's signature, AFX.

DESIGN PRINCIPLES

From their experience with their first class library, the AFX team developed a number of design principles that they used in the creation of the MFC library. Based on discussions with members of the original AFX team, we've derived the following design principles. The first version of the MFC library was built by following these principles. Subsequent versions are built on and extend the following basic principles:

- Simplify the process of building Windows-based applications.

- Incorporate existing Windows paradigms and objects.

- Adopt native API concepts, coding styles, and function names.

- Avoid defining new programming paradigms.

- Simplify complex API features to make them more accessible, even to beginning programmers.

- Ensure that the library is sufficiently extensible to incorporate new features and capabilities of Windows as these are developed.

Perhaps the most important goal of the AFX team was to simplify the process of building Windows-based applications. Although this seems like an obvious goal, the first class library created by the AFX team didn't satisfy this requirement. One way that MFC simplifies development is by handling administrative overhead for you. With the MFC library, code that your SDK-based applications must handle — for example, message loops and window procedures — is automatically handled for you and hidden from view. Unlike a Windows program in C, an MFC program doesn't even require an entry point. (In Windows, *WinMain* is the name of the entry point rather than *main*.) MFC provides a WinMain entry point that is automatically linked to your application.

In Old AFX, the development team created unnecessary overhead by building a new set of programming models. For MFC, they adopted the principle of incorporating existing Windows paradigms and objects. This helped make MFC a compact, efficient class library. It also helped MFC reach the design goal of being no more than 5% slower than a native SDK application — in some cases, MFC applications are faster!

In building MFC, the development team adopted concepts, coding styles, and function names from the native API to enhance understanding of the framework by experienced SDK programmers. If you or members of your development team already have Windows SDK programming experience, that experience will help you learn MFC programming. Even if everyone on your team is new to Windows programming, however, you'll still benefit. Many books, magazines, and sample applications are available on the subject of Windows programming. Even though many of these resources don't cover MFC-specific issues, because MFC closely mirrors the native API, most Windows reference material will help you in your MFC development efforts. For example, the help database for the native Windows API has been extremely useful to our MFC coding efforts, because it is more complete than the MFC help files.

One lesson the AFX team learned from their experience building Old AFX was to avoid defining new programming paradigms. In their words, their goal was to create "evolution not revolution." The most basic classes in MFC are thin layers that encapsulate native Windows API functions. Additional capabilities and functions provided by MFC rely on the base classes for all the work they do, which is another way of saying that they rely on the programming models found in the native Windows API.

Although the MFC developers avoided inventing new paradigms to replace existing Windows programming paradigms, they didn't hesitate to provide support for useful features when such support didn't already exist in the operating system. For example, the Document/View Architecture clearly represents an enhancement to the native API. The term *Document/View Architecture* describes a set of classes that simplify the process of mapping some data (a document) into one or more different graphical representations (the views) in a window or on a printed page. For example, spreadsheet data could be displayed as rows and columns of numbers or as a bar chart. In this example, a single data source produces two different visual representations. The Document/View Architecture forms the foundation for MFC's support for the *Compound Document Architecture*, a term that describes the data sharing capabilities of Windows' Object Linking and Embedding (OLE) support.

An important service provided by MFC is represented by the principle of simplifying complex API features to make them more accessible even to beginning programmers. The clearest example of this is the support provided by MFC for system features such as OLE and Open Database Connectivity (ODBC) support. But this principle is realized in many other places, making MFC programming much more accessible than SDK programming ever was.

The final principle is Microsoft's promise for the future. MFC was designed to be extensible to incorporate new features and capabilities of Windows as these are developed. You can commit your development efforts to MFC with confidence because Microsoft promises to continue developing it to encapsulate new API and operating system enhancements as they become available. In prior versions, MFC bridged the gap between Win16 and Win32 development efforts. The latest version incorporates API features that Microsoft introduced with Windows 95. Future versions of MFC will, no doubt, ease the move to future operating systems from Microsoft, such as Cairo, the promised upgrade to Windows NT 3.5.

KEY STRUCTURAL ELEMENTS

Certain implementation details shape MFC almost as much as the design principles. We call these details *structural elements* because they run through the structure of the entire class library. Your understanding of these elements will help you understand the rest of MFC. As appropriate, we'll also cover some practical coding considerations during this discussion.

The glue that holds together the major pieces of a C++ class library is *inheritance*. Inheritance allows for the creation of new types from an existing type without changing the original — or *base* — type. (See Chapter 6 for details about classes and inheritance.) Most MFC classes inherit from CObject, so we'll start by discussing that class. A few MFC classes *don't* inherit from CObject, however, and we'll describe these and explain why they stand alone. Finally, we'll explain why MFC can be considered a stateless class library.

The CObject base class

A brief glance at the various hierarchy charts of MFC reveals a common base class: *CObject*. The composition of this class — its member functions, overloaded operators, and single static data member — describes qualities shared by almost every other class in MFC. In other words, once you understand CObject, you've taken the first step toward understanding *all* MFC classes. Incidentally, CObject's implementation demonstrates some sound coding practices that are worth noting if you ever plan to implement your own class library.

The simplest way to summarize the contribution of this base class is that it helps make MFC — and all applications based on MFC — more robust and easier to debug. For example, the CObject::AssertValid member function checks the validity of an object, and CObject::Dump( ) helps you debug code by displaying the contents of an object. Even the parts of CObject that at first might not seem directly related to debugging support — for example, the memory allocators and de-allocators — play a role in affirming the proper operation of an MFC-based program.

To fully understand CObject, it helps to examine the class declaration. Listing 9-1 contains the declaration of CObject as it appears in AFX.H. CObject contains nine member functions (five of which are virtual), five overloaded operators, and a single static data member. In C++, static data members are allocated like C global variables — that is, for the life of a program. Unlike other class data members, however, they aren't allocated for each object that is created. CObject's single static data member is a structure of type CRuntimeClass, which contains various data items that are used to support the operation of CObject-derived classes. For CObject's member functions and overloaded operators, we've grouped the work they do into four categories: memory allocation, serialization, diagnostic support, and basic object architecture.

Listing 9-1
The Declaration of CObject in AFX.H

```
class CObject
{
public:

// Object model (types, destruction, allocation)
    virtual CRuntimeClass* GetRuntimeClass() const;
    virtual ~CObject();  // virtual destructors are necessary

    // Diagnostic allocations
    void* AFX_CDECL operator new(size_t, void* p);
    void* AFX_CDECL operator new(size_t nSize);
    void AFX_CDECL operator delete(void* p);

#ifdef _DEBUG
    // for file name/line number tracking using DEBUG_NEW
    void* AFX_CDECL operator new(size_t nSize, LPCSTR lpszFileName,
                                 int nLine);
#endif
```

```
        // Disable the copy constructor and assignment by default so
        // you will get compiler errors instead of unexpected behavior
        // if you pass objects by value or assign objects.
protected:
    CObject();
private:
    CObject(const CObject& objectSrc);          // no implementation
    void operator=(const CObject& objectSrc);   // no implementation

// Attributes
public:
    BOOL IsSerializable() const;
    BOOL IsKindOf(const CRuntimeClass* pClass) const;

// Overridables
    virtual void Serialize(CArchive& ar);

        // Diagnostic Support
    virtual void AssertValid() const;
    virtual void Dump(CDumpContext& dc) const;

// Implementation
public:
    static AFX_DATA CRuntimeClass classCObject;
#ifdef _AFXDLL
    static CRuntimeClass* PASCAL _GetBaseClass();
#endif
};
```

For run-time type checking support, call this function

CObject's sole data member is a static data member.

Memory allocation (and de-allocation) support is provided by three *new* operators and the single *delete* operator. Because the C++ compiler supplies new and delete operators, you might wonder why CObject has its own. The reason is to distinguish between object and non-object allocations. For example, you can call AfxDoForAllObjects( ) to enumerate all CObject-derived objects, and the CMemoryState memory leak detection class contains a DumpAllObjectsSince( ) member that creates a list of all CObject-derived objects that have been allocated but not freed.

In this way, help for diagnosing memory allocation problems is built into the memory allocation routines. To avoid the overhead that's incurred, you'll disable this support when building a *release version* of an MFC program. During program development, however, you'll enable this support by building *debug versions* that will help you find problems such as memory leaks, bad pointers, and buffer overflows.

A *memory leak* refers to an object that has been allocated but never de-allocated. Such problems are particularly insidious for programs that must run continuously, because all system memory is eventually consumed and a crash results. It might take two days or two months, but it *will* happen. When enabled, the diagnostic support displays the object type and the size of all allocated objects. To help you focus on where you need to plug the leak, it can even tell you the filename and the line number of the code that allocated the object. A simple method for detecting leaks is to call AfxDumpMemoryLeaks( ) immediately before exiting your program. You'll get a quick list of all the objects that you've forgotten to free.

Bad pointers and buffer overflows are caught by the creation of empty space between allocated objects. These spaces are filled with known values, so problems with bad pointers can be easily detected by checking the contents of the empty spaces. Free blocks are also initialized with a known value. When you suspect that a bug is caused by either a bad pointer or a buffer overflow, you can validate the free store by calling AfxCheckMemory( ). To help catch problems as soon as they occur, you can also ask MFC to run regular checks.

Diagnostic support for objects created from CObject-derived classes appears automatically because such objects inherit the CObject::new( ) and CObject::delete( ) operators. But non-CObject-derived classes also get this support, because MFC globally overloads the new and delete operators. (See Chapter 16 for details on MFC's memory allocation and diagnostic support.)

You might notice that the _DEBUG symbol controls whether one of CObject's new operators is declared. Microsoft's Integrated Development Environment (IDE) makes a distinction between building a release version and building a debug version. When building the debug version, the compiler and the linker work together to include all symbols that are needed to run the debugger. Diagnostic support is also enabled. As part of this process, the IDE defines the _DEBUG symbol. By contrast, the IDE tries to maximize performance and minimize code size by stripping out extraneous details from the release version.

CObject's IsSerializable( ) and Serialize( ) member functions support a feature called *persistence*. Persistence is the capability for a class to read and write its objects to and from a data stream such as a disk file. The technique of reading and writing such objects is called *serialization*. To support the serialization of CObject data, MFC provides the CArchive class.

The fact that support for serialization is present in MFC's most basic class might imply that *any* MFC object can be treated as a persistent object. Although it's true that you can derive new classes from CObject and get support for persistence by writing a little more code, very few of MFC's native classes (13 of 132 total) incorporate this feature.

Although CObject's memory operators support diagnostic services in addition to their memory allocation roles, other CObject members exist solely for their diagnostic support. Considering how much software development time is spent in tracking down bugs, it makes sense that CObject tries to help you cut down on the time you spend identifying some of the more common types of errors. CObject's diagnostic support takes three forms: runtime type checking, object validation, and object dumping.

Type checking is the capability to verify that data types are used in a consistent, valid way. C++ is a strongly typed language, and C++ compilers routinely perform *compile-time* checking for consistent type usage. For example, a C++ compiler flags an error for code such as the following:

```
class Dog
{
    int nBarkCount;
};

Dog * pDog;
int * pCat;

pCat = pDog;      // C++ compiler complains.
```

Although compile-time checking catches *some* errors, it can be defeated by casting. For example, we can coerce the compiler to accept the following statement without even a warning:

```
pCat = (int *)pDog;     // C++ compiler stays quiet.
```

Because of the high value placed on the compiler's capability for catching type mismatch errors, many experienced C and C++ programmers avoid the use of casts. In his book *The Design and Evolution of C++*, the creator of the C++ language, Bjarne Stroustrup, goes so far as to call casts "one of the ugliest features of C and C++."

Still, casting is sometimes unavoidable — particularly when you have a pointer to a base class that you want to use to access members of a derived class. In this case, casting allows you to coerce the pointer to behave as you want. You'll probably want to add type checking to guard against getting a wrong pointer type.

An example of a case in which casting is required in an MFC program involves accessing the application object, the outermost container that holds all other objects in your application. From anywhere in your application, you can get a pointer to that object by calling AfxGetApp( ), which returns a pointer to a CWinApp (CWinApp *). So far, so good.

But suppose you create a new class that's based on CWinApp, to which you add your own data and function members. Here's an example:

```
class DApp : public CWinApp
{
    int nCountOfBugs;
};
```

Without a cast, the following line of code causes a compiler error:

```
DApp * pApp = AfxGetApp();
```

By adding a cast, you can force the compiler to let you do what you want:

```
DApp * pApp = (DApp *)AfxGetApp();
```

However, this change opens up the *possibility* that at some time in the future, we'll have a hidden time bomb if the type returned by this function isn't the expected type. (Incidentally, we're not saying that Microsoft plans to change AfxGetApp( ) — just that any cast hides mismatched return types.) Because we forced the compiler to be quiet, its compile-time type checking is disabled. We are stuck with two choices: leave the time bomb to be found by future development teams, or find a way to fix it.

MFC provides a dynamic type-checking feature with which we can catch this error at runtime. When this feature is enabled for a CObject-derived class, we can call a function that does the checking for us. (See the accompanying sidebar for details on setting up dynamic type checking.) The checking is based on our overriding the CObject::IsKindOf( ) function, which checks whether a pointer references a specific type and returns a Boolean (True/False) value to let us know the outcome.

The MFC source files make extensive use of this capability to help catch type mismatch errors. Here's a line of code that will catch the error we described in our example:

```
ASSERT(pApp->IsKindOf(RUNTIME_CLASS(DApp)));
```

Runtime Type Checking in CObject-Derived Classes

CObject's primary role in MFC is to help you create robust applications. One way it does this is by providing runtime type checking. Although it provides similar capabilities, MFC's runtime type checking does not use the proposed C++ Run-Time Type Information (RTTI) language extensions.

To get MFC's support for runtime type checking, you add a static data member and a new member function to each class that you want to check. MFC provides macros that help streamline this process. Incidentally, the Visual C++ AppWizard automatically generates the necessary macros for classes derived from MFC base classes. If you scan through an AppWizard-generated program, you'll see some of the macros that we are describing.

To add runtime type checking to a CObject-derived class, you add two macros. You add the DECLARE_DYNAMIC macro to the class declaration. This macro takes a single parameter, the class name. Here's an example:

```
class TypeSafe : CObject
{
    DECLARE_DYNAMIC(TypeSafe);
};
```

This macro adds a static data member to the class of type CRuntimeClass for holding class type information. The name of the data member is the word *class* added to the class name. In our example, the data member is classTypeSafe. The macro also adds a member function called GetRuntimeClass(), which returns a pointer to the data member.

The declaration references two new class members, but it's up to the IMPLEMENT_DYNAMIC macro to actually provide an implementation. This macro takes two parameters: the name of the class and the base class. Here's how you would use this macro for the class in our example:

```
IMPLEMENT_DYNAMIC(TypeSafe, CObject);
```

When defining a dynamic class, you'd put this macro anywhere in a C++ (.CPP) source file. That's because this macro contains static data definitions and an actual function definition. In AppWizard code, this tends to be near the top of the source file so it's readily apparent, but it can appear anywhere in a C++ source file.

The call to TypeSafe::GetRuntimeClass() returns a pointer to classTypeSafe, the static data member of type CRuntimeClass, which the macros added to the class. Among its

Continued

Continued from previous page

other fields, this data structure contains a text string with the name of the class and the size of the object (in bytes). You could perform type checking by verifying that these two values are what you expect.

However, an even easier way to perform type checking is by checking the address of the CRuntimeClass data structure. It is, after all, a static data structure, so only one instance will be present. MFC provides a macro for fetching a pointer to this structure, RUNTIME_CLASS. For example, the following code fetches the address of our class runtime type information:

```
CRuntimeClass * prtti = RUNTIME_CLASS(TypeSafe);
```

The CObject::IsKindOf() function provides a handy way to check whether a particular pointer is of the desired type. To support type checking with derived classes, this function walks the inheritance tree until it encounters CObject. The following code checks the type of a TypeSafe pointer in a type safe way:

```
TypeSafe * pts = (TypeSafe *)GrabPointer();
if (pts->IsKindOf(RUNTIME_CLASS(TypeSafe)))
{ /* Type is correct. */
}
else
{ /* Incorrect type. */
}
```

To assist in our debugging, we could also use the ASSERT macro to flag the error for us:

```
ASSERT(pts->IsKindOf(RUNTIME_CLASS(TypeSafe)));
```

When we've built a program containing this line in Debug mode, this macro checks for the proper type at runtime. If the test fails, a message box is displayed showing the name of the source file and the source line number. On Release builds, the ASSERT() macro is empty, so no code is generated and no check is performed.

To take advantage of runtime type checking, you don't need to define your own IsKindOf() function, because the one in CObject works with any CObject-derived class. Every RUNTIME_CLASS-tagged function has a static data member of type CRuntimeClass. What makes a class unique is the address of the static data member. The call to IsKindOf() fails gracefully even when a class isn't tagged for runtime type checking.

Continued

> *Continued from previous page*
>
> Incidentally, if you're wondering whether MFC runtime type checking supports derived classes, it does. A member of CRuntimeClass, IsDerivedFrom(), points to the base class of a given CObject-derived class. For complete runtime type checking, runtime type checking must be enabled for each base class.
>
> Microsoft's MFC team used runtime type checking extensively within the MFC sources to help flag improper use of MFC classes. You should consider using this feature to help avoid troublesome and hard-to-find type mismatch errors.

Although it's not a particularly attractive line of code, it is quite effective in displaying a big, ugly message box similar to the example shown in Figure 9-1. Notice that the source filename and line number are shown to help you pinpoint the particular line of code. Incidentally, the check you place within an ASSERT() macro is made only for the debug version of your software and not for the release version. In the release version, ASSERT() doesn't create code. Rest assured that your users won't encounter an alarming message such as the one shown in Figure 9-1.

Figure 9-1
The message box that's displayed when ASSERT fails.

To get a better idea of how the ASSERT() macro works, create an AppWizard program and add this line of code to the InitInstance() function of the CWinApp-derived class:

```
ASSERT(FALSE);
```

This assertion always fails. When built for a Debug build, you'll see an error displayed like that in Figure 9-1.

Another way that CObject helps you diagnose problems is with AssertValid( ). This member function asks an object to check its own internal validity. To ensure that the object is in a known, stable state, you can call this function for objects created from any CObject-derived class. When you create your own CObject-derived classes, you'll want to check for consistency of your own data members. When you know that a specific CObject-derived object has become corrupt but you're not sure where or how this happened, you can insert calls to the object's AssertValid( ) function at strategic points throughout your program. This helps you narrow down — and hopefully pinpoint — the exact place in your code where the problem is occurring.

Even when an object's internal state is valid, you sometimes need help determining why two (or more) objects don't interact as you expected. Although you could examine their internal state using a tool such as a debugger, CObject provides an alternative. You can call a CObject-derived object's Dump( ) member function, which asks the object to write its contents — that is, the value of each data member — to a debugging stream. To figure out some types of bugs, you might have to call the Dump( ) member function for every object that's involved. A close examination of specific data members might reveal the whys and wherefores of the problem. When deriving new classes from existing MFC classes, you need to override Dump( ) to extend support for your own classes' data members. Within the overridden Dump( ) function, you call the base class Dump( ) function to allow base classes to dump their own data members.

Finally, several of CObject's member functions provide basic object architecture. They exist to ensure that derived classes behave in a consistent, reliable way, given the C++ method of defining classes. You don't get any additional functional capabilities from these member functions, but their presence does help you avoid some programming errors. For this reason, they serve as a useful model of practices you'll want to incorporate in your own class libraries. The members of interest here are: the destructor, ~CObject( ); the copy constructor, CObject( ); and the assignment operator, operator=( ).

CObject's destructor is declared in AFX.H in the following line of code:

```
virtual ~CObject(); //virtual destructors are necessary
```

The *virtual* keyword makes this a virtual function, and the comment highlights the fact that this is no accident. As discussed in Chapter 6, virtual functions in a base class define an interface. Often, base classes also provide a default implementation. Nonvirtual base class functions provide implementation only — that is, they are not intended to be overridden by derived classes.

If the role of a destructor is to clean up when objects are de-allocated, why have a *virtual* destructor? Because it is defined this way in MFC's most basic class, the destructor in every derived class is also forced to be virtual. (If a function is defined as virtual in a base class, it's always virtual for all derived classes — even if the *virtual* keyword is omitted.) When objects are de-allocated, every destructor is called, starting with the destructor in the current class and working back to CObject. Because all destructors are properly called, you ensure that cleanup is handled properly for your objects. (For more details on virtual destructors, see item 14, pp. 42-48, in Scott Meyer's book, *Effective C++*. Addison-Wesley, 1992.)

If CObject's destructor was *not* virtual, derived classes wouldn't automatically get virtual destructors. This would create problems when objects are de-allocated. The destructor for the current class would get called, but the destructors for any base classes would not be called. Because destructors often hold important cleanup code, such a problem might cause system-wide memory leaks that would threaten the stability of your MFC programs. When building your own class libraries, you should avoid this problem by making sure that your base classes have virtual destructors.

CObject's copy constructor and assignment operators are declared with private scope in the following lines from AFX.H:

```
private:
   CObject (const CObject& objectSrc);  // no implementation
   void operator=(const CObject& objectSrc); // no implementation
```

Just to refresh your C++ skills a bit, an object's copy constructor is called when a copy is made of the object. For example, a simple assignment statement calls the copy constructor to ensure that the newly created copy is a correct duplicate of the original:

```
CRect rect1;
CRect rect2(rect1);  // Copy constructor called here.
```

The preceding statement calls the copy constructor. However, because the copy constructor is hidden for CObject-derived classes, the compiler won't let you do even the following simple assignment:

```
CWnd window1;
CWnd window2(window1);  // Compiler error.
```

In MFC terms, if you have a window, you can't create a new window by means of the assignment statement. As a CObject-derived object, when an instance of a CWnd is created, a window must be wrapped within it to have a fully valid CWnd object. This seems like a powerful — and potentially useful — capability, so why does MFC get in our way?

The reason has to do with complications that can arise from implicit uses of the copy constructor. The complication for a CWnd-derived class is that the copy constructor creates a duplicate object. But does that mean a second window is created? And if not, which is the correct "wrapper" object for the window? In almost every case, parameter passing should simply pass a reference to the window object, not create an entirely new window.

When you make a function call in C or C++, parameters are passed with "call-by-value," which means that a *copy* of the value is passed to the caller. In C++, this is true for native types such as int, long, and char, as well as for custom types — that is, objects that are created from classes you define. So, if we call a function using an object, the copy constructor is called to create a duplicate of our object on the stack:

```
CRect rect;
IsGoodRect (rect)
```

MFC prevents you from using call-by-value with CObject-derived types. It does this by hiding CObject's copy constructor from you. Instead of making a copy of the object, you must refer to such objects using a pointer (call-by-reference). CObject-derived objects are usually referenced using pointers (which implies that they are usually allocated dynamically rather than being created as local or global objects). If you try to pass a CObject-derived object itself as a parameter in a function call — rather than a pointer to the object — you are using the object incorrectly. The compiler prevents your mistake by generating an error message (although the message doesn't help you figure out how to correct the problem).

Within CObject, the assignment operator, operator=, is also hidden from view. The compiler flags code such as the following example as an error:

```
CObject data, object;
data = object;
```

The compiler complains that the operator= function is unavailable. This makes sense, because it has been explicitly hidden (declared as private) from view.

As in the previous example, CObject-derived objects cannot be passed by value. Instead, the correct way to refer to such objects is with a pointer:

```
CObject * data, object;
data = &object;
```

To restate the major principle involved: *CObject-derived objects require the use of pointer semantics.* The handling of the copy constructor and the overloading of operator=( ) highlight a key point about CObject-derived objects: in general, they are meant to be referenced with pointers. To check the identity of a CObject-derived object, for example, you compare pointers. In MFC, this is called *pointer semantics.*

For objects created from classes that are *not* derived from CObject, you check their identity by checking the value within the object, rather than by simply comparing pointers. Also, such classes don't hide the copy constructor or operator=( ). You are free to copy such objects by value, which is referred to as *value semantics.*

Although the vast majority of MFC classes are derived from CObject, a few solitary classes are not. These classes make up a set of utility classes that play an important role in holding and passing state information. Let's take a look at some of the characteristics of the MFC classes that are *not* derived from CObject.

Non-CObject-derived classes

Although only 22 of the MFC library's 132 classes are not derived from CObject, you'll use these classes quite often. This fact alone makes it worthwhile for you to pursue a basic understanding of the non-CObject-derived classes. In addition, understanding this set of classes from a design-oriented viewpoint will help you decide when to base your own classes on CObject and when they should stand alone.

Pointer Semantics and Value Semantics

One key difference between CObject-derived classes and other classes is that CObject-derived classes use *pointer semantics* and the other classes use *value semantics*. An understanding of the difference between the two will help you better understand both types of classes and simplify the writing of code that correctly uses each type.

Put simply, the difference between the two types of semantics involves where the object data resides. When you create an object that has value semantics, the data resides entirely in the object. You can freely create new instances of the object, knowing full well that no loose object fragments or inconsistencies are being created. Native C/C++ data types all use value semantics:

```
int aNumber = 10;
int AnotherNumber = aNumber;
```

Objects created by non-CObject-derived classes use value semantics. For example, you can use objects created from MFC's CString character string class similar to the way that C++ integers are used (something that can't be done with character arrays in C):

```
CString aString = "A string";
CString AnotherString = aString;
```

After these two lines of code are executed, two CString objects exist. Each object is complete and doesn't need the other copy to operate properly.

The various CObject-derived classes use pointer semantics because a given instance of an object is incomplete. CWnd is an example of a CObject-derived class in MFC. A fully initialized instance of CWnd encapsulates a window (that is, an instance of the rectangular user-interface object that appears on the display screens of Windows 95 systems). To maintain consistency between the MFC heap and the operating system, there is a one-to-one correspondence between instances of CWnd and instances of operating system windows.

The operator=() is hidden in CObject-derived classes to force the compiler to reject the following types of operations, which create logical inconsistencies:

```
CWnd aWindow = CWnd();
CWnd AnotherWindow = aWindow;
```

Continued

Continued from previous page

To do the right thing, the operator=() would have to cause the creation of a new instance of the operating system window. MFC doesn't do this because most code simply wants to refer to an existing window without instantiating a new one.

The bottom line is one easy-to-follow rule: use pointers for objects that are created from CObject-derived classes. With other classes, you can use pointers or create new instances of objects, as best suits your purpose.

In terms of resources consumed, these classes take less memory than CObject-derived classes because they don't have the overhead required for classes that contain virtual member functions. Of course, the overhead is quite small — one 4-byte pointer — so this not a truly compelling reason to avoid using CObject as a base class. But when you need binary compatibility with existing C data types, you want to avoid virtual functions because that 4-byte pointer gets inconveniently placed at the beginning of the data structure. And from a practical point of view, some of these classes — most notably CRectTracker — provide handy features that you can use in any MFC-based program.

Table 9-1 lists the MFC library classes that are not derived from CObject. These classes are from many different parts of the class library, and they have widely differing uses. Classes in this set are used for everything from wrapping native Windows API data structures to supporting features specific to the MFC library.

We're not going to discuss each of these classes in detail; such descriptions are more appropriate in the context of individual MFC topics. Instead, we're going to provide a brief sampling of each class — in some cases, to show why these classes are not CObject-derived, and in others, because these classes are so useful that you'll want to learn about them as soon as possible.

Three non-CObject-derived classes are wrappers for native Win32 data structures: CRect, CPoint, and CSize. The native structures — RECT, POINT, and SIZE — could have been used by themselves, but the designers of MFC decided to enhance these classes with a few C++ niceties. A variety of constructors, several useful member functions, and some overloaded operators help simplify some otherwise tedious chores.

Table 9-1

The 22 MFC Classes That Are Not Derived from CObject

MFC Class	Description
CArchive	Used to serialize CObject-based classes.
CCmdUI	Supports enabling and disabling of menu items and control bar buttons.
CCreateContext	Supports MFC's Document/View architecture by connecting classes. These classes are used for opening files dynamically with CDocument-derived classes, displaying data in windows supported by CView-derived classes, and placing those windows inside other windows built from CFrameWnd-derived classes.
CDataExchange	Supports dialog box data exchange and data validation.
CDockContext	Supports dockable toolbars.
CDumpContext	Supports MFC diagnostic facilities in dumping and displaying the contents of an object.
CFieldExchange	Used by MFC's ODBC database classes.
CFileStatus	Holds file system file status (file size and other attributes).
CHandleMap	Provides a look-up table for mapping MFC objects to native WinAPI objects.
CMemoryState	Provides diagnostic support for memory snapshots and leak detection.
COleDataObject	Serves as a wrapper for native OLE data transfer via the clipboard and OLE drag/drop. (In native OLE terms, this is a wrapper for IDataObject.)
COleDispatchDriver	Serves as a wrapper for native OLE IDispatch automation support.
CPoint	Serves as a wrapper for the native Windows system POINT structure. Holds an (x,y) pair.
CPrintInfo	Provides support for Print and Print Preview capabilities.
CRecentFileList	Holds a list of recently accessed files.
CRect	Serves as a wrapper for the native Windows system RECT structure. Holds two (x,y) pairs.
CRectTracker	Simplifies creation of stretchable rectangles. CRectTracker is provided as an OLE helper class, but it is usable in any MFC program.
CRuntimeClass	For CObject-derived classes that use dynamic runtime information, this structure is used to define a static data structure holding various class attribute details (runtime type information, serialization information, and diagnostic helpers).
CSize	Serves as a wrapper for the native Windows system SIZE structure. Holds a pair of integers used for rectangle extents (cx, cy).
CString	A character string class that supports dynamic character strings, along with a host of useful capabilities.
CTime	Holds time and date information.
CTimeSpan	Holds time duration.

One important reason why the MFC developers *didn't* base these classes on CObject was so that their binary layout would faithfully replicate the layout of the native Win32 structures. For example, the developers wanted to ensure that MFC's CPoint would exactly mimic the Win32 POINT so that programmers could use one structure in place of the other when calling the native system functions. To understand how basing an MFC class on CObject would change its binary layout, consider the current layout shared by the Win32 POINT and the MFC CPoint:

```
struct tagPOINT {
    LONG x;
    LONG y;
    };
```

If CPoint was derived from CObject, its *binary* layout would resemble the following:

```
class CPoint : public CObject {
    VOID * pVtbl; // Implicit - inherited from CObject
    LONG x;
    LONG y;
    };
```

The presence of virtual functions in CObject causes the C++ compiler to create a virtual function table and to place a pointer to that table in the object's data. Even if derived classes don't define their own virtual classes, all base class virtual functions are inherited, which means this pointer would be present.

When designing your own classes, you'll want to avoid deriving from CObject when you want to maintain *binary compatibility* with some set of data structures that are already in use somewhere. A class that is stand-alone also occupies a little less memory and therefore is less expensive to instantiate.

CString is another class that is not derived from CObject. CString objects provide better support for strings than character arrays. At the same time, because a CString object looks just like a pointer to a character array, any function that expects a char * will accept a CString without any fuss.

The list of ways that CString improves on char[] is quite long, but a few examples should help stir your imagination. For one thing, CString objects are dynamically sized, so you never have to allocate character arrays for the worst-case scenario. As shown in the following example, appending strings is easy with a set of string concatenation operators:

```
CString cs1 = "Hello ";
CString cs2 = "World";
CString cs3 = cs1 + cs2;
```

Because every CString knows its own length (which is stored as a data member), it's also easy to query string length:

```
int cb = cs1.GetLength();
```

As shown in this example, this feature is implemented as an *inline* function that references the length value stored in the object (as opposed to calling strlen( ), for example).

CRectTracker is another class worth learning about, particularly if you plan to write graphics-intensive code. This class makes it easy to create stretchable rectangles — that is, rectangles that can be easily moved and resized by the user. You can choose from different styles for the border and the interior, and handles can be created to highlight the places where users can click and resize the rectangle. Although this class was originally created as a helper object for in-place active OLE objects, it isn't tied to OLE in any particular way. Therefore, you can use it to highlight any graphical object that you create.

As you build your MFC applications, you'll define classes (and structures) for your own purposes. For some tips on when to derive from CObject and when to create stand-alone classes, see the sidebar, "When to Derive from CObject." It's time now to turn our attention to the final structural element that affects every MFC class you work with: the stateless nature of MFC classes.

A stateless class library

In conversations with one of the authors, members of Microsoft's MFC development team described MFC as a "stateless class library." A cursory look at the MFC include files shows that MFC classes *do* retain state — that is, they do have data members. The developer meant that MFC classes don't have data members holding state information that is redundant with the state that is kept by the operating system.

When to Derive from CObject

As you use MFC to build applications, you'll define a wide variety of your own data types. An issue that will come up is whether you should base your own classes on CObject. Here are some guidelines to help you decide.

In some cases, the choice will be easy because you'll simply be deriving from existing MFC classes. Whatever the base class does, your new class will follow. For example, every MFC program creates a CWinApp-derived class, and because this class is based on CObject, so is your derived class. However, neither CRect nor CPoint are based on CObject, so your new classes inherit an independent streak when you derive from these classes.

For classes that are not directly derived from existing MFC classes, however, the choice will require a bit of thought. In general, CObject classes are helpful for handling "complex" objects. Here are some cases in which you will typically want to derive your class from CObject:

- The class contains large objects or non-C++ objects. For performance reasons, very large objects are more efficiently handled via pointer semantics and therefore should be derived from CObject. If the class encapsulates a non-C++ object — just as MFC's CWnd holds an MS-Windows window — then deriving from CObject is appropriate. A litmus test is whether making a copy of an existing object still refers to

the original object or truly represents an entirely separate and distinct object. In other words, value semantics suggest non-CObject inheritance and pointer semantics suggest CObject inheritance.

- You are creating an abstract class that will be the base class for a family of derived classes. The dynamic runtime type checking support of CObject will simplify debugging and detecting type errors.

- You are creating a wrapper class for a data object that resides elsewhere. Although this alone is not sufficient reason for deriving from CObject (because you can follow pointer semantics without CObject), a wrapper class probably also meets the first two criteria in this list.

- You plan to serialize the object. This alone is not sufficient reason for deriving from CObject, because as long as the object is contained in an object that is created from a CObject-derived class, you'll tap into MFC's support for persistence. However, because the need to serialize is combined with the need to contain other objects, inheritance from CObject is a good idea.

On the other hand, you'll probably avoid deriving from CObject when you are creating "simpler" classes. In the following

Continued

Continued from previous page

cases, you'll probably want to make the class stand alone:

- Members of the class contain only simple data types.

- You want to avoid the overhead of virtual function tables.

- You need to make your class binary compatible with an existing data type (perhaps a type used by a DLL). CRect, CPoint, and CSize are all examples of MFC classes that were defined to be binary compatible with native Windows system structures (RECT, POINT, and SIZE).

- The operation of value semantics is consistent with the way you plan to use the class — that is, an object is complete by itself and, therefore, can be copied to create a separate and distinct object.

- You need multiple inheritance between CObject-derived classes and your own classes. Runtime type checking does not properly detect type information when multiple inheritance is used between two CObject-derived classes.

The primary reason for this approach is to prevent the problems that can occur when the operating system state disagrees with the class library state. Such problems are similar to those that arise if you use two clocks: if one clock is wrong, you never really know what time it is. In the same way, extra work is required to maintain the accuracy of redundant data. Of course, this doesn't mean that the system's state information isn't available to you. On the contrary, numerous functions allow you to get — and set — system state. And as a last resort when an MFC class doesn't seem willing to get or set some piece of system state, you can always call native Win32 functions.

To ensure that your code doesn't fall victim to the problems associated with holding stale data, you should consider taking the approach used by the MFC developers. That is, when you need some piece of state information, make a function call rather than storing your own copy of that piece of state information.

From a purely object-oriented point of view, the presence of system state information is like the presence of protected data in a C++ base class. And certainly the operating system maintains private data that is inaccessible to you. The net result is that all MFC data members are public data members — a fact that may worry some object-oriented design engineers who prefer more private data as proof of encapsulation. The Win32 API does a fine job of encapsulating the data that needs to be hidden from an MFC program.

MFC Library Support for Windows

A common way to look at a class library is by examining the class hierarchy. However, the MFC class hierarchy is so big that the on-line help database splits it into six parts. And even though the hierarchy charts show only inheritance, this isn't always the most important relationship to understand when you are trying to use a class library's classes.

For a developer using a class library such as MFC, class hierarchy charts don't answer some fundamental questions, such as:

- Where does program execution begin?
- Which are the important classes that I should completely understand?
- What other relationships exist between classes?
- Do objects created by some classes naturally contain objects created by other classes?

To help answer these and other questions, we're going to describe some of the fundamental ways that MFC supports Windows programming.

We'll start by discussing WinMain( ), the entry point Microsoft defines for Windows programs. Every Windows program has a WinMain( ) function, and MFC provides one so that you'll never have to write your own. Although it isn't a complicated function, a close look at the WinMain( ) provided by MFC reveals a lot about the operation of every implementation of Windows. For one thing, in every implementation, messages drive the user interface and the scheduling of applications.

Our examination of WinMain( ) will also focus on practical issues, such as how to initialize your MFC application and how to perform application-level cleanup. We'll also show you some of the wonders that MFC provides for you — for example, message loops, and the opportunity to perform idle-time processing.

Finally, we'll examine the application object class, CWinApp. It serves as the outermost container for all other objects. Among the objects it contains, for example, is a pointer to your application's main window. Let's begin by browsing through the source code MFC provides you for WinMain( ).

THE WINMAIN() ENTRY POINT

Although most of MFC is part of one class or another, several important functions don't belong to any class. One such function is WinMain( ), which is the designated entry point to a Windows program. Windows replaces the standard C main function with WinMain( ), which passes some environment-specific parameters. MFC provides WinMain( ) primarily because much of the initialization required by a typical Windows program is fairly standard. You're free to provide your own WinMain( ) function; if you do, however, you need to be sure that you perform the start-up and clean-up code that MFC requires.

Listing 9-2 shows WinMain( ) as it is defined in WINMAIN.CPP (in a default installation, the source file is located at \msvc20\mfc\src\ winmain.cpp). Although the source file shows the name as _tWinMain, that's just the name of a symbol defined in TCHAR.H. As part of Visual C++'s support for different character sets, the actual function called is WinMain( ) when compiled for the ANSI character set and wWinMain( ) when compiled for Unicode support.

Listing 9-2
MFC's WinMain() Entry Point

```
_tWinMain(HINSTANCE hInstance, HINSTANCE hPrevInstance,
    LPTSTR lpCmdLine, int nCmdShow)
{
    ASSERT(hPrevInstance == NULL);

    int nReturnCode = -1;
    CWinApp* pApp = AfxGetApp();

    // AFX internal initialization
    if (!AfxWinInit(hInstance, hPrevInstance, lpCmdLine, nCmdShow))
```

```
            goto InitFailure;

    // App global initializations (rare)
    ASSERT_VALID(pApp);
    if (!pApp->InitApplication())
        goto InitFailure;
    ASSERT_VALID(pApp);

    // Perform specific initializations
    if (!pApp->InitInstance())
    {
        if (pApp->m_pMainWnd != NULL)
        {
            TRACE0("Warning: Destroying non-NULL m_pMainWnd\n");
            pApp->m_pMainWnd->DestroyWindow();
        }
        nReturnCode = pApp->ExitInstance();
        goto InitFailure;
    }
    ASSERT_VALID(pApp);

    nReturnCode = pApp->Run();
    ASSERT_VALID(pApp);

InitFailure:
    AfxWinTerm();
    return nReturnCode;
}
```

Always override InitInstance to do your initialization.

Calls MFC message loop.

SDK programmers will recognize the WinMain( ) function and its parameters because it's also required for Windows programs in C. During the development of an MFC-based program, you probably won't spend any time looking at this function (though you'll often see it when starting the debugger). However, you should understand what it does, because this is where every MFC program starts its execution. We'll start by describing each of WinMain( )'s parameters. Then, we'll summarize what WinMain( )'s 29 lines of code tell us about MFC (and Windows) programming.

WinMain() parameters

WinMain( )'s first two parameters are of type HINSTANCE, which identifies an *instance handle*. In Windows programming, *handles* are integers that identify native WinAPI objects. The term *instance* identifies an executable file in memory, though an instance handle is valid only in the context of the process in which the file has been mapped. Several Win32 functions require an instance handle, which identifies the executable file of the code making the call.

WinMain( )'s first parameter, hInstance, identifies the current instance, and hPrevInstance is the previous instance. In the Win16 API, this tells a program whether any previous copies of itself are presently running. With "old" Windows, when memory was extremely scarce, the idea was to simplify the process of sharing memory objects between instances. Although sharing seemed like a good idea, sharing also made it difficult for the system to properly clean up unused objects, which meant there was a possibility of memory leaks.

In the Win32 API, hPrevInstance is *always* NULL. To make sure this is the case, MFC's WinMain( ) raises an assertion if it's not:

```
ASSERT(hPrevInstance == NULL);
```

The presence of hPrevInstance is a relic of MFC's support for the Win16 API. Although Win16 programs used to check this value for the presence of a previous instance, that test won't work in a Win32 program.

The third parameter to WinMain( ) is lpCmdLine, an LPTSTR (basically a char *). Windows programs don't get their command line with a count of parameters and an array of pointers — argc and argv — though the compiler secretly creates an __argc and __argv for those programs that need it. Instead, the pointer refers to a simple string. Incidentally, the command line does *not* include the name of the program that's running, such as happens on UNIX systems.

WinMain( )'s last parameter is nCmdShow. This parameter indicates how a Windows program should display its main window: either as an icon, as a full-screen maximized window, or as a normal, open window. To make the main window visible in the desired way, a typical MFC program takes this value and calls CWnd::ShowWindow( ).

WinMain() local variables

MFC's WinMain( ) has a local variable, nReturnCode, which is used to hold the process return value. This integer value can be used to communicate with the process that started the execution of a program. There are no standard ways to use this value — that is, none of the implementations of Windows do anything with this value. However, parent processes can query the return code by calling a Win32 function, GetExitCodeProcess( ).

An MFC program terminates by calling a special MFC helper function, AfxPostQuitMessage( ), that terminates the program and carries the return value to the WinMain( ) function.

WinMain( ) creates a second local variable, pApp, of type CWinApp *. WinMain( ) checks the validity of pApp four times with the following statement:

```
ASSERT_VALID(pApp);
```

For a debug build, this macro displays an error dialog box if any of the following conditions are true:

- The pointer is NULL.
- The pointer holds an invalid address.
- The object being referenced is invalid in any detectable way.

This is an example of your CObject tax dollars at work. (The release build does no checking; it assumes that you've already removed all program bugs during the development process.)

A cursory examination of WinMain( ) reveals one reason why this object is validated so often: the pointer is used to call various CWinApp member functions. What's not immediately obvious, however, is the requirement that every MFC program must have a CWinApp-derived object created as a global object. Like a C global variable, a C++ global object is defined outside the scope of all functions.

WinMain() initialization and termination processing

WinMain( ) calls two Afx functions: AfxWinInit( ), which initializes the MFC program; and AfxWinTerm( ), which cleans up at the end. You don't need to be too concerned about what these functions do, but a quick look will show you how much effort MFC saves. In particular, MFC is ready to handle a variety of situations that you might not have anticipated — for example, running MFC on an Apple Macintosh, or embedding your MFC code in a dynamic link library (DLL).

Of particular interest within WinMain( ) are four CWinApp member functions: InitApplication( ), InitInstance( ), ExitInstance( ), and Run( ). To build an MFC program, you must create a new class that's derived from CWinApp. All four of the functions called by WinMain( ) are *virtual* functions, which means you *can* replace them. In practice, however, you'll probably override only one of them: InitInstance( ).

The first two of these four CWinApp functions are initialization functions. Because of the way in which Windows sets the value of hPrevInstance before calling WinMain( ), Win16 programs are able to differentiate between *per-application* initialization and *per-instance* initialization. But because Win32 programs always see a NULL value for hPrevInstance, a Win32 program can't differentiate between per-application and per-instance initialization. As such, we simply use one, InitInstance( ), in Win32 programs. The ExitInstance( ) function provides a place for performing program cleanup. In general, cleanup code is more appropriately placed in the destructor of the class that overrides CWinApp. However, it's hard to ignore the nice symmetry between the InitInstance( ) and ExitInstance( ) functions.

Message handling and application scheduling

Of the four CWinApp functions that are called by WinMain( ), the most important — and certainly the most complex — is CWinApp::Run( ). It contains the *message loop*, an (almost) infinite loop that runs for the life of a program to poll the system for user input to a program's windows. Because it's a virtual function, you can provide your own message loop if you'd like. But you'll want to take a close look at the core message loop so that you understand what it's doing for you. If you don't override it, CWinApp::Run is called; it then calls CWinThread::Run, which appears in Listing 9-3. This function is found in the file \mfc\src\thrdcore.cpp.

Listing 9-3
The MFC Message Loop

```
// main running routine until thread exits
int CWinThread::Run()
{
    ASSERT_VALID(this);

    // for tracking the idle time state
    BOOL bIdle = TRUE;

    // acquire and dispatch messages
    //until a WM_QUIT message is received.
    for (;;)
    {
        // phase1: check to see if we can do idle work
```

```
LONG lIdleCount = 0;
while (bIdle &&
    !::PeekMessage(&m_msgCur, NULL, NULL, NULL, PM_NOREMOVE))
{
    // call OnIdle while in bIdle state
    if (!OnIdle(lIdleCount++))
        bIdle = FALSE; // assume "no idle" state
}

// phase2: pump messages while available
do
{
    // pump message, but quit on WM_QUIT
    if (!PumpMessage())
        return ExitInstance();

    // reset "no idle" state after pumping "normal" message
    if (!bIdle && IsIdleMessage(&m_msgCur))
        bIdle = TRUE;

} while (::PeekMessage(&m_msgCur, NULL, NULL, NULL,
                        PM_NOREMOVE));
}

ASSERT(FALSE);  // not reachable
}
```

Cousin to the ::GetMessage( ) function.

Fetches a program's messages.

It's called an *infinite* message loop because of the for (;;) statement, and we like to joke that it runs forever and burns itself into your system's RAM. The larger loop contains two smaller loops. As indicated by the comments, phase 1 handles "idle work," while phase 2 "pumps messages" (user input) from the system into your application. Of course, the loop doesn't run forever; the receipt of a WM_QUIT message in the phase 2 loop exits the function via a simple return statement.

The phrase *idle work* refers to processing time that's not related to user input. For example, you might perform a sort, query a hardware device, or clean up leftover data. You tap into this processing time by overriding the OnIdle( ) function in your application class (the one that's derived from CWinApp). Support for this capability goes back to the earliest versions of Windows, when it was used by the print spooler to sneak tiny bits of processing time. Today, you can use the idle-time feature of Windows to do background processing in both the Win16 and the Win32 APIs. Of course, if your programs run only in Win32, you'll probably rely on threads for background processing.

Phase 2 of the message loop, the "message pump," queries the various system queues for messages. The priority of its operation is summarized in Table 9-2.

Table 9-2
Priority of Events in Handling Windows System Messages

Event	Description
Arrival of interthread SendMessage() messages	Highest priority. The Win32 SendMessage() function delivers messages directly to a window procedure, and its use is therefore analogous to a direct call to the window procedure. To prevent catching your program in the middle of processing one message, interthread SendMessage() messages are delivered only when a thread enters the known state of querying for new messages. You should note that these messages are still delivered directly to the window procedure and not through the message pump.
PostMessage receipt	Second-highest priority. The Win32 PostMessage() function allows a program to add messages to the message queue by placing messages in a thread's private message queue. Although an application can send any type of message via this mechanism, Windows itself sends only a few types of messages this way, including translated characters (WM_CHAR) and dynamic data exchange (DDE) messages.
WM_QUIT	Third highest priority. Application shutdown occurs when this message is received. The MFC framework usually generates this message when an application's main window is closed. To shut down an application, you can call AfxPostQuitMessage() directly (though you should consider this only as a last resort).
Hardware queue	Fourth highest priority. Mouse and keyboard input are received at interrupt time and are placed in a hardware event queue. The resulting messages are read from the queue in the order received.
WM_TIMER	Fifth highest priority. Timers created by calling SetTimer() have a relatively low priority. They are not intended to represent "realtime" passage of time, but rather that a minimum amount of time has passed. For interrupt-level timers, use the multimedia timer function, timeSetEvent(). For details, see the Win32 API documentation or the help database.
WM_PAINT	Sixth highest priority. This message represents a request to redraw the contents of a window. It has low priority because the video display has historically been the slowest device in the system. (We discuss this message in Chapter 13.)
Sleep	Lowest priority. When there's nothing to do, a thread goes to sleep and waits for useful input to come its way.

Two queues are of interest: the application's private queue and the hardware event queue. The other types of events represent state bits that are kept by the system on a per-thread basis.

Some developers might wonder why the WM_TIMER message is *not* an interrupt-level timer. The reason is mostly historical. Messages tend to arrive synchronously. If a timer message arrives while another message is being processed, it might catch your code in an unstable state. As a result, timers were also made synchronous. At a multimedia developers meeting at Microsoft in 1989, some game developers asked Microsoft to stop this hand-holding — some might say "arm-tying" — and trust developers to properly handle asynchronous timers. The result was the multimedia timer — represented by the Win32 timeSetEvent( ) function — which is truly asynchronous.

The message loop

The message handling part of the message loop is contained in CWinThread::PumpMessage( ), which is called in phase 2 of the message loop. The essential portions of this function are summarized as follows:

```
::GetMessage (&m_msgCur, NULL, NULL, NULL)
if (!PreTranslateMessage(&m_msgCur))
{
    ::TranslateMessage(&m_msgCur);
    ::DispatchMessage(&m_msgCur);
}
```

Reads queued messages.

Sends messages to window procedures.

In most cases, the use of the C++ global scope operator (::) in a function call made in the MFC source code means that a native Win32 function is being called. This example shows three such calls. The fourth call, to PreTranslateMessage( ), is to a virtual function that has been implemented in several MFC classes. This last function gives several MFC objects the opportunity to tweak the system's processing in the middle of this message loop. Usually, it simply enables keyboard accelerator commands. Let's look at the other three functions, which form the core of a typical Windows message loop.

The Win32 GetMessage( ) function does two things: it polls for a new message, and it tells the system that the preceding message has been processed. Under Windows 3.1, this function serves as the multitasking switcher. Under OS/2, a similar function — WinGetMsg( ) — is the switcher for OS/2 user-interface threads. In all implementations —

Windows 3.x, OS/2, Windows 95, and Windows NT — you cause problems if you don't call this function on a regular basis.

The seriousness of the problem depends on the robustness of the operating system's user interface. In Windows 3.x, the following code hangs the user interface for the entire system:

```
// Don't do this - hangs Windows 3.1 (system-wide).
// In Windows 95 and Windows NT, it hangs only the
// user interface of the associated thread (other
// programs' user-interface threads still run).
while (GetMessage(&msg, 0, 0, 0))
{
    while (1);
}
```

This example requires a local reboot to terminate the offending program and restore the user interface to proper operation.

On Windows 95 and Windows NT, this code hangs the user interface for the associated thread, but the user interfaces for all other threads continue to operate normally. Incidentally, a similar code fragment in an OS/2 Presentation Manager program causes the entire system's user interface to hang, similar to what happens in Windows 3.x:

```
hab = WinInitialize(...);
WinCreateMsgQueue(...)
// Don't do this - hangs OS/2
// user interface (system-wide)
while (WinGetMsg(&msg, 0, 0, 0))
{
    while (1);
}
```

Setting aside the abnormal case in which messages *aren't* queried, message receipt means permission to execute. We consider a message to be akin to a time slice for user-interface threads. This design allows the user interface of all versions of Windows (and OS/2!) to be highly responsive to user input. Implementations of Windows that support pre-emptive scheduling — for example, Windows 95 and Windows NT — always give a priority boost when undelivered messages are queued.

The MSG data structure

In the MFC message loop, message information is read into the m_msgCur structure. The m_ prefix indicates that the data item is a class data member (and not, for example, a local or global variable). A quick execution of the Search|Find in Files... command in the Integrated Development Environment (IDE) shows that this member appears in CWinThread and is of type MSG. This Win32 structure is defined as follows in OBJBASE.H:

```
typedef struct tagMSG
  {
  HWND hwnd;
  UINT message;
  WPARAM wParam;
  LPARAM lParam;
  DWORD time;
  POINT pt;
  } MSG;
```

The six values in this structure represent all the data associated with a single message. Taken together, these values make up a single unit of user input to a Windows program. The first member, hwnd, is a window handle that identifies the system window with which the input is associated.

The second member, message, is an unsigned integer that contains a coded message value. You'll see that many such messages have symbolic names that begin with a WM_ prefix — for example, WM_PAINT, WM_TIMER, WM_CHAR.

The third and fourth members, wParam and lParam, are 32-bit, unsigned integers that provide additional message details. Their meaning depends on the message. For example, mouse messages pack two 16-bit mouse coordinate values into lParam. On the other hand, keyboard input messages place key codes into wParam. As an interesting historical note, the *w* and *l* at the beginning of these parameter names stand for *word* and *long*. In the Win16 API, wParam was 16 bits and lParam was 32 bits. Both are 32 bits in Win32, so the prefixes have lost their meaning. The names have been retained for the sake of compatibility with older code.

The final two members, time and pt, provide the time and mouse location when a message was placed in the queue. Although you can look at these values, they typically are not used by Windows programs or by class libraries such as MFC. Windows uses these values internally before GetMessage( ) copies the entire data structure into the application-supplied buffer.

Application message handling

After GetMessage( ) fills m_msgCur, the various PreTranslateMessage( ) functions are called. We say "various," because quite a few MFC classes have a member with this name. This call gives various parts of the class library the opportunity to examine precooked keyboard messages. This is required to support dialog boxes (see Chapter 12) and keyboard accelerator commands (see Chapter 11).

The message loop reads in all messages for all windows in a program; the messages are then distributed to the specific window object that corresponds to the Windows system window. (There is actually a message queue per thread and not per program, but we're ignoring the issue of threads here to focus on windows and messages.) By overriding the PreTranslateMessage( ) function, an object can intercept mouse and keyboard input before it is transferred to its destination window.

The call to TranslateMessage( ) converts raw keyboard messages (WM_KEYDOWN and WM_SYSKEYDOWN) into "cooked" character input messages (WM_CHAR and WM_SYSCHAR). For details about when to use cooked versus raw keyboard messages, see Chapter 14, "Mouse and Keyboard Input." OS/2 programmers might notice that the message loops in OS/2 Presentation Manager programs don't make a similar call. The reason is that OS/2 delivers only cooked character messages.

The call to DispatchMessage( ) sends cooked messages to a function called a window procedure. Windows programs in C must provide these *call-back functions* to receive and process messages. MFC provides a standard window procedure in AfxWndProc( ). In turn, that function calls the appropriate window object, where the message is received by the corresponding CWnd::WindowProc( ) function. This function takes care of parsing the wParam and lParam values for each message. Then, it calls member functions in CWnd-derived classes for handling of individual messages.

A last word on WinMain()

In summary, MFC's WinMain( ) function handles application start-up, clean-up, and message processing. Most of the life of an MFC program is spent within the CWinThread::Run( ) function. The (almost) infinite loop in this function turns the crank that runs the engine of a Windows program. The engine pumps Windows system messages into a program, where they are handled by individual windows. When the engine is running at idle, it allows a program to have tiny bits of idle-time processing via the OnIdle( ) member function. By overriding this function, you can get idle-time processing in both Win16 and Win32 programs.

Threads offer a more robust mechanism for idle-time processing in Win32 programs running on Windows 95 and Windows NT.

The WinMain( ) function provided by MFC makes extensive use of an application object. This global object is created from a CWinApp-derived class. To fill in some of the details about what the application object is and what it does, we'll conclude this chapter by examining an MFC class that you must use in every MFC program: the application class, CWinApp.

THE APPLICATION OBJECT: CWINAPP

An application object is the outermost container in an MFC-based program. For any object, if you start looking at which object contains that object, you eventually end up at the application object. You *must* create an application object as a global object for your program, or WinMain( ) won't execute. You can create *only one* application object, because CWinApp complains if you try to create a second one. With the exception of a few global variables that MFC creates, every other object resides either in the application object itself, or within an object that is ultimately contained by the application object.

The application object holds the parameters that are passed to WinMain( ): instance handles, the program command line, and the ShowWindow( ) parameter. The application object also contains the application's main window, which earns this title because the application itself terminates when the main window is closed. Table 9-3 summarizes the more important CWinApp data members.

Table 9-3

Important CWinApp Data Members

Data Member	Description
CWnd * m_pMainWnd	The application's main window.
int m_nCmdShow	The value that is passed to ShowWindow to make an application's main window visible.
MSG m_msgCur	The last queued message received.
LPTSTR m_lpCmdLine	The program's command line.
LPCTSTR m_pszAppName	The application's name as displayed in the main window's caption bar.

CWinApp contains quite a few data members in addition to those shown in Table 9-3. We haven't listed all of them here because many are placeholders for features we'll discuss later in this book (such as the Document/View architecture, which we cover in Chapter 15), or because they provide support for more advanced features that are to be covered in future books in this programming series (OLE and ODBC, for example).

Figure 9-2 shows the relationship between CWinApp and the three classes from which it inherits: CObject, CCmdTarget, and CWinThread.

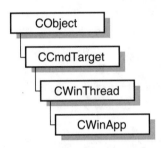

Figure 9-2
The relationship between CWinApp and its base classes.

Because CWinApp is derived from CObject, application objects inherit the various CObject characteristics. For example, you'll refer to application objects using pointer semantics instead of value semantics (as discussed earlier in this chapter). Because application objects can have dynamic runtime type information, you can validate pointers and avoid wrong casts. (This relates back to the example we gave earlier for making sure that any casts applied to the return value from AfxGetApp( ) don't hide a type mismatch error.)

By contrast, the things that CWinApp inherits from CCmdTarget are a bit more exciting. From this class, application objects gain the capability to receive WM_COMMAND messages. These messages are sent to a program's window in response to a user's selection of a menu item. This is a useful enhancement that MFC provides over SDK programming for Windows. In an SDK program, menu messages are sent to a window. However, it doesn't make sense for certain menu selections to be associated with a window because they are of interest to the entire application — for example a request to close the application, open a new window, or provide context-sensitive help.

MFC lets you delegate the task of responding to individual menu item selections to any object created from a CCmdTarget-derived class. For example, the request to close an application (File|Exit) might go to the application object. You might delegate the opening of a new window to a frame window that also has the task of holding all open windows. To handle context-sensitive help, you might create a help object that serves as a central dispatcher for your entire application. (We'll see how to handle menu command input in Chapter 11.)

CWinApp's third base class, CWinThread, represents a *thread*. This operating system object was not available in Windows 3.1 (or earlier). It was introduced to Windows programmers in the Win32 API of Windows 95 and Windows NT. As discussed in Chapter 2, threads are the unit of scheduling in both Windows 95 and Windows NT. From a purely object-oriented design perspective, CWinApp derives from CWinThread because *all applications are threads* — that is, a new application *always* has a thread for its own use.

The application object is the only global object required in an MFC program, and it serves as the outermost container for the entire program. It holds data — and provides services — that are potentially interesting to every part of your MFC-based program. To simplify access, the AfxGetApp( ) function lets you get a pointer to your application object from anywhere in your program. Here's a line of code taken from an MFC program:

```
DApp * pApp = (DApp *)AfxGetApp();
```

Because this function returns a CWinApp *, we cast to coerce the proper type. Otherwise, we wouldn't have access to the data members and member functions of our CWinApp-derived class.

Although every MFC program has an application object, its presence as a *global* object might worry you. In particular, experienced C programmers avoid creating global variables. After all, such variables consume memory for the life of a program and, because they are visible to the entire program, are vulnerable to misuse. Because global variables have a global scope, an overuse almost inevitably creates name clashes in which two parts of a program independently define a variable with a name such as FirstName. If the compiler didn't complain about such duplication, two unwitting users of the same variable might overwrite each other's data.

With all the reasons to avoid using global variables, it's odd that MFC programs *must* have a global application object. Aside from a few global variables that MFC creates for its own use, however, the number of global variables is actually quite small. Also, a CWinApp-derived application object earns the right to exist for the duration of a program's execution simply because of the central role it plays.

If C++ is still fairly new to you, remember that the constructor of a C++ global object runs before a program's entry point (main( ) in a character-based C program and WinMain( ) in a Windows C or C++ program). It seems to break the rules about where a program's execution starts. At a minimum, it certainly isn't what Kernighan and Ritchie promised in their book, *The C Programming Language*!

Mapping this concept into the context of an MFC program, the application object's constructor runs *before* WinMain( ). This should help convince you that — more than global variables in C — C++ global objects have an exalted status. As a practical point, you should avoid calling into the rest of your application from your application object's constructor. Instead, you should simply initialize your application object's data members. You're asking for trouble if you try anything fancy here, because the rest of your MFC program hasn't yet been properly initialized.

Within an MFC program, the initial code to be called is the InitInstance( ) function in your CWinApp-derived class. (We ignore InitApplication( ) because it is handled inconsistently between Win16 and Win32. Where the cost is low, compatibility between the two APIs is worth pursuing.) More precisely, when you override this virtual function in your MFC programs, you've defined your program's entry point. Although it's true that other code runs first — specifically, the application object's constructor and MFC's own WinMain( ) — InitApplication( ) provides the first point at which you have control over your program's destiny.

As defined in AFXWIN.H, the CWinApp class has 70 member functions. Of these, 19 are virtual functions and therefore, from a strictly C++ perspective, can be considered candidates for overriding. A quick glance at the source files or the help database reveals a hodgepodge of functions that have been collected to create this class.

One way to get a handle on this class is by exploring the entries in the help database. You'll find CWinApp members described in terms of six categories: command handlers, construction/destruction, data members, initialization, operations, and overrideables. We're not going to explore this class in any depth here; instead, we'll refer to individual CWinApp members as appropriate throughout this book. If you're curious about this class, feel free to click your way through the help database or leaf through the printed documentation. Taking the time to peruse reference material will always help you become more familiar with new and interesting system features.

This concludes our look at the basics of the MFC class library. The other chapters in this part of the book focus on practical tasks involved in getting various parts of an MFC-based Windows program to work. The next chapter covers the creation of windows, the most basic type of user-interface object. Later in this part, we'll cover other user-interface objects, including menus and toolbars (Chapter 11) and dialog boxes (Chapter 12). Once you have a program's user interface in place, you'll want to think about drawing inside a window (Chapter 13), and receiving mouse and keyboard input from the user (Chapter 14).

10 Creating Windows

*T*he windows created by a Microsoft Windows program are clearly its most important user-interface objects. If a program is to communicate with a user, it *must* create at least one window. This is not to say that you can't have a program without a window. In fact, it's not only possible but quite common to run a process that has no user interface. However, a window is required if your program is going to interact with a user on the system's graphical display screen.

In addition to providing the communications channel between a program and a user, a window organizes all the other user-interface objects you might want to use. If you want a menu, it must be attached to a window. The same is true for cursors, carets, icons, toolbars, message bars, and scroll bars. In fact, several of these objects — toolbars, message bars, and scroll bars — are themselves windows.

A typical window has two parts: a client area and a nonclient area. *Client area* refers to the rectangular area that the system reserves for your use within the window. Your application is the client, so, as the developer, it's your job to manage the client area. By *manage*, we mean that your program is responsible for creating a graphical representation of any data that is to be displayed in the client area. In addition, your program must receive and process all mouse or keyboard input that the user directs to the client area.

As its name suggests, the *nonclient area* is everything outside of the client area. The Windows system automatically manages this area for you. Among the components that can reside in the nonclient area are the caption bar, the system menu, the application menu, the sizeable border, and the scroll bars. Most components of the nonclient area are optional. In fact, it's quite possible to create a window *without* a non-client area. Which parts to include is one of the decisions that you make when creating a window. Figure 10-1 identifies the parts of a window that's "fully loaded" with the various components of the nonclient area.

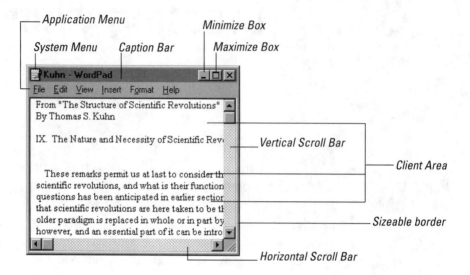

Figure 10-1
The components of a window.

This chapter discusses the creation and control of windows. Because your first task in creating a window in an MFC program is deciding which class to use, we'll start with a look at the types of window classes that MFC provides. Next, we'll discuss the details of creating windows. When you build an MFC program, you're likely to run Microsoft's MFC code generator program, AppWizard. Because the code created by the AppWizard hides some of the window creation details, we're going to replace AppWizard code with our own window creation code. In particular, we'll create a simple frame window. And finally, we'll discuss the use of messages to control the behavior of windows.

In all of this, we are ignoring a topic that is nonetheless quite important: user-interface design. That's not our focus here; instead, we are focusing on the mechanics of creating and maintaining windows. Let's start, then, with a look at the available windowing classes in the MFC library.

MFC Window Classes

Before you can create a window, you must decide which type of window you want. The MFC library gives you a head start by providing 40 different window classes. Figure 10-2 shows the portion of the MFC class hierarchy chart that contains these classes.

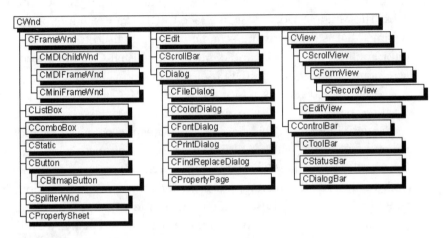

Figure 10-2

The MFC windowing class hierarchy.

With so many choices, how do you pick the right window class? Should all your classes derive from CWnd, the most basic MFC class? Or is there a more suitable base class on which to build your own window classes? We'll provide some tips later in this chapter to help you get started. Some of the classes are so complex that they require more in-depth coverage, which we'll provide in other chapters. In the next few pages, we'll provide some ideas for making sense of MFC's 40 windowing classes.

Once you've picked an MFC windowing class, you can do one of two things with it: You can either use the class directly (that is, instantiate an object of that type), or you can derive a new class to create the exact type of window that you need. (If you need to brush up on deriving new classes, please refer to Chapter 6.)

This discussion revolves around the fact that each window tends to fall into one of two categories, depending on the role it plays: *container windows*, which organize the elements of a program's user interface; and *data windows*, which appear inside container windows and hold user data for viewing or editing. From a purely mechanical point of view, you could think of a program's user interface as an arrangement of container windows and data windows. We must admit, however, that this simple viewpoint doesn't address the more complicated and difficult issues involved in deciding *which* windows to use, and *where* they should be arranged.

As an aside, it's worth mentioning that you can create a fairly complex hierarchy of windows by layering container windows and data windows. The Multiple Document Interface (MDI) is an example of window layering. MDI is a windowing scheme commonly used to build complex editor applications. (For example, Microsoft's Visual C++ Integrated Development Environment [IDE] uses MDI windowing.)

We've divided our discussion of available MFC windowing classes into three parts. We start by examining CWnd, the class at the head of the window hierarchy. This class encapsulates the native API window as well as all of the native API functions that manipulate windows. Next, we'll discuss the MFC classes that serve primarily as container windows. In the MFC hierarchy chart, container windows are represented by two base classes — CFrameWnd and CDialog — and all the other classes that are derived from these two types. Finally, we'll discuss the MFC classes that provide data windows. This group includes all the CWnd-based classes — including dialog box controls — not used for container windows.

CWND: THE NATIVE SYSTEM WINDOW

CWnd is the class designed specifically to wrap around the native Windows API window. CWnd has a single data member, m_hWnd, which is the handle to the contained window. (In this case, we are using the term *contained* in an object-oriented programming sense, not as it relates to container windows and data windows.) When you create a native system object, Windows provides a handle for identifying the object. As such, it makes sense that CWnd would contain the system window handle. CWnd has dozens of member functions, most of which are little more than wrapper functions for the windowing functions of the Windows API.

If you wanted to, you could instantiate CWnd and have it create a Windows window. What you'd get is a generic, do-nothing window.

Well, "do-nothing" is slightly overstating the point; the components of the nonclient area of the window would work. After all, the system manages the nonclient-area parts of a window. For example, if the window had a sizeable border, you could use the border to change the size of the window. The window's system menu (assuming it had one) would function properly. Similarly, the window's caption bar could be used to move the window. However, the client area — that part of the window in which you draw your data — would be empty. All keyboard input (except input processed by the system) would be ignored. Mouse input to the client area would also be ignored.

Rather than instantiating CWnd, you're more likely to derive a new class from it. Of course, such a class will inherit all of the properties of CWnd, which means, first and foremost, that objects of this type will contain a window. You can manipulate this window using all the functions that your new class inherits from CWnd — that is, all of the windowing functions of the Windows API. Although you can derive a new windowing class from CWnd, you'll do so only after making certain that none of MFC's other windowing classes can do the job.

As shown in the hierarchy chart in Figure 10-2, CWnd is the base class for all of MFC's windowing classes. It achieves this exalted position by being the least capable windowing class in MFC. Its importance rests in the fact that it unifies MFC's other windowing classes — just the role you'd expect from a base class in a class hierarchy. From a practical perspective, you'll want to understand this class primarily for what it tells you about all of MFC's other windowing classes.

As shown in Figure 10-3, CWnd itself has base classes. CWnd is derived from CCmdTarget, which serves as the base class for all classes that can receive user commands. We'll explore this class more fully in Chapter 11. There are several sources for user commands, including menus, accelerator tables, and toolbars. (CCmdTarget also supports OLE automation, a topic that is beyond the scope of this book.)

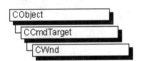

Figure 10-3
CWnd's two base classes.

From the point of view of a window, the capability to receive command messages isn't one of MFC's major improvements over the native Windows API because a Windows window could always receive command messages. From the point of view of every other class that derives from CCmdTarget, however, this is a significant improvement over the native API. MFC uses CCmdTarget to broaden the scope of objects that can receive user commands. As a result, an MFC program can distribute command notifications to any object created from a CCmdTarget-derived type. The task of satisfying a user command can be delegated to the object that most logically should do the work. Naturally, windows are included as possible recipients of menu commands (as well as other types of commands).

The CCmdTarget class is derived from CObject, which is the most basic object in the MFC hierarchy. As described in Chapter 9, most of what CObject brings to MFC classes is help in building more robust applications. For example, you can add diagnostic checks that use the runtime type information feature of CObject. Code such as the following example verifies that a pointer refers to a CWnd-type object (and not to any other type of object):

```
ASSERT(pWnd->IsKindOf(RUNTIME_CLASS(CWnd)));
```

Here are two ways to call another test that ensures that the window object itself is internally valid:

```
pWnd->AssertValid(); // Called from outside object.
ASSERT_VALID(this);  // Called from inside member function.
```

Although writing this code might seem tedious, the payback is more robust software. The MFC development team included several thousand assertions like these in MFC — approximately 5% of the lines in the library's sources. You benefit from these assertions when you call a library function using an invalid argument and cause an assertion to fail. You immediately know which line of code you should examine (although it might take some time to figure out *why* there is a problem).

Another quality that CWnd inherits from CObject is the use of pointer semantics. As described in Chapter 9, *pointer semantics* means that you must use a *pointer* when referring to a CWnd object in a function call.

You *cannot* pass a copy of the object to another function. MFC specifically hides the copy constructor, the C++ element that would allow such copying. All CObject-derived classes use pointer semantics to enforce the one-to-one correspondence between a C++ object and some Windows system object. In the case of CWnd, there's a one-to-one mapping between CWnd objects and Windows windows. By using pointer semantics, you avoid the problems that could otherwise arise from having duplicate objects with no clear delineation regarding which object should clean up the window. Cleanup is simple with pointer semantics; when a CWnd object is destroyed, the associated Windows system window is also destroyed.

Although you might not often (if ever) make direct use of CWnd, this class provides important capabilities to the classes that are derived from it — and from its two base classes, CCmdTarget and CObject. To help you decide how particular classes will be useful to you, let's turn our attention to the CWnd-derived classes, starting with those you'll use to build container windows.

CONTAINER WINDOW CLASSES

Container windows give structure to a program's user interface. As such, their primary job is very important, but somewhat unexciting; container windows exist to manage the windows they contain. An application's top-level container window is the first window the application creates at startup. After that main window closes, the application itself typically shuts down and is cleaned out of memory.

There are two basic types of containers: frames and dialogs. MFC's CFrameWnd class — and the classes that derive from it — supports frame windows. MFC's CDialog class — and the classes that are derived from CDialog — supports dialogs (or dialog boxes). As shown in Figure 10-4, Microsoft's AppWizard tool lets you choose between *three* different containers when it asks you to pick the type of application you want to create. However, this doesn't contradict our statement that there are two types of containers. Two AppWizard types — single document and multiple document — use frame windows.

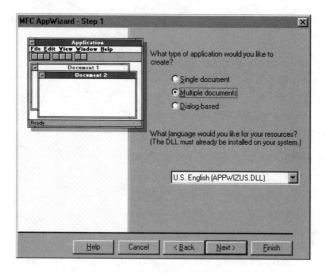

Figure 10-4

AppWizard lets you choose to create one of three types of applications. The first two create frame windows; the last creates a dialog box.

Frame container windows

The most important role played by a frame window is as the main window in an application. As shown in Table 10-1, MFC provides five different frame window classes. As containers, frames are more flexible than dialogs because frames can hold a wider variety of objects, including menus and various types of control bar windows (toolbars, status bars, dialog bars). Frames can also hold all the various types of data windows, which in an MFC Doc/View application typically means a view window. But frames can hold other types of data windows, including dialog box controls. As we'll discuss in the following section, dialogs can hold only a specialized type of data window known as a dialog box control.

With the exception of the OLE frame, all frame windows have a system menu and a caption bar. This allows users to close frame windows (using the system menu) and move frame windows (with the caption bar). Figure 10-5 illustrates four of MFC's five types of frame windows (we have omitted the OLE in-place active frame because it's beyond the scope of this book).

Table 10-1
MFC's Five Frame Window Classes

Class	Description
CFrameWnd	The main window for a single document application
CMDIFrameWnd	The main window for a multiple document application (that is, an MDI application)
CMDIChildWnd	A container window embedded in a CMDIFrameWnd window for an MDI application
CMiniFrameWnd	A free-floating tool palette frame
COleIPFrameWnd	An Object Linking and Embedding (OLE) in-place active frame for use by OLE server applications

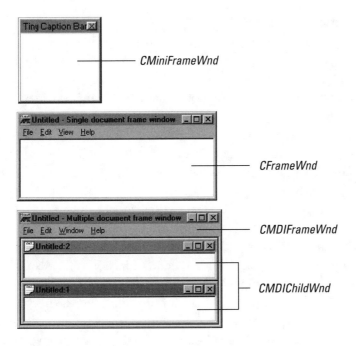

CMiniFrameWnd

CFrameWnd

CMDIFrameWnd

CMDIChildWnd

Figure 10-5
Four of MFC's five available types of frame windows.

When you ask AppWizard to create a single document application, it creates a CFrameWnd-derived window to serve as your application's main window. AppWizard ties this window into a Document/View application.

We'll cover some of the basics of the Document/View model later in this chapter. Chapter 15 provides an in-depth discussion of how it works.

On the other hand, if you ask AppWizard to build a multiple document (that is, MDI) application, it creates a CMDIFrameWnd for your application's main window. It also uses the CMDIChildWnd class as the internal container for different data editing and viewing windows.

The last two types of windows are more specialized. The CMiniFrameWnd class lets you create a frame window with a half-height caption bar. You probably won't use this as an application's main window. Instead, you'll use a window of this type for a floating toolbar. The last class, COleIPFrameWnd, is part of MFC's support for the in-place editing feature of Windows' OLE data sharing standard.

Dialog box container windows

Dialog boxes are simpler than frames, because dialogs typically contain only a specific type of data window, *dialog box controls*. Figure 10-6 shows two typical dialog boxes. You could certainly use a dialog box as your application's main window, a choice that AppWizard provides when you don't want a Document/View application. The user interface of a Visual Basic application typically consists solely of dialog boxes.

A key point to remember about dialog boxes is that they — and the controls contained within them — *are* windows. Therefore, anything you can do to any other type of window, you can do to a dialog box or a dialog box control. This point is made clear by the class hierarchy of MFC, in which CDialog is derived from CWnd. However, it's easy to forget this relationship because windows and dialog boxes are discussed using different terms and they are controlled using different function calls. Also, in some environments — the Apple Macintosh, for example — dialog box controls themselves are *not* windows, but are implemented as special case parts of windows. In Microsoft Windows, dialog boxes are windows, and the controls contained within dialog boxes are windows. Both have equal status with other types of data windows.

From a functional point of view, a dialog box is basically a form. Each control contained in a dialog box is a field for viewing or editing some item of data. Six types of dialog box controls provide a fairly wide range of editing capabilities. Edit controls let users edit text. List box and combo box controls let users pick from lists. Check boxes give users on/off control, and radio buttons let users make a mutually exclusive selection. After using a dialog box, a user typically accepts the input by clicking a button labeled OK or discards the input by clicking another button labeled Cancel. In Chapter 12, we'll introduce you to the basics of creating dialog boxes.

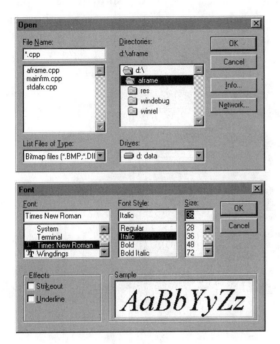

Figure 10-6
Examples of typical dialog boxes.

Before building your own dialog box from scratch, you should check to see whether Windows provides one that meets your needs. Of MFC's 15 dialog classes, you use only one when building a custom dialog box: CDialog. The other 14 dialog classes are basically wrappers around Windows' built-in dialogs. These classes fall into two camps: OLE dialogs and general-purpose, common dialogs. The OLE dialogs are those that are derived from COleDialog.

The general-purpose, common dialogs provide a variety of useful services. File I/O support, which is provided by CFileDialog, gets a filename from the user for performing a File | Open... or a File | Save As... operation. Support for allowing the user to control graphics output is provided by a color selection dialog (CColorDialog) and a font picker dialog

(CFontDialog). Print setup and control is provided by CPrintDialog, and support for text search and replace is provided by CFindReplaceDialog.

CPropertyPage and CPropertySheet support what are sometimes called *tabbed dialogs*. Known more correctly as *property sheets*, these are best described as compound dialogs. Figure 10-7 shows an example of a property sheet. Instead of forcing the user to return to a menu to select multiple dialog boxes, a property sheet groups all relevant sets of dialog box controls into a single, tabbed dialog.

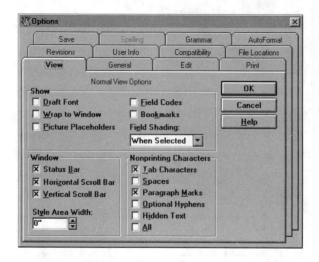

Figure 10-7
A property sheet allows you to group related sets of dialog box selections.

This discussion of container windows covers only half of MFC's available window classes. All the other windows are called *data windows*. These are the windows that are held and managed by frame and dialog containers. Data windows are discussed in the following section.

DATA WINDOW CLASSES

We use the term *data windows* to refer to the windows that are contained by frames and dialogs to hold some piece of user data. At different places in this book, we'll cover almost every type of data window provided by MFC. To give you a better idea of what is available, let's look at some qualities that are common to all data windows. This discussion is divided into three parts: control bars, view windows, and dialog box control windows.

Control bars

Control bars, represented by the classes that derive from CControlBar, are ornaments for frame windows. Microsoft's code-generation utility, AppWizard, can automatically generate a toolbar and a status bar for you (in step 4 of AppWizard's six steps). Control bars are not available in the native Windows API without a lot of work, and so represent another way that MFC makes your life a little easier.

MFC's CStatusBar class supports the creation of a status bar window at the bottom edge of a frame window. The simplest status bar gives you a small text window for echoing messages to the user. For example, MFC automatically displays helpful text when the user browses — that is, moves the mouse over — menu bar items or toolbar buttons. You can also add indicators to a status bar, letting the user know the status of the Caps Lock, Num Lock, and Scroll Lock keys.

A toolbar, produced by MFC's CToolBar class, displays a set of buttons that are typically aliases for menu items. MFC's toolbar is dockable. When a toolbar's docking is enabled, a user can move that toolbar to any edge of the containing window frame. An application can also create multiple toolbars and let the user choose which ones to display and which ones to hide. We'll cover the creation and control of toolbars in Chapter 11.

CDialogBar is a special type of toolbar that can hold dialog box controls. In this respect, dialog bars are like tiny dialog boxes that are attached to the sides of frame windows. Dialog bars differ from dialog boxes in that a dialog bar remains visible but a user typically dismisses a dialog box before continuing to work with the data in the application's main window. We'll cover the creation and use of dialog bars more fully in Chapter 12, after we've discussed the creation of dialog boxes.

View windows

View windows are those windows that are created from a CView-derived class. They are the "view" portion of the Document/View architecture that AppWizard supports in its single- and multiple-document applications (which we'll discuss later in this chapter). View windows provide a graphical representation of some piece of data. In doing so, they also make the data available for viewing or editing. An important aspect of MFC's Doc/View design is that a single block of data can be simultaneously represented by multiple different views.

When a data object is larger than a window, users expect to be able to use scrolling to control which part of the data is visible. The CScrollView class supports scrollable views, providing horizontal and vertical scroll bars that give the user control over which part of a data object is visible.

When a data object is best represented by a dialog box, the CForm-View class provides views that are defined in the same way that dialog boxes are defined. Like dialog boxes, form views use dialog box controls — for example, edit controls, list boxes, and buttons — to provide standard fields for editing data. CRecordView, a more specialized version of this class, connects the values in the form to fields in a database that follows the Open Database Connectivity (ODBC) specification.

Dialog box controls

The classes that wrap around dialog box controls are the final type of support that MFC provides for data windows. MFC has seven such classes. CStatic wraps around the system static controls, which allow for the display of static text, rectangles, icons, and other non-editable objects. CButton wraps around system button windows, and supports pushbuttons, check boxes, and radio buttons. CBitmapButton connects a bitmap to an owner-draw pushbutton. The CListBox and CComboBox classes wrap around these two types of system list controls. A combo box combines a list box with an edit control (or a static text control). MFC's CScrollBar wraps around the system's scroll bar control and the CEdit class wraps around the system's text editing controls.

Now that we're done with our whirlwind tour of MFC's available window classes, it's time to look at the window creation process. In the next two sections, we'll focus on creating a simple frame (CFrameWnd-derived) window.

Creating a Simple Frame Window

In the preceding section, we discussed available MFC window types. To introduce you to the process of window creation, we're going to show you what's involved in creating a CFrameWnd-derived frame window.

CFrameWnd has two member functions for creating windows: Create( ) and LoadFrame( ). We'll look at both of them, and then we'll discuss frame window creation in an AppWizard-generated program.

In almost every case, you'll build your MFC applications by first running AppWizard. Unless you're building a dialog box style application, you'll have to work with AppWizard's code that supports the Document/View (or Doc/View) architecture. Although this code is reasonably understandable, the window creation process is hidden from you. Because an understanding of the window creation process will help you better understand the rest of the user interface, we're going to strip away the Doc/View support in the code that's generated by AppWizard, and add back the minimum code needed to create a window. This is not to minimize the role of Doc/View, which is a central feature of MFC, but there will be cases in which you don't need its support. To help you recognize those situations, we'll start by describing what MFC's Doc/View architecture provides you.

AppWizard's Document/View Architecture

Two ideas are at the heart of MFC's Doc/View architecture. First, data comes from *documents*. Second, users view and edit their data through the filter of a *view*. Users may wish to view and edit a particular document's data in many different ways. For example, a word-processing document could appear in outline or full-text form, and a table of numbers could appear as a bar graph or as a line graph. Each of these represents a different view. The presence of multiple views doesn't change the fact that there is a single document. At the heart of Doc/View, then, is the separation of a data source (the document) from the user interface to the data (the view).

In Doc/View, the responsibility for managing user data — that is, reading from disk and writing to disk — is assigned to CDocument (and CDocument-derived) objects. Although the archetypal data might reside in a flat file, CDocument can be modified to accommodate other types of data, such as records read from a database, and images read from a scanner.

One important file format that Doc/View supports is that of *compound files*. These files have a format that's often described as "a file system within a file," because the logical structure of the file mimics the hierarchical file system structure of operating systems such as MS-DOS and Unix. Microsoft introduced compound files using the structured storage implementation of Object Linking and Embedding (OLE) version 2.0. OLE 2.0 uses this standard file format to simplify the process of sharing data between applications. However, the file format can also be used for non-OLE applications (a subject we won't cover in this book). Microsoft has publicly stated that compound files will be the standard file format for Cairo, the code name for a future version of Windows NT, and to allow the operating system itself to peek into your files.

Although the document classes hold and manage data, the view classes — the classes that are based on CView — display the data and possibly make it available for editing. Because a single document can have several graphical representations, the relationship between CDocument and CView can be (but doesn't have to be) a one-to-many relationship. If you glance at the MFC hierarchy chart, you'll notice that CView classes are derived from CWnd, which means that *views are windows*. In other words, one way to think of a view is as the user interface to some data. It's more than that, though, because print preview and document printing are supported by the view classes.

The Doc/View architecture is held together by *document templates*. A document template is a type of object that creates frame windows and view windows as your application needs them. You'll probably notice that when AppWizard creates a Doc/View application, it adds code to program initialization that registers a document template. For this task, AppWizard relies on two CDocTemplate-derived classes: CSingleDocTemplate for creating a single document application, and CMultiDocTemplate for creating a multiple document application.

Next, the AppWizard-generated code calls for the creation of a new, open document. In doing so, the document template creates the required frame window and view window. Because the application initialization and creation code is hidden inside the Doc/View support, you don't have to worry about startup. To see it happening, you can use the debugger to trace into the call to CWinApp::OnFileNew( ) at the end of the program initialization that takes place in the AppWizard-generated InitInstance( ).

Among the more useful features of MFC's Doc/View support are the many tasks that are done for you. Because the framework takes care of all the standard file operations — that is, opening and saving files — all you need to worry about is identifying the data that is to be read from and written to disk. On the windowing side, you get your choice of single document or multiple document windowing, either of which is handled automatically. The obvious benefit of MFC's Doc/View support is that it saves you time — once you understand how it works.

Of course, you won't need — or want — Doc/View support for every application you build. For one thing, Doc/View assumes that you have a block of data to manage, which might not be the case. Even if you do have a block of data, Doc/View also assumes that at some time you will want to view that data in different ways. If both of these assumptions are valid, the standard application that's built by AppWizard will provide a good starting point for creating your application.

However, all is not lost if you *aren't* interested in building applications that have these characteristics. It's not too hard to strip out the Doc/View support that AppWizard provides. For example, perhaps you are going to build a utility program that has no state and only one view. Or maybe you're going to build (yet another) calculator. In the following sections, we are going to present as our first MFC program AFRAME, a simple MFC program in which the Doc/View support has been stripped out. The remaining code shows you what is involved in creating a frame window, which is one of the goals of this chapter. But first, let's take a detailed look at how you create a window using MFC classes.

TWO-STEP WINDOW CONSTRUCTION

Window creation in MFC is a two-step process. First, you instantiate (allocate) a C++ object; then, you initialize the object. The C++ object can be created from CWnd, which will give you a stripped down, minimal window, or from any class that is derived from CWnd. (Remember that CWnd is the MFC class that wraps around a native system window. In OOP terms, a CWnd object *is a* system window. Therefore, objects created from classes that are derived from CWnd are also Windows windows.)

One of the challenges to learning about a class library is that functions are implemented in layers. Once you have some experience using MFC, you'll see how this layering often helps you fine-tune the operation of a particular class. This layering affects window creation because there are two functions you can call for the second step of window initialization. The lower-level function, CFrameWnd::Create( ), lets you control some important Windows API features. The higher-level function, CFrameWnd::LoadFrame( ), hides some of these messy details. So that you have the complete picture, we're going to start with the lower-level function, and discuss the higher-level function later.

Here's a code fragment that shows the two-step window creation process:

```
// Step 1: Allocate C++ object.
CFrameWnd * pwnd = new CFrameWnd();

// Step 2: Initialize the object.
pwnd->Create(NULL,            // Class name.
             "A Frame Window"); // Title bar text.
```

This code creates a CFrameWnd window, suitable for use as the main window in an application. For some details on why window creation requires two steps, see the sidebar, "An MFC Design Point." Let's examine these two steps in more detail.

Step 1: Allocate the C++ object

The first step in creating a window is to allocate a C++ object. Our example creates a C++ frame window object from MFC's CFrameWnd class:

```
// Step 1: Allocate C++ object.
CFrameWnd * pwnd = new CFrameWnd();
```

The constructor takes no parameters, which is a common practice for MFC object constructors. If you examine the MFC source files, you'll see that the constructor in almost every MFC object simply initializes its data members and returns.

We suggest that you follow this approach in your object constructors. Although you might be tempted to rush ahead and initialize everything in sight — opening files, allocating memory, connecting to the network, and so on — doing so will make it difficult to provide effective error handling. Besides, what's your rush? As described in the following section, creating windows involves several initialization steps. You'll want to make sure that you understand the various steps so you can properly position your own initialization code. As you'll see, this rarely involves doing much in the class constructor.

An MFC Design Point

Creating a window in MFC involves two steps: instantiation (or allocation) of a C++ object, and initialization of the object. The two-step process for creating a window in MFC mirrors the two-step process that is used to create just about every other MFC object. The allocation of the object simply sets aside memory for MFC state information. The second step is necessary to properly initialize the object and provide it with complete functional capabilities.

For most types of objects, a native Windows system object isn't created until the second step. For example, the only thing that happens when you allocate a CWnd object is that the memory gets allocated. The actual Windows API window isn't created until you initialize the object by calling some CWnd class function.

You might wonder why the MFC developers didn't combine these two steps into one. There are two reasons: one is a C++ limitation; the other is a design choice.

First, a C++ constructor doesn't provide a return value, the mechanism you'd typically rely on to detect failure. Although you can use several techniques for catching constructor errors, including the use of separate error variables and the use of exceptions, such methods would complicate the object creation process. This leads to the second reason: to simplify application development, MFC was designed with a "sensible subset" of C++ (refer to Chapter 9 for details about the design principles that guided the MFC developers).

Although you might find the two-step process somewhat cumbersome, it is simple to code for, simple to understand, and simple to debug. An extra line of object initialization code is a small price to pay for such benefits.

Step 2: Initialize the object

In the second step in the window creation process, object initialization, quite a bit more happens than in the first step. Not only do you have a few more choices to make, but this is the step during which a "real" (operating system) window is created. Here's the code from our previous example:

```
// Step 2: Initialize the object.
pwnd->Create(NULL,              // Class name.
             "A Frame Window"); // Title bar text.
```

Among other things, this function calls a WinAPI function, Create-WindowEx( ), which creates a system window.

Although the CFrameWnd::Create( ) function normally takes eight parameters, we get away with passing two because the other six have default values (a great C++ feature!). To help you better understand window creation, let's take a look at all the parameters that this function accepts. Create( ) is defined as follows:

```
BOOL
Create( LPCTSTR lpszClassName,
        LPCTSTR lpszWindowName,
        DWORD dwStyle = WS_OVERLAPPEDWINDOW,
        const RECT& rect = rectDefault,
        CWnd* pParentWnd = NULL,
        LPCTSTR lpszMenuName = NULL,
        DWORD dwExStyle = 0,
        CCreateContext* pContext = NULL );
```

Before cataloging the role of each parameter, a brief mention of the return type, BOOL, is necessary. This Boolean value will be nonzero (that is, True) when a window is successfully created, and zero (that is, False) when window creation fails. For example, window creation could fail if the system's limit on the number of windows (approximately 1,500 for Windows NT and over 3,000 for Windows 95) has been exceeded. If you override certain initialization functions — namely PreCreateWindow and the OnCreate message handler — you can force a failure yourself.

The first parameter, lpszClassName, takes a character string name of the Windows' system window class. (The data type, LPCTSTR, means "long pointer to const character string.") Although you might expect to find a value such as "CWnd" or "CFrameWnd," in fact, the type of class that this parameter refers to has nothing to do with MFC or C++ classes. Instead, the term *class* refers to a simple way to store window attributes. Among the values stored in a window class are user-interface objects to associate with a window, including a default menu, icons, cursors, and the color that is used for blanking the window. Unlike a C++ class, a Windows system class doesn't have any sort of inheritance. In fact, most of what it does is buried within the work that MFC does for you. Therefore, you can almost get by without even knowing that a window class is there. However, a few window attributes can be modified only by defining a new Windows window class.

The second parameter, lpszWindowName, is a character string for the window. This text is ignored by some types of windows — for example, list boxes. The primary use of this parameter is for windows that have caption bars (a quality that is controlled by the next field we'll discuss), in which the text is used as the window caption. Other types of windows use this field in other ways. For example, a pushbutton uses the text for its button label (which might be OK or Cancel). The text you supply for this parameter becomes the initial window text. After a window is created, you can always change the text by calling CWnd::SetWindowText( ).

The third parameter, dwStyle, is a flag field containing 20 different flags that you can set. Table 10-2 summarizes the available flags and groups them into five basic categories (the table actually lists 22 flags, because WS_OVERLAPPEDWINDOW and WS_POPUPWINDOW are compound flags). Let's discuss the available style flags, one group at a time.

Table 10-2
Window Creation Style Flags

Category	Flag	Description
Window Type		
	WS_CHILD	A window that always resides in the pixels of another window (its parent window).
	WS_OVERLAPPED	A window that always has a system menu and a caption bar. Overlapped windows can go anywhere on the display screen.
	WS_OVER-LAPPEDWINDOW	A (WS_OVERLAPPED) overlapped window with the following nonclient-area components: a caption bar, a system menu, a thick border (for resizing the window), a minimize box, and a maximize box.
	WS_POPUP	A free-floating window, similar to an overlapped window. But pop-up windows don't have to have caption bars, and overlapped windows always do. The most common use of pop-up windows is for dialog boxes.
	WS_POPUP-WINDOW	A (WS_POPUP) dialog box window with a border.
Nonclient Area		
	WS_BORDER	A thin border that cannot be used to resize the window.
	WS_CAPTION	A caption bar.
	WS_DLGFRAME	A double border that used to be the standard for dialog boxes. It has no caption bar, which means the user cannot move it. An extended style, WS_EX_DLGMODALFRAME, is the border style more commonly used for dialog frames today. We discuss the extended styles in Table 10-3.

(continued)

Table 10-1 (continued)

Category	Flag	Description
	WS_HSCROLL	A horizontal scroll bar along the bottom of the window.
	WS_VSCROLL	A vertical scroll bar along the right edge of the window.
	WS_MAXIMIZEBOX	A maximize box.
	WS_MINIMIZEBOX	A minimize box.
	WS_SYSMENU	A system menu.
	WS_THICKFRAME	A thick frame, which can be grabbed with the mouse and used to resize windows.
Initial State		
	WS_DISABLED	The window cannot receive either mouse or keyboard input.
	WS_MAXIMIZE	The size of the window fills the display screen.
	WS_MINIMIZE	The window is closed and only an icon shows where the window used to be.
	WS_VISIBLE	The window is accessible on the system desktop. This bit must be set for a user to see a window; forgetting to set it is a common programming mistake.
Clipping		
	WS_CLIPCHILDREN	Requests that the system not draw on the windows contained within the current window.
	WS_CLIPSIBLINGS	Requests that the system not draw on the sibling windows of the current window.
Controls		
	WS_GROUP	In a dialog box, identifies groups of radio buttons. More about this in Chapter 12.
	WS_TABSTOP	In a dialog box, identifies controls that will get control when the user presses the Tab key. More about this in Chapter 12.

The first group of style values defines the type of window. The Windows system supports three window types: overlapped (WS_ OVERLAPPED), pop-up (WS_POPUP), and child (WS_CHILD). Put simply, overlapped windows are for top-level container frames, pop-up windows are for dialogs, and child windows are used for all other types of windows. What we previously referred to as *data windows* — that is, control bars, views, and dialog box controls — are always created as child (WS_CHILD) windows.

Two values in this table, WS_OVERLAPPEDWINDOW and WS_POPUPWINDOW, aren't new style flags. Instead, they combine a window type with style flags commonly used for that window type. For example, WS_POPUPWINDOW is defined as:

```
WS_POPUP | WS_BORDER | WS_SYSMENU
```

WS_OVERLAPPEDWINDOW is defined as:

```
WS_OVERLAPPED | WS_CAPTION | WS_SYSMENU | WS_THICKFRAME | WS_MINIMIZEBOX |
WS_MAXIMIZEBOX
```

The | operator, as you might already know, is the Boolean bitwise OR operator. It combines the flags — each of which occupies a single bit — to create a compound value in a single memory location.

Next are the style values that describe which nonclient-area components a window should have. Figure 10-8 shows the relationship between the style value and the resulting part of a window. Incidentally, frame (overlapped) windows always have a caption bar and a system menu, so you don't need to specify these styles when creating a CFrameWnd-type window.

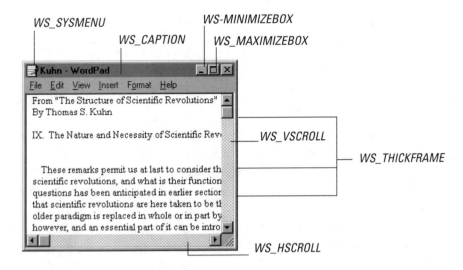

Figure 10-8
Window styles and nonclient-area window components.

The next group of values describes the initial state of a window when it is created. For example, you can control whether a window is minimized as an icon (WS_MINIMIZED), or maximized to fill the screen (WS_MAXIMIZED). Making a window initially disabled (WS_DISABLED) prevents the window from accepting any mouse or keyboard input. A modal dialog box disables its parent window to force the user to interact with the dialog. The WS_VISIBLE style bit tells Windows that the window can join the other visible windows where the user can see them. However, it's possible that a user might not see the window even though this bit is set. For example, the window might be covered by another window. If this bit is not set, however, the user cannot see the window. Forgetting to include this bit when creating windows is a common mistake. To complicate matters, although you don't have to set this bit for common types of windows such as frames and dialogs, you must set it for other types of windows, including certain data windows.

Another common mistake is to specify the WS_VISIBLE style bit, but forget to include the type of window. Remember to specify a window type — either WS_CHILD, WS_OVERLAPPED, or WS_POPUP — when you create a window.

The fourth parameter to CFrameWnd::Create( ), rect, defines the initial location and size of the window you're creating. The data type of the parameter is a reference to a RECT, which is defined as:

```
typedef tagRECT
{
    LONG left;
    LONG top;
    LONG right;
    LONG bottom;
} RECT;
```

It's worth noting that MFC defines a slightly more capable rectangle in CRect, a class that is derived from RECT. Although you can use either type, you might find that you occasionally need the extra rectangle handling member functions that CRect provides, and decide to use that type instead of RECT.

It's also worth noting that for WS_OVERLAPPED windows, you can specify a magic number, rectDefault, which tells the window manager to determine the location and size of the window in a "reasonable" manner. For the other two types of windows, WS_CHILD and WS_POPUP, you can't use this magic number. Instead, you must provide the desired location and size in "real" coordinates.

The fifth parameter, pParentWnd, is a pointer to a CWnd-derived window that is to serve as the parent of the window that is being created. This is an important field for all the contained data windows you create, though you'll sometimes define a parent for a container window as well. A data window — or more specifically, a WS_CHILD window — *must* have a parent. Such windows live in the pixels of their parent, and without a parent the window creation process fails.

In most cases, the top-level frame windows and dialog box windows won't have a parent. (Or, more correctly, the system desktop will be their parent.) However, you might decide that you want certain types of behavior that comes with the parent-child relationship. For example, parent windows are always "behind" their child windows. When you minimize a parent window, the child window also disappears. When you destroy a parent window, all child windows are destroyed along with it. Whatever their type, connecting a pair of windows as parent and child forces them to play together and to stay together.

The sixth parameter to CFrameWnd::Create( ), lpszMenuName, is a pointer to a character string with the name of the menu that is to be connected to the frame window. As we'll discuss in greater detail in Chapter 11, menus are defined by creating resources. Resources are a data type stored in a special file that usually has the extension .RC. The string that is passed here specifies the name of the menu resource that defines the menu that you want Windows to create and attach to your window. The default NULL value means "don't create a menu."

As a side note, resources — such as menus — can be identified by either strings or integer values. In fact, the Visual C++ tools tend to create integer IDs. So, how do you pass an integer value to a string (char *) parameter? By casting. The Windows API provides a helper macro that casts an integer ID to a string value: MAKEINTRESOURCE( ). For example, here are two possible resource ID strings:

```
char * pMenuString = "MyMenu";
char * pMenuInteger = MAKEINTRESOURCE(100);
```

The seventh parameter, dwExStyle, is an extension to the 20 flags you set in the third parameter, dwStyle. Table 10-3 summarizes the available "extended styles" and what they do.

Table 10-3

Window Creation Extended Style Flags

Flag	Description
WS_EX_DLGMODALFRAME	An alternative to the WS_DLGFRAME dialog border style, this style bit specifies both a double border and a caption bar that allows the user to move, but not resize, a dialog when it's covering something important.
WS_EX_NOPARENTNOTIFY	Child (WS_CHILD) windows tend to be like human children: they constantly jabber to their parents. (Child windows send messages when they are created or destroyed, on receipt of mouse messages, and so on.) Setting this style bit tells your child windows not to jabber.
WS_EX_ACCEPTFILES	This style bit specifies that a window will accept drag-and-drop files from the Windows 3.x File Manager or the Windows 95 Explorer.
WS_EX_TOPMOST	This style bit puts a window "on top of" every other window on the display screen. (When multiple windows have this style bit set, the most recently accessed window becomes the topmost of the topmost windows.)
WS_EX_TRANSPARENT	This style bit makes a window transparent, allowing it to grab mouse and keyboard events without covering the graphic display of another window. The Pen Windows system uses this bit to intercept pen input that can then be converted into a form more readily understood by underlying windows.

The eighth and last field, pContext, points to a CCreateContext structure. This structure defines key values in an application's Doc/View architecture, such as which window type to use as an application frame window, which type to use for view windows, and which document type to use. You won't usually fill in this field yourself. Instead, you'll leave it to the Doc/View support classes that fill this field automatically when creating a frame window that supports Doc/View.

Because the two-step process — object creation and then initialization — is such a common theme in MFC, the on-line help database identifies the initialization functions for each class. For most classes, the help database does a good job of pointing out the particular class function that connects an object to a Windows system object. It's odd, then, that the help database falters a bit when describing the two windowing classes we've been discussing, CWnd and CFrameWnd. In particular, the lists of initialization functions have too many entries.

Hungarian Naming

Throughout this book, you've undoubtedly noticed the unique naming convention that Microsoft uses for data types, parameter names, and variables. The convention used to create data type names such as LPCTSTR and parameter names such as lpszClass-Name is called *Hungarian naming*.

The Hungarian naming style was created by Charles Simonyi, a Microsoft programmer of Hungarian descent. While writing a doctoral dissertation on the subject of programmer productivity, he observed that programmers spend a lot of time deciding on symbolic names for variables, functions, and symbolic constants. So, he devised an approach to help speed up this process.

But Hungarian naming does more than simply provide you with some clever tricks for creating variable names. It also provides a shorthand method for identifying the contents of a data item. Using Hungarian naming can be a bit tricky at first, but if you stick with it, you'll find it can help you avoid common type mismatch errors. Although it's true that the compiler can catch these errors for you, you save even more time if you avoid such mistakes in the first place.

If your entire development team adopts Hungarian naming — or a similar scheme — everyone will benefit by being able to more easily read each other's code. As you work on building the legacy systems of tomorrow, you'll want to do everything you can to reduce inconsistencies and enhance the ease with which your code can be maintained. A programmer at Microsoft remarked to one of the authors that he briefly joined the Excel development team and, thanks to the strict Hungarian naming used on that project, was quickly able to understand Excel's data types and make a contribution to a portion of that program's code.

Even if you don't adopt Hungarian naming for your own coding, a familiarity will help you read the sample programs in this book as well as the source code to MFC itself. And because it's something of a standard among many Windows programmers, familiarity with Hungarian naming will also allow you to read sample programs that you find in other books, in magazines, and on bulletin board systems.

The key to Hungarian naming of variables is a set of abbreviations for different data types. Table 10-4 shows a set of Hungarian prefixes that we use. In addition to describing a variable's type, some abbreviations also hint at a variable's use. This is one reason why some types — for example, int — have several prefixes.

Continued

Continued from previous page

Table 10-4

Common Hungarian Prefixes

C/C++ Data Type	Hungarian Abbreviation	Description
char	ch	Character
char []	ach (or)	Character array
	rgch (or)	
	sz	
int	c	Count
int	cb	Count of bytes
int	cc (or)	Count of characters
	cch	
int	cx, cy	Count of x or y
(general case)	c<type>	Count of <type>
int	i	Index
int	n	Number
*	p	Pointer
char *	pch	Character pointer
(general case)	p<type>	Pointer to <type>
long	l	Signed long value
RECT	r	Windows rectangle
POINT	pt	Windows point

For quick and dirty variable names such as for a local variable, it's often convenient to use an abbreviation by itself. A more complete Hungarian name is created by adding an abbreviation as a prefix to one or more descriptive words. Here are some examples:

```
// Fetch filename.
char achName[FILE_SIZE_MAX];
GetFileName(achName);

// Get pointer to extension.
int ccName = lstrlen (achName);
char * pchExt = (char *)0;
```

Continued

Continued from previous page

```
    for (int i=ccName-1; i >= 0; i—)
    {
        if (achName[i] == '.')
        {
            pchExt = &achName[i];
            break;
        }
    }
```

In this example, the *ach* abbreviation identifies achName as a character array. The *Name* portion describes the array's contents. Notice how *ach* helps differentiate between an *array* of characters and a *count* of characters, such as is stored in ccName. This example shows one style of Hungarian naming, in which prefixes are lowercase and additional descriptive words mix upper- and lowercase.

It's worth noting that Hungarian is a style of naming, and not a standard. For example, no ANSI or ISO committee has defined an approved set of prefixes. Although we've shown the set that we use most often, we make no claim that it's the best, nor do we insist that you use this (or any other) set.

The developers of MFC use Hungarian naming, but they have adopted a convention that you might call Hungarian++. All class data members have the prefix m_ before the Hungarian prefix. For example, a Windows program in C might create a variable such as the following to hold a window handle:

```
    HWND hwnd;
```

Another possibility might be:

```
    HWND hWnd;
```

(Yes, you will see *w* in both upper- *and* lowercase letters. Remember, Hungarian is a *style*, not a law.) The data member in MFC's CWnd that holds the native API window handle has the following name:

```
    HWND m_hWnd;
```

MFC always uses the prefix C for C++ classes, such as CWnd, CWinApp, CObject, and CDialog. It's not exactly Hungarian, because only a single prefix is used. But knowing this will help you distinguish class names from other types.

Continued

Continued from previous page

For all the programs in this book, we'll use a Hungarian style that (we hope) you'll find consistent and easy to follow. However, we have deliberately chosen to deviate from some "standards" used by the MFC class library. Instead of *C* for class names, we'll use *D* (for *derived*) when a class is derived from an MFC class and *T* (or no prefix at all) for types that are not based on MFC classes. Here's an example of a class derived from MFC's CWinApp:

```
class DApp : public CWinApp
{
...
```

This should help you distinguish sample code classes from MFC base classes.

For data members, rather than the m_ prefix of the MFC classes, we use a d_ (data member) prefix. We aren't trying to create a new standard; we simply want to promote easy reading of the code that we provide.

With CWnd, for example, only four of the thirteen functions that the help database lists as initialization functions actually connect a C++ object to a windows system object: Create( ), CreateEx( ), Attach( ), and SubclassWindow( ). You'll use the first two most of the time, because they create the actual system window. You'll use the third member — Attach( ) — for the rare case in which a window has been created by a direct call to the Windows API. The Attach( ) function wraps an MFC CWnd object around such windows, allowing you to convert a Windows system window into a CWnd window. You would do this when you want to call CWnd member functions to control a window. The SubclassWindow( ) function does everything Attach( ) does, and it also creates a message map to allow you to intercept messages sent to a window (we'll cover messages and message maps in more detail later in this chapter). Among the five CFrameWnd functions listed in the help database as initialization functions, only two actually create a Windows system object: Create( ) and LoadFrame( ).

In our previous example, we used Create( ) to connect a system window to a CFrameWnd object. This function is almost identical to CWnd::Create( ), which is why we spent so much time describing each parameter. But when you create a frame window, you'll probably use the other CFrameWnd initialization function, LoadFrame( ). This is a higher-level function that simplifies the connection of user interface objects (such as menus, accelerators, and icons) to a frame window. It then calls CFrameWnd::Create( ) to handle the final creation step. To help you understand all the work that LoadFrame( ) does for you, let's examine it in greater detail.

INITIALIZING A FRAME WINDOW WITH LOADFRAME()

Although MFC's Doc/View support automatically creates a frame window for you, you won't always use Doc/View. When creating a window yourself, you could initialize the window with CFrameWnd::Create( ). However, this function does only minimal work for you. To get the most possible work for the least amount of code when you are not building a Doc/View application, you should initialize frame windows by calling CFrameWnd::LoadFrame( ).

One of the most useful features of this function is that it automatically connects various user interface objects to your frame window, with little effort on your part. You simply make sure that your user interface objects are defined using the same resource ID in your resource script file. Because AppWizard does this for you, to a certain extent you don't even have to worry about this step. However, to make sure that you understand what MFC is automatically doing for you, we're going to describe the role of resources in greater detail. Then, we'll examine all the parameters and options that LoadFrame( ) provides.

The role of resources

Although we are focusing on how resources are used by frame windows, they actually play a much larger role in Windows programs in general and in MFC programs in particular. MFC was set up by its developers to use resource data in extremely clever ways, assuming, of course, that your resources are set up properly. For example, menu templates and string data are types of resources. If you assign the same integer ID (for example, 1234) to a menu item (such as File|Open...) and a string (such as "Opens an existing document or template"), MFC automatically displays the string in the status bar when the user browses that particular menu item. Let's take a closer look at the role played by resources.

Simply put, a resource is a read-only data object that you define in a special place, *the resource script file*. The filename for this file has the .RC extension. AppWizard creates this file for you and references it in your project file. Table 10-5 lists all of Windows' predefined resource types with built-in API/MFC support. However, new resource types (formats) can be defined by the application (a topic covered in Chapter 15). At program build time, resource data is bound into a program's executable file.

Table 10-5
Windows' Available Resource Types

Type	Description
Accelerator Table	Defines keyboard commands, such as Ctrl-C for Edit|Copy (see Chapter 11).
Bitmap	Supports the storage of a graphic image as an array of pixel values.
Cursor	Small graphic images used to track mouse movement (see Chapter 14).
Dialog Box Template	Used in the creation of dialog boxes. The template describes the types of controls to create, as well as their location and size. The template also defines the initial size and location of the dialog box itself (see Chapter 12).
Font	Tables of character glyphs that are used to render character data on a graphic device.
Icon	A 16-pixel-by-16-pixel or 32-pixel-by-32-pixel graphic image used to represent a minimized window. You should provide both sizes in Windows 95, because the Shell will display the smaller one in the caption bar. (There's also a rumor that a 48-by-48 icon for high-resolution devices is on the way.)
Menu Template	Defines a menu (see Chapter 11).
String Table	Holds character strings.
Version	Holds program version information.

Because resources are *read only*, the operating system's memory manager can make certain assumptions about how resources should be handled to optimize memory usage. For example, in a low-memory situation, a resource doesn't have to be written to a page file; instead, it can be purged from memory. When it's needed again, the system can read it again from the program's executable file. Historically speaking, this capability was very important to the earliest versions of Windows (versions 1.x and 2.x), which had to run in less than 1 megabyte of memory. Even with the abundance of inexpensive memory today, though, efficient memory use by PC operating systems helps users get more out of their systems. (After all, no one wants to add another 4 megabytes to even one system, not to mention the thousands of systems that a large corporation typically owns.)

Resources also play a role in the process of *localizing* a software product for different markets — for example, creating French and German versions. If you have multilingual plans for your software, one approach for supporting this feature involves making sure that all strings are stored as resources. By doing so, you can avoid asking your translators to read through and change your C++ code, with all the possibilities of error that can result. Instead, you simply hand them the resource script file.

From a functional point of view, five resource types hold data that is used in constructing an application's user interface: accelerator tables, cursors, dialog box templates, icons, and menu templates. Applications use accelerator tables and menus to receive command input from the user. Cursors and icons are graphic images; cursors echo mouse movement, and icons show a minimized window. Dialog box templates define the size and location of all elements that make up a dialog box.

As for the other four types of resources, two — bitmaps and fonts — hold graphic data used by Windows' GDI subsystem. String tables hold character strings that you access with an integer ID. The version resource provides a standard means by which installation programs can identify the version number of an executable file.

When you initialize a frame window by calling LoadFrame( ), MFC checks for the presence of four resources: an accelerator table, an icon, a menu template, and a string table. (We've already mentioned the roles of the first three resources. The frame window gets its window caption from the string table.) If these resources are present, they are loaded and associated with the frame window. The only requirement for making this work is that the four resources must share a common resource ID. In fact, this ID is LoadFrame( )'s first parameter. Let's take a look at all of this function's parameters.

The parameters to LoadFrame()

Although we started out by showing you CFrameWnd::Create( ) as the function for initializing a frame window object, you'll probably call Load-Frame( ) for this task. In addition to calling CFrameWnd::Create( ) to create the Windows window, LoadFrame( ) also connects four resource objects to the frame. As described in the preceding section, the four resources are: an accelerator table, an icon, a menu, and a window title from the string table. Before showing you a program that demonstrates the use of this function, we'll discuss all of LoadFrame( )'s parameters. This function is defined in the help database as follows:

```
BOOL
LoadFrame( UINT nIDResource,
           DWORD dwDefaultStyle = WS_OVERLAPPEDWINDOW |
                                       FWS_ADDTOTITLE,
           CWnd* pParentWnd = NULL,
           CCreateContext* pContext = NULL );
```

The return value is similar to the return value for CFrameWnd::Create( ). This Boolean value is True for success and False for failure. In fact, the only time that LoadFrame( ) fails is when its call to Create( ) fails. (We provided details about when CFrameWnd::Create( ) fails earlier in this chapter.)

The first parameter, nIDResource, is an integer (UINT actually stands for unsigned integer) that identifies the resource objects that are to be connected to a frame window.

The second parameter, dwDefaultStyle, defines the window creation styles to be used when creating a window. As discussed earlier in this chapter, the style field holds flags that define the characteristics of a window. The predefined system flags have names with the prefix WS_ (window style). The various frame-window-specific styles have names that start with the prefix FWS_ (frame window style). The following table summarizes the CFrameWnd-specific window style flags:

Flag	*Description*
FWS_ADDTOTITLE	In a Doc/View application, this flag causes the top-level frame window to append the document name to the application name in the frame window's title bar. For example, if this flag is set and an application called Editor is working on a file named DATA.DAT, the title bar would read Editor - DATA.DAT. (In Windows 95, MFC sets the FWS_PREFIXTITLE flag.)
FWS_PREFIXTITLE	When used with the FWS_ADDTOTITLE flag in Doc/View applications, this flag changes the caption of a top-level frame window to display the document name before the application name. For example, if this flag is set and an application named Editor is working on a file named DATA.DAT, the title bar would be DATA.DAT - Editor.
FWS_SNAPTOBARS	This flag adjusts the frame window size to the size of the contained toolbars. This is useful, for example, in floating palettes.

The fourth parameter, pContext, supports Doc/View applications. This is a pointer to a CCreateContext object, which identifies — among other things — the document, view, and frame window classes that are currently in use.

AFRAME: A SIMPLE FRAME WINDOW

We've been describing all of the various pieces that go into the creation of a window, and now it's time to put this code in the context of a working program. Just as you'll probably do, we'll start with an AppWizard-generated program. Then, we'll modify the program by removing the code that handles window creation — that is, the Doc/View support. In our final step, we'll add back the code required to create a simple frame window.

Although Doc/View can be very useful, it is not required for every application. Just to be completely clear: you can create complete MFC applications that have no hint of Doc/View support. If you're building utility programs — a calculator or a clock, for example — you don't need Doc/View. But even large, complex applications can be built without Doc/View support. With that in mind, here are the steps you take to create a simple MFC frame window that doesn't require Doc/View support.

Figure 10-9 shows the frame window that is created by our sample program, AFRAME. To create this program, we start with an AppWizard-generated program. We then modify that program to strip out its Doc/View support, and we add support for creating a frame window.

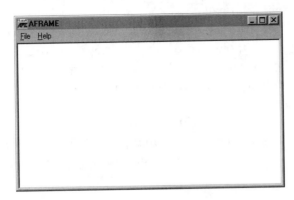

Figure 10-9
The window created by AFRAME is a CFrameWnd-derived window.

Here's an overview of the steps we'll take in creating our AFRAME program:

1. Create an AppWizard program. Test the program by building it and running it.
2. Remove the Doc/View support code from the main program file, AFRAME.CPP.
3. Add window creation code to InitInstance( ).
4. Make the frame window constructor public.
5. Remove unneeded source files from the project list (DOC.CPP and VIEW.CPP).
6. Modify the message map to eliminate unneeded messages.
7. Modify resources to eliminate all unneeded items.
8. Rebuild the ClassWizard database.

Step 1: Run AppWizard to create the program

To start AppWizard, we select the Visual C++ IDE's File|New... command. To build a new project, we select Project as the file type. For all of AppWizard's configuration dialog boxes — six in all — we select the simplest options: single document application, no database support, no OLE support, no toolbars or status bars, and no print preview or 3D control support.

AppWizard suggests source filenames that start with the first five letters of your application name (AFRAM in our case). This approach is useful if you store multiple projects in a single directory. Because we put projects in their own directories, however, we modify filenames and class names to suit our own tastes. You can do this from the screen that AppWizard puts up for the sixth program definition step.

One advantage of using a consistent set of class names is that you can easily cut and paste code between different projects. The following table shows the class names that AppWizard suggested, and what we changed them to:

Class	AppWizard-Suggested Name	Our Name
Application Object class	CAframeApp	DApp
Frame Window class	CMainFrame	DMainFrame
Document class	CAframeDoc	DDoc
Document class files	AFRAMDOC.H and AFRAMDOC.CPP	DOC.H and DOC.CPP
View class	CAframeView	DView
View class files	AFRAMVW.H and AFRAMVW.CPP	VIEW.H and VIEW.CPP

Here's the New Project Information that AppWizard displays before creating AFRAME's starting point:

```
Application type of AFRAME:
     Single Document Interface Application targeting:
         Win32

Classes to be created:
     Application: DApp in AFRAME.h and AFRAME.cpp
     Frame: DMainFrame in mainfrm.h and mainfrm.cpp
     Document: DDoc in doc.h and doc.cpp
     View: DView in view.h and view.cpp

Features:
     + MSVC Compatible project file (AFRAME.mak)
     + Uses shared DLL implementation (MFC30.DLL)
     + Localizable text in U.S. English
```

After we click the Finish button, AppWizard spins a set of source files. After AppWizard creates a new project, the first thing we always do is build an executable file and make sure it runs properly. (We've found that running out of disk space is the only reason a new program might fail. Still, it's a good idea to make sure you're starting with a working program.) To build the program, select the IDE's Project|Build command. To run the program, select Project|Execute.

Step 2: Remove Doc/View support

The second step involves removing Doc/View support from our program's main program file, AFRAME.CPP. We start by commenting out all of the initialization code from DApp::InitInstance( ). We also comment out references to the two include files, doc.h and view.h, because we won't need these files anymore.

Step 3: Add window creation code

The third step is to add the window creation code:

```
// Step 1: Allocate C++ window object.
DMainFrame * pFrame;
pFrame = new DMainFrame();

// Step 2: Initialize window object.
pFrame->LoadFrame(IDR_MAINFRAME);

// Make window visible
pFrame->ShowWindow(m_nCmdShow);

// Assign frame as application's main window
m_pMainWnd = pFrame;
```

In addition to the two steps we've discussed previously — allocating the C++ object, and then initializing the object — two other steps are required. First, we make the window visible, and then we attach the frame to the application object.

As the comments indicate, the CWnd::ShowWindow( ) call makes the frame window visible. To be visible at creation time, windows must be created with the WS_VISIBLE style bit. Although we could specify this style value to replace the default style flags of WS_OVERLAPPEDWINDOW | FWS_ADDTOTILE, we don't this. Instead, Windows makes our main window visible by passing the m_nCmdShow parameter to our program's WinMain entry point. Often, this value is simply SW_SHOWNORMAL for a regular, visible window. Sometimes, however, the value is SW_MINIMIZE, which produces a window that's initially minimized. (These values have a prefix of SW_ because they are parameters passed to the Microsoft Windows *ShowWindow( )* function.) When a user starts a program while pressing the Shift key, Windows passes the SW_MINIMIZE parameter to tell a program that it should start minimized. Otherwise, programs start up in "normal" mode.

Incidentally, you might be wondering where you can find WinMain( ) — the entry point to every Windows program. If you look through the AppWizard-generated code, you *won't* find it. Unless you define one yourself, every MFC program uses the one provided by MFC (we described it in some detail in the preceding chapter). MFC's WinMain( ) function connects to an AppWizard-generated program at the InitInstance( ) member of the CWinApp-derived class. In AFRAME, this appears in the source file AFRAME.CPP.

MFC's application object class, CWinApp, contains the m_pMainWnd
data member of type CWnd *. If we assign a NULL value to this field,
MFC assumes that something is wrong and automatically terminates the
application. By defining this field, you give MFC permission to shut
down the application when that window is destroyed. And so we duti-
fully make this assignment, which properly connects our frame window
to our program's application object.

Step 4: Make the DMainFrame constructor public

The fourth step is to make public the constructor to our frame window
class, DMainFrame. The Doc/View code usually instantiates objects of
this type using runtime type information magic that calls the constructor
even though it's defined as protected. Because we're instantiating it
directly, we modify the declaration — in MAINFRM.H — as follows:

```
public:
    DMainFrame();
```

Step 5: Clean up the project list

The fifth step is to eliminate unneeded source files from the project list.
We do this by selecting Project|Files... and removing DOC.CPP and
VIEW.CPP. Because we disabled the Doc/View support (during the second
step in this process), we don't need either file.

Step 6: Clean up the message map

The sixth step is to comment out unneeded message map entries. As
we'll discuss shortly, a message map is a data structure that is set up to
help MFC decide which system messages it should intercept for you. We
need to comment out these two message map entries from AFRAME.CPP,
because without Doc/View, our program won't need File|New or
File|Open... support:

```
// Standard file based document commands
// ON_COMMAND(ID_FILE_NEW, CWinApp::OnFileNew)
// ON_COMMAND(ID_FILE_OPEN, CWinApp::OnFileOpen)
```

Step 7: Clean up resources

The seventh step is to remove unneeded resource data. The AppWizard
creates six different resources: an accelerator table, a dialog box, an

icon, a menu, a string table, and a version detail resource. The only resource that might cause confusion is the menu, because some menu commands — notably File|New and File|Open — display error messages when selected. It's a simple matter to remove all menu items that don't apply to our program. The only two commands that we'll leave in AFRAME are File|Exit and Help|About.... By removing the other resources, we cut down the size of the resulting executable file. We can also erase the accelerator table, because none of the keyboard commands are useful for our program. In addition, we can remove most of the string table entries.

Step 8: Rebuild the ClassWizard database

The final step is to rebuild the ClassWizard's class database. ClassWizard, a tool we'll describe shortly, edits message maps. But because we've removed two classes, the ClassWizard can get confused. To get ClassWizard to rebuild the class database, you start by deleting the file AFRAME.CLW, which contains the ClassWizard database.

To rebuild the ClassWizard database, you open the resource (.RC) file by clicking on it in the Visual C++ IDE. With the resource window open, start the ClassWizard by selecting the Project|ClassWizard... menu item. Because the class database has been erased, you'll see a message box asking whether you want to rebuild the database. Choose Yes. When asked to select the classes, click the Add All button, and then click OK. The ClassWizard rebuilds the class database and shows you its message map editing window. We'll discuss the ClassWizard after we've discussed message handling in more detail. The program source files appear in Listings 10-1 through 10-9.

Listing 10-1
AFRAME.H

```
// AFRAME.h : main header file for the AFRAME application
//

#ifndef __AFXWIN_H__
    #error include 'stdafx.h' before including this file for PCH
#endif

#include "resource.h"        // main symbols
```

```
/////////////////////////////////////////////////////////////////////////
// DApp:
// See AFRAME.cpp for the implementation of this class
//

class DApp : public CWinApp
{
public:
    DApp();

// Overrides
    // ClassWizard generated virtual function overrides
    //{{AFX_VIRTUAL(DApp)
    public:
    virtual BOOL InitInstance();
    //}}AFX_VIRTUAL

// Implementation

    //{{AFX_MSG(DApp)
    afx_msg void OnAppAbout();
        // NOTE - the ClassWizard will add and remove member functions here.
        //    DO NOT EDIT what you see in these blocks of generated code !
    //}}AFX_MSG
    DECLARE_MESSAGE_MAP()
};


/////////////////////////////////////////////////////////////////////////
```

Listing 10-2
AFRAME.CPP

```
// AFRAME.cpp : Defines the class behaviors for the application.
//

#include "stdafx.h"
#include "AFRAME.h"

#include "mainfrm.h"
// #include "doc.h"  // Remove Doc/View support [ply]
// #include "view.h" // Remove Doc/View support [ply]

#ifdef _DEBUG
#undef THIS_FILE
static char BASED_CODE THIS_FILE[] = __FILE__;
#endif
```

```
/////////////////////////////////////////////////////////////////////
// DApp

BEGIN_MESSAGE_MAP(DApp, CWinApp)
    //{{AFX_MSG_MAP(DApp)
    ON_COMMAND(ID_APP_ABOUT, OnAppAbout)
        // NOTE - ClassWizard adds and remove mapping macros here.
        //     DO NOT EDIT these blocks of generated code!
    //}}AFX_MSG_MAP
    // Standard file based document commands
    // ON_COMMAND(ID_FILE_NEW, CWinApp::OnFileNew)
    // ON_COMMAND(ID_FILE_OPEN, CWinApp::OnFileOpen)
END_MESSAGE_MAP()

/////////////////////////////////////////////////////////////////////
// DApp construction

DApp::DApp()
{
    // TODO: add construction code here,
    // Place all significant initialization in InitInstance
}

/////////////////////////////////////////////////////////////////////
// The one and only DApp object

DApp theApp;

/////////////////////////////////////////////////////////////////////
// DApp initialization

BOOL DApp::InitInstance()                              An MFC program's
{                                                      entry point
/*  // BEGIN: Remove Doc/View support

    // Standard initialization
    // If you are not using these features and wish to reduce the size
    //  of your final executable, you should remove from the following
    //  the specific initialization routines you do not need.

    LoadStdProfileSettings(); // Load standard INI file options (including MRU)

    // Register the application's document templates.  Document templates
    //  serve as the connection between documents, frame windows and views.

    CSingleDocTemplate* pDocTemplate;
    pDocTemplate = new CSingleDocTemplate(
        IDR_MAINFRAME,
        RUNTIME_CLASS(Doc),
        RUNTIME_CLASS(DMainFrame),        // main SDI frame window
        RUNTIME_CLASS(View));
    AddDocTemplate(pDocTemplate);
```

```
    // create a new (empty) document
    OnFileNew();

    if (m_lpCmdLine[0] != '\0')
    {
        // TODO: add command line processing here
    }

*/  // END: Remove Doc/View support

    // Step 1: Allocate C++ window object.
    DMainFrame * pFrame;
    pFrame = new DMainFrame();

    // Step 2: Initialize window object.
    pFrame->LoadFrame(IDR_MAINFRAME);

    // Make window visible
    pFrame->ShowWindow(m_nCmdShow);

    // Assign frame as application's main window
    m_pMainWnd = pFrame;

    return TRUE;
}

/////////////////////////////////////////////////////////////////////
// DAboutDlg dialog used for App About

class DAboutDlg : public CDialog
{
public:
    DAboutDlg();

// Dialog Data
    //{{AFX_DATA(DAboutDlg)
    enum { IDD = IDD_ABOUTBOX };
    //}}AFX_DATA

// Implementation
protected:
    virtual void DoDataExchange(CDataExchange* pDX); // DDX/DDV support
    //{{AFX_MSG(DAboutDlg)
        // No message handlers
    //}}AFX_MSG
    DECLARE_MESSAGE_MAP()
};

DAboutDlg::DAboutDlg() : CDialog(DAboutDlg::IDD)
{
    //{{AFX_DATA_INIT(DAboutDlg)
    //}}AFX_DATA_INIT
}
```

```
void DAboutDlg::DoDataExchange(CDataExchange* pDX)
{
    CDialog::DoDataExchange(pDX);
    //{{AFX_DATA_MAP(DAboutDlg)
    //}}AFX_DATA_MAP
}

BEGIN_MESSAGE_MAP(DAboutDlg, CDialog)
    //{{AFX_MSG_MAP(DAboutDlg)
        // No message handlers
    //}}AFX_MSG_MAP
END_MESSAGE_MAP()

// App command to run the dialog
void DApp::OnAppAbout()
{
    DAboutDlg aboutDlg;
    aboutDlg.DoModal();
}


/////////////////////////////////////////////////////////////////////////
// DApp commands
```

Listing 10-3
MAINFRM.H

```
// mainfrm.h : interface of the DMainFrame class
//
/////////////////////////////////////////////////////////////////////////////

class DMainFrame : public CFrameWnd
{
public:
    // Made 'public' to allow us to instantiate
    // (used to be 'protected') — [ply]
    DMainFrame();
protected: // create from serialization only

    DECLARE_DYNCREATE(DMainFrame)

// Attributes
public:

// Operations
public:

// Overrides
    // ClassWizard generated virtual function overrides
    //{{AFX_VIRTUAL(DMainFrame)
    //}}AFX_VIRTUAL
```

```
// Implementation
public:
    virtual ~DMainFrame();
#ifdef _DEBUG
    virtual void AssertValid() const;
    virtual void Dump(CDumpContext& dc) const;
#endif

// Generated message map functions
protected:
    //{{AFX_MSG(DMainFrame)
    afx_msg int OnCreate(LPCREATESTRUCT lpCreateStruct);
    //}}AFX_MSG
    DECLARE_MESSAGE_MAP()
};
```

///

Listing 10-4
MAINFRM.CPP

```
// mainfrm.cpp : implementation of the DMainFrame class
//

#include "stdafx.h"
#include "AFRAME.h"

#include "mainfrm.h"

#ifdef _DEBUG
#undef THIS_FILE
static char BASED_CODE THIS_FILE[] = __FILE__;
#endif

/////////////////////////////////////////////////////////////////////////////
// DMainFrame

IMPLEMENT_DYNCREATE(DMainFrame, CFrameWnd)

BEGIN_MESSAGE_MAP(DMainFrame, CFrameWnd)
    //{{AFX_MSG_MAP(DMainFrame)
    ON_WM_CREATE()
    //}}AFX_MSG_MAP
END_MESSAGE_MAP()

/////////////////////////////////////////////////////////////////////////////
// DMainFrame construction/destruction
```

A message map for AFRAME's frame window.

```
DMainFrame::DMainFrame()
{
    // TODO: add member initialization code here

}

DMainFrame::~DMainFrame()
{
}

/////////////////////////////////////////////////////////////////////////
// DMainFrame diagnostics

#ifdef _DEBUG
void DMainFrame::AssertValid() const
{
    CFrameWnd::AssertValid();
}

void DMainFrame::Dump(CDumpContext& dc) const
{
    CFrameWnd::Dump(dc);
}

#endif //_DEBUG

/////////////////////////////////////////////////////////////////////////
// DMainFrame message handlers

int DMainFrame::OnCreate(LPCREATESTRUCT lpCreateStruct)
{
    if (CFrameWnd::OnCreate(lpCreateStruct) == -1)
        return -1;

    // TODO: Add your specialized creation code here

    return 0;
}
```

Handler for WM_CREATE message

Listing 10-5
STDAFX.H

```
// stdafx.h : include file for standard system include files,
//   or project specific include files that are used frequently, but
//       are changed infrequently
//

#include <afxwin.h>         // MFC core and standard components
#include <afxext.h>         // MFC extensions
```

Listing 10-6
STDAFX.CPP

```
// stdafx.cpp : source file that includes just the standard includes
//    AFRAME.pch will be the pre-compiled header
//    stdafx.obj will contain the pre-compiled type information

#include "stdafx.h"
```

Listing 10-7
RESOURCE.H

```
//{{NO_DEPENDENCIES}}
// Microsoft Visual C++ generated include file.
// Used by AFRAME.RC
//
#define IDR_MAINFRAME               128
#define IDD_ABOUTBOX                100

// Next default values for new objects
//
#ifdef APSTUDIO_INVOKED
#ifndef APSTUDIO_READONLY_SYMBOLS
#define _APS_NEXT_RESOURCE_VALUE    130
#define _APS_NEXT_CONTROL_VALUE     1000
#define _APS_NEXT_SYMED_VALUE       101
#define _APS_NEXT_COMMAND_VALUE     32771
#endif
#endif
```

Normally, you don't edit this file as text, but from graphical editors in IDE.

Listing 10-8
AFRAME.RC

```
//Microsoft Visual C++ generated resource script.
//
#include "resource.h"

#define APSTUDIO_READONLY_SYMBOLS
/////////////////////////////////////////////////////////////////////////////
//
// Generated from the TEXTINCLUDE 2 resource.
//
#include "afxres.h"


/////////////////////////////////////////////////////////////////////////////
#undef APSTUDIO_READONLY_SYMBOLS
```

```
#ifdef APSTUDIO_INVOKED
/////////////////////////////////////////////////////////////////////////
//
// TEXTINCLUDE
//

1 TEXTINCLUDE DISCARDABLE
BEGIN
    "resource.h\0"
END

2 TEXTINCLUDE DISCARDABLE
BEGIN
    "#include ""afxres.h""\r\n"
    "\0"
END

3 TEXTINCLUDE DISCARDABLE
BEGIN
    "#include ""res\\AFRAME.rc2""  // non-Visual C++ edited resources\r\n"
    "\r\n"
    "#define _AFX_NO_SPLITTER_RESOURCES\r\n"
    "#define _AFX_NO_OLE_RESOURCES\r\n"
    "#define _AFX_NO_TRACKER_RESOURCES\r\n"
    "#define _AFX_NO_PROPERTY_RESOURCES\r\n"
    "#include ""afxres.rc""  \011// Standard components\r\n"
    "\0"
END


/////////////////////////////////////////////////////////////////////////
#endif    // APSTUDIO_INVOKED


/////////////////////////////////////////////////////////////////////////
//
// Icon
//

IDR_MAINFRAME           ICON    DISCARDABLE     "res\\AFRAME.ico"

/////////////////////////////////////////////////////////////////////////
//
// Menu
//

IDR_MAINFRAME MENU PRELOAD DISCARDABLE
BEGIN
    POPUP "&File"
    BEGIN
        MENUITEM "E&xit",                       ID_APP_EXIT
    END
    POPUP "&Help"
    BEGIN
```

```
            MENUITEM "&About AFRAME...",                ID_APP_ABOUT
    END
END


/////////////////////////////////////////////////////////////////////
//
// Dialog
//

IDD_ABOUTBOX DIALOG DISCARDABLE  34, 22, 217, 55
STYLE DS_MODALFRAME | WS_POPUP | WS_CAPTION | WS_SYSMENU
CAPTION "About AFRAME"
FONT 8, "MS Sans Serif"
BEGIN
    ICON            IDR_MAINFRAME,IDC_STATIC,11,17,20,20
    LTEXT           "AFRAME Version 1.0",IDC_STATIC,40,10,119,8
    LTEXT           "Copyright \251 1995",IDC_STATIC,40,25,119,8
    DEFPUSHBUTTON   "OK",IDOK,176,6,32,14,WS_GROUP
END


/////////////////////////////////////////////////////////////////////
//
// Version
//

VS_VERSION_INFO VERSIONINFO
 FILEVERSION 1,0,0,1
 PRODUCTVERSION 1,0,0,1
 FILEFLAGSMASK 0x3fL
#ifdef _DEBUG
 FILEFLAGS 0x1L
#else
 FILEFLAGS 0x0L
#endif
 FILEOS 0x4L
 FILETYPE 0x1L
 FILESUBTYPE 0x0L
BEGIN
    BLOCK "StringFileInfo"
    BEGIN
        BLOCK "040904B0"
        BEGIN
            VALUE "CompanyName", "\0"
            VALUE "FileDescription", "AFRAME MFC Application\0"
            VALUE "FileVersion", "1, 0, 0, 1\0"
            VALUE "InternalName", "AFRAME\0"
            VALUE "LegalCopyright", "Copyright \251 1995\0"
            VALUE "LegalTrademarks", "\0"
            VALUE "OriginalFilename", "AFRAME.EXE\0"
            VALUE "ProductName", "AFRAME Application\0"
            VALUE "ProductVersion", "1, 0, 0, 1\0"
        END
    END
    BLOCK "VarFileInfo"
    BEGIN
```

```
          VALUE "Translation", 0x409, 1200
      END
END



/////////////////////////////////////////////////////////////////
//
// String Table
//

STRINGTABLE PRELOAD DISCARDABLE
BEGIN
  IDR_MAINFRAME "AFRAME\n\nAFRAME\n\n\nAFRAME.Document\nAFRAME Document"
END

STRINGTABLE PRELOAD DISCARDABLE
BEGIN
    AFX_IDS_APP_TITLE       "AFRAME"
END


#ifndef APSTUDIO_INVOKED
/////////////////////////////////////////////////////////////////
//
// Generated from the TEXTINCLUDE 3 resource.
//
#include "res\AFRAME.rc2"   // non-Visual C++ edited resources

#define _AFX_NO_SPLITTER_RESOURCES
#define _AFX_NO_OLE_RESOURCES
#define _AFX_NO_TRACKER_RESOURCES
#define _AFX_NO_PROPERTY_RESOURCES
#include "afxres.rc"        // Standard components

/////////////////////////////////////////////////////////////////
#endif     // not APSTUDIO_INVOKED
```

Listing 10-9
AFRAME.RC2

```
//
// AFRAME.RC2 - resources Microsoft Visual C++ does not edit directly
//

#ifdef APSTUDIO_INVOKED
    #error this file is not editable by Microsoft Visual C++
#endif //APSTUDIO_INVOKED


/////////////////////////////////////////////////////////////////////
// Add manually edited resources here...

/////////////////////////////////////////////////////////////////////
```

AppWizard generated all nine source files for AFRAME (as well as an icon file, AFRAME.ICO, which is not shown here). AFRAME has four include files, three C++ source files, and two resource script files. There are so many files because AppWizard creates a C++ source-file/include-file pair for each class it defines. (One exception is a dialog class for the application's About box, which AppWizard puts with the application object class.)

As shown in the following example, AppWizard generates comment lines to tell you what it's doing and to provide hints about what you can do in the code:

```
DApp::DApp()
{
  // TODO: add construction code here,
  // Place all significant initialization in InitInstance
}
```

As you get to know MFC better, you won't need such comments. Fortunately, you can remove many of them by making a selection in AppWizard before the code is generated.

The AppWizard-generated code contains numerous macros, such as BEGIN_MESSAGE_MAP( ) and ON_COMMAND( ). In the next section, we'll describe the macros that are related to message maps. The message map is an important data structure in the control of an MFC program. Some of the macros appear within comment lines, including AFX_VIRTUAL( ) and AFX_MSG( ). Commented macros are hidden from the C++ compiler, but are used by ClassWizard, a helper utility that simplifies the creation of your MFC source code. We'll describe this tool when we discuss message maps.

The Visual C++ editor usually doesn't display resource data as text, which is what you see in AFRAME.RC and AFRAME.RC2. Instead, as shown in Figure 10-10, the resource data is summarized for you in a window in the IDE. By clicking individual resource items, you can open various graphical editor windows. Behind the graphical editor is the resource script file in text form.

One of the C++ files, STDAFX.CPP, and its include file, STDAFX.H, might seem short — so short, in fact, that you might be tempted to eliminate them altogether. Resist the temptation, though, because these files provide precompiled header support. These files cause the compiler to create a 2MB file on disk for storing preprocessor symbols in precompiled form. As described in the accompanying sidebar, this can significantly reduce your compile time.

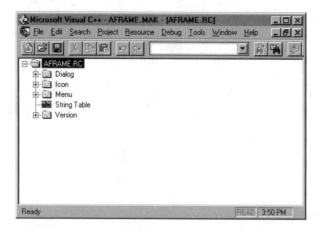

Figure 10-10
The Visual C++ resource summary window.

Precompiled Headers Produce Faster Compiles

When you compile an MFC source file, a single preprocessor directive — for example, #include <stdafx.h> — causes approximately 850K worth of include files to get loaded into memory and processed.

This data must be loaded because the MFC programming interface is defined in these files. However, the contents of these files don't change between builds. In other words, the compilation process involves redundant — and time-consuming — tasks.

To speed up the compiling process, the Microsoft Visual C++ environment supports *precompiled headers*. A precompiled header file is stored on disk during one run of the compiler, so that it can be reused during subsequent compiler runs. In theory, storing the preprocessor results from one compiler run could cut down on overall program rebuild time.

To convince ourselves that precompiled headers really work, we ran some tests. The Microsoft Visual C++ tools provide two different types of precompiled header support:

Continued

Continued from previous page

automatic and per-file. We didn't notice any performance improvement for automatic pre-compiled headers, but we found a significant difference with per-file precompiled headers (the type AppWizard sets up for you). The following table shows how long it took to build AFRAME on a Gateway 2000 system equipped with a 66MHz Intel-486 CPU:

Description	Per-File Precompiled Headers	Elapsed Time
Project|Rebuild All	No	90 sec.
Project|Build (change aframe.h)	No	58 sec.
Project|Rebuild All	Yes	95 sec.
Project|Build (change aframe.h)	Yes	27 sec.

As shown in this table, the fastest way to build AFRAME is by using precompiled headers with the Project\|Build command. Before we address this best-case scenario, it's worth discussing some of the other results. First, with or without precompiled headers, the Project\|Build command is always faster than Project\|Rebuild All. This may be obvious, but we often observe beginners using the two commands interchangeably, even though one is clearly faster. The Project\|Rebuild All command runs every tool on every source file, while Project\|Build command runs only those tools that are necessary to update the files that have changed.

In comparing the times for the two Rebuild All cases, the use of a precompiled header slows down the build process by a few seconds. The difference between these two cases — approximately 5 seconds — is the time required for storing precompiled header data to disk. Because a typical development scenario doesn't involve a complete rebuild for every small program change, the cost of a few seconds to build the initial precompiled header file is an investment in time that you'll subsequently recover.

Once the precompiled header file is built, you save time during normal builds. In our test, precompiled headers cut the program build time in half. Whether the results are as dramatic for larger programs remains to be seen. Anything that cuts down on tool time is well worth using.

Although the code created by AppWizard creates a bare-bones application, the window that this code creates doesn't really do anything. Whether you're using Doc/View — with its frame and view windows — or you've substituted your own window as we did for AFRAME, the window that's created doesn't have much personality. A window gets its personality by responding to *messages* that it receives from the system. Some messages notify a window of mouse and keyboard input. Other messages let the window know about changes to itself — for example, being moved, resized, or minimized to an icon. To help you add sparkle to the life of a window, the following section explores messages in a little more detail. We'll also cover the MFC data structure that is used to connect a message to its corresponding code: a *message map*.

Window Control and Messages

Once you've created a window, your next step is deciding which messages the window will process. When you are creating a Microsoft Windows program, much of the user-interface programming work involves writing code that responds to various messages. As we first discussed in Chapter 2, the *message* is the unit of input to a window.

From the slightly different perspective of application scheduling, a message is like a processor time slice because the receipt of a message means access to processor time. This is not to say that a message is the same thing as a time slice, because the two are, in fact, dramatically different. You can, for example, have a thread that receives no messages but gets plenty of time slices. Such a thread would avoid creating windows and in general make no calls to user-interface functions. If a thread makes any calls that interact with the display screen — user-interface calls or even graphics calls — then its access to time slices will be dependent on the thread getting messages for windows that it creates.

There are many different types of messages. For example, messages are generated when a user types with the keyboard or clicks a mouse button. Other messages are received when a window is created, resized, moved, or closed. And when things happen to different user interface objects — cursors, menus, or dialog box controls, for example — the window that owns the objects receives messages indicating that an event of potential interest has occurred. A window ignores unimportant messages and intercepts those that are important for making the window behave in the desired manner. Message handling is the centerpiece of programming for the Microsoft Windows user interface.

MESSAGE MAPS

When building MFC programs, AppWizard and ClassWizard set up data structures known as *message maps* to capture messages. A message map is an array that connects message values and class member functions. The MFC message-handling mechanism uses your message map to deliver messages to the correct class member function.

Message maps are created on a per-class basis. Every MFC class that receives messages requires a message map. AFRAME, our sample program, has separate message maps for each of three classes: the application class (DApp), the frame window class (DMainFrame), and the dialog box class (DAboutDlg). Here is DApp's message map, which appears in AFRAME.CPP:

```
BEGIN_MESSAGE_MAP(DApp, CWinApp)
    //{{AFX_MSG_MAP(DApp)
    ON_COMMAND(ID_APP_ABOUT, OnAppAbout)
        // NOTE - the ClassWizard will add and remove
        // mapping macros here.
        // DO NOT EDIT what you see in these blocks
        // of generated code!
    //}}AFX_MSG_MAP
    // Standard file based document commands
    // ON_COMMAND(ID_FILE_NEW, CWinApp::OnFileNew)
    // ON_COMMAND(ID_FILE_OPEN, CWinApp::OnFileOpen)
END_MESSAGE_MAP()
```

As shown in this example, message maps consist entirely of macros, which are defined in the MFC include files. The macro that is *not* commented out in this example connects the Help|About... menu selection (which is represented by the ID_APP_ABOUT menu item code) to the DApp::OnAppAbout( ) function. (To disable Doc/View support in AFRAME, we comment out the two ON_COMMAND( ) macros.)

The connection that message maps provide between classes is similar to C++ class inheritance, though it is implemented using a different mechanism. (C++ inheritance uses C++ virtual function tables; MFC class inheritance uses MFC message maps.) Notice in this message map that the BEGIN_MESSAGE_MAP( ) macro refers to two classes: DApp and CWinApp. When MFC's default message handler is searching for a handler for a particular message, it first searches the current class. If none is found, a base class — as defined in the message map macro — is searched. This continues until the CCmdTarget message map is reached.

Although this message dispatch mechanism parallels C++ inheritance, its proper operation relies on your supplying the correct name of the base class in the message map macro.

As mentioned in the AppWizard-generated comments, you should avoid editing anything between the pair of commented lines that contain the AFX_MSG_MAP( ) macros. (In fact, these aren't macros because the compiler never sees them — but because they use macro syntax and macro uppercase naming convention, we call them macros.) Instead, you'll use ClassWizard, a tool that Microsoft ships with Visual C++, to modify the contents of message maps. If you want ClassWizard to ignore message map entries that you have created, you place the entries outside these two macros. In fact, that's what AppWizard has done with the two ON_COMMAND macros near the end of this example.

Each message map entry has an associated message-handler function. Message-handler functions are member class functions which are called when a particular message is received. When ClassWizard generates a message map entry — which we'll discuss shortly — it also generates the required message-handler function. Here's an example of an empty message handler created by ClassWizard to handle the WM_CHAR message:

```
void DView::OnChar(UINT nChar, UINT nRepCnt, UINT nFlags)
{
    // TODO: Add your message-handler code here and/or call default

    CView::OnChar(nChar, nRepCnt, nFlags);
}
```

As shown in this example, ClassWizard provides comment lines to give you hints about the code that you need to provide.

Let's see what's involved with editing message maps using the Visual C++ ClassWizard.

EDITING MESSAGE MAPS WITH CLASSWIZARD

The Visual C++ ClassWizard tool automates the process of modifying AppWizard-generated code. As shown in Figure 10-11, the tabs at the top of this tool describe the different types of information that can be edited. After selecting the *Message Maps* tab, you can use ClassWizard to add message-handling code to MFC's various message-handling classes.

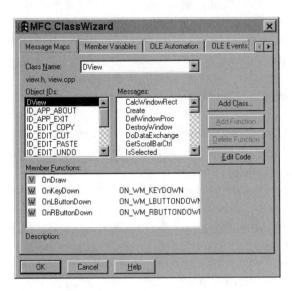

Figure 10-11
The ClassWizard, shown ready to add a message to AFRAME's main frame window class.

Selecting a function to add

When editing a message map with ClassWizard, you start by selecting a class from the Class Name combo box. After you select a class, the names of various types of objects are displayed in the Object ID list box. The first item in this list is always the class itself, which is the most interesting item. We say this because this first choice selects which class — and therefore which source files — will be modified by ClassWizard.

Other items in the Object ID list box are menu items (for frames, views, and application objects) or dialog box controls (for dialog boxes). ClassWizard helps you associate menu item selections with different types of objects in your application, and it lets you associate dialog box controls with the dialog box in which they are contained.

We'll cover menu items in Chapter 11 and dialog box controls in Chapter 12, so for now we'll skip further mention of those types of object

IDs. Instead, let's consider the case that's the most interesting from the point of view of overall message handling in an MFC program: getting messages for the class itself, which is the first item in the Object ID list. When you choose a class from the Object ID list box, ClassWizard fills the Messages list box with two possible types of entries: virtual functions and Windows system messages.

The virtual functions in the Messages list box are class member functions that can be overridden. ClassWizard knows enough about the various classes to determine which member functions can safely be replaced. Any functions that you shouldn't override are hidden from you by ClassWizard. Incidentally, the Messages list box title is misleading because xC++ virtual functions are *not* messages. This list is perhaps better described by the phrase *Prospective Member Functions* (though this title is probably too long for the ClassWizard window).

The other entries in the Messages list box truly are messages; they are Windows system messages. These messages have names with a WM_ prefix. In this example of Hungarian naming, *WM* stands for *windowing message*. If you run ClassWizard and scan the Messages list box, you'll see names such as WM_ACTIVATE, WM_CREATE, WM_KEYDOWN, and WM_MOVE.

There are more than 250 messages defined in the Windows API (and a few more that MFC defines for its own uses). However, ClassWizard simplifies matters by showing only the messages that apply to a specific window type. For example, it shows you only 44 messages for frame windows and 25 messages for view windows. Among the messages that it hides are system messages that you probably won't want to handle anyway. (To handle messages not listed by ClassWizard, select the Class Info tab and change the "Message Filter" for the particular window class.)

Even with ClassWizard's filtering, it still takes time to learn about the dozens of virtual functions and messages from which you can choose. Various Visual C++ tools can help you learn about messages. One such utility is SPY++, a program that lets you listen to a window's message traffic (we introduced SPY++ at the end of Chapter 2). Another resource is the help database. While highlighting a particular virtual function or message name, it's a simple matter to click ClassWizard's Help button — or you can press F1 — which queries the MFC help database for the selected item. Although the help database sometimes selects the wrong entry — displaying, for example, CButton::Create( ) when you really wanted CFrameWnd::Create( ) — it's a simple matter to redirect its search to the correct entry.

Adding and deleting functions

After selecting a virtual function (or message) from the Messages list box, you tell ClassWizard to create code by clicking the Add Function button. ClassWizard displays a small symbol in the Messages list box as a reminder that you've requested a handler. However, ClassWizard doesn't actually generate any code until you click the OK button or the Edit Code button. Only then does it create include file (.H) function declarations and C++ source file (.CPP) function definitions.

The name that ClassWizard selects for the functions it creates depends on the type of handler. There are three types of handlers, each of which has a slightly different naming convention: virtual function overrides, WM_COMMAND message handlers, and non-WM_COMMAND message handlers. The virtual function overrides are the simplest, because the generated function has the same name as the base class function.

For WM_COMMAND (menu command) message handlers, ClassWizard displays a dialog box prompting for a name. At the same time, it suggests a name. For example, the name it suggests for the Edit|Copy command is OnEditCopy. We prefer changing this to CmdEditCopy, because this name makes it clear that this is a command handler. And for the command update handler, it suggests a name such as OnUpdateEditCopy, which we always change to something shorter like UpdEditCopy. We like to reserve the *On* prefix — taking a Hungarian-like approach — for the third type of functions.

The third type of function names are for noncommand messages. These are for Windows API commands that start with a WM_ prefix — for example WM_CREATE, WM_MOUSEMOVE, WM_CHAR. For these functions, Class-Wizard doesn't give you a choice, but plugs in a standard set of names. For example, it creates OnCreate (for WM_CREATE), OnMouseMove (for WM_MOUSEMOVE), and OnChar (for WM_CHAR). It uses these predefined names because they correspond to message map macros (which you can see in AFXMSG_.H, in \msvc20\mfc\include). These tips should help you more readily understand where ClassWizard gets its function names.

If you click the Delete Function button *before* you click OK or Edit Code, ClassWizard removes the request from the Messages list. You can tell this has happened because ClassWizard removes the symbol from the

Messages list. On the other hand, ClassWizard complains if you ask it to remove a function for which code is already generated. In such cases, ClassWizard tells you that it won't remove any code from your C++ source files. It seems that Microsoft doesn't want to take any chances with accidentally deleting chunks of your valuable code, so you must do that manually. However, ClassWizard will remove the appropriate item from your class declaration and from the associated message map.

The capability to override base class functions is — according to Bjarne Stroustrup — the characteristic that makes C++ object oriented. But when you override a function, you might still need to call the base function so that it can handle the inner details that make the class work properly. When ClassWizard generates code for you, the code includes calls to base member functions. This is true for virtual functions that the code overrides as well as for message-handler functions. To operate correctly, the base class for a message-handler function often needs to receive a particular message. In addition to calling such functions, ClassWizard-generated code includes a comment line that indicates the relationship between your code and the calling base member functions. Your code might come before the call to the base class member or after it. ClassWizard comment lines help you make the right choice.

In the following section, we'll take a closer look at the specific messages that ClassWizard lets you handle. If you're interested in learning more about the specific code that ClassWizard creates, refer to the accompanying sidebar. Although it's not absolutely essential that you know these details, you'll sometimes need to bypass ClassWizard. In such cases, knowing what ClassWizard does can help you determine what you need to do yourself.

FRAME WINDOW MESSAGES

To help you pick specific messages that you might want to handle in a frame window, Table 10-6 lists commonly handled window messages. We've split these messages into four categories: action requests, hardware input, window notifications, and queries. Although ClassWizard also lets you override base class virtual functions, we're not going to discuss those here because most virtual functions have highly specialized uses.

As mentioned, the 14 messages in Table 10-6 are the most commonly handled messages in a typical window. Let's examine the four categories of messages.

You must handle an *action request message* carefully, if you choose to handle it at all. With these messages, the system is asking you to perform a specific task. If the message is mishandled, you break your window. For a better understanding of how these messages should be handled, you can start by examining the MFC source files for exact details on default implementations. We'll talk about one of these messages, WM_PAINT, in much greater detail in Chapter 13 when we discuss drawing in a window.

The *hardware input messages* let you know about mouse and keyboard input. Although most of these messages are fairly straightforward, there are a few quirks. For example, WM_KEYDOWN messages inform you of keystrokes, while WM_CHAR messages inform you of character input. As we'll discuss in greater detail in Chapter 14, the two sets of messages have considerable overlap. But a little patience — and a utility such as SPY++ — will help unravel the mystery.

Window *notification messages* let you know that something has happened. No action is required on your part when, for example, a window is moved (WM_MOVE) or its client area changes size (WM_SIZE). Peter Eden, an expert Windows programmer, suggests that you can clarify the meaning of each notification message by adding a 'D' (or 'ED') to its name — for example, WM_CREATED, WM_DESTROYED, WM_MOVED, and WM_SIZED. The point is simply that you don't send such messages to create, destroy, move, or resize a window. Instead, you make a function call, and the system responds by letting the object know that something has happened to the window.

The system sends *query messages* to ask a window its opinion on a subject. For example, if a window has an opinion on whether the system should shut down, the WM_QUERYENDSESSION message lets the window make its opinion known. These messages typically can be ignored, because the default handlers usually respond in a reasonable manner.

The Code That ClassWizard Creates

Although source code generators are not a new tool to software developers, you probably want to know the nature of *any* changes that are made to your code. Even if you aren't worried about whether ClassWizard makes any mistakes, you should still know what this tool does. After all, you might need to create code for a particular case that ClassWizard doesn't handle.

In particular, ClassWizard doesn't know how to deal with ranges of menu items or ranges of controls. For example, it might make sense to handle six different menu command selections within a single function. MFC provides the ON_COMMAND_RANGE() macro to help you, but ClassWizard doesn't know about this macro. In this section, we'll cover the background information you need for figuring out how to create code that supports this capability. We'll also dig a little deeper to satisfy the curiosity of those who always want to know a little bit more.

Two other capabilities that are not handled by ClassWizard are *private messages* and *registered messages*. The basic idea behind a private message is that you can define a message that allows one part of your program to communicate with another part. A registered message is similar to a private message, except it's used for *interapplication* message communication. That is, you can define a message that you register with the system. Other applications can get that message value from the system and use it to communicate with your program. Because ClassWizard doesn't support either feature, you'll have to modify your MFC code yourself if you need to use these capabilities.

Only a little experimentation is needed to figure out how ClassWizard adds entries to a class message map. In this example, we'll add support for the WM_CREATE message to AFRAME's frame window class, DMainFrame. ClassWizard creates code in three places: in the class declaration (MAINFRM.H), in the class implementation (MAINFRM.CPP), and in the class message map (MAINFRM.CPP).

In the class declaration, ClassWizard adds a line to declare the OnCreate() function:

```
class DMainFrame : public CFrameWnd
{
...
    //{{AFX_MSG(DMainFrame)
    afx_msg int OnCreate(LPCREATESTRUCT lpCreateStruct);
    //}}AFX_MSG
    DECLARE_MESSAGE_MAP()
};
```

Continued

Continued from previous page

ClassWizard inserts the code between the comment lines containing the two AFX_MSG macros. ClassWizard relies on these comment lines to mark the boundaries of what it can change.

The first part of this new code, afx_msg, is a macro that expands to... nothing! It's simply a placeholder for future use by the MFC development team. The rest of the new code is a typical function declaration. But without ClassWizard's help, you might wonder how you'd come up with the correct return type, function name, and parameter type. The simplest answer is to look in the MFC help database. By searching for *WM_ messages*, you can access a table that details for each message type the appropriate message map entry (a subject we'll explore shortly) and the required function prototype.

As a side note, AppWizard adds a DECLARE_MESSAGE_MAP() macro to the declaration of every class that needs a message map. This macro creates the following code:

```
private:
    static const AFX_MSGMAP_ENTRY _messageEntries[];
protected:
    static AFX_DATA const AFX_MSGMAP messageMap;
    virtual const AFX_MSGMAP* GetMessageMap() const;
```

In other words, one function and two data members are added to the class. (Another version of this macro adds *two* functions for dynamically linking to MFC, a detail we're going to overlook.) These declarations set up a mechanism by which the MFC message-handling code accesses two pointers: a pointer to the message map for the current class, and a pointer to the message map for the base class.

ClassWizard's second modification is to generate code for the declared function. For our example, the WM_CREATE message, ClassWizard declares the OnCreate() function, which is defined as follows:

```
int DMainFrame::OnCreate(LPCREATESTRUCT lpCreateStruct)
{
    if (CFrameWnd::OnCreate(lpCreateStruct) == -1)
        return -1;

    // TODO: Add your specialized creation code here

    return 0;
}
```

Continued

Continued from previous page

One of ClassWizard's nice features is that it calls the base class (if necessary), and then adds a comment where you are to add your own code. If a message has a return value, ClassWizard's code usually makes it easy to figure out what should be returned. As shown in this example, the WM_CREATE message returns 0 for success and -1 for failure.

The third modification that ClassWizard makes is to the class message map. The message map connects a message-handling class to MFC's message-handling mechanism. After we add the WM_CREATE message for the DMainFrame class, here is AFRAME's message map:

```
BEGIN_MESSAGE_MAP(DMainFrame, CFrameWnd)
    //{{AFX_MSG_MAP(DMainFrame)
    ON_WM_CREATE()
    //}}AFX_MSG_MAP
END_MESSAGE_MAP()
```

A reference to a simple macro, ON_WM_CREATE(), creates the required message map entry. When a window of this type receives a WM_CREATE message, MFC scans the message map until it finds the appropriate entry that tells it to call DMainFrame::OnCreate().

To help you better understand how this simple set of macros supports message handling, let's dissect each macro. As with the earlier declaration, the presence of the pair of commented macros — in this case, AFX_MSG_MAP() — helps ClassWizard find the right place to add code. These simple macros expand to quite a bit of code and data.

AppWizard provides the BEGIN_MESSAGE_MAP() and END_MESSAGE_MAP() macros. The start of a message map, BEGIN_MESSAGE_MAP(), expands into the following code:

```
const AFX_MSGMAP* DMainFrame::GetMessageMap() const
{
    return &DMainFrame::messageMap;
}

AFX_DATADEF const AFX_MSGMAP DMainFrame::messageMap =
{
    &CFrameWnd::messageMap,
    &DMainFrame::_messageEntries[0]
};

const AFX_MSGMAP_ENTRY DMainFrame::_messageEntries[] =

    {
```

Continued

Continued from previous page

When a message is received, the MFC message-handling mechanism calls DMain-Frame::GetMessageMap(), which returns a pointer to a structure filled with two more pointers. One of these pointers references the current class message map; the other pointer references the message map of the base class. The end of this macro marks the start of an array, the details of which are provided by the other macros in the message map.

What MFC is looking for, then, is a pointer to an array of structures. ClassWizard adds one macro for each message that is to be handled by a class. Each macro adds one entry to the structure. Our example has one macro, ON_WM_CREATE(). This macro expands as follows:

```
{  WM_CREATE, // Windows message
   0,
   0,
   0,
   AfxSig_is, // How to call function
   (AFX_PMSG)(AFX_PMSGW)\
   (int (AFX_MSG_CALL CWnd::*)(LPCREATESTRUCT))\
   OnCreate  // Function
},
```

This is all that MFC needs to pass a WM_CREATE message to the OnCreate() member of a class. MFC's message-handling code searches the array of structures, looking for a specific message entry. When one is found, MFC calls the corresponding function. When an entry isn't found, the message-handling code searches for a handler in the base class. If no entries are found in any MFC class message map, MFC ultimately calls the Windows system default handler, DefWindowProc().

The message map concludes with the END_MESSAGE_MAP() macro. When expanded, this macro creates a terminating entry to the message map array:

```
   {0, 0, 0, 0, AfxSig_end, (AFX_PMSG)0 }
};
```

This informs the MFC message map search code that there are no more entries in the message map. When an entry can't be found in one message map, MFC's message-handling code continues searching base classes. When none can be found, it calls CWnd::Default(). Although you *can't* override this function (because it's a nonvirtual function), you *can* override CWnd::DefWindowProc(), which is called by Default().

The message map itself is simply a data structure that MFC uses to search for member functions in message-handling classes. AppWizard sets up the basic framework for message handling. ClassWizard then fine-tunes the message handling, adding or deleting message-handling code as necessary.

Table 10-6

Frame Window Messages You're Likely to Handle

Category	Message	Description
Action Requests		Messages that require you to do something; otherwise, an object in the window might appear to be "broken." However, if you ignore a message, the default handlers will do the right thing.
	WM_CLOSE	A request to destroy the window (this calls CWnd::DestroyWindow()). Before destroying the window, however, you should make sure that it's safe to do so. For example, you might need to save user data, detach a network connection, or close a database. You'll often query the user before performing such actions.
	WM_PAINT	A request to draw (or redraw) the contents of a window's client area. The system does not store the image in a window's client area. This message asks an application to draw the original contents of a window at window creation time, and then redraw the contents whenever the window is covered or uncovered (the image is said to be damaged or invalidated).
Hardware Input		Messages that let you know of mouse and keyboard input.
	WM_CHAR	Some key sequence was pressed (a combination of WM_KEYDOWN messages) to produce a printable character.
	WM_KEYDOWN	A key on the keyboard was pressed. Note that some keys are nonprinting — for example, Ctrl, Shift, Alt, F1, F2. To capture printable characters, see WM_CHAR.
	WM_KEYUP	A key on the keyboard was released. A WM_KEYDOWN message is always followed by a WM_KEYUP message.
	WM_LBUTTONDBLCLK	The user has double-clicked the primary (typically left) mouse button while the mouse cursor is in the window's client area.

Category	Message	Description
	WM_LBUTTONDOWN	The user has single-clicked the primary mouse button while the mouse cursor is in the window's client area.
	WM_LBUTTONUP	The user has released the primary mouse button while the mouse cursor is in the window's client area.
	WM_MOUSEMOVE	The mouse cursor has moved in the window's client area.
Window Notifications		These messages inform your window of changes to its own state.
	WM_CREATE	A window of a class has been created. This is the time to initialize all the parts of a window (such as toolbars and status bars), because this is the first time that the Windows system window is alive and well.
	WM_DESTROY	A window of this class has been destroyed. This is the time to clean up anything created during the life of a Window.
	WM_MOVE	A window has moved.
	WM_SIZE	The size of a window's client area has changed.
Queries		The system sends these messages to ask questions. Because default handlers provide reasonable responses, no answers are required.
	WM_QUERYEND-SESSION	When the user shuts down the system, this message is sent to every top-level window in the system. It essentially asks whether shutdown is acceptable. If any window objects, shutdown is aborted. This and the WM_CLOSE message are the normal times for determining whether to save file data, close communications channels, and otherwise get ready to sleep. After you receive this message, you'll receive a WM_ENDSESSION, which lets you know whether shutdown is acceptable.

Something to Try

One of our technical reviewers, John Thorson at Microsoft, suggested we conclude this chapter by giving you a chance to add some message-handling code to a program. We know you're probably itching to write some code, so fire up your compiler and give the following a try.

Modify AFRAME — or a Doc/View application created by AppWizard — to add some message handlers. With the exception of the WM_PAINT message, you can add message handlers for any of the messages without creating problems (we'll explain in Chapter 13 why the paint message requires special handling). If you add message handlers to a Doc/View application, be sure to add them to the view — that is, the CView-derived — window class. The view covers the frame window, which prevent some messages from getting through to frame window message handlers.

Here are some suggestions for how to respond to various messages. In response to the WM_SIZE message, call the ::MessageBeep() function to make a noise. Here's a code fragment that does that:

```
void DView::OnSize(UINT nType, int cx, int cy)
{
    CView::OnSize(nType, cx, cy);

    ::MessageBeep(MB_OK);
}
```

In response to the WM_MOUSEMOVE message, echo the location of the mouse cursor in the frame window's caption bar. This code shows how to do that:

```
void DView::OnMouseMove(UINT nFlags, CPoint point)
{
    // Create a character string with mouse location.
    CString strCaption;
    strCaption.Format("Mouse Move Message: (%d,%d)", point.x, point.y);

    // Fetch pointer to main window.
    CFrameWnd * pWnd = (CFrameWnd *)AfxGetApp()->m_pMainWnd;

    // Modify window caption.
    pWnd->SetWindowText(strCaption);

    CView::OnMouseMove(nFlags, point);
}
```

Continued

Continued from previous page

For any of the other messages, call MFC's AfxMessageBox() function to display a message box. Here, for example, is one way to echo the key that caused a WM_CHAR message to be generated:

```
void DView::OnChar(UINT nChar, UINT nRepCnt, UINT nFlags)
{
    // Create character string containing character message.
    CString strChar;
    strChar.Format("The following key was struck: >> %c <<", nChar);

    // Display message box.
    AfxMessageBox(strChar);

    CView::OnChar(nChar, nRepCnt, nFlags);
}
```

Conclusion

Windows are the most important user-interface objects in Microsoft Windows. Every other user-interface object either *is* a window or can function properly only if it is connected to a window. Our primary goals for this chapter were to show you how to create a window, and to provide you with enough details to help you make the right decisions in your MFC software development projects.

We started by discussing all of MFC's available window classes. Before you can create a window, you must first decide which type of window you want. We divide MFC's windows into two types: container windows and data windows. Containers can be either frame (CFrameWnd-derived) windows or dialog (CDialog-derived) windows. For data windows, MFC provides control bars, views, and dialog box controls.

In most cases, you'll use AppWizard to build the starting code for your applications. AppWizard lets you choose between a dialog-based application and a single- or multiple-document Doc/View application. Because MFC's Doc/View classes create windows for you, they hide the actual window creation process. Our sample program, AFRAME, solves this problem by stripping out Doc/View support and showing you the steps required to add back the creation of a simple frame window. In addition to helping you understand window creation, AFRAME can also serve as a starting point for applications that don't require Doc/View support.

Once you've created a window with an MFC class, the next step is to fine-tune its behavior to reflect the needs of your application. You control the behavior of the window by overriding virtual functions and creating message response functions. Of these two steps, the most common approach is to respond to particular messages that the window receives.

Although it's possible to modify the source code manually, you'll probably use ClassWizard. This utility simplifies the process of overriding virtual functions and defining message handlers by spinning the basic code for you. Along the way, it also shows you the available choices to help you decide which of Windows' 200-plus messages to handle and which functions can be overridden in the MFC classes.

We didn't spend much time in this chapter describing individual messages and class functions that can be overridden. Throughout the following chapters, as we explore different types of user-interface objects and different system features, we'll describe the roles of various messages and class functions in greater detail. For example, you'll learn more about the important role that the WM_COMMAND message plays for menus, as well as how WM_PAINT supports drawing in a window, and how mouse and keyboard input messages are handled.

Now that we've covered the creation of windows, we're ready to explore ways in which commands can be received from a user. The Windows system provides two means for receiving commands: menus and accelerator key definitions. MFC adds a third mechanism, toolbars. All three types of objects help answer a simple question: What does the user want to do now?

11 Responding to Command Input

*I*n the preceding chapter, we identified windows as the most important user-interface objects in Microsoft Windows. The prize for second most important user-interface object probably belongs to menus. After all, every user relies on menus to figure out the available commands. The importance of menus is reflected in the number of menu support functions in the Windows API. And MFC doesn't get in the way of fine-tuning menus to meet the needs of your users.

In this chapter, we'll cover available MFC support for three user-interface objects used to receive command input: menus, accelerator tables, and toolbar buttons. After all, the first thing a user does when an application's window is displayed is to tell the application what to do — which involves using one of these three command input mechanisms. We'll show you how to get these user-interface objects ready to do your users' bidding.

Even casual users of Microsoft Windows know that a menu bar appears at the top of an application's main window. With Windows 95, Microsoft is promoting the use of per-object *context menus* that appear when the user clicks the right mouse button. Our sample program will show you how easy it is to create these menus.

An accelerator is a keystroke that a program interprets as a command. From your program's perspective, the results of a menu selection and an accelerator keystroke are identical because Windows generates identical messages for both. You can connect the two in the mind of a user by displaying the accelerator name in the menu, next to the equivalent menu item. For example, you'll often see Ctrl+V next to the Paste command in an Edit menu. Although both types of commands are connected in the user's mind, from a programming perspective the two are defined separately.

Specifically, menus are defined using menu resources, and accelerators are defined with accelerator resources.

The toolbar is the third type of command input device. Toolbars are windows with buttons that allow users to issue commands with a single mouse click. This makes toolbar commands somewhat more accessible to users, because menus require at least two mouse clicks (or a mouse click and drag). Because they occupy screen space, however, toolbars should be used for only the most commonly requested commands. For the same reason, most users want to be able to hide unwanted toolbars. AppWizard automatically provides this capability in the toolbars it creates for you. We'll show you how to create additional toolbars as well as how to show them and hide them as desired.

MFC provides another user-interface object that is often associated with command input: status bars. A status bar is typically a window at the bottom of an application's main window. A status bar displays text messages so that users know the current status of an application. As part of its support for command input, MFC automatically displays helpful tips in the status window when the user browses menu items or toolbar buttons.

In this chapter, we'll examine each of these user-interface objects. We'll start with the two that Windows provides — menus and accelerators — and then explore the two that MFC provides — toolbars and status bars. The best way to learn about these four user-interface objects is to study code samples. Fortunately, you can quickly get a sample of each by asking AppWizard to create some starter code for you.

Creating and Controlling Menus

When AppWizard creates a Doc/View application for you, it provides a default menu (or a pair of default menus when building a multiple-document application). In this section, we'll work through some of the steps you might take to change that menu to one that's more suitable for your application.

Similar to an operating system's file system, menus are defined as hierarchies. In both cases, the hierarchies consist of two basic types of entities. A file system has subdirectories and files, and menus have pop-up menus (sometimes called submenus) and menu items. Subdirectories are used by the file system to organize files and other subdirectories. Pop-up menus organize menu item groups and other pop-up menus.

Editing a Menu Resource

A menu resource lives in a resource script (.RC) file, along with an application's other resources. To access the resource file, open (or select) the project (.MAK) file, and then double-click the resource file. The Visual C++ IDE displays a summary of available resource types and available resources.

The resource summary list shows all the types of resources available in your application — for example, bitmaps, dialogs, icons, menus, a string table, and a version resource. When you double-click Menu, a list of menu resources is displayed. To open a particular menu resource in the menu editor, double-click its name in this list. (If you're using an App-Wizard-generated resource list, the name of your main menu will be IDR_MAINFRAME.) The selected menu resource is displayed in the menu editor.

From the menu editor, you can open the Menu Item Properties dialog box. This dialog box lists all the details of individual menu items. It also allows you to change any detail of a menu. To see this important user-interface object, double-click any menu item displayed in the menu editor.

Figure 11-1 shows the Menu Item Properties dialog box. Let's explore each field of this dialog in some detail. It's worth taking the time to understand these fields because each one reveals quite a bit about the menu support that Windows and MFC provide.

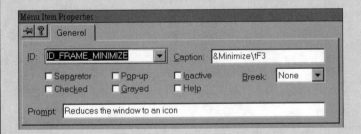

Figure 11-1
The Menu Item Properties dialog lets you edit menu details.

When the Menu Item Properties dialog is displayed, the first thing you'll probably want to do is make sure it doesn't disappear unexpectedly. To make it remain in place, click the thumbtack icon in the dialog's top-left corner. Our only complaint about this feature is that when you are done editing a menu, the dialog continues to be displayed. It's a minor annoyance, however, because the dialog provides such a clear picture of what goes into a menu.

Continued

Continued from previous page

With the thumbtack in place, the help button is worth exploring the first few times you use the menu editor. The help button is the question mark next to the thumbtack. Clicking this button summons the MFC help database to display details about all of the fields in the Menu Item Properties dialog box. This help screen provides a useful summary of the role played by each of the dialog's fields. (You can also open this help screen by pressing F1.)

Of the dialog's 10 fields, the most influential is the Pop-up check box. By clicking this check box, you define an item to be a submenu. A submenu can contain its own set of menu items, as well as more submenus. Windows lets you nest submenus as deeply as you'd like (the deepest we went before getting bored was 62 submenus). Overly deep menus tend to annoy users, so you'll want to limit the depth of your submenus to one or possibly two layers.

If you check the Pop-up check box, three fields are disabled: ID, Separator, and Prompt. When this check box is cleared, you are defining a typical menu item. In other words, you can create two types of items in menus: nested pop-up menus and menu items. Let's explore the other nine fields in the Menu Item Properties dialog box, starting with those that you use to define a menu item.

When you're defining a menu item, three fields play the most important roles: ID, Caption, and Prompt. To make sure that you're getting what you want, you need to check all three carefully when creating a menu item. This is true even for the ID field, which is automatically provided for you by the menu editor. Let's examine each of these three fields, starting with the ID.

When you are creating a new menu item, you start with one of two fields in the Menu Item Properties dialog box: the ID or the Caption. You start with the ID when creating a menu item using one of MFC's predefined identifier values. You use a predefined value for commands that the MFC framework may handle for you. For example, the ID for File I New is ID_FILE_NEW, the ID for Edit I Cut is ID_EDIT_CUT, and the ID for Window I New is ID_WINDOW_NEW. For a complete list of these predefined identifier values, see AFXRES.H, the MFC include file in which all of its default resource IDs are defined.

To create a menu item for which MFC has no built-in support, you start by selecting the blank menu item and entering a menu item name in the Caption field. As you type the caption, the menu editor instantly modifies the menu to show you the results of your changes. If you enter the caption first, the menu editor defines an ID value for you (to see the symbolic name, click another menu item, and then click back on the item you're creating). If you don't like the name of the ID that the menu editor supplies, you can always define your own name by typing over the supplied name.

Continued

Continued from previous page

As you might notice, the menu editor follows the convention of using the ID_ prefix at the beginning of command ID names. If you don't like the name (or the convention), it's a simple matter to type in a new symbolic name.

When filling in the Caption field, you will want to give some thought to a menu item's *keyboard mnemonic*. A keyboard mnemonic defines the keyboard interface to a menu item (or a pop-up menu). The mnemonic comes into play when the user activates a menu by holding the Alt key while pressing the underlined letter, or mnemonic, for that menu. For example, because of keyboard mnemonics, the File|Open command can be selected with the Alt-F-O key combination — that is, by holding down the Alt key and pressing F O. To a user, keyboard mnemonics are similar to accelerator keystrokes. From a programming perspective, however, they differ in that mnemonic support comes from the menu system. Accelerators, as you'll see in this chapter, are defined in an accelerator table. To define a mnemonic, insert an ampersand (&) before the letter that is to be underlined. To insert an ampersand in your menu text, insert two ampersands (&&) in the Caption field.

The third field you should always fill in when defining a menu item is the Prompt field. You use this field to enter a character string that you want displayed in the status bar when the user browses over (without selecting) a menu item. Even though you fill in this field in the menu editor, the string itself isn't stored as part of the menu resource. Instead, an entry is made in the string table resource, with the string ID set to the same value as the menu item command ID.

The Prompt field has two parts: the status bar string and the tool tip string. You already know about the status bar string. The tool tip string isn't used with a menu item, but rather applies to another command input device: toolbar buttons. A tool tip string is displayed when the mouse cursor pauses over a toolbar button. As shown in the following example (which shows the prompt value that MFC creates for the File|Exit command), you separate the two parts with a newline (\n) character:

```
Quit the application; prompts to save documents\nExit
```

The Separator check box creates a blank, half-height menu item consisting of a separator bar. These objects visually divide the contents of a pop-up menu.

The Checked, Grayed, and Inactive check boxes set a menu item's initial state. Although Windows applications in C use these fields, MFC programs rely on a more dynamic

Continued

Continued from previous page

mechanism for controlling the state of a menu item. When we discuss modifying menu items later in this chapter, you'll see that MFC defines a new message, CN_UPDATE_COMMAND_UI, for managing menu check marks and the enabling and graying of menu items.

The Help check box is supposed to force menu items on the main menu bar to be right-justified. In an older version of Windows (version 2.0), this was the standard. Newer versions of Windows (including Windows 95) filter out this option if it's defined in a menu resource. In other words, this check box appears to have no effect. If you really want this feature, you must add the MF_HELP flag to a menu item programmatically. Otherwise, menus are always left-justified.

The last field in the Menu Item Properties dialog box is the combo box labeled Break. It has three settings: None, Column, and Bar, with a default of None. Figure 11-2 shows examples of menus that use the Column and Bar settings. The Column flag causes a top-level menu bar to wrap to the next line; the same flag causes pop-up menus to have a new column. The Bar selection does the same thing as the Column selection, except that it draws a border between the two columns.

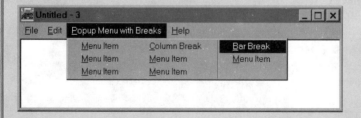

Figure 11-2
Menus can have column breaks and bar breaks.

    There are several ways to create a menu. The most common way is to define the menu at program build time using a menu resource. As we discussed in the preceding chapter, when a frame window is initialized, MFC's frame window class creates several user-interface objects from resource data. Included among these objects are accelerator tables and menus. Both are identified by a resource ID that is passed as the first parameter to CFrameWnd::LoadFrame( ). Visual C++ provides a set of resource editing tools, including a graphical menu editor for editing a menu's contents. The sidebar later in this section provides some tips on editing a menu using the menu editor.

Each menu item has two essential elements: a string name (such as "Copy") and an integer command ID (3, for example). In a menu resource, each menu item needs a unique command ID. By generating unique IDs for your menu items, the Visual C++ resource editor ensures that this requirement is met. It also creates a symbolic constant by combining the pop-up menu name with the menu item name. For example, in the BASEMENU sample program that appears later in this chapter, the menu editor creates the name ID_MENU_ENABLE for the Enable command in our pop-up menu named Menu.

After you've created a menu resource, you need to run the ClassWizard to create code for each menu item. As you'll see, ClassWizard treats each menu item as a separate user-interface object (listed in the Object ID list box). For each menu item, you have to decide which class should handle that item. Then, you have to decide whether you want code for the COMMAND menu message, the UPDATE_COMMAND_UI menu message, or both. To help you make these choices, the following section details the meaning of these two messages.

MENU MESSAGES

The menu resource is nothing more than a data structure that defines how the system should construct a menu. MFC automatically connects a menu to a frame window when the menu resource ID is provided. But MFC cannot automatically decide how a program should respond to menu item selections (aside from default handling provided in AppWizard-generated code). That's your job, and it is accomplished by the handling of menu messages.

Types of menu messages

For menu items, ClassWizard lets you choose between two messages: COMMAND and UPDATE_COMMAND_UI. Within the MFC source files, these messages have slightly different names: WM_COMMAND and CN_UPDATE_COMMAND_UI.

A WM_COMMAND message means that a user has selected a menu item (or an accelerator key or a toolbar button). This message is a request from the user for action, and some response is expected. As such, you must provide a WM_COMMAND message handler for each

menu item in your menus. If MFC cannot find a WM_COMMAND handler
for a given menu item, that menu item is grayed (disabled) and made
unavailable to the user. Here's an example of an empty WM_COMMAND
handler function created by ClassWizard:

```
void DMainFrame::OnMenuEnable()
{
    // TODO: Add your command handler code here
}
```

On the other hand, handling of the CN_UPDATE_COMMAND_UI
message is entirely optional. This message is a request from MFC to
update the appearance of individual menu items. For example, you might
place a check mark next to a menu item, gray out a menu item, or enable
a menu item. Here's an example of a CN_UPDATE_COMMAND_UI
message handler that does it all:

```
void DMainFrame::OnUpdateCheckedMenuItem(CCmdUI* pCmdUI)
{
    // Set check mark if d_bMenuChecked is TRUE,
    // Otherwise clear check mark.
    pCmdUI->SetCheck(d_bMenuChecked);

    // Enable if d_bMenuEnable is TRUE,
    // Otherwise gray out.
    pCmdUI->Enable(d_bMenuEnable);
}
```

As shown in this code fragment, you are passed a pointer to a
CCmdUI object. You control the menu item state by calling CCmdUI
member functions.

A single message, WM_COMMAND, lets you know that the user wants
some work done. You just need to make sure that a message-handler
function is ready to do the work. If you've already built Windows programs in C, be forewarned that this is the only similarity between MFC
and Windows API menu message handling. For a perspective on some of
the differences, see the accompanying sidebar.

MFC allows other objects besides window objects to handle messages.
This is an improvement over SDK-style programming, in which windows
are the only objects that receive messages of any kind. To take advantage
of this feature, you need to know which other objects can receive messages. You also need to know in what order MFC queries objects for command message handlers. In other words, you need to know how MFC
routes command messages. That's our next topic for discussion.

Menu Messages in the Windows API and MFC

If you've been writing SDK-style programs in C, you have a slightly different view of menus than that which is provided by MFC. For one thing, the Windows API defines *four* menu-related messages, not two. Table 11-1 summarizes how MFC handles Windows API messages.

Table 11-1
The Four Menu-Related Messages and MFC's Handling of Each Type

Windows API Message	MFC Message	Comments
WM_INITMENU	none	The user has started the menu system. The MFC base classes ignore this message, but you are not prevented from handling it.
WM_INITPOPUPMENU	CN_UPDATE_COMMAND_UI	This Windows API message lets a pop-up menu initialize all of its menu items. MFC figures out which menu items are in a pop-up menu and sends its message to individual menu item handlers. This allows individual menu items to be checked, grayed, enabled, or whatever. MFC's frame window class checks to make sure that a handler is present for the WM_COMMAND message for each menu item. If not, the menu item is automatically grayed (disabled).
WM_MENUSELECT	none	The Windows API message lets a program know when the user browses through a particular menu item. In MFC, the CFrameWnd class grabs the native system message and displays a text message in the status bar (if one is present). All you need to do is make sure that you provide a Prompt string for each menu item.
WM_COMMAND	WM_COMMAND	In both the Windows API and MFC, this message means that the user has chosen a command. In MFC, commands can come from menus, accelerator keystrokes, or toolbar buttons. If a window doesn't handle a command message, MFC routes that message to other objects for handling.

Menu message routing

Most of the messages that you handle in an MFC program are directed at one object type: a window. This follows the model used by the Windows API, and — given the types of messages — it seems to make sense. After all, windowing messages such as WM_CREATE, WM_MOVE, and WM_SIZE notify us that a window has been created, moved, or sized. In the Windows API and in MFC, only a window object is interested in such events. In addition, nonwindowing messages — for example, mouse and keyboard messages — direct data to a particular window, and therefore cannot be rerouted without creating confusion.

MFC departs from the Windows API in its handling of the two menuing messages. When an application creates a menu command, the frame window holding a menu doesn't have to process every menu message (although it usually handles some). Instead, the work can be delegated to message handlers within objects that own the resources to which the command applies. Among the candidates for handling menu messages are CCmdTarget-derived classes, which include windows (such as view windows), and application (CWinApp-derived) objects. In a Doc/View application, document objects and view objects (which are windows) are also candidates for handling menu messages.

Although any CCmdTarget-derived class *can* receive menu messages, in fact, menu messages take a specific path when they are routed. Table 11-2 lists the order that MFC uses to check the message maps when delivering command messages for non-Doc/View applications, single-document Doc/View applications, and multiple-document Doc/View applications.

If MFC's command message routing isn't to your liking, you can define your own priorities and send command messages to any object. However, you will have to override the OnCmdMsg( ) command message routing functions in several classes. Before doing this, you'll want to spend some time reviewing the MFC source files to make sure that your changes are in synch with the base classes. In particular, look for the default OnCmdMsg( ) handlers in the following classes: CView, CDocument, CFrameWnd, and CMDIFrameWnd. (You could also override PreTranslateMessage( ) to get the same result.)

Although it isn't likely that you'll modify the routing of menu messages, you will probably need to dynamically modify menus at one time or another. In the next section, we'll cover some of the possibilities for runtime changes to menus. We won't provide in-depth coverage of every capability; we'll just introduce the basics and give you an idea of what is possible.

Table 11-2
Routing of Command Messages for Different Application Types

Application Type	Base Class	Comments
Non-Doc/View	CFrameWnd	Frame window gets first crack at messages.
	CWinApp	The application object is handled second.
Single-document interface (SDI) Doc/View	CView	The active view is checked first for menu handlers.
	CDocument	The document of the active view comes next.
	CSingleDocTemplate	The document template of the active view is third.
	CFrameWnd CWinApp	The frame window comes next. The application object comes last.
Multiple-document interface (MDI) Doc/View	CView	The currently active view is checked first for menu handlers.
	CDocument	The document of the active view comes next.
	CMultiDocTemplate	The document template for the active view comes third.
	CMDIChildFrame	The child frame comes next, although this class relies on the CFrameWnd (its base class) implementation.
	CMDIFrameWnd CWinApp	The parent frame window is next. The application object is last.

DYNAMIC MENU OPERATIONS

In general, any change you can make to a menu in the menu editor can also be made dynamically at runtime. For example, you can create menus from scratch, add menu items, or remove menu items. Certain menu features — for example, owner-draw menu items and custom bitmap check marks — are accessible *only* at run time. (An owner-draw menu item contains a graphic image — such as a bitmap, or geometric figure drawn using calls to GDI — instead of a text string.)

Although MFC provides a menu class (CMenu), AppWizard's code doesn't use this class to create a menu. Instead, the Windows API supports the simultaneous creation of a window with a menu. When creating a Windows window, MFC's CFrameWnd class requests the creation of a menu. In the process, it also creates a bit of an object-oriented design paradox. Although a CFrameWnd *logically* contains a CMenu, it *physically* contains no CMenu data type.

Although you won't use CMenu to create the menu that is attached to your program's frame window, you'll use it extensively for dynamic menu operations. To get a CMenu pointer to the menu that is connected to a window, you call CWnd::GetMenu( ):

```
// Fetch pointer to main menu.
CMenu * pmenu = GetMenu();
```

You might notice another twist to the paradox we mentioned. This line of code fetches a pointer to an object that we never created. What's happening? The short answer, on which we'll soon elaborate, is that MFC creates a CMenu for us while adding it to a temporary object storage list.

For now, we're going to examine some of the issues involved in making dynamic modifications to menus. We'll start with the most common task you'll probably need: modifying the contents of an existing pop-up menu.

Changing an existing pop-up menu

Using a CMenu pointer from CWnd::GetMenu( ), we can do such things as inserting a new pop-up menu between the File menu and the Help menu. That's a subject we'll explore a bit later in this chapter.

For now, we're interested in a more common operation: adding menu items to and removing menu items from an existing pop-up menu. For this, we need another CMenu * pointer — in this case, to one of our submenus. As shown in the following lines of code, we use CMenu::GetSubMenu( ) to get a submenu pointer:

```
CMenu * pmenu = GetMenu();
CMenu * pmSub = pmenu->GetSubMenu(1);
```

CMenu::GetSubMenu( ) is defined as follows:

```
CMenu* GetSubMenu( int nPos)
```

The sole parameter, *nPos*, is a zero-based index to the submenu that we want to access.

Table 11-3 summarizes some common CMenu functions for modifying (or simply querying) the contents of a menu.

Table 11-3
A Basic Set of CMenu Class Functions for Modifying and Querying a Menu

Function	Description
AppendMenu()	Adds a new menu item to the end of an existing menu or to a new pop-up menu.
CheckMenuItem()	(Rarely called.) Sets or clears the menu check mark. In place of this function, you should provide an UPDATE_COMMAND_UI handler.
GetMenuItemID()	Queries a menu item's command ID.
GetMenuString()	Queries a menu item's text label.
EnableMenuItem()	Enables and disables menu items (only works if CFrameWnd:: m_b-AutoMenuEnable is set to FALSE). In place of this function, you should provide an UPDATE_COMMAND_UI handler.
InsertMenu()	Inserts a new menu item at a specified offset within an existing menu.
RemoveMenu()	Deletes a specific menu item.

For example, using the (pmSub) submenu pointer from our previous example, we can append a new menu item to an existing submenu like this:

```
pmSub->AppendMenu (MF_STRING,          // Menu flag
                   ID_MENU_ADDMENUITEM, // Command id.
                   "Add Menu &Item");   // Menu string.
```

Although the MFC help database describes the parameters for you, let's take a closer look at the declaration for CMenu::AppendMenu( ):

```
BOOL AppendMenu( UINT nFlags,
                 UINT nIDNewItem = 0,
                 LPCTSTR lpszNewItem = NULL);
```

The first parameter, nFlags, is a flag field for specifying the state of the menu item you create. Many menu modification functions use these flags, so we've summarized them for you in Table 11-4. When appending a menu item, you'll always choose one of the five flags from the group labeled "Type of Menu Item," at the beginning of the table. Common settings include MF_STRING, which creates a menu item identified by a string; MF_SEPARATOR, which adds a menu item separator bar; and MF_POPUP, which creates a new pop-up menu.

The meaning of the second parameter, nIDNewItem, depends on whether you're inserting a new menu item or a new pop-up menu (indicated by MF_POPUP in nFlags). If you're inserting a menu item, this parameter holds an integer command ID for the menu item. If you're inserting a new pop-up menu, this field is the menu handle of the menu to be inserted. (As you'll see, you use the value of CMenu::m_hMenu for this field.)

The meaning of the last parameter, lpszNewItem, depends on what type of item you're inserting. It's either a pointer to a character string for an MF_STRING item, or a unique item identifier for an MF_OWNERDRAW item.

You should note that when you dynamically create menu items, MFC doesn't know how to display help strings in the status window. (Recall that MFC does this automatically for static menu resources, using strings that you enter in the menu editor's Prompt field.) To enable this feature for dynamically created menu items, override CFrameWnd::GetMessageString( ) with your own version of GetMessageString( ). For dynamically created menu items, you supply the required strings. For statically created menu items, call the default handler which reads in the correct string from the string table.

Although the menu modification techniques that we've been describing certainly work as advertised, we've glossed over an important issue. We started out by saying that an MFC program doesn't create a CMenu object for its menu, but we clearly are using a CMenu object to change the menu. Where did this object come from? And who will delete the object when we're done with it? The answer to these questions is addressed in the accompanying sidebar, "MFC's Permanent and Temporary Handle Maps."

By adding menu items on the fly, your programs can be responsive to changes in the user's environment. Dynamic menu items are commonly used to update the lists of most recently used files, which often appear in File menus. Sometimes, you only know at runtime how many dynamic menu items you're going to create. To simplify the receipt of command notifications for such items, MFC lets you create command handlers for a range of command IDs. Unfortunately, ClassWizard doesn't (yet) support this feature. The following section shows you how it's done manually.

Table 11-4

Menu Flags Used as Parameters to Many CMenu Class Functions

Category	Menu Flag	Description
Type of Menu Item	MF_BITMAP	A menu item with a bitmap image instead of a string.
	MF_OWNERDRAW	A menu item that relies on the application to draw its contents. This is more flexible than MF_BITMAP for embedding graphic images in a menu.
	MF_POPUP	A pop-up menu.
	MF_SEPARATOR	A half-height space with a line for visually dividing groups of menu items.
	MF_STRING	A menu item or a pop-up menu (MF_POPUP) with a string.
Check State	MF_CHECKED	A check mark is displayed.
	MF_UNCHECKED	No check mark is displayed.
Enabled State	MF_DISABLED	The menu is not available to the user.
	MF_ENABLED	The menu is available to the user.
	MF_GRAYED	The menu is not available to the user *and* it appears grayed out. This makes more sense than MF_DISABLED, which doesn't give the user a visual cue about its state.
Menu Break	MF_MENUBREAK	At a menu item with this flag, the menu changes direction. For example, a menu bar menu — which normally travels in a horizontal direction — wraps to a new line; and a pop-up menu — which normally travels in a vertical direction — wraps to start a new column.
	MF_MENUBARBREAK	The same as MF_MENUBREAK, except that in pop-up menus a line is drawn to separate columns.
Identifying Menu Items	MF_BYCOMMAND	Pick menu items with the command ID.
	MF_BYPOSITION	Pick items with a zero-based offset in the current menu.

MFC's Permanent and Temporary Handle Maps

To bridge the gap between MFC objects and Windows API objects, MFC maintains a set of look-up tables, called *handle maps*. When we introduced the MFC library in Chapter 9, we mentioned that CObject-derived classes use *pointer semantics* instead of *value semantics*. So, to access an object created from a CObject-derived class, you need a pointer to the object.

In simplest terms, Windows uses handles to identify objects, and MFC uses pointers. The origin of pointer semantics was primarily for maintaining a one-to-one ratio between Windows system objects (windows and menus, for example) and C++/MFC objects (such as CWnd and CMenu objects). And while we identify a C++ object with a pointer, a Windows system object is always identified by a *handle*. Remember, a handle is a number that uniquely identifies a particular object. The meaning of the number is known only to the part of the system that issued the handle. Internal to the operating system, a handle might be a pointer or an index, but to the outside world it's just a number.

MFC uses handle maps to identify the C++ object that corresponds to a given Windows object handle. After all, when MFC calls Windows API functions, it cannot use the C++ object; MFC must use a handle. And when the Windows system libraries communicate back to MFC, they also use handles. Although MFC can easily figure out the handle from a C++ object (after all, it's usually one of the first data members), a little extra work is required for MFC to convert a system handle to a C++ pointer. To assist in this task, MFC creates handle maps.

MFC creates handle maps for two user-interface objects (windows and menus) and for seven graphic output objects (bitmaps, brushes, device contexts, fonts, palettes, pens, and regions). The creation of handle maps and handle map entries is handled transparently most of the time by individual MFC objects as needed.

In a few cases, such as when merging existing Windows API code into an MFC application, you'll find that you have to convert system handles to MFC object pointers. Each of the MFC classes that wrap Windows API objects has member functions that can help with this task. For example, CWnd::Attach() connects a CWnd object to an existing system window and creates the proper handle map entry. CWnd::Detach() deletes a window handle entry from the MFC handle maps.

MFC creates two types of handle maps: permanent and temporary. A *permanent handle map* exists for Windows API objects that are created via an MFC class. For example, when you initialize a CFrameWnd object by calling CFrameWnd::Create() or

Continued

Continued from previous page

CFrameWnd::LoadFrame(), an entry is made in the permanent handle table. When you delete an MFC object that has a permanent handle table entry, the object knows that it can also destroy the corresponding Windows API object.

Programmers who are experienced with SDK-style programming might wonder why an alternative mechanism wasn't chosen. In particular, why does MFC use handle tables for windows instead of window extra bytes? (Window extra bytes are a fixed number of extra bytes allocated by Windows on a per-window basis.) The reason is that predefined window types — such as dialog box controls — already use window extra bytes. Microsoft designed MFC to be able to wrap around preexisting classes. If MFC tried using window extra bytes with a window that already used window extra bytes, there would be a conflict.

MFC's automatic destruction of Windows system objects can cause you untold grief if you don't understand some of the subtler implications. In particular, you should avoid creating CObject-derived objects as local variables. At the end of the function — when the local objects go out of scope — the destructor will be called, which will destroy the Windows API object. The following code fragment taught this lesson to one of the authors:

```
// DON'T DO THIS!!! — When local variable goes out
// of scope, Windows API object is destroyed.
CMenu cm;
cm.LoadMenu(IDR_POPUP_MENU);

// The append operation will be short-lived...
CMenu * pmenu = GetMenu();
pmenu->AppendMenu(MF_POPUP, (UINT)cm.m_hMenu, "Popup");
```

With one important change, this code fragment could work properly. The only reason the object is destroyed is because CMenu::~CMenu() finds the object in the permanent handle map. By calling CMenu::Detach(), you disconnect the handle map entry and avoid this particular headache.

On the other hand, for objects that are not created via an MFC class, MFC has a *temporary handle map*. MFC creates an entry in the temporary handle map for objects that it must create on the fly to wrap Windows system objects. Such objects are very short-lived, though, because all entries to the temporary handle map are deleted during idle time processing. For this reason, you'll always reference temporary objects using pointers that are created as local variables. This way, you avoid the problem of having a pointer to an object that has been automatically deleted.

Continued

Continued from previous page

Every MFC function that wraps Windows API objects has the two functions we've described: Attach() and Detach(). There's also a third function, FromHandle(), which is a universal "get pointer from handle" function. This function first searches a permanent handle map, and then the temporary handle map. If no entry is found in either map, an object is created and an entry is made in the temporary handle map.

Here's an example that clarifies when an entry is made in the temporary handle map. The menu function we've been discussing, CWnd::GetMenu(), calls CMenu::FromHandle(). When you call this function in an AppWizard-generated program — which loads a menu from a resource — MFC automatically creates a CMenu for you. To ensure that you have complete access to this object, MFC adds an entry to the temporary handle map. Your access to the object will last at least until your program fetches its next message, because cleanup is handled at idle time.

So, how does MFC determine when things are idle? Idle time occurs only when you're not in the middle of handling a message. Idle time is a Windows API artifact that was first created long ago to provide printer spooling support (for Windows 1.01, which perhaps should now be renamed Windows 85). Idle time occurs whenever the user pauses a moment and allows all message queues to empty. Even the busiest worker on the slowest machine must pause sometime, whether it's to answer a phone, talk to a friend, or just think. A blink is all it takes for an idle moment to occur, at which time MFC frees the C++ objects (but *not* the Windows API objects) that are referenced in temporary handle maps.

To summarize: when you allocate and initialize an object yourself, MFC creates a permanent handle map entry. When you fetch a pointer to an object that you have never allocated, MFC creates an object and a temporary handle map entry.

Handling menu command ranges

If you dynamically create menu items, you need to provide command handlers. Although you could use ClassWizard to "dummy up" a set, you don't always know how many command handlers you need to create. For such situations, MFC lets you handle a range of command IDs with a single command handler. Because ClassWizard can't deal with a range of command IDs, you must write the code by hand that ClassWizard would otherwise create for you.

Your first concern is picking a range of command IDs that doesn't interfere with existing command IDs. This table summarizes how the available command ranges are used by ClassWizard in particular and the

MFC framework in general. As shown in this table, what's left for your use is a range of IDs from 0x9000 (36864) to 0xDFFF (57343):

Range	Description
0x8000–0x8FFF	ClassWizard uses this range for application-defined menus.
0x9000–0xDFFF	This range of command IDs is available for your use.
0xE000–0xFFFF	MFC uses this range for its own purposes.

Next, you need to add a function to the class declaration. Class-Wizard creates three pieces of code for every message: an include file declaration, a message map definition, and a function definition. Here's an example of a function declaration for a message-handling function that can handle a range of command IDs:

```
class DMainFrame : public DFrame
{   ...
    void OnCommandRange (UINT id);
    ...
};
```

The next piece is the message map entry, which MFC's message-handling mechanism must have to be able to find your function. To create this message map entry, you need to add an ON_COMMAND_RANGE( ) message map macro between the boundaries of a BEGIN_MESSAGE_MAP( ) and END_MESSAGE_MAP( ) pair. This message map macro takes three parameters: start of range, end of range, and function:

```
ON_COMMAND_RANGE(ID_MIN, ID_MAX, OnCommandRange);
```

The final piece is the function definition itself. It takes a single parameter, which is the command ID for a selected menu item. Here's an example:

```
void DMainFrame::OnCommandRange (UINT id)
{
    switch (id)
    {
        case ID_DYNA_COMMAND_1: ...
        case ID_DYNA_COMMAND_2: ...
        ...
    }
}
```

Once you understand the basics, dynamic changes to existing menus are fairly straightforward. In most cases, however, you'll rely on static menus — that is, menus built from menu resources — to inform your users about their command options. One important type of menu doesn't appear on a menu bar menu but does rely on menu resources for its definition: context menus. We'll show you how to create them in the following section.

CREATING CONTEXT MENUS

With Windows 95, Microsoft is promoting the creation of *context menus*. A context menu — sometimes called a *pop-up menu* — is not connected to the menu bar. Instead, it is displayed when the user selects an object and then clicks with the secondary (usually the right) mouse button. (It's also possible to simultaneously select an object and summon a context menu with just a single click of the secondary mouse button.) The Visual C++ IDE already makes extensive use of this type of menu, as do many other commercially available applications. Starting with Windows 95, the operating system itself uses context menus for handling numerous routine operations. To fit into this environment, you should consider adding them to your applications as well.

Instead of clicking the right mouse button, a user can also summon a context menu using a keystroke. The Applications key shown in Figure 11-3 appears on newer, Windows 95-compatible, 104-key keyboards, such as the Microsoft Natural keyboard. On keyboards that are so equipped, users can open a context menu by pressing the Applications key. To accommodate users whose keyboards are not equipped with this key, applications should define the Shift-F10 accelerator for summoning context menus.

Figure 11-3
The Applications key is marked with this symbol on newer, Windows-95-compatible keyboards.

Figure 11-4 shows the context menu from BASEMENU, a sample program you'll see later in this chapter. A single CMenu member function,

TrackPopupMenu( ), makes a context menu appear anywhere you'd like. But first, you need to create the menu object itself. To reflect the process you'll probably use when working with a context menu, we've divided the following discussion into three parts: menu creation, menu use, and menu cleanup.

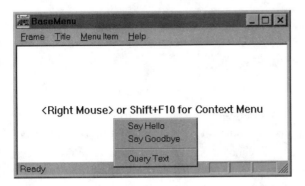

Figure 11-4

A context menu typically appears in response to a click of the right-hand button on the mouse.

Like most other MFC objects that wrap Windows API objects, two steps are required for creating a fully functioning object. First, you allocate a C++ object, and then you initialize the object. These lines of code from BASEMENU show one way to create and initialize a CMenu object:

```
// Allocate CMenu for context menu.
d_pmenuContext = new CMenu();
if (!d_pmenuContext) return -1;

// Initialize CMenu (connect menu to MFC menu object).
BOOL bSuccess = d_pmenuContext->LoadMenu(IDR_CONTEXT);
if (!bSuccess) return -1;
```

This code fragment is from a function that expects a return value of -1 on failure (the handler function for the WM_CREATE message). Allocation involves the new operator. Initialization involves a call to CMenu::Load-Menu( ), which takes as its only parameter a menu resource identifier.

Once it's created and initialized, the context menu is ready to appear whenever you want to see it. From the user's perspective, you want to see this menu when the user clicks the right mouse button. The following WM_RBUTTONDOWN message handler displays the context menu for our BASEMENU program:

```
void DMainFrame::OnRButtonDown(UINT nFlags, CPoint point)
{
    // Convert client coordinate to screen coordinates.
    ClientToScreen(&point);

    // Display context menu at mouse location.
    CMenu * psubmenu = d_pmenuContext->GetSubMenu(0);
    psubmenu->TrackPopupMenu(TPM_LEFTALIGN  | // Flags
                             TPM_RIGHTBUTTON,
                             point.x,          // x-coord.
                             point.y,          // y-coord.
                             this);     // "this" window.

    CFrameWnd::OnRButtonDown(nFlags, point);
}
```

The second of the two parameters to OnRButtonDown( ), point, gives the location of the mouse in client-area coordinates. But TrackPopup-Menu( ) expects screen coordinates, so we call CWnd::ClientToScreen( ). This function converts from client-area coordinates (the origin in the top-left corner of client area) to screen coordinates (the origin in the top-left corner of the screen).

Most of the parameters to CMenu::TrackPopupMenu( ) are reasonably straightforward. However, the last parameter is worth discussing. When the context menu appears, a stream of messages is generated that must be sent to some window or another. The pointer *this*, in the context of a CFrameWnd-derived class, identifies the window that should receive the menu messages.

The final step that you'll need to consider is how to clean up a context menu when you're done using it. BASEMENU simply deletes the CMenu object when we're done using it. Like all other entries in the permanent handle map table, when the object is destroyed, the system object is destroyed and the handle map entry is erased. Although you might delete the menu object in any of several different places, BASEMENU does it in the destructor for the window frame object:

```
DMainFrame::~DMainFrame()
{
    if (d_pmenuContext)
        d_pmenuContext->DestroyMenu();
}
```

You should keep the following tips in mind when using the menu editor to define context menus. For menu strings, don't include a mnemonic or accelerator hints. Also, when you use the menu editor to build your menu items, put them within a pop-up menu, as shown in Figure 11-5. In other words, make sure that you don't put your menu items in the top-level menu bar.

Figure 11-5
When creating a context menu in the resource editor, put all of the menu items in a pop-up menu.

As part of the Windows 95 user-interface standard, Microsoft recommends using the right mouse button for context menus. Users will expect this feature, and you put yourself at a disadvantage if you don't make use of it. The use of context menus is also a recommended feature if you want your software to meet the certification requirements for the Windows 95 logo.

Menus are the most obvious command input device, but they aren't the only one. Keyboard accelerators provide another mechanism by which users can issue commands to your program. In particular, experienced users prefer working with keyboard accelerators for more commonly used commands, simply because they are quicker than choosing commands from menus. The next section will help you understand the ins and outs of keyboard accelerators.

Enabling Keyboard Accelerators

An accelerator, sometimes known as a keyboard shortcut, lets a user issue a command using keyboard input. The Windows API provides the accelerator table resource for holding sets of accelerator key definitions. AppWizard provides an accelerator table when it generates a single- or multiple-document application. If a frame (CFrameWnd) window is initialized by calling CFrameWnd::LoadFrame( ), the accelerator table is automatically connected to the frame window.

One source of information about accelerators (and other user-interface objects) is Microsoft's *Windows 95 User Interface Design Guide*. Microsoft created this guide to promote consistency among Windows 95 applications. In particular, the guide recommends against creating keyboard commands "as the only way to access a particular operation." In fact, the guide refers to accelerators as "shortcuts," a reminder that they provide an alternative — not a substitute — for other command input mechanisms such as menus and toolbars.

History underscores the supporting role that accelerators are supposed to play. When Microsoft started to build Windows back in 1983, accelerator keys were not part the system's original design. Reflecting the influence of other GUI systems such as the Xerox Star and the Apple Macintosh, early Windows had a mouse- and menu-centered design. Microsoft added support for accelerators only after getting feedback from software companies that keyboard commands were important to users. From the earliest days of Windows, Microsoft realized that its success was dependent on the Windows software that was developed by third parties.

The addition of accelerator key support helped balance Microsoft's user-interface design philosophy for Windows. In its earliest days, Windows was mouse-centric. The addition of keyboard commands gave equal status to mouse and keyboard input. From that point, Microsoft started encouraging software developers to take the same approach in their application software. With its windows, menus, and dialog boxes, Windows provides users the freedom to choose whether they want to use the mouse or the keyboard for controlling standard user-interface objects. That's worth remembering as you design and develop the user interface for your Windows-based software.

Our exploration of keyboard accelerators starts with a general discussion of keyboard input. Next, we'll cover the creation of keyboard accelerators using the accelerator table editor. To help you figure out which keys to use and which ones to avoid, we'll provide some guidelines for appropriate accelerator key assignment. Then, we'll examine the Windows API mechanisms behind accelerators, and show you how to dynamically install an accelerator table. To complete our discussion of accelerator tables, we'll take a look at BASEMENU, a sample program that has both a menu and an accelerator table.

ABOUT KEYBOARD INPUT

The *Windows 95 User Interface Design Guide* defines clear categories of keyboard input: text keys, access keys, mode keys, and shortcut keys. The design guide uses the term *shortcut keys* to refer to accelerator keys. Let's examine each of these four types of keyboard input, paying special attention to the relationship between accelerator keys and one other category of keys.

The term *text keys* refers to printable characters — that is, upper- and lowercase letters, numbers, punctuation marks, and other symbols. Nothing in MFC or the Windows API prevents you from using text keys for command keys. If you've spent much time in a character-based, mainframe world, you have probably encountered this type of command key. Coming from that background, simple text commands seem natural. But this practice is inconsistent with the user-interface style that has evolved for Windows. Put simply, users expect that letter and number keys will generate printable letters and numbers.

The design guide's second category of keyboard input is access keys. An access key (sometimes called a *mnemonic*) is an alphanumeric key which, when pressed in combination with the Alt key, accesses a pop-up menu, a menu item, or a dialog box control. Adding an access key to a menu or a dialog box control isn't difficult; a simple ampersand (&) identifies the access key to the system, and Windows just makes them work. You need to make sure that your accelerator keys don't conflict with access keys. The simplest solution is to avoid defining accelerator keys that take the form of the Alt key plus a letter or number key.

Mode keys, the third type of keyboard input, have a significant effect on possible accelerator key combinations. As defined in Chapter 4 of the design guide, mode keys "change the actions of other keys (or other input devices)." There are two subcategories of mode keys: toggle keys and modifier keys. Toggle keys are somewhat of an artifact from the IBM PC family of computers. A standard Windows-compatible keyboard has three toggle keys: Caps Lock, Num Lock, and Scroll Lock.

For our discussion of accelerator keys, the second subcategory of mode keys — modifier keys — is more important. Although there are a few single-key accelerators (function keys, for example), the presence of modifier keys multiplies the number of key combinations that are available for defining accelerator keys. The standard 101-key keyboard defines three modifier keys: Shift, Ctrl, and Alt.

Microsoft has defined a specification for a new, 104-key keyboard in which the basic 101-key layout is enhanced with three new keys: two Windows keys (sporting the Windows logo) and an Applications key (shown earlier in Figure 11-3). The Windows key is an additional modifier key. Its use is reserved for the operating system.

The final category is the shortcut keys, or accelerators. Any keys that are not included in the other categories are available for use as single-key accelerators. This group includes the function keys (F1, F2, and so on) and the cursor movement keys (Home, the up-arrow key, and so on). With these keys and the modifier-plus key combinations, you have a wide range of choices for creating accelerator keys. Let's look at the mechanics of defining an accelerator key assignment.

DEFINING ACCELERATOR KEYS

Defining an accelerator key involves two basic steps. First, you need to create an accelerator table resource. The accelerator table resource defines the key codes and the command ID that will result when a user presses the accelerator key. Then, you need to advertise the availability of the key combination to the user. For key combinations that match menu item selections, you do this by modifying the menu item text. Let's look at what's involved in each of these steps.

Creating an accelerator table resource

The Visual C++ IDE has a built-in accelerator table editor. Just like the menu editor, the accelerator table editor provides access to a properties dialog which lets you edit individual items. To open the Accel Properties dialog, which is shown in Figure 11-6, double-click any accelerator. To make this dialog stick around, click the thumbtack icon.

By clicking the question mark button in the Accel Properties dialog, you can obtain details about each control. The accelerator table itself has three columns: ID, key, and type. These correspond roughly to the four sets of fields in the Accel Properties dialog box. You'll probably need only a little experimentation to feel comfortable with creating and editing accelerator entries. To fill in some of the gaps, though, let's look at each set of accelerator properties, starting with the command ID.

Figure 11-6
The accelerator table editor displaying the Accel Properties dialog box.

The command ID identifies the command code that is passed — via a WM_COMMAND message — when a user presses an accelerator key. The command list is filled with values from your program's RESOURCE.H file, along with a set of MFC's predefined values from AFXRES.H. When you define an accelerator, be sure that its command ID matches the command ID for the corresponding menu item. By doing so, you only have to provide a single command handler function that works for both menu input and accelerator input.

The Key field identifies the keyboard key for the accelerator. For alphanumeric characters, you simply type the number or letter. For non-printable characters, you use virtual key codes. As you scroll through the combo box that's connected to this field, you'll see that it contains 72 virtual key codes, each with a VK_ prefix. For example, VK_F1 is the virtual key code for the F1 function key, and VK_DOWN is the virtual key code for the down-arrow key.

If you're not sure which virtual key code to use, the simplest solution is to click the Next Key Typed button. You can then press a modifier-key combination that you want to use for your accelerator, and the accelerator editor will automatically fill in the correct entries for the Key, Modifiers, and Type fields in the Accel Properties dialog.

You choose the modifier key for your accelerator by clicking one of the check boxes in the Modifiers field. The design guide recommends that you use the Ctrl key as a modifier before the others. In addition, you should avoid using the Alt key with an alphanumeric accelerator because it might conflict with a menu access key. Even if you find Alt-alphanumeric-key combinations that don't conflict with your menu access keys, the access keys in internationalized versions often differ.

The Type field gives you a choice between ASCII and VirtKey. Almost every accelerator key should be a virtual key, because these transcend the different types of keyboards used around the world. However, you'll occasionally have to define an ASCII accelerator, most notably for using punctuation marks (for example, <, >, or /) as commands. Selecting the ASCII option in the Type field lets you define character — instead of keyboard key — commands. The ASCII Type lets you differentiate between upper- and lowercase letters. However, even though it's possible, for example, to have an 'A' command that differs from an 'a' command, you should avoid this practice. After all, users expect case-insensitive commands.

Creating accelerator menu hints

To let users know about your accelerator keys, you'll want to advertise them. The best place for doing this is next to the corresponding menu item. Following the menu item name within a menu resource, you simply insert a tab character (\t) and the accelerator key name. For example, the standard accelerator for the Edit|Paste menu item is Ctrl+V. The following menu resource entry shows how the hint for this accelerator is included in the Edit|Paste menu item:

```
&Paste\tCtrl+V
```

In some cases, your accelerator keys don't correspond to menu item selections. To make sure that your users can take advantage of these accelerator keys, you should add a help database entry.

You know how to create accelerator keys and how to add hints within menus, but you still need to figure out which keys to use for keyboard commands. We cover this subject in the following section.

SELECTING APPROPRIATE KEYBOARD ACCELERATORS

When you define keyboard accelerators, be sure to use standard accelerator key combinations that are consistent with other Windows applications. Table 11-5 summarizes the standard Windows keyboard commands. Two of the five categories in this table are implemented for you by the operating system (system commands) or by an MFC class (CMDIFrameWnd implements the MDI accelerator keys). The rest are up to you to implement in your own accelerator table. You'll want to be aware of all of them, however, to avoid defining an accelerator that conflicts with standard Windows keyboard commands.

Microsoft's design guide provides suggestions to help you pick a reasonable set of accelerator keys. We've reproduced those guidelines here for your convenience (from the *Windows 95 User Interface Design Guide*, Chapter 4, Microsoft Corporation, 1994):

- Assign single keys where possible because these keystrokes are the easiest for the user to perform.

- Make modifier-letter-key combinations case-insensitive.

- Use Shift-key combinations for actions that extend or complement the actions of the key or key combination used without the Shift key. For example, Alt-Tab switches windows in a top-to-bottom order. Shift-Alt-Tab switches windows in reverse order. However, avoid Shift-text keys, because the effect of the Shift key may differ for some international keyboards.

- Use Ctrl-key combinations for actions that represent a larger-scale effect. For example, in text editing contexts, Home moves to the beginning of a line, Ctrl-Home moves to the beginning of the text. Use Ctrl-key combinations for access to commands where a letter key is used — for example, Ctrl-B for bold. Remember that such assignments might only be meaningful for English-speaking users.

- Avoid Alt-key combinations, because they may conflict with the standard keyboard access for menus and controls. The Alt-key combinations — Alt-Tab, Alt-Esc, and Alt-spacebar — are reserved for system use. Alt-numeric-key combinations enter special characters.

- Avoid assigning shortcut keys defined in the design guide to other operations in your software. For example, if Ctrl-C is the shortcut for the Copy command and your application supports the standard copy operation, don't assign Ctrl-C to another operation.

- Provide support for allowing the user to change the shortcut key assignments in your software, when possible.

- Use the Esc key to terminate a function in process or to cancel a direct manipulation operation. It is also usually interpreted as the shortcut key for a Cancel button.

Table 11-5

Standard Keyboard Commands in Microsoft Windows

Category	Keystroke	Description
System Commands	Ctrl-Alt-Del	Local reboot in Windows 3.1. Logon/logoff in Windows 95 and Windows NT.
	Alt-Tab	Select the next active application.
	Alt-Esc	Select the next active application.
	Ctrl-Esc	Display the Start menu on Windows 95. (Display the Task List on Windows 3.1).
	Alt-Spacebar	Open the windows' system menu.
	PrtScr	Make a snapshot of the display screen and place it on the clipboard.
	Alt-PrtScr	Make a snapshot of the currently active window and place it on the clipboard.
	Alt	Activate or deactivate the application menu bar.
	Alt-Enter	Toggle DOS windows into and out of full screen text mode.
Application Modes	Esc	Cancel the current mode or operation.
	Enter	In dialog boxes, the same action as a mouse click on the default pushbutton.
	Tab	In a dialog box, select the next control.
	Alt-F4	Close the currently active top-level window.
	Applications key	Display a context menu (on Windows 95-compatible, 104-key keyboards).
	Shift-F10	Display a context menu.
	F1	Summon application help.
	Shift-F1	Summon context help.
File Commands	Ctrl-N	FileNew.
	Ctrl-O	FileOpen...
	Ctrl-P	FilePrint...
	Ctrl-S	FileSave.

Category	Keystroke	Description
Clipboard Commands	Ctrl-Z	Edit|Undo.
	Alt-Backspace	Edit|Undo (for backward compatibility with Windows 3.x).
	Ctrl-X	Edit|Cut.
	Shift-Del	Edit|Cut (for backward compatibility with Windows 3.x).
	Ctrl-C	Edit|Copy.
	Ctrl-Ins	Edit|Copy (for backward compatibility with Windows 3.x).
	Ctrl-V	Edit|Paste.
	Shift-Ins	Edit|Paste (for backward compatibility with Windows 3.x).
Multiple-Document Interface (MDI) Commands	Ctrl-F4	Close the document window that is currently active (CMDIFrameWnd handles this).
	Ctrl-F6	Activate the next document window (CMDIFrameWnd handles this).
	Shift-Ctrl-F6	Activate the previous document window (CMDIFrameWnd handles this).

Once you've selected the accelerator keys for your application, you have to decide whether to put them all in a single accelerator table or spread them out between multiple accelerator tables. For small- to medium-sized applications, a single accelerator table is sufficient. For larger, more complex applications working with several different types of data, you might find that you need several accelerator tables. The following section explores the issues involved in using multiple accelerator tables in an MFC application.

MULTIPLE ACCELERATOR TABLES

The use of multiple accelerator tables allows you to divide up the work that's to be done, and it gives you greater flexibility in enabling different keyboard command sets. MFC's Doc/View classes take advantage of this capability to support multiple accelerator tables. But we're avoiding Doc/View for now, so we'll show you how to use multiple accelerator tables in a non-Doc/View application. (Incidentally, we are avoiding Doc/View so that we can focus on MFC fundamentals, not because there's anything wrong with it. Once you grasp MFC fundamentals, Doc/View is simpler to understand and use.) To help you understand what's required, we'll start with a review of how the native Windows API provides accelerator support.

Native Windows API accelerator support

For all that accelerators do for you, the Win32 API has only six accelerator functions. (The scarcity of native API functions is one reason why you *don't* find a CAccelerators class in MFC.) The most important features are provided by two of these accelerator functions: LoadAccelerators( ) and TranslateAccelerator( ). LoadAccelerators( ) creates a RAM-resident accelerator table from an accelerator resource. The second function, Translate-Accelerator( ), tests whether a particular keyboard message corresponds to an accelerator table command entry.

In a Windows program written in C, you would call the load function to create the accelerator table and then call the translate function from your program's message loop. As we described in Chapter 9, MFC provides the message loop that every MFC-based program uses. The message loop in the thread class's CWinThread::Run( ) function calls CWinThread::PumpMessage( ), which does the following:

```
::GetMessage(&m_msgCur, NULL, NULL, NULL);
if (!PreTranslateMessage(&m_msgCur))
{
    ::TranslateMessage(&m_msgCur);
    ::DispatchMessage(&m_msgCur);
}
```

In this code fragment, the three functions with the global scope operators (::) are native Windows API functions. The fourth function, Pre-TranslateMessage( ), is the name of an overloaded function that appears in several MFC classes. These functions exist for one primary reason: to check for accelerator keys. To experienced Windows API programmers, this is a familiar message loop, with the exception that Translate-Accelerator( ) is usually called instead of PreTranslateMessage( ).

By the way, the function's name comes from the fact it is called before ::TranslateMessage( ). This latter function — which we'll discuss further in Chapter 14 — takes raw keyboard (virtual key) messages and turns them into cooked ASCII character input. For accelerator keys to be handled properly, they must be raw. Also, if a particular message is associated with an accelerator, the caller returns TRUE, and no further processing is required. Otherwise, the normal message loop functions are called.

The following MFC classes have a PreTranslateMessage( ) member:

CControlBar
CDialog
CFormView
CFrameWnd
CMDIChildWnd
CMDIFrameWnd
CPropertyPage
CPropertySheet
CWinApp
CWinThread
CWnd

Although all of them have this member, not all can support an accelerator table. In some cases — such as with CWinApp and CWinThread — the base member function simply calls the corresponding member in the windowing classes. This implies that accelerator tables can be used only by window classes. However, this limitation is not a design feature of MFC; it is a trait that MFC inherits from the native Windows API.

The basic flow of messages is from the innermost data window to the outermost container window. The command is handled by whichever window first claims it. In a single-document Doc/View application, the view window gets the first chance to handle an accelerator, followed by the frame window. In a multiple-document Doc/View application, the sequence progresses from the view window to the child frame, and then to the parent frame. In our Doc/View-free world, our BASEMENU sample program has only one window — a frame window — which alone among the MFC objects can receive accelerator key commands.

Let's take a closer look at the mechanics of providing accelerator tables to MFC's windowing classes.

Connecting a new accelerator table to a windowing class

To connect an accelerator table to a window class, you start by loading the accelerator table into memory. You'll do this sometime during the initialization of your window — PreCreateWindow( ) is a good choice. Incidentally, this function gets its name from the fact that it is called before ::CreateWindow( ), the native Win32 function that creates a Windows system window.

You load an accelerator table into memory by calling ::LoadAccelerators( ), which is defined as follows:

```
HACCEL LoadAccelerators(
    HINSTANCE  hinst,        // EXE file instance handle
    LPCTSTR  lpTableName); // Accelerator table name
```

The first parameter, the instance handle, identifies who you are in this system. This is passed to your program's WinMain( ) entry point. The second parameter is the accelerator table name, which you specified in the resource file.

The following code fragment loads an accelerator table named IDR_VIEW_COMMMANDS:

```
HINSTANCE hInst = AfxGetResourceHandle();
LPCTSTR lpID = MAKEINTRESOURCE(IDR_VIEW_COMMMANDS);
HACCEL d_hAccel = LoadAccelerators (hInst, lpID);
```

The AfxGetResourceHandle( ) function helps make sure that we get the correct instance handle — for code in an application as well as in a dynamic link library. The MAKEINTRESOURCE( ) macro converts the accelerator table's integer ID into a character string, which is the type required by the function. The return value, d_hAccel, is a Windows system handle that gives our program access to the accelerator table in memory.

Once an accelerator table is loaded into memory, the next step is to make sure it is called at the right time. This is a simple matter of overloading the PreTranslateMessage( ) function in a CWnd-derived class. Here's a sample implementation that does just that:

```
BOOL DWindowingClass::PreTranslateMessage(MSG * pMsg)
{
    if (d_hAccel == NULL)
        return FALSE;  // we didn't process

    return ::TranslateAccelerator(m_hWnd, d_hAccel, pMsg);
}
```

To illustrate the command input techniques we've been describing — menus and accelerator tables — the following section introduces the BASEMENU program.

SAMPLE PROGRAM: BASEMENU

BASEMENU demonstrates a few of the more common command input techniques you'll use in Windows programming. For example, it has a static menu, it does a few dynamic menu operations, and it has a context menu. It also has an accelerator table, with a few commands that we've selected to give quicker access to command selections. You'll find the source files to BASEMENU in Listings 11-1 through 11-6.

Listing 11-1
BASEMENU.H

```
// BaseMenu.h : main header file for the BASEMENU application
//

#ifndef __AFXWIN_H__
    #error include 'stdafx.h' before including this file for PCH
#endif

#include "resource.h"        // main symbols

/////////////////////////////////////////////////////////////////////////////
// DApp:
// See BaseMenu.cpp for the implementation of this class
//

class DApp : public CWinApp
{
public:
    DApp();

// Overrides
    // ClassWizard generated virtual function overrides
    //{{AFX_VIRTUAL(DApp)
    public:
    virtual BOOL InitInstance();
    //}}AFX_VIRTUAL

// Implementation

    //{{AFX_MSG(DApp)
    afx_msg void OnAppAbout();
        // NOTE - the ClassWizard will add and remove member functions here.
        //    DO NOT EDIT what you see in these blocks of generated code !
    //}}AFX_MSG
    DECLARE_MESSAGE_MAP()
};


/////////////////////////////////////////////////////////////////////////////
```

Listing 11-2
BASEMENU.CPP

```cpp
// BaseMenu.cpp : Defines the class behaviors for the application.
//

#include "stdafx.h"
#include "BaseMenu.h"

#include "mainfrm.h"

#ifdef _DEBUG
#undef THIS_FILE
static char BASED_CODE THIS_FILE[] = __FILE__;
#endif


/////////////////////////////////////////////////////////////////////////////
// DApp

BEGIN_MESSAGE_MAP(DApp, CWinApp)
    //{{AFX_MSG_MAP(DApp)
    ON_COMMAND(ID_APP_ABOUT, OnAppAbout)
        // NOTE - the ClassWizard will add and remove mapping macros here.
        //      DO NOT EDIT what you see in these blocks of generated code!
    //}}AFX_MSG_MAP
    // Standard file based document commands
    ON_COMMAND(ID_FILE_NEW, CWinApp::OnFileNew)
    ON_COMMAND(ID_FILE_OPEN, CWinApp::OnFileOpen)
END_MESSAGE_MAP()


/////////////////////////////////////////////////////////////////////////////
// DApp construction

DApp::DApp()
{
    // TODO: add construction code here,
    // Place all significant initialization in InitInstance
}


/////////////////////////////////////////////////////////////////////////////
// The one and only DApp object

DApp theApp;


/////////////////////////////////////////////////////////////////////////////
// DApp initialization

BOOL DApp::InitInstance()
{
    // Step 1: Allocate C++ window object.
    DMainFrame * pFrame;
    pFrame = new DMainFrame();
```

```
    // Step 2: Initialize window object.
    pFrame->LoadFrame(IDR_MAINFRAME);

    // Make window visible
    pFrame->ShowWindow(m_nCmdShow);

    // Assign frame as application's main window
    m_pMainWnd = pFrame;

    return TRUE;
}

/////////////////////////////////////////////////////////////////////////////
// CAboutDlg dialog used for App About

class CAboutDlg : public CDialog
{
public:
    CAboutDlg();

// Dialog Data
    //{{AFX_DATA(CAboutDlg)
    enum { IDD = IDD_ABOUTBOX };
    //}}AFX_DATA

// Implementation
protected:
    virtual void DoDataExchange(CDataExchange* pDX);    // DDX/DDV support
    //{{AFX_MSG(CAboutDlg)
        // No message handlers
    //}}AFX_MSG
    DECLARE_MESSAGE_MAP()
};

CAboutDlg::CAboutDlg() : CDialog(CAboutDlg::IDD)
{
    //{{AFX_DATA_INIT(CAboutDlg)
    //}}AFX_DATA_INIT
}

void CAboutDlg::DoDataExchange(CDataExchange* pDX)
{
    CDialog::DoDataExchange(pDX);
    //{{AFX_DATA_MAP(CAboutDlg)
    //}}AFX_DATA_MAP
}

BEGIN_MESSAGE_MAP(CAboutDlg, CDialog)
    //{{AFX_MSG_MAP(CAboutDlg)
        // No message handlers
    //}}AFX_MSG_MAP
END_MESSAGE_MAP()
```

```
// App command to run the dialog
void DApp::OnAppAbout()
{
    CAboutDlg aboutDlg;
    aboutDlg.DoModal();
}


/////////////////////////////////////////////////////////////////////////////
// DApp commands
```

Listing 11-3
MAINFRM.H

```
// mainfrm.h : interface of the DMainFrame class
//
/////////////////////////////////////////////////////////////////////////////

class DMainFrame : public CFrameWnd
{
public:
    DMainFrame();
protected: // create from serialization only
    DECLARE_DYNCREATE(DMainFrame)

// Attributes
public:
    BOOL    d_bCheckState;  // Check state of Menu|This Item.
    BOOL    d_bEnableState; // Enable state of Menu|This Item.
    CMenu * d_pmenuContext; // Right-mouse button menu.

// Operations
public:
    void ShowContextMenu(CPoint& point);

// Overrides
    // ClassWizard generated virtual function overrides
    //{{AFX_VIRTUAL(DMainFrame)
    //}}AFX_VIRTUAL

// Implementation
public:
    virtual ~DMainFrame();
#ifdef _DEBUG
    virtual void AssertValid() const;
    virtual void Dump(CDumpContext& dc) const;
#endif

protected:  // control bar embedded members
    CStatusBar  m_wndStatusBar;
```

```
    // Generated message map functions
protected:
    //{{AFX_MSG(DMainFrame)
    afx_msg int OnCreate(LPCREATESTRUCT lpCreateStruct);
    afx_msg void OnPaint();
    afx_msg void OnRButtonDown(UINT nFlags, CPoint point);
    afx_msg void OnContextMenu();
    afx_msg void OnFrameMinimize();
    afx_msg void OnFrameTop();
    afx_msg void OnMenuAppend();
    afx_msg void OnMenuCheck();
    afx_msg void OnMenuEnable();
    afx_msg void OnMenuThis();
    afx_msg void OnUpdateMenuThis(CCmdUI* pCmdUI);
    afx_msg void OnTitleBye();
    afx_msg void OnTitleHello();
    afx_msg void OnTitleQuery();
    //}}AFX_MSG
    DECLARE_MESSAGE_MAP()
};

//////////////////////////////////////////////////////////////////////////
```

Listing 11-4
MAINFRM.CPP

```
// mainfrm.cpp : implementation of the DMainFrame class
//

#include "stdafx.h"
#include "BaseMenu.h"

#include "mainfrm.h"

#ifdef _DEBUG
#undef THIS_FILE
static char BASED_CODE THIS_FILE[] = __FILE__;
#endif

//////////////////////////////////////////////////////////////////////////
// DMainFrame

IMPLEMENT_DYNCREATE(DMainFrame, CFrameWnd)

BEGIN_MESSAGE_MAP(DMainFrame, CFrameWnd)
    //{{AFX_MSG_MAP(DMainFrame)
    ON_WM_CREATE()
    ON_WM_PAINT()
    ON_WM_RBUTTONDOWN()
```

```
        ON_COMMAND(ID_CONTEXT_MENU, OnContextMenu)
        ON_COMMAND(ID_FRAME_MINIMIZE, OnFrameMinimize)
        ON_COMMAND(ID_FRAME_TOP, OnFrameTop)
        ON_COMMAND(ID_MENU_APPEND, OnMenuAppend)
        ON_COMMAND(ID_MENU_CHECK, OnMenuCheck)
        ON_COMMAND(ID_MENU_ENABLE, OnMenuEnable)
        ON_COMMAND(ID_MENU_THIS, OnMenuThis)
        ON_UPDATE_COMMAND_UI(ID_MENU_THIS, OnUpdateMenuThis)
        ON_COMMAND(ID_TITLE_BYE, OnTitleBye)
        ON_COMMAND(ID_TITLE_HELLO, OnTitleHello)
        ON_COMMAND(ID_TITLE_QUERY, OnTitleQuery)
        //}}AFX_MSG_MAP
END_MESSAGE_MAP()

/////////////////////////////////////////////////////////////////////
// arrays of IDs used to initialize control bars
static UINT BASED_CODE indicators[] =
{
    ID_SEPARATOR,              // status line indicator
    ID_INDICATOR_CAPS,
    ID_INDICATOR_NUM,
    ID_INDICATOR_SCRL,
};

/////////////////////////////////////////////////////////////////////
// DMainFrame construction/destruction

DMainFrame::DMainFrame()
{
    d_bCheckState  = FALSE; // Start menu item unchecked.
    d_bEnableState = TRUE;  // Start menu item enabled.
}

DMainFrame::~DMainFrame()
{
    // Delete CMenu context menu object.
    if (d_pmenuContext)
        delete d_pmenuContext;
}

/////////////////////////////////////////////////////////////////////
// DMainFrame diagnostics

#ifdef _DEBUG
void DMainFrame::AssertValid() const
{
    CFrameWnd::AssertValid();
}

void DMainFrame::Dump(CDumpContext& dc) const
{
    CFrameWnd::Dump(dc);
}
```

```
#endif //_DEBUG

/////////////////////////////////////////////////////////////////////
// DMainFrame helper functions

//-----------------------------------
// Display context menu at indicated client area location.
void DMainFrame::ShowContextMenu(CPoint& point)
{
    // Convert client coordinate to screen coordinates.
    ClientToScreen(&point);

    // Display context menu at mouse location.
    CMenu * psubmenu = d_pmenuContext->GetSubMenu(0);
    psubmenu->TrackPopupMenu(TPM_LEFTALIGN  |  // Flags.
                             TPM_RIGHTBUTTON,
                             point.x,         // x-coord.
                             point.y,         // y-coord.
                             this);           // "this" window.
}

/////////////////////////////////////////////////////////////////////
// DMainFrame message handlers

//-----------------------------------
// WM_CREATE handler.
int DMainFrame::OnCreate(LPCREATESTRUCT lpCreateStruct)
{
    if (CFrameWnd::OnCreate(lpCreateStruct) == -1)
        return -1;

    if (!m_wndStatusBar.Create(this) ||
        !m_wndStatusBar.SetIndicators(indicators,
          sizeof(indicators)/sizeof(UINT)))
    {
        TRACE0("Failed to create status bar\n");
        return -1;      // fail to create
    }

    // Allocate CMenu for context menu.
    d_pmenuContext = new CMenu();
    if (!d_pmenuContext) return -1;

    // Initialize CMenu (connect WinAPI menu to CMenu).
    BOOL bSuccess = d_pmenuContext->LoadMenu(IDR_TITLE);
    if (!bSuccess) return -1;

    return 0;
}

//-----------------------------------
// WM_PAINT handler.
void DMainFrame::OnPaint()
{
    CPaintDC dc(this); // device context for painting
```

```
        // Calculate client area center point.
        int   x, y;
        RECT rClient;
        GetClientRect(&rClient);
        x = rClient.right  / 2;
        y = rClient.bottom / 2;

        // Calculate offset for centering text.
        CString cs = _T("<Right Mouse> or Shift+F10 for Context Menu");
        CSize cb = dc.GetTextExtent(cs, cs.GetLength());
        x -= cb.cx / 2;
        y -= cb.cy / 2;

        // Draw text.
        dc.TextOut(x, y, cs);


        // Do not call CFrameWnd::OnPaint() for painting messages
}

//-----------------------------------
// WM_RBUTTONDOWN handler.
void DMainFrame::OnRButtonDown(UINT nFlags, CPoint point)
{
    ShowContextMenu(point);

    CFrameWnd::OnRButtonDown(nFlags, point);
}

//-----------------------------------
// WM_COMMAND handler for Shift+F10 -or- Applications key.
void DMainFrame::OnContextMenu()
{
    // Display context menu at top right corner of window.
    CPoint point(10,10);
    ShowContextMenu(point);
}

//-----------------------------------
// WM_COMMAND handler for Frame|Minimize.
void DMainFrame::OnFrameMinimize()
{
    // Send ourselves a system message to minimize.
    PostMessage(WM_SYSCOMMAND, SC_MINIMIZE);
}

//-----------------------------------
// WM_COMMAND handler for Frame|Top Half Move.
void DMainFrame::OnFrameTop()
{
    // Ask system for dimensions of screen.
    UINT cxWidth  = GetSystemMetrics(SM_CXSCREEN);
    UINT cyHeight = GetSystemMetrics(SM_CYSCREEN);

    // Calculate top half of screen.
    cyHeight /= 2;
```

```
    // Move window.
    MoveWindow(0, 0, cxWidth, cyHeight, TRUE);
}


//-----------------------------------
// WM_COMMAND handler for Menu Item|Append Item.
void DMainFrame::OnMenuAppend()
{
    // Fetch menu bar object.
    CMenu * pmMain = GetMenu();

    // Fetch submenu object using relative menu position.
    //    0      1      2        3
    // [Frame][Title][Menu Item][Help]
    CMenu * pmSub = pmMain->GetSubMenu(2);

    // Append new menu item.
    pmSub->AppendMenu (MF_STRING, ID_MENU_THIS, _T("&This Item"));
}


//-----------------------------------
// WM_COMMAND handler for Menu Item|Check/Uncheck.
void DMainFrame::OnMenuCheck()
{
    // Toggle menu check state.
    d_bCheckState = (!d_bCheckState);
}


//-----------------------------------
// WM_COMMAND handler for Menu Item|Enable/Disable.
void DMainFrame::OnMenuEnable()
{
    // Toggle menu enable state.
    d_bEnableState = (!d_bEnableState);
}


//-----------------------------------
// WM_COMMAND handler for Menu Item|This Item.
void DMainFrame::OnMenuThis()
{
    AfxMessageBox (_T("This menu item merely waits for other\n"
                      "menu items to change its check state\n"
                      "and its enable state."));
}


//-----------------------------------
// CN_UPDATE_COMMAND_UI handler for Menu Item|This Item.
void DMainFrame::OnUpdateMenuThis(CCmdUI* pCmdUI)
{
    pCmdUI->SetCheck(d_bCheckState);
    pCmdUI->Enable(d_bEnableState);
}


//-----------------------------------
// WM_COMMAND handler for Title|Say Goodbye.
```

```
void DMainFrame::OnTitleBye()
{
    SetWindowText(_T("BaseMenu - Goodbye from BaseMenu"));
}

//-----------------------------------
// WM_COMMAND handler for Title|Say Hello.
void DMainFrame::OnTitleHello()
{
    SetWindowText(_T("BaseMenu - Hello from BaseMenu"));
}

//-----------------------------------
// WM_COMMAND handler for Title|Query Text.
void DMainFrame::OnTitleQuery()
{
    TCHAR achTitle[100];
    GetWindowText (achTitle, 100);

    AfxMessageBox(achTitle);
}
```

Listing 11-5
RESOURCE.H

```
//{{NO_DEPENDENCIES}}
// Microsoft Visual C++ generated include file.
// Used by BaseMenu.rc
//
#define IDD_ABOUTBOX                    100
#define IDR_MAINFRAME                   128
#define IDR_TITLE                       130
#define ID_FRAME_TOP                    32771
#define ID_FRAME_MINIMIZE               32772
#define ID_TITLE_HELLO                  32773
#define ID_TITLE_BYE                    32774
#define ID_TITLE_QUERY                  32775
#define ID_MENU_THIS                    32776
#define ID_MENU_CHECK                   32777
#define ID_MENU_ENABLE                  32778
#define ID_MENU_APPEND                  32779
#define ID_CONTEXT_MENU                 32780

// Next default values for new objects
//
#ifdef APSTUDIO_INVOKED
#ifndef APSTUDIO_READONLY_SYMBOLS
#define _APS_NEXT_RESOURCE_VALUE        131
#define _APS_NEXT_COMMAND_VALUE         32781
#define _APS_NEXT_CONTROL_VALUE         1000
#define _APS_NEXT_SYMED_VALUE           101
#endif
#endif
```

Listing 11-6
BASEMENU.RC

```
//Microsoft Visual C++ generated resource script.
//
#include "resource.h"

#define APSTUDIO_READONLY_SYMBOLS
/////////////////////////////////////////////////////////////////////////////
//
// Generated from the TEXTINCLUDE 2 resource.
//
#include "afxres.h"


/////////////////////////////////////////////////////////////////////////////
#undef APSTUDIO_READONLY_SYMBOLS


#ifdef APSTUDIO_INVOKED
/////////////////////////////////////////////////////////////////////////////
//
// TEXTINCLUDE
//

1 TEXTINCLUDE DISCARDABLE
BEGIN
    "resource.h\0"
END

2 TEXTINCLUDE DISCARDABLE
BEGIN
    "#include ""afxres.h""\r\n"
    "\0"
END

3 TEXTINCLUDE DISCARDABLE
BEGIN
    "#include ""res\\BaseMenu.rc2""  // non-Visual C++ edited resources\r\n"
    "\r\n"
    "#define _AFX_NO_SPLITTER_RESOURCES\r\n"
    "#define _AFX_NO_OLE_RESOURCES\r\n"
    "#define _AFX_NO_TRACKER_RESOURCES\r\n"
    "#define _AFX_NO_PROPERTY_RESOURCES\r\n"
    "#include ""afxres.rc""  \011// Standard components\r\n"
    "\0"
END

/////////////////////////////////////////////////////////////////////////////
#endif    // APSTUDIO_INVOKED


/////////////////////////////////////////////////////////////////////////////
//
// Icon
//
```

```
IDR_MAINFRAME           ICON    DISCARDABLE     "res\\BaseMenu.ico"

/////////////////////////////////////////////////////////////////////////////
//
// Menu
//

IDR_MAINFRAME MENU PRELOAD DISCARDABLE
BEGIN
    POPUP "&Frame"
    BEGIN
        MENUITEM "&Top Half Move\tF2",          ID_FRAME_TOP
        MENUITEM "&Minimize\tF3",               ID_FRAME_MINIMIZE
        MENUITEM SEPARATOR
        MENUITEM "E&xit",                       ID_APP_EXIT
    END
    POPUP "&Title"
    BEGIN
        MENUITEM "Say &Hello\tCtrl+H",          ID_TITLE_HELLO
        MENUITEM "Say &Good-bye\tCtrl+G",       ID_TITLE_BYE
        MENUITEM SEPARATOR
        MENUITEM "&Query Title Text\tCtrl+T",   ID_TITLE_QUERY
    END
    POPUP "&Menu Item"
    BEGIN
        MENUITEM "&This Item",                  ID_MENU_THIS
        MENUITEM SEPARATOR
        MENUITEM "&Check / Uncheck",            ID_MENU_CHECK
        MENUITEM "&Enable / Disable",           ID_MENU_ENABLE
        MENUITEM SEPARATOR
        MENUITEM "&Append Menu Item",           ID_MENU_APPEND
    END
    POPUP "&Help"
    BEGIN
        MENUITEM "&About BaseMenu...",          ID_APP_ABOUT
    END
END

IDR_TITLE MENU DISCARDABLE
BEGIN
    POPUP "&Title Context Menu"
    BEGIN
        MENUITEM "Say Hello",                   ID_TITLE_HELLO
        MENUITEM "Say Goodbye",                 ID_TITLE_BYE
        MENUITEM SEPARATOR
        MENUITEM "Query Text",                  ID_TITLE_QUERY
    END
END


/////////////////////////////////////////////////////////////////////////////
//
// Accelerator
//
```

```
IDR_MAINFRAME ACCELERATORS PRELOAD MOVEABLE PURE
BEGIN
    93,             ID_CONTEXT_MENU,        VIRTKEY, NOINVERT
    "G",            ID_TITLE_BYE,           VIRTKEY, CONTROL, NOINVERT
    "H",            ID_TITLE_HELLO,         VIRTKEY, CONTROL, NOINVERT
    "T",            ID_TITLE_QUERY,         VIRTKEY, CONTROL, NOINVERT
    VK_F10,         ID_CONTEXT_MENU,        VIRTKEY, SHIFT, NOINVERT
    VK_F2,          ID_FRAME_TOP,           VIRTKEY, NOINVERT
    VK_F3,          ID_FRAME_MINIMIZE,      VIRTKEY, NOINVERT
END


/////////////////////////////////////////////////////////////////////////
//
// Dialog
//

IDD_ABOUTBOX DIALOG DISCARDABLE  34, 22, 217, 55
STYLE DS_MODALFRAME | WS_POPUP | WS_CAPTION | WS_SYSMENU
CAPTION "About BaseMenu"
FONT 8, "MS Sans Serif"
BEGIN
    ICON            IDR_MAINFRAME,IDC_STATIC,11,17,20,20
    LTEXT           "BaseMenu Version 1.0",IDC_STATIC,40,10,119,8
    LTEXT           "Copyright \251 1995",IDC_STATIC,40,25,119,8
    DEFPUSHBUTTON   "OK",IDOK,176,6,32,14,WS_GROUP
END


/////////////////////////////////////////////////////////////////////////
//
// Version
//

VS_VERSION_INFO VERSIONINFO
 FILEVERSION 1,0,0,1
 PRODUCTVERSION 1,0,0,1
 FILEFLAGSMASK 0x3fL
#ifdef _DEBUG
 FILEFLAGS 0x1L
#else
 FILEFLAGS 0x0L
#endif
 FILEOS 0x4L
 FILETYPE 0x1L
 FILESUBTYPE 0x0L
BEGIN
    BLOCK "StringFileInfo"
    BEGIN
        BLOCK "040904B0"
        BEGIN
            VALUE "CompanyName", "\0"
            VALUE "FileDescription", "BASEMENU MFC Application\0"
            VALUE "FileVersion", "1, 0, 0, 1\0"
```

```
                VALUE "InternalName", "BASEMENU\0"
                VALUE "LegalCopyright", "Copyright \251 1995\0"
                VALUE "LegalTrademarks", "\0"
                VALUE "OriginalFilename", "BASEMENU.EXE\0"
                VALUE "ProductName", "BASEMENU Application\0"
                VALUE "ProductVersion", "1, 0, 0, 1\0"
            END
        END
        BLOCK "VarFileInfo"
        BEGIN
            VALUE "Translation", 0x409, 1200
        END
END




/////////////////////////////////////////////////////////////////////////////
//
// String Table
//

STRINGTABLE PRELOAD DISCARDABLE
BEGIN
    IDR_MAINFRAME           "BaseMenu"
END

STRINGTABLE PRELOAD DISCARDABLE
BEGIN
    AFX_IDS_APP_TITLE       "BaseMenu"
    AFX_IDS_IDLEMESSAGE     "Ready"
END

STRINGTABLE DISCARDABLE
BEGIN
    ID_INDICATOR_EXT        "EXT"
    ID_INDICATOR_CAPS       "CAP"
    ID_INDICATOR_NUM        "NUM"
    ID_INDICATOR_SCRL       "SCRL"
    ID_INDICATOR_OVR        "OVR"
    ID_INDICATOR_REC        "REC"
END

STRINGTABLE DISCARDABLE
BEGIN
    ID_FILE_NEW       "Create a new document\nNew"
    ID_FILE_OPEN      "Open an existing document\nOpen"
    ID_FILE_CLOSE     "Close the active document\nClose"
    ID_FILE_SAVE      "Save the active document\nSave"
    ID_FILE_SAVE_AS   "Save the active document with a new name\nSave As"
END

STRINGTABLE DISCARDABLE
BEGIN
    ID_APP_ABOUT  "Display program information, version & copyright\nAbout"
    ID_APP_EXIT   "Quit the application; prompts to save documents\nExit"
END
```

```
STRINGTABLE DISCARDABLE
BEGIN
    ID_FILE_MRU_FILE1 "Open this document"
    ID_FILE_MRU_FILE2 "Open this document"
    ID_FILE_MRU_FILE3 "Open this document"
    ID_FILE_MRU_FILE4 "Open this document"
END

STRINGTABLE DISCARDABLE
BEGIN
    ID_NEXT_PANE      "Switch to the next window pane\nNext Pane"
    ID_PREV_PANE      "Switch back to the previous window pane\nPrevious Pane"
END

STRINGTABLE DISCARDABLE
BEGIN
    ID_WINDOW_SPLIT    "Split the active window into panes\nSplit"
END

STRINGTABLE DISCARDABLE
BEGIN
    ID_EDIT_CLEAR      "Erase the selection\nErase"
    ID_EDIT_CLEAR_ALL  "Erase everything\nErase All"
    ID_EDIT_COPY       "Copy the selection and put it on the
Clipboard\nCopy"
    ID_EDIT_CUT        "Cut the selection and put it on the Clipboard\nCut"
    ID_EDIT_FIND       "Find the specified text\nFind"
    ID_EDIT_PASTE      "Insert Clipboard contents\nPaste"
    ID_EDIT_REPEAT     "Repeat the last action\nRepeat"
    ID_EDIT_REPLACE    "Replace specific text with different text\nReplace"
    ID_EDIT_SELECT_ALL "Select the entire document\nSelect All"
    ID_EDIT_UNDO       "Undo the last action\nUndo"
    ID_EDIT_REDO       "Redo the previously undone action\nRedo"
END

STRINGTABLE DISCARDABLE
BEGIN
    AFX_IDS_SCSIZE         "Change the window size"
    AFX_IDS_SCMOVE         "Change the window position"
    AFX_IDS_SCMINIMIZE     "Reduce the window to an icon"
    AFX_IDS_SCMAXIMIZE     "Enlarge the window to full size"
    AFX_IDS_SCNEXTWINDOW   "Switch to the next document window"
    AFX_IDS_SCPREVWINDOW   "Switch to the previous document window"
    AFX_IDS_SCCLOSE        "Close active window & prompt to save documents"
END

STRINGTABLE DISCARDABLE
BEGIN
    AFX_IDS_SCRESTORE  "Restore the window to normal size"
    AFX_IDS_SCTASKLIST "Activate Task List"
END
```

```
STRINGTABLE DISCARDABLE
BEGIN
    ID_FRAME_TOP       "Move frame window to top half of display screen"
    ID_FRAME_MINIMIZE "Reduces the window to an icon"
    ID_TITLE_HELLO     "Displays a hello message in the title bar"
    ID_TITLE_BYE       "Displays a good-bye message in the title bar"
    ID_TITLE_QUERY     "Queries the frame window for the current title text"
    ID_MENU_THIS       "This is the item to check, uncheck, enable, and disable"
    ID_MENU_CHECK      "Toggles the checkmark on the top menu item"
    ID_MENU_ENABLE     "Toggles the enable state on the top menu item"
    ID_MENU_APPEND     "Adds a new menu item to this menu"
END


#ifndef APSTUDIO_INVOKED
/////////////////////////////////////////////////////////////////////////////
//
// Generated from the TEXTINCLUDE 3 resource.
//
#include "res\BaseMenu.rc2"  // non-Microsoft Visual C++ edited resources

#define _AFX_NO_SPLITTER_RESOURCES
#define _AFX_NO_OLE_RESOURCES
#define _AFX_NO_TRACKER_RESOURCES
#define _AFX_NO_PROPERTY_RESOURCES
#include "afxres.rc"     // Standard components


/////////////////////////////////////////////////////////////////////////////
#endif    // not APSTUDIO_INVOKED
```

BASEMENU started as an AppWizard-generated Doc/View application. But like AFRAME in the previous chapter, we stripped out Doc/View support to focus solely on window creation. Here, of course, our focus is command input. BASEMENU has a menu, an accelerator, and a status bar.

BASEMENU menu creation

BASEMENU's static menu resource definition was created by AppWizard, it was edited by the menu editor, and it appears in BASEMENU.RC. Like every other resource, the menu resource for this program's main menu has an ID: IDR_MAINFRAME. Like many resource IDs, it is defined in RESOURCE.H. In the not-too-distant past, Windows programmers edited resource definitions by editing the text definition. With the Visual C++ menu editor, today's programmers are spared those pains. Over time, you will probably become more familiar with the text version of a menu definition. However, because the menu editor works so well, you don't have to worry about studying the resource file too closely.

To give you the whole story about menus, we could expose the menu creation process in a more visible fashion. Doing so would probably be more of a disservice than a favor, however, because a frame window and its menu are so tightly integrated. If you want to know the exact moment when the frame window's menu gets created, look in the CFrameWnd::LoadFrame( ) function that our program calls in DApp::InitInstance( ). The menu is created along with the window when the native API's CreateWindow( ) [or CreateWindowEx( )] function is called.

In Windows, the really interesting events — for example, a user making a menu selection — are reported to your program via messages. As such, locating and deciphering the message map are the keys to reading and understanding an MFC program. The message map is a kind of table of contents for how an MFC object will respond to system events. When the focus is on menus, the two most interesting events are WM_COMMAND and CN_COMMAND_UPDATE_UI messages.

Message handling in BASEMENU

BASEMENU has three message maps. One message map is for DApp, the CWinApp-derived application class. A second message map is for DMain-Frame, the CFrameWnd-derived frame window class. The third message map is for CAboutDlg, the class for the About... dialog box that App-Wizard creates. In our earlier discussion of menu message routing, we said that in a program such as this, menu messages are routed first to the frame window and then to the application object. It's worth pointing out that no menu messages are ever sent to the dialog box's message map, even if you define a WM_COMMAND message map entry. Although this makes sense from a design point of view, it's not obvious from simply reading the source files. Not all message maps are created equal.

In a typical MFC application, menu handling is split between several classes — DApp and DMainFrame in our sample program. Primarily for ease of reading, we've put all command handling in DMainFrame. But don't let this limitation in our example deter you from distributing menu command handling over a wider range of objects. Other samples in this book will show a more typical distribution of command handling responsibilities.

BASEMENU handles one CN_UPDATE_COMMAND_UI message. MFC sends this message to update two different types of menu states. One is the menu check mark, which can be set or cleared. The other is the enabled state, which can be set to grayed (disabled) or enabled. When the message handler is called, MFC provides a pointer to a CCmdUI object. When responding for a menu item, you should call CCmdUI::SetCheck( ) to modify the check state. A menu item's enabled state is controlled by the CCmdUI::Enable( ) function.

BASEMENU handles three messages that aren't directly related to command input: WM_CREATE, WM_RBUTTONDOWN, and WM_PAINT. The WM_CREATE message, which is handled by DMainFrame::OnCreate( ), is an important windowing message. This is the very first message that Windows sends to tell you that a window has been created. Like a C++ constructor, this is the time to initialize a window. BASEMENU connects a status bar to its window and creates a context menu. You'll want to keep this message in mind as the right time for initializing most Windows API objects that are contained in a window.

The WM_RBUTTONDOWN message indicates that the user has clicked the right mouse button in our window's client area. BASEMENU responds by displaying a context menu. We'll provide more details on mouse button input in Chapter 14.

The other message, WM_PAINT, is important for windows that want to display a graphic image. Because Windows is an event-driven environment, the contents of a window are often overwritten as the window is minimized and restored, or buried and then brought back to the surface of the window stack. The system sends a WM_PAINT message to ask a window to redraw its contents. In BASEMENU, we respond to this message by displaying the instructions that ask the user to click the right mouse button for a context menu. We'll cover more of the details of drawing in a window in Chapter 14.

If you carefully scan all of BASEMENU's message maps, you'll find that one of its menu items, ID_APP_EXIT, isn't handled. As mentioned previously, if a command handler isn't present, MFC automatically disables the menu item. But if you look in BASEMENU's File menu, you'll notice that the Exit menu item is enabled! Also, when you select the File|Exit command, the application does exit properly. However, BASEMENU doesn't handle this message, so it doesn't do anything to terminate the application. What's happening?

The simple explanation is that DApp's base class, CWinApp, handles the message. CWinApp's source files have an ID_APP_EXIT message map entry, and the entry references the CWinApp::OnAppExit( ) function. In the same way that a base class can have virtual functions with default implementations, a base class can also have default message-handling functions. Many MFC base classes have interesting message-handling defaults that simplify your life.

C++ inheritance and MFC message map inheritance

A word of caution is needed. Although C++ class inheritance and MFC message map inheritance seem closely related, they are two different mechanisms. You can't simply override message handlers. Instead, they require the creation of completely new message map entries in the derived class. For example, to handle the ID_APP_EXIT function in BASEMENU, you can't simply override CWinApp::OnAppExit( ).

When dispatching messages, MFC scans the message map for each class, one at a time. The message map is just a data structure — an array — that maps message values to class member functions. Although C++ function inheritance and MFC message map inheritance often parallel each other, they are not interchangeable.

Internationalization

Shipping software in different character sets to support different languages is becoming an issue for many software developers. BASEMENU uses a Visual C++ macro, _T( ), which is intended to support different character sets. While reviewing BASEMENU's source files, you might have encountered the _T( ) macro around text strings, as in the following example:

```
SetWindowText(_T("BaseMenu - Hello from BaseMenu"));
```

As we'll describe in Chapter 14, Windows has two basic character sets: an 8-bit extended ANSI character set and a 16-bit Unicode character set. The Visual C++ compiler can generate strings for both character sets, but Unicode strings must have an L prefix. When the string in the preceding example is compiled for Unicode, the string is seen by the compiler as:

```
L"BaseMenu - Hello from BaseMenu"
```

When compiled for the ANSI character set, on the other hand, the _T( ) macro disappears to produce a C compiler string that you expect:

```
"BaseMenu - Hello from BaseMenu"
```

A little effort in using this macro will help simplify your development efforts as you go international. Now, it's time to turn our attention to a third type of command input device: toolbars.

Creating and Controlling Toolbars

For a user, toolbars provide instant access to program commands. Rather than digging into a menu or remembering a keystroke, toolbars are right there to see. Because they occupy precious screen space, you'll want to make sure that your toolbars include the most frequently used commands. Large programs tend to have multiple toolbars for different user tasks. Even if your program has only a single toolbar, make sure you give the user the option of hiding it when it gets in the way.

From a programming perspective, a toolbar is a child window that displays a series of bitmap buttons. Once you create a toolbar and make it visible, you can all but ignore it because it generates the same message — WM_COMMAND — that menus and accelerators generate. However, you will want to synchronize toolbar command IDs with the command IDs in menus and accelerators.

The following sections cover several topics that can help you work with toolbars. We'll start with a quick look at the place of toolbars in the MFC hierarchy. Then, we'll cover some of the details involved in dynamically creating and modifying toolbars. We'll conclude by introducing CTRLBARS, a sample program that shows some toolbar programming techniques.

MFC CONTROL BARS

MFC's toolbar class, CToolBar, is one of several classes that create windows for receiving some kind of command input and displaying status information to the user. As shown in Figure 11-7, the base class for this group, known collectively as control bars, is CControlBar. This class is derived from CWnd.

This inheritance relationship has some very useful implications. For example, because all control bars are derived from CWnd, all control bars are connected to a Windows API window. As a result, all of the functional capabilities of CWnd — creating, moving, showing, and hiding windows — are available when you're working with control bars.

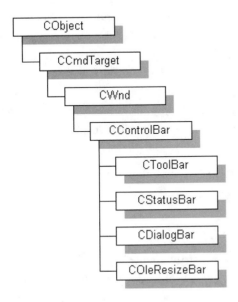

Figure 11-7
The place of toolbars in the MFC class hierarchy.

CToolBar has several sibling classes, including CStatusBar, CDialogBar, and COleResizeBar. When asked, AppWizard gladly creates a status bar by spinning code that creates a CStatusBar object. As mentioned in our discussion of menus, status bars sit at the bottom of a frame window and can display helpful information about menu choices. A status bar will also display helpful details about different toolbar buttons as the user moves the mouse cursor over the buttons.

The CDialogBar class creates dialog bars, which are a cross between a toolbar and a dialog box. A dialog bar can hold controls like a dialog box, but it stays visible in a frame window like a toolbar. We'll discuss this class further when we cover dialog boxes in Chapter 12.

The final MFC control bar is COleResizeBar, which supports resizing of in-place OLE objects, a subject that is beyond the scope of this book.

MFC toolbars (and dialog bars) are dockable. When this feature is enabled, a user can pick up a toolbar and move it to a different edge of a frame window. It is up to the frame window, however, to indicate which edges are acceptable docking sites. As an alternative, toolbars can also be moved away from any frame edge and left in a free-floating palette.

MFC toolbars also support *tool tips*. Tool tips are intended to help users understand the purpose of individual bitmap buttons. Users summon tool tip support — when it's enabled — by moving the mouse cursor over a toolbar button (without clicking the button). After a short wait, the tool tip — a brief word or phrase — appears in a tiny text window that hovers over the toolbar buttons.

To put toolbars to work in your MFC program, you must coordinate several items, including a bitmap resource, the toolbar itself, and the frame window. To help with this effort, the following section shows you how to create a toolbar of your own.

CREATING A TOOLBAR

AppWizard automatically generates a toolbar for you, but some of its features — for example, showing and hiding the toolbar — are buried in existing MFC classes. To give you a more complete picture of tool-bars, we're going to create a second toolbar. When we're done, our sample program, CTRLBARS, will show you how two toolbars can co-exist in the same program. From this, you'll see how easy it is to create additional toolbars.

Toolbar creation is a five-step process. First, you create a bitmap that holds the button images. Second, you build an array that maps your buttons to your program's command codes. Third, you write the code to create the toolbar and initialize it appropriately. Once the toolbar window is created, steps four and five involve connecting button images and command IDs to the toolbar. Once these minimum steps are accomplished, you can take other steps to fine-tune the behavior of your toolbar.

The first step, then, is to create a bitmap that holds all of the button images. You'll store the bitmap as a bitmap resource, which means you'll first open your project's resource (.RC) file. You create your bitmap button images in a row, using the bitmap editor, which is shown in Figure 11-8. The default size of each image is 16 pixels wide by 15 pixels high. Although you can use different sizes, a change from the default requires you to tell your toolbar object by calling CToolBar::SetSizes( ).

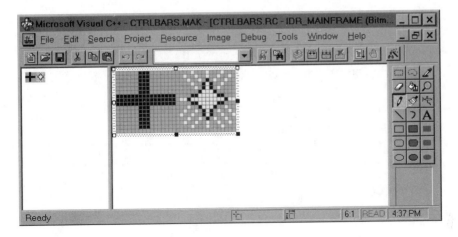

Figure 11-8

A toolbar bitmap in the bitmap editor.

The next step is to define an array of command codes that map button images to command IDs. As shown in the following example from CTRLBARS, this is an array of unsigned ints (UINT):

```
// toolbar buttons - IDs are command buttons
static UINT BASED_CODE buttons[] =
{
    // same order as in the bitmap 'bitmap1.bmp'
    ID_TOOLBAR_CREATE,
        ID_SEPARATOR,
    ID_TOOLBAR_SHOW
};
```

The two command codes are ID_TOOLBAR_CREATE and ID_TOOLBAR_SHOW. The other item, ID_SEPARATOR, adds a bit of spacing between these two buttons.

The third step is to create and initialize the toolbar object. As with other windows, you create a toolbar by first instantiating the object, and then calling an initialization function. Here's an example:

```
// Create C++ object and WinAPI window.
d_pToolbar2 = new CToolBar();
d_pToolbar2->Create(this, WS_CHILD | CBRS_TOP, 0x9100);
```

The initialization function, CToolBar::Create( ), overrides the base function CWnd::Create( ). As with other types of window objects, the style field — that is, the middle field — controls quite a few object attributes. This example has two style flags: WS_CHILD and CBRS_TOP.

The first style, WS_CHILD, is a standard windowing style that makes this a child window. The second style, CBRS_TOP, is a control-bar-specific style that puts the toolbar at the top of the frame window. Table 11-6 lists some other style flags that might be useful.

Table 11-6
Style Flags for Toolbar Windows

Flag	Description
WS_VISIBLE	Makes the toolbar window initially visible
CBRS_BOTTOM	Initially places the control bar at the bottom of the frame window
CBRS_FLYBY	Displays command descriptions in the status window when the mouse cursor pauses over buttons
CBRS_NOALIGN	Prevents repositioning of the control bar when its parent is resized
CBRS_TOOLTIPS	Displays tool tips when the mouse cursor pauses over buttons
CBRS_TOP	Initially places the control bar at the top of the frame window

Once the toolbar window is created, a few more initialization steps must be performed. For one thing, you need to connect the button images — which are stored in the bitmap resource — to your toolbar. You accomplish this by calling CToolBar::LoadBitmap( ), as in:

```
d_pToolbar2->LoadBitmap(IDR_TOOLS);
```

You also need to associate command IDs with buttons. As shown in the following example, you do this by calling CToolBar::SetButtons( ), with a pointer to the array created in step two:

```
d_pToolbar2->SetButtons(buttons, sizeof(buttons)/sizeof(UINT));
```

At this point, the toolbar is complete. However, you might still want to fine-tune the toolbar's operation in a few ways.

By default, a CToolBar toolbar can be moved only by program control. However, you can allow users to move the toolbar to other parts of the frame. To do so, you notify both the toolbar and the frame window. As shown in the following example, you do this by calling CToolBar::EnableDocking( ) and CFrameWnd::EnableDocking( ):

```
d_pToolbar2->EnableDocking(CBRS_ALIGN_ANY);
EnableDocking(CBRS_ALIGN_ANY);
```

Users can then dock and undock the toolbar. Or, under program control, you can dock the toolbar by calling CFrameWnd::DockControlBar( ), and you can undock the toolbar by calling CFrameWnd::FloatControlBar( ).

Once you create a toolbar, it remains attached to your frame window and works on its own. There aren't many things you'll need to do, except perhaps hide it or show it on demand. Let's see what this involves.

SHOWING AND HIDING TOOLBARS

The key point to keep in mind when showing or hiding a toolbar is that a toolbar is a window. In practice, this means that you'll rely more on CWnd member functions than on CToolBar functions.

Before you can show or hide a toolbar, it helps to know the current visibility state of the toolbar window. The WS_VISIBLE windowing style is the key to toolbar visibility. To query all of the style bits for a window, you call CWnd::GetStyle( ). This code fragment sets a flag based on the visibility of a toolbar window:

```
// Query current visibility.
BOOL bVisible = (d_pToolbar2->GetStyle() & WS_VISIBLE);
```

A call to CWnd::SetStyle( ) lets you change certain window styles; unfortunately, WS_VISIBLE is not one of them. Instead, you call CWnd::ShowWindow( ) and pass SW_HIDE to make the toolbar invisible and SW_SHOWNORMAL to make it reappear. The following code fragment toggles the visibility flag we queried in the previous example:

```
// Show or hide.
int nShow = (bVisible) ? SW_HIDE : SW_SHOWNORMAL;
d_pToolbar2->ShowWindow(nShow);
```

Whenever you programmatically change a toolbar, you must inform the frame window about the change. You do this by simply asking it to recalculate the positioning of control bars. You make this request by calling CFrameWnd::RecalcLayout( ), which takes no parameters:

```
// Reconfigure remaining toolbar items.
RecalcLayout();
```

The following section introduces a sample toolbar program that puts these toolbar creation and modification techniques into the context of a working program.

SAMPLE PROGRAM: CTRLBARS

As shown in Figure 11-9, our control bar sample program creates two toolbars and one status bar. A status bar and a toolbar are created along with the frame window. The second toolbar is created dynamically in response to menu command input. Both toolbars use a bitmap resource to define button images, and both use an array of command IDs to map buttons to commands. But if you compare the two toolbars, you'll notice some subtle differences between them.

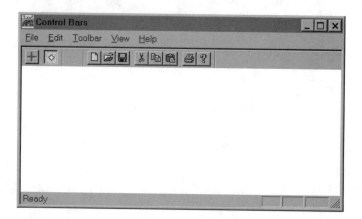

Figure 11-9
CTRLBARS with both toolbars and the status bar visible.

The biggest difference between the two toolbars involves the timing of when each becomes visible. The first toolbar, which is created during the WM_CREATE message processing of the frame window, uses default toolbar styles. These styles include the WS_VISIBLE style bit, which means the toolbar becomes visible when its parent — the frame window — becomes visible. We wait to create and display the second toolbar to demonstrate how you can explicitly control a toolbar. To make this toolbar visible on creation, it needs the WS_VISIBLE style bit [or a comparable call to ShowWindow( )], and the frame window needs to be notified with a call to CFrameWnd::RecalcLayout( ). Listings 11-7 through 11-12 contain the core parts of CTRLBARS.

Listing 11-7
CTRLBARS.H

```
// ctrlbars.h : main header file for the CTRLBARS application
//

#ifndef __AFXWIN_H__
    #error include 'stdafx.h' before including this file for PCH
#endif

#include "resource.h"        // main symbols

/////////////////////////////////////////////////////////////////////////////
// DApp:
// See ctrlbars.cpp for the implementation of this class
//

class DApp : public CWinApp
{
public:
    DApp();

// Overrides
    // ClassWizard generated virtual function overrides
    //{{AFX_VIRTUAL(DApp)
    public:
    virtual BOOL InitInstance();
    //}}AFX_VIRTUAL

// Implementation

    //{{AFX_MSG(DApp)
    afx_msg void OnAppAbout();
        // NOTE - the ClassWizard will add and remove member functions here.
        //    DO NOT EDIT what you see in these blocks of generated code !
    //}}AFX_MSG
    DECLARE_MESSAGE_MAP()
};


/////////////////////////////////////////////////////////////////////////////
```

Listing 11-8
CTRLBARS.CPP

```
// ctrlbars.cpp : Defines the class behaviors for the application.
//

#include "stdafx.h"
#include "ctrlbars.h"

#include "mainfrm.h"

#ifdef _DEBUG
#undef THIS_FILE
static char BASED_CODE THIS_FILE[] = __FILE__;
#endif

/////////////////////////////////////////////////////////////////////////////
// DApp

BEGIN_MESSAGE_MAP(DApp, CWinApp)
    //{{AFX_MSG_MAP(DApp)
    ON_COMMAND(ID_APP_ABOUT, OnAppAbout)
        // NOTE - the ClassWizard will add and remove mapping macros here.
        //     DO NOT EDIT what you see in these blocks of generated code!
    //}}AFX_MSG_MAP
    // Standard file based document commands
    ON_COMMAND(ID_FILE_NEW, CWinApp::OnFileNew)
    ON_COMMAND(ID_FILE_OPEN, CWinApp::OnFileOpen)
END_MESSAGE_MAP()

/////////////////////////////////////////////////////////////////////////////
// DApp construction

DApp::DApp()
{
    // TODO: add construction code here,
    // Place all significant initialization in InitInstance
}

/////////////////////////////////////////////////////////////////////////////
// The one and only DApp object

DApp theApp;

/////////////////////////////////////////////////////////////////////////////
// DApp initialization

BOOL DApp::InitInstance()
{
    // Step 1: Allocate C++ window object.
    DMainFrame * pFrame;
    pFrame = new DMainFrame();
```

```
    // Step 2: Initialize window object.
    pFrame->LoadFrame(IDR_MAINFRAME);

    // Make window visible
    pFrame->ShowWindow(m_nCmdShow);

    // Assign frame as application's main window
    m_pMainWnd = pFrame;

    return TRUE;
}

/////////////////////////////////////////////////////////////////////////////
// CAboutDlg dialog used for App About

class CAboutDlg : public CDialog
{
public:
    CAboutDlg();

// Dialog Data
    //{{AFX_DATA(CAboutDlg)
    enum { IDD = IDD_ABOUTBOX };
    //}}AFX_DATA

// Implementation
protected:
    virtual void DoDataExchange(CDataExchange* pDX);    // DDX/DDV support
    //{{AFX_MSG(CAboutDlg)
        // No message handlers
    //}}AFX_MSG
    DECLARE_MESSAGE_MAP()
};

CAboutDlg::CAboutDlg() : CDialog(CAboutDlg::IDD)
{
    //{{AFX_DATA_INIT(CAboutDlg)
    //}}AFX_DATA_INIT
}

void CAboutDlg::DoDataExchange(CDataExchange* pDX)
{
    CDialog::DoDataExchange(pDX);
    //{{AFX_DATA_MAP(CAboutDlg)
    //}}AFX_DATA_MAP
}

BEGIN_MESSAGE_MAP(CAboutDlg, CDialog)
    //{{AFX_MSG_MAP(CAboutDlg)
        // No message handlers
    //}}AFX_MSG_MAP
END_MESSAGE_MAP()
```

```
// App command to run the dialog
void DApp::OnAppAbout()
{
    CAboutDlg aboutDlg;
    aboutDlg.DoModal();
}


/////////////////////////////////////////////////////////////////////////////
// DApp commands
```

Listing 11-9
MAINFRM.H

```
// mainfrm.h : interface of the DMainFrame class
//
/////////////////////////////////////////////////////////////////////////////

class DMainFrame : public CFrameWnd
{
public:
    DMainFrame();
protected: // create from serialization only
    DECLARE_DYNCREATE(DMainFrame)

// Attributes
public:
    CToolBar * d_pToolbar2; // Pointer for dynamic toolbar.
    BOOL d_bToolbarVisible; // Flag for toolbar visibility.
// Operations
public:

// Overrides
    // ClassWizard generated virtual function overrides
    //{{AFX_VIRTUAL(DMainFrame)
    //}}AFX_VIRTUAL

// Implementation
public:
    virtual ~DMainFrame();
#ifdef _DEBUG
    virtual void AssertValid() const;
    virtual void Dump(CDumpContext& dc) const;
#endif

protected:  // control bar embedded members
    CStatusBar  m_wndStatusBar;
    CToolBar    m_wndToolBar;

// Generated message map functions
```

```
protected:
    //{{AFX_MSG(DMainFrame)
    afx_msg int OnCreate(LPCREATESTRUCT lpCreateStruct);
    afx_msg void OnToolbarCreate();
    afx_msg void OnToolbarShow();
    afx_msg void OnUpdateToolbarCreate(CCmdUI* pCmdUI);
    afx_msg void OnUpdateToolbarDestroy(CCmdUI* pCmdUI);
    afx_msg void OnUpdateToolbarShow(CCmdUI* pCmdUI);
    afx_msg void OnEditCopy();
    afx_msg void OnEditCut();
    afx_msg void OnEditPaste();
    afx_msg void OnEditUndo();
    afx_msg void OnFileNew();
    afx_msg void OnFileOpen();
    afx_msg void OnFileSave();
    afx_msg void OnFilePrint();
    //}}AFX_MSG
    DECLARE_MESSAGE_MAP()
};


/////////////////////////////////////////////////////////////////////////////
```

Listing 11-10
MAINFRM.CPP

```
// mainfrm.cpp : implementation of the DMainFrame class
//

#include "stdafx.h"
#include "ctrlbars.h"

#include "mainfrm.h"

#ifdef _DEBUG
#undef THIS_FILE
static char BASED_CODE THIS_FILE[] = __FILE__;
#endif

/////////////////////////////////////////////////////////////////////////////
// DMainFrame

IMPLEMENT_DYNCREATE(DMainFrame, CFrameWnd)

BEGIN_MESSAGE_MAP(DMainFrame, CFrameWnd)
    //{{AFX_MSG_MAP(DMainFrame)
    ON_WM_CREATE()
    ON_COMMAND(ID_TOOLBAR_CREATE, OnToolbarCreate)
    ON_COMMAND(ID_TOOLBAR_SHOW, OnToolbarShow)
    ON_UPDATE_COMMAND_UI(ID_TOOLBAR_CREATE, OnUpdateToolbarCreate)
```

```
        ON_UPDATE_COMMAND_UI(ID_TOOLBAR_SHOW, OnUpdateToolbarShow)
        ON_COMMAND(ID_EDIT_COPY, OnEditCopy)
        ON_COMMAND(ID_EDIT_CUT, OnEditCut)
        ON_COMMAND(ID_EDIT_PASTE, OnEditPaste)
        ON_COMMAND(ID_EDIT_UNDO, OnEditUndo)
        ON_COMMAND(ID_FILE_NEW, OnFileNew)
        ON_COMMAND(ID_FILE_OPEN, OnFileOpen)
        ON_COMMAND(ID_FILE_SAVE, OnFileSave)
        ON_COMMAND(ID_FILE_PRINT, OnFilePrint)
        //}}AFX_MSG_MAP
END_MESSAGE_MAP()


/////////////////////////////////////////////////////////////////////////////
// arrays of IDs used to initialize control bars

// toolbar buttons - IDs are command buttons
static UINT BASED_CODE buttons[] =
{
    // same order as in the bitmap 'bitmap1.bmp'
    ID_TOOLBAR_CREATE,
        ID_SEPARATOR,
    ID_TOOLBAR_SHOW
};

// toolbar buttons - IDs are command buttons
static UINT BASED_CODE Toolbar2Buttons[] =
{
    // same order as in the bitmap 'toolbar.bmp'
    ID_FILE_NEW,
    ID_FILE_OPEN,
    ID_FILE_SAVE,
        ID_SEPARATOR,
    ID_EDIT_CUT,
    ID_EDIT_COPY,
    ID_EDIT_PASTE,
        ID_SEPARATOR,
    ID_FILE_PRINT,
    ID_APP_ABOUT,
};

static UINT BASED_CODE indicators[] =
{
    ID_SEPARATOR,               // status line indicator
    ID_INDICATOR_CAPS,
    ID_INDICATOR_NUM,
    ID_INDICATOR_SCRL,
};


/////////////////////////////////////////////////////////////////////////////
// DMainFrame construction/destruction

DMainFrame::DMainFrame()
{
```

```
    d_pToolbar2 = 0;
    d_bToolbarVisible = FALSE;
}


DMainFrame::~DMainFrame()
{
}


int DMainFrame::OnCreate(LPCREATESTRUCT lpCreateStruct)
{
    if (CFrameWnd::OnCreate(lpCreateStruct) == -1)
        return -1;

    if (!m_wndToolBar.Create(this) ||
        !m_wndToolBar.LoadBitmap(IDR_MAINFRAME) ||
        !m_wndToolBar.SetButtons(buttons,
          sizeof(buttons)/sizeof(UINT)))
    {
        TRACE0("Failed to create toolbar\n");
        return -1;        // fail to create
    }

    // TODO: Delete these three lines if you don't want the toolbar to
    //   be dockable
    m_wndToolBar.EnableDocking(CBRS_ALIGN_ANY);
    EnableDocking(CBRS_ALIGN_ANY);
    DockControlBar(&m_wndToolBar);

    // TODO: Remove this if you don't want tool tips
    m_wndToolBar.SetBarStyle(m_wndToolBar.GetBarStyle() |
        CBRS_TOOLTIPS | CBRS_FLYBY);

    // Create a status bar.
    if (!m_wndStatusBar.Create(this) ||
        !m_wndStatusBar.SetIndicators(indicators,
          sizeof(indicators)/sizeof(UINT)))
    {
        TRACE0("Failed to create status bar\n");
        return -1;        // fail to create
    }

    return 0;
}

/////////////////////////////////////////////////////////////////////
// DMainFrame diagnostics

#ifdef _DEBUG
void DMainFrame::AssertValid() const
{
    CFrameWnd::AssertValid();
}
```

First toolbar created.

```
void DMainFrame::Dump(CDumpContext& dc) const
{
    CFrameWnd::Dump(dc);
}

#endif //_DEBUG

/////////////////////////////////////////////////////////////////////////////
// DMainFrame message handlers

//------------------------------------
// WM_COMMAND handler for Toolbar|Create menu item.
void DMainFrame::OnToolbarCreate()
{
    // Should only get here if we don't have a toolbar.
    ASSERT(d_pToolbar2 == 0);

    // Create C++ object and WinAPI window.
    d_pToolbar2 = new CToolBar();
    d_pToolbar2->Create(this, WS_CHILD | CBRS_TOP |
                              CBRS_TOOLTIPS | CBRS_FLYBY,
                        0x9100);

    // Get bitmap and connect to tool items.
    d_pToolbar2->LoadBitmap(IDR_TOOLS);
    d_pToolbar2->SetButtons(Toolbar2Buttons,
                      sizeof(Toolbar2Buttons)/sizeof(UINT));

    // Make toolbar dockable.
    d_pToolbar2->EnableDocking(CBRS_ALIGN_ANY);
    EnableDocking(CBRS_ALIGN_ANY);
    DockControlBar(d_pToolbar2);
}

//------------------------------------
// WM_COMMAND handler for Toolbar|Show menu item.
void DMainFrame::OnToolbarShow()
{
    ASSERT(d_pToolbar2 != 0);

    // Query current visibility.
    BOOL bVisible = (d_pToolbar2->GetStyle() & WS_VISIBLE);

    // Show or hide.
    int nShow = (bVisible) ? SW_HIDE : SW_SHOWNORMAL;
    d_pToolbar2->ShowWindow(nShow);

    // Reconfigure remaining toolbar items.
    RecalcLayout();

    // Store visibility state for later.
    d_bToolbarVisible = (!bVisible);
}

//------------------------------------
// ON_COMMAND_UPDATE_UI handler for Toolbar|Create menu item.
```

Second toolbar created.

Second toolbar shown or hidden.

Notify frame window.

```
void DMainFrame::OnUpdateToolbarCreate(CCmdUI* pCmdUI)
{
    pCmdUI->Enable(d_pToolbar2 == 0);
}


//-----------------------------------
// ON_COMMAND_UPDATE_UI handler for Toolbar|Show menu item.
void DMainFrame::OnUpdateToolbarShow(CCmdUI* pCmdUI)
{
    pCmdUI->Enable(d_pToolbar2 != 0);
    int nCheck = (d_bToolbarVisible) ? 1 : 0;
    pCmdUI->SetCheck(nCheck);
}

//-----------------------------------
// WM_COMMAND handler for Edit|Copy.
void DMainFrame::OnEditCopy()
{
    AfxMessageBox(_T("Edit|Copy command selected."));
}


//-----------------------------------
// WM_COMMAND handler for Edit|Cut.
void DMainFrame::OnEditCut()
{
    AfxMessageBox(_T("Edit|Cut command selected."));
}


//-----------------------------------
// WM_COMMAND handler for Edit|Paste.
void DMainFrame::OnEditPaste()
{
    AfxMessageBox(_T("Edit|Paste command selected."));
}


//-----------------------------------
// WM_COMMAND handler for Edit|Undo.
void DMainFrame::OnEditUndo()
{
    AfxMessageBox(_T("Edit|Undo command selected."));
}


//-----------------------------------
// WM_COMMAND handler for File|New.
void DMainFrame::OnFileNew()
{
    AfxMessageBox(_T("File|New command selected."));
}


//-----------------------------------
// WM_COMMAND handler for File|Open.
void DMainFrame::OnFileOpen()
{
    AfxMessageBox(_T("File|Open... command selected."));
}
```

```
//----------------------------------
// WM_COMMAND handler for File|Save.
void DMainFrame::OnFileSave()
{
    AfxMessageBox(_T("File|Save command selected."));
}

//----------------------------------
// WM_COMMAND handler for File|Save.
void DMainFrame::OnFilePrint()
{
    AfxMessageBox(_T("File|Print... command selected."));
}
```

Listing 11-11
RESOURCE.H

```
//{{NO_DEPENDENCIES}}
// Microsoft Visual C++ generated include file.
// Used by ctrlbars.rc
//
#define IDD_ABOUTBOX             100
#define IDR_MAINFRAME            128
#define IDR_TOOLS                129
#define ID_TOOLBAR_CREATE        32771
#define ID_TOOLBAR_SHOW          32772

// Next default values for new objects
//
#ifdef APSTUDIO_INVOKED
#ifndef APSTUDIO_READONLY_SYMBOLS
#define _APS_NEXT_RESOURCE_VALUE    130
#define _APS_NEXT_COMMAND_VALUE     32773
#define _APS_NEXT_CONTROL_VALUE     1000
#define _APS_NEXT_SYMED_VALUE       101
#endif
#endif
```

Listing 11-12
CTRLBARS.RC

```
//Microsoft Visual C++ generated resource script.
//
#include "resource.h"

#define APSTUDIO_READONLY_SYMBOLS
/////////////////////////////////////////////////////////////////////////////
//
// Generated from the TEXTINCLUDE 2 resource.
//
```

```
#include "afxres.h"


/////////////////////////////////////////////////////////////////////////////
#undef APSTUDIO_READONLY_SYMBOLS


#ifdef APSTUDIO_INVOKED
/////////////////////////////////////////////////////////////////////////////
//
// TEXTINCLUDE
//

1 TEXTINCLUDE DISCARDABLE
BEGIN
    "resource.h\0"
END

2 TEXTINCLUDE DISCARDABLE
BEGIN
    "#include ""afxres.h""\r\n"
    "\0"
END

3 TEXTINCLUDE DISCARDABLE
BEGIN
    "#include ""res\\ctrlbars.rc2""  // non- Visual C++ edited resources\r\n"
    "\r\n"
    "#define _AFX_NO_SPLITTER_RESOURCES\r\n"
    "#define _AFX_NO_OLE_RESOURCES\r\n"
    "#define _AFX_NO_TRACKER_RESOURCES\r\n"
    "#define _AFX_NO_PROPERTY_RESOURCES\r\n"
    "#include ""afxres.rc""  \011// Standard components\r\n"
    "\0"
END


/////////////////////////////////////////////////////////////////////////////
#endif    // APSTUDIO_INVOKED


/////////////////////////////////////////////////////////////////////////////
//
// Icon
//

IDR_MAINFRAME           ICON    DISCARDABLE     "res\\ctrlbars.ico"


/////////////////////////////////////////////////////////////////////////////
//
// Bitmap
//

IDR_TOOLS               BITMAP  MOVEABLE PURE   "res\\toolbar.bmp"
IDR_MAINFRAME           BITMAP  DISCARDABLE     "res\\bitmap1.bmp"


/////////////////////////////////////////////////////////////////////////////
//
```

```
// Menu
//

IDR_MAINFRAME MENU PRELOAD DISCARDABLE
BEGIN
    POPUP "&File"
    BEGIN
        MENUITEM "&New\tCtrl+N",              ID_FILE_NEW
        MENUITEM "&Open...\tCtrl+O",          ID_FILE_OPEN
        MENUITEM "&Save\tCtrl+S",             ID_FILE_SAVE
        MENUITEM SEPARATOR
        MENUITEM "&Print...",                 ID_FILE_PRINT
        MENUITEM SEPARATOR
        MENUITEM "E&xit",                     ID_APP_EXIT
    END
    POPUP "&Edit"
    BEGIN
        MENUITEM "&Undo\tCtrl+Z",             ID_EDIT_UNDO
        MENUITEM SEPARATOR
        MENUITEM "Cu&t\tCtrl+X",              ID_EDIT_CUT
        MENUITEM "&Copy\tCtrl+C",             ID_EDIT_COPY
        MENUITEM "&Paste\tCtrl+V",            ID_EDIT_PASTE
    END
    POPUP "&Toolbar"
    BEGIN
        MENUITEM "&Create",                   ID_TOOLBAR_CREATE
        MENUITEM "&Show",                     ID_TOOLBAR_SHOW
    END
    POPUP "&View"
    BEGIN
        MENUITEM "&Toolbar",                  ID_VIEW_TOOLBAR
        MENUITEM "&Status Bar",               ID_VIEW_STATUS_BAR
    END
    POPUP "&Help"
    BEGIN
        MENUITEM "&About ctrlbars...",        ID_APP_ABOUT
    END
END


/////////////////////////////////////////////////////////////////////////
//
// Accelerator
//

IDR_MAINFRAME ACCELERATORS PRELOAD MOVEABLE PURE
BEGIN
    "C",            ID_EDIT_COPY,         VIRTKEY, CONTROL, NOINVERT
    "N",            ID_FILE_NEW,          VIRTKEY, CONTROL, NOINVERT
    "O",            ID_FILE_OPEN,         VIRTKEY, CONTROL, NOINVERT
    "S",            ID_FILE_SAVE,         VIRTKEY, CONTROL, NOINVERT
    "V",            ID_EDIT_PASTE,        VIRTKEY, CONTROL, NOINVERT
    VK_BACK,        ID_EDIT_UNDO,         VIRTKEY, ALT, NOINVERT
    VK_DELETE,      ID_EDIT_CUT,          VIRTKEY, SHIFT, NOINVERT
```

```
    VK_INSERT,        ID_EDIT_COPY,        VIRTKEY, CONTROL, NOINVERT
    VK_INSERT,        ID_EDIT_PASTE,       VIRTKEY, SHIFT, NOINVERT
    "X",              ID_EDIT_CUT,         VIRTKEY, CONTROL, NOINVERT
    "Z",              ID_EDIT_UNDO,        VIRTKEY, CONTROL, NOINVERT
END


/////////////////////////////////////////////////////////////////////////
//
// Dialog
//

IDD_ABOUTBOX DIALOG DISCARDABLE  34, 22, 217, 55
STYLE DS_MODALFRAME | WS_POPUP | WS_CAPTION | WS_SYSMENU
CAPTION "About ctrlbars"
FONT 8, "MS Sans Serif"
BEGIN
    ICON            IDR_MAINFRAME,IDC_STATIC,11,17,20,20
    LTEXT           "ctrlbars Version 1.0",IDC_STATIC,40,10,119,8
    LTEXT           "Copyright \251 1995",IDC_STATIC,40,25,119,8
    DEFPUSHBUTTON   "OK",IDOK,176,6,32,14,WS_GROUP
END


/////////////////////////////////////////////////////////////////////////
//
// Version
//

VS_VERSION_INFO VERSIONINFO
 FILEVERSION 1,0,0,1
 PRODUCTVERSION 1,0,0,1
 FILEFLAGSMASK 0x3fL
#ifdef _DEBUG
 FILEFLAGS 0x1L
#else
 FILEFLAGS 0x0L
#endif
 FILEOS 0x4L
 FILETYPE 0x1L
 FILESUBTYPE 0x0L
BEGIN
    BLOCK "StringFileInfo"
    BEGIN
        BLOCK "040904B0"
        BEGIN
            VALUE "CompanyName", "\0"
            VALUE "FileDescription", "CTRLBARS MFC Application\0"
            VALUE "FileVersion", "1, 0, 0, 1\0"
            VALUE "InternalName", "CTRLBARS\0"
            VALUE "LegalCopyright", "Copyright \251 1995\0"
            VALUE "LegalTrademarks", "\0"
            VALUE "OriginalFilename", "CTRLBARS.EXE\0"
            VALUE "ProductName", "CTRLBARS Application\0"
```

```
                    VALUE "ProductVersion", "1, 0, 0, 1\0"
            END
    END
    BLOCK "VarFileInfo"
    BEGIN
        VALUE "Translation", 0x409, 1200
    END
END


/////////////////////////////////////////////////////////////////////////////
//
// String Table
//

STRINGTABLE PRELOAD DISCARDABLE
BEGIN
    IDR_MAINFRAME           "Control Bars"
END

STRINGTABLE PRELOAD DISCARDABLE
BEGIN
    AFX_IDS_APP_TITLE       "Control Bars"
    AFX_IDS_IDLEMESSAGE     "Ready"
END

STRINGTABLE DISCARDABLE
BEGIN
    ID_INDICATOR_EXT        "EXT"
    ID_INDICATOR_CAPS       "CAP"
    ID_INDICATOR_NUM        "NUM"
    ID_INDICATOR_SCRL       "SCRL"
    ID_INDICATOR_OVR        "OVR"
    ID_INDICATOR_REC        "REC"
END

STRINGTABLE DISCARDABLE
BEGIN
    ID_FILE_NEW             "Create a new document\nNew"
    ID_FILE_OPEN            "Open an existing document\nOpen"
    ID_FILE_CLOSE           "Close active document\nClose"
    ID_FILE_SAVE            "Save active document\nSave"
    ID_FILE_SAVE_AS         "Save active document with new name\nSave As"
    ID_FILE_PRINT           "Prints a file\nPrint"
END

STRINGTABLE DISCARDABLE
BEGIN
    ID_APP_ABOUT        "Display program information, version & copyright\nAbout"
    ID_APP_EXIT          "Quit application; prompt to save documents\nExit"
END

STRINGTABLE DISCARDABLE
```

```
BEGIN
    ID_FILE_MRU_FILE1          "Open this document"
    ID_FILE_MRU_FILE2          "Open this document"
    ID_FILE_MRU_FILE3          "Open this document"
    ID_FILE_MRU_FILE4          "Open this document"
END

STRINGTABLE DISCARDABLE
BEGIN
    ID_NEXT_PANE               "Switch to next window pane\nNext Pane"
    ID_PREV_PANE               "Switch to previous window pane\nPrevious Pane"
END

STRINGTABLE DISCARDABLE
BEGIN
    ID_WINDOW_SPLIT            "Split the active window into panes\nSplit"
END

STRINGTABLE DISCARDABLE
BEGIN
    ID_EDIT_CLEAR          "Erase the selection\nErase"
    ID_EDIT_CLEAR_ALL      "Erase everything\nErase All"
    ID_EDIT_COPY           "Copy selection to Clipboard\nCopy"
    ID_EDIT_CUT            "Cut the selection to Clipboard\nCut"
    ID_EDIT_FIND           "Find the specified text\nFind"
    ID_EDIT_PASTE          "Insert Clipboard contents\nPaste"
    ID_EDIT_REPEAT         "Repeat the last action\nRepeat"
    ID_EDIT_REPLACE        "Replace specific text with different text\nReplace"
    ID_EDIT_SELECT_ALL     "Select the entire document\nSelect All"
    ID_EDIT_UNDO           "Undo the last action\nUndo"
    ID_EDIT_REDO           "Redo the previously undone action\nRedo"
END

STRINGTABLE DISCARDABLE
BEGIN
    ID_VIEW_TOOLBAR            "Show or hide the toolbar\nToggle ToolBar"
    ID_VIEW_STATUS_BAR         "Show or hide the status bar\nToggle StatusBar"
END

STRINGTABLE DISCARDABLE
BEGIN
    AFX_IDS_SCSIZE             "Change the window size"
    AFX_IDS_SCMOVE             "Change the window position"
    AFX_IDS_SCMINIMIZE         "Reduce the window to an icon"
    AFX_IDS_SCMAXIMIZE         "Enlarge the window to full size"
    AFX_IDS_SCNEXTWINDOW       "Switch to the next document window"
    AFX_IDS_SCPREVWINDOW       "Switch to the previous document window"
    AFX_IDS_SCCLOSE            "Close active window & prompt to save documents"
END

STRINGTABLE DISCARDABLE
BEGIN
    AFX_IDS_SCRESTORE          "Restore the window to normal size"
    AFX_IDS_SCTASKLIST         "Activate Task List"
```

```
    END

    STRINGTABLE DISCARDABLE
    BEGIN
        ID_TOOLBAR_CREATE        "Creates a dynamic toolbar\nCreate Toolbar"
        ID_TOOLBAR_SHOW          "Show or hide dynamic toolbar\nHide/Show Toolbar"
    END


    #ifndef APSTUDIO_INVOKED
    /////////////////////////////////////////////////////////////////////////////
    //
    // Generated from the TEXTINCLUDE 3 resource.
    //
    #include "res\ctrlbars.rc2"  // non-Microsoft Visual C++ edited resources

    #define _AFX_NO_SPLITTER_RESOURCES
    #define _AFX_NO_OLE_RESOURCES
    #define _AFX_NO_TRACKER_RESOURCES
    #define _AFX_NO_PROPERTY_RESOURCES
    #include "afxres.rc"         // Standard components


    /////////////////////////////////////////////////////////////////////////////
    #endif     // not APSTUDIO_INVOKED
```

Summary

In this chapter, we've described three mechanisms for getting command input from the user: menus, accelerator tables, and toolbars. All three send the same message — WM_COMMAND — to notify your program of a command. All three also send a CN_UPDATE_COMMAND_UI message to ask whether a particular command is enabled or whether menu and toolbar items should be checked. As you've seen, most of the work in using these command input mechanisms is in setting them up.

In the next chapter, we're going to explore a third type of user-interface object: dialog boxes. The most common way to summon a dialog is by a menu command. In other words, dialogs can be thought of as a refinement to command input. For example, if a user selects a File|Open... command, a dialog box is needed to let the user select a particular file. Let's take a look, then, at Windows' third-most important user-interface object: the dialog box.

12 Dialog Boxes

*D*ialog boxes are the most intricate user-interface objects that you'll use in your Windows programs. Although a dialog box is simply a collection of windows, each type has its own quirks and eccentricities. With seven different types of windows, you have to deal with a lot of quirks. Because of the important role that dialogs play in Windows applications, you'll want to make sure that someone on your development team has mastered the subtle nuances of every type.

In this chapter, we'll cover the basics of using dialog boxes in an MFC application. We'll start with some background information that will help you become familiar with both the new terms you'll use and some of the choices you'll make when working with dialogs. Then, we'll cover the steps for building a dialog box. We'll conclude the chapter with a sample program, DIALOGS, which demonstrates five different types of dialog boxes.

Dialog Box Fundamentals

For some reason, dialogs have their own vocabulary, which might make it seem that they are radically different from other types of windows. Although the seven types of windows you use to build dialogs are each distinct types, they are still windows. Despite the unique behavior of each type, you'll get farther in your dialog box development if you remember one simple fact: *dialogs and dialog controls are windows*. To help get you started, the following sections define some basic terms that you'll encounter when dealing with dialog boxes.

WHAT IS A DIALOG BOX?

To a user, dialog boxes (or just plain dialogs) are the user-interface equivalent of printed forms. Although few users enjoy spending time staring at forms — for example, college applications, tax forms, product registration cards — forms do provide a standard means for handling information. In the same way, dialog boxes provide a somewhat humdrum, but very standard way for users to handle program data.

Because most dialogs are displayed in response to a menu selection, dialogs can be considered an extension to menu commands. After all, some commands are not complete by themselves. For example, consider a user request such as, "Computer, please open a file for me." A dialog box provides a standard way for a program to ask exactly *which* file the user wants to open. In effect, the dialog allows the computer to reply, "Certainly, user. Please fill out this form in triplicate, sign your name, and click the A-OK button."

But it's a little unfair to shove a dialog box at a user with no warning. For this reason, it has become common practice to notify the user that a particular menu selection will cause a dialog to appear. In particular, menu item names that end with an ellipsis (...) promise to provide dialogs when selected. Perhaps more importantly, menu items *without* an ellipsis promise not to bother the user with a dialog.

A programmer's perspective

From a programming perspective, the most important point to remember is that dialogs and dialog controls are windows. That is, a dialog box is a window, and each control inside a dialog box — an edit control, a push-button, or a list box, for example — is also a window. Although other environments — for example, the Apple Macintosh — implement controls as something other than windows, that's not the case in Microsoft Windows. The MFC class hierarchy clearly reflects this fact by its placement of all dialogs and all controls as classes derived from CWnd.

In practical terms, this means that anything you can do to a window, you can also do to a dialog box or a dialog box control. For example, in the same way that windows can be moved, resized, shown, hidden, enabled, and disabled, so can dialogs and controls. With its numerous window manipulation member functions, CWnd gives you many ways to fine-tune the operation of your dialogs and dialog controls. In fact, the only drawback is that the sheer number of CWnd member functions sometimes makes it hard to find the one you really want.

Dialog box message traffic

Because dialogs are windows, it's not surprising to find that — like windows — they operate by responding to messages. Where dialogs differ from other types of windows, however, is in the specific types of messages that are of interest. In particular, when dealing with other types of windows, you'll pay attention to a dozen or more types of messages. When working with dialogs, on the other hand, you'll usually be concerned with only two: WM_INITDIALOG and WM_COMMAND.

As its name suggests, the WM_INITDIALOG message tells you that it's time to initialize a dialog box. With other types of windows, you initialize the window in response to a WM_CREATE message. For example, the sample programs in the preceding chapter created toolbars in response to WM_CREATE. But when a dialog gets a WM_CREATE message, it is empty of all controls.

The receipt of a WM_INITDIALOG message tells you two things about a dialog. First, all of the controls have been built and are ready to be initialized. For example, an edit control might be filled with text, and a list box might be filled with strings. Second, you are guaranteed that the dialog itself isn't visible to the user when this message arrives. In other words, you can respond to this message and initialize your controls without fear that the user will see your dialog before you are ready to show it.

The other important message for dialog boxes, WM_COMMAND, is sent by controls to notify the dialog of interesting and useful events. When a control sends this message, it signs its name to the message along with a *notification code*. The notification code is the reason the message was sent. Each type of control has its own set of notification codes. For example, a button sends a BN_CLICKED notification to indicate that it has been clicked with the mouse. Edit controls send an EN_CHANGE code when the user adds or removes the edit control's text.

You might recall from the discussion in the preceding chapter that — just like dialog controls — menus send WM_COMMAND messages. And just like menu items, controls have IDs that allow the recipient to determine which object sent the message. In the unlikely event that you combine menus and controls in a single window (which is, after all, a fairly unusual thing to do), make sure you avoid unintentional overlap of IDs between menu items and dialog controls.

Your handling of the WM_COMMAND messages from dialog controls differs in one important way from your handling of those messages from menu items. A menu item sends a command message only on special occasions — that is, when the user selects a command. You should always respond to these messages. On the other hand, dialog controls send command messages at every possible opportunity. As such, you'll be more selective about how you respond to command messages from dialog controls. In fact, you'll probably ignore most of them.

MFC support for dialogs

When you are creating your own dialog boxes, the most important MFC class is CDialog. As shown in Figure 12-1, this is MFC's most basic dialog box class. When building your own, custom dialog boxes, you'll often derive new classes fromthis base class. Three of the five dialogs in this chapter's sample DIALOGS program define new classes that derive directly from CDialog.

Figure 12-1 also shows two other important MFC classes which are used to build property sheets (or *tabbed dialogs*). A property sheet (CPropertySheet) is a compound dialog box with multiple pages that can each be summoned by clicking a page tab. Individual property pages (CPropertyPage) hold groups of dialog box controls for updating a set of related fields.

Before building dialogs from scratch, you should review the set of prebuilt dialogs. The three classes that we've been discussing are used for building dialogs from scratch. But MFC has 13 other classes that wrap a set of prebuilt dialogs. These classes can give your dialogs lots of capabilities, with little coding required on your part.

MFC has two sets of prebuilt dialog classes. One set — the classes that derive from COleDialog — have specialized uses for building OLE compound document applications. Because we're not covering OLE programming issues in this book, we won't discuss this set of dialogs.

The remaining classes are referred to as *common dialogs*, because they provide functional capabilities that applications commonly need. Table 12-1 provides a summary of the common dialogs. The sample program at the end of this chapter will show how to use one of these classes, CFileDialog, to create a File|Open dialog box. The sample program in Chapter 13, FILELIST, shows how to create a font picker (CFontDialog) dialog.

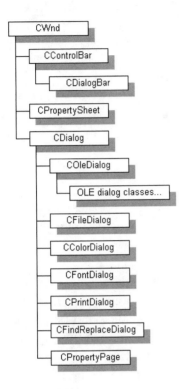

Figure 12-1

This fragment of the MFC class hierarchy shows all of the classes that relate to dialog boxes, including dialog bars and property sheets.

Table 12-1

Common Dialogs

Class	Description
CFileDialog	Two standard file operations, File|Open... and File|Save As..., both of which involve prompting a user for a filename
CColorDialog	Color picker dialog that shows a set of colors from which users can select
CFontDialog	Font picker dialog that shows users a list of available printer and display fonts, along with a sample of each font
CPrintDialog	Two standard print operations, File|Print... and File|Print Setup...
CFindReplaceDialog	Two search dialogs, one for a simple find operation and one for find and replace

A final class that's of interest in the context of dialogs is CDialogBar. If you check the MFC hierarchy, you'll notice that this class derives from CControlBar. Like the CToolBar class we discussed in the preceding chapter, CDialogBar creates a window that hangs on an edge of a frame window to generate commands. Although a toolbar displays only buttons, dialog bars can hold any type of dialog box control. We've waited until this chapter to discuss dialog bars because — even though they behave like toolbars — dialog bars are created and controlled in ways that more closely resemble regular dialog boxes.

WHAT IS A DIALOG BOX CONTROL?

If a dialog box is a form, then dialog box controls (or simply *controls*) are analogous to fields within a form. Windows provides the same flexibility for working with controls that it does for menus. That is, users can select controls using either the mouse or the keyboard. A simple mouse click is all that's needed to wake up a control. From the keyboard, the user can select controls using either the Tab key or an Alt-mnemonic-key combination.

Each type of control has a unique appearance and behavior, which you'll want to understand in order to provide the support that users expect from Windows applications. Each control knows how to make itself appear in the expected way, but producing the expected behavior requires some effort on your part. If you are not familiar with the standard behavior of controls, you should study the dialogs in the small applications that ship with Microsoft Windows. For details on user-interface standards for dialog box controls, you can refer to Chapter 7 of the *Windows 95 User Interface Design Guide*.

A programmer's perspective

From a programming perspective, controls — like dialogs — are windows. As we mentioned for dialogs, this means that you can manipulate controls using member functions of MFC's CWnd class. For example, to move, hide, show, enable, or disable a dialog box control, you call any of several CWnd member functions. Table 12-2 lists the CWnd member functions you'll typically call when working with controls.

Table 12-2

CWnd Member Functions Used with Dialog Box Controls

Function	Description
EnableWindow()	Toggle input to a control. Most controls respond by changing to a gray, mottled color to let users know they aren't available. This is particularly useful for pushbuttons and edit controls.
GetWindowText()	Query the text of any type of control except a list box.
GetWindowTextLength()	Query the length of text of any type of control except a list box.
MoveWindow()	Move any control to a new location.
SetFont()	Change the font used in a control.
ShowWindow()	Make a control visible or invisible.
SetWindowPos()	Move any control to a new location while also changing the Z-order, which changes the tab order. The tab order is the sequence in which controls are navigated when the user presses the Tab key.
SetWindowText()	Change the text of any type of control except a list box.

Perhaps the most important aspect of a control is that it behaves like a black box. In other words, it does its work and you don't have to worry about how it does it. For example, edit controls, which are used to edit text strings, just "know" how to do the right thing. When a user types, an edit control captures characters while displaying them in its window. When a user selects text with mouse input, an edit control grabs the mouse input and magically makes the correct letters appear selected. Controls are dependable, reliable, and independent little worker bees.

Although a control is self-sufficient, it doesn't do its job quietly. Instead, it sends a stream of reports to its parent window. The parent window, which is usually a dialog box, can ignore or use these reports as it sees fit. These reports are called *control notifications*, and they arrive as WM_COMMAND messages.

For example, buttons have two types of notifications: single mouse clicks and double mouse clicks. In most cases, a single-click is all that's needed for you to know that a button, such as an OK pushbutton, has been clicked and that it's time for a dialog to be dismissed. You can safely ignore the double-click notification if it's not of interest to you.

Each type of control has its own set of notification codes. The symbolic names for notification codes have a unique prefix for each class. For example, button notifications start with BN_. A single-click button notification is a BN_CLICKED notification code. When you're building your own, custom dialog boxes, the MFC ClassWizard helps you connect the available notification codes to the message map of a particular dialog box.

Available controls

Microsoft Windows has built-in support for six different types of dialog box controls: button, combo box, edit, list box, scroll bar, and static. Table 12-3 summarizes the available controls and the corresponding MFC classes.

Table 12-3

Microsoft Windows Dialog Box Controls and the Associated MFC Control Classes

Type of Control	MFC Class	Description
button	CButton and CBitmapButton	Three distinct type of buttons are supported: pushbuttons, check boxes, radio buttons. MFC adds support for a bitmap button, which displays a graphical image instead of a text label.
combo box	CComboBox	Combines two other types of controls: an edit control and a list box control. It's also available as a static control with a list box control.
edit	CEdit	A text entry field. You can have single- or multiline edit controls.
list box	CListBox	Displays a list of items. The default item type is a string, but owner-draw list boxes let you draw the contents for individual list box items.
scroll bar	CScrollBar	Two types are supported: vertical and horizontal. Provides a visual means for displaying and manipulating three numbers: a minimum, a maximum, and a current value.
static	CStatic	An output-only control, which can display a static text string, the outline of a rectangle, a filled rectangle, or an icon image.

One way that dialog boxes are distinct from other types of windows is that dialogs contain dialog box controls. Another difference involves the way in which applications choose to deploy dialog boxes, which brings up the subject of dialog box *modality*. To clarify what is meant by this term, let's take a moment to talk about the differences between modal and modeless dialog boxes.

MODAL DIALOG BOXES AND MODELESS DIALOG BOXES

When you create a dialog box, you have to decide whether to make it modal or modeless. At the programming level, this means choosing between two sets of functions for both creating and destroying dialogs. At the user level, the modality of a dialog box affects which other actions can be carried out in the application when the dialog box is visible.

A mode is an abstract term that refers to different states. People often refer to themselves as being in work mode, rest mode, or vacation mode. Few things are more upsetting than receiving a telephone call from a coworker who is in crisis mode when you're in rest mode or vacation mode. For some reason, such phone calls force you to revise *your* mode when perhaps the opposite — chill out mode — would be more appropriate for your colleague.

In the context of dialog boxes, the terms *modal* and *modeless* are somewhat misleading because a dialog always has a mode. What is usually called a *modal dialog box* is actually a dialog box in *exclusive mode*. And a *modeless dialog box* refers to a dialog box in *nonexclusive mode*. Let's take a closer look at each mode.

A modal dialog box operates in exclusive mode. Although a user can *see* an application's other user-interface objects — its main window, its menus, or its toolbars — when a modal dialog box is displayed, the user cannot *communicate* with those other objects. When it goes into its exclusive mode, a modal dialog box disables the other user-interface objects. For example, if a user attempts to interact with a menu, the only response from the system is a punitive "Beep." This reminds the user that the modal dialog has control of the application until the user dismisses the dialog.

For the sake of completeness, it's worth mentioning that there are two exclusive modes: application modal and system modal. When an application modal dialog is present, the user can still interact with other applications and is only prevented from working with other parts of the same application. When a system modal dialog box is present, the user is forced to respond to that dialog box, because everything else in the entire system is disabled. Although you need to know about both modes, you'll almost always create application modal dialog boxes. The exclusive nature of Windows' system modal dialog boxes is so thorough that it halts multitasking — something that rarely makes sense to do.

A modeless dialog box operates in nonexclusive mode. When such a dialog box is present, the user is free to interact with other user-interface objects. Menu items can be selected, and the main window can be resized, minimized to an icon, or even closed. In fact, except for the presence of dialog box controls, a modeless dialog box operates like any other window in an application.

From these descriptions, you might have the impression that modeless dialogs are somehow friendlier and more useful, and are therefore used more often than the less friendly, modal dialogs. In fact, just the opposite is true. Almost every dialog box that you encounter is modal.

Modal dialog boxes are more common because of the way dialog boxes are used. As a kind of extension to the menuing system, dialogs provide the data that applications need to complete a command. With modal dialogs, the rest of an application's user interface is put on hold until the user decides whether to go ahead with the command (by entering data into controls and clicking OK) or withdraw the request for the command (by clicking Cancel or pressing the Esc key).

Even though they are rare, modeless dialog boxes have their uses. One common example occurs in text search dialogs, which can continue a search after letting the user edit the text that's been found. Dialog bars provide another example. Although the dialog bar (CDialogBar) class is not — technically speaking — a dialog box (because it doesn't derive from CDialog), it can be thought of as a modeless dialog box.

Despite their differences, you create modal and modeless dialog boxes using the same basic steps. In the following section, we'll describe the five steps involved in creating any type of dialog box. We'll also point out the few differences that do exist in the process of creating modal and modeless dialogs.

Creating Dialog Boxes

In the not-too-distant past, programmers used graph paper to design dialog boxes, and then created them by entering text descriptions. Today, tools such as the Visual C++ dialog editor help you draw the dialog you want to create. Visual C++ has another helper, the ClassWizard, which plays several roles. Just as it does for other types of windows, ClassWizard edits the message map for a dialog box. To simplify the process of working with individual dialog box controls, it also helps you define dialog member variables.

Building a dialog box is a five-step process. First, you create a dialog box template. This is a blueprint that identifies which controls are to be included in the dialog and where each control should be placed. Next, you create a CDialog-derived class to handle all the message traffic for your dialog. This is an easy step because ClassWizard — the tool we use for editing message maps — will write the code for you.

With these two basic steps complete, the remaining three steps involve writing some code. In the third step, you write code that creates the dialog box, which usually happens in response to the selection of a menu item. At this point, you'll have a working (but empty) dialog, which will help you test and fine-tune the code you write during the last two steps in this process.

The fourth step is to add code to your CDialog-derived class to handle dialog box initialization. This means responding to the WM_INITDIALOG message by setting all the controls to their initial state. The last step is to write the code that responds to notification messages sent by controls. As you add the initialization code for each control, you'll want to stop and test the results to make sure they are what you expect.

To summarize, the dialog creation process involves five steps:

1. Creating a dialog template.
2. Creating a CDialog-derived class.
3. Creating the dialog box itself.
4. Adding message handling to initialize your dialog.
5. Adding handling for control notifications.

We should point out that the dialog development process is iterative. In other words, while you're working on the first few steps, you don't have to get everything perfect. If you subsequently find a better way to do something, you can always return to an earlier step, usually with minimal difficulty. Let's take a close look at each of the five steps in the process of creating a dialog box.

STEP 1: CREATING A DIALOG TEMPLATE

A dialog template describes the type and location of each control in a dialog box. Dialog templates are needed to create both modal and modeless dialog boxes. Dialog templates are stored inside dialog resources, in the same way that menu definitions are stored in menu resources. As shown in Figure 12-2, the Visual C++ tools include a dialog editor, which lets you define the contents of a dialog simply by drawing it.

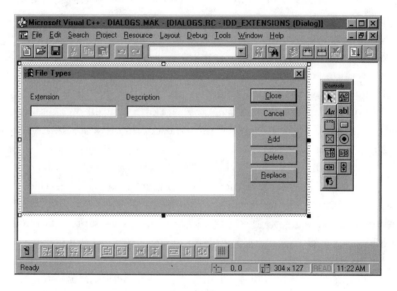

Figure 12-2
The dialog editor lets you define the contents of a dialog box by drawing the desired controls.

When your application creates a dialog box, it passes an identifier for the dialog resource to MFC, which in turn passes the ID to a Windows API function. This function reads the dialog template and creates a dialog frame and all of the desired controls. Although you could create a dialog on the fly, defining the dialog ahead of time in a dialog resource is much simpler. As you'll soon see, the dialog creation code is smart enough to resize every element of a dialog based on the display resolution. To create a dialog at runtime without the help of a dialog resource, you'd have to do a lot of work to make sure that the dialog has the same proportions on different display screens.

Let's take a closer look at what's involved in using the dialog editor. As you begin to experiment with this tool, you'll find that the dialog editor has a lot in common with the menu editor. In particular, you make extensive use of property sheets to change the attributes of individual controls and of the dialog box itself.

Creating a new dialog

To create a new dialog, you first open the resource script (.RC) file from the Visual C++ project window. Once the .RC file is open, either select the Resource|New... menu option, or click the Dialog resource item using your right mouse button, and select New Dialog from the pop-up menu that's displayed. To help you get started, the dialog editor creates a dialog with an OK button and a Cancel button.

To build on this starter dialog, you create new controls by clicking and dragging items from the Controls palette. The Controls palette has 11 buttons corresponding to the different types of controls. If you're not sure whether you're picking the right button, pause the mouse cursor over a button and wait for the tool tip text window to appear, telling you the purpose of that particular button.

Setting control properties

After adding a control to a dialog, you can set its properties by summoning a property sheet. You do this in much the same way that you summon a menu item property sheet — that is, you simply double-click the control. As shown in Figure 12-3, a property sheet contains a thumbtack icon, which lets you keep the property sheet around, and a help icon, which lets you access details about the meaning of different property sheet fields.

Figure 12-3

Double-clicking a control displays a property sheet — such as this one for pushbuttons — which lets you set a control's attributes.

The two most important control attributes are the control ID and the control caption. The dialog editor suggests a symbolic name for a control ID (such as IDC_BUTTON1), but you'll probably want to change this name to one that makes sense to you. You'll need to refer to the name in your program when you want to access that particular control.

Be careful when choosing a control caption, because the caption is the label that actually appears on the dialog. Like menu items, your control captions can display mnemonics that support keyboard navigation. To define a mnemonic, insert an ampersand (&) immediately before the character that is to be underlined in the caption. If you define a mnemonic for a control, a user can move to that control by pressing the Alt key in combination with the mnemonic key.

You need to consider a few issues when creating mnemonics for dialog controls. First, the OK and Cancel buttons already have keyboard equivalents (Enter and Esc), so don't add mnemonics for them. Also, captions aren't displayed for certain controls, such as list boxes, combo boxes, and scroll bars. To enable a mnemonic for one of these controls, you need to create a static text control with the desired mnemonic. Then, you need to associate the static control with the captionless control. When you set the tab order for the dialog (a topic we'll cover in the next section of this chapter), be sure to position the static text control *before* the captionless control.

In addition to the control ID and the caption, you may need to set various style fields. As you might recall from our discussion of window creation in Chapter 10, every window has a style field — that is, a flag field that determines the operating behavior of the window. Some styles, such as WS_CAPTION for a title bar and WS_VISIBLE for visibility, are generic for all types of windows. But window-specific styles are also available. For example, check boxes and radio buttons have a BS_LEFTTEXT style for putting the text on the left side of the button instead of the right side.

In the dialog editor, style fields are typically represented using a check box. Because these are specific to the different types of controls, you'll have to learn about them through experimentation and by reviewing the help database.

Four styles are common to every type of dialog control: visible, disabled, group, and tabstop. As the name suggests, the visible style flag indicates whether a control is initially visible. [At runtime, you can change visibility by calling CWnd::ShowWindow( ).]

The disabled style flag indicates whether a window can receive mouse and keyboard input from the user. When a control becomes disabled, it changes its appearance by graying itself to let the user know that it isn't a selection choice. [Once again, a function exists that lets you control this attribute at runtime: CWnd::EnableWindow( ).]

The other two common styles, group and tabstop, affect keyboard navigation between controls. The group style marks boundaries between groups of controls that can be navigated using arrow keys. Although you can set this style for any type of control, you'll only see its effect on buttons (pushbuttons, check boxes, and radio buttons). The most common type of button for grouping is radio buttons, because the Windows user-interface standard dictates that one and only one radio button in a group can be checked at any moment in time. Creating a group of radio buttons is helpful for users who prefer to cycle through a group of radio buttons using the arrow keys on the keyboard. It's particularly helpful when two sets of radio buttons are placed next to each other, and the group style at the start of each set marks the boundary between groups. To make sure that the groups behave in the way you expect, be sure to set the control tab order. And because the group style setting has no visual indicators, you'll need to create your own, perhaps using a static frame and static text.

The other style that affects keyboard navigation is the tabstop style. Setting this flag makes a control into a kind of bus stop for the user who is riding through your dialog using the Tab key like a city bus. To create the route map that the Tab key is to follow, you have to set the tab order. Otherwise, the default tab order is the order in which you create controls. Given the piecemeal manner in which dialogs are typically created, this can create quite a wild ride for the user who enjoys tabbing around your dialog.

Setting tab order

By setting the tab order, you can synchronize the visual layout of a dialog with the keyboard navigation order. The tab order is a nonissue for users who rely solely on the mouse to move around a dialog. But some users are mouse-phobic, and others have to work in environments that are hostile to mice (like the trading firm of one brokerage house we've heard about). Whatever the reason, you need to plan for keyboard-based navigation of your dialog boxes.

The default tab order is the order in which you create controls. So, if you carefully design your dialogs on paper and then create them in the order in which you expect tabbing to occur, you won't need to explicitly set the tab order. However, we suspect that most developers are neither that meticulous, nor even so lucky as to work on such stable, unchanging systems. The act of inserting even one new control into a dialog can force you to change the entire ordering of your dialog.

Fortunately, setting the tab order is easy. To see the current tab order, select the Layout|Tab Order menu item, or its associated accelerator key (Ctrl-D). The dialog editor tags each control with a number corresponding to its position in the current tab order. If you like the current ordering, you can cancel the command by clicking outside the dialog. Otherwise, you have to define the tab ordering for the entire dialog from start to finish. You do this by clicking the controls in the order you want the tabbing to be performed. (By the way, if you have very large dialogs and need a faster way to set the tab order, you can edit the resource script text file. The tab order corresponds to the order in which controls are listed in the dialog template.)

Setting dialog properties

In the same way that individual controls have property sheets, the dialog frame has its own property sheet. To access this property sheet, which is shown in Figure 12-4, simply double-click anywhere on the dialog box itself but outside the bounds of individual controls. The two property pages — General and Styles — let you fine-tune the dialog's operation.

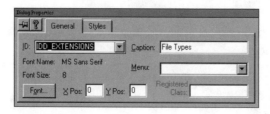

Figure 12-4

Set dialog properties, such as the dialog caption and the dialog style values, using the dialog property sheet.

Like controls, you can set a dialog's ID and its caption. You do this on the General property page. The dialog ID is actually the identifier for the entire dialog template. Although you need to use this identifier in your dialog creation code, the ClassWizard generates this code for you.

You use the Caption property to define the text you'd like to see displayed in the title bar of the dialog window. According to the *Windows 95 User Interface Design Guide*, a dialog's title should be the same as the command name that is used to summon the dialog. For example, if a dialog is displayed in response to the File | Open menu item, you should use the word *Open* as the dialog caption. To be consistent with other Windows applications, don't use *File Open* or even *Open....*

The dialog property sheet also lets you modify the font that is to be used in each dialog control. The default font is an 8-point font called MS Sans Serif, but you can easily create a huge dialog using 24-point Times New Roman, or a tiny dialog with 4-point Small Fonts, such as the examples we created in Figure 12-5.

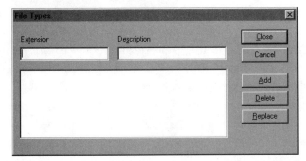

Figure 12-5
A dialog in two sizes: the larger one uses the default font, and the smaller one uses a font called 4-point Small Fonts.

You'll probably use the default font for most dialogs you create. We introduced the font changing example to help clarify how dialogs can work with different display adapters of differing resolutions. This is accomplished by the use of dialog box units in a dialog definition.

Dialog box units

The elements of a dialog box in a dialog box template are laid out using a special coordinate system known as *dialog box units*. As demonstrated in the preceding example, dialog box units scale with the dialog's font. Larger fonts translate into larger units, and smaller fonts translate into smaller units. The overall proportions of the dialog itself, however, stay the same.

We bring up the subject of dialog box units because the dialog editor displays coordinates in its status bar for the location and the size of the currently selected object. Both sets of coordinates are in dialog box units. Also, among the properties for a dialog are its initial (x,y) location. Once again, those coordinates are in dialog box units. Don't expect to see those coordinates except when you're working with dialogs.

There's another practical reason for mentioning dialog box units. Although the use of dialog box units does help dialogs to scale evenly between different screen resolutions, snags sometimes occur. You still need to test your dialogs at different resolutions. By testing at low resolutions, you can make sure the dialog doesn't suddenly grow too large for the screen. Testing at medium resolutions lets you check for boundary conditions and rounding errors. And testing at high resolutions lets you make sure that the location and size of your dialog are acceptable.

To help you understand the basic approach taken, here's how dialog box units are defined. One unit in the x-direction is equal to one-fourth of the average width of the letters in the font. One unit in the y-direction is equal to one-eighth of the font height.

You might sometimes need to convert between dialog units and device units. For example, you might want to draw something inside a dialog box or create a window on the fly between two resource-defined controls. The simple way to do this is by calling CDialog::MapDialogRect( ). This function converts a set of dialog box coordinates to the device units that are usually used to create and move windows.

Although we've gone into a lot of detail describing how to use the dialog editor, you'll probably find dialog templates easy to create. Don't forget, you can always return to this step if you want to fine-tune the appearance of your dialog. Once your dialog looks more or less the way you want it to, you're ready to move on to the next step: defining a CDialog-derived class to support your dialog.

STEP 2: CREATING A DIALOG CLASS

Like other resources, a dialog box template is little more than a data structure. To bring it to life, you need some code. For simple dialogs, the MFC CDialog class can handle all of the basics. All you need to do is create an instance of CDialog, pass the dialog template ID, and let CDialog handle the rest. Our sample DIALOGS program has an About... dialog box that shows how this is done.

To support a dialog that has anything more than an OK button and a Cancel button, however, you need to define a new dialog class. By doing so, you can provide custom initialization as well as custom handling of dialog control notifications. By using MFC's dialog data exchange (DDX) facility, you can also simplify the movement of data from your program to the dialog, and back again when the dialog disappears.

Assembling a dialog box class involves numerous details, which can make it a bit of a bother. Fortunately, one of the Visual C++ tools, Class-Wizard, simplifies the creation of a CDialog-derived class in several ways. First, ClassWizard can generate code for a basic CDialog-derived class, with only one or two mouse clicks on your part. It can also create and edit message maps for dialog boxes, just as it does for frame windows. Finally, ClassWizard helps you define member variables for your dialog class. In particular, it can generate member variables that connect to the different controls within a dialog box. As a result, you can set up the major part of the class framework with just a couple of mouse clicks!

Creating class code with ClassWizard

In less time than it will probably take you to read this paragraph, Class-Wizard can create the basic code for a dialog class. After you summon ClassWizard (by pressing Ctrl-W or selecting Project|ClassWizard), click the Add Class... button. As shown in Figure 12-6, ClassWizard displays the Add Class dialog. If you start ClassWizard from within the dialog editor, this dialog is automatically summoned for you.

Although five fields must be completed in the Add Class dialog, ClassWizard does its best to suggest the proper values for each field. The Class Name field is the only one you really have to create, because ClassWizard uses this name to create an include (.H) filename and a C++ source (.CPP) filename. For the Class Type field, you'll select CDialog, perhaps after scrolling through the other class types you can create. Finally, after making sure that the Dialog field has the name of your dialog resource, you click the Create Class button. ClassWizard generates your code upon exit from this dialog.

Figure 12-6
ClassWizard's Add Class dialog helps you define a new MFC dialog class.

The include file

The example in Listing 12-1 is an include file that ClassWizard generated for a CDialog-derived class named SomeDialog. It contains all of the basic elements needed for a C++ class declaration, as well as some of MFC's favorite elements. ClassWizard created some peculiar looking, commented macro lines that begin with //{{AFX_xxx. These are signposts that will later help ClassWizard find key parts of the include file.

Although you'll never have to modify these commented macro blocks by hand, it's helpful to know what they do. The AFX_VIRTUAL macros, which you've seen before, mark overridden virtual functions. Another familiar macro, AFX_MSG, marks the boundaries of message-handling functions. The set of macros that we haven't seen previously in this book is AFX_DATA. As we'll discuss in greater detail later in this chapter, these macros create the declarations for MFC's dialog data exchange, which is a fairly automatic mechanism for moving data into and out of a dialog box.

Listing 12-1

The ClassWizard-Generated Include File for the SomeDialog Class

```
// somedial.h : header file
//


/////////////////////////////////////////////////////////////////
// SomeDialog dialog

class SomeDialog : public CDialog
{
// Construction
public:
    SomeDialog(CWnd* pParent = NULL);    // standard constructor

// Dialog Data
    //{{AFX_DATA(SomeDialog)
    enum { IDD = IDD_DIALOG5 };
        // NOTE: the ClassWizard will add data members here
    //}}AFX_DATA


// Overrides
    // ClassWizard generated virtual function overrides
    //{{AFX_VIRTUAL(SomeDialog)
    protected:
    virtual void DoDataExchange(CDataExchange* pDX);//DDX/DDV support
     //}}AFX_VIRTUAL

// Implementation
protected:

    // Generated message map functions
    //{{AFX_MSG(SomeDialog)
        // NOTE: the ClassWizard will add member functions here
    //}}AFX_MSG
    DECLARE_MESSAGE_MAP()
};
```

The C++ source file

Listing 12-2 shows the C++ source code that ClassWizard generates for the CDialog-derived class. This class definition has a familiar MFC feature: a message map for handling messages that are sent to the dialog. But the class definition also includes something that we haven't discussed previously: two functions that are empty except for some of ClassWizard's commented out marker macros. Like the new macro in the include file, these macros are part of MFC's support for dialog data exchange. We'll explore that topic in detail when we discuss communicating with a control.

Listing 12-2

The ClassWizard-Generated C++ Source File for the SomeDialog Class

```cpp
// somedial.cpp : implementation file
//

#include "stdafx.h"
#include "AnApp.h"
#include "somedial.h"

#ifdef _DEBUG
#undef THIS_FILE
static char BASED_CODE THIS_FILE[] = __FILE__;
#endif


/////////////////////////////////////////////////////////////////////////
// SomeDialog dialog


SomeDialog::SomeDialog(CWnd* pParent /*=NULL*/)
        : CDialog(SomeDialog::IDD, pParent)
{
   //{{AFX_DATA_INIT(SomeDialog)
      // NOTE: the ClassWizard will add member initialization here
   //}}AFX_DATA_INIT
}


void SomeDialog::DoDataExchange(CDataExchange* pDX)
{
   CDialog::DoDataExchange(pDX);
   //{{AFX_DATA_MAP(SomeDialog)
      // NOTE: the ClassWizard will add DDX and DDV calls here
   //}}AFX_DATA_MAP
}


BEGIN_MESSAGE_MAP(SomeDialog, CDialog)
   //{{AFX_MSG_MAP(SomeDialog)
      // NOTE: the ClassWizard will add message map macros here
   //}}AFX_MSG_MAP
END_MESSAGE_MAP()


/////////////////////////////////////////////////////////////////////////
// SomeDialog message handlers
```

With the minimal code in place to support a dialog box, this is a good time to check our work. To do that, we need to write the code that brings up a dialog box. Because dialogs most often appear in response to menu selections, this usually means that we need to create a menu item and a menu handler.

STEP 3: CREATING THE DIALOG BOX

With a dialog box template and the code for a bare-bones dialog class, you have the minimum needed to make a real dialog appear. When you create the dialog, all of the controls that you have defined for the dialog are displayed — at least the ones for which the visible style bit is set to True. Once created, most controls have some minimal functional capability. For example, check boxes and radio buttons click on and off. Similarly, the OK and Cancel buttons are smart enough to be able to make the dialog disappear.

The automatic operation of controls is an important feature of dialogs, with the benefit that you can get started with only a little coding. In object-oriented programming terms, each control encapsulates core capabilities in a simple package. The amount of code you need to write depends on how much initialization you want to do and how much you want to coordinate the activities of different controls with each other.

In the bare-bones dialog that we've created so far, none of the controls contain initial values. For example, edit controls have no text to edit, check boxes are unchecked, radio buttons are unselected, and the lists in your list boxes are empty. Unless you've used the *initial values* feature of the dialog editor, combo boxes are also empty. Part of what it takes to create dialogs, then, is initialization code that sets the starting values in your controls.

Our bare-bones dialog also has no intercontrol coordination. For example, when you select a filename from a list box in a File|Open dialog, the name is also copied to an edit control. All of these tasks must be performed by your dialog box code. Another feature of a File|Open dialog is that a double-click on a valid file in the File list box is the same thing as selecting that filename and clicking the OK button. Controls aren't smart enough to coordinate such activities on their own. They need help from the dialog box class, which acts like a traffic cop, moving data where it needs to go.

Both of these features — initialization and intercontrol data flow — are important to your finished dialog. But when you start building a dialog, you don't need to put every last piece in place before checking your work. We're going to postpone coverage of what it takes to fine-tune controls, and look instead at the steps that are required to get a dialog up and running. We'll start by describing what it takes to create a modal dialog box, and then we'll look at how the creation of modeless dialogs differs.

Creating a modal dialog box

As with most MFC objects, creation of a modal dialog box is a two-step process. First, you need to instantiate a C++ object. Then, you initialize the object. For the dialog that ClassWizard created for us a little earlier, here's what you do:

```
SomeDialog dlg;
int nResult = dlg.DoModal();
if (nResult == IDOK)
{ /* User clicked OK button or pressed Enter key. */
}
else
{ /* User clicked Cancel button, pressed Esc key, or error. */
}
```

Nothing much happens during allocation. In this example, as a local object, our dialog object is allocated on the stack. Of course, if the dialog holds other state information that you want to use elsewhere in your program, you can dynamically allocate the dialog object and hold a pointer for as long as you need the object.

Although allocation is simple, dialog initialization — which is handled by CDialog::DoModal( ) — is fairly involved. This call creates a modal dialog box and displays it. But this function does more than initialize the dialog; it creates its own little world in which the modal dialog box can run.

Once the modal dialog is created and displayed, a message loop starts waiting for user input. From the discussion in Chapter 9, you might recall that message loops are the mechanism by which a Microsoft Windows program receives mouse and keyboard input. Input that is received by a modal dialog is dispatched to the designated control for processing. This continues until the user dismisses the dialog — perhaps by clicking the OK button. At that point, the modal dialog's private message loop terminates and program control returns to the function that called CDialog::DoModal( ). Incidentally, you won't find the private message loop for a modal dialog in the MFC sources; instead, the message loop is hidden within the Windows API function libraries.

As we mentioned previously, a modal dialog box runs in exclusive mode. This means that other user-interface objects are disabled. For example, before the modal dialog appears, the parent window is disabled — that is, all mouse input and keyboard input are shut off. This effectively disables the application's menus, scroll bars, and other frame window devices. In addition, the application's accelerator keys don't work because they rely on the operation of the Main message loop in CWinThread::Run( ). After all, input is funneled through the message loop owned by the modal dialog box and not by MFC's normal message loop. This exclusive-mode operation continues until the user dismisses the modal dialog, at which point everything returns to "normal."

Creating a modal dialog box is only half of the modal dialog box story. You also need to understand how a modal dialog box gets dismissed. You need to dismiss a modal dialog box to escape its exclusive mode and allow your users to continue working with your application. As part of this process, a modal dialog tells its caller whether the user dismissed the dialog with an OK button or a Cancel button.

Dismissing a modal dialog box

Although a user could spend minutes or even hours laboring over a dialog, all changes should be ignored if the dialog is dismissed with a click of the Cancel button. As a result, the most important piece of information you need to get from a modal dialog is whether to worry about change requests. The two basic return values from CDialog::DoModal( ) are IDOK and IDCANCEL. The first return value says "use the changes," and the second says "lose them."

You can have other return values, but to get them you must understand where the return value comes from. To understand this, let's look at how CDialog shuts down a dialog. When the user clicks the OK button, the default handler for this — CDialog::OnOK( ) — does the following (it does a few other things, but we'll ignore them for now):

```
void CDialog::OnOK()
{
    EndDialog(IDOK);
}
```

The call to CDialog::EndDialog( ) dismisses a modal dialog. It also stores away the value that is to be used as the return value for CDialog::DoModal( ). For other return values besides IDOK and IDCANCEL, you need to call CDialog::EndDialog( ) yourself instead of calling CDialog::OnOK( ) or its companion, CDialog::OnCancel( ).

The two key CDialog functions for modal dialogs are DoModal( ), which creates a modal dialog, and EndDialog( ), which dismisses a modal dialog. As detailed in the following sections, you'll use two other functions when creating and dismissing modeless dialog boxes.

Creating a modeless dialog box

You use almost the same steps to build a modeless dialog as you do for a modal dialog box. The most important differences are in how you create and dismiss modeless dialogs. Otherwise, you can use the same dialog template, as well as the same dialog class code (with only some minor changes). Even the way that initialization and control notification are handled — two steps we haven't discussed yet — are the same for modal and modeless dialogs.

As with most MFC objects, you'll use a two-step process to create a modeless dialog: allocation of the C++ object, followed by initialization. An important difference for modeless dialogs is that you can't allocate the C++ object as a local object. A local C++ object works for modal dialogs because they run in exclusive mode. However, because modeless dialogs don't spin within a message loop, program control returns immediately after initialization. When the stack is cleaned up, the modeless dialog object is also cleaned up.

Let's look at a code fragment that's suitable for creating a modeless dialog box. Because a local variable won't work for a modeless dialog box, we define a pointer to a CDialog-derived class:

```
DDlg * d_pdlgModeless;
```

The simplest way to summon a modeless dialog box involves our usual two steps:

```
d_pdlgModeless = new DDlg();
d_pdlgModeless->Create(DDlg::IDD, this);
```

Although this code fragment does cause a modeless dialog box to appear, it has a few problems. For one thing, because a modeless dialog runs in nonexclusive mode, whatever we did to trigger this code — for example, a menu item selection — can still occur. This isn't necessarily a problem, but we probably don't want to create a *second* modeless dialog box. In most cases, it makes sense to summon the first one. If our dialog already exists, we could do this by calling SetActiveWindow( ).

But this solution has problems of its own. Chief among them is how to figure out whether the dialog already exists. For example, if we simply determine whether the pointer d_pdlgModeless points to a valid object, we won't know whether the user has dismissed the window, unless we do something like explicitly overwriting the pointer when the window closes. That's not a bad solution, but a more robust one is simply to check whether a valid window is attached to this object. Although no MFC function does this, a native Windows API function — IsWindow( ) — fits the bill nicely. If you pass a window handle to this function, it returns True for a valid window handle.

The following example is a slightly more robust piece of code for creating a modeless dialog. It has the added advantage that it also handles some of the interesting side cases. If the dialog is already present, it is made active. If our object was previously allocated but then dismissed, this code recognizes it and does the right thing:

```
if (d_pdlgModeless && ::IsWindow(d_pdlgModeless ->m_hWnd))
    {
        d_pdlgModeless->SetActiveWindow();
    }
    else
    {
        d_pdlgModeless = new DDlg();
    }

    if (!::IsWindow(d_pdlgModeless->m_hWnd))
    {
        d_pdlgModeless->Create(DDlg::IDD, this);
    }
```

An unstated assumption in this code is that d_pdlgModeless will be NULL before we encounter this code for the first time. The constructor of the object that contains the modeless dialog — for example, a DMainFrame — is a good place to satisfy this assumption:

```
d_pdlgModeless = 0;
```

Aside from the exclusive nature of modal dialogs, the other major difference between modal and modeless dialogs is in how you dismiss a modeless dialog box. The following section shows you how it's done.

Dismissing a modeless dialog box
You use a different approach to dismiss a modeless dialog box because you don't need to disable its exclusive mode. Instead, because it's just a regular window, you call CWnd::DestroyWindow( ). It's that simple. When the dialog window is destroyed, all of the contained controls —

its child windows — are also destroyed. This automatic clean-up mechanism is part of the windowing support that's built into the Windows API.

An issue that might concern you is letting the parent window know that the modeless dialog is gone. With their exclusive mode, modal dialogs don't face this issue. But the nonexclusive mode means that a modeless dialog can disappear unbeknownst to its parent window. There are several ways to solve this. By calling IsWindow( ) from any point in your program, you can query whether a WinAPI window exists for a C++ window object. You could also set the pointer to the dialog object to NULL, and check that pointer when you need to know. A third alternative is to send a message to the parent window at the exact moment when the dialog closes. We'll demonstrate this third technique with the progress bar modeless dialog in our sample DIALOGS program, which you'll find later in this chapter.

Once you're sure that you can get a dialog box to appear — whether it's a modal dialog or a modeless dialog — the next step is to write some code to initialize the contents of individual dialog controls. This work is always done when the dialog receives a WM_INITDIALOG message.

STEP 4: HANDLING DIALOG INITIALIZATION

It's important to consider how you're going to initialize every type of data object you work with. When dealing with a complex object such as a dialog box, you must pay special attention to timing because initialization often involves multiple stages. With dialogs — that is, with CDialog-derived objects — initialization takes place in three stages: in the class constructor, in response to a WM_CREATE message, and in response to a WM_INITDIALOG message.

Constructor initialization

From the perspective of C++ development, you'll only initialize class data members in the class constructor. Although it's possible to do almost anything in a constructor (except call virtual functions of derived classes), you should avoid such practices. Because constructors don't have a mechanism for returning a failure condition, anything that fails in a constructor goes unreported. (That is, unless you use exception handling. But we're going to ignore that option for now.)

In the constructor for a CDialog-derived class, you'll certainly initialize the data members that you define. In addition, however, you'll find that the ClassWizard generates code to initialize the data members that it creates. We'll discuss this more fully in the context of MFC's dialog data exchange (DDX) support, which we'll introduce later in this chapter. For now, let's look at the other places where we could initialize a dialog box.

WM_CREATE initialization

Because a dialog box is a window, it receives a WM_CREATE message when the window is created. As a result, you *could* do some form of initialization on your window. For example, when we created toolbars in Chapter 11, we created them in the frame window's WM_CREATE handler. But dialog boxes are different. In particular, the really interesting initialization deals with initializing dialog box controls. Although it is possible that you could respond to the WM_CREATE message to perhaps initialize dialog data structures, the more common initialization message occurs after all dialog box controls have been created: WM_INITDIALOG.

WM_INITDIALOG initialization

When you get the WM_INITDIALOG message, you're guaranteed that your dialog is in a particular state. First, by the time you get this message, the dialog frame has already been created. Second, every control in the dialog has been created and placed in its proper position. Finally, neither the dialog nor any control is visible. For that reason, you can fine-tune the appearance, the size, the location, or the contents of any or all of the controls in your dialog.

Dialog data exchange (DDX) support

Dialog data exchange (DDX) is a convenient MFC feature for automatically initializing controls. Although the concepts behind DDX are simple, understanding DDX can be difficult at first because the implementation is hidden from you. (By *hidden* we mean that it's not in your program files, but you can easily uncover specific details about how DDX works by browsing the MFC source files.)

Dialog data exchange is based on the idea that the state of most controls can be represented by simple variables. For example, check box state is either true or false, which corresponds to a BOOL variable set to True or False. To simplify the implementation of DDX support,

ClassWizard, automatically generates much of the required code. The only coding you do is to initialize the variables.

Dialog data exchange uses two of the three types of dialog object initialization: in the constructor and in response to a WM_INITDIALOG message. ClassWizard generates statements in the constructor to set the initial values for controls. As shown in the following example, these statements are bracketed with a pair of commented AFX_DATA_INIT( ) macros (we added the comments):

```
//{{AFX_DATA_INIT(SomeDialog)
m_EditValue = _T("");    // Initial CString value for edit control.
m_ComboValue = _T("");   // Initially selected item in combo box list.
m_ListValue = _T("");    // Initially selected item in list box.
m_CheckValue = FALSE;    // Initial BOOL value for check box.
m_ScrollValue = 0;       // Initial value for scroll bar.
//}}AFX_DATA_INIT
```

To set specific default values in these member variables, you can either modify the constructor directly or change them directly before calling DoModal( ).

The second part of initialization involves copying these values into the correct control during dialog box initialization. In your CDialog-derived class, ClassWizard generates a function called DoDataExchange( ). This function is called by CDialog::OnInitDialog( ). Here's a typical DoData-Exchange( ) function for the five controls in the previous example:

```
void SomeDialog::DoDataExchange(CDataExchange* pDX)
{
    CDialog::DoDataExchange(pDX);
    //{{AFX_DATA_MAP(SomeDialog)
    DDX_Text(pDX, IDC_BIGED, m_EditValue);
    DDX_CBString(pDX, IDC_COMBO1, m_ComboValue);
    DDX_LBString(pDX, IDC_LIST1, m_ListValue);
    DDX_Check(pDX, IDC_CHECK1, m_CheckValue);
    DDX_Scroll(pDX, IDC_SCROLLBAR1, m_ScrollValue);
    //}}AFX_DATA_MAP
}
```

Sandwiched between the commented AFX_DATA_MAP( ) macros are calls to a set of functions that copy data values from class member variables into controls.

DDX support actually provides two-way data transfer. As we've described, it sets an initial value for dialog controls at start-up. When a user clicks the OK button, the DDX mechanism copies values from controls back to member variables. For some of the simpler types of controls, that's all you need for moving data to and from a dialog box.

Setting up the DDX tables

Setting up DDX support for dialog controls is easy. First, you run Class-Wizard and select the Member Variables property page. On that page, select your dialog class from the Class combo box. ClassWizard shows you a list of controls in your dialog. Select the control for which you'd like a member variable, and click the Add Variable... button. As shown in Figure 12-7, ClassWizard displays the Add Member Variable dialog.

Figure 12-7
The Add Member Variable dialog automatically adds control member variables to a CDialog-derived class.

The Add Member Variable dialog has three fields, but the bottom one — Variable Type — lists the type of member variable to be created, and is informational only. The top field — Member Variable Name — lets you pick the name of the member variable that ClassWizard will add to your C++ class. The middle field — Category — is really the interesting one. For most types of controls, you have a choice between Value and Control.

If you pick the *Value* category, ClassWizard creates a simple data type that is used to perform the automatic, two-way data transfer that we described. For example, with an edit control, you'll get a CString member variable that is used for moving data to and from the edit control. At dialog initialization — in response to WM_INITDIALOG — controls with member variables from the Value category are automatically initialized.

Then, when the user clicks the OK button to close the dialog, the DDX mechanism reads the control values back into the member variables. (If the user clicks Cancel, no data is copied to the member variables.) So, the Values category sets up DDX for you.

On the other hand, if you pick the *Control* category, the member variable that ClassWizard creates is a pointer to that control type. For example, with an edit control, you'll get a CEdit * member variable. This variable (and its associated handle map entry) is automatically created and initialized for you. It gives you direct access to all the member functions of the MFC control class (CEdit, in this example). With this member variable, you can call CEdit::GetLineCount( ) to retrieve the number of lines in a multiline edit control. You could call CWnd::SetWindowText( ) to copy text into the control yourself, or CWnd::GetWindowText( ) to read a string back out (thereby duplicating what DDX does for you automatically).

It's worth pointing out that you can have *both* types for a given control. The Value variable copies data to and from the control for you. The Control variable provides a pointer to a class object for directly manipulating a control.

Limitations on DDX support

Although it provides a convenient way to move data into and out of dialog controls, DDX support does have limitations. When you reach these limits, you have to write your own code to manage certain controls. As shown in Table 12-4, only four of eight controls are completely supported by DDX initialization. Of the remaining four, two types are only partially supported — that is, you must create the lists in list boxes and combo boxes. The other two types — pushbuttons and radio buttons — are not supported at all.

Although ClassWizard's member variables provide a convenient means for accessing the controls in a dialog, it's not the only way. You can access dialog controls more directly by making a simple call and getting a valid class pointer to any control in a dialog.

Accessing controls without member variables

To access a control without a member variable, you call CWnd::GetDlg-Item( ). For example, here's how you can get a CEdit * pointer for an edit control with the control ID of ID_FIRSTNAME:

```
CEdit * pedFirst = (CEdit *)GetDlgItem(ID_FIRSTNAME);
```

Table 12-4

Available DDX Support for Dialog Box Controls

Control	DDX Support?	Details
check box	Yes	BOOL holds True or False value for the check box.
combo box	Partial	CString holds the string to select initially.
edit	Yes	CString holds the initial string.
list box	Partial	CString holds the string to select initially.
pushbutton	No	Not supported because pushbuttons hold no state.
radio button	No	Not supported because radio buttons must be configured as a group.
scroll bar	Yes	int value holds the initial scroll bar position.
static text	Yes	CString holds the initial string to be displayed in the static text control.

So, what good is this pointer to you? While this pointer is valid, it allows you to call member functions in CEdit, CWnd, CCmdTarget, or CObject. Please remember, though, that CWnd::GetDlgItem( ) creates an entry in MFC's temporary window handle map, which means you shouldn't hold onto this pointer between different messages.

We need to mention an important assumption that's made in this line of code. You're calling GetDlgItem( ) from a member function of the parent window object of the control. This is a somewhat obvious C++ programming issue, but if you're calling from outside a parent window function, you need a pointer to the parent window object. For example, if pDlg was a CDialog * to the parent window, the correct code would be:

```
CEdit * pedFirst = (CEdit *)pDlg->GetDlgItem(ID_FIRSTNAME);
```

Another assumption in this line of code is that ID_FIRSTNAME really refers to an edit control. If it doesn't, we could be in trouble. To make sure we point to the right type of object, we could add an assertion to flag an error. For example, the assertion in the second line of the following code will alert us during a Debug build if the returned pointer isn't a CEdit *:

```
CEdit * pedFirst = (CEdit *)pDlg->GetDlgItem(ID_FIRSTNAME);
ASSERT(pedFirst->IsKindOf(RUNTIME_CLASS(CEdit)));
```

The more controls you have, the more work you must do to initialize the controls. You have several choices for initializing the controls.

You can rely on dialog data exchange, you can directly access individual controls, or you can mix the two approaches. A little bit of experimentation will help you find the mix that works best for you.

Regardless of which method you use to initialize controls, the real work of getting a dialog to operate correctly is in responding to control notifications. The following section describes the basic mechanics of responding to dialog box control notifications.

STEP 5: HANDLING CONTROL NOTIFICATIONS

The last step in building dialog boxes is to write the code that responds to the individual control notification messages. When an event of interest happens to a control, the control notifies its parent window by sending a notification message. Like menu items, dialog controls send WM_COMMAND messages. However, a menu item has only one type of notification: that it's been selected. Controls send a much broader range of notification messages.

For example, the various buttons — that is, pushbuttons, check boxes, and radio buttons — have two notifications. One message indicates that the button has been clicked (BN_CLICKED), and the other indicates that the button has been double-clicked (BN_DOUBLECLICKED). How you respond to a particular event depends on the effect that you wish to produce. You will almost always respond to a BN_CLICKED message from a pushbutton, simply because users expect something to occur when they click a pushbutton. For example, a dialog might close, the screen color might change, or the text size and color might change.

The types of notifications that are available depend on the control type. For example, static text controls don't send any notifications. On the other hand, edit controls, list box controls, and combo box controls each can send a diverse set of notifications. Helpful references for notification codes are the Win32 API reference manual and the on-line help database (API32.HLP on the Visual C++ installation disks). The MFC help database is strangely silent on the subject of control notifications.

MFC dialog classes handle control notifications in the same way that other messages are handled — that is, via a message map. In Figure 12-8, ClassWizard is being used to edit the message map for a dialog from our sample DIALOGS program. (We'll describe this sample program in the next section of this chapter.)

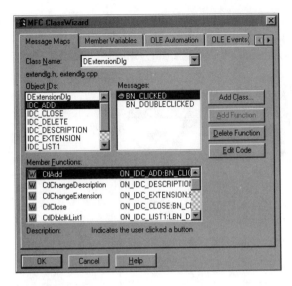

Figure 12-8
You can use the ClassWizard to add control notification handling functions to the message map of CDialog-derived classes.

When you select a control ID in the Object ID list box, ClassWizard displays the applicable notifications in the Messages list. To add a notification handling function for your dialog, select the appropriate notification in the Messages list, and click the Add Function button. ClassWizard generates a notification function for you and creates the appropriate entry in the dialog's message map.

To help you put together all of the dialog creation ideas that we've described in this chapter, the following section presents a sample program that displays five dialog boxes. Because dialogs are typically modal, this program has three modal dialogs and two modeless dialogs. In choosing the examples, we've tried to give you an idea of the range of possibilities that dialogs offer.

DIALOGS: Five Sample Dialog Boxes

Our sample DIALOGS program demonstrates some of the more common techniques for creating and controlling dialog boxes. As shown in Figure 12-9, when DIALOGS starts up, it displays a toolbar with four buttons that each summon a dialog box. Our fifth dialog in this sample program is the dialog bar that appears above the toolbar and below the menu. Table 12-5 summarizes the five dialogs in our sample DIALOGS program.

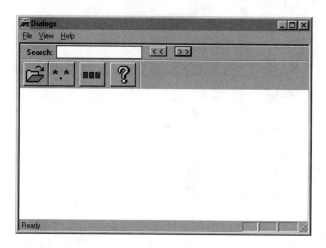

Figure 12-9

DIALOGS as it appears at program start-up.

Table 12-5

Dialog Boxes Created by the DIALOGS Program

Dialog	Description
About Box	The simplest of the five dialogs, the About box is even simpler than the one that's provided by AppWizard. It just instantiates MFC's CDialog without defining a new class.
FilelOpen Dialog	One of the system's common dialogs, it is used for getting the name of a file to open.
FilelType Dialog	A modal dialog box that's used to build a list of file extensions and descriptions. The output of this dialog becomes the input for the file list in the FilelOpen dialog.
Dialog Bar	Uses the CDialogBar class to put dialog box controls in a dialog bar on the frame window. Although CDialogBar doesn't derive from CDialog, we consider it to be more like a modeless dialog than toolbar.
Progress Bar	A modeless dialog box that displays a graphic representation of a progress bar. Instead of drawing the progress bar, we rely on text output using WingDings, the graphic image font. Along the way, this program shows how to dynamically change a control's font.

When you run DIALOGS, you might notice that the buttons on the toolbar are larger than normal. Instead of using the default 16 × 15 pixels for each button bitmap, we doubled their size so that each bitmap is 32 × 30. To make this work properly in the toolbar, we had to nearly double the size of each button. The default size is 24 × 22. We increased this to 42 × 38. To make such a change in your toolbars, you must call CToolBar::SetSizes, which takes two SIZE structures as parameters. Here's an example:

```
// Set bitmap button size.
SIZE szButton = {42,38};
SIZE szBitmap = {32,30};
m_wndToolBar.SetSizes(szButton, szBitmap);
```

DIALOG's complete program files are shown in Listings 12-3 through 12-12. Details about each type of dialog appear after the listings.

Listing 12-3
DIALOGS.H

```
// dialogs.h : main header file for the DIALOGS application
//

#ifndef __AFXWIN_H__
    #error include 'stdafx.h' before including this file for PCH
#endif

#include "resource.h"        // main symbols

/////////////////////////////////////////////////////////////////////////
// DApp:
// See dialogs.cpp for the implementation of this class
//

class DApp : public CWinApp
{
public:
    DApp();

// Overrides
    // ClassWizard generated virtual function overrides
    //{{AFX_VIRTUAL(DApp)
    public:
    virtual BOOL InitInstance();
    //}}AFX_VIRTUAL

// Implementation
```

```
    //{{AFX_MSG(DApp)
    afx_msg void OnAppAbout();
        // NOTE - the ClassWizard will add and remove member functions here.
        //    DO NOT EDIT what you see in these blocks of generated code !
    //}}AFX_MSG
    DECLARE_MESSAGE_MAP()
};


/////////////////////////////////////////////////////////////////////////
const UINT PM_PROGRESS_CLOSING = WM_USER;
```

"PM" stands for "private message."

Listing 12-4
DIALOGS.CPP

```
// dialogs.cpp : Defines the class behaviors for the application.
//

#include "stdafx.h"
#include "dialogs.h"

#include "progress.h"
#include "extendlg.h"
#include "mainfrm.h"

#ifdef _DEBUG
#undef THIS_FILE
static char BASED_CODE THIS_FILE[] = __FILE__;
#endif

/////////////////////////////////////////////////////////////////////////
// DApp

BEGIN_MESSAGE_MAP(DApp, CWinApp)
    //{{AFX_MSG_MAP(DApp)
    ON_COMMAND(ID_APP_ABOUT, OnAppAbout)
        // NOTE - the ClassWizard will add and remove mapping macros here.
        //    DO NOT EDIT what you see in these blocks of generated code!
    //}}AFX_MSG_MAP
    // Standard file based document commands
    ON_COMMAND(ID_FILE_NEW, CWinApp::OnFileNew)
    ON_COMMAND(ID_FILE_OPEN, CWinApp::OnFileOpen)
END_MESSAGE_MAP()

/////////////////////////////////////////////////////////////////////////
// DApp construction
```

```
DApp::DApp()
{
    // TODO: add construction code here,
    // Place all significant initialization in InitInstance
}

//////////////////////////////////////////////////////////////////////
// The one and only DApp object

DApp theApp;

//////////////////////////////////////////////////////////////////////
// DApp initialization

BOOL DApp::InitInstance()
{
    // Turn on support for 3-dimensional dialog box controls.
    Enable3dControls();

    // Set control text and control background colors.
    SetDialogBkColor( RGB(192, 192, 192), RGB(0, 0, 0) );

    // Step 1: Allocate C++ window object.
    DMainFrame * pFrame;
    pFrame = new DMainFrame();

    // Step 2: Initialize window object.
    pFrame->LoadFrame(IDR_MAINFRAME);

    // Make window visible
    pFrame->ShowWindow(m_nCmdShow);

    // Assign frame as application's main window
    m_pMainWnd = pFrame;

    return TRUE;
}

//////////////////////////////////////////////////////////////////////
// DApp commands

// App command to run the dialog
void DApp::OnAppAbout()
{
    CDialog aboutDlg(IDD_ABOUTBOX);
    aboutDlg.DoModal();
}
```

AppWizard-generated function calls.

Using CDialog directly to create a dialog box.

Listing 12-5
MAINFRM.H

```
// mainfrm.h : interface of the DMainFrame class
//
//////////////////////////////////////////////////////////////////////

class DMainFrame : public CFrameWnd
{
public:
    DMainFrame();
protected: // create from serialization only
    DECLARE_DYNCREATE(DMainFrame)

// Attributes
public:
    BOOL           d_bSearchBarVisible; // Search bar visibility flag.
    CDialogBar   * d_pDialogBar;  // Toolbar with dialog controls.
    CFileDialog  * d_pOpenFile;   // Ptr to OpenFile dialog.
    DExtensionDlg * d_pExtDlg;    // Ptr to file extension dialog.
    DProgress    * d_pdlgProgress; // Progress modeless dialog.

// Operations
public:

// Overrides
    // ClassWizard generated virtual function overrides
    //{{AFX_VIRTUAL(DMainFrame)
    //}}AFX_VIRTUAL

// Implementation
public:
    virtual ~DMainFrame();
#ifdef _DEBUG
    virtual void AssertValid() const;
    virtual void Dump(CDumpContext& dc) const;
#endif

protected:  // control bar embedded members
    CStatusBar  m_wndStatusBar;
    CToolBar    m_wndToolBar;

// Generated message map functions
protected:
    //{{AFX_MSG(DMainFrame)
    afx_msg int OnCreate(LPCREATESTRUCT lpCreateStruct);
    afx_msg void OnFileOpen();
    afx_msg void OnFileType();
    afx_msg void CmdViewSearchbar();
    afx_msg void UpdViewSearchbar(CCmdUI* pCmdUI);
    afx_msg void CmdProgress();
    afx_msg void OnTimer(UINT nIDEvent);
```

Automatically created on receipt of WM_CREATE message.

```
    //}}AFX_MSG
    afx_msg BOOL CmdSearchForward(UINT nID);
    afx_msg BOOL CmdSearchBackward(UINT nID);
    afx_msg LRESULT MsgProgressClosing(WPARAM wParam, LPARAM lParam);
    DECLARE_MESSAGE_MAP()
};

/////////////////////////////////////////////////////////////////////////

// ID of Search bar child window
const int ID_SEARCH_BAR = 0x9000;
```

Listing 12-6
MAINFRM.CPP

```
// mainfrm.cpp : implementation of the DMainFrame class
//

#include "stdafx.h"
#include "dialogs.h"

#include "extendlg.h"
#include "progress.h"
#include "mainfrm.h"

#ifdef _DEBUG
#undef THIS_FILE
static char BASED_CODE THIS_FILE[] = __FILE__;
#endif

/////////////////////////////////////////////////////////////////////////
// DMainFrame

IMPLEMENT_DYNCREATE(DMainFrame, CFrameWnd)

BEGIN_MESSAGE_MAP(DMainFrame, CFrameWnd)
    //{{AFX_MSG_MAP(DMainFrame)
    ON_WM_CREATE()
    ON_COMMAND(ID_FILE_OPEN, OnFileOpen)
    ON_COMMAND(ID_FILE_TYPE, OnFileType)
    ON_COMMAND(ID_VIEW_SEARCHBAR, CmdViewSearchbar)
    ON_UPDATE_COMMAND_UI(ID_VIEW_SEARCHBAR, UpdViewSearchbar)
    ON_COMMAND(ID_VIEW_PROGRESS, CmdProgress)
    ON_WM_TIMER()
    //}}AFX_MSG_MAP
    ON_COMMAND_EX(IDC_FORWARD, CmdSearchForward)
    ON_COMMAND_EX(IDC_BACK, CmdSearchBackward)
    ON_MESSAGE(PM_PROGRESS_CLOSING, MsgProgressClosing)
END_MESSAGE_MAP()
```

```
/////////////////////////////////////////////////////////////////////////
// arrays of IDs used to initialize control bars

// toolbar buttons - IDs are command buttons
static UINT BASED_CODE buttons[] =
{
    // same order as in the bitmap 'toolbar.bmp'
    ID_FILE_OPEN,
    ID_FILE_TYPE,
        ID_SEPARATOR,
    ID_VIEW_PROGRESS,
        ID_SEPARATOR,
    ID_APP_ABOUT,
};

static UINT BASED_CODE indicators[] =
{
    ID_SEPARATOR,              // status line indicator
    ID_INDICATOR_CAPS,
    ID_INDICATOR_NUM,
    ID_INDICATOR_SCRL,
};

/////////////////////////////////////////////////////////////////////////
// DMainFrame construction/destruction

DMainFrame::DMainFrame()
{
    d_pOpenFile   = 0;
    d_pExtDlg     = 0;
    d_pDialogBar  = 0;
    d_bSearchBarVisible = TRUE;
    d_pdlgProgress = 0;
}

DMainFrame::~DMainFrame()
{
    // Delete file open object.
    if (d_pOpenFile)
        delete d_pOpenFile;

    // Delete file extensions object.
    if (d_pExtDlg)
        delete d_pExtDlg;

    // Delete dialog bar object.
    if (d_pDialogBar)
        delete d_pDialogBar;

    // Delete progress dialog box.
    if (d_pdlgProgress)
        delete d_pdlgProgress;
}
```

```
//------------------------------------
// WM_CREATE message handler.
int DMainFrame::OnCreate(LPCREATESTRUCT lpCreateStruct)
{
    if (CFrameWnd::OnCreate(lpCreateStruct) == -1)
        return -1;

    // Create dialog bar object.
    d_pDialogBar = new CDialogBar();
    if (!d_pDialogBar)
        return -1;

    // Initialize dialog bar.
    d_pDialogBar->Create(this, IDD_SEARCHBAR, WS_CHILD | CBRS_TOP |
                         CBRS_TOOLTIPS | CBRS_FLYBY, ID_SEARCH_BAR);

    // Make dialog bar visible.
    d_pDialogBar->ShowWindow(SW_SHOWNORMAL);

    // Initialize tool bar.
    if (!m_wndToolBar.Create(this) ||
        !m_wndToolBar.LoadBitmap(IDR_MAINFRAME) ||
        !m_wndToolBar.SetButtons(buttons,
           sizeof(buttons)/sizeof(UINT)))
    {
        TRACE0("Failed to create toolbar\n");
        return -1;        // fail to create
    }

    // Set bitmap button size.
    SIZE szButton = {42,38};
    SIZE szBitmap = {32,30};
    m_wndToolBar.SetSizes(szButton, szBitmap);

    // Initialize status bar.
    if (!m_wndStatusBar.Create(this) ||
        !m_wndStatusBar.SetIndicators(indicators,
           sizeof(indicators)/sizeof(UINT)))
    {
        TRACE0("Failed to create status bar\n");
        return -1;        // fail to create
    }

    // TODO: Delete these three lines if you don't
    // want the toolbar to be dockable.
    m_wndToolBar.EnableDocking(CBRS_ALIGN_ANY);
    EnableDocking(CBRS_ALIGN_ANY);
    DockControlBar(&m_wndToolBar);

    // TODO: Remove this if you don't want tool tips
    m_wndToolBar.SetBarStyle(m_wndToolBar.GetBarStyle() |
        CBRS_TOOLTIPS | CBRS_FLYBY);
```

Dialog bar creation.

Toolbar creation.

Status bar creation.

```
// Create File|Open... dialog object.
d_pOpenFile = new CFileDialog (TRUE);
if (!d_pOpenFile)
    return -1;
```
*Create Open
File dialog.*

```
// Create File|Type... dialog object.
d_pExtDlg = new DExtensionDlg();
if (!d_pExtDlg)
    return -1;
```
*Create File Type
dialog.*

```
    return 0;
}

/////////////////////////////////////////////////////////////////////////////
// DMainFrame diagnostics

#ifdef _DEBUG
void DMainFrame::AssertValid() const
{
    CFrameWnd::AssertValid();
}

void DMainFrame::Dump(CDumpContext& dc) const
{
    CFrameWnd::Dump(dc);
}

#endif //_DEBUG

/////////////////////////////////////////////////////////////////////////////
// DMainFrame message handlers

//-----------------------------------
// WM_COMMAND handler for File|Open... menu item.
void DMainFrame::OnFileOpen()
{
    // Build list of file extensions.
    CStringList * psl = &d_pExtDlg->d_cslFileType;
    int nCount = psl->GetCount();
    ASSERT(((nCount/2)*2) == nCount);   // Must be even.
    CString csFilter;
    POSITION pos = psl->GetHeadPosition();
    while (pos != NULL)
    {
        csFilter += psl->GetNext(pos);
        csFilter += (TCHAR)'\0';
        csFilter += psl->GetNext(pos);
        csFilter += (TCHAR)'\0';
    }

    // Add all files selection.
    csFilter += _T("All Files (*.*)");
    csFilter += (TCHAR)'\0';
```
*Start of File|Open
handler.*

```
    csFilter += _T("*.*");
    csFilter += (TCHAR)'\0';

    // Assign string to OPENFILENAME member.
    d_pOpenFile->m_ofn.lpstrFilter = csFilter;

    // Display File.Open... dialog box.
    int iRet = d_pOpenFile->DoModal();

    // Ignore when user clicks [Cancel] button.
    if (iRet != IDOK)
        return;

    // Fetch fully-qualified file name.
    CString csFile = d_pOpenFile->GetPathName();
    AfxMessageBox(csFile);
}


//------------------------------------
// WM_COMMAND handler for File|Type... menu item.
void DMainFrame::OnFileType()
{
    d_pExtDlg->DoModal();
}


//------------------------------------
// WM_COMMAND handler for View|Search Bar menu item.
void DMainFrame::CmdViewSearchbar()
{
    // Toggle visibility flag.
    d_bSearchBarVisible = (d_pDialogBar->GetStyle() & WS_VISIBLE);
    d_bSearchBarVisible = !d_bSearchBarVisible;

    // Show or hide dialog bar window.
    int nShow = (d_bSearchBarVisible) ? SW_SHOWNORMAL : SW_HIDE;
    d_pDialogBar->ShowWindow(nShow);

    // Reorganize all toolbars.
    RecalcLayout();
}


//------------------------------------
// CN_UPDATE_COMMAND_UI handler for View|Search Bar menu item.
void DMainFrame::UpdViewSearchbar(CCmdUI* pCmdUI)
{
    int nCheck = (d_bSearchBarVisible) ? 1 : 0;
    pCmdUI->SetCheck(nCheck);
}


//------------------------------------
// WM-COMMAND handler for clicking >> button in dialog bar.
BOOL DMainFrame::CmdSearchForward(UINT nID)
{
```

*Display Open
File dialog.*

*Display File
Type dialog.*

*Hide or show
dialog box.*

>> button handler.

```
    // Fetch string from edit control.
    CEdit * pedSearch =
            (CEdit *)d_pDialogBar->GetDlgItem(IDC_SEARCHTEXT);
    TCHAR   ach[MAX_LEN];
    pedSearch->GetWindowText(ach, MAX_LEN);

    // Format string and display in a message box.
    CString cs;
    cs.Format(_T("Searching forward for [%s]..."), ach);
    AfxMessageBox(cs);

    return TRUE;
}

//-----------------------------------
// WM_COMMAND handler for clicking << button in dialog box.
BOOL DMainFrame::CmdSearchBackward(UINT nID)
{
    // Fetch string from edit control.
    CEdit * pedSearch =
            (CEdit *)d_pDialogBar->GetDlgItem(IDC_SEARCHTEXT);
    TCHAR   ach[MAX_LEN];
    pedSearch->GetWindowText(ach, MAX_LEN);

    // Format string and display in a message box.
    CString cs;
    cs.Format(_T("Searching backward for [%s]..."), ach);
    AfxMessageBox(cs);

    return TRUE;
}

//-----------------------------------
// Handle WM_COMMAND message for View|Test Progress Bar...
void DMainFrame::CmdProgress()
{
    // Start progress bar demo.
    if (!d_pdlgProgress)
    {
        d_pdlgProgress = new DProgress();
        d_pdlgProgress->Create(IDD_PROGRESS, this);
        SetTimer(1, 100, 0);
    }
    else
    {
        // Complain if user tries to start another demo.
        MessageBeep(MB_OK);
    }
}
```

<< button handling.

Activate progress bar.

Set timer for $1/10$ second.

```
//-----------------------------------
// Handle WM_TIMER message for advancing progress bar.
void DMainFrame::OnTimer(UINT nIDEvent)
{
    // Check for a valid object & valid window.
    if (d_pdlgProgress && ::IsWindow(d_pdlgProgress->m_hWnd))
    {
        // Increment by 5 percent each time.
        int nCount = d_pdlgProgress->GetPercent();
        nCount+=2;
        d_pdlgProgress->SetPercent(nCount);

        // When at or over 100%, we're done.
        if (nCount >= 100)
        {
            d_pdlgProgress->PostMessage(WM_KEYDOWN, VK_ESCAPE);
        }
    }
    else  // Destroy timer when valid object is gone.
    {
        KillTimer(1);
    }
}


//-----------------------------------
// Handle PM_PROGRESS_CLOSING message.
LRESULT DMainFrame::MsgProgressClosing(WPARAM wParam, LPARAM lParam)
{
    // Clear our pointer to progress bar.
    if (d_pdlgProgress)
    {
        delete d_pdlgProgress;
        d_pdlgProgress = 0;
    }

    return (LRESULT)0;
}
```

WM_TIMER handler for progress bar.

Delete C++ progress bar object.

File Type dialog include file.

Listing 12-7
EXTENDLG.H

```
// extendlg.h : header file
//

///////////////////////////////////////////////////////////////////////
// DExtensionDlg dialog

class DExtensionDlg : public CDialog
{
```

```
// Construction
public:
    DExtensionDlg(CWnd* pParent = NULL);    // standard constructor

// Dialog Data
    //{{AFX_DATA(DExtensionDlg)
    enum { IDD = IDD_EXTENSIONS };
    CButton       d_bnAdd;
    CButton       d_bnDelete;
    CButton       d_bnReplace;
    CEdit         d_edDescription;
    CEdit         d_edExtension;
    CListBox      d_listExtensions;
    //}}AFX_DATA

    CStringList d_cslFileType;  // List of file extensions.

// Overrides
    // ClassWizard generated virtual function overrides
    //{{AFX_VIRTUAL(DExtensionDlg)
    protected:
    virtual void DoDataExchange(CDataExchange* pDX);    // DDX/DDV support
    //}}AFX_VIRTUAL

// Implementation
protected:
    void CopyEditToListboxAt(int nIndex);
    void CopyListboxToStringList(CListBox &list, CStringList * psl);
    void SplitAtChar(CString& csIn, CString& csL, CString& csR, TCHAR tch);

    // Generated message map functions
    //{{AFX_MSG(DExtensionDlg)
    virtual BOOL OnInitDialog();
    afx_msg void CtlAdd();
    afx_msg void CtlClose();
    afx_msg void CtlDelete();
    afx_msg void CtlReplace();
    afx_msg void CtlDblclkList1();
    afx_msg void CtlDoubleclickedDelete();
    afx_msg void CtlChangeDescription();
    afx_msg void CtlChangeExtension();
    //}}AFX_MSG
    DECLARE_MESSAGE_MAP()
};

const int MAX_LEN = 255;
```

The data this dialog creates and edits is in this container class object.

Listing 12-8

EXTENDLG.CPP

File Type dialog implementation.

```cpp
// extendlg.cpp : implementation file
//

#include "stdafx.h"
#include "dialogs.h"
#include "extendlg.h"

#ifdef _DEBUG
#undef THIS_FILE
static char BASED_CODE THIS_FILE[] = __FILE__;
#endif

BEGIN_MESSAGE_MAP(DExtensionDlg, CDialog)
    //{{AFX_MSG_MAP(DExtensionDlg)
    ON_BN_CLICKED(IDC_ADD, CtlAdd)
    ON_BN_CLICKED(IDC_CLOSE, CtlClose)
    ON_BN_CLICKED(IDC_DELETE, CtlDelete)
    ON_BN_CLICKED(IDC_REPLACE, CtlReplace)
    ON_BN_DOUBLECLICKED(IDC_DELETE, CtlDoubleclickedDelete)
    ON_EN_CHANGE(IDC_DESCRIPTION, CtlChangeDescription)
    ON_EN_CHANGE(IDC_EXTENSION, CtlChangeExtension)
    ON_LBN_DBLCLK(IDC_LIST1, CtlDblclkList1)
    //}}AFX_MSG_MAP
END_MESSAGE_MAP()

/////////////////////////////////////////////////////////////////////////////
// DExtensionDlg dialog


DExtensionDlg::DExtensionDlg(CWnd* pParent /*=NULL*/)
    : CDialog(DExtensionDlg::IDD, pParent)
{
    //{{AFX_DATA_INIT(DExtensionDlg)
    //}}AFX_DATA_INIT
}

void DExtensionDlg::DoDataExchange(CDataExchange* pDX)
{
    CDialog::DoDataExchange(pDX);
    //{{AFX_DATA_MAP(DExtensionDlg)
    DDX_Control(pDX, IDC_REPLACE, d_bnReplace);
    DDX_Control(pDX, IDC_LIST1, d_listExtensions);
    DDX_Control(pDX, IDC_EXTENSION, d_edExtension);
    DDX_Control(pDX, IDC_DESCRIPTION, d_edDescription);
    DDX_Control(pDX, IDC_DELETE, d_bnDelete);
    DDX_Control(pDX, IDC_ADD, d_bnAdd);
    //}}AFX_DATA_MAP
}
```

```
/////////////////////////////////////////////////////////////////////////////
// DExtensionDlg helper functions.

//----------------------------------------
// Helper function to copy listbox contents to a string list.
void DExtensionDlg::CopyListboxToStringList(CListBox &list, CStringList * psl)
{
    CString csBuffer;
    CString csExt;
    CString csDesc;

    // Loop through strings in listbox.
    int nCount = list.GetCount();
    for (int i = 0; i < nCount; i++)
    {
        // Fetch next item from listbox.
        list.GetText(i, csBuffer);

        // Split string between description and extension.
        SplitAtChar(csBuffer, csExt, csDesc, (TCHAR)'\t');

        // Add to string list.
        psl->AddTail(csDesc);
        psl->AddTail(csExt);
    }
}


//----------------------------------------
// Helper function to split a CString into two CStrings.
void DExtensionDlg::SplitAtChar(CString& csIn, CString& csLeft,
                                CString& csRight, TCHAR tch)
{
    // Search for tab character.
    int iChar = csIn.Find(tch);
    int nRightLen = csIn.GetLength() - iChar - 1;

    // Split string at search character.
    csRight = csIn.Right(nRightLen);
    csLeft  = csIn.Left(iChar);
}


//----------------------------------------
// Helper function to copy contents of edit control to specific listbox item.
void DExtensionDlg::CopyEditToListboxAt(int nIndex)
{
    // Fetch extension string.
    CString csExt;
    d_edExtension.GetWindowText(csExt);

    // Fetch description string.
    CString csDesc;
    d_edDescription.GetWindowText(csDesc);
```

```
    // Combine text strings.
    CString csList = csExt;
    csList += _T("\t");
    csList += csDesc;

    // Add text string to listbox.
    nIndex = d_listExtensions.InsertString(nIndex, csList);

    // Make item currently selected.
    d_listExtensions.SetCurSel(nIndex);
}


//////////////////////////////////////////////////////////////////////////////
// DExtensionDlg message handlers

//-------------------------------------------
// Handle WM_INITDIALOG for File Extensions dialog.
BOOL DExtensionDlg::OnInitDialog()
{
    CDialog::OnInitDialog();

    // Create string list pointer with shorter name.
    CStringList * psl = &d_cslFileType;

    // Make sure string list has even number of items.
    int nCount = psl->GetCount();
    ASSERT(((nCount/2)*2) == nCount);

    // Set tab stop in listbox.
    int nTab[6];
    nTab[0] = 106;   // Hard-coded based on dialog box definition.
    nTab[1] = 116;
    nTab[2] = 126;
    nTab[3] = 136;
    nTab[4] = 146;
    nTab[5] = 156;
    d_listExtensions.SetTabStops(6, nTab);

    // Loop through all strings in CListStrings, adding to listbox.
    POSITION pos = psl->GetHeadPosition();
    while (pos != NULL)
    {
        // Get an empty CString.
        CString csFilter;
        csFilter.Empty();

        // Fetch description from next position.
        CString csTemp;
        csTemp = psl->GetNext(pos);

        // Concatenate file extension and file description, as in:
        //    "*.cpp"  +  "Tab"  +  "C++ source files"
```

Handle WM_INITDIALOG message.

```
            csFilter += psl->GetNext(pos);
            csFilter += _T("\t");
            csFilter += csTemp;

            // Add to listbox.
            d_listExtensions.AddString(csFilter);                    Initialize list box.
        }

        // Disable Add and Replace buttons.
        d_bnAdd.EnableWindow(FALSE);                                 Disable
        d_bnReplace.EnableWindow(FALSE);                             pushbuttons.

        // Refine controls depending on number of items in listbox.
        if (nCount > 0)
        {
            // Set listbox selection to first item.
            d_listExtensions.SetCurSel(0);
        }
        else
        {
            // Disable Delete button
            d_bnDelete.EnableWindow(FALSE);
        }

        return TRUE;
    }

    //----------------------------------------
    // Handle BN_CLICKED notification for Add button.
    void DExtensionDlg::CtlAdd()                                     Click Add button.
    {
        CopyEditToListboxAt(-1);

        // Empty contents of both text buffers.
        d_edExtension.SetWindowText(_T(""));
        d_edDescription.SetWindowText(_T(""));

        // Set focus to extensions control.
        d_edExtension.SetFocus();

        // Enable Delete button
        d_bnDelete.EnableWindow(TRUE);
    }

    //----------------------------------------
    // Handle BN_CLICKED notification for Close button.
    void DExtensionDlg::CtlClose()                                  Click Close button.
    {
        // Empty contents of list.
        d_cslFileType.RemoveAll();

        // Rebuild string list.
        CopyListboxToStringList(d_listExtensions, &d_cslFileType);
```

```
    CDialog::OnOK();
    return;
}


//---------------------------------------
// Handle BN_CLICKED notification for Delete button.
void DExtensionDlg::CtlDelete()                          Click Delete button.
{
    // Query currently selected item.
    int iItem = d_listExtensions.GetCurSel();
    if (iItem == LB_ERR)
    {
        ::MessageBeep(MB_OK);
        return;
    }

    // Delete listbox item.
    d_listExtensions.DeleteString(iItem);

    // Get number of items in listbox.
    int iLast = d_listExtensions.GetCount() - 1;

    // If Listbox is empty...
    if (iLast == LB_ERR)
    {
        // Disable Delete button when listbox is empty.
        d_bnDelete.EnableWindow(FALSE);

        // Give keyboard focus to extensions edit control.
        d_edExtension.SetFocus();
    }
    else
    {
        // Keep current selection near same spot as previously.
        int iNext = (iItem > iLast) ? iLast : iItem;
        d_listExtensions.SetCurSel(iNext);

        // Give keyboard focus to listbox.
        d_listExtensions.SetFocus();
    }
}
```
Keyboard focus gets set for next user operation.

```
//---------------------------------------
// Handle BN_CLICKED notification for Replace button.
void DExtensionDlg::CtlReplace()                         Click Replace button.
{
    // Query currently selected item.
    int iItem = d_listExtensions.GetCurSel();
    if (iItem == LB_ERR)
    {
        return;
    }
```

```
        // Delete currently selected string.
        d_listExtensions.DeleteString(iItem);

        // Move edit control data to listbox.
        CopyEditToListboxAt(iItem);

        // Empty contents of both text buffers.
        d_edExtension.SetWindowText(_T(""));
        d_edDescription.SetWindowText(_T(""));

        // Set focus to extensions control.
        d_edExtension.SetFocus();

        // Make new item in listbox the selected item.
        d_listExtensions.SetCurSel(iItem);
    }
```

Double-click treated like single click (one author's pet peeve — solved!)

```
//-----------------------------------------
// Handle BN_DOUBLECLICKED notification for Delete button.
void DExtensionDlg::CtlDoubleclickedDelete()
{
    // To handle situation when user is clicking like crazy,
    // interpret a double-click as a single click.
    CtlDelete();
}


//-----------------------------------------
// Handle EN_CHANGE notification for Description edit control.
void DExtensionDlg::CtlChangeDescription()
{
    // Calculate length of strings in edit controls.
    int nLen1 = d_edDescription.GetWindowTextLength();
    int nLen2 = d_edExtension.GetWindowTextLength();

    // Enable [Add] button when edit controls have text,
    // Otherwise disable it.
    BOOL bEnable = (nLen1 > 0 && nLen2 > 0) ? TRUE : FALSE;
    d_bnAdd.EnableWindow(bEnable);

    // Enable [Replace] button when edit controls have text,
    // AND when an item is currently selected.
    int nCurSel = d_listExtensions.GetCurSel();
    d_bnReplace.EnableWindow(bEnable && nCurSel != LB_ERR);
}
```

Enable/disable buttons as appropriate.

```
//-----------------------------------------
// Handle EN_CHANGE notification for Extension edit control.
void DExtensionDlg::CtlChangeExtension()
{
    // Handle changes same as other edit control.
    CtlChangeDescription();
}
```

```
//----------------------------------------------
// Handle LBN_DBLCLK double mouse click notification.
void DExtensionDlg::CtlDblclkList1()
{
    // Query currently selected item.
    int iItem = d_listExtensions.GetCurSel();
    if (iItem == LB_ERR)
    {
        return;
    }

    // Fetch currently selected description string
    CString csBuffer;
    CString csExt;
    CString csDesc;
    d_listExtensions.GetText(iItem, csBuffer);

    // Split string between description and extension.
    SplitAtChar(csBuffer, csExt, csDesc, (TCHAR)'\t');

    // Put strings into respective controls.
    d_edExtension.SetWindowText(csExt);
    d_edDescription.SetWindowText(csDesc);

    // Set focus to extensions control.
    d_edExtension.SetFocus();
}
```

Double-click on list box.

Listing 12-9
PROGRESS.H

Progress bar include file.

```
// progress.h : header file
//

/////////////////////////////////////////////////////////////////////////////
// DProgress dialog

class DProgress : public CDialog
{
// Construction
public:
    DProgress(CWnd* pParent = NULL);    // standard constructor

// Attributes
    int         d_nPercent;  // Percent complete (0 to 100).
    LOGFONT     d_lf;        // Windows API LOGFONT font descriptor.
    CFont     * d_pfont;     // MFC font object.
    LPTSTR      pstrBar;     // Holds characters for percent complete bar.
```

Use WingDings font to show progress.

```
        void SetPercent (int n);
        int  GetPercent ();
        void ResizeStatic(CStatic * pst);
        void CenterChildWindow(CWnd * pwndChild);

// Dialog Data
    //{{AFX_DATA(DProgress)
    enum { IDD = IDD_PROGRESS };
    //}}AFX_DATA

// Overrides
    // ClassWizard generated virtual function overrides
    //{{AFX_VIRTUAL(DProgress)
    protected:
    virtual void DoDataExchange(CDataExchange* pDX);    // DDX/DDV support
    //}}AFX_VIRTUAL

// Implementation
protected:

    // Generated message map functions
    //{{AFX_MSG(DProgress)
    virtual BOOL OnInitDialog();
    afx_msg HBRUSH OnCtlColor(CDC* pDC, CWnd* pWnd, UINT nCtlColor);
    //}}AFX_MSG
    void OnCancel();
    DECLARE_MESSAGE_MAP()
};
```

Listing 12-10
PROGRESS.CPP ————————————————————————▶

*Progress bar
implementation file.*

```
// progress.cpp : implementation file
//

#include "stdafx.h"
#include "dialogs.h"
#include "progress.h"

#ifdef _DEBUG
#undef THIS_FILE
static char BASED_CODE THIS_FILE[] = __FILE__;
#endif


/////////////////////////////////////////////////////////////////////////
// DProgress dialog

BEGIN_MESSAGE_MAP(DProgress, CDialog)
    //{{AFX_MSG_MAP(DProgress)
    ON_WM_CTLCOLOR()
```

```
    //}}AFX_MSG_MAP
    ON_COMMAND(IDCANCEL, OnCancel)
END_MESSAGE_MAP()

// PERCENT_MAX * PERCENT_PART = 100 (approx)
// Good pairs: (Max,Part) = (20,5) or (25,4) or (33,3) or (50,2) or (100,1)
const int PERCENT_MAX  = 50;  // == 100 percent.
const int PERCENT_PART =  2;  // == Our scaling factor.

///////////////////////////////////////////////////////////////////////////
// DProgress constructors and setup functions.

DProgress::DProgress(CWnd* pParent /*=NULL*/)
    : CDialog(DProgress::IDD, pParent)
{
    d_nPercent = 0;
    //{{AFX_DATA_INIT(DProgress)
    //}}AFX_DATA_INIT
}


void DProgress::DoDataExchange(CDataExchange* pDX)
{
    CDialog::DoDataExchange(pDX);
    //{{AFX_DATA_MAP(DProgress)
    //}}AFX_DATA_MAP
}

///////////////////////////////////////////////////////////////////////////
// DProgress helper functions.

//-----------------------------------------
// Helper function to set current percentage.
void DProgress::SetPercent (int nSetPercent)
{
    // Enforce 0-100 range for percent.
    if (nSetPercent < 0)   nSetPercent = 0;
    if (nSetPercent > 100) nSetPercent = 100;

    // Store current percent.
    d_nPercent = nSetPercent;

    // Calculate percent to closest 5%.
    int nPart = nSetPercent/PERCENT_PART;

    // Create pointer to end of string array.
    LPTSTR lpstr = pstrBar + (PERCENT_MAX - nPart - 1);

    CStatic * pstPercent = (CStatic *)GetDlgItem(IDC_PROGRESS);
    pstPercent->SetWindowText(lpstr);
}
```

Updates all required member and dialog state.

```
//----------------------------------------
// Helper function to return current percent.
int  DProgress::GetPercent ()
{
    return d_nPercent;
}


//----------------------------------------
// Resize static control to fit text.
void DProgress::ResizeStatic(CStatic * pst)
{
    // Calculate size of 100% string.
    CClientDC dc(this);
    dc.SelectObject(d_pfont);
    CSize szString = dc.GetTextExtent(pstrBar, PERCENT_MAX);
    szString.cx += (::GetSystemMetrics(SM_CXBORDER) * 4);

    // Query existing window size.
    RECT rStatic;
    GetWindowRect (&rStatic);

    // Set new size.
    pst->SetWindowPos(&CWnd::wndTop, 0, 0,
                      szString.cx, szString.cy, SWP_NOMOVE);
}


//----------------------------------------
// Resize static control to fit text.
void DProgress::CenterChildWindow(CWnd * pwndChild)
{
    // Get pointer to parent window.
    CWnd * pwndParent = pwndChild->GetParent();

    // Fetch parent size, then calculate center.
    CRect rParent;
    pwndParent->GetClientRect(&rParent);

    // Fetch child size.
    CRect rChild;
    pwndChild->GetWindowRect(&rChild);
    pwndParent->ScreenToClient(&rChild);

    // Calculate offset from parent to child.
    int cx = ((rParent.right + rParent.left)/2) -
             ((rChild.right  + rChild.left)/2);
    int cy = ((rParent.top    + rParent.bottom)/2) -
             ((rChild.top     + rChild.bottom)/2);

    // Apply offset to child rectangle.
    rChild.OffsetRect(cx, cy);

    // Move child to center of parent window.
    pwndChild->MoveWindow(rChild, FALSE);
}
```

At start-up, resize progress indicator for exact font.

At startup, center progress indicator window.

```
///////////////////////////////////////////////////////////////////////////////
// DProgress message handlers

//-----------------------------------------
// Handle WM_INITDIALOG initialization message.
BOOL DProgress :OnInitDialog()
{
    CDialog::OnInitDialog();

    // Fetch pointer to progress bar static control.
    CStatic * pstPercent = (CStatic *)GetDlgItem(IDC_PROGRESS);

    // Add a border to progress bar window.
    DWORD dwStyle = pstPercent->GetStyle();
    dwStyle |= WS_BORDER;
    ::SetWindowLong(pstPercent->m_hWnd, GWL_STYLE, dwStyle);

    // Calculate font width based on window size.
    RECT rChild;
    pstPercent->GetClientRect(&rChild);

    // Define a WinAPI logical font.
    d_lf.lfWidth  = rChild.right / PERCENT_MAX;
    lstrcpy(d_lf.lfFaceName, "WingDings");
    d_lf.lfHeight = 0;
    d_lf.lfEscapement = 0;
    d_lf.lfOrientation = 0;
    d_lf.lfWeight = 0;
    d_lf.lfItalic = 0;
    d_lf.lfUnderline = 0;
    d_lf.lfStrikeOut = 0;
    d_lf.lfCharSet = SYMBOL_CHARSET;
    d_lf.lfOutPrecision = 0;
    d_lf.lfClipPrecision = 0;
    d_lf.lfQuality = 0;
    d_lf.lfPitchAndFamily = 0;

    // Connect WinAPI font to CFont (MFC) font object.
    d_pfont = new CFont();
    if (!d_pfont)
    {
        DestroyWindow();
        return FALSE;
    }
    d_pfont->CreateFontIndirect(&d_lf);

    // Set up percent complete box to hold WingDing font.
    pstPercent->SetFont(d_pfont, FALSE);

    // Center dialog over frame window.
    CenterWindow();
```

Handle
WM_INITDIALOG.

Dynamic change to
window style.

```
    pstrBar = new TCHAR[PERCENT_MAX+1];
    if (!pstrBar)
    {
        DestroyWindow();
    }
    LPTSTR lp = pstrBar;
    for (int i = 0; i < PERCENT_MAX; i++, lp++)
        *lp = (TCHAR)'n';
    pstrBar[PERCENT_MAX] = (TCHAR)'\0';

    // Resize progress indicator and center over dialog.
    ResizeStatic(pstPercent);
    CenterChildWindow(pstPercent);

    return TRUE;
}


//-----------------------------------------
// Handle WM_CTLCOLOR message - what color are my children?
HBRUSH DProgress::OnCtlColor(CDC* pDC, CWnd* pWnd, UINT nCtlColor)
{
    // Call default handler to do most of the work.
    HBRUSH hbr = CDialog::OnCtlColor(pDC, pWnd, nCtlColor);

    // Draw blue blocks for progres indicator bars.
    pDC->SetTextColor(RGB(0, 0, 255));

    return hbr;
}


//-----------------------------------------
// Handle OnCancel event when user hits Escape key.
void DProgress::OnCancel()
{
    // Delete font.
    if (d_pfont)
    {
        delete d_pfont;
        d_pfont = 0;
    }

    // Tell parent that we're shutting down.
    CWnd * pMain = GetParent();
    pMain->PostMessage(PM_PROGRESS_CLOSING);

    // Destroy window.
    DestroyWindow();

    // Clean up percent bar string.
    delete [] pstrBar;
}
```

Allocate array of "100%" value — used to set progress indicator.

Create blue progress indicator.

Cancel progress bar.

Listing 12-11
RESOURCE.H

```
//{{NO_DEPENDENCIES}}
// Microsoft Visual C++ generated include file.
// Used by DIALOGS.RC
//
#define IDC_ADD                         3
#define IDC_DELETE                      4
#define IDC_REPLACE                     5
#define IDD_ABOUTBOX                    100
#define IDR_MAINFRAME                   128
#define IDD_EXTENSIONS                  130
#define IDD_SEARCHBAR                   131
#define IDD_PROGRESS                    132
#define IDC_EXTENSION                   1000
#define IDC_DESCRIPTION                 1001
#define IDC_LIST1                       1002
#define IDC_CLOSE                       1003
#define IDC_BACK                        1004
#define IDC_FORWARD                     1005
#define IDC_SEARCHTEXT                  1006
#define IDC_PROGRESS                    1007
#define ID_FILE_TYPE                    32771
#define ID_VIEW_SEARCHBAR               32772
#define ID_VIEW_PROGRESS                32773


// Next default values for new objects
//
#ifdef APSTUDIO_INVOKED
#ifndef APSTUDIO_READONLY_SYMBOLS
#define _APS_3D_CONTROLS                1
#define _APS_NEXT_RESOURCE_VALUE        133
#define _APS_NEXT_COMMAND_VALUE         32774
#define _APS_NEXT_CONTROL_VALUE         1008
#define _APS_NEXT_SYMED_VALUE           101
#endif
#endif
```

Listing 12-12
DIALOGS.RC

```
//Microsoft Visual C++ generated resource script.
//
#include "resource.h"

#define APSTUDIO_READONLY_SYMBOLS
/////////////////////////////////////////////////////////////////////////////
//
```

```
// Generated from the TEXTINCLUDE 2 resource.
//
#include "afxres.h"

/////////////////////////////////////////////////////////////////////////////
#undef APSTUDIO_READONLY_SYMBOLS


#ifdef APSTUDIO_INVOKED
/////////////////////////////////////////////////////////////////////////////
//
// TEXTINCLUDE
//

1 TEXTINCLUDE DISCARDABLE
BEGIN
    "resource.h\0"
END

2 TEXTINCLUDE DISCARDABLE
BEGIN
    "#include ""afxres.h""\r\n"
    "\0"
END

3 TEXTINCLUDE DISCARDABLE
BEGIN
    "#include ""res\\dialogs.rc2""  // non-Visual C++ edited resources\r\n"
    "\r\n"
    "#define _AFX_NO_SPLITTER_RESOURCES\r\n"
    "#define _AFX_NO_OLE_RESOURCES\r\n"
    "#define _AFX_NO_TRACKER_RESOURCES\r\n"
    "#define _AFX_NO_PROPERTY_RESOURCES\r\n"
    "#include ""afxres.rc""  \011// Standard components\r\n"
    "\0"
END


/////////////////////////////////////////////////////////////////////////////
#endif    // APSTUDIO_INVOKED


/////////////////////////////////////////////////////////////////////////////
//
// Icon
//

IDR_MAINFRAME           ICON    DISCARDABLE     "res\\dialogs.ico"

/////////////////////////////////////////////////////////////////////////////
//
// Bitmap
//

IDR_MAINFRAME           BITMAP  MOVEABLE PURE   "res\\toolbar.bmp"
```

```
///////////////////////////////////////////////////////////////////////////
//
// Menu
//

IDR_MAINFRAME MENU PRELOAD DISCARDABLE
BEGIN
    POPUP "&File"
    BEGIN
        MENUITEM "&Open...\tCtrl+O",              ID_FILE_OPEN
        MENUITEM "&Type...",                      ID_FILE_TYPE
        MENUITEM SEPARATOR
        MENUITEM "E&xit",                         ID_APP_EXIT
    END
    POPUP "&View"
    BEGIN
        MENUITEM "&Toolbar",                      ID_VIEW_TOOLBAR
        MENUITEM "&Status Bar",                   ID_VIEW_STATUS_BAR
        MENUITEM "&Search Bar",                   ID_VIEW_SEARCHBAR
        MENUITEM SEPARATOR
        MENUITEM "&Test Progress Bar...",         ID_VIEW_PROGRESS
    END
    POPUP "&Help"
    BEGIN
        MENUITEM "&About dialogs...",             ID_APP_ABOUT
    END
END


///////////////////////////////////////////////////////////////////////////
//
// Accelerator
//

IDR_MAINFRAME ACCELERATORS PRELOAD MOVEABLE PURE
BEGIN
    "O",              ID_FILE_OPEN,             VIRTKEY, CONTROL, NOINVERT
END


///////////////////////////////////////////////////////////////////////////
//
// Dialog
//
```

About dialog template.

```
IDD_ABOUTBOX DIALOG DISCARDABLE   34, 22, 172, 101
STYLE DS_MODALFRAME | WS_POPUP | WS_CAPTION | WS_SYSMENU
CAPTION "About Dialogs"
FONT 10, "Arial"
BEGIN
    ICON            IDR_MAINFRAME,IDC_STATIC,11,17,18,20
    LTEXT           "DIALOGS - sample dialog boxes.\n\nFoundations of Visual
```

```
                        C++ Programming for Windows 95\nby Paul Yao and Joseph Yao",
                                        IDC_STATIC,40,10,126,45
            LTEXT                   "Copyright \251 1995. All rights reserved.",IDC_STATIC,
                                        40,61,126,8
            DEFPUSHBUTTON           "OK",IDOK,70,80,32,14,WS_GROUP
        END
```

File Type dialog template.

```
        IDD_EXTENSIONS DIALOG DISCARDABLE  0, 0, 304, 127
        STYLE DS_MODALFRAME | WS_POPUP | WS_VISIBLE | WS_CAPTION | WS_SYSMENU
        CAPTION "File Types"
        FONT 8, "MS Sans Serif"
        BEGIN
            EDITTEXT                IDC_EXTENSION,7,24,95,13,ES_AUTOHSCROLL
            EDITTEXT                IDC_DESCRIPTION,112,24,117,13,ES_AUTOHSCROLL
            LISTBOX                 IDC_LIST1,7,46,222,65,LBS_USETABSTOPS |
                                        LBS_NOINTEGRALHEIGHT | WS_VSCROLL | WS_TABSTOP
            DEFPUSHBUTTON           "&Close",IDC_CLOSE,245,8,50,14
            PUSHBUTTON              "Cancel",IDCANCEL,245,25,50,14
            PUSHBUTTON              "&Add",IDC_ADD,245,50,50,14
            PUSHBUTTON              "&Delete",IDC_DELETE,245,67,50,14
            PUSHBUTTON              "&Replace",IDC_REPLACE,245,84,50,14
            LTEXT                   "Ex&tension",IDC_STATIC,8,12,42,8
            LTEXT                   "De&scription",IDC_STATIC,112,12,57,8
        END
```

Dialog bar template.

```
        IDD_SEARCHBAR DIALOG DISCARDABLE  0, 0, 176, 15
        STYLE WS_CHILD
        FONT 8, "MS Sans Serif"
        BEGIN
            PUSHBUTTON              "< <",IDC_BACK,121,2,16,10
            DEFPUSHBUTTON           " > >",IDC_FORWARD,144,2,16,10
            EDITTEXT                IDC_SEARCHTEXT,34,2,80,12,ES_AUTOHSCROLL
            LTEXT                   "Search:",IDC_STATIC,6,4,25,8
        END
```

Progress dialog template.

```
        IDD_PROGRESS DIALOG DISCARDABLE  0, 0, 250, 29
        STYLE WS_POPUP | WS_VISIBLE | WS_CAPTION
        CAPTION "Loading File.  Please Wait......"
        FONT 8, "Arial"
        BEGIN
            CONTROL "",IDC_PROGRESS,"Static",SS_LEFTNOWORDWRAP | WS_GROUP,4,7,243,13
        END


        /////////////////////////////////////////////////////////////////////////
        //
        // Version
        //

        VS_VERSION_INFO VERSIONINFO
         FILEVERSION 1,0,0,1
         PRODUCTVERSION 1,0,0,1
         FILEFLAGSMASK 0x3fL
```

```
#ifdef _DEBUG
 FILEFLAGS 0x1L
#else
 FILEFLAGS 0x0L
#endif
 FILEOS 0x4L
 FILETYPE 0x1L
 FILESUBTYPE 0x0L
BEGIN
    BLOCK "StringFileInfo"
    BEGIN
        BLOCK "040904B0"
        BEGIN
            VALUE "CompanyName", "\0"
            VALUE "FileDescription", "DIALOGS MFC Application\0"
            VALUE "FileVersion", "1, 0, 0, 1\0"
            VALUE "InternalName", "DIALOGS\0"
            VALUE "LegalCopyright", "Copyright \251 1995\0"
            VALUE "LegalTrademarks", "\0"
            VALUE "OriginalFilename", "DIALOGS.EXE\0"
            VALUE "ProductName", "DIALOGS Application\0"
            VALUE "ProductVersion", "1, 0, 0, 1\0"
        END
    END
    BLOCK "VarFileInfo"
    BEGIN
        VALUE "Translation", 0x409, 1200
    END
END



/////////////////////////////////////////////////////////////////////////////
//
// String Table
//

STRINGTABLE PRELOAD DISCARDABLE
BEGIN
    IDR_MAINFRAME          "Dialogs"
END

STRINGTABLE PRELOAD DISCARDABLE
BEGIN
    AFX_IDS_APP_TITLE      "Dialogs"
    AFX_IDS_IDLEMESSAGE    "Ready"
END

STRINGTABLE DISCARDABLE
BEGIN
    ID_INDICATOR_EXT       "EXT"
    ID_INDICATOR_CAPS      "CAP"
    ID_INDICATOR_NUM       "NUM"
    ID_INDICATOR_SCRL      "SCRL"
```

```
         ID_INDICATOR_OVR          "OVR"
         ID_INDICATOR_REC          "REC"
END

STRINGTABLE DISCARDABLE
BEGIN
     ID_FILE_OPEN                  "Open an existing file\nOpen"
END

STRINGTABLE DISCARDABLE
BEGIN
     ID_APP_ABOUT                  "Display program info, version, copyright\nAbout"
     ID_APP_EXIT                   "Quit application; prompt to save documents\nExit"
END

STRINGTABLE DISCARDABLE
BEGIN
     ID_FILE_MRU_FILE1             "Open this document"
     ID_FILE_MRU_FILE2             "Open this document"
     ID_FILE_MRU_FILE3             "Open this document"
     ID_FILE_MRU_FILE4             "Open this document"
END

STRINGTABLE DISCARDABLE
BEGIN
     ID_VIEW_TOOLBAR               "Show or hide the toolbar\nToggle ToolBar"
     ID_VIEW_STATUS_BAR            "Show or hide the status bar\nToggle StatusBar"
END

STRINGTABLE DISCARDABLE
BEGIN
     AFX_IDS_SCSIZE                "Change the window size"
     AFX_IDS_SCMOVE                "Change the window position"
     AFX_IDS_SCMINIMIZE            "Reduce the window to an icon"
     AFX_IDS_SCMAXIMIZE            "Enlarge the window to full size"
     AFX_IDS_SCNEXTWINDOW          "Switch to the next document window"
     AFX_IDS_SCPREVWINDOW          "Switch to the previous document window"
     AFX_IDS_SCCLOSE               "Close active window and prompt to save documents"
END

STRINGTABLE DISCARDABLE
BEGIN
     AFX_IDS_SCRESTORE             "Restore the window to normal size"
     AFX_IDS_SCTASKLIST            "Activate Task List"
END

STRINGTABLE DISCARDABLE
BEGIN
     IDC_BACK                      "Search to beginning of file\nBackward Search"
     IDC_FORWARD                   "Search to end of file\nForward Search"
     IDC_SEARCHTEXT                "Type in text to find\nSearch Text"
END
```

```
STRINGTABLE DISCARDABLE
BEGIN
    ID_FILE_TYPE            "Create extensions for File Open dialog\nAdd Types"
    ID_VIEW_SEARCHBAR       "Show or hide the search bar\nToggle Search Bar"
    ID_VIEW_PROGRESS        "Run progress bar from start to end\nProgress Bar"
END


#ifndef APSTUDIO_INVOKED
/////////////////////////////////////////////////////////////////////////////
//
// Generated from the TEXTINCLUDE 3 resource.
//
#include "res\dialogs.rc2"   // non-Microsoft Visual C++ edited resources

#define _AFX_NO_SPLITTER_RESOURCES
#define _AFX_NO_OLE_RESOURCES
#define _AFX_NO_TRACKER_RESOURCES
#define _AFX_NO_PROPERTY_RESOURCES
#include "afxres.rc"         // Standard components


/////////////////////////////////////////////////////////////////////////////
#endif     // not APSTUDIO_INVOKED
```

Like all of the other programs we've described in this part of the
book, we started with an AppWizard-generated program. Because we're
ignoring MFC's Doc/View support, we removed that code. What's left is
a simple menu in a simple frame window that creates five dialogs.

USING CDIALOG DIRECTLY: AN ABOUT... BOX

Figure 12-10 shows DIALOG's About... box. We included this dialog primarily because we wanted to show you the smallest amount of work that
would be required to display a dialog. Although AppWizard can automatically generate a simple About... box for you, ours is even simpler.

Most of the effort in creating the About... box involves building a
dialog box template that displays some details about this program. We
also changed the dialog font to 10-point Arial — just a bit larger than
the default 8-point MS Sans Serif font. Displaying this dialog involves
two lines of code in DIALOG's application object (in DIALOGS.CPP):

```
void DApp::OnAppAbout()
{
    CDialog aboutDlg(IDD_ABOUTBOX);
    aboutDlg.DoModal();
}
```

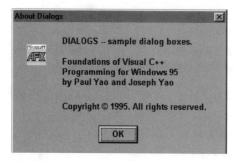

Figure 12-10
DIALOG's About... box with a 10-point Arial font.

So little work is required simply because CDialog does so much. In particular, it handles the one notification that is of interest to our program — the user clicking the OK button.

USING COMMON DIALOGS: FILE|OPEN

Building your own Open File dialog like the example shown in Figure 12-11 would take at least several hundred lines of code. Fortunately, as discussed earlier in this chapter, the Windows API includes support for eight commonly used dialogs. As a result, only minimal effort is required to produce an attractive, fully functional dialog. And as Microsoft continues to improve and refine Windows, these common dialogs will also be upgraded. For example, if you built a program to run in Windows 3.1 and you used the Open File dialog, your program automatically gained support for long filenames when they were introduced in Windows 95.

As part of its support for the Open File dialog, Windows 95 provides a default dialog box template. We mention this because you might have noticed that DIALOG's resource script doesn't have such a template. However, you can provide a template to be used in place of the system's dialog template. You just need to set a flag and provide the template ID when you create the common dialog.

Although the common dialogs are provided by the operating system, MFC defines a set of wrappers for each of them. We're going to cover only one of the eight common dialogs, but the pattern for using all of them is the same. You instantiate an MFC common dialog object, fill in data members as needed, and then call DoModal( ). The dialog is displayed, and you just wait for the results to come back after the user closes the dialog box.

Figure 12-11

The Open File dialog is one of eight common dialogs that provide a lot of dialog capability with only a little coding.

We've put the File|Open support in DIALOG's main window frame class, DMainFrame. It has a data member of type CFileDialog *, which holds a pointer that is initialized as follows (in MAINFRAME.CPP) when the frame window receives a WM_CREATE message:

```
// Create File|Open... dialog object.
d_pOpenFile = new CFileDialog (TRUE);
if (!d_pOpenFile)
    return -1;
```

Within CFileDialog, Microsoft has embedded a data structure of type OPENFILENAME. Because this is a Windows 95 data structure, it is better documented in the API32.HLP database than in the MFC help databases. You fill in this data structure to control the operation of the dialog box.

DIALOGS initializes this data structure before calling DoModal( ). One member of OPENFILENAME is lpstrFilter, which is defined as a LPCTSTR — a pointer to a const character string. This parameter actually expects a pointer to a compound string, which is a series of strings separated by NULL characters

The lpstrFilter parameter accepts a sequence of strings which the common dialog uses to initialize the *Files of Type* combo box. This combo box allows the user to specify which types of files the Open File dialog should list. For example, if the user selects All Files (*.*) from the Files of Type combo box, the Open File dialog will list all files in the current directory.

The lpstrFilter parameter actually accepts pairs of strings. The first string of each pair is a description, such as "All Files (*.*)." The second string in each pair uses wildcards — for example *.* — to select files that match the description. By defining several sets of these string pairs, you allow the user to filter which types of files are listed in the Filename list box. Here are some sample pairs:

Wildcard String	Description
.	All files
*.cpp	C++ source files
*.h	Include files
.c;.cpp;*.h	Any source file

Notice that the last item in this table has multiple wildcard strings, which are separated by semicolons.

To get its list of files, DIALOGS relies on a CStringList list of strings. DIALOGS provides another dialog box, the File|Type dialog, for the express purpose of editing this list of strings. We'll describe this dialog in the following section.

The Open File dialog is displayed when the user issues a File|Open command (via either the menu or the toolbar):

```
// Display File.Open... dialog box.
int iRet = d_pOpenFile->DoModal();
```

This creates a modal dialog box. As such, when this function returns, the value of iRet will be either IDOK — that is, accept the requested file — or IDCANCEL — ignore the results. CFileDialog provides several member functions for querying the results of calling this dialog. For example, GetPathName( ) gets the full path of the requested file, GetFileName( ) gets the filename without the path, and GetFileExt( ) gets only the file's extension.

Although the common Open File dialog provides a simple means for getting a filename, MFC provides an even simpler way. MFC's application class, CWinApp, has a member function called OnFileOpen( ) which displays a File|Open dialog. AppWizard sets up a call to CWinApp::OnFileOpen( ) as the command handler for the File|Open command.

If the user closes the File|Open dialog by clicking the OK button, CWinApp::OnFileOpen( ) calls OpenDocumentFile( ). The simpler technique for getting the name of a file to open is to override CWinApp::OpenDocumentFile( ), which passes a CString with the name of the file to open. Of course, using this support means that you have to be satisfied with its default parameters. However, if it meets your needs, you have all the features with less code.

The next dialog that we'll discuss is the modal dialog that is created to collect file type information for use by the Open File dialog.

CREATING A CUSTOM MODAL DIALOG: FILE|TYPE

Our next example, the File Type dialog, is more representative of the amount of code required to support a typical dialog box. It would be nice if all your dialog box development required as little code as our first two sample dialogs. But users expect some interaction between controls in even the simplest dialog.

We should mention that dialog development — like most user-interface creation — is an iterative process. Dialog capabilities tend to be added gradually as you discover new interactions between controls that make sense. Don't rush the process, because you probably won't think of every possible interaction that your users need in one sitting.

DIALOG's File|Type menu item opens the File Type dialog. As shown in Figure 12-12, this modal dialog box lets you build pairs of strings consisting of extension wildcards and description strings. As mentioned in the preceding section, the Open File dialog uses these strings to help the user locate specific file types.

As mentioned previously, most of the work in getting a dialog to work properly involves responding to dialog notifications. Table 12-6 summarizes the notifications that DIALOGS handles for the File Type dialog. Incidentally, the File Type dialog is created by the

DExtensionDlg class, which is declared in EXTENDLG.H and defined in EXTENDLG.CPP.

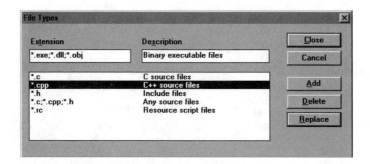

Figure 12-12
The File Type dialog lets the user edit the list of file extensions that appear in the Open File dialog's Files of Type list.

Dialog initialization

The sole purpose of this dialog is to create or update a list of character strings. MFC provides the CString class for holding simple character strings. A second MFC class, CStringList, holds a linked list of CString strings. The primary job of the File Type dialog is to allow a user to easily edit a list of string pairs that are used by the Open File dialog.

When the File Type dialog receives a WM_INITDIALOG message, it fills the list box with the strings from the string list. The list box has been flagged (in the dialog editor) to support tabs, so a set of list box tabs is set up to simplify the display of strings in separate columns. Finally, various pushbuttons are disabled to help the user distinguish enabled features from disabled features.

As shown in this example from the initialization for our DIALOGS program's File Type dialog, you set the tab stops in a list box by calling the CListBox::SetTabStops( ) function:

```
// Set tab stop in list box.
int nTab[6];
nTab[0] = 106;  // Hard-coded based on dialog box definition.
nTab[1] = 116;
nTab[2] = 126;
nTab[3] = 136;
nTab[4] = 146;
nTab[5] = 156;
d_listExtensions.SetTabStops(6, nTab);
```

Table 12-6

The Eight Notifications Handled by the File Type Dialog

Control	Notification	Description
Add button	BN_CLICKED	When the user clicks the Add button, CtlAdd() is called. This function moves items from the edit controls into the list box.
Close button	BN_CLICKED	When the user clicks the Close button, Ctl-Close() is called. This function moves the data from the list box into the CStringList used by the program to initialize the Open File dialog.
Delete button	BN_CLICKED	When the user clicks the Delete button, CtlDelete() is called. This function deletes the item that's currently selected in the list box.
Replace button	BN_CLICKED	When the user clicks the Replace button, CtlReplace() is called. This function deletes the currently selected list box item, and creates a new list box item using the data from the two edit controls.
Delete button	BN_DOUBLE-CLICKED	When the user double-clicks the Delete button, CtlDoubleclickedDelete() is called. This function calls CtlDelete(), and simply serves as a backup when the user is clicking the mouse very quickly.
Description edit control	EN_CHANGE	When any change occurs in the description edit control, CtlChangeDescription() is called. This function enables and disables various buttons in the dialog, depending on the state of the edit controls.
File extension edit control	EN_CHANGE	When any change occurs in the file extension edit control, CtlChangeExtension() is called. This function calls CtlChange-Description() to enable and disable push-buttons, as necessary.
List box	LBN_DBLCLK	When the user double-clicks the list box control, the CtlDblclkList1() function is called. This function copies the contents of the list box to the two edit controls.

Although hard-coded values are usually frowned upon, they seem quite appropriate for this example.

The units used for tab stops are dialog box units. As mentioned previously, dialog box units are based on the font that's used for the dialog. Therefore, although we have hard-coded values, they will scale appropriately with the different sizes of the font. If we subsequently decide to change our dialog template, we can also change this table of hard-coded values. Whether you agree with our little programming shortcut, there are two points you should remember about this example. First, this example shows how easy it is to set tab stops in a list box. Second, you need to remember that tabs are set in dialog box units — and not in pixels.

Another task that's performed during the dialog's initialization is the disabling of various pushbuttons. We do this to prevent the user from picking an invalid operation. Because a disabled pushbutton displays gray text, a user can easily see at a glance which buttons are available and which are not. As shown in the following code, you disable a pushbutton by calling CWnd::EnableWindow( ), with its sole parameter set to FALSE:

```
// Disable Add and Replace buttons.
d_bnAdd.EnableWindow(FALSE);
d_bnReplace.EnableWindow(FALSE);
```

To enable a pushbutton, you simply call the same function, with its parameter set to TRUE.

Two and possibly three of the dialog's pushbuttons are disabled during dialog initialization. During its normal operation, the dialog continually enables and disables these pushbuttons, depending on the state of the various controls. For example, when either edit control is blank, both the Add button and the Replace button are disabled. When the dialog's list box is entirely empty, the Delete button is disabled to let the user know that it's not available.

Adding an item to the list

To give you a clearer sense of how the dialog operates, let's consider a simple interaction: a user adding items to the list. We'll describe each user action and explain how the notifications create changes in the state of the dialog.

When the dialog is first displayed, the user can immediately start typing in the control in the upper-left corner of the dialog — that is, the edit control labeled Extension. This happens because the keyboard focus goes to the first nonstatic control in the dialog. In this instance, *first* means the first to be created, which is the same as the tab order.

After the dialog has started, we'll sometimes move the keyboard focus to a particular window by calling CWnd::SetFocus( ). But we only do this when the user clicks one of three pushbuttons: Add, Remove, or

Delete. You should avoid making arbitrary changes to the keyboard focus, because the user should control where input is to go.

As the user types into each edit control, the controls let the parent window know by sending EN_CHANGE notifications. Our sole interest is in making sure that the Add and Replace buttons are enabled when there is text in *both* edit controls. To check for the presence of text, we call CWnd::GetWindowTextLength( ). The Replace button has an additional restriction: It should be enabled only when an item is selected in the list box. To check this, we call CListBox::GetCurSel( ). The following lines of code perform these two tests:

```
// Calculate length of strings in edit controls.
int nLen1 = d_edDescription.GetWindowTextLength();
int nLen2 = d_edExtension.GetWindowTextLength();

// Enable [Add] button when edit controls have text,
// Otherwise disable it.
BOOL bEnable = (nLen1 > 0 && nLen2 > 0) ? TRUE : FALSE;
d_bnAdd.EnableWindow(bEnable);

// Enable [Replace] button when edit controls have text,
// AND when an item is currently selected.
int nCurSel = d_listExtensions.GetCurSel();
d_bnReplace.EnableWindow(bEnable && nCurSel != LB_ERR);
```

Once there is some text in both edit controls, the user can create a list box entry by clicking the Add button (or pressing Alt-A). This triggers a BN_CLICKED notification, which is mapped to our dialog's CtlAdd( ) member function. A string from each edit control is fetched with calls to CWnd::GetWindowText( ), and the two strings are concatenated, with a tab character between them. The combined string is then put in the list box by calling CListBox::InsertString( ).

After the strings are copied from the edit controls to the list box, we still need to take care of a few chores. First, the edit controls must be cleared out. Next, control of the keyboard — that is, the focus — is set to the first edit control. Finally, the Delete button is enabled because it's now possible to delete the entry that was created. Our code does have a bit of a redundancy. We enable the Delete button every time an entry is created — and not just the first time. Although this might waste a few processor cycles, the extra work is benign. Here's the code that handles our extra chores:

```
// Empty contents of both text buffers.
d_edExtension.SetWindowText(_T(""));
d_edDescription.SetWindowText(_T(""));

// Set focus to extensions control.
d_edExtension.SetFocus();

// Enable Delete button
d_bnDelete.EnableWindow(TRUE);
```

It seems as though you can always find another refinement that you could make to a user interface, and this dialog box is no exception. If this dialog were to be used for entering long lists of extension-description pairs, we would want to enable the Enter key. To do that, the dialog requires only a slight modification.

In a dialog, the Enter key is connected to the default pushbutton. The default pushbutton is the button for which the BS_DEFPUSHBUTTON style bit is set. (Regular pushbuttons have the BS_PUSHBUTTON style.) A user can easily identify the default pushbutton in a dialog because it has a thicker border than the other pushbuttons.

In our dialog, the Close button is the default pushbutton, because it's always enabled. However, by calling CButton::SetButtonStyle( ), we can make the Add button the default pushbutton. By making the Add button the default pushbutton when it becomes enabled, our dialog allows a user to enter text and quickly press the Enter key. When the Add button becomes disabled, it's a simple matter to restore default processing to the Close button.

In the next section, we'll explore the shutdown phase of our dialog. During shutdown, the results of our dialog are returned to the caller.

Dialog box shutdown

A user can dismiss the File Type dialog in any of several ways. A user can accept the changes by clicking the Close button or by pressing the Enter key. Changes can be rejected by clicking the Cancel button or by pressing the Esc key. Because CDialog has a default message handler, you don't have to deal with cancellations unless you want to do something special.

When the user accepts the changes, control passes to our dialog's CtlClose( ) notification handler. Here's the code for that function:

```
void DExtensionDlg::CtlClose()
{
    // Empty contents of list.
    d_cslFileType.RemoveAll();

    // Rebuild string list.
    CopyListboxToStringList(d_listExtensions, &d_cslFileType);

    CDialog::OnOK();
    return;
}
```

The data member d_cslFileType is a CStringList, which is a type of container for holding linked lists of CStrings. If the user really wants to accept the changes, we have to get rid of the current items in the list before adding a new set. CStringList::RemoveAll( ) takes care of that.

Our helper function, CopyListboxToStringList( ), loops through the list of strings. After dissecting extensions from descriptions, it adds the new strings to the string list. As mentioned previously, this set of strings will be used as a source of wildcards for the File Open dialog.

When all is said and done, we call the base class handler, CDialog::OnOK( ), which shuts down our dialog for us. Of course, we could do this just as easily. But it makes sense to call the default handler because this allows our application to keep up with future changes to Microsoft Windows and MFC.

The next user-interface object that we'll discuss is half dialog box and half toolbar: it's a dialog bar. Like a toolbar, a dialog bar sits on the edge of a window to provide extra support for command input. Like a dialog box, a dialog bar is defined using a dialog template. When you create a dialog bar, its controls send notification messages to their parent window. Let's see what's involved in creating a dialog bar.

CREATING A CONTROL BAR

To define a dialog bar, you start by creating a dialog box template. Unlike other dialog templates, however, you won't have an OK button or even a Cancel button. You don't need these buttons because the dialog bar sits and waits on the side of — for example — your application's frame window. Figure 12-13 shows the example control bar from our DIALOGS program. Like a modeless dialog box, a control bar is quite content to run in nonexclusive mode.

Figure 12-13
This control bar from the DIALOGS program contains one edit control and two pushbutton controls.

Although it's certainly possible to derive a new class when you create a dialog bar, for most purposes you can simply instantiate a CDialogBar object. For example, here is the code that DIALOGS uses to create its dialog bar:

```
// Create dialog bar object.
d_pDialogBar = new CDialogBar();
if (!d_pDialogBar)
    return -1;

// Initialize dialog bar.
d_pDialogBar->Create(this, IDD_SEARCHBAR, WS_CHILD | CBRS_TOP |
                     CBRS_TOOLTIPS | CBRS_FLYBY, ID_SEARCH_BAR);

// Make dialog bar visible.
d_pDialogBar->ShowWindow(SW_SHOWNORMAL);
```

Dialog bars are a little shy, so you should avoid specifying the visibility style bit at creation time. In other words, leave out the WS_VISIBLE bit in the call to CDialogBar::Create( ). And in the dialog box template, be sure to uncheck the Visible style bit. Otherwise, creation will mysteriously fail. (The Debug version will raise an assertion to let you know that something is wrong.) This shyness is caused by the fact that dialog bars don't want to be caught half ready to serve users. Once it's created, a dialog bar is happy to make an appearance — which we request in the preceding example with our call to CWnd::ShowWindow( ).

Like controls in regular dialog boxes, controls in a dialog bar send notification messages to the dialog bar's parent window. In our case, the notification messages are sent to DIALOG's frame window. Unfortunately, the ClassWizard doesn't know how to set up a message handler for the dialog bar's controls. To handle notifications, we need to declare a member function in the include file, define a message map entry, and define the actual function in a C++ source file.

Here's how the two member functions from DIALOG's DMainFrame class are declared (in Listing 12-5, MAINFRM.H):

```
afx_msg BOOL CmdSearchForward(UINT nID);
afx_msg BOOL CmdSearchBackward(UINT nID);
```

Unlike a menu command handler, this one has a parameter for communicating the control notification code. For example, our buttons could send a BN_CLICKED or a BN_DOUBLECLICKED.

Because this is a little different from a regular command handler, you don't use the standard ON_COMMAND( ) macro. Instead, you use ON_COMMAND_EX( ), which takes into account the additional parameter:

```
ON_COMMAND_EX(IDC_FORWARD, CmdSearchForward)
ON_COMMAND_EX(IDC_BACK, CmdSearchBackward)
```

Finally, you define a function with a prototype like the following function:

```
BOOL DMainFrame::CmdSearchForward(UINT nID);
```

The BOOL return value will be True for command messages that you handle and False for messages that you pass on to other handlers. (Chapter 11 provides more details about WM_COMMAND message routing.)

DIALOG's dialog bar doesn't do much; it just displays a dummy message box that says "Searching for...," along with the text string in the edit control. However, the code is useful for showing how to get a pointer to a control that's on a dialog bar. It works a little differently than in a regular dialog class.

To get a pointer to a control on a dialog bar, you call GetDlgItem( ). However, you must call this function through the control's parent window — which is the dialog bar, and not your frame window. When we created the dialog bar, we got back d_pDialogBar, a CDialogBar pointer. Here's how we can call to get a CEdit pointer to the edit control in our dialog bar:

```
CEdit * pedSearch =
        (CEdit *)d_pDialogBar->GetDlgItem(IDC_SEARCHTEXT);
```

Other than the additional notifications — and slightly different notification functions — dialog bars are very much like toolbars. It's now time to take a look at the fifth and last dialog box that DIALOGS creates — a modeless dialog box that displays a progress bar.

CREATING A CUSTOM MODELESS DIALOG: PROGRESS BAR

Figure 12-14 shows DIALOG's progress bar. For now, it runs off a timer to simulate what might happen during a long operation. But it can also be easily modified to run in other circumstances.

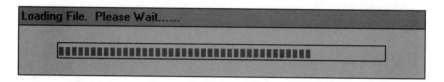

Figure 12-14
DIALOG's progress bar is a modeless dialog box that keeps a user updated with a program's internal processing.

The progress bar has a simple dialog box template containing a single, static text control. However, it uses the control in some interesting ways that you might find helpful in other situations. For example, the control uses a different font than the normal dialog fonts. Also, the progress indicator bars are displayed in a bright blue (which is not readily apparent in Figure 12-14) that is typically used for progress indicators.

Changing the font is a matter of creating a CFont object and passing it to the control by calling CWnd::SetFont( ). We'll explore fonts more fully in Chapter 13. For now, the important point is that we select a symbol font named WingDings. It just so happens that a lowercase *n* in this font looks a lot like a square box — enough so that it can easily pass for a box in a progress bar.

Changing the color of a control is also fairly simple. Most of the interactions between a control and its parent window occur through a notification embedded in a WM_COMMAND message. However, controls can also send their parents a WM_CTLCOLOR message. Here's the code that handles this message for our progress bar:

```
HBRUSH DProgress::OnCtlColor(CDC* pDC, CWnd* pWnd, UINT nCtlColor)
{
    // Call default handler to do most of the work.
    HBRUSH hbr = CDialog::OnCtlColor(pDC, pWnd, nCtlColor);

    // Draw blue blocks for progress indicator bars
    pDC->SetTextColor(RGB(0, 0, 255));

    return hbr;
}
```

Controls send the WM_CTLCOLOR message right before they draw. In effect, the child window asks, "What color do you want me to be?" In our case, we tell the child, "Bright blue." Notice that we first call the default handler, in case the system wants to set up other attributes. But we get the last word as we change the text color to blue.

Most of this work on the progress bar is done while the dialog is being set up — that is, in response to the WM_INITDIALOG message. Once the dialog is created, a single function, SetPercent( ), lets a caller control the current setting of the progress bar. A caller can also find out the current setting by calling GetPercent( ).

One important issue for modeless dialog boxes is clean-up. With a modal dialog box, the clean-up issue is simple; nothing else happens until the dialog is through. On the other hand, you have to let the parent window know when a modeless dialog goes away. Our progress bar accomplishes this by sending a private message — PM_PROGRESS_ CLOSING — when it closes. Because ClassWizard doesn't know how to handle private messages, we had to write the code for this task.

In the past several chapters, we've been focusing our attention on user-interface objects. Having covered the big three — windows, menus, and dialogs — we're going to turn our attention to I/O issues.

In the following chapter, we cover the creation of graphic output. We'll focus on text output, because it's the most common type in typical applications. But we'll cover enough of the basics to help you start exploring the creation of other types of graphics. That's the output part. As for input, Chapter 14 will give you a complete look at what it takes to handle mouse and keyboard input in a CWnd-derived window.

13 Introduction to GDI and Text Drawing

Graphics programming is such a vast topic that whole books have been dedicated to the subject (some of which are listed in the Recommended Reading section at the end of this book). But to get some useful work done, you don't need to know everything about creating graphic output. In fact, most programmers who are building basic business applications need to know only the ground rules. Once you've mastered these fundamentals, you can pick up additional topics and techniques as your needs warrant.

This chapter provides the basic set of ground rules for creating text in a window. We'll start with a brief overview of GDI. We'll also describe — in very broad terms — GDI's other types of output (raster and vector graphics) as well as the three other types of devices and pseudodevices that GDI supports.

From there, we'll delve into a wide range of programming topics that cover drawing messages, data structures, and function calls. The chapter concludes with FILELIST, a program that opens text files and displays their contents in a scrollable window. Along the way, we'll also refer to ECHOFILL, another sample program that isn't printed in the book but is included on the accompanying disk. This program shows an interesting side effect of the way in which the WM_PAINT message is handled.

An Overview of GDI

GDI, the Graphics Device Interface, is one of three dynamic link libraries that form the core of Microsoft Windows. GDI handles all of the graphic output from a Windows program. When a drawing package creates a circle, when a word-processing program sends a page of text to a printer, when a screen saver flashes fancy graphics, all of these operations use GDI services to create their output.

Windows itself uses GDI to draw the various parts of the user interface. When you see a window, a menu, or a dialog, each of these has been drawn with calls to GDI. GDI is even responsible for the mouse cursor, which seems to float above the other objects on the display screen.

GDI's presence in the system provides you with high-level drawing functions that allow you to produce interesting graphics effects with little effort. For example, it's easy to draw text in a multitude of sizes and colors. You can move and manipulate bitmaps with just a few calls. You can produce sophisticated vector drawings without having to fuss over the math they might otherwise require. All of this comes with a minimum of code because GDI defines the programming interface and — through a large set of device drivers — provides uniform results across a large number of devices.

In the following sections, we're going to introduce you to the types of graphic output that GDI can produce. We'll also discuss the types of devices that GDI supports. And we'll introduce you to the device context, an important data structure that connects a program to a device and lets it control the appearance of graphic output.

TYPES OF GRAPHIC OUTPUT

GDI functions let a program create three types of graphic output: text, raster graphics, and vector graphics. Figure 13-1 shows examples of each type. Although these categories might seem arbitrary, they aren't. At the device driver level, each type has its own set of entry points and ways of operating. At the programming interface, a program controls the appearance of each type using slightly different sets of drawing attributes. By understanding the distinctions between these three types, you can often avoid the confusion that is sometimes caused by inconsistencies in the handling of each type.

Let's look at each of the three types of graphic output that GDI can produce, starting with text.

Text

8-point MS Serif Bold
10-point Courier New Italic
12-point Arial Regular
14-point Times New Roman Bold Italic

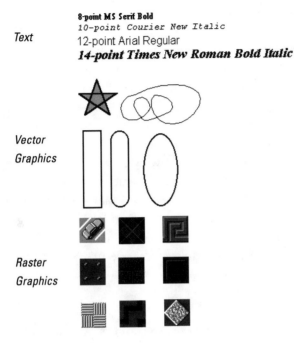

Vector
Graphics

Raster
Graphics

Figure 13-1

GDI functions make it possible for a program to create text, raster graphics, and vector graphics.

Text as graphics

An irony of Windows programming is that, although GDI simplifies the creation of raster and vector graphics, it's harder to create text output in a Windows program than in a character-based program. This was first pointed out to one of the authors by David Durant, one of the first people to teach Windows programming outside of Microsoft. By *harder*, we mean that quite a few more lines of code are required to get similar results. It's harder to create text because text is treated as graphics.

Why is handling text as graphics difficult? Perhaps an example will help explain why. Calling the C-runtime function printf( ) for text output is simple. You don't have to worry about the color of the text. You don't have to worry about the font. In most cases, you don't even worry about *where* the text appears — because it simply shows up on a "next line" or a "next" character position.

Text requires more work in Windows because you can control more aspects than you were ever able to in the character-based world. Do you want red text? No problem. Need 18-point, bold letters? You can choose from a large set of such letters. Are you planning to create shadowed effects by drawing the same text overlapping itself by just a pixel or two? You certainly can't do any of that in a character-based environment, but you can do all of it in Windows.

As an example of text as graphics, consider the fact that Windows 95 itself uses text to draw the ornaments of a window. The minimize box, the maximize box, and the close box are all characters from the Marlett font. Because previous versions of Windows used bitmaps for these ornaments, the switch to a TrueType font — which is scalable — gives Windows 95 the flexibility of allowing users to change the caption bar size. For the extra work that fonts require, the added benefit is greater flexibility in controlling the resulting output.

Raster graphics

GDI's second type of graphic output is raster graphics. A raster graphics function operates on data stored in arrays called *bitmaps*. The most obvious example of a bitmap is projected onto the display screen of a computer when the power is on. A standard VGA monitor's 640 × 480 image is little more than a bitmap that the display adapter hardware makes visible on the display screen. Part of Windows' support for raster graphics is the capability to create *offscreen* bitmap images. Like the image on your display screen, such bitmaps can hold all kinds of graphic data.

Other examples of raster graphics are icons and cursors, which you add to a program by editing the resource file. Window movement on the display screen is yet another example of raster graphics. When the user picks up a window and moves it to another location on the display screen, a raster graphics function picks up the rectangle of pixels at the source and moves it to the destination rectangle.

Windows' user interface also makes use of raster graphics in other ways. For example, most of the pixels in a typical Windows application are drawn by making raster graphics function calls. In particular, all of the white (or background color) space that's not text in a window is drawn by calling the PatBlt( ) — pattern-fill bit-boundary block transfer — function. The thin lines that make up window borders are also drawn using this pattern fill function, with the destination rectangle set to draw a very thin pattern.

Because the data on the display screen is stored in arrays of raster data, bitmaps are useful for caching complex graphical objects for fast-display screen drawing. You can build complex drawings ahead of time — either on the fly or at program build time — so the bitmap image is ready and waiting. Whether the image is a cartoon character, a logo, or some other complex symbol, it can be quickly copied from the bitmap cache to your display screen, as needed. The only problem with bitmaps is the space that they consume, both in RAM and on disk. For example, a screen-size, 640×480, 8-bit-per-pixel, 256-color bitmap occupies approximately 300K. To ensure that your bitmaps are worth the space they consume, you'll want to cache only your most commonly drawn graphical objects.

One very practical use of raster data involves capturing screen shots for documentation purposes. This capability is useful for creating everything from application's design document to end-user documentation. The PrtScr key copies the entire screen to the clipboard. A slight variation, Alt-PrtScr, copies only the top-level window. From the clipboard, these bitmap images can then be pasted to a word-processing document. For example, that's how we created all the screen shots that you see in this book.

Vector graphics

In the context of GDI, the term *vector graphics* refers to the drawing functions that create lines and filled figures. GDI has a whole set of functions for drawing straight lines, curves, polygons, pie wedges, and rectangles. You can call these functions with any raster or text function to mix text and graphics in any way that suits you.

When most people think of *graphics*, they think of geometric shapes. It's ironic, then, that very few vector graphics functions are called by Windows 95 when it draws the user interface. Instead, menus, dialogs, and all parts of windows are drawn using only text and raster graphics calls. Even though a window border looks like a straight line and therefore might seem to involve vector graphics calls, in fact, window borders are drawn with raster graphics calls.

Aside from drawing packages, most applications don't make much use of GDI's vector graphics. There's nothing wrong with these functions, it's just that most business uses are text-based. And for complex images, most programs use bitmaps (or icons).

Another reason for the lack of vector graphics is that most program-mers are still fairly new to graphics programming. Prior to programming for Windows, many programmers worked in a character-based environment such as MS-DOS or Unix. In the midst of learning the new ways of think-ing that graphical, event-driven programming requires, these programmers often can't take the time to explore the use of vector graphics.

As time passes and more programmers have the opportunity to work with vector graphics functions, we expect this to change. For example, vector graphics calls might be used to draw polygons around groups of related objects, with the effect of more directly connecting these objects in a user's mind. The TreeView list box in Windows 95, for example, shows how vector graphics can be used to highlight the connections between data.

GDI's three types of graphic output — text, raster, and vector — com-bine to provide numerous choices for creating a wide range of visual effects. To make the most of each type requires a bit of imagination. For example, most programmers don't typically think of text as graphics. But the window ornaments in Windows 95 show one way that this can be done. The progress dialog box in the DIALOGS sample program in the preceding chapter shows another use of text as graphics. That program uses WingDings, a symbol font, to create the little boxes in a progress bar. In many cases, less-obvious techniques such as these can allow your applications to provide lots of capabilities with only a little bit of code.

Let's take a look at the types of devices that GDI can support.

GDI Devices

Built-in support for text, raster graphics, and vector graphics isn't required for a graphics device to be a GDI device. Some devices *can* do it all — most notably printers that use Adobe's Postscript language and printers that use the Microsoft At Work print technology. But the vast majority of graphics devices — that is, display adapters and printers — don't have anywhere near this sophistication.

The only requirement for being a GDI device is the capability to turn on a pixel. Beyond that, GDI can do most of the work of decomposing drawing requests into a simpler form. It's up to each device driver to tell GDI exactly what that specific device can and cannot do. The driver passes GDI a set of device capability bits that GDI uses to modify its drawing requests.

On devices with limited capabilities, GDI does most of the drawing work. Using its built-in drawing simulations, GDI can convert all text and vector calls into raster data. Although raster data occupies more space than higher-level drawing functions, this is offset by the benefit of being able to render highly complex GDI drawings on even the least capable device.

For more capable devices, GDI does less of the work. After all, if a device can handle a drawing request — perhaps using special hardware — GDI puts less demand on the system's CPU. Also, higher-level drawing requests take much less memory and disk space, providing even greater improvement in overall system throughput.

The capability to work on a wide range of devices is one reason why Microsoft calls GDI a device-independent graphics package. If a drawing capability doesn't exist on the device itself, GDI steps in with a software simulation to create a reasonable result. If a device does have a built-in capability, GDI gets out of the way and lets the user enjoy the speed advantage of hardware-based graphics.

The types of devices supported by GDI can be divided into two categories: physical devices and pseudodevices. John Butler, a member of the original GDI design team, first pointed out this distinction to one of the authors. We think it's a useful distinction because it helps clarify GDI's device-independent nature. It also points to another aspect of GDI: that a single set of drawing calls can be used to draw on both physical and logical drawing surfaces.

Physical devices

From an application's point of view, there are two basic physical devices: display screens and printers. When drawing on a display screen, an application is always drawing inside a window. The window manager makes sure that the drawing from one application doesn't accidentally spill over into the windows that belong to other applications.

GDI enforces window boundaries using a feature known as *clipping*. Clipping is the definition of drawing boundaries. The most obvious drawing boundaries are the borders of windows, which the system manages for you. In addition, you can create your own drawing boundaries by creating your own *clipping regions*. For example, you might use this capability to create a brick wall between the drawings done by two different parts of an application without creating additional windows.

In the same way that clipping serves to enforce boundaries between drawings on the display screen, GDI uses another technique — *spooling* — to enforce the boundaries between drawings done to the printer. Although the Windows implementation of spooling might differ from that of other operating systems, the principle is the same. Print jobs are stored until the printer is ready to receive them.

When sending output to a printer, you must make some special considerations, such as the paper size, the orientation, and the available fonts. But you'll use the same set of GDI functions whether you're drawing on the display screen or on a printer. In practical terms, this means that you can write a single piece of drawing code for both types of devices.

Pseudodevices

Pseudodevices provide a way to store pictures. GDI has two types of pseudodevices: bitmaps and metafiles. When he used the term *pseudodevice*, Butler was referring to the fact that the API gives both of these storage devices the same respect that it gives a physical device. But bitmaps and metafiles obviously aren't devices in the traditional sense. Aside from the RAM or the disk space in which they are stored, they have no physical hardware. They are, in effect, software simulations of a logical device.

A bitmap is an array of picture elements. In the same way that you can call GDI functions to draw on the display screen or on the printer, you can call GDI functions to draw on a bitmap. Although a bitmap simulates a raster drawing surface, you aren't limited to using only raster graphics calls. Instead, you can make any text, raster graphics, or vector graphics drawing calls to draw on a bitmap.

GDI's second type of pseudodevice is the metafile. While a bitmap is an array of pixels, metafiles are lists of drawing calls. Like bitmaps, metafiles store pictures. Bitmaps hold the pixels that are drawn after a function call. Metafiles capture GDI function calls *before* any pixels are illuminated. A metafile is basically a recording of a set of drawing calls, including parameters, that can be played back to create a picture on any other GDI device.

To give you a better idea of what's in a metafile, we should point out that there is nothing intrinsically graphical about capturing function call parameters. You could, for example, create a similar mechanism to log calls made to the C-runtime string routines. After a program runs, you might have a list containing several thousand references to "strcpy( )," "strcat," and other functions, along with the parameters used. We're not sure what good this would do, because you wouldn't know the meaning of all those parameters without some additional data. However, when you record GDI drawing call in a metafile, you have a very good chance of re-creating your original picture when you replay the metafile.

The record-and-playback nature of metafiles provides a great deal of flexibility for storing pictures. However, that flexibility comes at a cost. For complicated pictures, drawing is slower with a metafile than with a comparable bitmap. The drawback to bitmaps, though, is that they tend to consume quite a bit of memory. To decide which pseudodevice you should use, you must study both and decide when the tradeoffs make one more useful to you than the other.

Whenever you draw to any GDI device — whether it is a physical device or a pseudodevice — you always need access to a data structure called a device context (DC). In fact, a handle to a device context is always the first parameter to a GDI drawing call in the native API.

MFC wraps GDI's DC into a set of C++ classes. This includes CDC and the CDC-derived classes. Many of the members of these classes are simple inline wrapper functions around native GDI drawing calls. Let's turn our attention to understanding the role played by device contexts as well as how the MFC classes support them.

THE DEVICE CONTEXT

A *device context* — also known as a *DC* — is a data structure that GDI creates to represent a device connection. For example, to draw on the display screen, a Windows program must have a DC for the display. And to create output on a printer, yet another DC is required — this one created specifically for the printer. If the same program also wants to create output in a metafile and a bitmap, a third and a fourth DC are required. The role of a DC, then, is to provide a connection between a program and either a physical device or a pseudodevice.

In addition to providing a device connection, a DC holds a collection of drawing attribute settings. For example, one drawing attribute in the DC is the text color. When a text drawing function is called, the function refers to the text color attribute to determine the correct color for the text.

You can change any drawing attribute at any time by calling specific GDI functions. For example, the SetTextColor( ) function sets the text color. For every attribute-setting function, there is a comparable attribute query function. For example, to find out the current text color settings, you call GetTextColor( ).

DC DRAWING ATTRIBUTES

Table 13-1 summarizes the 25 attributes that GDI stores in a DC. The table indicates which drawing attributes affect each of the three types of graphic objects. The Comments column provides details about default settings and how to change each attribute. The functions that are mentioned in Table 13-1 are member functions of CDC, the MFC class that wraps the GDI device context.

Table 13-1

Drawing Attributes That GDI Stores in a Device Context

Attribute	Text	Raster	Vector	Comments
Arc direction			X	Default=Counterclockwise. Determines whether arcs are drawn in a clockwise (AD_CLOCKWISE) or counterclockwise (AD_COUNTER-CLOCKWISE) direction. Set by calling SetArcDirection().
Background color	X	X	X	Default=RGB(255,255,255) — that is, white. Used for the background of normal text, in color-to-monochrome bitmap conversions, and for the background of styled (non-solid) pens and hatched brushes. Set by calling SetBkColor().
Background mode	X	X	X	Default=OPAQUE. Turns use of background color ON (OPAQUE) or OFF (TRANSPARENT). Set by calling SetBkMode().
Bounds rectangle	X	X	X	Default=Disabled. When enabled, tells GDI to keep track of the area into which it has drawn. Control with SetBoundsRect().
Brush		X	X	Default=White brush. Defines the interior color of closed figures. In MFC, create a CBrush object, and then select it into the DC by calling SelectObject().

Attribute	Text	Raster	Vector	Comments
Brush origin			X	Default=(0,0). Sets the point in device space to align a brush. Necessary only for hatched and dithered brushes, because only these types can have misalignments. Set by calling SetBrushOrg().
Clipping region	X	X	X	Default=Entire drawing surface. Defines drawing boundaries. Set by creating a clipping region (CRgn) and selecting it into a DC (SelectClipRgn()).
Color adjustment		X		Default=No adjustment. Defines the changes to bitmaps stretched with calls to StretchBlt() and StretchDIBits(). Set by calling SetColorAdjustment().
Current position	X		X	Default=(0,0). An (x,y) pair originally created to assist in line drawing. Enable for text by calling SetTextAlign() with the TA_UPDATECP flag. Set attribute by calling SetCurrentPosition().
Drawing mode			X	Default=R2_COPYPEN. Determines how Boolean operators are used when vector graphics are drawn. Set by calling SetROP2().
Font	X			Default=System font. Determines which set of graphic figures are used for drawing text. In MFC, set by creating a CFont object and connecting it to a DC by calling SelectObject().
Graphics mode	X	X	X	Default=GM_COMPATIBLE. Determines whether GDI ignores world transform and other Win32 enhancements (Windows 3.1 compatible) or whether these are used (GM_ADVANCED). Set by calling SetGraphicsMode().
Mapping mode	X	X	X	Default=MM_TEXT. Controls much of coordinate mapping. In the default mode, one logical unit equals one device unit. Set by calling SetMapMode().

(continued)

Table 13-1 (continued)

Attribute	Text	Raster	Vector	Comments
Miter limit			X	Default=10.0. Determines how much miter (pointiness) to allow in a join of a geometric line before capping off the corner. (Note: This setting only affects lines drawn with pens that have the PS_JOIN_MITER style.) Set by calling SetMiterLimit().
Palette	X	X	X	Default=System palette. Supported only by certain devices, it gives applications control over how the physical color table, or palette, is set. To use this attribute, create a CPalette object and connect to a device by calling SelectPalette().
Pen			X	Default=Black pen. Used by vector graphics functions to draw the borders of geometric figures such as rectangles and pie wedges, as well as for drawing straight and curved lines. Set by creating a CPen object and connecting to a device by calling SelectObject().
Polygon filling mode			X	Default=Alternate. Determines how the interior spaces of complex, overlapping polygons are to be filled. With a five-pointed star, for example, should the center be filled or not? The default, ALTERNATE, means *No*. The other choice, WINDING, means *Yes*. Change by calling SetPolyFillMode().
StretchBlt mode		X		Default=BLACKONWHITE. Determines how pixels are removed when a bitmap is shrunk using the StretchBlt() API. Set by calling SetStretchBltMode().
Text alignment	X			Default=TA_LEFT I TA_TOP. Determines the alignment between text drawing coordinates and the resulting text box. Default is upper-left, but eight other alignments are possible. Set by calling SetTextAlign().
Text color	X			Default=RGB(0,0,0) — that is, black. Determines the foreground color of pixels. (See also the background color attribute). Set by calling SetTextColor().

Attribute	Text	Raster	Vector	Comments
Text extra spacing	X			Default=0. Determines how many pixels are to be padded into each character cell in a string. Used to expand a string to fill a margin. Set by calling SetTextCharacterExtra().
Text justification	X			Default=(0,0). Determines how many pixels to pad into *break characters* (that is, spaces) to help a line of text fill out a margin. Set by calling SetTextJustification().
Viewport extent	X	X	X	Default=(1,1). Used with a mapping mode of MM_ISOTROPIC or MM_ANISOTROPIC. Helps scale a drawing by modifying the device coordinate side of the scaling ratio. Set by calling SetViewportExt().
Viewport origin	X	X	X	Default=(0,0) — that is, the upper-left corner of device space. Moves the origin around the device space. Set by calling SetViewportOrg().
Window extent	X	X	X	Default=(1,1). Used with a mapping mode of MM_ISOTROPIC or MM_ANISOTROPIC. Scales a drawing by modifying the world coordinate side of the scaling ratio. Set by calling SetWorldExt().
Window origin	X	X	X	Default=(0,0). Moves the origin around the world coordinate space. Set by calling SetWindowOrg().

The default DC settings provide a good starting place for drawing. The best way to learn about GDI drawing is by writing small programs that draw a few simple objects. As you begin to experiment with new drawing functions, you won't have to make many changes to DC attributes to get reasonable results. Once you have a clearer understanding of how various drawing functions work, you can begin to explore the role of individual drawing attributes.

To help you get started, we're going to turn our attention to topics related to drawing in a window. Although our ultimate goal is to cover text drawing in depth, you'll find that much of the same material also applies to raster and vector graphics calls.

Drawing Text in a Window

In this section, we'll cover some of the topics you need to understand to draw text in a window. To tap the full power of GDI, you'll eventually want to explore sending output to the printer as well as how to use bitmaps and metafiles. You'll also want to learn more about raster and vector graphics, which both provide useful ways to enhance the capabilities of any graphics program. But the road to other devices and to other types of graphic output starts with the simple step of drawing text in a window. Let's get started.

THE WM_PAINT MESSAGE

For drawing in a window, the most important message is WM_PAINT. In simplest terms, this message asks a window to redraw its contents. There are many reasons why you might get this message. For example, another window might open on top of your window and overwrite its contents. Or, a user might decide to "unminimize" a previously minimized window. Or, it might simply be that your program is just starting up.

Whatever the reason for a window getting a WM_PAINT message, the system can't re-create the contents of a window's client area. A member of the original Windows development team, Mark Cliggett, related to us that the team considered various ways that the system might be able to store window data. One possibility was to take a snapshot of a window before it was covered by other windows. The sheer amount of memory required for this approach made it an unworkable solution.

In the character-based world, a screen full of data can be stored in a tiny, 2K buffer. In the graphics world of Windows, however, a 256-color, 640×480 window needs 300K. With several applications running, a megabyte or more would be quickly eaten up. This was too high a price to pay for the first version of Windows, when system memory totaled only one megabyte! With Windows 95 targeted to run in 4 megabytes, a megabyte of window snapshots is still too much memory for too little benefit.

Even if memory wasn't a problem, however, another problem remains. If the system stores window snapshots and any part of a window's data changed, the cache would be worthless. In such a situation, the application would have to redraw the contents of the window anyway. As a result, all of the memory and all of the processor time spent saving the snapshot would be wasted.

The WM_PAINT message is the solution to the problem of keeping the state of a window up to date. Windows makes every application entirely responsible for maintaining the contents of its windows. The WM_PAINT message provides the mechanism by which the system tells you that it's time to refresh a window. All you have to do is make sure that your program retains whatever state information it needs for accomplishing this task.

Setting up a WM_PAINT handler is easy with ClassWizard. You simply start ClassWizard, select the appropriate class, and click on WM_PAINT in the Messages list box. Here's an example of the empty paint-handling code that ClassWizard creates:

```
void DMainFrame::OnPaint()
{
    CPaintDC dc(this); // device context for painting

    // TODO: Add your message handler code here

    // Do not call CFrameWnd::OnPaint() for painting messages
}
```

In addition to spinning an empty paint-handling function for you, ClassWizard gives you two bonuses. First, it instantiates a CPaintDC, which is a special type of DC for handling paint messages. Second, a friendly comment reminds you that you should not call the message-handling function in the base class. This is important, because you might expect that this message — like so many others — would need a call to the base class member.

The ClassWizard-generated code provides an instance of a CPaintDC object. A quick look at the MFC class hierarchy reveals that this class is derived from CDC, which is the MFC class that wraps around GDI's device context. As we mentioned earlier in this chapter, the device context is a connection to a GDI device. With a CPaintDC in hand, you access the device — that is, query its state and send it graphic output — by making calls to CPaintDC member functions.

Table 13-2 shows the relationship between MFC's device context classes and GDI devices. Things seem slightly skewed toward the display, which has three device context classes. Because we're focusing our attention on the display screen, let's discuss these three classes.

Table 13-2

Relationship Between MFC's Device Context Classes and GDI Devices

Device	CDC-Derived Class
Display	CPaintDC, CClientDC, CWindowDC
Printer	CDC
Bitmap	CDC
Metafile	CMetaFileDC

The three types of display DC classes reflect three different ways to draw in a window. One of these, CWindowDC, allows you to draw anywhere in a window, including a window's nonclient areas. Recall that the nonclient area includes the caption bar, the system menu, the menu bar, the scroll bars, and the border. This isn't a terribly interesting device context, because the system always manages the nonclient area on our behalf. If you had tried to draw in the nonclient area of a Windows 3.x (or earlier) application, it would have been broken by the way that Windows 95 handles the nonclient area. To avoid incompatibilities with future versions of Windows, you'll want to avoid this type of drawing.

Another of the display DC classes, CClientDC, lets you draw in a window's client area. Although this might seem more like the type of drawing you'll be doing, it's actually only used for special situations. For example, this is the type of DC to use if you want to draw in response to a mouse click or keyboard input. We'll take a brief look at this DC later in this chapter, but mostly we'll be suggesting that you use it only with great care.

The most important display DC class is CPaintDC. This class lets you draw in a window's client area during a very special time — that is, in response to a WM_PAINT message. Let's see some of the other ways that a painting DC is special.

A PAINTING DC

Compared to other DCs, a painting DC (CPaintDC) is special for one reason: clipping. Earlier in this chapter, we mentioned that clipping is the creation of drawing boundaries. The most visually obvious example of clipping is a window. The window manager creates a boundary that happens to coincide with the window border. If you ever see pixels stray out of the clipping boundary — that is, outside a window's border — the cause is a bug within GDI or within the device driver.

A painting DC is special because the window manager sets up clipping around the specific portions of a window that are invalid. To help you better visualize what we mean by this, we've written ECHOFILL, a program that demonstrates the concept of clipping. The inspiration for ECHOFILL comes from a program written by Kim Crouse, a former Microsoft University instructor. Figure 13-2 shows ECHOFILL after its main window has been enlarged twice: once using the right border, and once using the bottom border. A total of three WM_PAINT messages generated the pixels that are currently displayed in the client area.

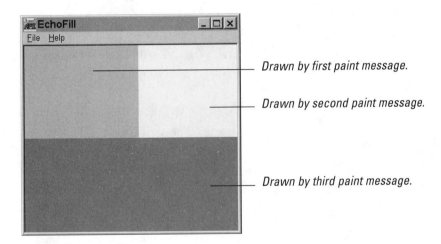

Figure 13-2
By trying to fill the entire client area in response to a WM_PAINT message, ECHOFILL echoes the clipping that is set up by the window manager. The three rectangles are the result of resizing the window twice.

The key to interpreting what you see in ECHOFILL's client area is the fact that ECHOFILL responds to each WM_PAINT message by trying to fill the *entire* client area with a different color. If it could do this, you'd see a single color filling the client area. But that's not what you see. Instead, three WM_PAINT messages created the three colored rectangles.

When ECHOFILL's window is first created, a paint message causes the entire window to be the same color. When the window is resized to the right, another paint message is generated. This time, however, only the newly exposed portion of the window is within the clipping area. As a result, the rectangle on the right appears. Then, when the window is resized using the bottom border, another paint message is generated. Once again, because only the exposed part of the window is included in the clipping area, only the bottom part of the window is painted.

The best way to understand what ECHOFILL is doing is to run the program, which you'll find on the disk that accompanies this book. If this is not convenient (books, after all, are still more portable than computers), take a look at the following fragment of code. One seemingly odd thing about this function is that it calls ExtTextOut( ), a text drawing function, to fill the window's client area with a solid color:

```
void DMainFrame::OnPaint()
{
    CPaintDC dc(this); // device context for painting

    // Query size of window's client area.
    CRect rClient;
    GetClientRect(&rClient);

    // Select next color for background
    ASSERT(iNextColor >= 0 && iNextColor < MAX_COLORS);
    dc.SetBkColor(crBackground[iNextColor]);

    // Fill client area with background color.
    dc.ExtTextOut(0, 0, ETO_OPAQUE, &rClient, 0, 0, 0);

    // Increment color index and wrap to start of range.
    iNextColor++;
    if (iNextColor >= MAX_COLORS) iNextColor = 0;
}
```

The reason why the window manager sets up clipping in such an odd manner is mostly a matter of history. The first versions of Windows ran on very slow computers (Intel 8088, 80286, and 80386). The display adapters were also very slow. To improve overall system performance, clipping for WM_PAINT messages limits the available pixels to only those that were damaged. In those days, video memory was so slow that you boosted drawing performance simply by refraining from touching video RAM.

With today's much faster processors and much faster display adapters, this time saving is no longer an issue, except on the slowest computers.

In fact, MFC all but disables this feature. We had to play some tricks with ECHOFILL so that it could more clearly show the paint clipping. And on Windows NT and Windows 95, support for *Full Drag* further changes the handling of window painting. The net effect of both changes is that you get WM_PAINT messages more often.

Faster hardware and more frequent paint requests don't change the underlying importance of the WM_PAINT message: It represents a request by the system to draw in a window. You don't know when this message will come or why. Regardless of the cause, you must be prepared to re-create whatever should be in your window's client area.

Now that you understand when to draw — that is, in response to a WM_PAINT message — and why this message occurs, it's time to examine two other drawing issues. First, we need to determine which coordinate system to use. Then, we need to know which functions to call.

Drawing coordinates

When a DC is first created, its default coordinates are pixel — or, device — units. As needed, you can modify the entire coordinate system to use inches, centimeters, or printer point units. You can also arbitrarily scale your drawings using *rubber sheet graphics*. But the default units, which we're going to use, are device units. In DC attribute terms, this is known as the MW_TEXT *mapping mode.*

The default origin — that is, coordinate (0,0) — is located in the upper-left corner of the drawing surface. On the display screen, this means the upper-left corner of the window's client area. On the printed page, it means the upper-left corner of whatever would be the top of the page. Just as you can change the coordinate system, you can also change the location of the origin. For our purposes, though, we're going to stick with the default origin.

The default direction of movement along the x- and y-axes is a little different from the Cartesian coordinate system you may have studied in school. Figure 13-3 shows the default orientation of both axes, along with the location of the origin in the window.

In a window, the default coordinate system is called *client-area coordinates*. Because the same coordinates are used for mouse input, client-area coordinates make it easy to match mouse clicks to objects you've drawn in your window.

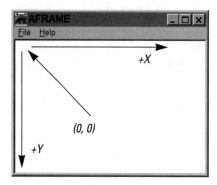

Figure 13-3

Client-area coordinates use device units, have the origin in the upper-left corner, and orient positive x toward the right and positive y toward the bottom.

Text drawing functions

As summarized in Table 13-3, GDI provides five text drawing functions.

Table 13-3

GDI Text Drawing Functions

Function	Description
DrawText()	Provides some text formatting while text is drawn. Among the 14 flags that set draw options, some control text alignment (for example, left, right, center, top). Another flag requests that tab characters be expanded to tab stops, and the DT_WORDBREAK flag requests enabling of word wrapping to produce multiple lines of text output.
ExtTextOut()	Draws a single line of text with three added features. First, you can specify a clipping rectangle to limit text to an arbitrary rectangle. Second, you can specify an opaque rectangle, which involves filling in a rectangle with the background text color. And third, you can control the spacing of characters by providing an array of character cell width values.
GrayString()	Creates mottled text, like that used in menus to show a disabled menu item.
TabbedTextOut()	Draws a line of text, just like TextOut(). The only difference is that you can define an array of tab stop positions for the support of tab characters.
TextOut()	Draws a single line of text.

To draw a single line of text, the easiest function to call is CDC::TextOut( ). This function is defined in two different ways:

```
BOOL TextOut( int x, int y, LPCTSTR lpszString, int nCount);
```

And:

```
BOOL TextOut( int x, int y, const CString& str );
```

Where:

- *x* and *y* are coordinates for positioning the text string. By default, text hangs below and to the right of this point.
- *lpszString* is a pointer to a character string.
- *nCount* is the count of characters in the string.
- *str* is a CString, which therefore contains both character string and string length information about the text that is to be drawn.

Here's an example of a WM_PAINT handling function that calls TextOut( ) to display the text "Hello Windows 95" at location (100,100):

```
void DMainFrame::OnPaint()
{
    CPaintDC dc(this); // device context for painting
    LPCTSTR pText = _T("Hello Windows 95");
    dc.TextOut(100, 100, pText, lstrlen(pText));
}
```

The _T( ) macro makes strings Unicode-aware.

Here's the same function, rewritten for the second form of TextOut( ):

```
void DMainFrame::OnPaint()
{
    CPaintDC dc(this); // device context for painting
    CString cs = _T("Hello Windows 95");
    dc.TextOut(100, 100, cs);
}
```

When specifying drawing coordinates in GDI drawing functions such as TextOut( ), remember that Windows 95 recognizes only 16 bits of significance. Even though you might pass a 32-bit int value, GDI under Windows 95 operates in only 16 bits (just like GDI did under Windows 3.x). Under Windows NT, however, all 32 bits of precision are recognized and supported. Unless you want your programs to run only on Windows NT, limit the range of your drawing coordinates to those that fit in 16-bit integers.

CDC::TextOut( ) draws a single line of text. In many cases, however, you want to draw multiple lines of text, which requires several calls to TextOut( ) with different coordinates for each call. Unlike text drawing in a character-oriented environment, drawing coordinates in GDI are something other than character cells (for now, pixels). To properly space the text that's drawn by different calls, you need to do some text coordinate calculation. We'll explore this subject in the following section.

TEXT COORDINATE CALCULATIONS

GDI provides several functions that are useful in the calculation of text coordinates. You need to use this set of functions because the spacing of text strings depends not only on the font specified by the user, but on the resolution of the target device. Before drawing any text, you need to ask GDI for the required text coordinate values.

Table 13-4 lists some of GDI's more useful text measurement functions. To help you understand these functions, we'll take a look at some of their more common uses. We'll start by discussing how to calculate point size, a common concern when working with text. We'll then describe how to get to the "next string" — whether it's on the same line as the current string, or the next line. Our last text coordinate topic is centering a line of text around a point.

Font point size

Even a casual user of word-processing programs knows that text is measured in *points*. One point is approximately 1/72.54 inches, which makes a point small, but not too small to be seen by the unaided eye. Windows uses a value of 1/72 inch for a point — a reasonable approximation for most uses. Common sizes for regular text range between 8 points and 12 points. Headlines can be anywhere from 14 points up to 24 or 36 points, or even larger. Text is usually measured by its height and not by its width, although in Windows you can request a font using either or both attributes.

As we mentioned earlier, our focus is on device units, which are the simplest to deal with. The basic formula for converting between device units and point size is as follows:

```
PointSize = (72 * DeviceUnits) / LogicalInch
```

Going the other way, here's the formula for converting points to device units:

```
DeviceUnits = (PointSize * LogicalInch) / 72
```

Incidentally, you'll probably want to use Windows' MulDiv( ) helper function rather than letting the compiler do the math. This function eliminates rounding and overflow errors that sometimes occur with plain integer arithmetic. Here's the previous formula written to use this function:

```
DeviceUnits = ::MulDiv(PointSize, LogicalInch, 72);
```

Table 13-4

Common GDI Text Coordinate Calculation Functions

Function	Description
GetCharWidth()	Gets a copy of the default character width values for a range of letters in the font currently selected in a DC.
GetDeviceCaps()	Gets various bits of device-specific data. In the context of text, LOGPIXELSY provides the number of pixels in a logical vertical inch. This is useful for calculating font point size.
GetTabbedTextExtent()	Like GetTextExtent(), this function gets the width and height that a character string would occupy when drawn with the font selected in a DC. This also takes into account tab settings.
GetTextExtent()	Gets the width and height that a given string would occupy when drawn with the font currently selected in a DC.
GetTextMetrics()	Gets a copy of the TEXTMETRIC data for the font currently selected in a DC. This data structure contains basic font measurement information.

We need to explain a few things about these formulas. First, the term *logical inch* refers to the number of pixels in an inch. It's called *logical* because of the way this measurement is defined for display screens. On display screens, a logical inch is usually larger than a physical inch. This helps ensure that 8-point fonts — which are typically the smallest size used — are readable. On printers, logical inches and physical inches are the same.

To obtain the logical inch for a particular device, you call CDC::GetDeviceCaps( ), the *device capabilities* function. GetDeviceCaps( ) takes a single parameter, an index of the capability to query. Two indices return logical inch values: LOGPIXELSX for movement in the x-direction, and LOGPIXELSY for movement in the y-direction. Because point size refers to the height of text — that is, its size along the y-axis — you use LOGPIXELSY to find out the logical inches for a given device:

```
LogicalInch = dc.GetDeviceCaps(LOGPIXELSY);
```

Another point worth mentioning is that our formulas use a ratio of 1:72 instead of the more accurate 1:72.54 ratio of points to inches. This rounding down is done because GDI in particular — and Windows in general — doesn't use any floating-point arithmetic. The reason is performance. Intel x86 processors prior to the 80486 lacked hardware support for floating-point arithmetic. Because floating-point arithmetic in software can be very slow, Windows uses integer arithmetic, which allows for faster operation and a reasonable degree of accuracy. Although this may change in future versions, for now Windows relies solely on integer arithmetic.

Next string, same line

You must sometimes split a single line of text between multiple text drawing calls [that is, multiple calls to TextOut( )]. This can happen for any number of reasons. It might simply be more convenient, given the way your data is stored. Or, you might want to display a line of text in which parts of the text use different drawing attributes. For example, displaying red text next to blue text requires *two* calls to TextOut( ). Using two fonts in the same line of text also requires two text drawing calls.

To calculate the position for the "next string," you call CDC::GetTextExtent( ). This function tells you both the width and height of a character string for the currently selected font. This function is defined as follows:

```
CSize GetTextExtent( LPCTSTR lpszString, int nCount ) const;
```

Where:

- *lpszString* is a pointer to the character string.
- *nCount* is the number of characters to include.
- The return value, CSize, is a structure with two members: *cx* is the width of the character string, and *cy* is the height.

For example, here's how you write "Hello Windows 95" on the same line using two calls to TextOut( ):

```
int x, y;
x = 100;
y = 100;
LPCTSTR pHello = _T("Hello ");
LPCTSTR pWin95 = _T("Windows 95");

// Draw first string.
dc.TextOut(x, y, pHello, lstrlen(pHello));

// Calculate size of first string.
CSize sizeString = dc.GetTextExtent(pHello, lstrlen(pHello));

// Adjust x-coordinate.
x += sizeString.cx;

// Draw second string.
dc.TextOut(x, y, pWin95, lstrlen(pWin95));
```

To preserve the space between the strings, the first string — "Hello" — ends with a space.

Next string, next line

Another common text calculation involves determining how much space to put between two lines of text. As a shortcut, we could use the return value from the function we looked at a moment ago, GetTextExtent( ). After all, this function provides both the width *and* the height of a character string. Here's how to use this function to calculate the spacing between two lines of text:

```
// Draw first string.
dc.TextOut(x, y, pHello, lstrlen(pHello));

// Calculate size of first string.
CSize sizeString = dc.GetTextExtent(pHello, lstrlen(pHello));

// Adjust y-coordinate.
y += sizeString.cy;

// Draw second string.
dc.TextOut(x, y, pWin95, lstrlen(pWin95));
```

Although this is workable for many situations, it's not the most accurate calculation. It takes into account the character cell height, but the font designer might have decided that more space is needed *between* lines of text. And if the font designer went to the trouble of defining additional pixels for interline spacing, it's worthwhile for you to use that spacing.

The term that font designers use for the space between lines of text is *external leading*. With its origins in the days when type was set by hand as tiny pieces of metal, the term *leading* refers to flat bars of metal that were placed between lines of text. It is considered *external* leading because it's not included — that is, it's outside of — the character cell height. Another term, *internal leading*, refers to intercharacter spacing that's been built into each character cell.

Both the internal and external leading values are stored in a TEXTMETRIC data structure. To get a copy of this data structure for a given font, you call CDC::GetTextMetrics( ). This function provides text metric data for the font that's currently selected in the DC. Here's an example of calling this function:

```
TEXTMETRIC tmSys;
dc.GetTextMetrics(&tmSys);
```

(As an aside, note that the data structure — TEXTMETRIC — is singular, while the function call — GetTextMetrics( ) — is plural. This annoying inconsistency has bubbled up from the native Windows API.)

To calculate the space between lines of text, you need to use two TEXTMETRIC members: character cell height and external leading size. For the text metric structure we just filled, here's how you calculate the value that must be added to the y-coordinate before drawing the next line:

```
int cyLineHeight = tmSys.tmHeight + tmSys.tmExternalLeading;
```

In our earlier example, we'd add this to the y-coordinate before drawing the second line of text:

```
// Adjust y-coordinate.
y += cyLineHeight;

// Draw second string.
dc.TextOut(x, y, pWin95, lstrlen(pWin95));
```

We've shown two ways to get the height of a character cell, and you might be wondering how this value relates to a font's point size. Watch out, they are probably not the same. We say "probably" because it's *possible* that they are the same. But to be absolutely sure, you must check another text metric value, the internal leading.

As we've discussed, *leading* is a fancy word for interline spacing. External leading is the space *not* included in the character cell height. Internal leading, on the other hand, is the space that *is* included in the character cell height. Dennis Adler, a font guru at Microsoft, pointed this out to one of the authors. To calculate the point size of a font, you subtract the value of the internal leading from the font height. In code terms, that means:

```
int DeviceUnits = tmSys.tmHeight - tmSys.tmInternalLeading;
```

The result of this calculation is the height of the character cells in device units. To convert this value to points, we need to take into account the device's logical inch. Using the size from the previous formula, here's how you get the font size in points:

```
int LogicalInch = dc.GetDeviceCaps(LOGPIXELSY);
int PointSize = ::MulDiv(72, DeviceUnits, LogicalInch);
```

Centering text

It's often useful to center a string of text over a particular point. For example, you might want to center a text label over a column of text. Or, you might want to center a label within another graphic object. Whatever the reason, when you need to solve problems like this, it's helpful to think of text as a graphic object. Like a birthday present, text comes in a box — which we sometimes call a *text box*.

By default, a character string hangs below and to the right of the text coordinate. As a result, the centering of text requires figuring out how to shift the control point up and to the left. The size of the shift is equal to one-half the size of the text box — that is, we shift the text up by one-half of the text box height, and to the left by one-half of the text box width. To show you what we mean, here's a code fragment that centers a text string over a given (x,y) point:

```
// The string.
CString cs = _T("Centered Line of Text");

// Calculate the shift up and to the left.
CSize size = dc.GetTextExtent(cs, cs.GetLength());
int xCentered = x - (size.cx/2);
int yCentered = y - (size.cy/2);

// Draw line of centered text
dc.TextOut(xCentered, yCentered, cs);
```

The techniques that we've been describing — working with multiple text fragments on one line, handling multiple lines of text, and centering text — are representative of the types of operations you'll apply to text in Windows. Although text requires a little more work in a graphical environment than in a character-based environment, the extra effort is worthwhile because you get complete control over the positioning and appearance of the resulting text.

We've covered the basics of drawing text in a window. The key message for window drawing is WM_PAINT. With the code that Class-Wizard generates, you get a CPaintDC object that provides the necessary link to the window in which you want to draw. By making GDI drawing calls through this object, you can create black text that appears in a window using the default, system font.

If you're itching to write some code, now would be a good time to start up Visual C++ and ask AppWizard to spin you a program. Here's a hint: you don't have to remove the Doc/View support to practice text drawing. If you take this shortcut, however, be sure to install your WM_PAINT handler for the view window and not for the frame window. This is important because the view window completely covers the client area of the frame window.

Now that we've covered the basics of text drawing, we're ready to explore some techniques for making our application a little more dynamic. For example, how do you generate a paint message? And what if you want to draw in response to another message besides WM_PAINT? Finally, how can you change the appearance of the text that you draw? These topics will be our focus for the following section and for the rest of this chapter.

Requesting a paint message

When we introduced the WM_PAINT message, we described it as the most important drawing message. We also noted that you can never know the cause of the message; your window might have changed size, or it might have been previously covered by another window. However, you don't really need to worry about the cause. You simply need to redraw whatever is in your window.

In some cases, however, the cause of a paint message isn't an external factor such as the user changing a window size. Instead, it's an internal factor that only you can recognize. For example, the user might have entered some additional text in a text input window. Or, the user might have added or removed a column of data from a spreadsheet window. Whatever the internal cause, when the data represented in the window changes, you need to generate a paint message.

To generate a paint message, you declare that the contents of the window are invalid. You can do this by calling a few different CWnd member functions. Of these, CWnd::Invalidate( ) is the simplest because it takes only a single parameter, a Boolean value that specifies whether to erase the background before drawing. This function declares the entire client area to be invalid:

```
// Force redraw of entire window — first erase contents.
Invalidate(TRUE);
```

Another function that generates paint messages is CWnd::Invalidate-Rect( ). This function lets you identify the specific rectangle to be redrawn. On slower hardware, this helps minimize screen flicker. On any hardware, you'll want to be conservative when you request a redraw, because too much screen flicker can annoy users. From an ergonomic point of view, such flicker causes fatigue — which not only annoys users but forces them to take more frequent breaks than might otherwise be necessary when using your software. Here's how to request a paint message for a particular rectangle:

```
// Text Coordinates.
int xText;
int yText;
...
// The string.
CString cs = _T("Invalidate area around this text string");

// Calculate size of text box.
CSize size = dc.GetTextExtent(cs, cs.GetLength());

// Define invalid rectangle and request paint message.
CRect r(xText, yText, xText + size.cx, yText + size.cy);
InvalidateRect(&r, TRUE);
```

Compared to other messages — for example, those that are associated with mouse or keyboard input — paint messages have a very low priority. After all, if more data comes in, additional paint messages might be necessary. When you declare a window to be invalid, the window might receive other messages before getting the WM_PAINT message.

In some cases, you need to raise the priority of a WM_PAINT message. To force an immediate paint message, you call CWnd::Update-Window( ). For example, you might need to do this if you've already called Invalidate( ) to request a redraw, but you also want to immediately draw on the updated window. It's not uncommon to declare part of a window invalid and then immediately force a paint message, as in:

```
InvalidateRect(&r, TRUE);
UpdateWindow();
```

But you should save this for cases in which you really need to have your window redrawn. Otherwise, as we mentioned earlier, you create too much screen flicker on slower display devices.

To summarize, when you want the image in a window to be changed, you invalidate the area in which the change will be seen. This area will be drawn during a subsequent WM_PAINT message. The UpdateWindow( ) call *does not* declare part of a window to be invalid. It simply accelerates repainting for invalidated areas. If no area is invalid, calls to UpdateWindow( ) have no effect on the contents of a window. Windows' conservative paint policy limits the drawing — via clip rectangles — to only the part of a window that is invalid.

We mentioned that calling UpdateWindow( ) forces an immediate repaint so that you can draw over a valid window. However, this makes sense only if you're drawing in response to some other message besides WM_PAINT. Let's talk about how you'd do this, and explore some of the issues you must address.

Drawing outside paint messages

In some cases, you need to draw in response to messages other than WM_PAINT. We should mention that one school of thought suggests that you draw *only* when you get a paint message. This centralizes your drawing code, which helps to make it more robust. This is a good goal to work toward.

However, to enhance a program's performance or its interactivity for the user, you might need to draw in response to other messages. For example, consider a text editing window. If such a program generated a paint message for every character typed, it would run very slowly (particularly noticeable on slower systems). The overhead associated with continually creating paint messages would use too much processing time.

Or, consider a drawing program that lets a user pick up a graphic object and move it around a window. As the object is moved, it must be redrawn to show the user its new, tentative location. Once again, creating a paint message for each new location would create too much overhead. For both of these cases, you'll want to draw in response to other messages besides the paint message.

However, a word of caution is needed here. If you draw and erase a temporary object — for example, a stretchable *rubber rectangle* — there's no problem. But if you draw more permanent objects, your painting code will have to know about those objects. After all, you don't know when a user will force a redraw of a window. All the user needs to do to make this happen is to minimize and then maximize your window. The same result occurs when another application's window is maximized over your window. When your application becomes the active application, you'll have to handle a paint message for your entire window. Any lack of synchronization between your paint and nonpaint drawing code will become painfully obvious to your users.

Setting aside these caveats and concerns, it's relatively easy to draw in response to other messages. Instead of using the CPaintDC — which is reserved for WM_PAINT drawing — you use a CClientDC object. The clipping for a CClientDC is set to the entire client area of a window. (Recall that clipping for a CPaintDC is set to just the *invalid* part of a window.) For example, here is how to say "Hello Windows 95," which is centered under the cursor, when the user clicks the left mouse button:

```
void DFrame::OnLButtonDown(UINT /*nFlags*/, CPoint point)
{
    CClientDC dc(this);

    CString cs = _T("Hello Windows 95");

    CSize size = dc.GetTextExtent(cs, cs.GetLength());
    int xCentered = point.x - (size.cx/2);
    int yCentered = point.y - (size.cy/2);

    dc.TextOut(xCentered, yCentered, cs);
}
```

So far, the sample code in this chapter has shown you how to fetch a DC and draw a line of text using the default DC attributes. The default settings are useful, but you'll eventually want to control some or all of the attributes that affect the appearance of text. We'll delve into those topics next.

Controlling the Appearance of Text

To change the appearance of text, you change one of the DC attributes that affect text. As summarized in Table 13-5, eight attributes affect the appearance or the positioning of text. The most effective way to understand the changes that a DC attribute controls is to see the text change in a real program. If your computer is handy, you might consider generating a tiny AppWizard program so that you can experiment with each attribute, as it is discussed. In a Doc/View application, don't forget that you'll want to paint in a view window.

Table 13-5

DC Attributes That Affect the Appearance of Text

Attribute	Description
Background color	Default=RGB(255,255,255), or white. Used for the background of normal text, in color-to-monochrome bitmap conversions, and for the background of styled (nonsolid) pens and hatched brushes. Set by calling SetBkColor().
Background mode	Default=OPAQUE. Turns use of background color ON (OPAQUE) or OFF (TRANSPARENT). Set by calling SetBkMode().
Current position	Default=(0,0). An (x,y) pair originally created to assist in line drawing. Enable for text by calling SetTextAlign() with the TA_UPDATECP flag. Set attribute by calling SetCurrentPosition().
Font	Default=System font. Determines which set of graphic figures are used for drawing text. In MFC, set by creating a CFont object and connecting to a DC by calling SelectObject().
Text alignment	Default=TA_LEFT	TA_TOP. Determines the alignment between text drawing coordinates and the resulting text box. Default is upper-left, but eight other alignments are possible. Set by calling SetTextAlign().
Text color	Default=RGB(0,0,0), or black. Determines the foreground color of pixels. (See also Background color). Set by calling SetTextColor().
Text extra spacing	Default=0. Determines how many pixels are to be padded into each character cell in a string. Used to expand a string to fill a margin. Set by calling SetTextCharacterExtra().
Text justification	Default=(0,0). Determines how many pixels to pad into *break characters* (that is, spaces) to help a line of text fill out a margin. Set by calling SetTextJustification().

In the following sections, we'll start by describing some of the more basic text attributes. Then, we'll spend quite a bit of time on the most important and most complicated text attribute, the font. Finally, we'll look at FILELIST, a sample program that reads a text file and displays its contents in a window. In addition to showing you how to open files and change fonts, this program demonstrates some other useful text output techniques, such as scrolling text.

BASIC TEXT ATTRIBUTES

Aside from the font, which we'll cover later, the two basic categories of text attributes are used to control the color and the positioning of text.

GDI color support

Before you can change the color of text, you need to understand how to specify color in GDI. The basic Windows data type for holding color values is COLORREF. The easiest way to define colors is by using the RGB( ) macro, which takes three parameters that define the red, green, and blue color components. For each color component, you specify a value in the range 0–255. For example, here are three color values — one each for red, green, and blue:

```
COLORREF crRed   = RGB(255, 0,  0);
COLORREF crGreen = RGB( 0,255, 0);
COLORREF crBlue  = RGB( 0, 0,255);
```

Although this might seem fairly straightforward, a number of factors make this more complex than it first seems. In GDI, these types of color references are called *logical colors*. Here, *logical* doesn't mean Boolean. Instead, this term is used to differentiate between logical colors and *physical colors*, which are the colors that a physical hardware device can actually display. A high-resolution, 16-million color device shouldn't have a problem displaying various combinations of red, green, and blue. But it's a different story for a black-and-white printer. How are these differences handled?

You should think about logical colors in terms of requests. If you request red and the device can produce red, you get what you asked for. If you request red and the device can't give you what you want, the device provides the closest possible match. That might mean black! To solve the problem of the black-and-white printer, you start by not asking for colors that aren't available. To find out the number of available colors, you call CDC::GetDeviceCaps( ), as in:

```
int nColors = dc.GetDeviceCaps(NUMCOLORS);
```

On color display screens, the system creates a default palette with 20 colors. For devices that support only 16 colors, only the first 16 of these 20 colors are used (the rest turn into white or gray). On devices that support more than 16 colors, these 20 form the default set that are available to applications. Listing 13-1 lists the standard RGB values for fetching these colors. (On the disk that accompanies this book, the ECHOFILL program uses these values. They are defined in MAINFRM.H.)

Listing 13-1
The 20 Standard RGB Values in the Default System Palette

```
// 16-color device support
const COLORREF g_crBlack      = RGB(  0,  0,  0);
const COLORREF g_crYellow     = RGB(255,255,  0);
const COLORREF g_crDkYellow   = RGB(128,128,  0);
const COLORREF g_crRed        = RGB(255,  0,  0);
const COLORREF g_crDkRed      = RGB(128,  0,  0);
const COLORREF g_crMagenta    = RGB(255,  0,255);
const COLORREF g_crDkMagenta  = RGB(128,  0,128);
const COLORREF g_crBlue       = RGB(  0,  0,255);
const COLORREF g_crDkBlue     = RGB(  0,  0,128);
const COLORREF g_crCyan       = RGB(  0,255,255);
const COLORREF g_crDkCyan     = RGB(  0,128,128);
const COLORREF g_crGreen      = RGB(  0,255,  0);
const COLORREF g_crDkGreen    = RGB(  0,128,  0);
const COLORREF g_crGray       = RGB(192,192,192);
const COLORREF g_crDkGray     = RGB(128,128,128);
const COLORREF g_crWhite      = RGB(255,255,255);

// Additional four colors for displays with more than 16 colors.
const COLORREF g_crLtYellow   = RGB(255,251,240);
const COLORREF g_crLtGreen    = RGB(192,220,192);
const COLORREF g_crLtBlue     = RGB(166,202,240);
const COLORREF g_crMedGray    = RGB(160,160,164);
```

On displays that support more than 16 colors, you can always define your own custom palette. When selected into a DC, this gives you access to a much wider range of colors. However, the use of palettes is beyond the scope of this book. The default palette serves nicely for all but the most demanding applications.

Text color

Now that you know how to use the RGB macros to pick colors, let's look at the three DC attributes that affect text color. These attributes are: text color, background color, and background mode. When you first get a DC, it contains the following default settings for these three values:

Text Color Attributes	Default Setting
Text color	Black text: RGB(0,0,0)
Background color	White background: RGB(255,255,255)
Background mode	Use the background color: OPAQUE

To set the color that is to be used for drawing the foreground pixels of text, you call CDC::SetTextColor( ). This function is defined as follows:

```
COLORREF SetTextColor( COLORREF crColor );
```

This function takes a color value as input, and returns the previous text color setting. For example, here's how to get red text:

```
dc.SetTextColor(RGB(255,  0,  0));
dc.TextOut (x, y, "This is red text", 16);
```

To set the color for background text pixels, call CDC::SetBkColor( ). This function is defined as follows:

```
COLORREF SetBkColor( COLORREF crColor )
```

As you may have surmised, the background pixels are those that are inside the text box but not part of letter strokes. Here's how you set the background color to black:

```
dc.SetBkColor(RGB(  0,  0,  0));
dc.TextOut (x, y, "This text has a black background", 32);
```

The final DC attribute that affects the color of text is the background mode. It's basically an on/off toggle for the background mode. The default setting, OPAQUE, tells GDI to use the background color. The alternate setting, TRANSPARENT, tells GDI not to use the background color in drawing text. You set the background mode by calling CDC::SetBkMode( ), which is defined as follows:

```
int SetBkMode( int nBkMode );
```

If you're interested in letting your users set the foreground or background colors, you'll probably want to use the Color Picker dialog. This is one of the common dialogs that is included as part of Windows 95. With just a few lines of code, you get a fully functioning dialog.

Text alignment

Text alignment describes the relationship between the (x,y) text coordinate and the text box. The default setting aligns the text below and to the right of the text coordinate.

To set the text alignment, you call CDC::SetTextAlign( ). This function takes a single parameter, a combination of the flags listed in Table 13-6. The flags in each column are mutually exclusive — that is, you take one flag from each column. The first row of Table 13-6 lists the default settings, which are also marked with an asterisk (*).

Table 13-6
Text Alignment Flags for CDC::SetTextAlign()

x-axis alignment	y-axis alignment	Update current position
TA_LEFT (*)	TA_TOP (*)	TA_NOUPDATECP (*)
TA_CENTER	TA_BASELINE	TA_UPDATECP
TA_RIGHT	TA_BOTTOM	

You might want to change the default settings if you're going to mix text of different sizes (or even the same size and different fonts) on the same line. The y-axis default alignment, TA_TOP, would yield strange results if you didn't adjust the y-axis values yourself. Here's how you set the text alignment to accommodate multifont drawing:

```
dc.SetTextAlign(TA_LEFT | TA_BASELINE);
```

It's also convenient to change the text alignment when you are trying to align the right side of text with another graphic object. Although you could tinker with the x-axis value, it's easier to set the alignment as follows:

```
dc.SetTextAlign(TA_RIGHT | TA_TOP);
```

Another situation in which you might want to change the text alignment is when you want to use the DC's current position value for text. The current position is an (x,y) coordinate pair that's typically used for vector graphics. However, you can use it for text when you set the TA_UPDATECP flag:

```
dc.SetTextAlign(TA_UPDATECP);
```

With this setting, the only coordinate used for text drawing is the current position. As each line of text is drawn, the position is updated so it's ready for the next text. You set the current position by calling CDC::MoveTo( ). Because it uses the TA_UPDATECP flag, the following code draws its text at (12,92) instead of at the coordinates specified in the TextOut( ) call:

```
// Request that text drawing use current position.
dc.SetTextAlign(TA_UPDATECP);

// Set current value of current position.
dc.MoveTo(12,92);

// Even though coordinates are specified here, they are ignored.
dc.TextOut(100, 200, "This text is not drawn at 100,200", 33);
```

Text justification

There are two final text attributes in our basic set: text justification and text extra spacing. Each of these helps you pad out lines of text. You'll pad out text lines to produce WYSIWYG (what-you-see-is-what-you-get) output. For the most part, this means that you tweak the display screen output to mimic the printed output.

To adjust the settings of these two attributes, you call CDC::SetTextJustification( ) and CDC::SetTextCharacterExtra( ), respectively. SetTextJustification( ) lets you specify the number of pixels to add to each space character. This setting represents additional room beyond what the font would normally use for spaces. If even more padding is needed, you call SetTextCharacterExtra( ) instead of SetTextJustification( ). SetText-CharacterExtra( ) adds extra pixels to every character (not just the space characters).

We should mention that these two drawing attributes date back to the very first version of Windows, and that other techniques for accomplishing the same results have since been added to Windows. For example, the ExtTextOut( ) function gives you complete control over the width of individual character cells. If you can take the time for the extra work it requires, it's well worth the results. The addition of TrueType fonts to Windows has also cut down on the differences between display screen fonts and printer fonts. An application that exclusively uses True-Type fonts can get reasonably close to WYSIWYG output with little or no character cell padding.

We've covered all the basic text attributes first because they are the simplest. In the following section, we direct our attention to the text attribute that has the greatest effect on the appearance of text, the font.

About Fonts

In this section, we'll cover the basics for creating and using fonts. The easiest approach for working with fonts is to use GDI's stock fonts. But to access a broader range of fonts that are installed in a typical Windows system, you'll need to create a CFont object.

What is a font?

A font is a collection of complex graphical images, of a single size and design, that are used to represent character data. Fonts are commonly identified by point size and by name, such as "Arial" or "Times Roman," and perhaps also by style. In common parlance, we refer to specific fonts using such terms as 18-point Times Roman, or 8-point bold Arial.

If you've never been exposed to the world of fonts, it can be quite a shock to learn that literally thousands of different fonts are available. Windows 95 ships with a basic set of fonts, but numerous font packs are sold to add to this set. And it's not at all uncommon for Windows applications to include even more fonts. For example, Corel Corporation's CorelDraw application ships with more than 800 fonts.

By default, Windows 95 ships with about a dozen basic fonts. Windows 95 includes a font preview utility — the character map program, CHARMAP — which lets you quickly see the fonts that are loaded in the system. In Figure 13-4, CHARMAP is displaying a basic set of characters from the Times New Roman font.

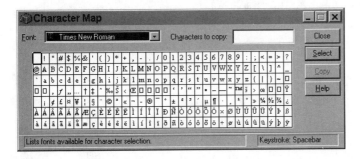

Figure 13-4

The CHARMAP character map program, showing the set of characters in the Times New Roman font.

Selecting a stock font

To select a font, you start by getting your hands on one. In an MFC program, this means having a properly initialized CFont object. The simplest way to get a font is to use one of the predefined stock fonts that Windows provides. The following example shows how to get one of the stock fonts:

```
CFont fontStock;
fontStock.CreateStockObject(ANSI_FIXED_FONT);
```

For details on other stock fonts, refer to the MFC documentation under CGd::Object.

Like every other drawing attribute, a font must be connected to a DC before it affects the appearance of any output. To connect a font to a DC, you call CDC::SelectObject( ). For example, this code fragment connects the font that we just created to a DC:

```
dc.SelectObject(&fontStock);
```

Until we select a different font into the DC, all text that we draw will appear using this font.

Fonts differ from other drawing attributes in an important way. Most attributes are simply numbers that are stored in the DC. Within the system, however, a font is its own object, and it has its own life separate from the DC. For every font object that you create, you need to make sure that you destroy the object when you're done using it. Otherwise, there is space wasted somewhere.

In practical terms, this means simply making sure that you destroy every CFont object that you create. The destructor to this class helps you make sure that no system memory is wasted. But how do you catch those CFont objects that you forget to delete? Fortunately, the Visual C++ tools can help you catch them. Just run the Debug build of your program in the debugger that's built into the Visual C++ development environment. When the program shuts down, you'll see a laundry list of objects that haven't been properly cleaned up.

We should mention that stock fonts aren't actually cleaned up even when you delete their CFont wrapper. The reason is that the system created those fonts for everyone to use.

Selecting nonstock fonts

To select a font other than a stock font, you have to submit a font request to GDI. One way to represent a font request is with the LOGFONT — logical font — data structure. To submit a font request to GDI, you fill in this data structure and pass it to a CFont initialization function, CFont::CreateFontIndirect( ). The term *indirect* in this function name refers to the fact that the function takes a pointer parameter. Another initialization function, CFont::CreateFont( ), takes a series of parameters that, when taken together, match LOGFONT.

A logical font is a lot like the logical color we described earlier in this chapter when we discussed setting text color. A logical font represents a logical request that GDI and the device driver use to figure out which specific *physical* font to use. In the same way that you can ask for red and get black, you might ask for 24-point Times New Roman and get 12-point Courier.

The problem of mismatched fonts has many solutions, including PANOSE font IDs, font enumeration, and applying your own font mapping algorithms. We won't go into them here, because they are not of general interest. But we have a few suggestions.

The simplest solution would be to always use the device default. A font that you can create using a stock font always provides the device default. It is generally a 10- or 12-point device font. Or, limit your choices to the dozen or so fonts that are built into Windows 95. This is the same general solution that we applied to the red-black color mismatch: Don't ask for something that the system doesn't have.

The following example is taken from this chapter's sample program, FILELIST. Two variables are declared in DMainFrame, the frame window class:

```
CFont  * d_pFont;   // Ptr to CFont object.
LOGFONT  d_lf;      // Current logical font.
```

The first variable, d_pFont, is a pointer to the CFont font object that FILELIST's main window creates and carries around. The second variable, d_lf, is a logical font structure that contains our font request.

The first step in creating a nonstock font is to fill in the LOGFONT request. During the constructor for DMainFrame, that data structure is filled as follows:

```
// Init desired font.
memset (&d_lf, 0, sizeof(LOGFONT));

// Initial font face name is Courier New.
lstrcpy (d_lf.lfFaceName, "Courier New");

// Initial font size is 10 pt.
// Get a screen DC.
CWindowDC dc(NULL);
int cyPixels = dc.GetDeviceCaps(LOGPIXELSY);
d_lf.lfHeight = (-1) * MulDiv(10, cyPixels, 72);
```

Negative font height requests height without internal leading — true point size.

As a general rule, we avoid calling functions in the constructor that might fail. After all, C++ provides no simple way to report such failures. Although we *could* set a failure flag in the object, that assumes that someone, somewhere will check the flag. Our experience is that, more often than not, this never gets done.

The font initialization step that might fail is the allocation of the CFont object. With the logical font structure defined, here's how we allocate the CFont object and pass our font request to GDI:

```
// Create a new font
d_pFont = new CFont();
d_pFont->CreateFontIndirect(&d_lf);
```

It's worth noting that GDI doesn't do much except make a copy of our request because the font request isn't yet associated with any specific GDI device. That association will be required before GDI lifts a finger to consider what we've requested.

Once the font object is created, you associate it with GDI device -- display screen, printer, metafile, or bitmap — by calling CDC::SelectObject( ). As with stock fonts, once our custom font object is connected to a DC, it affects all text drawn until a new font is selected. Here's how FILELIST selects our font into a DC during its paint message:

```
// Fetch a device context (dc) for "this" window.
CPaintDC dc(this);

// Select current font into DC.
dc.SelectObject(d_pFont);
```

The simplest way for a program to allow users to pick fonts is with the system's built-in Font Picker dialog box. This is one of Windows' common dialog boxes, like the Open File dialog we encountered in a previous chapter. You can see an example of the Font Picker dialog in our sample program, which we'll describe next.

FILELIST SAMPLE PROGRAM

In Figure 13-5, our sample FILELIST program is displaying one of its own program files using the 24-point Italic Times New Roman font. FILELIST demonstrates several useful text handling techniques, including the creation and use of fonts, the display of multiple lines of text, and the scrolling of text. Along the way, it uses two common dialog boxes: the Open File dialog for specifying a particular text file and the Font Picker dialog for selecting fonts. Listings 13-2 through 13-5 show the main program files for FILELIST.

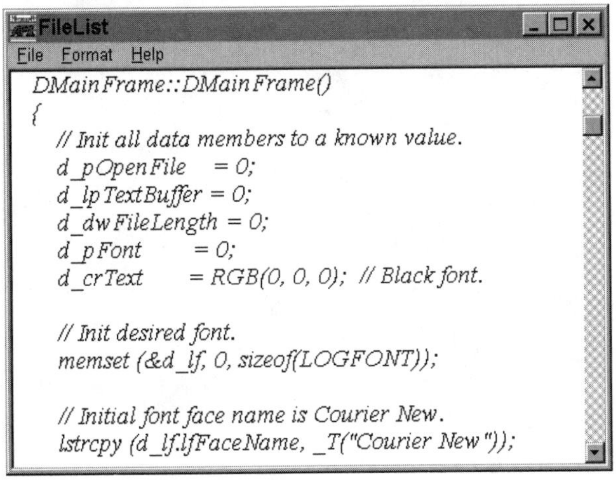

Figure 13-5
FILELIST displays the contents of text files in a requested font.

Listing 13-2
FILELIST.H

```
// filelist.h : main header file for the FILELIST application
//

#ifndef __AFXWIN_H__
    #error include 'stdafx.h' before including this file for PCH
#endif

#include "resource.h"        // main symbols

/////////////////////////////////////////////////////////////////////////////
// DApp:
// See filelist.cpp for the implementation of this class
//

class DApp : public CWinApp
{
public:
    DApp();

// Overrides
    // ClassWizard generated virtual function overrides
    //{{AFX_VIRTUAL(DApp)
```

```
    public:
    virtual BOOL InitInstance();
    //}}AFX_VIRTUAL

// Implementation

    //{{AFX_MSG(DApp)
    afx_msg void OnAppAbout();
        // NOTE - the ClassWizard will add and remove member functions here.
        //      DO NOT EDIT what you see in these blocks of generated code !
    //}}AFX_MSG
    DECLARE_MESSAGE_MAP()
};
```

//

Listing 13-3
FILELIST.CPP

```
// filelist.cpp: This program opens and displays text files.
//

#include "stdafx.h"
#include "filelist.h"

#include "mainfrm.h"

#ifdef _DEBUG
#undef THIS_FILE
static char BASED_CODE THIS_FILE[] = __FILE__;
#endif

////////////////////////////////////////////////////////////////////////
// DApp

BEGIN_MESSAGE_MAP(DApp, CWinApp)
    //{{AFX_MSG_MAP(DApp)
    ON_COMMAND(ID_APP_ABOUT, OnAppAbout)
        // NOTE - the ClassWizard will add and remove mapping macros here.
        //      DO NOT EDIT what you see in these blocks of generated code!
    //}}AFX_MSG_MAP
    // Standard file based document commands
    ON_COMMAND(ID_FILE_NEW, CWinApp::OnFileNew)
    ON_COMMAND(ID_FILE_OPEN, CWinApp::OnFileOpen)
END_MESSAGE_MAP()

////////////////////////////////////////////////////////////////////////
// DApp construction
```

```
DApp::DApp()
{
    // TODO: add construction code here,
    // Place all significant initialization in InitInstance
}

/////////////////////////////////////////////////////////////////////////////
// The one and only DApp object

DApp theApp;

/////////////////////////////////////////////////////////////////////////////
// DApp initialization

BOOL DApp::InitInstance()
{
    // Step 1: Allocate C++ window object.
    DMainFrame * pFrame;
    pFrame = new DMainFrame();

    // Step 2: Initialize window object.
    pFrame->LoadFrame(IDR_MAINFRAME);

    // Make window visible
    pFrame->ShowWindow(m_nCmdShow);

    // Assign frame as application's main window
    m_pMainWnd = pFrame;

    return TRUE;
}

/////////////////////////////////////////////////////////////////////////////
// CAboutDlg dialog used for App About

class CAboutDlg : public CDialog
{
public:
    CAboutDlg();

// Dialog Data
    //{{AFX_DATA(CAboutDlg)
    enum { IDD = IDD_ABOUTBOX };
    //}}AFX_DATA

// Implementation
protected:
    virtual void DoDataExchange(CDataExchange* pDX);    // DDX/DDV support
    //{{AFX_MSG(CAboutDlg)
        // No message handlers
    //}}AFX_MSG
    DECLARE_MESSAGE_MAP()
};
```

```
CAboutDlg::CAboutDlg() : CDialog(CAboutDlg::IDD)
{
    //{{AFX_DATA_INIT(CAboutDlg)
    //}}AFX_DATA_INIT
}

void CAboutDlg::DoDataExchange(CDataExchange* pDX)
{
    CDialog::DoDataExchange(pDX);
    //{{AFX_DATA_MAP(CAboutDlg)
    //}}AFX_DATA_MAP
}

BEGIN_MESSAGE_MAP(CAboutDlg, CDialog)
    //{{AFX_MSG_MAP(CAboutDlg)
        // No message handlers
    //}}AFX_MSG_MAP
END_MESSAGE_MAP()

// App command to run the dialog
void DApp::OnAppAbout()
{
    CAboutDlg aboutDlg;
    aboutDlg.DoModal();
}


/////////////////////////////////////////////////////////////////////////
// DApp commands
```

Listing 13-4
MAINFRM.H

```
// mainfrm.h : interface of the DMainFrame class
//
/////////////////////////////////////////////////////////////////////////
#include <afxtempl.h> // Connect to CArray template.

// Structure to track lines in text file.
class STRING
{
  public:
    LPTSTR pText;
    int    ccLen;
};

// This declaration uses the CArray template
// to provide a dynamic array of STRING records.
class StringArray : public CArray <STRING, STRING &>
{
```

```
  public:
    StringArray() {}
    STRING& operator=(STRING & s)
    {
        m_pData->pText = s.pText;
        m_pData->ccLen = s.ccLen;
        return *m_pData;
    }
};

const int g_nTabCount=25;
const int g_nTabStop=4;

class DMainFrame : public CFrameWnd
{
public:
    DMainFrame();
protected: // create from serialization only
    DECLARE_DYNCREATE(DMainFrame)

// Attributes
public:
    BOOL           d_bTabs;        // Respect tabs or not.
    CFileDialog *  d_pOpenFile;    // Ptr to OpenFile dialog.
    CFontDialog *  d_pSetFont;     // Ptr to Font Picker dialog.
    CFont  *       d_pFont;        // Ptr to CFont object.
    COLORREF       d_crForeground; // Foreground text color.
    COLORREF       d_crBackground; // Background text color.
    LOGFONT        d_lf;           // Current logical font.
    LPINT          d_pnTabs;       // Array of tab settings.
    LPTSTR         d_lpTextBuffer; // Ptr to text buffer.
    DWORD          d_dwFileLength; // File length.
    StringArray    d_saTextInfo;   // Array of string info.
    int            d_cLines;       // Count of lines in text.
    int            d_cyLineHeight; // Height of one line of text.
    int            d_clHeight;     // Window height line count.
    int            d_iTopLine;     // Index of top-most line.
    int            d_cyClient;     // Window client area height.
    int            d_cxLeftMargin; // Margin to left of text.

// Operations
public:
    void BuildStringArray();
    BOOL CreateNewFont();
    void ResetScrollValues();

// Overrides
    // ClassWizard generated virtual function overrides
    //{{AFX_VIRTUAL(DMainFrame)
    //}}AFX_VIRTUAL

// Implementation
```

```
public:
    virtual ~DMainFrame();
#ifdef _DEBUG
    virtual void AssertValid() const;
    virtual void Dump(CDumpContext& dc) const;
#endif

// Generated message map functions
protected:
    //{{AFX_MSG(DMainFrame)
    afx_msg void CmdFileOpen();
    afx_msg void CmdFormatFont();
    afx_msg void CmdFormatTabs();
    afx_msg void UpdFormatTabs(CCmdUI* pCmdUI);
    afx_msg int OnCreate(LPCREATESTRUCT lpCreateStruct);
    afx_msg void OnPaint();
    afx_msg void OnSize(UINT nType, int cx, int cy);
    afx_msg void OnVScroll(UINT nSBCode, UINT nPos, CScrollBar* pScrollBar);
    afx_msg void OnWinIniChange(LPCTSTR lpszSection);
    //}}AFX_MSG
    DECLARE_MESSAGE_MAP()
};


/////////////////////////////////////////////////////////////////////////
```

Listing 13-5
MAINFRM.CPP

```
// mainfrm.cpp : implementation of the DMainFrame class
//

#include "stdafx.h"
#include "filelist.h"

#include "mainfrm.h"

#ifdef _DEBUG
#undef THIS_FILE
static char BASED_CODE THIS_FILE[] = __FILE__;
#endif

/////////////////////////////////////////////////////////////////////////
// DMainFrame

IMPLEMENT_DYNCREATE(DMainFrame, CFrameWnd)

BEGIN_MESSAGE_MAP(DMainFrame, CFrameWnd)
    //{{AFX_MSG_MAP(DMainFrame)
    ON_COMMAND(ID_FILE_OPEN, CmdFileOpen)
```

```
    ON_COMMAND(ID_FORMAT_FONT, CmdFormatFont)
    ON_COMMAND(ID_FORMAT_TABS, CmdFormatTabs)
    ON_UPDATE_COMMAND_UI(ID_FORMAT_TABS, UpdFormatTabs)
    ON_WM_CREATE()
    ON_WM_PAINT()
    ON_WM_SIZE()
    ON_WM_VSCROLL()
    ON_WM_WININICHANGE()
    //}}AFX_MSG_MAP
END_MESSAGE_MAP()

/////////////////////////////////////////////////////////////////////////
// DMainFrame construction/destruction

DMainFrame::DMainFrame()
{
    // Init all data members to a known value.
    d_pOpenFile    = 0;
    d_lpTextBuffer = 0;
    d_dwFileLength = 0;
    d_pFont        = 0;

    // Init desired font.
    memset (&d_lf, 0, sizeof(LOGFONT));

    // Initial font face name is Courier New.
    lstrcpy (d_lf.lfFaceName, _T("Courier New"));

    // Initial font size is 10 pt.
    CWindowDC dc(NULL);
    int cyPixels = dc.GetDeviceCaps(LOGPIXELSY);
    d_lf.lfHeight = (-1) * MulDiv(10, cyPixels, 72);

    // Initial tab setting is OFF.
    d_bTabs = TRUE;

    // Tab table initially empty (set when font selected).
    d_pnTabs = 0;
}

DMainFrame::~DMainFrame()
{
    if (d_pFont) delete d_pFont;
    if (d_pnTabs) delete [] d_pnTabs;
    if (d_pOpenFile) delete d_pOpenFile;
    if (d_pSetFont) delete d_pSetFont;
}

/////////////////////////////////////////////////////////////////////////
//
// DMainFrame helper functions.
```

```
//------------------------------------------
// BuildStringArray - Parses text file to create a CString array.
void DMainFrame::BuildStringArray()
{
    // Scan buffer to calculate line count.
    LPTSTR lpNext = d_lpTextBuffer;
    LPTSTR lpEnd  = d_lpTextBuffer + d_dwFileLength - 1;
    *lpEnd = '\n';
    for (d_cLines = 0; lpNext < lpEnd; d_cLines++, lpNext++)
    {
        // Search for next <CR> character.
        lpNext = strchr(lpNext, '\n');

        // Discontinue if NULL encountered.
        if (lpNext == NULL) break;
    }

    // Set array size.
    d_saTextInfo.SetSize(d_cLines);

    // Scan buffer to build array of pointers & sizes.
    STRING string;
    lpNext = d_lpTextBuffer;
    for (int iLine = 0; iLine < d_cLines; iLine++)
    {
        // Char count for current line.
        string.ccLen = 0;
        string.pText = lpNext;

        // Loop to end-of-line.
        while ((*lpNext != '\n') && (*lpNext != '\r'))
        {
            lpNext++;           // Check next char.
            string.ccLen++;     // Increment length counter.
        }

        // Enter value in array.
        d_saTextInfo[iLine] = string;

        // Skip over <CR> <LF>
        lpNext += (2 * sizeof(char));
    }
}


//------------------------------------------
// CreateNewFont - Creates new CFont for use in drawing text.
BOOL DMainFrame::CreateNewFont()
{
    // Delete any previous font.
    if (d_pFont)
        delete d_pFont;
```

Creates array of character string pointers.

Creates new font and calculates all font-specific values.

```
    // Create a new font
    d_pFont = new CFont();
    if (!d_pFont) return FALSE;
    d_pFont->CreateFontIndirect(&d_lf);

    // Calculate font height
    CClientDC dc(this);
    TEXTMETRIC tm;
    dc.SelectObject(d_pFont);
    dc.GetTextMetrics(&tm);
    d_cyLineHeight = tm.tmHeight + tm.tmExternalLeading;

    // Calculate left margin.
    d_cxLeftMargin = tm.tmAveCharWidth * 2;

    // Rebuild tab setting table.
    if (d_pnTabs) delete [] d_pnTabs;
    d_pnTabs = new INT[g_nTabCount];
    for (int i=0; i<g_nTabCount; i++)
    {
        d_pnTabs[i] = d_cxLeftMargin + (i * g_nTabStop * tm.tmAveCharWidth);
    }

    return TRUE;
}


//----------------------------------------
// ResetScrollValues - Adjust scrolling for window size changes.
void DMainFrame::ResetScrollValues()
{
    // Set count of lines in window height.
    d_clHeight = d_cyClient / d_cyLineHeight;

    // Hide scroll bars when not needed.
    if (d_cLines <= d_clHeight)
    {
        SetScrollRange(SB_VERT, 0, 0, TRUE);
        d_iTopLine = 0;
        return;
    }

    // Adjust scroll range for new window size.
    SetScrollRange (SB_VERT, 0, d_cLines - d_clHeight, TRUE);

    // Adjust scroll thumb position.
    SetScrollPos(SB_VERT, d_iTopLine, TRUE);
}

/////////////////////////////////////////////////////////////////////////
// DMainFrame diagnostics
```

Calculate text scroll-dependent values for WM_SIZE message.

```
#ifdef _DEBUG
void DMainFrame::AssertValid() const
{
    CFrameWnd::AssertValid();
}

void DMainFrame::Dump(CDumpContext& dc) const
{
    CFrameWnd::Dump(dc);
}

#endif //_DEBUG

/////////////////////////////////////////////////////////////////////////////
// DMainFrame message handlers

//-----------------------------------------
// Handler for File|Open command message.
void DMainFrame::CmdFileOpen()
{
    // Display File.Open... dialog box.
    int iRet = d_pOpenFile->DoModal();

    // Ignore when user clicks [Cancel] button.
    if (iRet != IDOK)
        return;

    // Fetch fully-qualified file name.
    CString csFile = d_pOpenFile->GetPathName();

    // Open file in read-only mode.
    CFile cfData;
    if (!cfData.Open(csFile, CFile::modeRead))
    {
        AfxMessageBox(_T("Error Opening File"));
        return;
    }

    // Free previous buffer contents
    if (d_lpTextBuffer)
    {
        free(d_lpTextBuffer);
        d_lpTextBuffer=0;
    }

    // Calculate file size & allocate buffer.
    // Pad to avoid bad address reference.
    d_dwFileLength = cfData.GetLength() + sizeof(char);
    d_lpTextBuffer = (LPTSTR)malloc (d_dwFileLength);
    if (!d_lpTextBuffer)
    {
        AfxMessageBox(_T("Cannot Allocate Memory For File"));
        return;
    }
```

File/Open menu command handler.

```
    // Read Buffer.
    cfData.Read((LPVOID)d_lpTextBuffer, d_dwFileLength);

    // Empty buffer array.
    d_saTextInfo.RemoveAll();

    // Scan buffer for text line info.
    BuildStringArray();

    // "Index to top line displayed" = top of file.
    d_iTopLine = 0;

    // Recalculate scroll bar info.
    ResetScrollValues();

    // Request a WM_PAINT message to redraw window.
    Invalidate();
}


//-----------------------------------------
// Handler for Format|Font command message.
void DMainFrame::CmdFormatFont()
{
    // Display font picker dialog box.
    int iRet = d_pSetFont->DoModal();

    // Ignore when user clicks [Cancel] button.
    if (iRet != IDOK)
        return;

    // Rebuild font definition based on dialog selection.
    CreateNewFont();

    // Recalculate scroll bar info.
    ResetScrollValues();

    // Request a WM_PAINT message to redraw window.
    Invalidate();
}


//-----------------------------------------
// Handler for Format|Tabs command message.
void DMainFrame::CmdFormatTabs()
{
    // Toggle "respect tab" flag.
    d_bTabs = !d_bTabs;

    // Request a WM_PAINT message to redraw window.
    Invalidate();
}


//-----------------------------------------
// Handler for CN_UPDATE_COMMAND_UI message.
void DMainFrame::UpdFormatTabs(CCmdUI* pCmdUI)
{
```

Format/Font menu command handler.

Format Expand Tabs menu command handler.

Set/clear check mark

```
    // Display a checkmark if user wants to respect tabs.
    int nCheck = (d_bTabs) ? 1 : 0;
    pCmdUI->SetCheck(nCheck);
}


//------------------------------------
// WM_CREATE message handler.
int DMainFrame::OnCreate(LPCREATESTRUCT lpCreateStruct)
{
    // Send WM_CREATE to base class first...
    if (CFrameWnd::OnCreate(lpCreateStruct) == -1)
        return -1;

    // Create File.Open... dialog object.
    d_pOpenFile = new CFileDialog (TRUE);
    if (!d_pOpenFile)
        return -1;

    // Initialize file filter.
    d_pOpenFile->m_ofn.lpstrFilter = _T("All Source Files\0*.cpp;*.h;*.rc\0"
                                        "C++ Sources (*.cpp)\0*.cpp\0"
                                        "Include Files (*.h)\0*.h\0"
                                        "All Files (*.*)\0*.*\0");

    // Create Format.Font... dialog object.
    d_pSetFont = new CFontDialog(&d_lf, CF_SCREENFONTS);
    if (!d_pSetFont)
        return -1;

    // Create initial font object.
    if (!CreateNewFont())
        return -1;

    // Initialize application settings.
    OnWinIniChange("");

    // Indicate window creation is OK.
    return 0;
}


//------------------------------------
// WM_PAINT message handler.
void DMainFrame::OnPaint()
{
    // Fetch a device context (dc) for "this" window.
    CPaintDC dc(this);

    // Select current font into DC.
    dc.SelectObject(d_pFont);

    // Select text color.
    dc.SetTextColor(d_crForeground );
```

WM_CREATE handler.

Set systems-dependent attributes

WM_PAINT handler.

```
        // Select text background color.
        dc.SetBkColor(d_crBackground);

        // Figure out which lines to draw.
        int iLine = d_iTopLine;
        int cLastLine = d_iTopLine + d_clHeight + 1;
        cLastLine = min (cLastLine, d_cLines);

        // Loop through client area coordinates to draw.
        int cyLine = 0;
        while (iLine < cLastLine)
        {
            // Draw a line of text.
            LPTSTR lp = d_saTextInfo[iLine].pText;
            int    cc = d_saTextInfo[iLine].ccLen;

            // Drawing function depends on 'respect tabs' setting.
            if (d_bTabs && d_pnTabs != 0)
            {
                dc.TabbedTextOut(d_cxLeftMargin, cyLine, lp, cc,
                                 g_nTabCount, d_pnTabs, 0);
            }
            else
            {
                dc.TextOut(d_cxLeftMargin, cyLine, lp, cc);
            }

            // Increment various counts.
            cyLine += d_cyLineHeight;
            iLine++;
        }
}

//----------------------------------------
// WM_SIZE message handler.
void DMainFrame::OnSize(UINT nType, int cx, int cy)     WM_SIZE handler.
{
    // Notify base class of new window size.
    CFrameWnd ::OnSize(nType, cx, cy);

    // Save client area height.
    d_cyClient = cy;

    // Recalculate scroll bar info.
    ResetScrollValues();                        WM_VSCROLL
}                                               handler.

//----------------------------------------
// WM_VSCROLL message handler.
void DMainFrame::OnVScroll(UINT nSBCode, UINT nPos, CScrollBar* pScrollBar)
{
    // Temporary "new line" value.
    int iTop = d_iTopLine;
```

```
// Based on particular scroll button clicked, modify top line index.
switch(nSBCode)
{
    case SB_BOTTOM:
        iTop = d_cLines - d_clHeight;
        break;
    case SB_ENDSCROLL:
        break;
    case SB_LINEDOWN:
        iTop++;
        break;
    case SB_LINEUP:
        iTop-;
        break;
    case SB_PAGEDOWN:
        iTop += d_clHeight;
        break;
    case SB_PAGEUP:
        iTop -= d_clHeight;
        break;
    case SB_THUMBPOSITION:
        iTop = nPos;
        break;
    case SB_THUMBTRACK:
        iTop = nPos;
        break;
    case SB_TOP:
        iTop = 0;
        break;
}

// Check range of new index;
iTop = max (iTop, 0);
iTop = min (iTop, d_cLines - d_clHeight);

// If no change, ignore.
if (iTop == d_iTopLine) return;

// Pixels to scroll = (lines to scroll) * height-per-line.
int cyScroll = (d_iTopLine - iTop) * d_cyLineHeight;

// Define new top-line value.
 d_iTopLine = iTop;

// Scroll pixels.
ScrollWindow(0, cyScroll);

// Adjust scroll thumb position.
SetScrollPos(SB_VERT, d_iTopLine, TRUE);
}
```

```
//-------------------------------------------
// WM_WININICHANGE message handler.
void DMainFrame::OnWinIniChange(LPCTSTR lpszSection)
{
    CFrameWnd::OnWinIniChange(lpszSection);

    // Get new background & foreground colors in case these have changed.
    d_crForeground = GetSysColor(COLOR_WINDOWTEXT);
    d_crBackground = GetSysColor(COLOR_WINDOW);

    // Force redraw of window.
    Invalidate();
}
```

WM_WININICHANGE handler to fetch system colors.

Program design note

A word or two on the design of FILELIST is appropriate. Almost all of the work that this program does is contained in the main frame window (MAINFRM.H and MAINFRM.CPP). We've packed everything together because it's a small example and putting everything into one source file makes it easier to read than if it was scattered among multiple sources. However, we don't claim that this design will scale up elegantly if we continue to add features (and code size) to this program. It could probably use an object dedicated to managing the text data. Also, it might be helpful to have a division between the drawing code and the command input code.

It just so happens that those features are part of the Doc/View architecture that we've been avoiding for so long. In Chapter 15, we'll show you another version of this program that takes advantage of this natural division of labor between the parts of a program. Our work on this version hasn't been wasted, however, because we can use most of the basic code in a Doc/View version.

Common dialog boxes

FILELIST uses two of Windows' common dialog boxes, but we aren't going to discuss the use of those dialogs here. What's important for our current discussion is that the File Open dialog provides a filename that we use to open a file and read its contents. The Font Picker dialog provides a LOGFONT structure that is used to create the font request that we send to GDI.

Memory

Let's take a moment to look at how FILELIST manages its memory. When a file is open, FILELIST calls malloc( ) to carve out a file-size chunk of memory. After the entire contents of the file are read into this memory, we call our own BuildStringArray( ) helper function.

This function reads through the file data twice. The first time, it count the lines of text. The second time, it builds an array of type STRING. This structure is defined in MAINFRM.H as:

```
// Structure to track lines in text file.
class STRING
{
  public:
    LPTSTR pText;
    int    ccLen;
};
```

For each line in the buffer, we store a pointer to the string and a count of the characters in the string.

To manage access to each element of the array, we've defined a class called StringArray. It's basically a dynamic array defined with MFC's CArray container class template. This is declared in MAINFRM.H:

```
// This declaration uses the CArray template
// to provide a dynamic array of STRING records.
class StringArray : public CArray <STRING, STRING &>
{
  public:
    StringArray() {}
    STRING& operator=(STRING & s)
                    {m_pData->pText = s.pText;
                     m_pData->ccLen = s.ccLen;
                     return *m_pData;}
};
```

We covered templates briefly in Chapter 7, but this is our first opportunity to provide an example of a working template.

This template allows us to access the string pointer using common C/C++ array notation. For example, in response to a paint message, we access a pointer to a particular line of text using the following line:

```
LPTSTR lp = d_saTextInfo[iLine].pText;
```

We don't really use one of CArray's most helpful features: its capability to change the size of the array we access. But we chose it because it does automatic bounds checking (in the Debug build), which is something that the native C/C++ array notation doesn't provide.

Scrolling

Another feature that FILELIST implements is scrolling. The fundamental issue behind scrolling is that a scroll bar represents three numbers: a minimum, a maximum, and a current position. To scroll properly, the key question you must answer is this: Which number should be represented?

In FILELIST, the scroll bar represents the line of text that is currently at the top of the display window. The index to the current "top line" is stored in d_iTopLine, one of DMainFrame's member variables. All scroll bar handling — which is performed primarily in response to the WM_SIZE and WM_VSCROLL messages — does little more than update this single value. (Although it also manages the location of the scroll thumb.)

The net result of all the scrolling code becomes visible in response to the WM_PAINT message. And, as the following fragment shows, all of the drawing code relies on the top-line index, which is stored in d_iTopLine:

```
// Figure out which lines to draw.
int iLine = d_iTopLine;                            Scrollbar=tracked
int cLastLine = d_iTopLine + d_clHeight + 1;       value.
cLastLine = min (cLastLine, d_cLines);

// Loop through client area coordinates to draw.
int cyLine = 0;
while (iLine < cLastLine)
{
    // Draw a line of text.
    LPTSTR lp = d_saTextInfo[iLine].pText;
    int    cc = d_saTextInfo[iLine].ccLen;

    // Drawing function depends on 'respect tabs' setting.
    if (d_bTabs && d_pnTabs != 0)
    {
        dc.TabbedTextOut(d_cxLeftMargin, cyLine, lp, cc,
                         g_nTabCount, d_pnTabs, 0);
    }
    else
    {
        dc.TextOut(d_cxLeftMargin, cyLine, lp, cc);
    }

    // Increment various counts.
    cyLine += d_cyLineHeight;
    iLine++;
}
```

FILELIST has a menu item that toggles d_bTabs, the *respect-or-ignore-tabs* flag. This flag determines whether to draw the line of text using TextOut( ) (which ignores tabs) or TabbedTextOut( ) (which respects tabs).

Text attributes

And, of course, all of the painting code ultimately relies on the text attributes that are set prior to drawing. Fonts are created and destroyed at the exact moment when the user selects the font. At painting time, all we have to do is select the font and use it.

Summary

In this chapter, we've covered the basics of creating text output in a window. Most of what we've covered will also apply to other types of GDI devices, all of which you'll someday want to use for graphic output. What we've tried to present here, though, are the basics that are required for the more commonly needed operations.

In the next chapter, we'll explore mouse and keyboard input. Although each type of input has its own uses, what they have in common is the fact that Windows handles the low-level details of catching the input from each type of hardware and placing it in a queue. When your program is ready to receive the input, Windows sends it to your program in the form of — what else? — messages.

14

Mouse and Keyboard Input

*M*icrosoft's recently introduced image slogan is "Where do you want to go today?" Although this might initially seem more appropriate for a bus company than a software company, it starts to make sense if you think about it a bit. After all, transportation isn't a bad metaphor for the way a personal computer takes you where you haven't been before. New information, like a new place, can have elements that are at the same time disorienting, useful, and exciting.

If a PC is your mode of transportation, the mouse is like the steering wheel — moving your program's operation in new directions. And the keyboard is the engine, driven by piston-like fingers that transport the data from your mind to its destination. Whether a user is entering numbers into a spreadsheet or you are cranking out a C++ program, everything screeches to a halt when the fingers stop.

In this chapter, we'll show you how to handle mouse and keyboard input. For background, we'll discuss the various pieces of state that the system stores. Windows 95 uses the idea of *local input state* — a concept that Microsoft first introduced with Windows NT — to support both a multitasking scheduler and a view of input state that is compatible with previous versions of Windows.

Next, we'll look at the various ways that a program can use keyboard input. If desired, you can avoid dealing with low-level keyboard input by using user-interface objects such as edit controls. With this in mind, we're going to pay particular attention to the less obvious, but very important ways that an application must manage keyboard state. As part of this discussion, we will consider the keyboard focus, the keyboard caret, the selection state, and other user-interface constructs that are related to keyboard input.

From there, we'll look at mouse input. Again, you can avoid dealing with low-level mouse input by using higher-level user-interface objects. At a minimum, though, you'll want to manage state that's related to mouse input. Here, we'll consider such issues as the shape of the mouse cursor, the capture of mouse input, and the clipping of the mouse cursor to a specific clipping rectangle.

We'll conclude this chapter with GETTEXT, a sample program that builds on our FILELIST program from the preceding chapter. GETTEXT makes extensive use of mouse and keyboard input for the selection of text.

Input Basics and System State

The challenge to properly handling mouse and keyboard input in Windows is understanding and managing the context in which input occurs. The input itself is rather simple; you get several types of messages for both mouse and keyboard events. When you write code for keyboard input, you decide between two keyboard messages. The most critical mouse input is communicated by two or three mouse messages.

Once you've written the basic message-handling code, an even more important step awaits you. You need to write supporting code to make your application behave in a predictable and consistent manner. To accomplish this, you must understand the context of input messages — the unobvious, but critical ways that input interacts with application state, as viewed by both a user and Windows itself. Let's start by looking at the types of Windows input messages, and then study more closely the input state of first the keyboard and then the mouse.

INPUT AS MESSAGES

Most C programmers are used to getting input — particularly keyboard input — by polling the system via function calls. For example, the C-runtime library contains the getc( ) function, which reads the "next character" from standard input:

```
char ch = getc();
```

Windows doesn't use the notion of *standard input* for mouse and keyboard input; instead, it sends input to a program's windows as messages which get stored in a hardware input queue. Table 14-1 lists all of the Windows mouse and keyboard messages to which you'll respond when directly handling user input. Only half of these messages are intended for your use, because Windows itself handles the other half.

Table 14-1

Windows' Mouse and Keyboard Input Messages

Type of Message	Message	Description
Client Area Mouse Messages		Client-area messages are sent when the mouse cursor is over a window's client area, as determined by a WM_NCHITTEST message. These messages are for application use.
	WM_MOUSEMOVE	The cursor has moved over a window's client area.
	WM_LBUTTONDOWN	The left (primary) button has been pushed while the cursor is over the client area.
	WM_LBUTTONUP	The left (primary) button has been released.
	WM_RBUTTONDOWN	The right (secondary) button has been pushed while the cursor is over the client area.
	WM_RBUTTONUP	The right (secondary) button has been released.
	WM_MBUTTONDOWN	The middle button has been pushed while the cursor is over the client area.
	WM_MBUTTONUP	The middle button has been released.
Nonclient Area Mouse Messages		Nonclient-area messages are sent when a WM_NCHITTEST message determines that the mouse cursor is over a nonclient area of a window. Windows handles these messages.
	WM_NCMOUSEMOVE	The mouse has moved over a nonclient area of a window.

(continued)

Table 14-1 (continued)

Type of Message	Message	Description
	WM_NCLBUTTONDOWN	The left (primary) button has been pushed while the cursor is over the nonclient area.
	WM_NCLBUTTONUP	The left (primary) button has been released.
	WM_NCRBUTTONDOWN	The right (secondary) button has been pushed while the cursor is over the nonclient area.
	WM_NCRBUTTONUP	The right (secondary) button has been released.
	WM_NCMBUTTONDOWN	The middle button has been pushed while the cursor is over the nonclient area.
	WM_NCMBUTTONUP	The middle button has been released.
Mouse Cursor Messages		These messages help determine the correct shape for the mouse cursor. Windows usually handles these messages. Applications sometimes handle them as well, though this is less common.
	WM_NCHITTEST	A query message that asks, "Where in the window is the mouse cursor?" The NC in this query message doesn't mean that it's only for the nonclient area, although that is the system's primary interest. Instead, this message returns a hit-test code that identifies the cursor position in the window — for example, over a border, over a menu, or over the client area.
	WM_SETCURSOR	A request to change the shape of the mouse cursor based on the return value from a previously sent WM_NCHITTEST message.
Application Keyboard Messages		These messages are sent to a window that has the keyboard focus. These messages are for application use.
	WM_KEYDOWN	The user has pressed a keyboard key.
	WM_KEYUP	The user has released a keyboard key.

Type of Message	Message	Description
	WM_DEADCHAR	The user has pressed a nonprinting key associated with a diacritical mark (for example, an umlaut, an accent, a circumflex). In most cases, you can ignore this message, because the next WM_CHAR message will provide the correct character code.
	WM_CHAR	A prior WM_KEYDOWN message has been successfully translated to a printable character. This message carries the associated character code.
System Keyboard Messages		System keyboard messages are sent when one of two conditions is met: either the Alt key is down, or the window that has the focus is minimized. Windows usually handles these messages.
	WM_SYSKEYDOWN	The user has pushed a keyboard key when one of the two system key conditions is met.
	WM_SYSKEYUP	The user has released a keyboard key when one of the two system key conditions is met.
	WM_SYSDEADCHAR	The user has pushed a nonprinting key associated with a diacritical mark (for example, an umlaut, an accent, a circumflex) when one of the two system key conditions is met.
	WM_SYSCHAR	A prior WM_KEYDOWN message has been successfully translated to a printable character when one of the two system key conditions is met. This message carries the associated character code.
Keyboard Focus		The focus answers a simple question for the system: To which window should keyboard messages be directed? Only one window can own the keyboard at any time. These messages tell a window when it's getting or losing the focus. These messages are for application use.

(continued)

Table 14-1 (continued)

Type of Message	Message	Description
	WM_SETFOCUS	A window is gaining access to keyboard input.
	WM_KILLFOCUS	A window is losing access to keyboard input.
Top-Level Window Activation		The importance of activation in this context is its close association with keyboard focus. These messages are for application use, although Windows provides you with reasonable default handling.
	WM_ACTIVATE	A notification message that is sent to frame and dialog windows — or any other window without a parent — to notify them when they gain or lose activation. On losing activation, a window usually saves display state information. When reactivated, a window usually restores this state, which includes keyboard focus and selection state.
	WM_ACTIVATEAPP	A notification that is sent to all frame and dialog windows when activation is gained or lost to a window in another application (.EXE file).
	WM_MOUSEACTIVATE	A mouse query message that is sent when the user clicks the mouse in the window of an application that is not active. The response to this message determines whether the application should be made active. Also, the application can determine whether a normal mouse message should be sent or whether the mouse message should be eaten — that is, removed from the message stream. This is useful when, for example, a mouse message causes a window to be activated. The sole purpose of such mouse input is to change activation and not to change the window input state.

The really important keyboard messages

So that you don't get overwhelmed by the size of this message list, we should point out that mouse and keyboard input arrives via a very small number of messages. For keyboard input, two messages matter most. The WM_CHAR message tells you about visible characters (numbers, letters, punctuation, and so on). And WM_KEYDOWN tells you about nonvisible keys — for example, function keys and arrow keys.

Listing 14-1 is a code fragment that responds to a WM_CHAR message to echo characters as the user types them. To get a sense for how keyboard input is handled, you might want to take a moment to enter this code into an AppWizard-generated program. (You don't have to remove Doc/View support, but make sure you add this code to the view and not to the frame window.)

Listing 14-1
Handling the WM_CHAR Message

```
// Define a class member variable to save 'next character position'
class DView : public CView
...
    // Attributes
  public:
    CPoint ptCharacter;
...
};

// Initialize next character position.
DView::DView()
{
    ptCharacter.x = 0;
    ptCharacter.y = 0;
}

    ...

//---------------------------------
// Handler for WM_CHAR message.
void DView::OnChar(UINT nChar, UINT nRepCnt, UINT nFlags)
{
    // Fetch a client area DC and draw character.
    CClientDC dc(this);
    dc.TextOut(ptCharacter.x, ptCharacter.y, (LPCTSTR)&nChar, 1);

    // Query size of current character.
    CSize sizeTextBox;
    sizeTextBox = dc.GetTextExtent((LPCTSTR)&nChar, 1);
```

```
    // Advance location for next character position.
    ptCharacter.x += sizeTextBox.cx;

    CView::OnChar(nChar, nRepCnt, nFlags);
}
```

Although the code fragment in Listing 14-1 does echo characters, it's really only half of the story. We say this because when you draw in a window, you must also be prepared to handle the WM_PAINT message and re-create whatever should be in the window. For the sake of simplicity, we don't do that here. But to give you a sense of what it involves, we'd have to store the characters, perhaps in a CString object. In response to the WM_PAINT message, we would then redraw the entire string.

The really important mouse messages

To see how mouse input is handled, you might try adding the code from Listing 14-2 to an AppWizard-generated program. This code handles two of the three most important mouse messages: WM_LBUTTONDOWN and WM_MOUSEMOVE. (It ignores WM_LBUTTONUP.) A message box is displayed for the button click message. And in response to mouse move messages, the mouse location is displayed in the frame window's caption bar.

Listing 14-2
Sample Code for Handling Mouse Messages

```
void DView::OnLButtonDown(UINT nFlags, CPoint point)
{
    AfxMessageBox(_T("Left Mouse Button Down"));

    CView::OnLButtonDown(nFlags, point);
}

void DView::OnMouseMove(UINT nFlags, CPoint point)
{
    // Create a string containing the mouse location.
    CString str;
    str.Format(_T("Mouse location = (%d,%d)"), point.x, point.y);

    // Fetch pointer to frame window.
    DMainFrame * pFrame = (DMainFrame *)AfxGetApp()->m_pMainWnd;

    // Change caption to our string.
    pFrame->SetWindowText(str);

    CView::OnMouseMove(nFlags, point);
}
```

System messages

Windows uses about half of the defined input messages for nonclient-area objects. The mouse messages with names that contain the letters *NC* are messages that Windows handles for the nonclient-area components of a window. For example, Windows receives a WM_NCLBUTTON-DOWN message when a user selects a menu option, resizes a window frame, or minimizes a window. The differences between these actions depend on the mouse location when the mouse button is clicked.

The keyboard messages with names containing the letters *SYS* are for system use. For example, the WM_SYSKEYDOWN message is like WM_KEYDOWN, except the system message is sent when the Alt key is being pressed or when the window with the focus is minimized. Windows uses system key messages to support keyboard mnemonics — that is, the underlined letters that are used to navigate and select menu items and dialog box controls.

Application messages

The nonsystem mouse and keyboard messages are for application use — that is, they are for your use. With the help of ClassWizard, creating and responding to the basic set of messages is fairly straightforward. Later in this chapter, we'll describe some of the minor fine-tuning points that are necessary.

If you're the sort of person who learns best by doing, now is a good time to start AppWizard and ask it to spin a starting application for you. In response to keyboard messages, you might request a paint message [call CWnd::Invalidate( )], and during the paint code, simply draw the one character that's entered. Or, you might consider echoing the mouse location in a message box [call AfxMessageBox( )] when a mouse button is clicked.

The challenge of handling mouse and keyboard messages directly

Handling individual mouse and keyboard messages is easy, but putting them together in a coherent fashion takes a little more work. For example, consider what might be involved in creating a text editing window. Although this seems like a simple type of window to create, a wide range of state information — for example, current selection and current input location — must be maintained. Seemingly simple features such as word wrap aren't always so simple to implement. Then there are the memory management issues...

Fortunately, Windows provides you with two types of edit controls — one type for standard, single-font use, and the other for multiple-font, rich text use. Unless you're one of the few developers who need to create a word-processing program, you'll probably never have to build your own text editing window. Both types of edit controls provide most of the capabilities that applications typically need.

You don't have to be writing a WYSIWYG word-processing program to care about mouse and keyboard input. What you do have to manage, however, are the system settings that control the flow of mouse and keyboard input. Let's take a look at both of these sets, starting with keyboard input and then moving on to mouse input states.

KEYBOARD INPUT STATE

When you're sitting at your desk working, interruptions are a frustrating obstacle to your productivity. But you have to be able to deal with interruptions and return to the task at hand. The same is true for your software. In a highly interactive, multitasking environment such as Windows 95 or Windows NT, your program *will* be interrupted. To build a robust program, you must anticipate the ways that it will be interrupted. You have to plan ahead so that none of the interruptions cause inconsistencies in your program's operations.

In the context of keyboard input, interruptions take two forms: a change of window activation, and the associated change of keyboard focus. Let's see what each involves.

Window activation

The *active window* is the top-level window with which the user has chosen to work. Only *one* top-level window can be active at any moment, and its caption bar changes color to reflect its active state. The window manager also promotes the active window to the top of the *Z-order*, a term that refers to a metaphorical stacking of windows from the perspective of the user. The top of the Z-order is an exalted position, because it makes a window the most important in the system — for the moment, anyway.

We should first clarify what we mean by the term *top-level window*. This is a frame window or a dialog window that has no parent. You can also consider these windows to be children of the desktop.) In an MFC program, a top-level window is typically derived from CFrameWnd or CDialog — but a program normally has only one top-level window.

In the mind of a user, the top-level window represents the application. To access an application, a user activates a top-level window. To close an application, the user closes that window. To see a list of top-level windows in the system, all you have to do is bring up the Task Manager in Windows 95 (or the Task List in Windows 3.1 and Windows NT).

A user can activate a top-level window in other ways besides from the Task Manager. A keystroke combination, Alt-Tab, lets a user search for a new top-level window to activate. By clicking with the mouse, a user can activate an inactive application. Regardless of how it happens, a user has the right to bestow the blessings of activation on one application, while revoking them from another.

Despite the user's fickle behavior, an application must maintain its composure when activation is lost. To do this, an application records its own state, including the keyboard focus, the selection state of displayed objects, and various visual cues regarding application state. That state must be restored when activation is subsequently returned.

Like other important events, loss of activation is accompanied by messages — in this case, WM_ACTIVATE and WM_ACTIVATEAPP. The WM_ACTIVATE message tells a particular window that it has either gained or lost activation. The WM_ACTIVATEAPP message tells all frame and dialog windows when activation is either lost to or recovered from another application. Windows passes a flag with each of these messages to indicate whether activation is being gained or lost. Applications more commonly respond to the first message, WM_ACTIVATE, because it is most closely tied to events that should change the visual state of a window.

When activation is regained, a window gets a WM_ACTIVATE message with either the WA_ACTIVE flag or the WA_CLICKACTIVE flag (for activation related to mouse clicks). When one of these messages is received, the state that was saved upon deactivation must be restored. Windows lets you know about activations related to mouse clicks in case you want to set a flag to ignore the upcoming mouse message. After all, you'll probably hide some of your application's state when it is inactive. You don't want a mouse click that should simply reactivate your application to also change the rest of your application's state. When we discuss mouse state a bit later in this chapter, we'll talk about another message that can help solve this particular problem, WM_MOUSEACTIVATE.

The reason why you take such care in saving and restoring an application's state is simply because users expect it. For example, if a user selects a block of text in a word-processing program, the user expects that block to remain selected, even if another application becomes activated. When deactivated, a program should hide its selection state. Upon regaining activation, the word-processing program should pretend that the user never left and once again display the text as selected. Your program *will* be interrupted, so the only issue is what you can do to recover gracefully from interruptions.

Although you want to make it appear to users that nothing has changed in your application, quite a bit of work is associated with saving and restoring application state. Table 14-2 summarizes some of the points that you need to keep in mind when the activation changes.

Table 14-2

States to Be Saved when a Window Becomes Inactive

State	Comments
Keyboard Focus	When a frame or a dialog contains child windows, the keyboard focus must be properly reinstated to the correct child window. On losing activation, then, a window that contains child windows should record the identify of the child that has the keyboard focus. Note that this is automatically done for dialog boxes. You need to handle it only for frame windows.
Keyboard Caret	The caret is a keyboard pointer (called a cursor in other environments). Carets appear as rectangular, blinking squares that echo the "current location" of keyboard input. When a window loses focus, any existing caret must be destroyed. On regaining focus, the window must re-create the caret (if you want the window to have a caret).
Selection State	The selection state refers to objects that have been highlighted — typically by changing color. When a window becomes inactive, the selection state should be hidden. It should be shown when the window once again becomes the active window.
Mouse Cursor	Mouse cursors change shape when the mouse is moved over a window. In particular, the WM_SETCURSOR message — which you can handle yourself, if you'd like — is sent to a window requesting the correct cursor.
Color Palette	Ownership of the system palette is associated with the window that has the keyboard focus.

With the exception of the color palette, which is a more advanced programming topic, we'll discuss all of the items listed in this table in the remainder of this chapter. Let's see what's involved in handling changes related to the keyboard focus.

Keyboard focus

The *keyboard focus*, or simply the focus, identifies the specific window to which keyboard messages are sent. As the user types on the keyboard, each keystroke adds events to the hardware event queue. To prevent the queue from overflowing, the system must somehow unload these little hot potatoes. The focus window is the lucky window to which any and all keyboard messages are sent.

Windows does some default handling related to the saving and restoring of keyboard focus. When a top-level window becomes active — that is, in response to a WM_ACTIVATE message notifying a window that it is *receiving* activation — Windows' default handler gives that window the focus. And when a dialog box regains activation, the default handling is to return focus to the dialog box control that had the focus when activation was lost.

There's only one situation in which gaining the activation also requires you to set the focus. You need to set the focus in a frame window with child windows. Only the frame window automatically gets the focus on activation. If it makes more sense to direct input to one of the child windows, you must set the focus to the appropriate child window.

Sometimes, it also makes sense to set the focus in a dialog box. Our sample DIALOGS program in Chapter 12 provides an example. In the sample program's File Types dialog, when the user clicks the Add button, the focus is moved to the first edit control. This lets the user begin entering a new pair of strings in the two edit controls. Otherwise, the focus would remain on the Add button — which would require a user to move the focus using mouse or keyboard actions.

To move the focus, you call CWnd::SetFocus( ). Be careful to avoid confusing this function call with the WM_SETFOCUS message. The function sets the focus. The message — which is sent by the function — notifies a window that the focus has been acquired. The SetFocus( ) function also sends a message to the window losing the focus. This WM_KILLFOCUS message gives the window the bad news that its keyboard message receipt days are over — at least for now.

At any time, you can find out which window has the keyboard focus by calling CWnd::GetFocus( ). This function cannot see beyond the walls that divide applications, however, so the return value would be NULL for focus windows in other applications. We'll discuss this further when we explore local input state later in this chapter. For now, let's look at the input state that's associated with the mouse.

Mouse Input State

The mouse is somewhat more freewheeling than the keyboard. After all, the keyboard is locked onto the focus window, which in turn is a child of the currently active window. By contrast, the mouse cursor can easily race off to any window — regardless of whether it is the active window. The mouse can even change activation, which of course brings the focus from the old window to the new one.

To help you make sense of mouse input, we'll describe the key messages and input state that relate to mouse input. We'll start with the WM_MOUSEACTIVATE message, which asks a window whether a mouse click should change the window activation. Next, we'll describe how two messages — WM_NCHITTEST and WM_SETCURSOR — control the shape of the mouse cursor. Then, we'll describe when you should capture the mouse to reserve mouse input for a single window. We'll also touch briefly on cursor clipping — a technique you'll almost never use, though our coverage wouldn't be complete without it.

Mouse activation messages

At certain times, an application's activation is tied to mouse input. In particular, when a user clicks on an inactive top-level window, a WM_MOUSE-ACTIVATE message is sent to that window. You may want to reply to that message yourself, or you can let Windows' default handler reply. Windows' default reply is reasonable, but to fine-tune that reply, you'll want to understand the meaning of the WM_MOUSEACTIVATE message.

The first thing we need to mention about WM_MOUSEACTIVATE is that it is a *query*, and the system wants an answer. Note that WM_ACTIVATE — a message that might seem related — is a notification, not a query. The system doesn't care what you do with a notification; it's yours to respond to or to ignore. With a query message, on the other hand, the return value is very important because Windows pays close attention to your reply.

Table 14-3 lists possible return values for WM_MOUSEACTIVATE. Windows' default handler returns MA_ACTIVATE, which — as indicated in the table — tells Windows to activate the window that's been clicked. This reply also controls whether the mouse message — normally a WM_LBUTTONDOWN — gets delivered to the target window.

Table 14-3

Possible Return Values to the WM_MOUSEACTIVATE Message

Return Value	Meaning
MA_ACTIVATE	Allow the window to be activated and let it receive the mouse message.
MA_ACTIVATEANDEAT	Allow the window to be activated, but don't let it receive the mouse message.
MA_NOACTIVATE	Don't activate the window, but let it receive the mouse message.
MA_NOACTIVATEANDEAT	Don't activate the window, and don't let it receive the mouse message.

Your choice of a return value to this message allows you to more precisely reactivate your application. For example, consider a drawing package that uses mouse messages to draw squares. If the application is inactive, a mouse-click message probably just means that the user wants to activate the application. After all, the user doesn't want to draw spurious squares. The window could reply with MA_ACTIVATEANDEAT, which says to activate the window but then discard the mouse message.

The problem with ignoring the mouse messages is that *every* mouse message is ignored. Not only are client-area mouse messages ignored, nonclient-area messages also disappear. This has the unfortunate side effect that nonclient-area objects — for example, menus — don't receive the mouse click.

For results that are closer to what you want, you should probably reply with MA_NOACTIVATE — as is done by Microsoft Word and Microsoft Excel. In response to mouse clicks, you must activate the window yourself. CWnd::ActivateWindow( ) does this nicely. But this means you'll probably also want to set a flag — presumably in a class member variable of a CWnd-derived class — specifying that subsequent mouse messages should be ignored. Otherwise, the click message could have unwanted side effects, such as drawing spurious objects or changing the selection state.

For just this one message, you need to consider quite a few issues. Each choice puts a slightly different spin on how an application appears to a user. And this message is just one of the many events you must handle. Let's look at another set of mouse-related messages that affect system state: the messages that change the shape of the mouse cursor.

Mouse cursor messages

As the mouse cursor flies over different windows, it broadcasts a constant stream of messages. The results of these messages allow Windows to set the mouse cursor to the correct shape. These messages are sent to whichever window happens to lie under the mouse cursor, and not just the active window or even the focus window.

The first message, WM_NCHITTEST, is a query. With this message, Windows is asking the window to identify which part of the window the cursor is above. Windows is not looking for coordinates. Instead, it is asking for a hit-test code that indicates whether the cursor is over, for example, the client area or the caption bar. Figure 14-1 illustrates the hit-test codes that are associated with the different parts of a window.

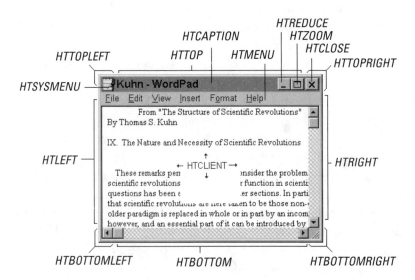

Figure 14-1

The hit-test codes expected back from the WM_NCHITTEST query message.

Moving a Window with a Mouse Hit-Test Trick

Here's a quick and easy coding trick that lets a user move a window by clicking (and then dragging) from anywhere in a window's client area. As you know, a user typically moves a window by clicking the caption bar and dragging. But not all windows have a caption bar. This trick allows a user to move such a window by clicking in the client area of the window. The trick is based on how the WM_NCHITTEST message tells windows about where the user has clicked the mouse.

To perform this trick, you simply return HTCAPTION — the hit-test code for the window's caption area — when the request refers to the client area. The following MFC code fragment does this:

```
UINT DMainFrame::OnNcHitTest(CPoint point)
{
    // Convert screen coordinates to client area coordinates.
    CPoint ptClient = point;
    ScreenToClient(&ptClient);

    // Query client area rectangle.
    CRect rClient;
    GetClientRect(&rClient);

    // When the point lies within the client area,
    // say it's in the caption.
    if (rClient.PtInRect(ptClient))
    {
        return HTCAPTION;
    }

    // Be sure to call the default handler for
    // nonclient-area mouse messages.
    return CFrameWnd::OnNcHitTest(point);
}
```

A few items in this code fragment deserve explanation. For one thing, the coordinates passed to this message are *screen coordinates*. Like client-area coordinates, these are pixel units. However, the origin (0,0) is located in the upper-left corner of the *screen* (rather than in the upper-left corner of the *client area*). The call to CWnd::ScreenToClient() converts the screen coordinates to client-area coordinates.

To determine whether the indicated point lies within the client area, this fragment calls CRect::PtInRect(). This is a fairly straightforward routine, once you know that you find it in CRect.

Perhaps the most important point to be made about this code is that it calls the default handler if we don't handle the message. We do this because we don't want to worry about the hit testing for every other part of the window.

Our sample GETTEXT program uses the other mouse cursor message, WM_SETCURSOR. To give you a better idea of how the hit-test message works, the accompanying sidebar describes how you can allow the user to move a window based on your reply to the WM_NCHITTEST message. The Windows Clock program uses this trick, and you can use it in your own programs.

If you run the message eavesdropping utility, SPY++, you'll notice that every hit-test message is followed by a WM_SETCURSOR message. This latter message is a request for the window to install the appropriate cursor. To install your own cursor, you call a native Windows API function, ::SetCursor( ). Because this is a native API function (without an MFC equivalent), you won't find it documented in the MFC manuals or the help database. Instead, you need to refer to the Win32 API manuals or the Win32 help database.

The close relationship between these two messages is underscored by the fact that one of the parameters to the WM_SETCURSOR message is a hit-test code. You could define your own hit-test codes — at least in theory — as long as you avoided the range of values that Windows uses. You would pass values from your own range of hit-test codes to indicate where in the window the cursor is located, and then check for your own values in response to the cursor setting message.

Although this is a somewhat elegant solution, we recommend against it. Because of the incompatibilities that it could create with future versions of Windows (however unlikely), we avoid defining new codes that Windows might misinterpret. Instead, if we want a window to have sub-window areas with different cursors for each, we install those cursors in response to the WM_SETCURSOR message. After checking for the HTCLIENT hit-test code, we install our cursor. When the hit-test code indicates that the cursor is over another part of the window, we pass that on to the default handler. You'll see an example of this in the GETTEXT sample program, later in this chapter.

Capturing the mouse

From time to time, you have to ask the mouse to give its full attention to a single window. You do this by *capturing the mouse*. Although you might think that "mouse capture" somehow limits the movement of the cursor, it doesn't. (That happens when you *clip the cursor*, a subject that we'll address shortly.) Instead, capturing the mouse forces all mouse messages to be sent to a single window. Here's the real kicker: the window that has captured the mouse continues to get mouse input *even when the cursor is not over the window.*

So, when does a window want to grab the mouse's full attention? This is necessary when one mouse message — typically the left button down message (WM_LBUTTONDOWN) — starts a multiple-mouse-message action. Examples include drag and drop, dragging to select multiple items (such as multiple lines in a word processor), and dragging to draw.

If the mouse flew off without letting you know about the button up message, it could — in the words of Microsoft's Mark Cliggett — "leave your application in an indeterminate state." After all, when a multiple-mouse-message action starts, you'll probably set some flags to indicate that the action is taking place. You want to avoid having such actions get terminated in midstride. In other words, capturing the mouse is necessary to force the mouse to stay in touch until it finishes what it has started.

To understand mouse capture, it helps to see it in action. Run almost any application and bring up the File Open dialog box. The mouse can be captured by two dialog box controls: list boxes and edit controls. Mouse capture takes place when you click to select an item in a list box or text in the edit control. After clicking in such controls, when you drag the mouse outside the border, you'll see the control scroll its contents. The scrolling is caused by mouse capture.

Another place you can see mouse capture work is within most text editing windows (including the Visual C++ editor). These windows scroll when you click in a window filled with text, and drag beyond the window border. These windows are only able to continue receiving mouse input — in the form of WM_MOUSEMOVE messages — because the mouse has been captured.

Now that you've seen it at work, you probably want to know how you can capture the mouse yourself. It's easy; you just call CWnd::SetCapture( ). As we mentioned, you typically do this in response to a mouse down message. To *release* the capture — something you must be sure to do — call CWnd::ReleaseCapture( ). A good time to release the mouse capture is in response to a button up message (WM_LBUTTONUP).

Here's some ClassWizard-generated code that shows a typical scenario for mouse capture and release. The mouse is captured when the left mouse button is clicked (in reply to the WM_LBUTTONDOWN message), and it is released when the left mouse button comes up (in reply to the WM_LBUTTONUP message):

```
void DMainFrame::OnLButtonDown(UINT nFlags, CPoint point)
{
    // Grab the mouse.
    SetCapture();

    CFrameWnd::OnLButtonDown(nFlags, point);
}

void DMainFrame::OnLButtonUp(UINT nFlags, CPoint point)
{
    // Release the mouse.
    ReleaseCapture();

    CFrameWnd::OnLButtonUp(nFlags, point);
}
```

Incidentally, when you capture the mouse, Windows doesn't send you any hit-test (WM_NCHITTEST) or cursor-setting (WM_SETCURSOR) messages. The assumption is that you already have complete control of the mouse, and that you will change the cursor when you need to. If you want to change the cursor during mouse capture, you would probably do so in response to WM_MOUSEMOVE, the only mouse message you get when the mouse is captured.

Mouse cursor clipping

Another facility that Windows lets you control is *mouse cursor clipping*. It's not something you'll do very often, but to complete our discussion of mouse state, we need to at least mention it. Mouse cursor clipping — like the clipping that GDI does for graphic drawings — involves the definition of a rectangle boundary. The mouse cursor can move only within its defined cursor clipping rectangle.

One example of cursor clipping is obvious when using Windows. Windows itself clips the cursor to the display screen. If it didn't, a user might accidentally send the cursor over the edge of the screen and into oblivion. We've seen some display drivers that have an option to allow the cursor to wrap around the left edge onto the right, and over the top of the screen onto the bottom. Although it's not our taste in mouse cursors, some users undoubtedly appreciate being able to do this.

So, why should a program clip the cursor? Obviously, it's necessary to prevent the user from moving the cursor outside a given area. For example, a security program might let the user move the cursor only around the password dialog box. We must confess that it's tough to come up with good examples of when to use cursor clipping, because we haven't liked the few places where we've seen it done. For example, the Paintbrush program in Windows 3.1 clips the cursor when you're drawing shapes such as bezier curves. We find it more annoying than useful.

Microsoft's MFC developers apparently agree with our assessment that this isn't a general-purpose function. They don't include the Windows API function that controls cursor clipping — ::ClipCursor( ) — in any MFC class. What's interesting, though, is that although MFC doesn't wrap this function in any of its own classes, it *does* clip the cursor in one specific circumstance. When resizing an OLE toolbar, the cursor is clipped to the parent window's client area. This is one use that makes sense to us, because the size of a child window should be limited by the size of the parent window.

In earlier versions of Windows, the input states that we've been describing — window activation, keyboard focus, mouse capture, and cursor clipping — were maintained on a global, systemwide basis. In Windows 95 and Windows NT, however, Microsoft's support for multiple threads would get tangled if input state was global. This is one of the problems with the user interface in the OS/2 Presentation Manager. Although it's a great programming environment, the operating system itself suffers the same scheduling entanglements as older versions of Windows.

To overcome this scheduling problem, input state in Windows 95 and Windows NT is maintained on a local, per-thread basis. (For the sake of simplicity, though, we'll consider the simple, single-threaded case, which allows us to consider input state on a per-program basis.) This is referred to as *local input state*, and it is the next topic we are going to cover.

LOCAL INPUT STATE

The term *local input state* refers to the model used by the developers of Windows 95 and Windows NT to describe how a program's input state is viewed by the operating system. This is usually not an issue for most development projects, unless you need to query or modify the input state of one program (or thread) from another program (or thread). That requires a little more work. You might also be faced with this issue if you wrote code for earlier versions of Windows, which did not use this input model.

Earlier versions of Windows used a model that might be called a *global input state* model. In simple terms, input state — like keyboard focus and window activation — used to be stored on a global, systemwide basis. This made a lot of sense when Windows was, essentially, a single-threaded system (although it was still a *multitasking* system because multiple programs could be present in memory at the same time).

With global input state, any program can query or modify input state at any time. For example, in Windows 3.x, any program can find out which window has the keyboard focus. Such a program can even steal the focus, although in practice few programs do this because users neither expect nor want programs to randomly change input state.

In a local input state system, all of the input states that we've discussed in this chapter are kept on a per-program (actually, on a per-thread) basis. That includes the following input state:

- Window activation
- Keyboard focus
- Mouse cursor
- Mouse capture
- Cursor clipping

The importance of local — as opposed to global — input state is that it represents a change from earlier versions of Windows. In particular, Win16 code sometimes assumes that a query for the current focus window always returns a valid window handle. Such code, when ported to Win32, will sometimes get a NULL value if the program that's querying isn't the foreground application. The system's input state is invisible to applications that don't have the local input state.

With global input state, an application could set the focus or the activation to a window in another application. This can't happen with local input state. If you try to set input state in another application, the system ignores your request. In addition, although it's possible to set (or query) your own application's input state at any time, changes aren't visible to the user until your application owns the foreground window.

FOREGROUND WINDOW

When Microsoft introduced the idea of local input state into the various Windows operating systems, they had to preserve some connection to global input state. Even if for no other reason, this is necessary because the Task Manager needs to be able to identify which window the user is using. The Task Manager also needs to activate an application; by definition, this can't be accomplished by simply changing local input state.

The single piece of input state that Windows 95 and Windows NT maintain on a global, systemwide basis is the *foreground window*. The foreground window identifies the top-level window which — from the perspective of a user — is currently active in the system. Of course, there are function calls for setting and querying the foreground window. To select a new foreground window, you call CWnd::SetForeground-Window( ). And to query the current foreground window, you call CWnd::GetForegroundWindow( ).

The preceding discussion of keyboard and mouse input state provides important background for the proper use and control of keyboard and mouse input. In the following sections, we'll focus first on keyboard input, and then on mouse input. Our objective is to help you understand the system operation so that you can easily integrate keyboard and mouse input into your own Windows application software.

Keyboard Input

The handling of individual keyboard messages is fairly straightforward. Once you know which message(s) to look for, it's a simple matter to set up the message handling that springs into action when a particular key is pressed. You'll probably package keyboard commands as accelerators, which we discussed in Chapter 11. As command input, accelerators generate WM_COMMAND messages.

For keyboard input not handled by an accelerator table, you'll choose either the WM_KEYDOWN message or the WM_CHAR message to detect keyboard input. In this section, we'll describe the differences between these two messages as well as when you'll choose one over the other.

We're also going to cover some of the less obvious aspects of keyboard input. We'll start with a look at how the keyboard hardware's scan codes are translated into visible character codes. Then, we'll discuss general user-interface issues that relate to keyboard input; namely, what to do when a window gets the keyboard focus. Finally, we'll touch on the three different character sets that you may encounter when building Windows applications.

TRANSLATION OF KEYBOARD INPUT

As depicted in Figure 14-2, keyboard data undergoes two translations. The first is performed by the keyboard device driver when it converts scan codes into virtual key (WM_KEYDOWN) messages. Next, applications call a Windows API function, ::TranslateMessage( ), which filters virtual key messages for printable characters. When printable characters are found, Windows generates an entirely new message, WM_CHAR, and adds it to the message stream.

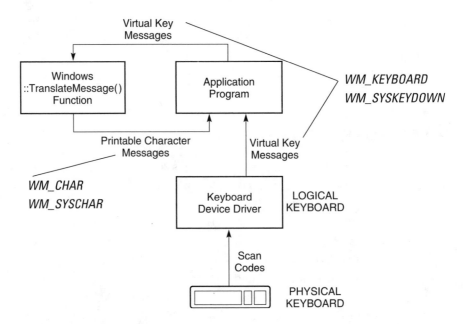

Figure 14-2

This diagram depicts the conversion of keyboard data from scan codes to virtual key codes to printable characters.

How much of this translation process do you really need to understand? That depends on your needs. If you spent a lot of time as an MS-DOS programmer, you probably want to know how Windows enhances the basic keyboard scan codes that are created by MS-DOS interrupts. If you plan to support international versions of your Windows software, you'll certainly want to know how Windows handles the different keyboards that are used around the world. Even if these two issues aren't important for your purposes, you should at least know when to use each of the two types of keyboard messages.

Keyboard data starts with the keyboard, so that's where we'll begin.

The physical keyboard

Keyboards haven't changed much since the first IBM-PCs were shipped back in the summer of 1981. Those first machines shipped with an 83-key keyboard. In 1984, IBM introduced the 84-key keyboard with the IBM-AT computer (the SysReq key was added). IBM subsequently introduced the 101/102-key keyboard, which mostly duplicated existing keys. That keyboard has become the standard for IBM-compatible computers.

At Fall Comdex in 1994, Microsoft introduced the Microsoft Natural Keyboard. In addition to sporting a curvy, ergonomic design, this keyboard adds two keys to the standard set. (One of the authors used this keyboard while writing many of the chapters in this book.) As you'll recall from our discussion of keyboard accelerators in Chapter 11, the two new keys are the Applications key and the Windows key.

The Applications key is intended for application use; it summons context menus. And in Windows 95, Windows itself responds to the Windows key by displaying the Task Manager. Both represent relatively minor, but useful additions to keyboard operation. However, it's too early to say whether other keyboard manufacturers will adopt these new keys.

Getting keyboard input to an MS-DOS program often involves an intimate knowledge of how a low-level keyboard code, known as a *scan code*, is generated. Although C-runtime functions translate keyboard input for you, MS-DOS programmers who opt for high performance will grab keyboard scan codes directly. Scan codes are not related to any character set; instead, they are a set of 8-bit codes that indicate which key has been pressed. For example, the key that generates a *Y* on a U.S.-English keyboard has a scan code of 15 hex. It doesn't take too much imagination — or code — to build a table for converting scan code data to ASCII characters. That's what many MS-DOS programmers must do.

Intimate knowledge of the keyboard was required because MS-DOS programmers have to ignore about half of the scan codes that are generated. Each key on the keyboard actually has *two* scan codes. One indicates that a key has been pressed, and the other indicates that the key has been released. The difference between the two scan codes is 80 hex. For example, the *Y* key that we discussed a moment ago sends a scan code of 15 hex when pressed and 95 hex when released. Of these two, the down transition is more interesting. When reading scan codes, the up transition — which has the sign bit set — is usually ignored.

One problem with scan codes is that they are a very hardware-dependent, low-level type of input. To properly perform scan code conversion, you must take into account the keyboard that is currently installed on the system. Most types of keyboards are distinguished on the basis of language or, in some cases, country.

One example, the Swiss-German keyboard, takes into account both language and country. On that keyboard, the *Z* key and the *Y* key are reversed from what they are on the U.S.-English keyboard. As a result, an MS-DOS program that relies on scan code conversions according to the U.S.-keyboard layout won't work correctly in Switzerland without some modification.

When we say that keyboard scan codes are hardware dependent, we really mean that they are dependent on the way keys are laid out differently to follow various cultural conventions. For a scan-code-dependent program that could work worldwide, approximately two dozen different translation tables are required. And that's only taking into account the keyboards that use the Roman alphabet. For other keyboards, such as Russian Cyrillic, Arabic, and the various Asian keyboards, a whole new set of problems arise.

In addition to being hardware dependent, scan codes are so low level that they don't take into account keyboard state, such as the Shift key or the Caps Lock key. As a result, considerable effort is required to simply detect the difference between an upper- and a lowercase letter. For example, a scan-code-dependent program can't tell the difference between *Y* and *y* without a lot of extra work. Scan codes aren't case sensitive because keyboards aren't case sensitive.

Windows has different solutions for each of these two problems. To avoid relying on country-specific keyboard layouts, Windows keyboard drivers convert scan codes into a standard set of *virtual key codes*. This set of keys make up what is sometimes called the *Windows logical keyboard*. To solve the problem of keyboard state, Windows provides a helper function to convert virtual key codes into printable characters. This latter conversion creates the distinction between upper- and lowercase that we rely on when reading text.

The Windows logical keyboard

The logical keyboard is an abstraction that serves to hide differences between keyboards in countries that use Roman characters. You won't see a keyboard layout for the logical keyboard anywhere in the Windows documentation. What you will see, however, are the definitions for virtual key (VK_) codes. It's the job of the keyboard device driver to convert hardware-specific scan codes into virtual key codes.

In particular, Windows calls the keyboard driver to convert raw hardware scan codes into virtual key codes. These virtual key codes are sent to applications as messages. Because there are two scan codes per keyboard key — that is, a "key pressed" code and a "key released" code — there are also two messages per key. The WM_KEYDOWN message indicates that a keyboard key has been pressed, and the WM_KEYUP message indicates that a key has been released.

Although virtual key messages solve one problem with scan codes, they don't solve the second problem. The problem they solve is that you don't have to worry about different keyboards. The device driver does whatever translation is necessary to produce a uniform set of key codes.

The problem that still exists, however, is that virtual key codes are fairly low level. In particular, you have to do a lot of work to decide whether letters are upper- or lowercase. And virtual key codes aren't influenced by changes to shift key states, which include the Shift, Ctrl, and Alt keys. Virtual key codes also ignore the state of the Caps Lock, Num Lock, and Scroll Lock keys.

Although they don't provide enough information to get character input, virtual key codes are suitable for use as accelerator key codes. As you may recall from the discussion in Chapter 11, there are two types of accelerators: VIRTKEY and ASCII. We recommend that you always use VIRTKEY, which — as the name suggests — corresponds to virtual keys. The other type of accelerator, ASCII, is created from the other type of keyboard message, which we're going to discuss next.

Printable character messages

The Windows API contains a function for converting between virtual key code messages and WM_CHAR messages. We call these the "printable character messages," because most are uppercase letters, lowercase letters, numbers, or punctuation marks. That is, they correspond to characters that you can see on the display screen and send to the printer.

The ::TranslateMessage( ) function is the Windows API function that converts virtual key messages into WM_CHAR messages. Unless you've written Windows SDK programs, you've probably never seen this function. And because MFC calls this function for you in its message loop, you don't ever have to worry about it.

What's important is that this function adds WM_CHAR messages to your application's message queue. Every WM_CHAR message that you receive will be preceded by a WM_KEYDOWN message and followed by a WM_KEYUP message. You get printable character input from the WM_CHAR message, and you can safely ignore the associated virtual key messages.

If you ignore WM_KEYDOWN messages, why does Windows bother sending them to you? This message is for all the keys that *don't* have a corresponding printable character. We should mention that such keystrokes seem more like commands than data, and the easiest way to handle keyboard commands is with an accelerator table. However, you can't always use an accelerator table. In particular, it's something of a convention that only one accelerator table is active at any point in time. That accelerator table would be the one for an application's frame window. All other windows must process low-level keyboard input directly, without the benefits that accelerator tables provide.

Table 14-4 lists the virtual key codes for keys that don't create printable characters. When you can't create accelerator table entries, you'll rely on the WM_KEYDOWN message to detect when these keys have been pressed.

To summarize, keyboard input starts as scan codes. A Windows keyboard driver converts these codes to a hardware-independent form: virtual key codes. Typically, Windows applications then send the virtual key code messages to a Windows API function that generates WM_CHAR character messages when printable characters are typed. For nonprintable characters — such as function keys and navigation keys — you must rely on the WM_KEYDOWN virtual key message.

Table 14-4

Virtual Key Codes for Keys That Don't Produce Printable Characters

Key	Virtual Key Code
Alt	VK_MENU
Application	VK_APPS
Ctrl	VK_CONTROL
Del	VK_DELETE
Down-arrow	VK_DOWN
End	VK_END
F1	VK_F1
F2	VK_F2
F3	VK_F3
F4	VK_F4
F5	VK_F5
F6	VK_F6
F7	VK_F7
F8	VK_F8
F9	VK_F9
F10	VK_F10
F11	VK_F11
F12	VK_F12
Home	VK_HOME
Ins	VK_INSERT
Left-arrow	VK_LEFT
Pause	VK_PAUSE
PgDn	VK_NEXT
PgUp	VK_PRIOR
PrtScr	VK_SNAPSHOT
Right-arrow	VK_RIGHT
Shift	VK_SHIFT
Up-arrow	VK_UP

Now that you understand the types of keyboard input messages that Windows will send you, it's time to address input issues related to application state. Toward that end, the following section describes how an application lets the user know that a window has the keyboard focus. This can be done using several techniques, which we call echoing the keyboard focus.

ECHOING KEYBOARD FOCUS

When you build support for keyboard input into a window, you must provide a visual cue that lets the user know when that support is enabled. Because a window gets keyboard input when it has the focus, the proper time for displaying those visual cues is when the window gets the focus. It follows, then, that you should disable the visible signs of the focus when the window loses the focus.

To help you build windows that display the proper visual cues, the following sections describe three ways that a window can advertise its ownership of the focus. We'll start with a look at creating carets, which are Windows' keyboard pointers. Then, we'll talk about focus rectangles, something you'll see in dialog box controls but which can also be displayed in other types of windows. Finally, we'll talk about the relationship between a window's selection state and the keyboard focus.

Creating and maintaining keyboard carets

A caret is a blinking bitmap that lets the user know where keyboard input will have an effect. In other operating systems, such as Unix and MS-DOS, a keyboard pointer is called a cursor. But because the cursor in Windows is the mouse pointer, in Windows we refer to keyboard pointers using the slightly more obscure name of *carets*.

Table 14-5 lists the eight CWnd member functions that create and manage carets. This group of functions is fairly small and easy to understand. The challenge with carets revolves around timing issues, such as when to create, show, hide, and destroy carets.

You create a caret when a window gets the keyboard focus. Although you might be tempted to create it earlier, you should resist the temptation. After all, you only need a caret to echo the results of keyboard input. And without the focus, you don't have any keyboard input. In addition to creating the caret, you need to position it within your window and make it visible. Here's a fragment of code that does the right thing in response to a WM_SETFOCUS message:

```
//------------------------------
// Handler for WM_SETFOCUS message.
void DMainFrame::OnSetFocus(CWnd* pOldWnd)
{
    // First call default handler.
    CFrameWnd::OnSetFocus(pOldWnd);
```

```
    // Create, position, and make caret appear.
    CreateSolidCaret(0, d_cyLineHeight);
    SetCaretPos(d_ptCaretLocation);
    ShowCaret();
}
```

Just as you create a caret when you get the focus, the logical time
to destroy the caret is when you lose the focus. In response to the
WM_KILLFOCUS message, you'll first hide the caret, and then destroy it.
Here's a code fragment that shows how this is done:

```
//--------------------------------
// Handler for WM_KILLFOCUS message.
void DMainFrame::OnKillFocus(CWnd* pNewWnd)
{
    CFrameWnd::OnKillFocus(pNewWnd);

    // Query and save current caret position.
    d_ptCaretLocation = GetCaretPos();

    // Eliminate caret.
    HideCaret();
    DestroyCaret();
}
```

Table 14-5
CWnd Member Functions for Creating and Managing Carets

Function	Description
CreateCaret()	Creates a caret using a bitmap that you provide. The accompanying sidebar provides a fun example of using a bitmap caret.
CreateGrayCaret()	Creates a solid gray caret using the size you specify.
CreateSolidCaret()	Creates a solid black caret using the size you specify.
GetCaretPos()	Returns the location of the caret. Because of local input state in Windows 95 and Windows NT, you can only find the location of a caret if it's contained within a window that's created by the calling thread.
DestroyCaret()	Destroys a caret. To avoid putting your application in an unknown state, destroy the caret when you lose the keyboard focus (and create a caret when you gain the keyboard focus).
HideCaret()	Makes a caret invisible.
SetCaretPos()	Moves a caret to a position in a window. When a window containing a caret is scrolled, the caret gets scrolled with the window data.
ShowCaret()	Makes a caret visible.

The only other caret issue involves drawing outside of normal WM_PAINT drawing. If a caret is in a window, you must hide the caret before any non-WM_PAINT drawing. Otherwise, you might overwrite the caret. When the non-WM_PAINT drawing is done, you can restore the caret. Here's a code fragment that shows what we mean:

```
//--------------------------------
// Handler for WM_CHAR message.
void DMainFrame::OnChar(UINT nChar, UINT nRepCnt, UINT nFlags)
{
    CSize sizeTextBox;

    // Fetch caret position.
    CPoint pt = GetCaretPos();

    // Hide caret before fetching DC.
    HideCaret();

    // Drawing in non-WM_PAINT message.
    // Bracket required to force DC to disappear.
    {
        CClientDC dc(this);
        dc.TextOut(pt.x, pt.y, (LPCTSTR)&nChar, 1);
        sizeTextBox = dc.GetTextExtent((LPCTSTR)&nChar, 1);
    }

    // Advance caret position.
    pt.x += sizeTextBox.cx;
    SetCaretPos(pt);

    // Display caret.
    ShowCaret();
}
```

This code fragment actually does more than just hide the caret. It shows how you respond to the WM_CHAR message to both draw the character that's typed and advance the caret. As discussed in the preceding chapter, such drawn objects won't be a permanent part of a window's contents unless they are also drawn in response to the WM_PAINT message. Because our code makes no provision for saving the text anywhere, this isn't done. (When you understand why this code fragment is "broken," you truly understand the meaning of the WM_PAINT message.)

To test your caret creation code, be sure to force the focus to switch away from your program. Do this by activating the Task Manager (Ctrl-Esc), or by activating any other application that's currently running. When you switch away, the caret should disappear without a trace.

When you switch back, the caret should be in the same place it was before you switched focus.

The keyboard caret is called the "keyboard pointer" because it shows users the exact point in a window at which keyboard input will have an effect. Users expect to be able to navigate carets around a window through the use of the arrow keys. Another way to echo the keyboard focus is with a focus rectangle, which we discuss next.

Simulating a VCR Clock with a Keyboard Caret

Figure 14-3 shows a tiny sample program that we've included with the source code that accompanies this book. The program is called VCRCLOCK, and it's meant to poke fun at the clocks in videocassette recorders. Like the clock in this "sophisticated" software simulation, VCR clocks seem to always show 12:00. Like typical VCR clocks, ours blinks continuously.

The blinking "12:00" is a keyboard caret, created from a bitmap that is stored in the program as a bitmap resource. In case you forget what makes carets so special, think of this program. After all, the caret is the only user-interface object in Windows that blinks, in the same way that the clock on a VCR is often its only indicator that blinks.

Figure 14-3
The VCRCLOCK program shows how you can use a bitmap to create a large caret that simulates the clock in a videocassette recorder.

Focus rectangles

A focus rectangle provides an alternative to a caret for signaling the keyboard focus location. Unlike carets, focus rectangles don't blink. Instead, they provide subtle highlighting that draws a user's eye to a particular part of a window. Whether you use a focus rectangle or a caret depends on what you are trying to highlight. The most common examples of focus rectangles occur in dialog boxes. For all non-edit controls, focus rectangles are drawn as the user moves the focus — via the Tab key or the mouse — to the different controls in the dialog. Figure 14-4 shows a focus rectangle around a check box control.

Figure 14-4

In a dialog box, a focus rectangle such as this one around the check box indicates the location of the keyboard focus.

Focus rectangles aren't solely for dialog box controls, although this is the most obvious and most common use. You can use them anywhere a caret just doesn't seem right. One difference between focus rectangles and carets is that carets are always solid rectangles. Focus rectangles, on the other hand, are hollow, and they wrap around other objects. If you need to echo the focus in a way that is solid or blinking, you want a caret. For a subtler, hollow pointer, try a focus rectangle instead.

Drawing a focus rectangle is extremely easy. You simply call MFC's CDC::DrawFocusRect( ) function. The following example shows how to draw a focus rectangle around a block of text:

```
//-------------------------------
// Handler for WM_LBUTTONDOWN message.
void DMainFrame::OnLButtonDown(UINT nFlags, CPoint point)
{
    CClientDC dc(this);

    // Draw a line of text at mouse cursor location.
    CString str;
    str.Format("There is a focus rectangle around this text");
    dc.TextOut(point.x, point.y, str);

    // Calculate width and height of text.
    CSize sizeText = dc.GetTextExtent(str, str.GetLength());

    // Calculate a margin around the focus rectangle.
    int cxMargin = GetSystemMetrics (SM_CXBORDER) * 4;
    int cyMargin = GetSystemMetrics (SM_CYBORDER) * 1;

    // Calculate size of focus rectangle.
    CRect rTextBox;
    rTextBox.left    = point.x - cxMargin;
    rTextBox.top     = point.y - cyMargin;
```

```
        rTextBox.right  = point.x + sizeText.cx + cxMargin;
        rTextBox.bottom = point.y + sizeText.cy + cyMargin;

        // Draw a focus rectangle around a block of text.
        dc.DrawFocusRect(&rTextBox);

        CFrameWnd::OnLButtonDown(nFlags, point);
    }
```

This code fragment draws a focus rectangle in response to a
WM_LBUTTONDOWN message. We show this simply as an example of
how to call CDC::DrawFocusRect( ). But the truth of the matter is that
button messages aren't the events that typically trigger the drawing of
focus rectangles.

You're more likely to draw the focus rectangle when a window gets
the focus. The reason should be obvious: That's when you are certain
that your window has the focus. And, as you may recall from our earlier
discussion, this means that you draw a focus rectangle in response to a
WM_SETFOCUS message. Here's a fragment of code taken from an MFC
program that shows how to do this:

```
//------------------------------
// Handler for WM_SETFOCUS message.
void DMainFrame::OnSetFocus(CWnd* pOldWnd)
{
    CFrameWnd::OnSetFocus(pOldWnd);

    CClientDC dc(this);

    // Draw focus rectangle when we get the focus.
    CRect rFocus;
    rFocus.left   = d_ptFocusRect.x;
    rFocus.top    = d_ptFocusRect.y;
    rFocus.right  = d_ptFocusRect.x + d_cxIcon;
    rFocus.bottom = d_ptFocusRect.y + d_cyIcon;
    dc.DrawFocusRect(&rFocus);
}
```

If you draw a focus rectangle, you must be sure to erase it. Because
a focus rectangle exists just to show focus ownership, the logical time to
erase a focus rectangle is when the window loses the focus. Interestingly
enough, a focus rectangle is erased by calling the exact same function
that drew it in the first place: CDC::DrawFocusRect( ). The following
code fragment erases the focus rectangle we drew a moment ago. This
is done in response to — what else? — the WM_KILLFOCUS message:

```
//------------------------------
// Handler for WM_KILLFOCUS message.
void DMainFrame::OnKillFocus(CWnd* pNewWnd)
{
    CFrameWnd::OnKillFocus(pNewWnd);

    CClientDC dc(this);

    // Hide focus rectangle when we lose the focus.
    CRect rFocus;
    rFocus.left   = d_ptFocusRect.x;
    rFocus.top    = d_ptFocusRect.y;
    rFocus.right  = d_ptFocusRect.x + d_cxIcon;
    rFocus.bottom = d_ptFocusRect.y + d_cyIcon;
    dc.DrawFocusRect(&rFocus);
}
```

You might find it a bit puzzling that the same code can erase *and* draw a focus rectangle. To explain how this is possible, we need to describe how CDC::DrawFocusRect( ) works. This function uses Boolean arithmetic to invert a set of pixels. To draw a focus rectangle, pixels are inverted. To erase the same focus rectangle, the same pixels are inverted again, which completely and effectively erases the focus rectangle. This is often referred to as a Boolean operation and it makes use of GDI's Boolean *raster operations* (or *ROP codes*).

So far, we've described how you make a focus rectangle appear when you get a WM_SETFOCUS message, and how you make it disappear in response to a WM_KILLFOCUS message. But there's one more message that can affect the health and well-being of a focus rectangle. To provide complete support for a focus rectangle, you must redraw the focus rectangle in response to the WM_PAINT message.

You need to draw a focus rectangle when handling a WM_PAINT message for the same reason that you draw any other object in a window's client area. You can't determine ahead of time when some outside event will damage the contents of a window's client area. It might be as simple as a screen saver that automatically starts after 10 minutes of idle time. Whatever the reason, you draw a focus rectangle with the same function we described earlier, CDC::DrawFocusRect( ). With WM_PAINT, however, you must first determine whether the window has the focus. If it doesn't, you don't draw the focus rectangle. Only if it has the focus do you draw the focus rectangle. Here's a WM_PAINT handler that first checks for the presence of the focus before drawing a focus rectangle:

```
//-----------------------------
// Handler for WM_PAINT message.
void DMainFrame::OnPaint()
{
    CPaintDC dc(this); // device context for painting

    // Only draw focus rectangle if our window has focus.
    if (GetFocus() == this)
    {
        // Calculate coordinate
        CRect rFocus;
        rFocus.left   = d_ptFocusRect.x;
        rFocus.top    = d_ptFocusRect.y;
        rFocus.right  = d_ptFocusRect.x + d_cxIcon;
        rFocus.bottom = d_ptFocusRect.y + d_cyIcon;

        // Draw actual focus rectangle.
        dc.DrawFocusRect(&rFocus);
    }
}
```

Both types of focus-echoing mechanisms — carets and focus rectangles — are relatively easy to create and use. But a third issue — the selection state — is closely related to the keyboard focus. By *selection state*, we mean the display of objects selected by a user in a window. To support Windows' standards for user-interface activity, selection state must be visible only when a window has focus. At all other times, the selection state of objects must be hidden.

Selection state and keyboard focus

With Windows applications, a common mode of operation involves *noun-verb* operations. This means that the user first selects an object, and then chooses the action to take on that object. For example, to change the formatting of a word in a word-processing program, the user first selects the word, and then chooses the Format command. Although this mode of operation is obvious to experienced Windows users, the opposite — that is, verb-noun operation — is quite common in character-based environments.

Objects can be selected using either the mouse or the keyboard. Regardless of how it's done, Windows programs change the color of selected objects to help users distinguish them from other objects. An example is shown in Figure 14-5. We touched on this subject briefly in the previous chapter when we discussed picking text colors. As you might recall, you fetch the colors to use by calling ::GetSysColor( ) with the appropriate color indices. Then, you perform a bitwise exclusive OR to determine the color of selected text. This is summarized in the following lines of code:

```
COLORREF d_crForeground = GetSysColor(COLOR_WINDOWTEXT);
COLORREF d_crBackground = GetSysColor(COLOR_WINDOW);
COLORREF d_crSelectFore = d_crForeground ^ 0x00ffffff;
COLORREF d_crSelectBack = d_crBackground ^ 0x00ffffff;
```

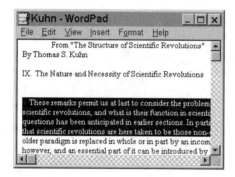

Figure 14-5

The selection of this text — white letters on a black background — should appear only when the window has the focus.

In general, when a window loses the keyboard focus, it should hide its selection. When focus is restored, the window should again show the selection. We say "in general" because there are a few situations in which a window will still show its selection state even though it has lost the focus. In particular, two windows might need to simultaneously display the selected state. For details, see the *Windows 95 User Interface Design Guide*.

To get a sense for when to show selection state and when to hide it, run some of the popular Windows applications. If you watch closely, you'll see that numerous small visual cues indicate changes in activation and focus. Some of these — for example, the change in caption bar color — are handled by Windows. Other state changes — such as the three we've discussed here — must be handled by your application. But rather than dictate hard-and-fast rules, we should point out that the most important criterion is what works for your users.

Before moving on to mouse input, the final keyboard topic we're going to cover is character sets. We'll define the available character sets and describe when and where they may affect your development efforts.

WINDOWS CHARACTER SETS

A *character set* is a convention that describes how character codes are displayed on a graphic display device. The character codes themselves are introduced into a program through disk files or character messages. And, of course, they are displayed on display screens and in printed output by calling various GDI (or in MFC terms, CDC) text drawing functions. When working with Windows, you may eventually encounter four character sets in one way or another. They are: the OEM character set, the ANSI character set, double-byte character sets (DBCSs), and the Unicode character set.

The OEM (MS-DOS) character set

The term *OEM character set* actually refers to any hardware-specific character set. For example, the VGA adapter has characters burned into ROM. This type of hardware-specific character set is what most programmers have in mind when they use the term *OEM character set*. But as noted by Ed Mills, a member of the original GDI team, OEM really means the "unknown character set." It is unknown because every printer and plotter — and every display screen adapter — can have its own set of characters.

Although it is *possible* for each device to have a unique character set, in practice, most OEM character sets share common elements. First, the OEM character sets for phonetic languages all are 8-bit character sets and therefore can hold a maximum of 255 characters. (Asian languages such as Chinese, Japanese, and Korean use multiple bytes to represent larger numbers of characters. Second, all share a common set of characters in the range of character codes between 0×20 and $0 \times 7e$. Outside that range, you'll find considerable variation.

To manage the differences outside the common range, IBM introduced the concept of a *code page*. Each variation has its own unique ID. For example, code page 437 is the default for computers built for use in the United States. To users (and programmers) in the United States, that is the character set most commonly associated with the term *OEM char-acter set*. Figure 14-6 shows the characters that Windows recognizes as belonging to this character set. Other code pages that have been defined include code page 850 — a "multilingual" set — and code pages for Arabic, Russian Cyrillic, French Canadian, and Portuguese. Outside the United States, the term *OEM character set* refers to whatever default code page is installed on the graphics display adapter.

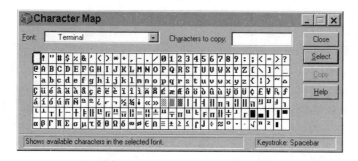

Figure 14-6

The character map program showing the characters in the OEM/MS-DOS character set.

The term *OEM character set* is derived from the fact that one set of Microsoft's customers are *original equipment manufacturers*, or OEMs. These are companies that build personal computers or personal com-puter hardware. In the personal computer arena, one of these OEM customers — IBM — took the lead in defining new code pages. IBM built the first MS-DOS computer — creating a product category that is sometimes still referred to as "IBM-compatible personal computers." From the perspective of graphic output, however, Microsoft considers all hardware-specific character sets — including those on printers and plotters — to fall under the umbrella term *OEM character set*.

In the context of Windows programming, we prefer to use the term *MS-DOS character set* instead of OEM character set. We're more inter-ested in the character set used by MS-DOS to support the file system than in variations for different printers or plotters. For such graphic devices, a Windows-specific device driver hides the native character set. Instead, the character sets on all graphic devices follow the Windows character set (which we'll discuss shortly).

IBM defined the MS-DOS character set for use in a character-based world. Standard ASCII values occupy the positions between values 0×20 and $0 \times 7f$ (the first three rows in Figure 14-6). Immediately following this range are some vowels with diacritical marks — that is, circumflexes, umlauts, and various accent marks. The range following standard ASCII also contains various graphical characters, such as line segments that can be combined to form simple line graphics, Greek characters, and mathematical symbols. Beyond that range (and not shown in the figure) are interesting characters such as smiley faces, and other vaguely useful symbols.

This is of interest to Windows programmers because MS-DOS programs use the MS-DOS character set. A Windows program that imports raw text data might need to ask a user about the text source. If OEM characters (outside the range of common values) were somehow included, such characters might be incorrectly interpreted. (The reason will be clear shortly when we explore Windows' ANSI character set.)

The other major reason why a Windows programmer might care about the MS-DOS character set is because it's the character set used by the FAT file system. This is the file system that Microsoft first introduced with MS-DOS in the early 1980s. It's still in use today, and, in fact, is the one file system that is accessible by every version of Windows (we include here Windows 3.x, Windows 95, and Windows NT). Filenames, directory names, and disk volume names are all written using the MS-DOS character set in the FAT file system.

With Windows 95, Microsoft is introducing some enhancements to the file system. One enhancement is support for long filenames. To the user, a filename can be as long as 255 characters. (And complete file paths can be up to 260 characters long.) For compatibility with earlier versions of MS-DOS and Windows, however, a *short name* is also created and stored using the MS-DOS character set.

Another Windows 95 enhancement involves changes to the file I/O functions. Although Win16 programmers have to worry about matching file I/O functions to the proper character set, in Windows 95 all file I/O functions for Win32 programs use the Windows character set by default. [Windows 95 also lets you control this by calling SetFileApisToOEM( ) and SetFileApisToANSI( ).]

Although the OEM (or MS-DOS) character set has always been of peripheral concern to Windows programmers, another character set has dominated the landscape for Win16 programmers. We are referring to the 8-bit ANSI (or Win/ANSI) character set, which Windows has always used for keyboard messages sent to 16-bit Windows programs. This is also the primary character set for Win32 programs running under Windows 95. And even though it's *not* the primary character set for Windows NT (that honor belongs to Unicode), the Win/ANSI character set is fully supported by Windows NT. Let's try to understand why Microsoft decided to introduce a new character set with its Microsoft Windows operating system.

The ANSI (Win/ANSI) character set

The characters in the ANSI character set are shown in Figure 14-7. When Microsoft first created Windows, the American National Standards Institute — ANSI — had defined standards for character sets. Most notable among these is ASCII (the American Standard Code for Information Interchange). In a sense, Windows uses what might be considered just another MS-DOS code page. What's different, as we'll soon describe, is that this character set provides more flexibility than almost any other 8-bit character set for supporting an international set of characters.

Figure 14-7
The character map program showing the characters in the Win/ANSI character set.

Windows' ANSI character set is sometimes called the Win/ANSI — or just plain Windows — character set. That helps connect it inextricably with Microsoft Windows. If you compare the MS-DOS and Win/ANSI character sets, you'll notice that the first three lines — that is, the range between 0×20 and $0 \times 7e$ — are identical. This reflects the U.S.-centric nature of both character sets. Programmers in the U.S. often overlook the differences between these character sets, because written English doesn't use diacritical (accent) marks over vowels.

The most important improvement that the Windows character set makes over the MS-DOS character set can be seen in the character map's sixth and seventh rows. The Win/ANSI character set has a wide variety of vowels, with every combination of vowel and diacritical mark that's used in the Roman alphabet. With the Windows character set, a machine that's equipped with — for example — a Swiss-German keyboard can create files that can be properly read, modified, and printed on a computer equipped for any other country or language (assuming the Roman alphabet is used). You can't do that with the MS-DOS character set, because the various character sets don't all have the same diacritical marks.

Win/ANSI is the primary character set for Windows 95. This means several things. First, all function calls that accept text strings expect Win/ANSI characters. Also, character input (that is, WM_CHAR) messages hold character codes in the Win/ANSI character set. This means that any character strings in data files will probably use this character set.

However, Win/ANSI isn't the only character set to consider. In particular, the Windows NT operating system supports Unicode as its primary character set. Let's discuss what this means in terms of the Win32 API and your Windows 95 development efforts.

The Unicode character set

Although the Win/ANSI character set solves some problems with the sharing of data files, it doesn't solve all of them. For example, it's very difficult to put Russian and Arabic into the same data file and have both sets of text print out properly (each requires a different code page). Even if the users of your software never combine multiple languages, the process of creating localized versions of your software for different language markets will be greatly simplified if your software can handle character data in a uniform manner. And handling character data in a uniform manner is what Unicode is all about.

Unicode is a 16-bit character set that is designed as a *universal* character set. It solves the problem of sharing data between different language groups, because all the major alphabets of the world are represented in Unicode. It's a sort of United Nations for character sets, where the world's characters all come together for the common goal of simplifying electronic communication.

From a software development perspective, the key benefit of Unicode is that it simplifies the process of creating software for use in different languages. To prepare software for other languages, you will always have to modify the visible text strings in menus, dialogs, message boxes, help files, and so on. But by using Unicode, you don't have to modify the *infrastructure* for parsing text strings. There is one simple reason for this: every character occupies exactly 16 bits.

Microsoft adopted Unicode as the primary character set for Windows NT, its high-end Windows operating system. Because Unicode contains all of the characters in the OEM and ANSI character sets, Windows NT can support MS-DOS and Windows programs that rely on those character sets. This is an essential part of the support that Windows NT provides for backward compatibility with MS-DOS and Win 16 Windows application software.

The relationship between Windows 95 and Unicode is not as straightforward. In particular, the default character set in Windows 95 is Win/ANSI. Windows 95 provides only limited support for Unicode. Win32 function calls under Windows 95 expect ANSI character strings for character string pointer parameters. And character codes in character messages (WM_CHAR) are also ANSI characters. In a Unicode-aware application, on the other hand, Windows sends character messages using the Unicode character set.

Although Unicode is not its native character set, Windows 95 can convert strings between Unicode and ANSI. This is necessary because the resources in a Win32 program that contain strings — that is, menus, dialogs, and string tables — are stored using Unicode. When such resources are loaded to run in Windows 95, they are converted to ANSI. When loaded to run in Windows NT, they are used as is.

The other reason why Windows 95 must be able to convert between Unicode and ANSI involves the file system. Although the "MS-DOS-visible," short filenames are stored using the OEM character set, long filenames are stored in Unicode. The Unicode filenames are only visible to MS-DOS programs that call extensions to the MS-DOS interrupts specifically provided to support long filename file I/O functions.

The 32-bit OLE (Object Linking and Embedding) libraries are yet another example of a Windows 95 feature that uses Unicode. The 16-bit libraries, which were first built for Windows 3.1, use the ANSI character set. But the 32-bit libraries, which also support OLE on both Windows 95 and Windows NT, use only Unicode.

When building a Win32 program, you must decide whether to use Unicode or ANSI as your program's default. Although it is possible to mix Unicode and ANSI in a single program, you still need to decide which will be the default. Out of the box, Visual C++ 2.x sets the ANSI character set as the default. You need to make some minor changes in order to specify the Unicode character set as the default for Win32 applications that are built with Visual C++. These changes are detailed in the accompanying sidebar. By choosing the Unicode character set for your Win32 program, you get only limited support when running on Windows 95.

Compiling an Application for Unicode Support

We were able to compile and run our MFC programs to use the Unicode character set by following instructions in Chapter 12 of the *Visual C++ Programming Techniques* reference manual. For your convenience, here is a summary of the steps we took.

Out of the box, the Visual C++ compiler builds programs that store strings using the ANSI character set. Overriding this default is fairly simple. You define a _UNICODE symbol before any statement that references an include file, as in:

```
#define _UNICODE
```

Although you could define this in every source code file, it's easier to change one setting. In the Visual C++ development environment, choose the Projects|Settings... menu item. From the Project Settings property sheet, choose the C/C++ setting tab. Then, from the Category list, add _UNICODE to the Preprocessor Definitions edit control. Remove the definition for _MBCS, which requests *multibyte character set* support.

The next step is to define a new entry point. The entry point for ANSI applications is _WinMain@16. For Unicode applications, you must define wWinMainCRTStartup as the application entry point. You don't define a new function, because Microsoft provides one in a linker library. Instead, in the Project Settings property sheet, select the Link tab and the Output category. Enter the Unicode entry point name in the edit control labeled Entry Point Symbol.

Continued

Continued from previous page

You might find, as we did, that you need to install new linker libraries and dynamic link libraries from the Visual C++ install disks (or the CD-ROM) to make this work. For example, we copied MFC30UD.LIB into \msvc20\mfc\lib and MFC30UD.DLL into the system directory (\WIN95\SYSTEM). Otherwise, you get both linker errors and runtime errors. Although you can simply copy the files from the CD-ROM, the Visual C++ Setup program also provides an option that copies all required static and dynamic link libraries for you.

One last step — which we've already been taking in all of the samples in this book — is to mark every literal string as a Unicode string. To request that the compiler use Unicode with a character string, you prefix the string with an *L*, as in:

```
lstrcpy (achHello, L"Hello World");
```

To help you switch between the two character sets, the _T() macro forces literal strings to follow whatever default you've chosen. This macro uses Unicode when _UNICODE is defined; otherwise, it uses ANSI. Here's a more portable version of the previous line of code:

```
lstrcpy (achHello, _T("Hello World"));
```

Your use of this macro still allows you to define Unicode strings by explicitly including the *L*, or ANSI strings by omitting it.

Unicode-aware Win32 programs must be run on Windows NT to get full Unicode support. If you try to run a Unicode Win32 program on Windows 95, you'll find that the program won't run.

Windows NT supports both ANSI and Unicode applications by providing two entry points for every function that takes a character string pointer parameter. Evidence of this can be found in the Win32 include files (which are located in \msvc20\include). For example, GDI's TextOut function is defined as follows in WINGDI.H:

```
WINGDIAPI BOOL  WINAPI TextOutA(HDC, int, int, LPCSTR, int);
WINGDIAPI BOOL  WINAPI TextOutW(HDC, int, int, LPCWSTR, int);
#ifdef UNICODE
#define TextOut   TextOutW
#else
#define TextOut   TextOutA
#endif // !UNICODE
```

In other words, the meaning of TextOut depends on whether Unicode is being used. When Unicode is used, TextOutW is called (the *W* stands for *wide character set*). When ANSI is used, TextOutA is called.

There are few simple answers as to whether you should use Unicode or ANSI for your Win32 programming projects. On the one hand, Unicode makes a lot of sense if Windows NT is the target operating system. Unicode gives you the benefit of a universal character set on a not-yet universal operating system. But Unicode-aware applications won't run on Windows 95, which is likely to become the more widespread version of Windows.

In the short term, if you are creating a Win32 program that you're targeting for Windows 95, it looks like a simple choice to use the ANSI character set. But don't make that choice too hastily, because certain Unicode functions are supported under Windows 95. It's not complete API support, but it might be enough to help you avoid total reliance on ANSI.

To decide whether it's worth the effort to take the slightly more difficult route of using Unicode on Windows 95, you have to decide how important the international software market is for your application. After all, certain types of software probably won't ever be international — for example, utilities created for in-house use at a company that has operations in only one country. But if any part of your prospective installed base spans different languages (or even different countries), you might want to consider the internationalization help that Unicode provides.

If you decide to build your Win32 programs using the ANSI character set, the good news is that you can run on both Windows 95 and Windows NT. You will pay a slight performance penalty on Windows NT, however, because every ANSI character string must be converted to Unicode, and vice-versa. And to create localized versions of your software — particularly for the Japanese, Chinese, Korean, Russian, or Arabic markets — you have your work cut out for you.

We suspect that most developers of Win32 applications will choose ANSI character set support. Localization costs are often far from the minds of developers facing the bigger challenge of building a new piece of software. And the ANSI character set works fine for most of the world's languages. Where it fails, however, is for languages that have more than 256 symbols. These languages are handled by Windows' double-byte character set support.

Double-byte character set (DBCS) and multibyte character set (MBCS)

Windows' double-byte character set support is provided for three languages — Chinese, Japanese, and Korean — that use more than 256 characters in writing. The writing systems used for all three languages have their roots in the Chinese written language. Chinese scholars mention the existence of more than 50,000 individual symbols, although only about 10,000 symbols are used for data processing needs.

Although it's officially called the double-byte character set, DBCS support actually mixes one- and two-byte characters. For this reason, some developers refer to this as multibyte character set (MBCS) support. As you might imagine, the mixture of one- and two-byte characters often creates problems when parsing strings. When dealing with DBCS languages, for example, you cannot blindly loop through a character string by incrementing an array index, as in:

```
char ach[MAX_TEXT_SIZE];
char achNextChar;
int cbSize = FetchString(ach);
for (int i = 0; i < cbSize; i++)
{
    achNextChar = achNextChar[i];
    ...
}
```

Instead, you must examine the contents of individual strings to check for single- versus double-byte character codes.

The mouse and keyboard provide you with a direct connection to the user. For that reason, the primary challenge in properly handling the input is to cover all of the odd interactions between input devices and application state. As you'll see in our sample GETTEXT program, mouse-support routines can be used in many ways for keyboard input, and vice-versa. Most important, though, is that you provide consistent behavior to the user. It's a time-consuming and tedious task, as is demonstrated by the length of the sample program relative to the functional capabilities that it produces. But this is the level of consistency that users have come to expect in applications that are built for GUI systems.

GETTEXT: Scrolling and Selecting Text

We created the GETTEXT program, shown in Figure 14-8, to show you some basic techniques for supporting both mouse and keyboard interaction. We've integrated the two because that's generally a more difficult task than handling only one or the other. Although users typically employ *either* the mouse *or* the keyboard for a given task, they might decide to switch in the middle of a task. And your application software must be prepared to handle that switch.

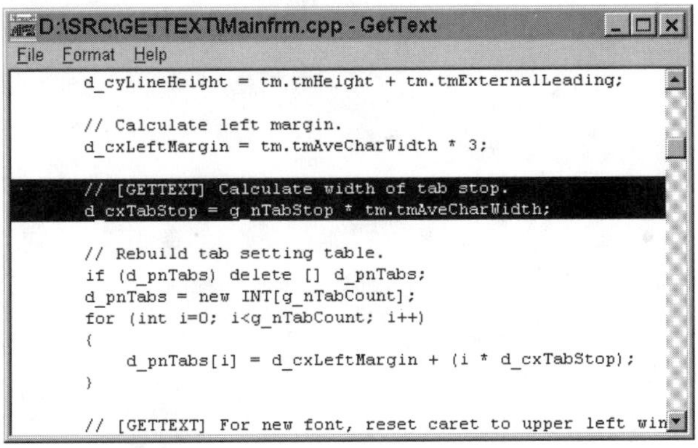

Figure 14-8
GETTEXT is shown selecting some lines of text. This sample program supports the extending of a selection while scrolling, the display of a keyboard caret, and the combining of caret movement and scrolling.

The GETTEXT program takes as its starting point the FILELIST program from Chapter 13. We chose this program because we needed some data to manipulate. As you may recall, FILELIST reads a text file and displays the file in a scrolling window. But that program doesn't handle any mouse and keyboard input. To demonstrate some common interaction techniques, our GETTEXT program handles both mouse and keyboard input.

GETTEXT is roughly twice as long as FILELIST. To help you quickly identify the code that was created for GETTEXT, new lines of code and new functions are preceded by comment lines that start with [GETTEXT]. As you browse through the code, it will be readily apparent what's new with GETTEXT and what was part of the original FILELIST program. Listings 14-3 through 14-8 contain the core source files for GETTEXT.

Listing 14-3
GETTEXT.H

```
// gettext.h : main header file for the GETTEXT application
//

#ifndef __AFXWIN_H__
    #error include 'stdafx.h' before including this file for PCH
#endif

#include "resource.h"        // main symbols

/////////////////////////////////////////////////////////////////////////////
// DApp:
// See gettext.cpp for the implementation of this class
//

class DApp : public CWinApp
{
public:
    DApp();

// Overrides
    // ClassWizard generated virtual function overrides
    //{{AFX_VIRTUAL(DApp)
    public:
    virtual BOOL InitInstance();
    //}}AFX_VIRTUAL

// Implementation

    //{{AFX_MSG(DApp)
    afx_msg void OnAppAbout();
        // NOTE - the ClassWizard will add and remove member functions here.
        //      DO NOT EDIT what you see in these blocks of generated code !
    //}}AFX_MSG
    DECLARE_MESSAGE_MAP()
};


/////////////////////////////////////////////////////////////////////////////
```

Listing 14-4
GETTEXT.CPP

```
// GetText.cpp: This is an enhancement to the FILELIST program
//              of Chapter 11. This program demonstrates mouse
//              and keyboard interaction techniques. Using the
//              mouse, lines of text can be selected, and the
```

```
//                caret can be moved. Keyboard input is used to
//                move the caret and to control scrolling.
//

#include "stdafx.h"
#include "gettext.h"

#include "mainfrm.h"

#ifdef _DEBUG
#undef THIS_FILE
static char BASED_CODE THIS_FILE[] = __FILE__;
#endif

/////////////////////////////////////////////////////////////////////////////
// DApp

BEGIN_MESSAGE_MAP(DApp, CWinApp)
    //{{AFX_MSG_MAP(DApp)
    ON_COMMAND(ID_APP_ABOUT, OnAppAbout)
        // NOTE - the ClassWizard will add and remove mapping macros here.
        //    DO NOT EDIT what you see in these blocks of generated code!
    //}}AFX_MSG_MAP
    // Standard file based document commands
    ON_COMMAND(ID_FILE_NEW, CWinApp::OnFileNew)
    ON_COMMAND(ID_FILE_OPEN, CWinApp::OnFileOpen)
END_MESSAGE_MAP()

/////////////////////////////////////////////////////////////////////////////
// DApp construction

DApp::DApp()
{
    // TODO: add construction code here,
    // Place all significant initialization in InitInstance
}

/////////////////////////////////////////////////////////////////////////////
// The one and only DApp object

DApp theApp;

/////////////////////////////////////////////////////////////////////////////
// DApp initialization

BOOL DApp::InitInstance()
{
    // Step 1: Allocate C++ window object.
    DMainFrame * pFrame;
    pFrame = new DMainFrame();

    // Step 2: Initialize window object.
    pFrame->LoadFrame(IDR_MAINFRAME);
```

```cpp
    // Make window visible
    pFrame->ShowWindow(m_nCmdShow);

    // Assign frame as application's main window
    m_pMainWnd = pFrame;

    // [GETTEXT] Check for file name on command line.
    if (m_lpCmdLine[0] != '\0')
    {
        CString strFile;
        strFile = &m_lpCmdLine[0];
        pFrame->OpenTextFile(strFile);
    }

    return TRUE;
}


/////////////////////////////////////////////////////////////////////////
// CAboutDlg dialog used for App About

class CAboutDlg : public CDialog
{
public:
    CAboutDlg();

// Dialog Data
    //{{AFX_DATA(CAboutDlg)
    enum { IDD = IDD_ABOUTBOX };
    //}}AFX_DATA

// Implementation
protected:
    virtual void DoDataExchange(CDataExchange* pDX);    // DDX/DDV support
    //{{AFX_MSG(CAboutDlg)
        // No message handlers
    //}}AFX_MSG
    DECLARE_MESSAGE_MAP()
};

CAboutDlg::CAboutDlg() : CDialog(CAboutDlg::IDD)
{
    //{{AFX_DATA_INIT(CAboutDlg)
    //}}AFX_DATA_INIT
}

void CAboutDlg::DoDataExchange(CDataExchange* pDX)
{
    CDialog::DoDataExchange(pDX);
    //{{AFX_DATA_MAP(CAboutDlg)
    //}}AFX_DATA_MAP
}
```

```
BEGIN_MESSAGE_MAP(CAboutDlg, CDialog)
    //{{AFX_MSG_MAP(CAboutDlg)
        // No message handlers
    //}}AFX_MSG_MAP
END_MESSAGE_MAP()

// App command to run the dialog
void DApp::OnAppAbout()
{
    CAboutDlg aboutDlg;
    aboutDlg.DoModal();
}


/////////////////////////////////////////////////////////////////////////////
// DApp commands
```

Listing 14-5
MAINFRM.H

```
// mainfrm.h : interface of the DMainFrame class
//
/////////////////////////////////////////////////////////////////////////////
#include <afxtempl.h> // Connect to CArray template.

// Structure to track lines in text file.
class STRING  // : public CObject
{
  public:
    LPTSTR pText;
    int    ccLen;
};

// This declaration uses the CArray template
// to provide a dynamic array of STRING records.
class StringArray : public CArray <STRING, STRING &>
{
  public:
    StringArray() {}
    STRING& operator=(STRING & s)
                        {m_pData->pText = s.pText;
                         m_pData->ccLen = s.ccLen;
                         return *m_pData;}
};

const int g_nTabCount=25;
const int g_nTabStop=4;

class DMainFrame : public CFrameWnd
{
```

```
public:
    DMainFrame();
protected: // create from serialization only
    DECLARE_DYNCREATE(DMainFrame)

// Attributes
public:
    BOOL          d_bTabs;          // Respect tabs or not.
    CFileDialog * d_pOpenFile;      // Ptr to OpenFile dialog.
    CFontDialog * d_pSetFont;       // Ptr to Font Picker dialog.
    CFont   *     d_pFont;          // Ptr to CFont object.
    COLORREF      d_crForeground;   // Foreground text color.
    COLORREF      d_crBackground;   // Background text color.
    LOGFONT       d_lf;             // Current logical font.
    LPINT         d_pnTabs;         // Array of tab settings.
    LPTSTR        d_lpTextBuffer;   // Ptr to text buffer.
    DWORD         d_dwFileLength;   // File length.
    StringArray   d_saTextInfo;     // Array of string info.
    int           d_cLines;         // Count of lines in text.
    int           d_cyLineHeight;   // Height of one line of text.
    int           d_clHeight;       // Window height line count.
    int           d_iTopLine;       // Index of top-most line.
    int           d_cyClient;       // Window client area height.
    int           d_cxLeftMargin;   // Margin to left of text.

    // [GETTEXT] New attributes.
    BOOL          d_bCapture;       // Mouse capture flag.
    BOOL          d_bMouseActive;   // Whether mouse click activated window.
    BOOL          d_bTimerStarted;  // Mouse move timer started.
    BYTE          d_bchFirstChar;   // First character in char width table.
    COLORREF      d_crSelectFore;   // Selected object foreground color.
    COLORREF      d_crSelectBack;   // Selected object background color.
    CPoint        d_ptCaret;        // Location of keyboard caret.
    HCURSOR       d_hcrIBeam;       // Text area I-Beam.
    HCURSOR       d_hcrLArrow;      // Left arrow for drag/drop.
    HCURSOR       d_hcrRArrow;      // Right arrow for left margin.
    int           d_cxTabStop;      // Width of a tab stop.
    int           d_cxAveCharWidth; // Average width of a character.
    int           d_nFocusMode;     // Current selection and/or focus state.
    int           d_nSelectFirst;   // Index of first selected line.
    int           d_nSelectLast;    // Index of last selected line.
    LPINT         d_piCharWidth;    // Table of character widths.
    UINT          d_nTimerID;       // ID of mouse move select timer.

// Operations
public:
    void BuildStringArray();
    BOOL CreateNewFont();
    void ResetScrollValues();
    // [GETTEXT] New operation for opening file from command line.
    void OpenTextFile(CString strFile);

    // [GETTEXT] New operations for caret handling.
    void MoveCaret(int nLine, int nChar);
```

```
    void MoveCaretChar(int nCharCount);
    void MoveCaretClick(CPoint ptHit);
    int  QueryClickChar(int iLine, CPoint point);
    int  QueryClickLine(CPoint point);

    // [GETTEXT] New operations for selection handling.
    void GetSelectedRect(CRect * prSelected);
    void InvertLines(int nFirst, int nLast);

// Overrides
    // ClassWizard generated virtual function overrides
    //{{AFX_VIRTUAL(DMainFrame)
    //}}AFX_VIRTUAL

// Implementation
public:
    virtual ~DMainFrame();
#ifdef _DEBUG
    virtual void AssertValid() const;
    virtual void Dump(CDumpContext& dc) const;
#endif

// Generated message map functions
protected:
    //{{AFX_MSG(DMainFrame)
    afx_msg void CmdFileOpen();
    afx_msg void CmdFormatFont();
    afx_msg void CmdFormatTabs();
    afx_msg void UpdFormatTabs(CCmdUI* pCmdUI);
    afx_msg int OnCreate(LPCREATESTRUCT lpCreateStruct);
    afx_msg BOOL OnEraseBkgnd(CDC* pDC);
    afx_msg void OnKeyDown(UINT nChar, UINT nRepCnt, UINT nFlags);
    afx_msg void OnKillFocus(CWnd* pNewWnd);
    afx_msg void OnLButtonDblClk(UINT nFlags, CPoint point);
    afx_msg void OnLButtonDown(UINT nFlags, CPoint point);
    afx_msg void OnLButtonUp(UINT nFlags, CPoint point);
    afx_msg void OnMButtonDown(UINT nFlags, CPoint point);
    afx_msg int OnMouseActivate(CWnd* pDesktopWnd, UINT nHitTest, UINT message);
    afx_msg void OnMouseMove(UINT nFlags, CPoint point);
    afx_msg void OnNcLButtonDown(UINT nHitTest, CPoint point);
    afx_msg void OnNcRButtonDown(UINT nHitTest, CPoint point);
    afx_msg void OnPaint();
    afx_msg void OnRButtonDown(UINT nFlags, CPoint point);
    afx_msg BOOL OnSetCursor(CWnd* pWnd, UINT nHitTest, UINT message);
    afx_msg void OnSetFocus(CWnd* pOldWnd);
    afx_msg void OnSize(UINT nType, int cx, int cy);
    afx_msg void OnTimer(UINT nIDEvent);
    afx_msg void OnVScroll(UINT nSBCode, UINT nPos, CScrollBar* pScrollBar);
    afx_msg void OnWinIniChange(LPCTSTR lpszSection);
    //}}AFX_MSG
    DECLARE_MESSAGE_MAP()
};
```

```
///////////////////////////////////////////////////////////////////////

// [GETTEXT] Flags (for d_nFocusMode) indicate WM_SETFOCUS action required.
const int FOCUS_EMPTY  = 0;  // No file currently open (hide caret).
const int FOCUS_CARET  = 1;  // Caret visible (no selection).
const int FOCUS_SELECT = 2;  // Selection visible (hide caret).
```

Listing 14-6
MAINFRM.CPP

```cpp
// mainfrm.cpp : implementation of the DMainFrame class
//

#include "stdafx.h"
#include "gettext.h"

#include "mainfrm.h"

#ifdef _DEBUG
#undef THIS_FILE
static char BASED_CODE THIS_FILE[] = __FILE__;
#endif

///////////////////////////////////////////////////////////////////////
// DMainFrame

IMPLEMENT_DYNCREATE(DMainFrame, CFrameWnd)

BEGIN_MESSAGE_MAP(DMainFrame, CFrameWnd)
    //{{AFX_MSG_MAP(DMainFrame)
    ON_COMMAND(ID_FILE_OPEN, CmdFileOpen)
    ON_COMMAND(ID_FORMAT_FONT, CmdFormatFont)
    ON_COMMAND(ID_FORMAT_TABS, CmdFormatTabs)
    ON_UPDATE_COMMAND_UI(ID_FORMAT_TABS, UpdFormatTabs)
    ON_WM_CREATE()
    ON_WM_ERASEBKGND()
    ON_WM_KEYDOWN()
    ON_WM_KILLFOCUS()
    ON_WM_LBUTTONDBLCLK()
    ON_WM_LBUTTONDOWN()
    ON_WM_LBUTTONUP()
    ON_WM_MBUTTONDOWN()
    ON_WM_MOUSEACTIVATE()
    ON_WM_MOUSEMOVE()
    ON_WM_NCLBUTTONDOWN()
    ON_WM_NCRBUTTONDOWN()
    ON_WM_PAINT()
    ON_WM_RBUTTONDOWN()
    ON_WM_SETCURSOR()
```

```
    ON_WM_SETFOCUS()
    ON_WM_SIZE()
    ON_WM_TIMER()
    ON_WM_VSCROLL()
    ON_WM_WININICHANGE()
    //}}AFX_MSG_MAP
END_MESSAGE_MAP()

/////////////////////////////////////////////////////////////////////////////
// DMainFrame construction/destruction

DMainFrame::DMainFrame()
{
    // Init all data members to a known value.
    d_pOpenFile    = 0;
    d_lpTextBuffer = 0;
    d_dwFileLength = 0;
    d_pFont        = 0;

    // Init desired font.
    memset (&d_lf, 0, sizeof(LOGFONT));

    // Initial font face name is Courier New.
    lstrcpy (d_lf.lfFaceName, _T("Courier New"));

    // Initial font size is 10 pt.
    CWindowDC dc(NULL);
    int cyPixels = dc.GetDeviceCaps(LOGPIXELSY);
    d_lf.lfHeight = (-1) * MulDiv(10, cyPixels, 72);

    // Initial tab setting is OFF.
    d_bTabs = TRUE;

    // Tab table initially empty (set when font selected).
    d_pnTabs = 0;

    // [GETTEXT] Set to a known value.
    d_cLines       = 0;

    // [GETTEXT] Set initial caret position.
    d_ptCaret = CPoint(0,0);

    // [GETTEXT] NULL pointer for later initialization.
    d_piCharWidth = 0;

    // [GETTEXT] Width of a tab stop.
    d_cxTabStop = 0;

    // [GETTEXT] Initialize WM_SETFOCUS action.
    d_nFocusMode = FOCUS_EMPTY;

    // [GETTEXT] Set mouse activation to 'OFF'.
    d_bMouseActive = FALSE;
```

```
        // [GETTEXT] Initialize selected line counters.
        d_nSelectFirst = -1;
        d_nSelectLast  = -1;

        // [GETTEXT] Timer flag.
        d_bTimerStarted = FALSE;
        d_nTimerID = 0;
}


DMainFrame::~DMainFrame()
{
        if (d_pFont) delete d_pFont;
        if (d_pnTabs) delete [] d_pnTabs;
        if (d_piCharWidth) delete [] d_piCharWidth;
        if (d_pOpenFile) delete d_pOpenFile;
        if (d_pSetFont) delete d_pSetFont;
}


/////////////////////////////////////////////////////////////////////////////
//
// DMainFrame helper functions.

//-----------------------------------------
// BuildStringArray - Parses text file to create a CString array.
void DMainFrame::BuildStringArray()
{
        // Scan buffer to calculate line count.
        LPTSTR lpNext = d_lpTextBuffer;
        LPTSTR lpEnd  = d_lpTextBuffer + d_dwFileLength - 1;
        *lpEnd = '\n';
        for (d_cLines = 0; lpNext < lpEnd; d_cLines++, lpNext++)
        {
                // Search for next <CR> character.
                lpNext = strchr(lpNext, '\n');

                // Discontinue if NULL encountered.
                if (lpNext == NULL) break;
        }

        // Set array size.
        d_saTextInfo.SetSize(d_cLines);

        // Scan buffer to build array of pointers & sizes.
        STRING string;
        lpNext = d_lpTextBuffer;
        for (int iLine = 0; iLine < d_cLines; iLine++)
        {
                // Char count for current line.
                string.ccLen = 0;
                string.pText = lpNext;

                // Loop to end-of-line.
                while ((*lpNext != '\n') && (*lpNext != '\r'))
                {
```

```
            lpNext++;             // Check next char.
            string.ccLen++;      // Increment length counter.
        }

        // Enter value in array.
        d_saTextInfo[iLine] = string;

        // Skip over <CR> <LF>
        lpNext += (2 * sizeof(char));
    }
}


//-----------------------------------------
// CreateNewFont - Creates new CFont for use in drawing text.
BOOL DMainFrame::CreateNewFont()
{
    // Delete any previous font.
    if (d_pFont)
        delete d_pFont;

    // Create a new font
    d_pFont = new CFont();
    if (!d_pFont) return FALSE;
    d_pFont->CreateFontIndirect(&d_lf);

    // Calculate font height
    CClientDC dc(this);
    TEXTMETRIC tm;
    dc.SelectObject(d_pFont);
    dc.GetTextMetrics(&tm);
    d_cyLineHeight = tm.tmHeight + tm.tmExternalLeading;

    // Calculate left margin.
    d_cxLeftMargin = tm.tmAveCharWidth * 3;

    // [GETTEXT] Calculate width of tab stop.
    d_cxTabStop = g_nTabStop * tm.tmAveCharWidth;

    // Rebuild tab setting table.
    if (d_pnTabs) delete [] d_pnTabs;
    d_pnTabs = new INT[g_nTabCount];
    for (int i=0; i<g_nTabCount; i++)
    {
        d_pnTabs[i] = d_cxLeftMargin + (i * d_cxTabStop);
    }

    // [GETTEXT] For new font, reset caret to upper left window corner.
    d_ptCaret = CPoint(d_cxLeftMargin,0);

    // [GETTEXT] If we have focus, recreate and move caret.
    if (GetFocus() == this)
    {
        HideCaret();
        DestroyCaret();
```

```
            CreateSolidCaret(0, d_cyLineHeight);
            SetCaretPos(d_ptCaret);
            ShowCaret();
        }

        // [GETTEXT] Rebuild character width table for newly selected font.
        if (d_piCharWidth) delete [] d_piCharWidth;

        // [GETTEXT] Calculate size of new width table and allocate.
        int nCharCount = tm.tmLastChar - tm.tmFirstChar + 1;
        d_piCharWidth = new INT[nCharCount];

        // [GETTEXT] Query GDI for character width data.
        dc.GetCharWidth(tm.tmFirstChar, tm.tmLastChar, d_piCharWidth);

        // [GETTEXT] Record 1st char to use in using char width table
        d_bchFirstChar = tm.tmFirstChar;

        // [GETTEXT] Store average character width for tab stop handling.
        d_cxAveCharWidth = tm.tmAveCharWidth;

        return TRUE;
}


//----------------------------------------
// [GETTEXT] Helper function to open a file.
void DMainFrame::OpenTextFile(CString strFile)
{
        // Display hourglass cursor.
        BeginWaitCursor();

        // Open file in read-only mode.
        CFile cfData;
        if (!cfData.Open(strFile, CFile::modeRead))
        {
            AfxMessageBox(_T("Error Opening File"));
            return;
        }

        // Free previous buffer contents
        if (d_lpTextBuffer)
        {
            free(d_lpTextBuffer);
            d_lpTextBuffer=0;
        }

        // Calculate file size & allocate buffer.
        // Pad to avoid bad address reference.
        d_dwFileLength = cfData.GetLength() + sizeof(char);
        d_lpTextBuffer = (LPTSTR)malloc (d_dwFileLength);
        if (!d_lpTextBuffer)
        {
```

```
        AfxMessageBox(_T("Cannot Allocate Memory For File"));
        return;
    }

    // Read Buffer.
    cfData.Read((LPVOID)d_lpTextBuffer, d_dwFileLength);

    // Empty buffer array.
    d_saTextInfo.RemoveAll();

    // Scan buffer for text line info.
    BuildStringArray();

    // "Index to top line displayed" = top of file.
    d_iTopLine = 0;

    // Recalculate scroll bar info.
    ResetScrollValues();

    // [GETTEXT] Set focus mode to "use caret".
    if (d_nFocusMode == FOCUS_EMPTY)
    {
        d_nFocusMode = FOCUS_CARET;
        OnSetFocus(this);
    }

    // [GETTEXT] Move Caret to beginning of text file.
    MoveCaret(0,0);

    // [GETTEXT] Set selection state 'off'.
    d_nSelectFirst = -1;
    d_nSelectLast  = -1;

    // [GETTEXT] Modify frame window title.
    UpdateFrameTitleForDocument(strFile);

    // Request a WM_PAINT message to redraw window.
    Invalidate();

    // Restore normal cursor.
    EndWaitCursor();
}

//----------------------------------------
// ResetScrollValues - Adjust scrolling for window size changes.
void DMainFrame::ResetScrollValues()
{
    // Set count of lines in window height.
    d_clHeight = d_cyClient / d_cyLineHeight;

    // Hide scroll bars when not needed.
    if (d_cLines <= d_clHeight)
    {
```

```
                SetScrollRange(SB_VERT, 0, 0, TRUE);
                d_iTopLine = 0;
                return;
            }
        else
            {
                // Adjust scroll range for new window size.
                SetScrollRange (SB_VERT, 0, d_cLines - d_clHeight, TRUE);

                // Adjust scroll thumb position.
                SetScrollPos(SB_VERT, d_iTopLine, TRUE);
            }
    }


//////////////////////////////////////////////////////////////////////////
// DMainFrame diagnostics

#ifdef _DEBUG
void DMainFrame::AssertValid() const
{
    CFrameWnd::AssertValid();
}

void DMainFrame::Dump(CDumpContext& dc) const
{
    CFrameWnd::Dump(dc);
}

#endif //_DEBUG

//////////////////////////////////////////////////////////////////////////
// DMainFrame message handlers

//-----------------------------------------
// Handler for File|Open command message.
void DMainFrame::CmdFileOpen()
{
    // [GETTEXT] Hide all focus related settings.
    OnKillFocus(this);

    // Display File.Open... dialog box.
    int iRet = d_pOpenFile->DoModal();

    // Ignore when user clicks [Cancel] button.
    if (iRet != IDOK)
        return;

    // Fetch fully-qualified file name.
    CString strFile = d_pOpenFile->GetPathName();

    // [GETTEXT] Open and parse text file.
    OpenTextFile(strFile);
```

```
    // [GETTEXT] Set focus mode to "use caret".
    d_nFocusMode = FOCUS_CARET;
    OnSetFocus(this);
}

//-----------------------------------------
// Handler for Format|Font command message.
void DMainFrame::CmdFormatFont()
{
    // Display font picker dialog box.
    int iRet = d_pSetFont->DoModal();

    // Ignore when user clicks [Cancel] button.
    if (iRet != IDOK)
        return;

    // Rebuild font definition based on dialog selection.
    CreateNewFont();

    // Recalculate scroll bar info.
    ResetScrollValues();

    // Request a WM_PAINT message to redraw window.
    Invalidate();
}

//-----------------------------------------
// Handler for Format|Tabs command message.
void DMainFrame::CmdFormatTabs()
{
    // Toggle "respect tab" flag.
    d_bTabs = !d_bTabs;

    // Request a WM_PAINT message to redraw window.
    Invalidate();
}

//-----------------------------------------
// Handler for CN_UPDATE_COMMAND_UI message.
void DMainFrame::UpdFormatTabs(CCmdUI* pCmdUI)
{
    // Display a checkmark if user wants to respect tabs.
    int nCheck = (d_bTabs) ? 1 : 0;
    pCmdUI->SetCheck(nCheck);
}

//-----------------------------------------
// WM_CREATE message handler.
int DMainFrame::OnCreate(LPCREATESTRUCT lpCreateStruct)
{
    // Send WM_CREATE to base class first...
    if (CFrameWnd::OnCreate(lpCreateStruct) == -1)
        return -1;
```

```
        // Create File.Open... dialog object.
        d_pOpenFile = new CFileDialog (TRUE);
        if (!d_pOpenFile)
            return -1;

        // Initialize file filter.
        d_pOpenFile->m_ofn.lpstrFilter = _T("All Source Files\0*.cpp;*.h;*.rc\0"
                                            "C++ Sources (*.cpp)\0*.cpp\0"
                                            "Include Files (*.h)\0*.h\0"
                                            "All Files (*.*)\0*.*\0");

        // Create Format.Font... dialog object.
        d_pSetFont = new CFontDialog(&d_lf, CF_SCREENFONTS);
        if (!d_pSetFont)
            return -1;

        // Create initial font object.
        if (!CreateNewFont())
            return -1;

        // Initialize application settings.
        OnWinIniChange(_T(""));

        // [GETTEXT] Load cursors
        d_hcrIBeam  = ::LoadCursor(NULL, IDC_IBEAM);
        d_hcrLArrow = ::LoadCursor(NULL, IDC_ARROW);
        d_hcrRArrow = AfxGetApp()->LoadCursor(IDC_RARROW);
        if (d_hcrIBeam == NULL || d_hcrRArrow == NULL)
            return -1;

        // Indicate window creation is OK.
        return 0;
    }


//----------------------------------------
// [GETTEXT] Handler for WM_ERASEBKGND message.
BOOL DMainFrame::OnEraseBkgnd(CDC* pDC)
{
    // Select text background color.
    pDC->SetBkColor(d_crBackground);

    // Figure out which lines of text need blanking out.
    int iLine = d_iTopLine;
    int cLastLine = d_iTopLine + d_clHeight + 1;

    // Modify text colors based on selection state.
    int iSelectMin = -1;
    int iSelectMax = -1;
    if (d_nFocusMode == FOCUS_SELECT && GetFocus() == this)
    {
        // Get order of selected lines straight .
        int nSelectLow  = min (d_nSelectFirst, d_nSelectLast);
        int nSelectHigh = max (d_nSelectFirst, d_nSelectLast);
```

```
        if (!(nSelectLow > cLastLine || nSelectHigh < d_iTopLine))
        {
            // Figure out which lines to draw selected.
            iSelectMin = max (nSelectLow, d_iTopLine);
            iSelectMax = min (nSelectHigh, cLastLine);
        }
    }

    // Initialize first rectangle to erase.
    CRect rClient;
    GetClientRect(&rClient);
    int yClientBottom = rClient.bottom;
    rClient.bottom = rClient.top + d_cyLineHeight;

    // Loop through lines in client area.
    int cyLine = 0;
    while (rClient.top <= yClientBottom)
    {
        // Set background to "selected" colors.
        if (iLine == iSelectMin)
        {
            pDC->SetBkColor(d_crSelectBack);
        }

        // Erase background (uses 'background' color in DC)
        pDC->ExtTextOut(0, 0, ETO_OPAQUE, &rClient, 0, 0, 0);

        // Set background to "normal" colors.
        if (iLine == iSelectMax)
        {
            pDC->SetBkColor(d_crBackground);
        }

        // Increment various counts.
        iLine++;
        rClient.top    += d_cyLineHeight;
        rClient.bottom += d_cyLineHeight;
    }

    // Don't call the default handler, since it
    // erases the wrong (white always) color.
    // ++++ NO: return CFrameWnd::OnEraseBkgnd(pDC);

    return TRUE;
}

//------------------------------------------
// [GETTEXT] WM_KEYDOWN message handler.
void DMainFrame::OnKeyDown(UINT nChar, UINT nRepCnt, UINT nFlags)
{
    switch(nChar)
    {
        case VK_HOME:
```

```
                // Ctrl+Home means go to start of document.
                if (::GetKeyState(VK_CONTROL) < 0)
                {
                    // Scroll to start of document
                    OnVScroll(SB_TOP, 0, 0);
                    MoveCaret(0,0);
                }
                else
                {
                    // Move to start of current line.
                    int iLine = QueryClickLine(d_ptCaret);
                    MoveCaret(iLine, 0);
                }
                break;
            case VK_END:
                // Ctrl+End means go to end of document.
                if (::GetKeyState(VK_CONTROL) < 0)
                {
                    // Scroll to end
                    OnVScroll(SB_BOTTOM, 0, 0);
                    MoveCaret(d_cLines-1,0);
                }
                else
                {
                    // Move to end of current line.
                    int iLine = QueryClickLine(d_ptCaret);
                    int iChar = d_saTextInfo[iLine].ccLen;
                    MoveCaret(iLine, iChar);
                }
                break;
            case VK_UP:
                {
                    CPoint ptCaret;
                    ptCaret = GetCaretPos();
                    ptCaret.y -= d_cyLineHeight;
                    MoveCaretClick(ptCaret);
                }
                break;
            case VK_DOWN:
                {
                    CPoint ptCaret;
                    ptCaret = GetCaretPos();
                    ptCaret.y += d_cyLineHeight;
                    MoveCaretClick(ptCaret);
                }
                break;
            case VK_LEFT:
                MoveCaretChar(-1);
                break;
            case VK_RIGHT:
                MoveCaretChar(+1);
                break;
            case VK_PRIOR: // [PgUp] key.
                {
```

```
                    CPoint ptCaret;
                    ptCaret = GetCaretPos();
                    HideCaret();
                    OnVScroll(SB_PAGEUP, 0, 0);
                    ShowCaret();
                    SetCaretPos(ptCaret);
                }
                break;
        case VK_NEXT:   // [PgDn] key.
                {
                    CPoint ptCaret;
                    ptCaret = GetCaretPos();
                    HideCaret();
                    OnVScroll(SB_PAGEDOWN, 0, 0);
                    ShowCaret();
                    SetCaretPos(ptCaret);
                }
                break;
    }

    CFrameWnd::OnKeyDown(nChar, nRepCnt, nFlags);
}


//-----------------------------------------
// [GETTEXT] WM_KILLFOCUS message handler.
void DMainFrame::OnKillFocus(CWnd* pNewWnd)
{
    CFrameWnd::OnKillFocus(pNewWnd);

    switch(d_nFocusMode)
    {
        case FOCUS_EMPTY:
            break;
        case FOCUS_CARET:
            // Query and save current caret position.
            d_ptCaret = GetCaretPos();

            // Eliminate caret.
            HideCaret();
            DestroyCaret();
            break;
        case FOCUS_SELECT:
            InvertLines(d_nSelectFirst, d_nSelectLast);
            break;
    }
}


//-----------------------------------------
// [GETTEXT] WM_LBUTTONDBLCLK message handler.
void DMainFrame::OnLButtonDblClk(UINT nFlags, CPoint point)
{
    // Our pet peeve - Ignoring a second keystroke that looked
    // like a double-button click.
```

```
    // Our solution - Handling the double-click message and
    // calling the single-click handler.
    OnLButtonDown(nFlags, point);
}


//-----------------------------------------
// [GETTEXT] WM_LBUTTONDOWN message handler.
void DMainFrame::OnLButtonDown(UINT nFlags, CPoint point)
{
    // If we're activating with button click,
    // activate window and ignore mouse message.
    if (d_bMouseActive)
    {
        SetActiveWindow();
        d_bMouseActive = FALSE;
        return;
    }

    // Hide results of previous focus mode.
    switch (d_nFocusMode)
    {
        case FOCUS_CARET:
            HideCaret();
            break;
        case FOCUS_SELECT:
            InvertLines(d_nSelectFirst, d_nSelectLast);
            d_nSelectFirst = -1;
            d_nSelectLast  = -1;
            break;
    }

    // Set focus mode based on mouse location.
    d_nFocusMode = (point.x < d_cxLeftMargin) ? FOCUS_SELECT : FOCUS_CARET;

    // Make results of new focus mode known to user.
    switch(d_nFocusMode)
    {
        case FOCUS_EMPTY:
            break;
        case FOCUS_CARET:
            {
                int nLine = QueryClickLine(point);
                int nChar = QueryClickChar(nLine, point);
                MoveCaret(nLine, nChar);
                ShowCaret();
            }
            break;
        case FOCUS_SELECT:
            {
                // Figure out where mouse was clicked.
                d_nSelectFirst = QueryClickLine(point);
                d_nSelectLast  = d_nSelectFirst;
```

```
                        // Highlight that line.
                        InvertLines(d_nSelectFirst, d_nSelectLast);

                        // Capture the mouse.
                        SetCapture();
                        d_bCapture = TRUE;
                    }
                    break;
        }

    CFrameWnd::OnLButtonDown(nFlags, point);
}

//-----------------------------------------
// [GETTEXT] Handler for WM_LBUTTONUP message.
void DMainFrame::OnLButtonUp(UINT nFlags, CPoint point)
{
    // Release the mouse (captured during WM_LBUTTONDOWN)
    if (d_bCapture)
    {
        ReleaseCapture();
        d_bCapture = FALSE;
    }

    // Kill the timer (started during WM_MOUSEMOVE)
    if (d_bTimerStarted)
    {
        KillTimer(d_nTimerID);
        d_bTimerStarted = FALSE;
    }

    CFrameWnd::OnLButtonUp(nFlags, point);
}

//-----------------------------------------
// [GETTEXT] Handler for WM_MBUTTONDOWN message.
void DMainFrame::OnMButtonDown(UINT nFlags, CPoint point)
{
    // If we're activating with button click,
    // activate window and ignore mouse message.
    if (d_bMouseActive)
    {
        SetActiveWindow();
        d_bMouseActive = FALSE;
        return;
    }
}

//-----------------------------------------
// [GETTEXT] WM_MOUSEACTIVATE message handler.
int DMainFrame::OnMouseActivate(CWnd* pDesktopWnd, UINT nHitTest, UINT message)
{
```

```
        d_bMouseActive = TRUE;

        return MA_NOACTIVATE;
}


//-----------------------------------------
// [GETTEXT] Handler for WM_MOUSEMOVE message.
void DMainFrame::OnMouseMove(UINT nFlags, CPoint point)
{
        // Pay attention to mouse moves only in select mode.
        if ((!d_bCapture) || (d_nFocusMode != FOCUS_SELECT))
        {
            CFrameWnd::OnMouseMove(nFlags, point);
            return;
        }

        // Fetch current line selected.
        CRect rClient;
        GetClientRect(&rClient);
        point.x = 1;
        if (!rClient.PtInRect(point))
        {
            // Scroll if above or below client area.
            if (point.y < rClient.bottom)
            {
                OnVScroll(SB_LINEUP, 0, 0);
                point.y = rClient.top;
            }
            else
            {
                OnVScroll(SB_LINEDOWN, 0, 0);
                point.y = rClient.bottom - 1;
            }

            // Also, start timer to speed up scrolling.
            if (!d_bTimerStarted)
            {
                d_bTimerStarted = TRUE;
                d_nTimerID = SetTimer(1, 50, 0);
            }
        }

        // Get current line.
        int iNextLine = QueryClickLine(point);

        // Ignore if we've already selected.
        if (iNextLine == d_nSelectLast)
            return;

        // Figure direction from First => Last line.
        int nFirstLast = (d_nSelectFirst > d_nSelectLast) ? -1 : +1;
        if (d_nSelectFirst == d_nSelectLast) nFirstLast =   0;
```

```
    // Figure direction from First => Next line.
    int nFirstNext = (d_nSelectFirst > iNextLine) ? -1 : +1;
    if (d_nSelectFirst == iNextLine) nFirstNext = 0;

    // Figure direction from Last => Next line.
    int nLastNext = (d_nSelectLast > iNextLine) ? -1 : +1;

    // First case: extending the current selection.
    if ((nFirstLast == 0)
        || ((nFirstLast == nFirstNext) && (nFirstNext == nLastNext)))
    {
        InvertLines(d_nSelectLast+nLastNext, iNextLine);
    }

    // Second case: backtracking (erasing) previous lines.
    else if ((nFirstNext == 0)
            || (nFirstLast == nFirstNext) && (nFirstLast != nLastNext))
    {
        InvertLines(d_nSelectLast, iNextLine+nFirstLast);
    }

    // Third case: crossing over anchor (first) line: backtrack AND extend.
    else if ((nFirstNext == nLastNext) && (nFirstNext != nFirstLast))
    {
        // Erase to backtrack.
        InvertLines(d_nSelectLast, d_nSelectFirst+nFirstLast);

        // Extend in new direction.
        InvertLines(d_nSelectFirst+nFirstNext, iNextLine);
    }

    // Update last selection to current line.
    d_nSelectLast = iNextLine;
}


//-----------------------------------------
// WM_NCLBUTTONDOWN message handler.
void DMainFrame::OnNcLButtonDown(UINT nHitTest, CPoint point)
{
    // If we're activating with button click,
    // activate window and ignore mouse message.
    OnMButtonDown(nHitTest, point);

    CFrameWnd::OnNcLButtonDown(nHitTest, point);
}


//-----------------------------------------
// [GETTEXT] Handler for WM_NCRBUTTONDOWN message.
void DMainFrame::OnNcRButtonDown(UINT nHitTest, CPoint point)
{
    // If we're activating with button click,
    // activate window and ignore mouse message.
    OnMButtonDown(nHitTest, point);
}
```

```
//----------------------------------------
// WM_PAINT message handler.
void DMainFrame::OnPaint()
{
    // Fetch a device context (dc) for "this" window.
    CPaintDC dc(this);

    // Select current font into DC.
    dc.SelectObject(d_pFont);

    // [GETTEXT] - Only draw foreground text pixels.
    dc.SetBkMode(TRANSPARENT);

    // Select text color.
    dc.SetTextColor(d_crForeground );

    // Figure out which lines to draw.
    int iLine = d_iTopLine;
    int cLastLine = d_iTopLine + d_clHeight + 1;
    cLastLine = min (cLastLine, d_cLines);

    // [GETTEXT] Modify text colors based on selection state.
    int iSelectMin = -1;
    int iSelectMax = -1;
    if (d_nFocusMode == FOCUS_SELECT && GetFocus() == this)
    {
        // Get order of selected lines straight .
        int nSelectLow  = min (d_nSelectFirst, d_nSelectLast);
        int nSelectHigh = max (d_nSelectFirst, d_nSelectLast);

        if (!(nSelectLow > cLastLine || nSelectHigh < d_iTopLine))
        {
            // Figure out which lines to draw selected.
            iSelectMin = max (nSelectLow, d_iTopLine);
            iSelectMax = min (nSelectHigh, cLastLine);
        }
    }

    // Loop through client area coordinates to draw.
    int cyLine = 0;
    while (iLine < cLastLine)
    {
        // Draw a line of text.
        LPTSTR lp = d_saTextInfo[iLine].pText;
        int    cc = d_saTextInfo[iLine].ccLen;

        //   [GETTEXT] Set to "selected" colors.
        if (iLine == iSelectMin)
        {
            // Select text color.
            dc.SetTextColor(d_crSelectFore );
        }
```

```
        // Drawing function depends on 'respect tabs' setting.
        if (d_bTabs && d_pnTabs != 0)
        {
            dc.TabbedTextOut(d_cxLeftMargin, cyLine, lp, cc,
                             g_nTabCount, d_pnTabs, 0);
        }
        else
        {
            dc.TextOut(d_cxLeftMargin, cyLine, lp, cc);
        }

        // [GETTEXT] Set to "normal" colors.
        if (iLine == iSelectMax)
        {
            // Select text color.
            dc.SetTextColor(d_crForeground );
        }

        // Increment various counts.
        cyLine += d_cyLineHeight;
        iLine++;
    }
}


//-----------------------------------------
// [GETTEXT] Handler for WM_RBUTTONDOWN message.
void DMainFrame::OnRButtonDown(UINT nFlags, CPoint point)
{
    // If we're activating with button click,
    // activate window and ignore mouse message.
    OnMButtonDown(nFlags, point);
}


//-----------------------------------------
// [GETTEXT] WM_SETCURSOR message handler.
BOOL DMainFrame::OnSetCursor(CWnd* pWnd, UINT nHitTest, UINT message)
{
    if (nHitTest != HTCLIENT)
    {
        return CFrameWnd::OnSetCursor(pWnd, nHitTest, message);
    }

    // Query cursor location and convert to client area coordinates.
    CPoint ptCursor;
    ::GetCursorPos(&ptCursor);
    ScreenToClient(&ptCursor);

    // Calculate rectangle around selected lines of text.
    CRect rSelected;
    GetSelectedRect(&rSelected);

    // Cursor => Right Arrow if cursor in right margin.
    // Cursor => Left Arrow if cursor over selected text.
```

```
        // Cursor => I-Beam for text selection.
        if (ptCursor.x <= d_cxLeftMargin)        ::SetCursor(d_hcrRArrow);
        else if (rSelected.PtInRect(ptCursor))  ::SetCursor(d_hcrLArrow);
        else                                     ::SetCursor(d_hcrIBeam);

        return TRUE;
}


//----------------------------------------
// [GETTEXT] WM_SETFOCUS message handler.
void DMainFrame::OnSetFocus(CWnd* pOldWnd)
{
    CFrameWnd::OnSetFocus(pOldWnd);

    switch(d_nFocusMode)
    {
        case FOCUS_EMPTY:
            break;
        case FOCUS_CARET:
            // Create, position, and make caret appear.
            CreateSolidCaret(0, d_cyLineHeight);
            SetCaretPos(d_ptCaret);
            ShowCaret();
        case FOCUS_SELECT:
            InvertLines(d_nSelectFirst, d_nSelectLast);
            break;
    }
}


//----------------------------------------
// WM_SIZE message handler.
void DMainFrame::OnSize(UINT nType, int cx, int cy)
{
    // Notify base class of new window size.
    CFrameWnd ::OnSize(nType, cx, cy);

    // Save client area height.
    d_cyClient = cy;

    // Recalculate scroll bar info.
    ResetScrollValues();
}


//----------------------------------------
// [GETTEXT] Handler for WM_TIMER message.
void DMainFrame::OnTimer(UINT nIDEvent)
{
    // Query cursor location and convert to client area coordinates.
    CPoint ptCursor;
    ::GetCursorPos(&ptCursor);
    ScreenToClient(&ptCursor);
```

```
    // Query client area.
    CRect rClient;
    GetClientRect (&rClient);

    // Compare cursor location to client area.
    if (rClient.PtInRect(ptCursor))
    {
        // Kill timer and go home.
        KillTimer(d_nTimerID);
        d_bTimerStarted = FALSE;
    }
    else
    {
        // Send fake mouse move messages to force scrolling.
        OnMouseMove(0, ptCursor);
    }


    CFrameWnd::OnTimer(nIDEvent);
}


//-----------------------------------------
// WM_VSCROLL message handler.
void DMainFrame::OnVScroll(UINT nSBCode, UINT nPos, CScrollBar* pScrollBar)
{
    // [GETTEXT] Ignore if scroll bars not present. No scrolling possible.
    int nMinPos, nMaxPos;
    GetScrollRange(0, &nMinPos, &nMaxPos);
    if (nMinPos == nMaxPos)
        return;

    // Temporary "new line" value.
    int iTop = d_iTopLine;

    // Based on particular scroll button clicked, modify top line index.
    switch(nSBCode)
    {
        case SB_BOTTOM:
            iTop = d_cLines - d_clHeight;
            break;
        case SB_ENDSCROLL:
            break;
        case SB_LINEDOWN:
            iTop++;
            break;
        case SB_LINEUP:
            iTop-;
            break;
        case SB_PAGEDOWN:
            iTop += d_clHeight;
            break;
        case SB_PAGEUP:
            iTop -= d_clHeight;
```

```
                break;
            case SB_THUMBPOSITION:
                iTop = nPos;
                break;
            case SB_THUMBTRACK:
                iTop = nPos;
                break;
            case SB_TOP:
                iTop = 0;
                break;
        }

        // Check range of new index;
        iTop = max (iTop, 0);
        iTop = min (iTop, d_cLines - d_clHeight);

        // If no change, ignore.
        if (iTop == d_iTopLine) return;

        // Pixels to scroll = (lines to scroll) * height-per-line.
        int cyScroll = (d_iTopLine - iTop) * d_cyLineHeight;

        // Define new top-line value.
        d_iTopLine = iTop;

        // Scroll pixels.
        ScrollWindow(0, cyScroll);

        // Adjust scroll thumb position.
        SetScrollPos(SB_VERT, d_iTopLine, TRUE);
}


//----------------------------------------
// WM_WININICHANGE message handler.
void DMainFrame::OnWinIniChange(LPCTSTR lpszSection)
{
    CFrameWnd::OnWinIniChange(lpszSection);

    // Get new "normal" background & foreground colors.
    d_crForeground = GetSysColor(COLOR_WINDOWTEXT);
    d_crBackground = GetSysColor(COLOR_WINDOW);

    // [GETTEXT] Get new "selected" colors (in 7 easy steps).

    // 1. Create an offscreen DC (compatible with display screen).
    CDC dcBitmap;
    dcBitmap.CreateCompatibleDC(NULL);

    // 2. Query current device details.
    CClientDC dcScreen(this);
    int nPlanes = dcScreen.GetDeviceCaps(PLANES);
    int nBitCount = dcScreen.GetDeviceCaps(BITSPIXEL);
```

```
    // 3. Create a tiny bitmap and connect to the DC from step #1.
    CBitmap bm;
    bm.CreateBitmap(2, 2, nPlanes, nBitCount, 0);
    CBitmap * pbmOld = dcBitmap.SelectObject(&bm);

    // 4. Set up rectangle for bitmap surface.
    CRect rBitmap = CRect(0, 0, 3, 3);

    // 5. Find foreground color inverse (we're looking for d_crSelectFore).
    dcBitmap.SetBkColor(d_crForeground);
    dcBitmap.ExtTextOut(0, 0, ETO_OPAQUE, &rBitmap, 0, 0, 0);
    dcBitmap.InvertRect(&rBitmap);
    d_crSelectFore = dcBitmap.GetPixel(1,1);

    // 6. Find background color inverse (we're looking for d_crSelectBack).
    dcBitmap.SetBkColor(d_crBackground);
    dcBitmap.ExtTextOut(0, 0, ETO_OPAQUE, &rBitmap, 0, 0, 0);
    dcBitmap.InvertRect(&rBitmap);
    d_crSelectBack = dcBitmap.GetPixel(1,1);

    // 7. Disconnect bitmap from DC to help GDI clean up properly.
    dcBitmap.SelectObject(pbmOld );

    // Force redraw of window.
    Invalidate();
}
```

Listing 14-7
CARET.CPP

```
// caret.cpp : Caret handling helper functions.
//

#include "stdafx.h"
#include "gettext.h"

#include "mainfrm.h"

#ifdef _DEBUG
#undef THIS_FILE
static char BASED_CODE THIS_FILE[] = __FILE__;
#endif

//-----------------------------------------
// [GETTEXT] MoveCaret moves the caret to a particular line and character.
void DMainFrame::MoveCaret(int iLine, int iChar)
{
    // Ignore if we don't have any lines of text
    if (d_cLines == 0)
        return;
```

```
        // Check that line and character indices are in range.
        ASSERT (iLine >= 0 && iLine <= d_cLines);
        ASSERT (iChar >= 0 && iChar <= (d_saTextInfo[iLine].ccLen));

        // Get pointer to text string and count of characters.
        LPTSTR lp = d_saTextInfo[iLine].pText;
        int    cc = d_saTextInfo[iLine].ccLen;

        // Figuring which line is simple math.
        CPoint ptCaret;
        ptCaret.y = (iLine - d_iTopLine) * d_cyLineHeight;

        // Figuring which character requires a loop and some simple math.
        ptCaret.x = d_cxLeftMargin;
        for (int ich = 0; ich < iChar; ich++)
        {
            // If a tab character...
            if (lp[ich] == '\t')
            {
                // Tabs enabled...
                if (d_bTabs)
                {
                    ptCaret.x += d_cxTabStop;
                }
                else // ... Tabs disabled.
                {
                    ptCaret.x += d_cxAveCharWidth;
                }
            }
            else // ...not a tab character.
            {
                ptCaret.x += d_piCharWidth[lp[ich] - d_bchFirstChar];
            }
        }

    SetCaretPos(ptCaret);
    d_ptCaret = ptCaret;
}

//-----------------------------------------
// [GETTEXT] MoveCaretChar moves caret by a relative amount.
void DMainFrame::MoveCaretChar(int nCharCount)
{
    // We're not equipped to handle moves greater than ABS(1).
    ASSERT ((nCharCount == -1) || (nCharCount == 1));

    // Handle empty buffer situation.
    if (d_cLines == 0)
        return;

    // Query caret indices: (line offset, character offset)
    int iLine = QueryClickLine(d_ptCaret);
    int iChar = QueryClickChar(iLine, d_ptCaret);
```

```
    // Query length of current line.
    int ccLine = d_saTextInfo[iLine].ccLen;

    // [LeftArrow] at start of line.
    if ((nCharCount <= 0) && (iChar == 0))
    {
        // Cannot move before first line.
        if (iLine == 0)
        {
            ::MessageBeep(0);
            return;
        }

        iLine -= 1;
        iChar = d_saTextInfo[iLine].ccLen;

        // Scroll if we need to.
        if (iLine < d_iTopLine)
            OnVScroll(SB_LINEUP, 0, 0);
    }

    // [RightArrow] at end of line.
    else if ((nCharCount >= 0) && (iChar == ccLine))
    {
        // Cannot move beyond last line
        if (iLine == (d_cLines-1))
        {
            ::MessageBeep(0);
            return;
        }

        iLine += 1;
        iChar = 0;

        // Scroll if we need to.
        int yCaretBottom = d_ptCaret.y + (d_cyLineHeight * 2);
        CRect rClient;
        GetClientRect(&rClient);
        if (rClient.bottom < yCaretBottom)
            OnVScroll(SB_LINEDOWN, 0, 0);
    }

    // Adjust caret character index.
    else
    {
        iChar += nCharCount;
    }

    MoveCaret(iLine, iChar);
}

//----------------------------------------
// [GETTEXT] MoveCaretClick simulates a mouse click to move the caret.
```

```
void DMainFrame::MoveCaretClick(CPoint ptHit)
{
    CRect rClient;
    GetClientRect(&rClient);

    // Scroll UP if top of caret is above top of client area.
    if (ptHit.y < 0)
    {
        // Prevent scrolling above top line.
        if (d_iTopLine <= 0)
        {
            ::MessageBeep(0);
            return;
        }

        // Scroll requested line into view.
        OnVScroll(SB_LINEUP, 0, 0);

        // Adjust hit point to take scrolling into account.
        ptHit.y += d_cyLineHeight;
    }

    // Scroll DOWN if bottom of caret is below bottom of client area.
    if ((ptHit.y + d_cyLineHeight) > rClient.bottom)
    {
        // Prevent scrolling below last line.
        if (d_iTopLine >= (d_cLines - d_clHeight))
        {
            ::MessageBeep(0);
            return;
        }

        // Scroll requested line into view.
        OnVScroll(SB_LINEDOWN, 0, 0);

        // Adjust hit point to take scrolling into account.
        ptHit.y -= d_cyLineHeight;
    }

    // Give ourselves a mouse click.
    OnLButtonDown(0, ptHit);
}


//----------------------------------------
// [GETTEXT] QueryClickChar fetches index to character where caret goes.
int DMainFrame::QueryClickChar(int iLine, CPoint point)
{
    // Easy special case: left margin click means start of line.
    if (point.x <= d_cxLeftMargin || d_cLines == 0)
        return 0;

    // Get pointer to text string and count of characters.
    LPTSTR lp = d_saTextInfo[iLine].pText;
    int    cc = d_saTextInfo[iLine].ccLen;
```

```
    // Loop until a hit.
    int ich;
    int x = d_cxLeftMargin;
    int xPrev = x;
    for (ich = 0; ich <= cc; ich++)
    {
        // Check for passing the character cell.
        if (x >= point.x)
        {
            // Compare point to middle of previous character cell.
            if ((xPrev + x) / 2 >= point.x)
            {
                ich-;
            }

            // Character to right of caret location.
            return ich;
        }

        // Store previous char cell for 1/2 cell calculation.
        xPrev = x;

        // If a tab character...
        if (lp[ich] == '\t')
        {
            // Tabs enabled?
            int xTabWidth = (d_bTabs) ? d_cxTabStop : d_cxAveCharWidth;
            x += xTabWidth;
        }
        else // ...not a tab character.
        {
            // Avoid reading past end of array.
            if (ich < cc)
            {
                // Increment x-value by last character width.
                x += d_piCharWidth[lp[ich] - d_bchFirstChar];
            }
        }
    }

    // Beyond end of line means caret goes after last character.
    return cc;
}

//----------------------------------------
// [GETTEXT] QueryClickLine converts client area point to line number.
int DMainFrame::QueryClickLine(CPoint point)
{
    // Figure out range of lines to check.
    int iLine = d_iTopLine;
    int cLastLine = d_iTopLine + d_clHeight + 1;
    cLastLine = min (cLastLine, d_cLines);
```

```
    // Initialize hit test rectangle to client area size.
    CRect rTextLine;
    GetClientRect(&rTextLine);
    // Can't deal outside client area.
    ASSERT(rTextLine.PtInRect(point));
    rTextLine.bottom = d_cyLineHeight;

    // Loop through lines in window doing hit testing.
    // NOTE: Since every line is the same height,
    //        we could easily optimize this loop.
    for (int i=iLine; i < cLastLine; i++)
    {
        // Test for a hit.
        if (rTextLine.PtInRect(point))
        {
            return i;
        }

        // If no hit, increment test rectangle and try again.
        rTextLine.top    += d_cyLineHeight;
        rTextLine.bottom += d_cyLineHeight;
    }

    // User clicked below bottom line. Set pick to last line.
    return cLastLine - 1;
}
```

Listing 14-8
SELECT.CPP

```
// select.cpp : Line selection helper functions
//

#include "stdafx.h"
#include "gettext.h"

#include "mainfrm.h"

#ifdef _DEBUG
#undef THIS_FILE
static char BASED_CODE THIS_FILE[] = __FILE__;
#endif

//----------------------------------------
// [GETTEXT] Query rectangle around currently selected lines of text.
void DMainFrame::GetSelectedRect(CRect * prSelected)
{
    // If nothing selected, return an empty rectangle.
    if (d_nFocusMode != FOCUS_SELECT)
    {
        prSelected->SetRectEmpty();
```

```
        return;
    }

    // Order by min/max.
    int nMinSelect = min(d_nSelectFirst, d_nSelectLast);
    int nMaxSelect = max(d_nSelectFirst, d_nSelectLast);

    // Initialize left and right sides of selection rectangle.
    CRect rSelected;
    rSelected.left  = -32000;
    rSelected.right =  32000;

    // Set top line.
    rSelected.top    = (nMinSelect - d_iTopLine)     * d_cyLineHeight;
    rSelected.bottom = (nMaxSelect - d_iTopLine + 1) * d_cyLineHeight;

    // Query client area.
    CRect rClient;
    GetClientRect(&rClient);

    // Get intersection of client area with selected rectangle.
    prSelected->IntersectRect(&rSelected, &rClient);
}

//-----------------------------------------
// [GETTEXT] Invert set of lines using brute force CDC::InvertRect() func-
tion.
void DMainFrame::InvertLines(int nFirst, int nLast)
{
    // Get order straight.
    int nLow  = min (nFirst, nLast);
    int nHigh = max (nFirst, nLast);

    // Initialize first rectangle to invert.
    CRect rClient;
    GetClientRect(&rClient);
    rClient.top = (nLow - d_iTopLine) * d_cyLineHeight;
    rClient.bottom = rClient.top + d_cyLineHeight;

    // Fetch DC with client area clipping.
    CClientDC dc(this);

    // Loop from first to last, inverting as we go.
    while (nLow <= nHigh)
    {
        // Invert rectangle.
        dc.InvertRect(&rClient);

        // Update all relevant indexes and coordinates.
        nLow++;
        rClient.top    += d_cyLineHeight;
        rClient.bottom += d_cyLineHeight;
    }
}
```

GETTEXT demonstrates two focus-related input techniques: managing a caret and managing selection state. In this chapter, we've covered the basics of handling carets and showing selection. But to see how involved input state can really get, you have to look at a program such as GETTEXT. Using a simple metric — lines of code — FILELIST has about 500 lines of code for reading and displaying a text file. GETTEXT triples that amount with around 1,500 lines for caret and selection management code (in MAINFRM.CPP, CARET.CPP, and SELECT.CPP). And GETTEXT's selection code is relatively simple because it handles only lines of text and not parts of lines.

We point this out, not to scare you off, but to give you an idea of the effort involved with low-level mouse and keyboard input. In anticipation of the day when you have to tell your manager how long it will take to implement the mouse and keyboard portion of an input window, keep in mind the myriad tiny issues that GETTEXT demonstrates.

In any MFC program, message maps serve as a table of contents that details how various windows behave. Table 14-6 summarizes the different messages that are handled by GETTEXT's frame window.

Table 14-6

Message Handling in GETTEXT's Frame Window

Message	Description
CmdFileOpen	Handles the File|Open command to display the File Open dialog, open a file, and read in its contents.
CmdFormatFont	Handles the Format|Font command to display the Font Picker dialog.
CmdFormatTabs	Handles the Format|Tabbed Text menu item, which toggles expanding of tabs.
UpdFormatTabs	Controls the check mark on the Format|Tabbed Text menu item.
WM_CREATE	Performs all CFrameWnd initialization that might possibly fail. All other initialization goes in CFrameWnd's constructor.
WM_ERASEBKGND	Erases the window background in support of text selection. From within SPY++, it seems as though this message always comes after the WM_PAINT message. Actually, the CPaintDC constructor calls ::BeginPaint(), a Windows API function that sends this message.
WM_KEYDOWN	Handles scrolling and caret movement.
WM_KILLFOCUS	Stores application state and hides the caret or selection state.

Message	Description
WM_LBUTTONDBLCLK	One author's pet peeve. This message is sent to a window when two mouse clicks occur in close succession. The effect is that a window seems to ignore user input. That's not polite, especially when it's a simple matter to call the WM_LBUTTONDOWN handler.
WM_LBUTTONDOWN	Resets the caret/selection handling code. First, it hides whatever we had. Then, based on the mouse location, it moves the caret or selects a line of text.
WM_LBUTTONUP	Releases the mouse capture, which was obtained in WM_LBUTTONDOWN when selecting text. Also kills the timer that's started in response to WM_MOUSEMOVE when selecting text and the mouse is outside of the client area.
WM_MBUTTONDOWN	Activate the window, because we decline activation when we get the WM_MOUSEACTIVATE message.
WM_MOUSEACTIVATE	This message says the user has clicked in our window when it's not active. We decline activation, but ask for the mouse message. We also set a flag so that we can ignore the very next mouse message that we receive.
WM_MOUSEMOVE	This message is solely for selecting new lines of text. See the discussion later in this chapter about what selection involves.
WM_NCLBUTTONDOWN	See the discussion of the WM_MBUTTONDOWN message.
WM_NCRBUTTONDOWN	See the discussion of the WM_MBUTTONDOWN message.
WM_PAINT	Draws lines of text. In the FILELIST implementation, background erasure was handled by Windows' default. GETTEXT only draws foreground pixels for text (which is why the background mode is set to TRANSPARENT). The background pixels are handled during WM_ERASEBKGND message.
WM_RBUTTONDOWN	See the discussion of the WM_MBUTTONDOWN message.
WM_SETCURSOR	Sets the mouse cursor based on the location of the mouse.
WM_SETFOCUS	Based on GETTEXT's current focus state, either does nothing, creates a caret, or inverts selected lines of text. All of this is undone when the focus is lost (see the discussion of the WM_KILLFOCUS message).
WM_SIZE	Updates the scroll bar, possibly showing or hiding the scroll bar.
WM_TIMER	Handles the timer message that's received in support of scrolling selections. This occurs during a selection when the user moves outside (above or below) the client area.
WM_VSCROLL	Scrolls the window contents. Because this is also called by the caret and selection code, a check is made to verify that scroll bars are present before scrolling.
WM_WININICHANGE	Lets a program know that the user has changed a system setting from the Control Panel. The two settings that interest GETTEXT are the foreground text color and the background window color. GETTEXT also synthesizes its own selection colors (foreground and background) so that its background colors match those produced by CDC::InvertRect().

Although some people say that code should speak for itself, we are going to speak for the code we've created in GETTEXT. In particular, we want to help you make use of the techniques that GETTEXT demonstrates. Toward that end, we're going to touch on some of the reasons why we made choices that we did. We'll start with a look at setting the mouse cursor. Then, we'll discuss managing the cursor. Finally, we'll examine the issues related to selecting multiple objects — which, in this context, means lines of text.

SETTING THE CLIENT AREA MOUSE CURSOR

One of the most obvious ways to give the user feedback is with the shape of the mouse cursor. GETTEXT uses four cursors: the hourglass "wait" cursor while a file is being opened and parsed, a text I-beam cursor for normal text selection, the normal way and a reverse arrow for selecting lines of text.

Of the three cursors, the hourglass cursor is the easiest to display because MFC provides two helper functions. One function, BeginWait-Cursor( ), displays the hourglass cursor. The other function, EndWait-Cursor( ), returns the cursor to its normal shape. Both functions are called during the long time it takes to read and parse a file — which GETTEXT handles in DMainFrame::OpenTextFile( ).

We should point out that this is not the only way to display an hourglass cursor. You could also do this by handling the WM_SETCURSOR message. If a program needs to interact with the user — that is, retrieve any type of message — while still displaying the hourglass cursor, you *must* respond to the WM_SETCURSOR solution. Windows sends a constant stream of these messages to each window, causing a continual updating of each window's cursor. (To see this for yourself, run SPY++.)

The other cursors — the I-beam, the reverse arrow, and the forward arrow — are loaded at window creation time. The I-beam is a system-supplied cursor, and it is displayed when the cursor is over most parts of the window. The reverse-arrow cursor is displayed only when the cursor moves to the window's left margin. And the forward-arrow cursor is displayed when the mouse is over lines that have been selected (highlighted) by user input. This presumably tells the user that the data is ready to be grabbed by the mouse for operations such as drag-and-drop.

Based on the location of the mouse, GETTEXT displays one of these three cursors in response to the WM_SETCURSOR message. The function call for displaying cursors is a Windows API function, SetCursor( ). For example, here is the line of code that displays the right-arrow cursor:

```
::SetCursor(d_hcrRArrow);
```

DISPLAYING A CARET

Much of our time in creating GETTEXT was spent assembling the pieces that support caret creation and movement. The level of effort required is somewhat ironic given that a caret is such a tiny sliver of pixels. But carets must be precisely aligned to the surrounding graphic objects (which are, in the case of GETTEXT, lines of text). In addition, users expect carets to have default behavior — such as line wrapping — that requires lots of code to support.

Adding and destroying a caret

To get support for a keyboard caret, the easy part is creating the caret. In response to the WM_SETFOCUS message, GETTEXT creates a caret by calling CWnd::CreateSolidCaret( ). Next, the caret is moved by calling CWnd::SetCaretPos( ). And finally, it's made visible by calling CWnd::ShowCaret( ).

The other side of caret creation is caret cleanup. When a window loses the focus — which has already happened when you get a WM_KILLFOCUS message — that's the time to destroy the caret. Before you can destroy a caret, however, it must be hidden. This is accomplished by calling CWnd::HideCaret( ). Only then can the caret be cleaned up — which GETTEXT does by calling CWnd::DestroyCaret( ).

Because the caret is scaled for the current font, it must also be destroyed and re-created when the font changes. Otherwise, you might have a tiny caret next to a large font, or vice-versa. Fortunately, GET-TEXT uses the same font for all of the text in the window. If we were to build a multifont text window, we'd change the caret size when moving between blocks of different-sized text.

The actual font changes are performed in DMainFrame::CreateNew-Font( ), which destroys the old font, creates a new font, and then queries the system for font metric information. The existing caret is then destroyed and a new one created; in the process, every Windows API caret function is called:

```
// [GETTEXT] If we have focus, recreate and move caret.
if (GetFocus() == this)
{
    HideCaret();
    DestroyCaret();
    CreateSolidCaret(0, d_cyLineHeight);
    SetCaretPos(d_ptCaret);
    ShowCaret();
}
```

Although it is not strictly necessary, we check for the presence of the focus because we want to avoid strange side effects that might arise from changing the caret when we *don't* have the focus.

Moving the caret

Once we're sure that the caret is being properly created and destroyed, the next thing we need to do is move the caret. Ultimately, either the mouse or the keyboard can be used to move the caret. We wrote the mouse code first because it's the quickest and easiest to get going. We also anticipated that we could call the caret-handling mouse code from our caret-handling keyboard code because — when moving between lines of text — our code must allow the caret to jump into the middle of a line. That's precisely what the mouse is set up to allow.

Moving the caret with mouse input is a two-step process. First, we identify the line on which the user is clicking. This is relatively easy, because every line in our text buffer is the same height. If we think of each line as a simple rectangle, we can call CRect::PtInRect( ) on each line that's currently in the window. Within GETTEXT, we implement a function that does all of this for us and returns an index to the selected line. This function is DMainFrame::QueryClickLine( ).

The next step is to figure out which specific characters are under the mouse cursor. This is slightly more difficult because we have to take into account *proportionally spaced fonts*. These are fonts in which character widths vary among the different characters that make up the font. For example, the uppercase *W* is typically wider than the lowercase *l*.

To figure out where the mouse was clicked in a line of proportionally spaced text, some calculation is necessary. To simplify matters, we ask GDI for a table of character width values for every character in the font by calling CDC::GetCharWidth( ). With that table in hand, it's an easy task to add up character width values until we find out where the mouse was clicked.

With mouse support for caret movement in place, we proceed to set up keyboard support. On the surface, this seems easy to do; you simply call CWnd::SetCaretPos( ). But several nonlinear conditions require careful thought if they are to be handled properly. For example, no movement is allowed beyond the start of the file or the end of the file. Also, wrapping must occur at the ends of lines. When wrapping backward, the caret must move to the end of the preceding line. When wrapping forward, the caret must move to the beginning of the next line. You can probably think of many other special cases. When you start adding up these different possibilities, it's easy to see how this could turn into a runaway session of coding for special cases.

We solved this problem by creating the state-transition table shown in Table 14-7. This tool can be very helpful for solving certain types of programming problems that have just a few states and inputs that combine to create different types of results. In this example, 7 states and 4 inputs combine to produce 28 possible results. Because of duplication, the state table shows that we have to write code for only eight distinct transitions.

Table 14-7

State-Transition Table Describing Caret Movement

State	ArrowUp	ArrowRight	ArrowDown	ArrowLeft
File Start	Error	CharRight	ClickDown	Error
Line Start	ClickUp	CharRight	ClickDown	PrevLine
Line Middle	ClickUp	CharRight	ClickDown	CharLeft
Line End	ClickUp	NextLine	ClickDown	CharLeft
File End	ClickUp	Error	Error	CharLeft
Window Top	Scroll, ClickUp	CharRight	ClickDown	CharLeft
Window End	ClickUp	CharRight	Scroll, ClickDown	CharLeft

Some of the notation in this state-transition table might require explanation. With the term *Error*, we mean that a user error has occurred and we can ignore the input. We make a beep sound on the system speaker to warn the user, but nothing else is required. The ClickUp and ClickDown transitions are handled by simulating a mouse click. In particular, this simplifies the problems of proportionally spaced fonts. After all, we already solve that problem with the caret-handling mouse code. Reusing it simplifies our caret-handling keyboard code.

Within GETTEXT, we boiled down the eight results into three helper functions: MoveCaret( ), MoveCaretChar( ), and MoveCaretClick( ). The first function, MoveCaret( ), positions the caret in terms of lines and character cells. It doesn't handle any scrolling; that must be done elsewhere. The second function, MoveCaretChar( ), moves a caret within a given line. Although it's smart enough to move the caret forward or backward by a line, it can't handle moving — and possibly scrolling — more than one line at a time. And the third function, MoveCaretClick( ), was created to handle moving the caret up or down based on mouse clicks. However, it also works pretty well when moving the caret in response to the up-arrow or down-arrow keys.

At the end of a development project, some of our friends at Microsoft participate in an activity called a *postmortem*. After a project is complete, the postmortem provides an opportunity to record details about lessons learned, and to make suggestions about possible changes for the next version. In creating a postmortem report for our GETTEXT program, we would recommend putting all of the caret-handling code into its own class. That way, our caret class could be reused and applied to manage carets for other types of input windows. There are also transitions between caret-handling mode and text-selection mode. We don't claim that this program is 100% bug-free, but it is enough to give you an idea of the important issues that need to be addressed.

SELECTING TEXT

Our final comments on GETTEXT involve the selecting of text. We limited our text selection to handling *lines of text* rather than *blocks of characters*. But it shouldn't take too much imagination to adapt the line selection logic to the creation of your own character selection code.

Selecting text: the left mouse button

All selection starts when the user clicks the left mouse button. But because that button also moves the caret, GETTEXT checks the mouse location before putting itself into *text selection mode*. Here's the line of code — which is taken from the WM_LBUTTONDOWN handler — that does this:

```
// Set focus mode based on mouse location.
d_nFocusMode = (point.x< d_cxLeftMargin) ? FOCUS_SELECT:FOCUS_CARET;
```

To convert a mouse click into a line index, GETTEXT calls QueryClick-Line( ), one of its own helper functions. With that information, it then changes the appearance of the line to make it look "selected" by calling:

```
// Highlight that line.
InvertLines(d_nSelectFirst, d_nSelectLast);
```

Drawing selected text

A close study of the WM_LBUTTONDOWN text-selection code will show that we're doing something that's a little tricky. We're drawing in response to a message *other than* the WM_PAINT message. This is tricky because, as we mentioned in our discussion of WM_PAINT in Chapter 13, you must make sure that the non-WM_PAINT drawing code is perfectly synchro-nized with the WM_PAINT drawing code. Otherwise, all sorts of strange results can occur.

It took quite a bit of effort — measured both in lines of code and in hours of work — to get these two synchronized. In lines-of-code terms, FILELIST has about 54 lines between handling WM_PAINT and WM_WININICHANGE. This latter message retrieves the proper text colors — foreground as well as background — for drawing text.

When we were done enhancing the original code from FILELIST, GETTEXT had 178 lines — more than *three times* the text drawing code of FILELIST. In addition to the WM_PAINT and WM_WININICHANGE messages, we added support for one more message: WM_ERASEBKGND.

The role of the WM_ERASEBKGND message is to erase a win-dow's background. Windows' default handling normally does just the right thing — that is, filling the window with the correct window eras-ing color. But the "correct" color, as defined in the Control Panel, is usually white.

Windows' default background color creates a slight problem when you're working with selected text. With unselected, "normal" text, things work fine. The erase message fills the background, and the paint message fills the foreground. But selected text has a different background color from normal text. So the problem with using the default background color for selected text is that the user sees the screen blink during a paint message.

The reason why GETTEXT has so much code for handling selected text is to avoid this annoying blink. It touches pixels as few times as possible, setting them to the correct color the first time. This requires a lot of work in the WM_PAINT code, and elsewhere.

Different Types of Background Color

Depending on its context, the term *background color* can have several different meanings. One meaning is associated with the WM_ERASEBKGND message that GETTEXT handles. When a window gets this message, Windows wants the client area to be filled with a particular color. That color is often white, but the user can set the default "Window Color" to any other value from the Control Panel. To get an RGB triplet for the default color, you call ::GetSysColor() with a COLOR_WINDOW index. In fact, this is what GETTEXT does when it gets a WM_WININICHANGE message:

```
d_crBackground = GetSysColor(COLOR_WINDOW);
```

The term background color also refers to a GDI attribute that gets set into a device context. When drawing, you set this attribute by calling CDC::SetBkColor(). This drawing attribute affects three types of drawn objects: text background, hatched (nonsolid) brushes used to fill areas, and styled (nonsolid) pens used to draw lines. (This attribute also plays a role when converting between monochrome and color bitmaps.)

Although the two meanings differ, they are not entirely incompatible. It just so happens that GETTEXT sets the GDI background color attribute when it responds to the WM_ERASEBKGND message:

```
// Select text background color.
pDC->SetBkColor(d_crBackground);
```

Continued

Continued from previous page

But don't get thrown off by our use of this attribute. In fact, we could have written other drawing code that didn't use the background color at all! It would have been less confusing, but it also would have been slightly less efficient.

The only reason why GETTEXT sets the background color attribute is because of a wonderful feature of GDI's ExtTextOut() function. When called with the ETO_OPAQUE flag, this function fills a rectangular drawing area with the background color as set in the DC. Here, for example, is the line of code from GETTEXT's frame window that — in responding to the WM_ERASEBKGND message — does the actual work of erasing the contents of the window:

```
// Erase background (uses 'background' color in DC)
pDC->ExtTextOut(0, 0, ETO_OPAQUE, &rClient, 0, 0, 0);
```

A more traditional Windows API approach to filling a window with a background color is to create a brush (CBrush) object of the desired color. Then, you can fill the client area by calling CDC::FillRect(). In one sense, this is better than the text background color approach because brush colors can be *dithered*.

Dithering is a clever technique of filling an area with alternating pixels to make the user think that a device has lots more colors than it really has. For example, alternating blue and white pixels looks like light blue. Dithering works pretty well for filling random areas.

But GDI only uses dithering for vector graphics. When drawing text, GDI *only* uses solid colors. This is true for foreground colors as well as background colors. Because of dithering, we can't rely on a GDI brush to produce the same color as the DC's background color provides when drawing text. This is another benefit — aside from less code and faster actual drawing — that we get by using ExtTextOut(). Because it's a text drawing function, it works in a text-compatible way.

Extra work for non-WM_PAINT selected text drawing

When GETTEXT draws selected text in response to WM_LBUTTON-DOWN and WM_MOUSEMOVE messages, it must be careful to avoid touching any pixels twice. This is necessary because selected lines are not drawn — that is, no GDI text drawing function is actually called. Instead, rectangular areas of the screen are *inverted*. If any area is inverted the wrong number of times, the result would be garbage on the screen. Text is inverted *once* to be selected, and it's inverted again to return to normal.

GETTEXT's DMainFrame::InvertLines( ) function accepts line numbers as its input and determines which actual pixels to invert. It then inverts lines of text by calling InvertRect( ), a GDI function which is wrapped in MFC as the inline CDC::InvertRect( ) function. This function calls through the device driver to invert blocks of pixels at a time, and for that reason is very fast.

But there is a price to pay for that speed. When drawing selected text in response to a WM_PAINT message, GETTEXT must do some extra work to ensure that the colors it uses match the inverted colors. Although this might seem like a simple task, it's not.

A simple way to get inverted colors is by querying the system for the user's color preferences and doing some math to derive an inverted color. For example, these four lines of code provide a reasonable set of foreground and background colors for both normal and selected text:

```
COLORREF d_crForeground = GetSysColor(COLOR_WINDOWTEXT);
COLORREF d_crBackground = GetSysColor(COLOR_WINDOW);
COLORREF d_crSelectFore = d_crForeground ^ 0x00ffffff;
COLORREF d_crSelectBack = d_crBackground ^ 0x00ffffff;
```

This is the code fragment that we presented earlier in this chapter as the way to get the required colors. One sign of the reasonableness of this approach is that some successful shipping applications — namely Microsoft Word and Microsoft Excel — apparently use it.

This won't work for our sample program because GETTEXT uses the fast screen invert function, InvertRect( ). This function relies on the device driver to determine what constitutes the correct opposite for a given color. To reliably know the opposite color for a given system color, GETTEXT has to ask. It does so by actually drawing with the given colors, inverting them, and then asking for the RGB triplets of the resulting colors.

The seven steps that GETTEXT takes to request and receive the correct inverted colors are as follows (the original appears in MAINFRM.CPP, in the WM_WININICHANGE message handler):

```
// Get new "normal" background & foreground colors.
d_crForeground = GetSysColor(COLOR_WINDOWTEXT);
d_crBackground = GetSysColor(COLOR_WINDOW);

// [GETTEXT] Get new "selected" colors (in 7 easy steps).

// 1. Create an offscreen DC (compatible with display screen).
CDC dcBitmap;
```

```
dcBitmap.CreateCompatibleDC(NULL);

// 2. Query current device details.
CClientDC dcScreen(this);
int nPlanes = dcScreen.GetDeviceCaps(PLANES);
int nBitCount = dcScreen.GetDeviceCaps(BITSPIXEL);

// 3. Create a tiny bitmap and connect to the DC from step #1.
CBitmap bm;
bm.CreateBitmap(2, 2, nPlanes, nBitCount, 0);
CBitmap * pbmOld = dcBitmap.SelectObject(&bm);

// 4. Set up rectangle for bitmap surface.
CRect rBitmap = CRect(0, 0, 3, 3);

// 5. Find foreground color inverse (store in d_crSelectFore).
dcBitmap.SetBkColor(d_crForeground);
dcBitmap.ExtTextOut(0, 0, ETO_OPAQUE, &rBitmap, 0, 0, 0);
dcBitmap.InvertRect(&rBitmap);
d_crSelectFore = dcBitmap.GetPixel(1,1);

// 6. Find background color inverse (store in d_crSelectBack).
dcBitmap.SetBkColor(d_crBackground);
dcBitmap.ExtTextOut(0, 0, ETO_OPAQUE, &rBitmap, 0, 0, 0);
dcBitmap.InvertRect(&rBitmap);
d_crSelectBack = dcBitmap.GetPixel(1,1);

// 7. Disconnect bitmap from DC to help GDI clean up properly.
dcBitmap.SelectObject(pbmOld );
```

It creates a bitmap, draws on the bitmap, inverts the colors, and then queries the resulting color. The color query function, CDC::GetPixel( ), returns the exact color value that will match the inverted color selected by InvertRect( ).

Text selection and mouse movement

Depending on what type of selection you want to support and how sophisticated you want to be, selecting multiple lines of text using the mouse can involve other messages besides WM_LBUTTONDOWN. One such message is WM_MOUSEMOVE. Another message is the WM_TIMER message.

GETTEXT allows for the selection of multiple text lines, which is accomplished using both of these messages. In a click-drag operation, the mouse move message (WM_MOUSEMOVE) tells GETTEXT that the user wants to select a range of items. At first glance, support for extending a single selection to multiple items is simple. You just add new items as the user moves the mouse. However, several complications can arise.

One such complication is part of all mouse input handling. When the mouse moves between two points, not every point in the window is hit. In particular, when the mouse moves quickly, the coordinates retrieved from mouse move messages could be fairly widely dispersed. So, a problem you always face in any click-drag operation is that you might be working with an incomplete set of mouse points in the selection set.

To solve this problem, you need to think through the ways you can interpolate the missing data. In GETTEXT, with its linear list of lines, it's fairly easy. The line on which the mouse first clicks is the anchor for the selection. As the mouse moves over other lines, every line between the anchor point and the current mouse position is included in the selection set.

Another problem with tracking and responding to mouse movement is that users don't always move the mouse in predictable ways. For example, while selecting five lines of text, a user might accidentally select six or seven lines. You need to be forgiving and allow them to cut back on the set of selected lines. Or, a user might start selecting lines of text in one direction (say, upward), only to have a change of heart and start selecting in the other — downward — direction. Once again, your interactive mouse selection code must be able to add and remove items as the user fidgets with the mouse.

To solve the fidgety-user problem, you need to think through all of the possible ways that input might arrive. If you think of only the obvious or even the more desirable input streams, you leave yourself wide open to user fidgeting. Even when you think you've covered all possible cases, there will always be a few more that elude you for the longest time. Persistence and patience will pay off.

Yet another problem can occur if the user starts to scroll and then moves the mouse outside the client area. As mentioned earlier in this chapter, capturing the mouse helps you get a steady stream of input. All you need is a way to put this input to work for you.

As GETTEXT shows, one way to solve this problem is by setting a timer. As long as the mouse is outside (above or below) the client area, automatic scrolling is automatically performed. Support for a combination of selection and scrolling is one feature that users expect, and GETTEXT shows you the basic steps involved in implementing this capability for your own applications.

Summary

In contrast to its support for graphic output and user-interface objects, Windows' support for mouse and keyboard input is fairly low-level. You are notified of individual keyboard keystrokes — that is, down and up transitions — as well as individual mouse move and mouse button transitions. This gives you a great deal of flexibility for shaping your software's user interface, but it requires a lot of work on your part if it is to be handled robustly.

The chapters in this part of the book were written to provide coverage of the core ways in which Microsoft's MFC class library encapsulates the Windows API. But MFC is not limited to just a set of user-interface and graphics classes. In the next part, we're going to explore how MFC provides support for key architectural features that you'll need for building complete, fully functional applications.

IV Application Architecture

We use the term *architecture* to refer to the major design elements that affect the organization and operation of a program. In a good design, each architectural element is able to play several roles. In doing so, each element adds coherence and integrity to the software's operation. An analogy can be drawn to the world of physical architecture. For example, the flying buttresses in a Gothic cathedral such as Notre Dame in Paris play both a structural role and an aesthetic role. They provide the support for the massive clerestory columns of stone, and they contribute to the visual statement that stone — like the human spirit — can float on air.

We chose the particular topics that are covered in this part of the book because we believe they will play a role in many MFC applications. We don't claim that every topic will be useful to every reader, because your key design elements will depend on what your particular software needs to accomplish. But we believe that these topics are general enough to provide something for every reader. They constitute what might be considered "advanced" topics, because to take advantage of these suggestions, a programmer must be familiar with the material covered in earlier sections in this book.

Chapter 15 covers MFC's support for a Document/View style of application. This is an important topic for those readers who are building file-based editing applications. It also provides a foundation for OLE support. However, not every application needs Document/View features (or even OLE features). That's why we've postponed discussion of this topic until now.

Every application makes use of memory, and Chapter 16 discusses architectural issues related to the management of system and application memory. On the one hand, a program could get by with simply using the C++ new operator. On the other hand, as an application's need for memory grows, so will the need for making crucial memory design decisions. In Chapter 16, we provide a framework for making those decisions.

CHAPTER

15

Document/View Architecture

*M*FC's Document/View (or just Doc/View) architecture provides a framework for building applications that manage disk-based data. Among the types of programs that benefit from this approach are editors, file viewers, and database query front ends. Even programs for handling data streams that aren't disk-based — such as terminal emulation programs, real-time data acquisition programs, and games — can benefit from MFC's Doc/View support.

AppWizard, the Visual C++ code generator, makes it easy to create a Doc/View application. When you create either a single- or a multiple-document application, you get an empty Doc/View application. (On the other hand, the dialog-based applications that AppWizard creates don't use Doc/View.)

Once you have an empty Doc/View application, what steps do you take to complete your application? Although AppWizard makes it easy to *create* a Doc/View application, a little more effort is needed to understand how Doc/View works as well as how to modify App-Wizard-generated code to suit your purposes. It's not overly complex, but much of MFC's work is hidden in the default behavior of the various MFC classes.

To learn about MFC's support for Doc/View, we traced into the class library code using a debugger. If you can spare the time, this is a great way to get the inside scoop on exactly what is happening. And you can apply this approach to learning about other MFC topics in particular and any software system in general. If you have questions about Doc/View after you read this chapter, a trip into Debugger-land could solve your mysteries. To help you make this trip, this chapter includes a section on using a debugger to explore the MFC class libraries.

To save you a journey to the bottom of the Doc/View classes, we'll share the results of our own trips. We'll start with an overview of the elements that make up the Doc/View architecture. After a brief detour to explore the use of the debugger, we'll discuss some of the "next steps" you might take once AppWizard has generated a Doc/View application for you. Finally, we'll show you two Doc/View examples, HASAVIEW and HASVIEWS, single- and multiple-document Doc/View implementations of the FILELIST program from Chapter 13.

An Overview of Doc/View

MFC's Doc/View architecture manages the relationship between a single type of data and the multiple ways in which the data might be made available to users. Figure 15-1 shows one way you can visualize this relationship. In this example, the data source is perhaps an array of numbers such as you might find in a spreadsheet program. Two possible views for this type of data are shown: as a spreadsheet grid and as a graph.

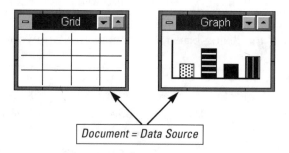

Figure 15-1

The Doc/View architecture delegates the management of data to a document object, and the visual presentation of the data to view objects.

In this arrangement, the *document* is a data source. The most common type of document is a disk-based file. But that's not the only type of data source. For example, a document could receive its data through a communications port or over a network. Regardless of the source, the management of that data is encapsulated within the document object.

The view, on the other hand, provides the visual display — in a window or on a printed page — of data to the user. In this example, a single document has two views and therefore can be displayed in two different forms: as a spreadsheet and as a bar graph. As implemented in MFC, a single view provides output both to the display screen and to the printer. In this chapter, we focus solely on displaying the view on the display screen.

As an aside, it's worth mentioning that MFC's implementation of Doc/View is not the first of its kind. Smalltalk-80 has Model/View/Controller support, which divides an application's tasks among data management (the model), representations of the data (the views), and user-input management (the controller). The tasks that Smalltalk handles using its view and controller are lumped together by MFC into a view.

WHY USE DOC/VIEW?

The most important feature that Doc/View provides is the separation of data handling from data display. With these two important tasks encapsulated in a standard way into two types of objects, the work of each is greatly simplified. Rather than mixing both types of code together, each stands alone. In general, Doc/View is most useful for any application in which significant amounts of data must be managed, or the display of data involves significant complexity.

Another important Doc/View feature is that the various MFC classes provide lots of help for common Doc/View actions. For example, the handling of files — selecting, opening, and closing — is handled entirely by the class library framework. All you have to do is read and write the bytes you need from the data stream that's provided. This type of support means that less time is spent rewriting the same code that typically must be written for this type of application, and more time can be spent on application-specific code.

Another Doc/View feature is print preview support. Users want to see the results of their work on screen before sending output to the printer. To build this support yourself would take several months and thousands of lines of code. Using MFC's built-in support saves you the time and effort of writing the code yourself.

Do you absolutely need to use Doc/View support to build an MFC application? We certainly don't think so. If you've read through Part III of this book, you've already seen quite a few examples of MFC applications that were built without Doc/View support. Although most were admittedly simple programs, they demonstrate that nothing in the Windows user interface requires Doc/View.

In some cases, use of Doc/View probably *doesn't* make sense. In general, you'll *avoid* Doc/View when you are building applications that are not data-oriented. Utility programs, such as a clock, probably won't be implemented with Doc/View. Visual C++ ships with ZoomIn, a screen magnification program in which Doc/View isn't used because it doesn't make sense. Another category of programs that would not use Doc/View are those with nonstandard user interfaces, such as Microsoft's Bob.

Those are the basic ideas behind Doc/View. It's basically a set of classes that help to separate the work of data management from that of data representation. To take advantage of this simple design, you need to understand some of its implementation details. Providing you with that understanding is our goal for the rest of this chapter.

MFC Doc/View Classes

Table 15-1 summarizes the MFC classes that play a direct role in supporting Doc/View applications. We've divided this group into three sets: class factory classes, primary classes, and support classes. Although you won't directly use every class, a general familiarity will help you understand some of your choices. As for the support classes, if nothing else, a basic understanding will help you read the MFC source files.

Most of the classes and data types in Table 15-1 are probably new to you. Of course, CFrameWnd — the frame window class — is an old friend to most MFC programmers. And although it's not an old friend, CView is derived from CWnd, and so is a window. You've also previously seen CWinApp, the application object class. In addition to being required by every MFC application, it provides crucial parts of MFC's Doc/View support.

Table 15-1

MFC Classes That Support Doc/View Applications

Set	Class	Description
Class Factory		Coordinates the creation and connection of Doc/View parts.
	CDocTemplate	Pure virtual base class. Has default implementation and defines the interfaces needed for a document template.
	CSingleDocTemplate	Supports Doc/View in Single-Document Interface (SDI) windowing operation. This class inherits from CDocTemplate.
	CMultiDocTemplate	Supports Doc/View in Multiple-Document Interface (MDI) windowing operation. This class inherits from CDocTemplate.
Primary Doc/ View Classes		Play a direct role in the management and display of data.
	CDocument	Manages the storage of data in memory. For applications with disk-based data, this class handles the movement of data between memory and disk.
	CView	Provides the user interface to the data stored in a CDocument-derived class.
	CFrameWnd, CMDIChildWnd, CMDIFrameWnd	Organizes user-interface objects such as view windows, toolbars, and menus.
	CWinApp	Holds a list of document templates and provides default handling of basic file operations (FileINew, FileIOpen, and FileIClose).
Support Classes and Data Types		Used by other classes.
	CArchive	Serialization class used by CDocument to aid in moving data to and from data files.
	CString	General-purpose character string class. (Its use is *not* limited to Doc/View.)
	CPtrList	A container class used by various Doc/View classes to hold lists of pointers. For example, CWinApp holds a list of pointers to document templates. The multi-document template class has a list of open documents. The document class holds a list of associated views.
	POSITION	A surrogate for a void * that MFC uses to hold its place in a CPtrList.

The application object

MFC's support for Doc/View applications starts with CWinApp, the application object class. This class provides basic file I/O support for opening and saving file-based data. Although it's up to a document object to actually read and write the data, the application object provides help in the selecting and opening of files.

Part of CWinApp's file I/O support is a set of dialogs that are displayed when the user selects the File|New, File|Open, or File|Save As... commands. When the user requests a new, empty document, CWinApp's default handler calls the appropriate classes to produce an empty CDocument-derived object and an associated CView window for viewing the data.

The handling of the File|New command can get a little involved when a single application supports several types of documents. An example of this occurs in the Visual C++ IDE itself. In response to the File|New command, Visual C++ displays a dialog similar to the example in Figure 15-2. This dialog is provided automatically by MFC's application object class, which is smart enough to know when an application can work with more than one type of file.

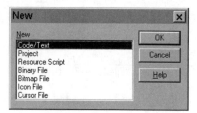

Figure 15-2

An example of a File|New dialog displayed by the Visual C++ IDE, which itself is a Doc/View application.

Another type of dialog that CWinApp supports is the dialog that's displayed in response to the File|Open command. CWinApp's default handler displays a File Open dialog with a complete set of file extensions for the different types of files that can be opened. The Visual C++ IDE uses a slightly modified version of the default handler to add support for the different ways in which a program file can be open (text, binary, and so on).

As part of its File|New and File|Open handlers, CWinApp maintains a list of the application's document templates. When handling a File|New request, CWinApp builds a list of available objects. From this list, the user can choose which type of new document is to be created. And as part of its File|Open support, CWinApp also walks the document template list to determine which file extension choices should be available to the user.

CWinApp holds a list of document templates, which are CDocTemplate-derived objects that know how to assemble the parts that make up Doc/View support for a given application. For applications that support several types of data files — represented by the addition of document templates to the application object — CWinApp prompts for the type of document.

View classes

The user-interface component of a Doc/View application is provided by one of the several types of view classes. The most important aspect of views is that *views are windows*. A view can never stand by itself; instead, it must always be created as a child of another window. Among other reasons, the creation of views as (WS_CHILD) child windows is part of MFC's support for in-place editing windows for OLE-enabled applications. The parent of a view window is usually a frame (CFrameWnd or derived) window. In the context of OLE support, the parent of a view window can be an OLE in-place aware frame window.

Because a view is a window, it can receive windowing messages just like any other CWnd-derived class. For example, a view window can receive mouse and keyboard messages. One of the sample applications that ships with Visual C++ is SCRIBBLE, which demonstrates how Doc/View support can be used to create a simple drawing program. SCRIBBLE accepts mouse input to create line drawings. The sample programs that we provide at the end of this chapter — HASAVIEW and HASVIEWS — show how keyboard messages can be received by a view. In these examples, keyboard input controls the scrolling of individual view windows.

As shown in the fragment of the MFC class hierarchy chart in Figure 15-3, MFC provides several CView-derived classes. They provide support for scrolling (CViewScroll), for the display of dialog box controls (CFormView), and for the display of database records (CRecordView).

There's even a view class wrapped around Windows' edit control which lets you build a simple, notepad-like text editor (CEditView).

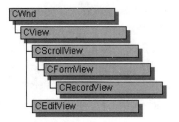

Figure 15-3
When building a Doc/View application, you use these CView-derived classes to build your views.

Although the predefined views are useful in some cases, they do have limitations that relate to their 16-bit heritage. For example, the scrolling view supports scrolling over a range of only 64K values. When displaying a list of 10-point text on a typical VGA screen, for example, that sets a maximum of 2,000 lines of text that can be scrolled. To put this into perspective, the largest MFC source file — WINCORE.CPP — is 3,000 lines long.

The text editor view, CEditView, has a similar limitation. Because the Windows 95 edit control is implemented entirely in 16-bit code, the largest data file that can be read and edited is 64K. Although this is large enough for many purposes, you must go elsewhere for help editing larger blocks. One place you might look for help is in the rich edit control, which ships with Windows 95. This is not supported in the current version of MFC as of this writing, although Microsoft plans to add this support in a future version.

When building a Doc/View application, you must specify a view class to be used. This could be a predefined view class, such as CEditView, or — as will most likely be the case — a new class you define that is derived from CView. As we've mentioned, the key to working with a view is remembering that views are Windows windows. Almost everything that we said about windows in Part III of this book applies to views.

View windows differ from regular windows in one respect: the handling of drawing code. The base CView class handles some of the behind-the-scenes work to render a graphic image on either a display screen or a

printer. From our discussion in Chapter 13, you might recall that Windows
sends a WM_PAINT message to tell a window when it's time to draw.
There isn't a comparable WM_PRINT message to create printed output,
but in CView-derived windows the two tasks are managed by a single,
higher-level virtual function: OnDraw( ). In a view window, rather than
handling the WM_PAINT message, you'll override OnDraw( ). The result is
a single function for output to both the display screen and the printer.

To convince yourself that a view is a window, this would be a good
time to write some simple Doc/View code. After you start Visual C++,
crank up the AppWizard. (That is, select File|New, and ask for a new
project. Then, work through the six wizard windows, requesting either a
single- or a multiple-document application.) You'll see that AppWizard
already overrides CView::OnDraw( ) for you:

```
/////////////////////////////////////////////////////////
// DSampleView drawing

void DSampleView::OnDraw(CDC* pDC)
{
    DSampleDoc* pDoc = GetDocument();
    ASSERT_VALID(pDoc);

    // TODO: add draw code for native data here
}
```

One of the differences between drawing in a view and drawing in a
window is that you don't have to create your own DC. You might recall
that drawing a single line of text in a non-view window involves
responding to the WM_PAINT message with code such as this:

```
void DSomeWindow::OnPaint()
{
    CPaintDC dc(this); // device context for painting

    CString str = "Hello Windows 95";
    dc.TextOut(10, 10, str);

}
```

You don't do this in a view because the base CView code fetches a
DC for you. It might be a CPaintDC, and it might be a CDC for a printer.
Although you can find out, you usually won't care. After all, if you can
produce a single body of code for both devices, so much the better. In
terms of creating an accurate representation of some data, issues such as

color, available fonts, and device capabilities are more important than whether a device is a display screen or a printer.

Here is an OnDraw( ) function that draws a line of text both in a window and on the printed page:

```
void DSampleView::OnDraw(CDC* pDC)
{
    DSampleDoc* pDoc = GetDocument();
    ASSERT_VALID(pDoc);

    CString str = "Hello Windows 95";
    pDC->TextOut(10, 10, str);
}
```

There's a strictly C++ language difference between how the OnPaint( ) and OnDraw( ) functions access the DC object. As shown in this example, OnDraw( ) receives a pointer to a CDC object. As such, the object is accessed using the points-to (->) operator rather than the dot (.) operator, which OnPaint( ) handlers normally use.

Notice the call to GetDocument( ) in our tiny OnDraw( ) function. This gets a pointer to the document object that is associated with our view window. Even though our code doesn't use the resulting pDoc pointer, you'll often need to grab this pointer in view window code. This is necessary because — according to the Doc/View way of thinking — a view has no data. Instead, it relies on a document object to hold all the data that it needs.

Before continuing, we should clarify what we mean when we say that "a view has no data." As C++ objects, views can of course have data members. For example, our HASAVIEW program defines several view-based data members, which serve to fine-tune the graphic presentation of the data.

But a view won't hold any of the application state that might typically be stored in a file on disk or in a database. Instead, the job of holding persistent data belongs to a document object. To underscore that design choice, the MFC definition for CView itself includes a single data member — a pointer to the associated document object:

```
CDocument* m_pDocument;
```

Let's take a look at the class from which document objects get their characteristics: MFC's CDocument class.

Document classes

The role of a document object is to provide a data source. As mentioned earlier, view classes don't hold any application data; instead, they rely on document objects for data. In C++ terms, the document object considers view objects to be a *friend* class. After all, documents trust view objects to read their data for display in a window. The trust goes even deeper, though, because view objects in many cases will also change the data that's stored in the documents. Although the word *view* might suggest that this object only looks at the data, it can do much more than that. A view provides the user interface which allows a user to add to, modify, update, and even delete the data in a document object.

A document/view pair is a team. One manages storage, the other manages graphic presentation and user input. One is called on to load and save data, the other to display and edit the data. A typical scenario involves a CDocument-derived object that reads the contents of a disk file into memory, setting up whatever RAM-based structures are needed for optimal access. Then, a set of CView-derived view objects — friends (in the C++ sense) with the document — read and manipulate that data.

You can think of a document object as providing a means for moving data between memory and disk. View objects don't know how the data is stored, and they don't care to know. They totally rely on — and fully trust — the document objects to do the right thing in providing the data when it's needed. From the perspective of a view object, a document object is a type of virtual storage device. In many cases, the document object is a logical encapsulation of disk-based data.

But a document object is more than just a wrapper for a file — a task that is already provided by CFile. Instead, it's a complete abstraction of a data source that hides where the data is coming from. And even though a document object could make its data available to its views by means of something as simple as a pointer, that doesn't have to be the case. For example, a document object could provide an interface to its data in the form of a set of function calls that return pointers to data in 4K increments.

This abstraction of an MFC document as a data source allows you to play some interesting tricks. For example, maybe the source of data is a communications port rather than a disk file. Maybe the source of data is the Windows clipboard or another process in the system. Perhaps it's even a process running on another computer that the document object communicates with over a network. From the perspective of the view, it doesn't make a difference.

The amount of cooperation between a given document and a given view object depends on how they are designed. It doesn't take too much imagination to conceive of a document object that is very particular about which data it allows to be seen by any given view. Instead of exposing data pointers, a document object might expose only member functions. Views might call one set of member functions to draw, another set to query basic document statistics, and still a third set to allow limited changes to the document's contents.

Regardless of the specific protocol that is chosen for communicating between a document and a view, the point remains that a document object manages data. Whether it loads the data all at once or a little at a time is up to the document. Whether it provides free access to any and all comers, or only to a select few with the right security codes, is a decision that is made within the document object. And, as we've already mentioned, the document object implementor decides which data source the document uses.

The default data source for MFC document objects is a regular file. The less a data source looks like the kind of data file that MFC expects to see, the more work you have to add to the basic support that MFC provides. CDocument goes so far as to open a file for you and pass a reference to an object through which the file's data can be accessed. A single function, Serialize( ), handles both the reading from and the writing to a document's data file.

When AppWizard spins a Doc/View application, it provides an empty Serialize( ) function as part of the CDocument-derived class code. Here is the code that AppWizard provides, including its comments that let you know what is expected:

```
void DSampleDoc::Serialize(CArchive& ar)
{
    if (ar.IsStoring())
    {
        // TODO: add storing code here
    }
    else
    {
        // TODO: add loading code here
    }
}
```

Within this basic framework, you have two choices. You can either read all of the required data from the file, or write all of the required data to the file.

Exactly how this is done is a function of the single parameter that's passed to Serialize( ), that is, the reference to a CArchive object. This class is basically a wrapper for a CFile object. Let's take a moment to consider the role of the CArchive class in handling a document's data.

The CArchive class

MFC's CArchive class implements C++ streams that are wrapped around an MFC file object (CFile). This class is used by the default CDocument implementation to read and write the entire contents of a disk file. CDocument handles the opening and closing of the requested files. The reading and writing of specific data bytes are handled by document-specific Serialize( ) functions in CDocument-derived classes.

In a Doc/View application, the document object creates a CArchive when a file is opened or closed. Of course, this occurs when the user selects the File|Open command or the File|Save command. Although the application object (CWinApp) usually handles these menu selections, one of two CDocument functions is eventually called. CDocument::OnOpen-Document( ) is called to open a file, and CDocument::OnSaveDocument( ) is called to save a document.

Both of these functions open a file, create a CArchive, and then call the document's Serialize( ) function. A document-specific serialization function is required, because MFC doesn't have any default handling for the reading or writing of different types of data files. Upon a return from the call to Serialize( ), the file is closed.

CDocument's default handling of file data assumes that entire files are both written and read at a single stroke. If you prefer a more incremental approach, you need to provide the handling yourself. But if you can work with this one-shot approach to file I/O, CDocument's defaults are for you.

Perhaps the simplest way to access an archive is by using the C++ streams approach. This involves using two of CArchive's operators: << and >>. When writing to the archive, you use the << operator, as in:

```
int nValue;
ar << nValue; // Write value to archive.
```

And when you write to the data stream, you use the >> operator, as in:

```
int nValue;
ar >> nValue; // Read value from archive.
```

Among the advantages of using streams for file I/O is the utter simplicity of these operators. In addition, these operators have polymorphic implementations that can automatically take care of type-specific details. If you've already used C++ streams, you know that these operators read and write the correct number of bytes based on the data type. For example, the following statements write out the correct number of bytes to the given archive stream:

```
char  ch = 'W';
short nShort = 95;
long  nLong = 95;

ar << ch;      // Writes 1 byte.
ar << nShort;  // Writes 2 bytes.
ar << nLong;   // Writes 4 bytes.
```

Fetching these values at some later point is as easy as reversing the direction of the operator:

```
ar >> ch;      // Reads 1 byte.
ar >> nShort;  // Reads 2 bytes.
ar >> nLong;   // Reads 4 bytes.
```

But you aren't limited to using C++ streams to save and restore document object state. If you'd like, you can bypass the buffered stream and read and write directly to the CFile object. CFile basically provides a C++ wrapper around C-runtime file I/O routines (although on Windows 95, CFile actually wraps Win32 file I/O calls).

The primary difference between a CArchive and a CFile object is that the CArchive does its own buffering. CFile, on the other hand, makes direct calls to the Windows file I/O functions, which do only a minimal amount of data buffering. They correspond to what C programmers call *low-level* file I/O routines.

To use a CFile object from within a document's serialization function, you first call CArchive::GetFile( ) to get a CFile pointer. You then make calls that look a lot like C-runtime file I/O calls. You call CFile::Seek( ) to position the file pointer, CFile::Read( ) to read in data, and CFile::Write( )

to write out data. To ensure that every last byte has been written out, there's CFile::Flush( ).

Clearly, this approach makes sense if you're porting existing code that uses the C-runtime libraries. It's a simple matter to retrofit your code to use CFile instead. Of course, this assumes that you will do your own buffering when dealing with large volumes of data. Otherwise, you risk serious problems with performance.

The Doc/View class that brings all the others together — and the one that we're going to discuss next — is the document template.

Document template classes

A document template is an object that has as its primary purpose the creation of other objects. First among these are CView-derived objects and CDocument-derived objects. In some cases, document templates also create a frame window to hold a view window (most notably in multiple-document interface applications). In most cases, though, what a document template creates is limited to a data storage object (CDocument-derived) and a window to show the data (CView-derived).

Document templates solve a problem that isn't adequately addressed in C++: how to write code to instantiate a class that hasn't been written yet. For example, it's relatively easy to create an object of a known type using the new operator:

```
CWhatever * pOne = new CWhatever();
```

But how do you write code to create an instance of something that isn't yet defined? What we need is something along the lines of:

```
<CFutureWhatever> * pDoc = new <CFutureWhatever>();
```

In the world of object-oriented design, this type of object is sometimes called a *Factory Method* or a *Virtual Constructor*. Such objects allow a class framework such as MFC to define the handling for certain categories of classes — for example, document and view classes — without having access to the specific class definition. (For an in-depth discussion, refer to the book *Design Patterns*, written by the "gang of four," Gamma, Helm, Johnson, and Vlissides, which we mention in the Recommended Reading list.) This is analogous to the way that C++ template classes allow for the manipulation of new types of data objects using existing code.

MFC's single-document template class (CSingleDocTemplate) supports the creation of an application that can open only a single document at a time. Nothing prevents a user from running multiple copies of a program, but the individual copies can each have only one document. Even with only one document, though, it's still possible to create and display multiple views. In the realm of Windows' user-interface design, this is sometimes called the Single-Document Interface (SDI).

By contrast, the multiple-document template (CMultiDocTemplate) can simultaneously support multiple documents in a single application. This supports a windowing scheme called the Multiple-Document Interface. This approach is not quite as old as Windows, though it does date back to the version of Microsoft Excel that was first introduced in the days of Windows 2.0 (circa 1987).

MDI windowing provides a standard way for a single application to manage multiple data windows. And, as the name suggests, multiple different documents can also be displayed within the multiple data windows. In fact, diverse relationships between windows and data are possible. In the simplest case, a single window could display a single data set. Two (or more) windows can display data from the same data set. Or, a dozen windows could display data from a half-dozen different data sets. The number of documents, and the number of corresponding windows, is entirely up to the user.

The only problem with MDI-style windowing is that it can be very confusing to users. Microsoft's studies in its usability labs indicate that users of MDI applications often disable MDI operation by maximizing a single data window. The result resembles an SDI window, which then brings into question whether MDI is in fact a reasonable model to support. In the short term, simply because of inertia, the answer is probably yes. In the longer term, though, as Microsoft's *document-centric* vision of computing becomes more widespread, continued use of MDI is not a certainty.

Document templates make extensive use of resources — that is, the data definitions within the application's resource script (.RC) file. For example, the default file extensions for a Doc/View application are stored in the string table. Other resource types — that is, menus, icons, and accelerator tables — can also be implemented for individual document templates. Let's take a moment to consider some of the ways that MFC's Doc/View features use Windows' resource data.

DOC/VIEW'S USE OF RESOURCES

As mentioned earlier in this book, a *resource* is a read-only data object. Windows provides built-in support for several types of resources. In addition, as we'll describe in Chapter 16, applications can define their own custom resource types.

MFC's Doc/View classes use resource data to fine-tune the definition of a document template's operation. We should first mention that although both SDI and MDI applications use resources, the MDI case is more interesting, because MFC lets specific types of data files — as represented by a document template — have their own menus, accelerator tables, and string table entries.

Just as a single identifier, IDR_MAINFRAME, identifies all of a frame window's resources, a single identifier is used for a document template. AppWizard creates the resource ID name, based on the application name. For HASVIEWS, our MDI sample Doc/View application, the identifier is IDR_HASVIETYPE.

The string table entry for a document type is especially complex. As described in the MFC documentation in the entry for the function CDocTemplate::GetDocString( ), it consists of seven substrings. With each substring separated by an "\n," such an entry includes the window title, the default file extensions, and some OLE registration database values.

Another Doc/View resource type is a per-document menu. When the user switches activation from one document type to another, MFC has the capability to switch to a new menu. This capability is useful when different command sets are needed for different document types.

There is also the capability to implement a per-document accelerator table. Although the AppWizard doesn't create one for you, it's a simple matter to create your own. The only trick is that you must use the right name when you define a document-specific set of accelerator keystrokes.

Document-type-specific icons are another type of resource used in Doc/View support. These are particularly useful in an MDI Doc/View application. When a particular document is minimized, its icon is displayed.

Now that you've seen the basic components of MFC's Doc/View support, you're undoubtedly ready to look at some working examples. Among MFC programmers, the classic sample program is SCRIBBLE, which Microsoft includes with Visual C++ (look in \MSVC20\SAMPLES\ MFC\SCRIBBLE). Among the sample programs that accompany this book, we provide two more examples. HASAVIEW is a single-document application, and HASVIEWS is a multiple-document application. These two sample programs are described in more detail later in this chapter.

Before we get to them, however, we're going to take a detour and explore a tool that will help you learn about MFC as well as help you find bugs in the MFC software that you write. We are referring to the debugger. If you're a developer who uses debuggers all the time, you might have already figured out how to use the tool that's built into the Visual C++ IDE. If not, we hope you find our mini-tutorial helpful for learning the basics of this useful tool.

One of the most effective ways to learn about a large piece of software, such as the MFC library, is to look at the software's source code. But that can sometimes be as interesting as looking at someone else's vacation photos. Somehow, someone else's experiences — whether they're having fun at play or having fun at work writing code — aren't as interesting as your own.

There is, however, a marvelous tool that can help bring someone else's software to life: a source-level debugger. We think it's a shame that many developers don't use this tool, because it can work wonders in finding certain categories of bugs. But to be fully effective, you must first learn to use it, and then regularly practice using it. If you're among the two-thirds of developers who avoid using a debugger, read the next section to learn how you can use one to explore MFC's murky depths.

Exploring Doc/View with the Debugger

When speaking at conferences or conducting workshops, we often ask groups of programmers about their experiences using source-level debugging tools. In general, we find that only about one-third of programmers use such tools on a regular basis. If you're among that group, you've probably already discovered the Visual C++ debugger and have mapped your knowledge of other tools to this one. If so, you might choose to only skim this section.

This section is written for the majority of programmers, who generally avoid using source-level debugging tools. We're going to proceed slowly, giving tips on what makes for a successful debugging session.

We're also going to cover the use of common keyboard commands, a fairly small set that provides a lot of capabilities. If you've been intimidated by source-level debugging tools before, we invite you to spend a little time learning how to use a tool that could save you a tremendous amount of time in the long run. And who knows, you might even find that it's fun.

Diving into a Debugger

Using a debugger to trace into a large piece of software, such as the MFC class library, is a lot like scuba diving. If you've never been scuba diving, you wear a body suit that keeps you warm and dry. You carry bulky air tanks on your back, and you put a two-way *regulator* in your mouth that provides air when you inhale and leaks air when you exhale. Getting used to breathing while underwater takes some time, because even the best (nonfish) swimmers are in the habit of holding their breath underwater. Finally, you wear equipment for buoyancy control, including weights around your waist to keep you down and an inflatable life vest to bring you up.

Like swimming in unknown waters, you can immediately become disoriented when you first trace into someone else's code. So, you must move carefully. If you wander too far, you'll be hopelessly lost in all the twisting, turning passages. Although a debugger might not put you in physical danger — for example, you won't run out of oxygen — the ensuing discomfort and downright claustrophobia might make you swear off any future debugging adventures. That would be too bad, because there's so much the debugger can help you learn.

Simple Debugging: Tracing into WinMain()

For your first debugging trips, plan your location very carefully. A good place to start is at WinMain( ), the MFC function that serves as the entry point for every program. It happens to be located in \MSVC20\MFC\SRC\WINMAIN.CPP. Try tracing from there into the call to your own InitInstance( ) function. It's an easy trip to make. The added advantage is that familiarity with this section of code — and its various side passages — will help you better understand the operation of MFC in particular and of Windows in general.

To get completely comfortable with this section of MFC code, you must make several trips through WinMain( ). On the first trip, go directly from WinMain( )'s first instruction to the point at which it calls InitInstance( ). To help you make this trip, Listing 15-1 contains a fragment of WinMain( ), in which we've added comments to direct you away from trouble and toward your destination. We mark the way by using the old-fashioned /*...*/ comments, which should be easy to distinguish from the new-style // comments used by the MFC developers. Be forewarned that things are never as they first appear. Innocent-looking macros can lead to large, unexpected side routes.

Listing 15-1
A Diving Map of WinMain's Inland Waterways

```
/*
 * Diver - the F8 key starts the debugger and takes you here.
 */
_tWinMain(HINSTANCE hInstance, HINSTANCE hPrevInstance,
          LPTSTR lpCmdLine, int nCmdShow)
{
    /*
     * Diver - Innocent macro
     */
    ASSERT(hPrevInstance == NULL);

    /*
     * Diver - Place cursor on variable and press Shift-F9
     *            for "Quick Watch" support. See how the value
     *            changes as the instruction is executed. But only
     *            when variable is "in-scope", that is, when
     *            execution control is within function braces.
     */
    int nReturnCode = -1;

    /*
     *Diver - Somewhat involved function. Avoid on first dive.
     */
    CWinApp* pApp = AfxGetApp();

    // AFX internal initialization
    /*
     * Diver - Very involved function, avoid on first dive. But
     *            come back and trace through to see all of the things
     *            that the MFC library does for you to fine-tune
     *            itself to work well with Windows.
```

```
    */
    if (!AfxWinInit(hInstance, hPrevInstance, lpCmdLine, nCmdShow))
        goto InitFailure;

    // App global initializations (rare)
                        /*
    ASSERT_VALID(pApp);  * Diver - Warning! Very complex macro.
                        */
    if (!pApp->InitApplication())  /* Diver - Simple function. */
        goto InitFailure;
    ASSERT_VALID(pApp);

    // Perform specific initializations
    /*
     * Diver - Trace into function on first dive by pressing F8 key.
     */
    if (!pApp->InitInstance())
    {
        if (pApp->m_pMainWnd != NULL)
        {
            TRACE0("Warning: Destroying non-NULL m_pMainWnd\n");
            pApp->m_pMainWnd->DestroyWindow();
        }
        nReturnCode = pApp->ExitInstance();
        goto InitFailure;
    }
    ASSERT_VALID(pApp);

    /*
     * Diver - On later dive, trace into following function to
     *          see message loop and idle-time handling provided
     *          by MFC.
     */
    nReturnCode = pApp->Run();
    ASSERT_VALID(pApp);

InitFailure:
    AfxWinTerm();
    return nReturnCode;
}
```

You don't have to look far to find the Visual C++ debugger, because it's provided as part of the development environment. Although you might have worked with other compilers that have separate debuggers — including earlier Microsoft compilers — that's not the case here. As you trace into various source files, those files are displayed in regular text editing windows. You have to be careful to avoid making changes that you don't intend to make — particularly to the MFC source files themselves! To start debugging, you only have to open an MFC project.

DEBUGGER KEYBOARD COMMANDS

To operate the debugger, you can either issue keyboard commands or choose menu items. Our personal preference is for keyboard commands, because they are faster and easier to use, once you've learned them. In particular, one debug command — setting a breakpoint with F9 — has no easy menu equivalent. (Instead of a simple menu command, you have to work with a clumsy dialog.)

For your first debugging session, all you need are three debugging commands: F5, F8, and F10. You can get started with just this small set because these are the primary commands for controlling program execution. Table 15-2 summarizes these and a few other commands that we like to use. Let's take a moment to discuss these three keys.

Table 15-2

Commonly Used Debugger Keyboard Commands

Keystroke	Description
F5	Go. Run the program until it terminates or until a breakpoint is encountered.
F8	Step Into. Single step an individual source code instruction. When an instruction is a function call, step into that function to its first instruction. (*Stay at the same depth or go deeper.*)
F9	Toggle Breakpoint at Cursor. Turns breakpoints on or off at the current keyboard cursor position.
F10	Step Over. Single step an individual source code instruction. Treat a function call like any other source code instruction — execute it and continue to next one. (*Swim no deeper.*)
Shift-F9	Quick Watch. Display the value of the variable under the keyboard cursor.
Shift-F7	Step Out. Run the program until control is returned to the caller of the current function. (This is the opposite of Step Into. In scuba terms, inflate the life vest a wee bit to float out of the current function.)

The F8 key is the Step-Into key. When you press this key, the debugger executes one source-level instruction. That's the *step* part of the command. As far as stepping *into* anything, that happens when the source-level instruction contains a function call. In that case, control is passed to the called function. In scuba terms, think of this as staying at the same depth (for noncall instructions) or going deeper (for calling functions). Figure 15-4 shows the relationship between the Step-Into command and a related command, Step-Over.

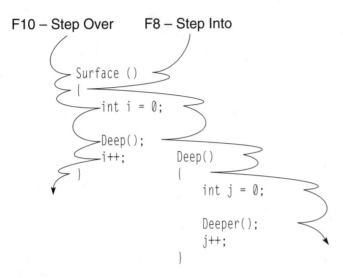

Figure 15-4
The relationships between two debugger step commands and function calls.

Pressing the F10 key issues the Step-Over command. Like the Step-Into command, this command causes the debugger to execute individual source-level instructions. It differs from Step-Into when the source code contains a function call. In that case, the call is executed but control is maintained within the current function. In scuba terms, this is the *swim-no-deeper* command.

The F5 key is the Go! command. It tells the debugger to start (or resume) normal program execution. If you become hopelessly confused, this command lets the program continue running. Be careful, though. Control won't be returned to the debugger until either of two conditions occurs: the program terminates, or a breakpoint is encountered.

This isn't really a problem when you're just casually tracing into some program, because it's quite common to start a program a dozen times or more during a debugging session. But it can cause difficulties if your attention is focused on some particularly interesting problem in some dark corner of a program. If you get lost, you might have to do a lot of work to re-create that scenario during another debugging session.

Now would be a good time to stop reading and to start experimenting with using the debugger to trace through WinMain( )'s execution. You'll use a combination of the three keys we've just described. In particular, the F8 (Step-Into) command key starts the debugger (there's a momentary pause when the debugger first starts) and steps you into WinMain( ). A small, yellow arrow in the left margin shows the instruction that's about to be executed. When you are just starting the debugger, don't press the F5 (Go!) key unless you've set a break point. We'll show you how to do that in a moment.

Another useful command is the Step-Out command, which is issued with the Shift-F7 key. When you're tracing into called functions, you sometimes go too far. Or, you might slip into a set of twisting, turning calls that MFC packs into some of its macros. That's when the Step-Out command is particularly useful. This command is a complementary function to Step-Into. It tells the debugger to continue program execution until control is returned to the function that called the current function. It can help you escape some otherwise too-tight corners.

Several commands let you define *breakpoints*. As the name suggests, these are places in your program where execution automatically stops. Judicious use of breakpoints is an important skill to master when using a debugger. A bit later in this section, we'll identify some breakpoints you can set to help you learn more about MFC's Doc/View classes. One way you can define breakpoints is by selecting the Debug|Breakpoints... menu command and fussing with the ensuing dialog box. This is the only way to access all six types of breakpoints that Visual C++ supports.

The quickest way to access the most common type of breakpoint, Break At Location, is by pressing the F9 command key. Incidentally, this key command isn't referenced in any menu item, so it will be harder to remember than the other commands we're discussing in this section. But it's worth whatever trouble it takes for you to remember it, because it's so much faster than using the dialog box.

Setting breakpoints can be a little quirky because of the relationship between source code instructions and machine code instructions. You can position the cursor anywhere in a source file, but not every source line has associated machine code instructions. If the debugger is running when you set a breakpoint, the debugger places the breakpoint at the next valid source instruction.

However, in some cases, you'll set a breakpoint when the debugger isn't running. Although the Visual C++ tools will let you do this, when the debugger starts up, it scans all breakpoints and modifies those that don't fall on valid breakpoint lines. To let you know that it has made these changes, you'll see a message like the example shown in Figure 15-5. Don't be alarmed; the debugger is just letting you know that it has made some changes for you.

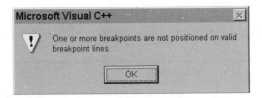

Figure 15-5
The debugger displays this message on start-up to let you know that it has moved some breakpoints for you.

Another useful command is Quick Watch, which you issue by pressing Shift-F9. This command asks the debugger to display the contents of a memory location. You specify which one to show by moving the keyboard cursor within the bounds of a variable name. When you press Shift-F9, a window is opened to show you the current values. Incidentally, you can only read local variables when program execution has stopped in such a way that the variables are still in scope. If it's not in scope, the debugger tells you that your symbol could not be found.

DIVING INTO THE DOC/VIEW CLASSES

Table 15-3 provides some suggestions about where you can set breakpoints to learn more about how MFC's Doc/View support works. You can set these breakpoints for any Doc/View program, including this chapter's two sample programs, HASAVIEW and HASVIEWS. Or, you can start the AppWizard code generator and have it spin you a new program.

Regardless of which MFC sample you choose, you can learn a lot by tracing through the MFC source files. You'll see how the Microsoft developers make use of the ASSERT( ) macro to validate assumptions that they've made in their code. You'll also see extensive use of the ASSERT_VALID( ) macro to ensure that a pointer references a valid piece of memory. In many cases, an assertion will stop you cold. It may take some time to figure out why you were stopped, but once you fix the problem, the result is that you have made your software more robust.

Table 15-3

Suggested Locations for Setting Breakpoints When Diving into the Doc/View Classes with the Debugger

Function	Source File	Comments
CWinApp:: AddDocTemplate()	APPUI.CPP	Shows how CWinApp adds a new document type to its CPtrList list of document templates.
CWinApp::OnFileNew()	APPDLG.CPP	Shows how CWinApp walks its list of templates to choose a particular file type.
CMultiDocTemplate constructor	DOCMULTI.CPP	Shows how the document template loads a menu and an accelerator resource for use by files of a particular type.
CMDIFrameWnd:: LoadFrame()	WINMDI.CPP	Shows the similarities between an MDI frame and a regular frame window.
CFrameWnd:: LoadFrame()	WINFRM.CPP	Shows the key elements of window creation, especially the use of resource data (the string table, the menus, the icons) and the use of the Windows API window class. Provides many opportunities to examine strings using the Shift-F9 Quickwatch command. Warning: This involves miles of passages, so be sure to plan several trips to cover all aspects.
CWinApp:: OnFileOpen()	APPDLG.CPP	Shows how the framework fetches a filename for you. And if you trace through the various OpenDocumentFile() functions, you'll see much of the default object creation code at work. In particular, the multiple-document implementation lets you see a lot of dynamic object creation — that is, calls to CObject::CreateObject(). This is the virtual constructor that we've mentioned in this chapter.

You'll also pick up new techniques that you can use in your own programs. For example, MFC uses data types in ways that you might not otherwise encounter — for example, CString, POSITION, and TCHAR for mixing ASCII and Unicode support, and CDumpContext in Dump( ) member functions. And you'll encounter various functions — such as AfxMessageBox( ) — that are quite useful but might otherwise be difficult to learn about.

If you've found some satisfaction in using the debugger to explore MFC's shallower regions, perhaps you'll be encouraged to use this tool more often. We hope this happens, because it's only by use that you acquire greater skill with the debugger. Over time, you'll instinctively learn when it makes sense to rely on a debugger to inspect a particular piece of code.

Now, let's take a look at our sample Doc/View applications.

Two Doc/View Samples

To really show how Doc/View operates, we needed a program that worked with some data. So, we added Doc/View support to our FILELIST program from Chapter 13. The actual approach we used was to run AppWizard to build a Doc/View framework. Then, using the magic of cut-and-paste, we used the FILELIST source files to create our new sample programs.

We created two versions of the Doc/View FILELIST. One is HASAVIEW, a single-document application, which is shown in Figure 15-6. The other one, HASVIEWS, is the multiple-document version, which is shown in Figure 15-7. Because the two programs are virtually identical, this section of the book includes the listings for only the more complicated, multiple-document version, HASVIEWS. The source files for the single-document version are included with the source files that accompany this book. The program files for the MDI version, HASVIEWS, appear in Listings 15-2 through 15-9.

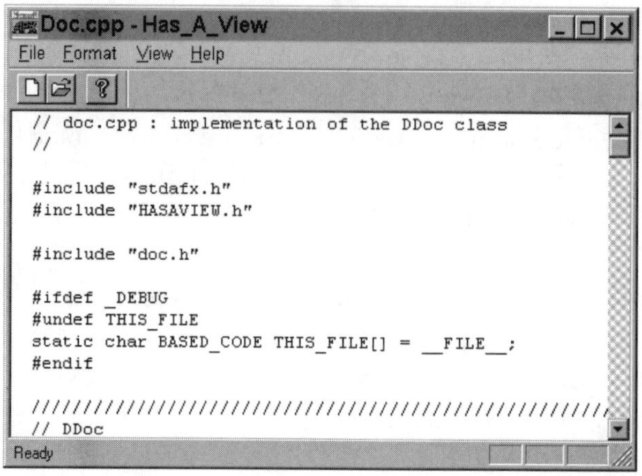

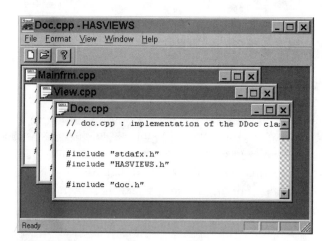

Figure 15-6

HASAVIEW, a single-document version of FILELIST.

Figure 15-7

HASVIEWS, a multiple-document version of FILELIST.

Listing 15-2

HASVIEWS.H

```
// HASVIEWS.h : main header file for the HASVIEWS application
//

#ifndef __AFXWIN_H__
    #error include 'stdafx.h' before including this file for PCH
#endif
```

```
#include "resource.h"        // main symbols

/////////////////////////////////////////////////////////////////////////
// DApp:
// See HASVIEWS.cpp for the implementation of this class
//

class DApp : public CWinApp
{
public:
    DApp();

// Overrides
    // ClassWizard generated virtual function overrides
    //{{AFX_VIRTUAL(DApp)
    public:
    virtual BOOL InitInstance();
    //}}AFX_VIRTUAL

// Implementation

    //{{AFX_MSG(DApp)
    afx_msg void OnAppAbout();
        // NOTE - the ClassWizard will add and remove member functions here.
        //    DO NOT EDIT what you see in these blocks of generated code !
    //}}AFX_MSG
    DECLARE_MESSAGE_MAP()
};


/////////////////////////////////////////////////////////////////////////
```

Listing 15-3
HASVIEWS.CPP

```
// HASVIEWS.cpp : Defines the class behaviors for the application.
//

#include "stdafx.h"
#include "HASVIEWS.h"

#include "mainfrm.h"
#include "doc.h"
#include "view.h"

#ifdef _DEBUG
#undef THIS_FILE
static char BASED_CODE THIS_FILE[] = __FILE__;
#endif
```

```
///////////////////////////////////////////////////////////////////////////
// DApp

BEGIN_MESSAGE_MAP(DApp, CWinApp)
    //{{AFX_MSG_MAP(DApp)
    ON_COMMAND(ID_APP_ABOUT, OnAppAbout)
        // NOTE - the ClassWizard will add and remove mapping macros here.
        //     DO NOT EDIT what you see in these blocks of generated code!
    //}}AFX_MSG_MAP
    // Standard file based document commands
    ON_COMMAND(ID_FILE_NEW, CWinApp::OnFileNew)
    ON_COMMAND(ID_FILE_OPEN, CWinApp::OnFileOpen)
END_MESSAGE_MAP()


///////////////////////////////////////////////////////////////////////////
// DApp construction

DApp::DApp()
{
    // TODO: add construction code here,
    // Place all significant initialization in InitInstance
}


///////////////////////////////////////////////////////////////////////////
// The one and only DApp object

DApp theApp;

///////////////////////////////////////////////////////////////////////////
// DApp initialization

BOOL DApp::InitInstance()
{
    // Standard initialization
    // If you are not using these features and wish to reduce the size
    //  of your final executable, you should remove from the following
    //  the specific initialization routines you do not need.

    Enable3dControls();

    LoadStdProfileSettings();  // Load standard INI file options

    // Register the application's document templates.  Document templates
    //  serve as the connection between documents, frame windows and views.

    CMultiDocTemplate* pDocTemplate;
    pDocTemplate = new CMultiDocTemplate(
        IDR_HASVIETYPE,
        RUNTIME_CLASS(DDoc),
        RUNTIME_CLASS(CMDIChildWnd),    // standard MDI child frame
        RUNTIME_CLASS(DView));
    AddDocTemplate(pDocTemplate);
```

```
    // create main MDI Frame window
    DMainFrame* pMainFrame = new DMainFrame;
    if (!pMainFrame->LoadFrame(IDR_MAINFRAME))
        return FALSE;
    m_pMainWnd = pMainFrame;

    // Create a new (empty) document
    // [HASVIEWS] - Disabled since an empty view makes no sense.
    OnFileNew();

    if (m_lpCmdLine[0] != '\0')
    {
        // TODO: add command line processing here
    }

    // The main window has been initialized, so show and update it.
    pMainFrame->ShowWindow(m_nCmdShow);
    pMainFrame->UpdateWindow();

    return TRUE;
}

/////////////////////////////////////////////////////////////////////////////
// CAboutDlg dialog used for App About

class CAboutDlg : public CDialog
{
public:
    CAboutDlg();

// Dialog Data
    //{{AFX_DATA(CAboutDlg)
    enum { IDD = IDD_ABOUTBOX };
    //}}AFX_DATA

// Implementation
protected:
    virtual void DoDataExchange(CDataExchange* pDX);    // DDX/DDV support
    //{{AFX_MSG(CAboutDlg)
        // No message handlers
    //}}AFX_MSG
    DECLARE_MESSAGE_MAP()
};

CAboutDlg::CAboutDlg() : CDialog(CAboutDlg::IDD)
{
    //{{AFX_DATA_INIT(CAboutDlg)
    //}}AFX_DATA_INIT
}

void CAboutDlg::DoDataExchange(CDataExchange* pDX)
{
    CDialog::DoDataExchange(pDX);
```

```
        //{{AFX_DATA_MAP(CAboutDlg)
        //}}AFX_DATA_MAP
    }

    BEGIN_MESSAGE_MAP(CAboutDlg, CDialog)
        //{{AFX_MSG_MAP(CAboutDlg)
            // No message handlers
        //}}AFX_MSG_MAP
    END_MESSAGE_MAP()

    // App command to run the dialog
    void DApp::OnAppAbout()
    {
        CAboutDlg aboutDlg;
        aboutDlg.DoModal();
    }


    /////////////////////////////////////////////////////////////////////////
    // DApp commands
```

Listing 15-4
MAINFRM.H

```
// mainfrm.h : interface of the DMainFrame class
//
/////////////////////////////////////////////////////////////////////////

class DMainFrame : public CMDIFrameWnd
{
    DECLARE_DYNAMIC(DMainFrame)
public:
    DMainFrame();

// Attributes
public:
// ============= Begin Attributes formerly in FILELIST =============
    COLORREF        d_crForeground; // Foreground text color.
    COLORREF        d_crBackground; // Background text color.
// ============= End Attributes formerly in FILELIST =============

// Operations
public:
    void InitColors();

// Overrides
    // ClassWizard generated virtual function overrides
    //{{AFX_VIRTUAL(DMainFrame)
    //}}AFX_VIRTUAL

// Implementation
public:
```

```
    virtual ~DMainFrame();
#ifdef _DEBUG
    virtual void AssertValid() const;
    virtual void Dump(CDumpContext& dc) const;
#endif

protected:  // control bar embedded members
    CStatusBar  m_wndStatusBar;
    CToolBar    m_wndToolBar;

// Generated message map functions
protected:
    //{{AFX_MSG(DMainFrame)
    afx_msg int OnCreate(LPCREATESTRUCT lpCreateStruct);
    afx_msg void OnWinIniChange(LPCTSTR lpszSection);
    //}}AFX_MSG
    DECLARE_MESSAGE_MAP()
};

/////////////////////////////////////////////////////////////////////////
```

Listing 15-5
MAINFRM.CPP

```
// mainfrm.cpp : implementation of the DMainFrame class
//

#include "stdafx.h"
#include "HASVIEWS.h"

#include "mainfrm.h"

#ifdef _DEBUG
#undef THIS_FILE
static char BASED_CODE THIS_FILE[] = __FILE__;
#endif

/////////////////////////////////////////////////////////////////////////
// DMainFrame

IMPLEMENT_DYNAMIC(DMainFrame, CMDIFrameWnd)

BEGIN_MESSAGE_MAP(DMainFrame, CMDIFrameWnd)
    //{{AFX_MSG_MAP(DMainFrame)
        // NOTE - the ClassWizard will add and remove mapping macros here.
        //    DO NOT EDIT what you see in these blocks of generated code !
    ON_WM_CREATE()
    ON_WM_WININICHANGE()
    //}}AFX_MSG_MAP
END_MESSAGE_MAP()
```

```
/////////////////////////////////////////////////////////////////////////
// arrays of IDs used to initialize control bars

// toolbar buttons - IDs are command buttons
static UINT BASED_CODE buttons[] =
{
    // same order as in the bitmap 'toolbar.bmp'
    ID_FILE_NEW,
    ID_FILE_OPEN,
        ID_SEPARATOR,
    ID_APP_ABOUT,
};

static UINT BASED_CODE indicators[] =
{
    ID_SEPARATOR,            // status line indicator
    ID_INDICATOR_CAPS,
    ID_INDICATOR_NUM,
    ID_INDICATOR_SCRL,
};

/////////////////////////////////////////////////////////////////////////
// DMainFrame construction/destruction

DMainFrame::DMainFrame()
{
}

DMainFrame::~DMainFrame()
{
}

int DMainFrame::OnCreate(LPCREATESTRUCT lpCreateStruct)
{
    if (CMDIFrameWnd::OnCreate(lpCreateStruct) == -1)
        return -1;

    if (!m_wndToolBar.Create(this) ||
        !m_wndToolBar.LoadBitmap(IDR_MAINFRAME) ||
        !m_wndToolBar.SetButtons(buttons,
          sizeof(buttons)/sizeof(UINT)))
    {
        TRACE0("Failed to create toolbar\n");
        return -1;      // fail to create
    }

    if (!m_wndStatusBar.Create(this) ||
        !m_wndStatusBar.SetIndicators(indicators,
          sizeof(indicators)/sizeof(UINT)))
    {
        TRACE0("Failed to create status bar\n");
        return -1;      // fail to create
    }
```

```
    // TODO: Delete these three lines if you don't want the toolbar to
    //   be dockable
    m_wndToolBar.EnableDocking(CBRS_ALIGN_ANY);
    EnableDocking(CBRS_ALIGN_ANY);
    DockControlBar(&m_wndToolBar);

    // TODO: Remove this if you don't want tool tips
    m_wndToolBar.SetBarStyle(m_wndToolBar.GetBarStyle() |
        CBRS_TOOLTIPS | CBRS_FLYBY);

    // [HASVIEWS] - Initialize application settings.
    InitColors();

    return 0;
}

/////////////////////////////////////////////////////////////////////////////
// DMainFrame helper functions
void DMainFrame::InitColors()
{
    d_crForeground = GetSysColor(COLOR_WINDOWTEXT);
    d_crBackground = GetSysColor(COLOR_WINDOW);
}

/////////////////////////////////////////////////////////////////////////////
// DMainFrame diagnostics

#ifdef _DEBUG
void DMainFrame::AssertValid() const
{
    CMDIFrameWnd::AssertValid();
}

void DMainFrame::Dump(CDumpContext& dc) const
{
    CMDIFrameWnd::Dump(dc);
}

#endif //_DEBUG

/////////////////////////////////////////////////////////////////////////////
// DMainFrame message handlers

void DMainFrame::OnWinIniChange(LPCTSTR lpszSection)
{
    CFrameWnd::OnWinIniChange(lpszSection);

    // Get new background & foreground colors in case these have changed.
    InitColors();

    // Force redraw of window.
    Invalidate();
}
```

Listing 15-6
VIEW.H

```
// view.h : interface of the DView class
//
/////////////////////////////////////////////////////////////////////////////

class DMainFrame;

class DView : public CView
{
protected: // create from serialization only
    DView();
    DECLARE_DYNCREATE(DView)

// Attributes
public:
    DDoc* GetDocument();
    DMainFrame* GetFrame();
// ============= Begin Attributes formerly in FILELIST =============
    BOOL           d_bTabs;        // Respect tabs or not.
    CFontDialog * d_pSetFont;     // Ptr to Font Picker dialog.
    CFont   *     d_pFont;        // Ptr to CFont object.
    LOGFONT        d_lf;           // Current logical font.
    LPINT          d_pnTabs;       // Array of tab settings.
    int            d_cyLineHeight; // Height of one line of text.
    int            d_clHeight;     // Window height line count.
    int            d_iTopLine;     // Index of top-most line.
    int            d_cyClient;     // Window client area height.
    int            d_cxLeftMargin; // Margin to left of text.
// ============= End Attributes formerly in FILELIST =============

// Operations
public:
    BOOL CreateNewFont();
    void ResetScrollValues();

// Overrides
    // ClassWizard generated virtual function overrides
    //{{AFX_VIRTUAL(DView)
    public:
    virtual void OnDraw(CDC* pDC);   // overridden to draw this view
    protected:
    virtual void OnUpdate(CView* pSender, LPARAM lHint, CObject* pHint);
    //}}AFX_VIRTUAL

// Implementation
public:
    virtual ~DView();
#ifdef _DEBUG
    virtual void AssertValid() const;
    virtual void Dump(CDumpContext& dc) const;
#endif

protected:
```

```
// Generated message map functions
protected:
    //{{AFX_MSG(DView)
    afx_msg void CmdFormatFont();
    afx_msg void CmdFormatTabs();
    afx_msg void UpdFormatTabs(CCmdUI* pCmdUI);
    afx_msg int OnCreate(LPCREATESTRUCT lpCreateStruct);
    afx_msg void OnKeyDown(UINT nChar, UINT nRepCnt, UINT nFlags);
    afx_msg void OnSize(UINT nType, int cx, int cy);
    afx_msg void OnVScroll(UINT nSBCode, UINT nPos, CScrollBar* pScrollBar);
    //}}AFX_MSG
    DECLARE_MESSAGE_MAP()
};

#ifndef _DEBUG  // debug version in view.cpp
inline DDoc* DView::GetDocument()
    { return (DDoc*)m_pDocument; }
#endif

///////////////////////////////////////////////////////////////////////////
```

Listing 15-7
VIEW.CPP

```
// view.cpp : implementation of the DView class
//

#include "stdafx.h"
#include "HASVIEWS.h"

#include "doc.h"
#include "view.h"
#include "mainfrm.h"

#ifdef _DEBUG
#undef THIS_FILE
static char BASED_CODE THIS_FILE[] = __FILE__;
#endif

///////////////////////////////////////////////////////////////////////////
// DView

IMPLEMENT_DYNCREATE(DView, CView)

BEGIN_MESSAGE_MAP(DView, CView)
    //{{AFX_MSG_MAP(DView)
    ON_COMMAND(ID_FORMAT_FONT, CmdFormatFont)
    ON_COMMAND(ID_FORMAT_TABS, CmdFormatTabs)
    ON_UPDATE_COMMAND_UI(ID_FORMAT_TABS, UpdFormatTabs)
```

```
        ON_WM_CREATE()
        ON_WM_KEYDOWN()
        ON_WM_SIZE()
        ON_WM_VSCROLL()
        //}}AFX_MSG_MAP
END_MESSAGE_MAP()

/////////////////////////////////////////////////////////////////////////////
// DView construction/destruction

DView::DView()
{
    // Init all data members to a known value.
    d_pFont         = 0;

    // Init desired font.
    memset (&d_lf, 0, sizeof(LOGFONT));

    // Initial font face name is Courier New.
    lstrcpy (d_lf.lfFaceName, _T("Courier New"));

    // Initial font size is 10 pt.
    CWindowDC dc(NULL);
    int cyPixels = dc.GetDeviceCaps(LOGPIXELSY);
    d_lf.lfHeight = (-1) * MulDiv(10, cyPixels, 72);

    // Initial tab setting is OFF.
    d_bTabs = TRUE;

    // Tab table initially empty (set when font selected).
    d_pnTabs = 0;
}

DView::~DView()
{
    if (d_pFont) delete d_pFont;
    if (d_pnTabs) delete [] d_pnTabs;
    if (d_pSetFont) delete d_pSetFont;
}

/////////////////////////////////////////////////////////////////////////////
//
// DView helper functions.

//-----------------------------------------
// CreateNewFont - Creates new CFont for use in drawing text.
BOOL DView::CreateNewFont()
{
    // Delete any previous font.
    if (d_pFont)
        delete d_pFont;

    // Create a new font
    d_pFont = new CFont();
```

```
    if (!d_pFont) return FALSE;
    d_pFont->CreateFontIndirect(&d_lf);

    // Calculate font height
    CClientDC dc(this);
    TEXTMETRIC tm;
    dc.SelectObject(d_pFont);
    dc.GetTextMetrics(&tm);
    d_cyLineHeight = tm.tmHeight + tm.tmExternalLeading;

    // Calculate left margin.
    d_cxLeftMargin = tm.tmAveCharWidth * 2;

    // Rebuild tab setting table.
    if (d_pnTabs) delete [] d_pnTabs;
    d_pnTabs = new INT[g_nTabCount];
    for (int i=0; i<g_nTabCount; i++)
    {
        d_pnTabs[i] = d_cxLeftMargin + (i * g_nTabStop * tm.tmAveCharWidth);
    }

    // Recalculate scroll bar info.
    ResetScrollValues();

    return TRUE;
}

//-----------------------------------------
// ResetScrollValues - Adjust scrolling for window size changes.
void DView::ResetScrollValues()
{
    // Set count of lines in window height.
    d_clHeight = d_cyClient / d_cyLineHeight;

    // [HASAVIEW] Get Doc pointer in type-safe way.
    DDoc * pDoc = (DDoc *)GetDocument();
    ASSERT(pDoc->IsKindOf(RUNTIME_CLASS(DDoc)));

    // Hide scroll bars when not needed.
    if (pDoc->d_cLines <= d_clHeight)
    {
        SetScrollRange(SB_VERT, 0, 0, TRUE);
        d_iTopLine = 0;
        return;
    }

    // Adjust scroll range for new window size.
    SetScrollRange (SB_VERT, 0, pDoc->d_cLines - d_clHeight, TRUE);

    // Adjust scroll thumb position.
    SetScrollPos(SB_VERT, d_iTopLine, TRUE);
}
```

```
//////////////////////////////////////////////////////////////////////
// DView drawing

void DView::OnDraw(CDC* pDC)
{
    DDoc* pDoc = GetDocument();
    ASSERT_VALID(pDoc);

    // Select current font into DC.
    pDC->SelectObject(d_pFont);

    // Fetch pointer to frame window, which holds desired drawing colors.
    DMainFrame * pFrame = GetFrame();

    // Select text color.
    pDC->SetTextColor(pFrame->d_crForeground );

    // Select text background color.
    pDC->SetBkColor(pFrame->d_crBackground);

    // Figure out which lines to draw.
    int iLine = d_iTopLine;
    int cLastLine = d_iTopLine + d_clHeight + 1;
    cLastLine = min (cLastLine, pDoc->d_cLines);

    // Loop through client area coordinates to draw.
    int cyLine = 0;
    while (iLine < cLastLine)
    {
        // Draw a line of text.
        LPTSTR lp = pDoc->d_saTextInfo[iLine].pText;
        int    cc = pDoc->d_saTextInfo[iLine].ccLen;

        // Drawing function depends on 'respect tabs' setting.
        if (d_bTabs && d_pnTabs != 0)
        {
            pDC->TabbedTextOut(d_cxLeftMargin, cyLine, lp, cc,
                               g_nTabCount, d_pnTabs, 0);
        }
        else
        {
            pDC->TextOut(d_cxLeftMargin, cyLine, lp, cc);
        }

        // Increment various counts.
        cyLine += d_cyLineHeight;
        iLine++;
    }
}


//////////////////////////////////////////////////////////////////////
// DView diagnostics
```

```
#ifdef _DEBUG
void DView::AssertValid() const
{
    CView::AssertValid();
}

void DView::Dump(CDumpContext& dc) const
{
    CView::Dump(dc);
}

DDoc* DView::GetDocument() // non-debug version is inline
{
    ASSERT(m_pDocument->IsKindOf(RUNTIME_CLASS(DDoc)));
    return (DDoc*)m_pDocument;
}
#endif //_DEBUG

DMainFrame* DView::GetFrame()
{
    DMainFrame * pFrame = (DMainFrame *)AfxGetApp()->m_pMainWnd;
    ASSERT(pFrame->IsKindOf(RUNTIME_CLASS(DMainFrame)));
    return pFrame;
}

/////////////////////////////////////////////////////////////////////////////
// DView message handlers

//----------------------------------------
// Handler for Format|Font command message.
void DView::CmdFormatFont()
{
    // Display font picker dialog box.
    int iRet = d_pSetFont->DoModal();

    // Ignore when user clicks [Cancel] button.
    if (iRet != IDOK)
        return;

    // Rebuild font definition based on dialog selection.
    CreateNewFont();

    // Recalculate scroll bar info.
    ResetScrollValues();

    // Request a WM_PAINT message to redraw window.
    Invalidate();
}

//----------------------------------------
// Handler for Format|Tabs command message.
void DView::CmdFormatTabs()
{
```

```
        // Toggle "respect tab" flag.
        d_bTabs = !d_bTabs;

        // Request a WM_PAINT message to redraw window.
        Invalidate();
    }

//-----------------------------------------
// Handler for ON_COMMAND_UPDATE_UI message for Format|Tabs command.
void DView::UpdFormatTabs(CCmdUI* pCmdUI)
{
        // Display a checkmark if user wants to respect tabs.
        int nCheck = (d_bTabs) ? 1 : 0;
        pCmdUI->SetCheck(nCheck);
    }

//-----------------------------------------
// WM_CREATE message handler.
int DView::OnCreate(LPCREATESTRUCT lpCreateStruct)
{
        if (CView::OnCreate(lpCreateStruct) == -1)
            return -1;

        // Create Format.Font... dialog object.
        d_pSetFont = new CFontDialog(&d_lf, CF_SCREENFONTS);
        if (!d_pSetFont)
            return -1;

        // Create initial font object.
        if (!CreateNewFont())
            return -1;

        return 0;
    }

//-----------------------------------------
// WM_KEYDOWN message handler.
void DView::OnKeyDown(UINT nChar, UINT nRepCnt, UINT nFlags)
{
        switch(nChar)
        {
            case VK_HOME:
                // Ctrl+Home means go to start of document.
                if (::GetKeyState(VK_CONTROL) < 0)
                {
                    // Scroll to start of document
                    OnVScroll(SB_TOP, 0, 0);
                }
                break;
            case VK_END:
                // Ctrl+End means go to end of document.
                if (::GetKeyState(VK_CONTROL) < 0)
                {
                    // Scroll to end
                    OnVScroll(SB_BOTTOM, 0, 0);
```

```
            }
            break;
        case VK_UP:
        case VK_LEFT:
            OnVScroll(SB_LINEUP, 0, 0);
            break;
        case VK_DOWN:
        case VK_RIGHT:
            OnVScroll(SB_LINEDOWN, 0, 0);
            break;
        case VK_PRIOR: // [PgUp] key.
            OnVScroll(SB_PAGEUP, 0, 0);
            break;
        case VK_NEXT:  // [PgDn] key.
            OnVScroll(SB_PAGEDOWN, 0, 0);
            break;
    }

    CView::OnKeyDown(nChar, nRepCnt, nFlags);
}


//----------------------------------------
// WM_SIZE message handler.
void DView::OnSize(UINT nType, int cx, int cy)
{
    CView::OnSize(nType, cx, cy);

    // Save client area height.
    d_cyClient = cy;

    // Recalculate scroll bar info.
    ResetScrollValues();
}


//----------------------------------------
// WM_VSCROLL message handler.
void DView::OnVScroll(UINT nSBCode, UINT nPos, CScrollBar* pScrollBar)
{
    // Temporary "new line" value.
    int iTop = d_iTopLine;

    // Temporary copy of document line count.
    int cLines = GetDocument()->d_cLines;

    // Based on particular scroll button clicked, modify top line index.
    switch(nSBCode)
    {
        case SB_BOTTOM:
            iTop = cLines - d_clHeight;
            break;
        case SB_ENDSCROLL:
            break;
        case SB_LINEDOWN:
            iTop++;
            break;
```

```
            case SB_LINEUP:
                iTop-;
                break;
            case SB_PAGEDOWN:
                iTop += d_clHeight;
                break;
            case SB_PAGEUP:
                iTop -= d_clHeight;
                break;
            case SB_THUMBPOSITION:
                iTop = nPos;
                break;
            case SB_THUMBTRACK:
                iTop = nPos;
                break;
            case SB_TOP:
                iTop = 0;
                break;
        }

    // Check range of new index;
    iTop = max (iTop, 0);
    iTop = min (iTop, cLines - d_clHeight);

    // If no change, ignore.
    if (iTop == d_iTopLine) return;

    // Pixels to scroll = (lines to scroll) * height-per-line.
    int cyScroll = (d_iTopLine - iTop) * d_cyLineHeight;

    // Define new top-line value.
     d_iTopLine = iTop;

    // Scroll pixels.
    ScrollWindow(0, cyScroll);

    // Adjust scroll thumb position.
    SetScrollPos(SB_VERT, d_iTopLine, TRUE);

    CView::OnVScroll(nSBCode, nPos, pScrollBar);
    }


//----------------------------------------
// Notification from CDocument that contents have
// changed (due to File|Open or File|New).
void DView::OnUpdate(CView* pSender, LPARAM lHint, CObject* pHint)
{
    // Reset "Index to top line displayed" = top of file.
    d_iTopLine = 0;

    // Recalculate scroll bar info.
    ResetScrollValues();

    // Force repaint.
    Invalidate();
}
```

Listing 15-8
DOC.H

```
// doc.h : interface of the DDoc class
//
/////////////////////////////////////////////////////////////////////////

#include <afxtempl.h> // Connect to CArray template.

// Structure to track lines in text file.
class STRING  // : public CObject
{
  public:
    LPTSTR pText;
    int    ccLen;
};

// This declaration uses the CArray template
// to provide a dynamic array of STRING records.
class StringArray : public CArray <STRING, STRING &>
{
  public:
    StringArray() {}
    STRING& operator=(STRING & s)
                        {m_pData->pText = s.pText;
                         m_pData->ccLen = s.ccLen;
                         return *m_pData;}
};

const int g_nTabCount=25;
const int g_nTabStop=4;

class DDoc : public CDocument
{
protected: // create from serialization only
    DDoc();
    DECLARE_DYNCREATE(DDoc)

// Attributes
public:
// ============ Begin Attributes formerly in FILELIST =============
    LPTSTR         d_lpTextBuffer; // Ptr to text buffer.
    DWORD          d_dwFileLength; // File length.
    StringArray    d_saTextInfo;   // Array of string info.
    int            d_cLines;       // Count of lines in text.
// ============== End Attributes formerly in FILELIST =============

// Operations
public:
    void BuildStringArray();

// Overrides
```

```
        // ClassWizard generated virtual function overrides
        //{{AFX_VIRTUAL(DDoc)
        public:
        virtual BOOL OnNewDocument();
        //}}AFX_VIRTUAL

    // Implementation
    public:
        virtual ~DDoc();
        virtual void Serialize(CArchive& ar);    // overridden for document i/o
    #ifdef _DEBUG
        virtual void AssertValid() const;
        virtual void Dump(CDumpContext& dc) const;
    #endif

    protected:

    // Generated message map functions
    protected:
        //{{AFX_MSG(DDoc)
            // NOTE - the ClassWizard will add and remove member functions here.
            //    DO NOT EDIT what you see in these blocks of generated code !
        //}}AFX_MSG
        DECLARE_MESSAGE_MAP()
    };


    //////////////////////////////////////////////////////////////////////
```

Listing 15-9
DOC.CPP

```
    // doc.cpp : implementation of the DDoc class
    //

    #include "stdafx.h"
    #include "HASVIEWS.h"

    #include "doc.h"

    #ifdef _DEBUG
    #undef THIS_FILE
    static char BASED_CODE THIS_FILE[] = __FILE__;
    #endif

    //////////////////////////////////////////////////////////////////////
    // DDoc

    IMPLEMENT_DYNCREATE(DDoc, CDocument)

    BEGIN_MESSAGE_MAP(DDoc, CDocument)
        //{{AFX_MSG_MAP(DDoc)
```

```
        // NOTE - the ClassWizard will add and remove mapping macros here.
        //    DO NOT EDIT what you see in these blocks of generated code!
    //}}AFX_MSG_MAP
END_MESSAGE_MAP()

/////////////////////////////////////////////////////////////////////////////
// DDoc construction/destruction

DDoc::DDoc()
{
    // Init all data members to a known value.
    d_lpTextBuffer = 0;
    d_dwFileLength = 0;
}


DDoc::~DDoc()
{
    // Free allocated buffer.
    if (d_lpTextBuffer)
    {
        free(d_lpTextBuffer);
    }
}


BOOL DDoc::OnNewDocument()
{
    if (!CDocument::OnNewDocument())
        return FALSE;

    // Free allocated buffer.
    if (d_lpTextBuffer)
    {
        free(d_lpTextBuffer);
        d_lpTextBuffer = 0;
    }

    // Reset file line length counter.
    d_dwFileLength = 0;

    // Reset count of lines.
    d_cLines        = 0;

    // Reset string array size.
    d_saTextInfo.RemoveAll();

    return TRUE;
}


/////////////////////////////////////////////////////////////////////////////
//
// DDoc helper functions.

//----------------------------------------
// BuildStringArray - Parses text file to create a CString array.
```

```
void DDoc::BuildStringArray()
{
    // Scan buffer to calculate line count.
    LPTSTR lpNext = d_lpTextBuffer;
    LPTSTR lpEnd  = d_lpTextBuffer + d_dwFileLength - 1;
    *lpEnd = '\n';
    for (d_cLines = 0; lpNext < lpEnd; d_cLines++, lpNext++)
    {
        // Search for next <CR> character.
        lpNext = strchr(lpNext, '\n');

        // Discontinue if NULL encountered.
        if (lpNext == NULL) break;
    }

    // Set array size.
    d_saTextInfo.SetSize(d_cLines);

    // Scan buffer to build array of pointers & sizes.
    STRING string;
    lpNext = d_lpTextBuffer;
    for (int iLine = 0; iLine < d_cLines; iLine++)
    {
        // Char count for current line.
        string.ccLen = 0;
        string.pText = lpNext;

        // Loop to end-of-line.
        while ((*lpNext != '\n') && (*lpNext != '\r'))
        {
            lpNext++;           // Check next char.
            string.ccLen++;     // Increment length counter.
        }

        // Enter value in array.
        d_saTextInfo[iLine] = string;

        // Skip over <CR> <LF>
        lpNext += (2 * sizeof(TCHAR));
    }
}

///////////////////////////////////////////////////////////////////////
// DDoc serialization

void DDoc::Serialize(CArchive& ar)
{
    if (ar.IsStoring())
    {
        // Should never get here because document files are read-only.
        ASSERT(FALSE);
    }
    else
```

```
        {
            // Free previous buffer contents
            if (d_lpTextBuffer)
            {
                free(d_lpTextBuffer);
                d_lpTextBuffer=0;
            }

            // Fetch CFile for accessing data.
            CFile * pfileData = ar.GetFile();

            // Calculate file size & allocate buffer.
            // Pad to avoid bad address reference.
            d_dwFileLength = pfileData->GetLength() + sizeof(char);
            d_lpTextBuffer = (LPTSTR)malloc (d_dwFileLength);
            if (!d_lpTextBuffer)
            {
                AfxMessageBox(_T("Cannot Allocate Memory For File"));
                return;
            }

            // Read Buffer.
            pfileData->Read((LPVOID)d_lpTextBuffer, d_dwFileLength);

            // Empty buffer array.
            d_saTextInfo.RemoveAll();

            // Scan buffer for text line info.
            BuildStringArray();

    }     /* [if (ar.IsStoring()) ] */
}

/////////////////////////////////////////////////////////////////////////
// DDoc diagnostics

#ifdef _DEBUG
void DDoc::AssertValid() const
{
    CDocument::AssertValid();
}

void DDoc::Dump(CDumpContext& dc) const
{
    CDocument::Dump(dc);
}
#endif //_DEBUG

/////////////////////////////////////////////////////////////////////////
// DDoc commands
```

The hardest part about taking a monolithic program such as FILELIST and converting it for Doc/View support was deciding which part went where. Very little new code was needed; in fact, we were able to delete the code that created the File Open dialog because CWinApp already provides this dialog.

We call FILELIST monolithic because most of the interesting code is in a single object: DMainFrame. Even though it's wrapped within an MFC class, this approach is similar to how C/SDK programs are often organized. When modifying the code for Doc/View support, we had to split some of the basic windowing code between HASVIEW's main frame class and its view class.

Although FILELIST's main frame class does all of its work, the main frame class in HASVIEWS does very little work. Aside from creating the status bar and the button bar (which is done using AppWizard-generated code), HASVIEWS' main window class keeps track of which colors to use when drawing text. Our reason for doing this requires a bit of explanation.

USER PREFERENCES AND THE WM_WININICHANGE MESSAGE

Through the Windows Control Panel, users control quite a few system attributes. These attributes include the fonts that are to be used in various places, and the colors that are to be used for various window elements, including window text. Whenever a change occurs, the system sends a WM_WININICHANGE message. The name of this message comes from the fact that these system attributes used to be stored in the WIN.INI file. (In Windows 95 and Windows NT, such values are stored in a database called the system registry.) On receipt of this message, the frame window queries the system — by calling GetSysColor( ) — to make sure that it has the most up-to-date values.

MFC's frame window class distributes the WM_WININICHANGE message to a wider audience than does Windows itself. Windows only sends this message to the top-level windows in an application. The default handling of CFrameWnd, on the other hand, is to distribute the message to all child windows. The net result is that every window in the system can know when it should query for changes to user-defined preferences.

In spite of the way that MFC distributes this message, HASVIEWS still handles it centrally. We do it this way because, from our perspective, a system attribute such as text color is an application-wide attribute that is best held in a central place. Within your own MFC window classes, it would be perfectly reasonable for you to handle this message on a per-window basis.

HASVIEWS DATA MANAGEMENT

One important practical issue was how to take FILELIST's data — all of which is in its frame window — and distribute it among the different Doc/View objects. To simplify matters, we copied *every* data member to *every* Doc/View class. Then, we commented out the data members that didn't belong in a particular class. By the time you see this code, those lines will have long been erased. But to show you what we mean, here's a code fragment taken from VIEW.H during the conversion process:

```
// ========== Begin Attributes formerly in FILELIST ===========
// -- App
// -- Frame
//     COLORREF     d_crForeground; // Foreground text color.
//     COLORREF     d_crBackground; // Background text color.
// -- Doc
//     LPTSTR       d_lpTextBuffer; // Ptr to text buffer.
//     DWORD        d_dwFileLength; // File length.
//     StringArray  d_saTextInfo;   // Array of string info.
//     int          d_cLines;       // Count of lines in text.
// -- View
    BOOL            d_bTabs;        // Respect tabs or not.
    CFontDialog *   d_pSetFont;     // Ptr to Font Picker dialog.
    CFont   *       d_pFont;        // Ptr to CFont object.
    LOGFONT         d_lf;           // Current logical font.
    LPINT           d_pnTabs;       // Array of tab settings.
    int             d_cyLineHeight; // Height of one line of text.
    int             d_clHeight;     // Window height line count.
    int             d_iTopLine;     // Index of top-most line.
    int             d_cyClient;     // Window client area height.
    int             d_cxLeftMargin; // Margin to left of text.
// -- Not needed
//     CFileDialog * d_pOpenFile; // Ptr to OpenFile dialog.
// ============== End Attributes formerly in FILELIST ==============
```

When deciding which data belongs in a class, a key issue involves splitting data members between view and document classes. From a purist's perspective, views shouldn't have any data. The document should own it all. But the purist's perspective isn't always the best. Instead, the deciding factor should be what works best.

For example, in our sample programs, we put the font (CFont) in the view. Because these are file viewing programs, we made the font a view attribute rather than a document attribute. By doing so, we can allow a user to — for example — open several copies of the same file and have each appear in a different font. But that's not always the "best" way to implement graphical attributes (some might argue that it's not even the best way in these programs).

In certain types of programs, fonts might be considered a document attribute. For example, when a user changes the font for a line of text in a word-processing program, the program normally attaches that attribute to the text. If the file is saved and restored, the attribute remains. And if a second window is opened, the line of text shows the same attribute in both windows. In such cases, the font is clearly a document attribute and, as such, should be stored in the document object.

Doc/View Notification

When the contents of a document have changed, the document class notifies all of its views. This allows each view to do whatever is necessary to revise its contents. The document does this by calling a CView-derived member function, DView::OnUpdate( ). Although we didn't have to write much new code when porting FILELIST to HASVIEWS, we did have to provide this function for our new view class.

Sometimes, the need for notification goes the other way. If a view makes a change to the document's contents, the view must tell the document. This allows the document to notify all the other views that things have changed. It also allows the document to set its "dirty" bit, so that the application can't shut down without properly saving the data. To notify a document that its contents have changed, views call CDocument::UpdateAllViews( ).

You might have noticed that HASVIEWS doesn't call this function. It doesn't need to, because it only reads data files; it doesn't allow any type of editing. But when you're writing Doc/View applications that modify document data, your views must call this function.

With its Document/View architecture, MFC provides a useful means for dividing the work of data storage and the user interface to that data. Not every application can take advantage of Doc/View support, but the ones that can will get a lot of work done for them with very little development effort on your part.

In the next chapter, we're going to explore another issue of importance to every MFC and Windows 95 application: memory. We'll cover all of the available types of memory, and we'll help you make choices related to how and where to store your application's data.

Windows 95 Memory Management

*M*emory is the currency of software. Without sufficient memory, software runs sluggishly or not at all. With enough memory, software operates properly and can do its assigned work. However, determining what is sufficient for a particular program depends on how the program spends the available memory. Although memory prices continue to fall, memory isn't free. Developers must decide on a realistic memory budget for their software, and then build software that can live within its means.

In this chapter, we'll cover every type of memory available to an MFC/Win32 program running on Windows 95. Just as there are many types of currency — for example, U.S. dollars, Swiss francs, and Japanese yen — there are many types of memory. In addition to cataloging what's available, we're going to describe when and why particular types of memory are useful in a typical MFC program. One thing is clear: even simple programs can require a world traveler's portfolio of different types of memory. Table 16-1 summarizes the types of memory available to an MFC/Win32 program.

For the most part, we'll ignore issues related to code, aside from mentioning that an executable file gets loaded as a Win32 memory mapped file. This is not to say that the memory that code occupies is somehow unimportant. On the contrary, issues such as fast start-up and other performance characteristics require a close study of how code occupies memory. For now, however, we focus on memory used for data.

Table 16-1

Types of Memory Available to MFC/Win32 Programs Running on Windows 95

Category	Type	Description
Compiler	Automatic	Local variables or local objects. Created on entry to a function using stack space, and freed on exit.
	Static	Global variables and global objects defined outside the scope of any function. Static data also includes string constants. Variables and objects defined using the *static* keyword also add to the store of static data. The lifetime of such data is the duration that its executable file is resident in memory.
	Class	Class member data refers to variables and objects allocated in an object due to the member data defined for a class. This data lives as long as the object in which it is contained. The data in local (stack) objects is allocated on entry to a function and cleaned up on exit. Data in global (static) objects exists while the executable file is in memory.
	Dynamically Allocated	Memory allocated with calls to malloc() or operator new(). For proper memory management, applications should call free() or operator delete() on all allocated data areas and objects.
Win16 Types	Global Heap	Memory allocated with calls to GlobalAlloc(). In Win16, this corresponds to an allocated segment. In Win32, such objects are allocated in a Win32 process heap [just like LocalAlloc()-allocated memory].
	Local Heap	Memory allocated with calls to LocalAlloc(). In Win16, this corresponds to a subsegment allocation. In Win32, such memory — like GlobalAlloc()-allocated memory — resides in a Win32 private heap.
	Resources	Read-only data defined in resource (.RC) files. Predefined types include menus, dialogs, and string tables. A program can also create custom resource types, using techniques that we'll describe in this chapter.
	Atoms	Strings stored in memory tables and accessed using a unique integer ID. Both the Win16 and the Win32 API include AddAtom(), FindAtom(), and DeleteAtom(). Internally, Windows uses atoms for registered clipboard formats and registered messages. Applications use the global atom table for dynamic data exchange (DDE) support. Global atom routines include GlobalAddAtom() and GlobalFindAtom().
	Window Extra Bytes	Windows creates instance data for each window created. Window extra bytes are private bytes in addition to what the system itself stores. Access these bytes using various Win16/Win32 API that we describe in this chapter.

Category	Type	Description
	Class Extra Bytes	Windows creates instance data for each defined window class (different from the C++/MFC window class). Class extra bytes are private bytes in addition to what the system stores in class data. Access these bytes using various Win16/Win32 API that we describe in this chapter.
	Properties	Attributes dynamically connected to windows. For example, you could create a COLOR attribute and attach a color index. Access by calling Win16/Win32 routines, SetProp(), GetProp(), and RemoveProp().
Win32 Private Memory	Private Pages	Allocates memory in page increments (4K in Windows 95, possibly larger in Windows NT) by calling VirtualAlloc(). This Win32 function also reserves ranges of addresses when called with the MEM_RESERVE flag.
	Win32 Private Heap	Memory allocated with calls to HeapAlloc(). Multiple heaps can be created in a Win32 process by calling HeapCreate(). Get a handle to the process default heap by calling GetProcessHeap().
	Thread Local Storage	Memory allocated on a per-thread basis. There are two types: dynamic thread local storage are allocated by calls to TlsAlloc(). Static thread local storage are allocated by the compiler.
Win32 Shared Memory	Shared Pages	Memory allocated with calls to MapViewOfFile(), which can also create a view into a memory mapped file depending on the file handle parameter. An invalid file handle value (–1) creates shared pages, and a valid file handle creates a memory mapped file.
	Shared Sections	Static (global) variables declared with __declspec(thread) define a shared section in an executable image. When loaded into memory, such variables are shared between processes in both Windows 95 and Windows NT programs.
	Memory Mapped Files	Shared pages connected to a process address space with calls to MapViewOfFile(). Note that this is the same API used to create shared pages.
	Executable Image	Executable (.EXE) file or dynamic link library (.DLL) file in memory.

This chapter is divided into three sections. First, we'll look at operating system memory management, which provides a high-level understanding of some fundamental issues. In the second and third sections of this chapter, we'll explore the topic of dynamic memory allocation, focusing first on private allocation and then on shared allocation. Although this is admittedly an artificial way to divide the subject, it serves to connect an operating system perspective to the types of memory that are available to applications.

In the first section of this chapter, we'll take a quick look at how the Intel-86 processors provide paged, 32-bit memory addressing. Then, we'll describe how Windows 95 uses the Intel memory features to provide a private, per-process address space. Much of the basic operation of memory management under Windows 95 will be familiar to developers who have worked with operating systems such as Unix, OS/2, and Windows NT. Because there is much to be gained by comparisons, we'll compare Windows 95 features to those provided by Windows NT. Our hope is to help developers more easily create Win32 executables that run well on both operating systems. We will complete our look at system memory management with a discussion of how Windows 95 manages cleanup of its various memory areas.

In the second section of this chapter, we'll look at a private memory allocation of a process. We'll start by describing how Win32 provides the capability to manage both the pages of virtual memory and the address space into which pages are mapped. Because the primary allocator for many MFC programs will be the default Visual C++ allocators, we'll next describe how these operate. Of particular interest to most developers should be a description of how to use the diagnostic support built into the various MFC allocators.

We'll continue our discussion of private memory allocation with a look at the various heap APIs that are supported. The Win32 API provides its own heap allocation API — lead by the HeapAlloc( ) function — but it also includes the two sets of Win16 allocation routines. The presence of these two allocation packages, which are lead by GlobalAlloc( ) and LocalAlloc( ), should be reassuring to developers who are familiar with the Win16 API. In particular, they will help in porting Win16 code to Win32. These routines provide at least one feature — support for moveable heap objects — that the native Win32 allocator does not. We will conclude our look at private memory allocation by describing some of the ways in which application memory can be connected to operating system objects. In that vein, two types are of interest: thread local storage and window extra bytes.

In the final section of this chapter, we'll discuss the sharing of memory between processes. Win32 provides interprocess memory sharing features in an unlikely place: as part of its memory mapped file I/O support. When you see how memory mapped files work, you'll find that it elegantly solves two problems at once: interprocess memory sharing and interprocess file sharing. After all, shared pages are shared pages. If the backing store is the system page file, you have shared memory. If the backing store is any other file in the file system, you have memory mapped file I/O. We conclude this section — and this chapter — with a look at creating custom resources (that is, resource types besides the system's predefined types).

Let's begin with a look at memory management from the perspective of the operating system.

System Memory Management

Perhaps the most important improvement that Windows 95 offers over earlier versions of Windows is its flat 32-bit addressing. A Win16 program running on Windows 3.x had to be chopped up into *segments*, blocks of memory ranging in size from 16 bytes to 64K. When building a Win16 program, developers must wrestle with the proper use of compiler keywords such as _near and _far to establish the proper framework for addressing. Developers writing to Win32 don't have to worry about these issues. Few developers leaving the Win16 API for a life of Win32 programming will miss the segmented addressing headaches they leave behind.

Windows 95 runs many types of programs, including MS-DOS programs, Win16 programs, and of course Win32 programs. For a complete picture of how the Intel-86 processors are able to do this, you must understand Intel's four addressing modes for its 32-bit x86 processors. These modes are: Real mode, 16-bit Protected mode, 32-bit Paged mode, and 16-bit Virtual 8086 mode. Because Win32 programs run in 32-bit Paged mode, our discussion focuses on this mode. For details on the other three memory addressing modes, see the Intel reference in the Recommended Reading list at the end of this book.

INTEL-86 32-BIT PAGED ADDRESSING MODE

The Win32 API was designed for processors that could support two memory features: 32-bit addressing and paged memory. Within the

Intel-86 family of processors, only Intel 80386 and later CPUs meet these requirements. Earlier processors — including the 8088 and the 80286 — don't meet the memory feature requirements of Win32 and therefore cannot run Windows 95.

Later members of this processor family — including the 80386, the i486, and the Pentium — meet both requirements. All of these processors support a single page size: 4K. As such, Win32 programs running under Windows 95 must work with this page size.

But don't assume that every Win32 implementation will have 4K pages. For example Digital's Alpha processor, a platform that runs Windows NT, has 8K pages. And Win32 was designed to accommodate other page sizes, including 16K pages and even 32K pages. If you create Win32 software that somehow relies on a 4K page size, you may create incompatibilities when running on a non-4K page processor.

The addressing scheme that we're going to describe is basically hard wired into the Intel processors. Because it represents a reasonable scheme for paged, virtual memory, this same approach is also used by Windows NT — even when running on non-Intel processors.

The three parts of a virtual address

Intel's 32-bit paged addressing works by dividing a 32-bit address into three parts. As shown in Figure 16-1, a 32-bit address has one 12-bit portion and two 10-bit portions. To help you understand how this works, we're going to start with the low-order 12 bits.

We start with the low-order 12 bits because they are the simplest to understand. They describe an offset into a single page of memory. We've already mentioned that a page is 4K, which makes sense given that two to the twelfth power is 4K (4,096). Individual pages are little more than arrays of bytes with 4K entries. Of course, a 12-bit address can't buy what it used to. To store any useful amount of data, multiple pages are needed.

We can access more pages by making use of the middle 10 bits in our 32-bit virtual address. Those 10 bits are used as an offset into a special memory page called a *page table*. A page table resides in a 4K memory page, and can refer to 1,024 other pages that each hold application code or data. Taken together, the 22 address bits can address 4MB of RAM. Although 4MB used to be a lot of memory, it isn't much anymore. To gain access to the full address space of the processor, we have to use the final 10 bits from the virtual address.

The high-order 10 bits of a 32-bit address are used as an index into yet another page table. But this page table is special, because it points to other page tables, rather than code or data pages. For this reason, it has a special name: a *page directory*. Like other page tables, page directories contain arrays of 32-bit values. In all, up to 1,024 page tables can be addressed from a given page directory. If you do the math, you'll see that a single page directory can reference up to 4GB of memory. As you may know, that is the size of the address space for 32-bit Intel-86 CPUs.

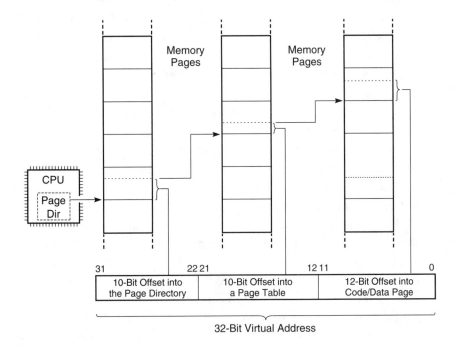

Figure 16-1
How Intel-86 processors convert a 32-bit virtual address into the three pieces used to address physical memory pages.

One question that may still concern you is how the addressing mechanism knows how to get started. That is, how does it know which page holds the page directory? The page directory is referenced in a special CPU register: the CR3 register. (There are also CR0, CR1, and CR2 registers, but their use is beyond the scope of this discussion.) The CPU relies on operating system software to manage the contents of this register. That is why different operating systems with different memory schemes can all run on Intel-86 processors. Among the operating systems that run on Intel processors are MS-DOS, 16-bit Windows 3.x, Windows NT, Unix, OS/2, and iRMX (an Intel operating system).

The translation lookaside buffer

Before we get into Windows-95-specific memory management issues, we need to make one more point about paged addressing. It might seem as though each access to an individual memory location requires access to *two* other memory locations: a page directory and a page table. That would make paged memory three times as costly to access as nonpaged memory.

This would be true, except that the processors maintain a cache — called the *translation lookaside buffer* (TLB) — which stores the most recently used page table entries. The size of the cache varies by individual processor, but is generally quite small. For example, a TLB on a 486 can cache up to 32 page table entries. In turn, these entries reference 128K of code or data.

This small number of cache entries proves to be sufficient in most cases because most software exhibits a trait called *locality of reference*. In other words — speaking in jest, of course — most software chases its own tail, running in circles while working on a tiny data set that tends to be close together. Cache hit rates of 98% and higher make performance problems related to memory addressing fairly rare, but not impossible.

Although most software tends to work in a way that the TLB can accommodate, there's no guarantee that *every* program will do so. From our description of how memory is addressed, it should be easy to write software that renders the TLB useless. For example, allocate 33 pages of RAM and then circulate among them in a round-robin style. A program based on such a memory access scheme would run noticeably slower than a program that respected the role of the TLB. Keep this in mind when designing the way your software arranges and accesses its memory.

WINDOWS 95 PER-PROCESS ADDRESS SPACE

So, how does Windows 95 create a private, per-process address space? At first blush, you might think that it updates the CPU's CR3 register on a context switch. Although Windows NT and other operating systems work that way, Windows 95 doesn't. Instead, Windows 95 sets up the

CR3 register once — during system initialization — and leaves it alone during normal system operation. A private, per-process address space on Windows 95 isn't set up by using the processor's CR3 register. Instead, Windows 95 plays some tricks during a context switch, setting up what Matt Pietrek calls (in the April 1995 edition of the *Microsoft Systems Journal*) a "memory context."

Windows 95 memory contexts

Windows 95 is less generous than Windows NT, which provides each process with a private address space. As we've mentioned elsewhere, part of the reason is that Windows 95 itself doesn't have a generous budget. Giving each process a private address space would cost a 4K page directory plus several 4K page tables per process. Running on a minimum budget of 4MB of memory, Windows 95 can't afford to spend memory too freely.

Instead, Windows 95 creates a single set of page tables. During a context switch between a thread in one process and a thread in another process, Windows 95 updates the page tables. The view that each process sees is what Pietrek calls a "memory context." Part of the address space consists of system dynamic link libraries (DLLs), which are shared by all processes. The page table entries that refer to this part of the address space — from 2GB to 4GB — don't ever have to change. Instead, during a context switch, the only page entries that have to change are those associated with private, per-process pages — that is, from 4MB to 2GB. As might be expected, the changes made by Windows 95 to the page tables appear to each process as the "magic" of the operating system. Each sees private data in one range of addresses, and shared memory in another.

Whatever tricks are played by the operating system, the processor's addressing mechanism stays the same. It's up to the operating system's memory manager to decide what memory should be made visible to which process. A particular code or data page can be mapped in the address space of a single process or into the address spaces of multiple processes. Windows 95 does both of these, thanks to the flexibility of the Intel processors.

For compatibility with Windows 3.x, Win16 programs on Windows 95 don't have a private address space. Instead, they run in a common address space. This allows for the type of memory sharing that Win16 programs are used to: free access to memory pointers, object handles, and memory handles. When converting Win16 programs to the Win32 API, any Win16-style memory sharing must be updated to support Win32-compatible sharing techniques.

Figure 16-2 shows a map of process memory for both Windows 95 and Windows NT. To a Win32 process, both look similar. This is no accident, because a similar memory layout helps a Win32 program run on either. But there are also subtle differences; some are barely worth noting and others are quite significant. We're going to discuss the similarities first, and then touch on key differences.

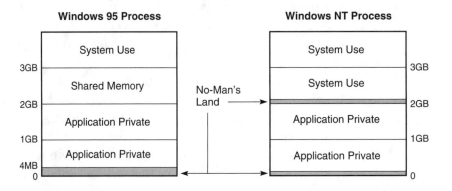

Figure 16-2
Memory maps comparing the address space of a Win32 process in Windows 95 and Windows NT.

Process memory similarities between Windows 95 and Windows NT

Windows 95 and Windows NT share a common executable file format for Win32 programs. This is significant because executable files in both operating systems are loaded as memory mapped files. As will be discussed later in this chapter, this mechanism relies on the virtual memory manager to connect a disk-based file with a range of memory addresses. Pages are read from disk only when the corresponding memory addresses are accessed.

The file format of a Win32 executable is called the *portable executable* format. It is one of several executable file formats created for various Microsoft operating systems. Table 16-2 summarizes the executable file formats used for other Microsoft operating systems. The *Signature* column identifies a two-letter code in the file header that identifies the specific type of an executable file.

Table 16-2
Executable File Formats Used by Various Microsoft Operating Systems

Executable File Type	Signature	Description
MS-DOS program	MZ	Mark Zbikowski's relocatable executable file format. Mark created the MS-DOS 2.0 executable file format, and made himself immortal by using his initials for the executable file signature.
Win16	NE	*New executable* files are segment-oriented Win16 programs. OS/2 1.x used the same file format for its 16-bit programs.
Win32	PE	*Portable executable* files are Win32 programs. This file format is used for Win32 programs built for Windows 95 and Windows NT.
Windows virtual drivers	LE	*Linear executable* files are 32-bit device drivers — sometimes called VxDs — introduced with Windows 3.0 and still used by Windows 95.

From the perspective of process address space, Windows 95 and Windows NT share another common trait: use of a *no-man's land* address range. These are invalid addresses which exist to help catch various types of pointer errors, in particular the use of NULL pointers. On Windows NT, there are two such areas, each of which is 64K. One is at the base of the address space (address 0 to 10000h). The other is at the top of the application's address space (from 7FFF0000 to 7FFFFFFF).

The Windows 95 no-man's land, on the other hand, is a single 4MB area at the bottom of the address space. Any attempt to access memory in this range causes a processor exception (as it also does on Windows NT). Both operating systems terminate any process with an unhandled exception. Hidden in the Windows 95 no-man's land are parts of Real-mode MS-DOS, as well as an area reserved for use by Win16 programs.

As an interesting side note, the no-man's land for Win16 programs is only 64K. This exists to help catch pointers which access segment 0. Other than this similarity, the memory view of Win16 programs is quite different from that seen by Win32 programs. For backward compatibility, a Win16 program running on Windows 95 has almost the same memory view as it does when running on Windows 3.1.

Another trait shared by Windows 95 and Windows NT is the way in which DLLs are mapped into the address space of a process. With both systems, application-specific DLLs get mapped into the range of addresses set aside for application-specific uses — that is, below 2GB.

The only exception on Windows 95 are system DLLs, which provide all of the functions that make up the Win32 API. These are loaded into the shared memory area between 2GB and 3GB. By their very nature, these DLLs are shared by all Win32 applications. As such, it makes sense that they reside in the part of the address space that's shared by all processes.

As you can see, there are some similarities between the way Windows 95 and Windows NT provide memory access to a Win32 process. Now, let's look at some of the differences.

Process memory differences between Windows 95 and Windows NT

The chief differences between Windows 95 and Windows NT involve security. Windows NT erects rigid barriers between processes. On the other hand, Windows 95 is more trusting, continuing the tradition started by MS-DOS and the various 16-bit versions of Windows. Although Windows 95 provides each process with a private address space, everything within the shared memory area is fully accessible.

The chief benefit that Windows 95 derives from this open, trusting approach is that it requires fewer resources than Windows NT. In the same way that a sophisticated building security system requires more resources — wiring, electricity, security guards, and cameras — so does a more secure operating system. Windows 95 was built to run on an 80386 processor with 4MB of RAM (although 8MB is probably more realistic). To support its silicon fortress, Windows NT needs at least an 80486 and 12MB of RAM. (Although once again more RAM — say 16MB to 24MB — makes a difference in overall performance.)

Windows NT requires more processor resources because the bulk of its GUI system is implemented outside the address space of a Win32 process. For example, each call to create a window or draw graphics issues requests that are implemented in a separate process and a separate address space from the calling process. The name of this process is the *Win32 Subsystem*. Running in a separate address space, core operating system components are safe from both accidental and deliberate tampering. The cost of this security is in performance — that is, more resources are required to get the same performance as on more open systems such as Windows 95.

Windows 95 places all system libraries within its 2GB to 3GB shared memory area. For better or worse, all of the system libraries are within easy reach of every Win32 (and Win16) program. When your Win32 program is running on Windows 95, it never takes more than a simple function call (plus perhaps a jump instruction) to reach the actual system functions. On Windows NT, there's typically a context switch between a function call and the code that actually does the work. (However, simple query functions on Windows NT are as fast as they are on Windows 95.)

Because it was designed with security in mind, Windows NT doesn't share memory lightly. For example, there is no common, shared memory area as in Windows 95. Instead, nothing gets shared that isn't explicitly assigned to be shared. This enhanced security also makes Windows NT more robust than Windows 95. You can have a higher degree of confidence that shared data isn't being viewed by someone who shouldn't see it.

On Windows 95, on the other hand, shared memory is allocated in the shared memory area, where it is immediately accessible to every process in the system. If security is an issue for you, this might be a problem. Except for knowing the address, nothing special is needed for a process to read or write data stored in the shared area. (And it's not hard to write a brute force routine that scans shared addresses for interesting tidbits.)

Setting aside security concerns, the different memory sharing approaches can create programming problems. (Security concerns are certainly important, but security isn't our focus here.) At issue is how to share memory between two Win32 programs that will run on both Windows 95 and Windows NT. You'll use the same APIs to access shared memory. So, what is different?

The differences arise from the fact that a shared object in Windows NT can be mapped to different addresses in different processes. Consider a 64K shared buffer. When made available to three different processes on Windows NT, it might get mapped to address 800000h in one process, to 850000h in a second process, and to 900000h in a third. Although you can try to map a shared object to a particular address, it's difficult and — depending on the size of the object and the contents of each address space — may be impossible. A single memory object can get mapped to different locations in different Win32 processes on Windows NT because each process address space is independent of every other process address space.

On Windows 95, a shared object created by one process is visible to every process, at the same address. As mentioned earlier, that address is always between 2GB and 3GB. When 2 — or even 200 — other Win32 processes access the shared memory, it is always at the same address on Windows 95.

At issue here is how you write a single Win32 program that will share memory properly on both operating systems. The short answer is to avoid passing addresses directly between Win32 programs, and to make sure to use the proper memory sharing APIs. Also, when writing memory sharing programs, be sure to test them on Windows NT. It is, after all, the fussier of the two operating systems. When we discuss memory sharing in more detail, we'll describe tricks for writing memory sharing code compatible on all Win32 platforms.

An important improvement over Windows 3.1 that both Windows 95 and Windows NT provide to Windows programmers involves system cleanup of memory. That's the next topic we'll discuss.

SYSTEM MEMORY CLEANUP

A problem shared by every 16-bit version of Windows — from version 1.01, released in 1985, to 3.11, released in 1993 — is the inability to clean up all allocated system memory. According to John Pollock, a member of the Windows 1.0 development team, this problem arises from what was, in retrospect, a bad design decision. Windows required applications to manage the creation and cleanup of objects allocated in system memory. When Win16 applications forget to delete objects, system memory is lost. On systems that operate continually for weeks or months without being rebooted, the behavior of such applications causes one of the various system heaps to become exhausted. The inevitable result is a system crash of one form or another.

To understand how Windows 95 and Windows NT solve this problem, it helps to understand why the problem occurred in the first place. The primary reason why Windows 3.1 (and earlier versions) didn't remove system objects from memory was to enable sharing of GDI drawing objects between programs. To solve the problem, the Win32 specification differs from Win16 in this one point: Win32 doesn't recognize the sharing of GDI objects between processes.

In 16-bit Windows, all GDI objects are designed to be freely shareable between programs. Shareable objects include bitmaps, brushes, DCs, fonts, metafiles, palettes, pens, and regions. Ironically, the reason for object sharing was to save memory; several cooperating programs could pool their GDI drawing objects, thereby reducing the load on GDI's heap. After all, six red pens consume more memory than a single red pen. To allow this sharing, Windows 3.1 leaves all leftover GDI drawing objects in memory. Other types of objects — including windows, menus, cursors, and icons — automatically get cleaned up at application termination time. Leftover GDI objects that aren't actually being shared represent memory forever lost in Windows (at least until Windows is restarted).

When running Win16 programs, Windows 95 and Windows NT continue to respect the rights of Win16 programs to share objects. This can cause a problem on these systems, because a buggy Win16 program can consume system resources and potentially harm the operation of Win32 programs. These operating systems defend themselves against wasteful Win16 programs in several ways.

Windows 95 and Windows NT delete leftover GDI objects from Win16 programs, but only when no Win16 programs are running. In this way, Windows 95 and Windows NT respect the sharing rights of Win16 programs. But when all Win16 programs have terminated, GDI objects created by 16-bit programs can be removed from memory. The effect of buggy, wasteful Win16 programs will diminish over time, as they are replaced by newer Win32 programs.

Windows 95 has a second defense, which seems like something Windows probably should have been doing all along. When either a Win16 program or a Win32 program attempts to create a GDI object, Windows 95 doesn't blindly create a new one, as was done in previous versions. Instead, it determines whether an object of that type already exists. If so, the previously created object is reused. A reference count ensures that objects aren't deleted prematurely. For example, if a program asks GDI to create a red pen and no red pen exists in the system, GDI creates one and returns a handle to that object. But if a red pen already exists, GDI increments the reference count to the existing red pen and lets the caller have a handle to the existing pen. Neither the original creator nor the new user need know that GDI is allowing objects to be shared.

Incidentally, the implicit sharing of GDI objects between programs on Windows 95 can cause spurious assertion messages with older versions of MFC. When an MFC program creates a GDI object — wrapped in an MFC CBitmap, CBrush, or CPen, for example — MFC Debug builds verify that handle values are unique. For example, if a program creates two red pens, Windows 95 provides the same handle for both pens. This behavior isn't expected by versions of MFC prior to version 3.1. In fact, these older versions of MFC check to make sure that handle tables contain no duplicate values. When duplicates are found, MFC displays an assertion — in the form of a large, ugly message box. You can ignore such messages (or upgrade to a version of MFC that is Windows-95-aware).

For programmers experienced with Win16 programming, the automatic cleanup provided for Win32 programs on Windows 95 and Windows NT is welcome relief. No longer do they need to worry about system crashes caused by exhausted system heaps. All objects exist on a per-process basis, and when a process terminates, its leftover objects are deleted.

Automatic cleanup of system objects comes at a slight cost: Win32 GDI objects can't be freely shared between processes in the way they could in Win16. If two programs each need to use a red pen, each program must create its own. Note that clipboard sharing of GDI objects — a set which includes metafiles and bitmaps — is fully supported in Win32 just as it was in Win16. Only the internal implementation has changed, which shouldn't affect normal clipboard use.

Automatic cleanup of leftover objects isn't an excuse for sloppy coding. All objects that you create should be accounted for. You have several means for checking your code to ensure that objects are cleaned up properly. One is built into MFC and the IDE debugger. Debug builds of MFC programs keep a list of all objects that have been allocated and destroyed. At program termination time, a list gets displayed of all leftover objects — what MFC calls *memory leaks* — which include system objects as well as all dynamically allocated chunks of memory. To see this list, you must run your program in a debugger, such as the IDE debugger, which can display the MFC's debugging messages. Another tool that detects leftover system objects — but not internally allocated data — is Nu-Mega's Bounds Checker.

One minor hitch in automatic cleanup involves global atoms. An atom is a unique integer ID that can be used to access a variable-length character string. The system libraries in both Windows NT and Windows 95 create atoms in the global atom table for registered system messages and registered clipboard formats. Because such values are shared between processes, they must reside in a shared memory area. Although both operating systems could clean up the global atom table, they don't. The good news is that the number of available atom values is large: about 1K atoms on Windows 95 and 16K atoms on Windows NT. And because duplicate strings create the same atom, you won't exhaust a heap by repeatedly running a program that registers the same string in the atom table but forgets to clean it up. Nonetheless, you'll want to keep in mind that this is one resource that the system doesn't manage perfectly.

One possible hitch for the global atom table is caused by applications that use Windows' dynamic data exchange (DDE). As you may know, this is a data sharing mechanism that involves messages (such as WM_DDE_DATA) sent between windows. DDE doesn't use atoms for the data being shared, but rather for human-readable data identifiers. (For example, a range of spreadsheet cells might be identified by the string "A12:C52".) If you're creating Windows programs that use low-level DDE to share data, make sure you destroy all atoms that you create. (Alternatively, use Windows' DDE-Management Library — DDEML — which properly handles the cleanup of the global atom table.)

At this point, our coverage of system memory management is complete. Next, we're going to explore all the types of private memory available for allocation by an application.

Process Private Memory

Although you might be tempted to stick with *new* as your memory allocator, it's not always the best choice. With large objects, for example, you get more control by using the native Win32 memory allocators. For performance-critical or hard real-time applications, you might decide to create per-class allocators. Bjarne Stroustrup recommends this for frequently used classes, in Chapter 10 of his book, *The Design and Evolution of C++*.

Even if operator new is your primary allocator, you might want to store the resulting pointer somewhere other than in a regular variable. In particular, the Win32 API provides memory *wallets* — window extra bytes and thread local storage — to tuck away data associated with operating system objects. Such nooks and crannies can help simplify the relationship between a program's data and operating system objects. Even if you never use these memory cubbyholes, learning about them will help you understand the operation of various user-interface objects. For example, dialog box controls — including edits, list boxes, combo boxes, and buttons — use window extra bytes to store control-specific data.

In the following sections, we'll describe every available place to store data that is private to a process. The relationship of each memory type to the other process-private memory is graphically depicted in Figure 16-3. Missing from that illustration are memory types allocated *outside* the address space of a process — meaning window extra bytes and thread local storage. Our focus in this section is private memory; we'll cover shared memory types later in this chapter.

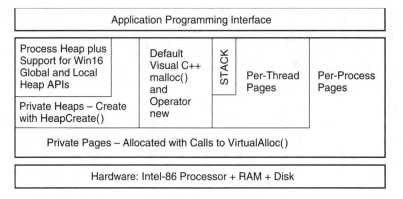

Figure 16-3
A layered view of every type of Win32 process-private memory.

This layered view shows the hardware on the bottom, and the connection to the application on the top. Although many types of memory are available, all ultimately rely on private pages that have been allocated in the process address space. In addition to providing per-process pages, Win32 allows for the creation of per-thread data. Finally, there is a set of APIs for heap allocation. Visual C++ provides its own default heap allocator that it builds on top of raw pages. In addition, the Win32 heap allocator provides basic heap support, and — for backward compatibility — supports both types of Win16 heap allocation functions.

Microsoft operating systems always seem to provide memory allocation APIs in pairs. For example, the 16-bit OS/2 API provides DosAllocSeg( ) to allocate segments and DosSubAlloc( ) to allocate subsegments. (Yes, Microsoft did create this portion of the OS/2 API.) Win16 provides a comparable pair of allocation routines, with GlobalAlloc( ) for allocating segments and LocalAlloc( ) for subdividing segments into smaller, subsegment-size chunks.

Win32 continues the tradition, providing VirtualAlloc( ) to allocate pages, and HeapAlloc( ) for subpage allocation. These are the first two types of memory we'll discuss. (We sometimes refer to dual sets of allocators as *biggie* and *teeny* allocators, because this captures the key difference between sets of allocators: granularity of allocated memory.)

We'll conclude our discussion of process-private memory with a brief look at ways to tie memory to operating system objects. Window extra bytes and properties allow data to be connected to windows. The two types of thread local storage connect data to threads — the unit of scheduling that's sometimes called lightweight processes — that run in the memory context of a Win32 process.

Let's begin, then, with a look at how process pages get allocated.

ALLOCATING PAGES

In the paged memory environment of Windows 95 (and Windows NT), all memory available to a Win32 process resides in paged memory, meaning it resides in one page or another. Several subpage allocators are supported. As pointed out to one of the authors by Lou Perazzoli, a member of the Windows NT development team at Microsoft, however, only two Win32 functions add new pages to the address space of a process. One function, VirtualAlloc( ), allocates private pages. The other function, MapViewOfFile( ), allocates shared pages. Every other allocator relies on these two — directly or indirectly — to provide memory pages.

The Win32 private page allocator is VirtualAlloc( ). In addition to allocating private-process pages, it has another role. It reserves memory address ranges without actually causing the consumption of any physical space — either in RAM-based pages or in disk-based page-file pages. This allows a program to reserve large address ranges, with no cost in terms of pages consumed. As needed, sets of memory pages can be mapped to the reserved address range. For example, tiny incremental portions of a large chunk of data from a gigabyte-sized database can be loaded into "real" memory as needed. To allocate a new page in a range of reserved addresses, a program calls this same function — VirtualAlloc( ) — to commit memory.

To allocate shared pages, a Win32 process calls MapViewOfFile( ). The name of this function is quite strange, but it reflects the function's dual role. On the one hand, MapViewOfFile( ) creates a view into a memory mapped file. On the other hand, it allocates shared pages — which is another way to describe a memory mapped file that also happens to be the system's paging file. We'll discuss the allocation of shared pages later in this chapter.

For now, our focus is process-specific page allocation. We'll start with a look at how VirtualAlloc( ) lets you reserve address space. Then, we'll discuss the allocation of pages. Finally, we'll touch on stack allocation in a Win32 program.

Reserving address space

Win32 allows you to manage your process address space. Most programmers don't think of the address space as a resource to be managed. After all, with billions of addresses, why be choosy? But, direct control of the address space can be helpful in some situations.

For example, it's helpful to manage the address space when you need to dynamically allocate a block of memory for a data object that might grow. Although it's not always necessary, keeping all of the parts of the object in contiguous memory simplifies data handling. To allow a block to grow in contiguous memory, however, most operating systems require you to preallocate memory beyond what you actually need.

Allocating more memory than you need is wasteful, but it's sometimes the easiest way to get what you need. Otherwise, when an object outgrows one piece of memory, it may need to be moved to a larger space. Moving large objects is expensive, in terms of processor time, and can fragment the address space. Of course, there are alternatives to preallocating too much space. You can move objects when they grow, and you can use linked lists to logically connect different data blocks. But that creates other problems such as list management overhead and bugs due to the complexity of data handling.

The Win32 API provides a much more elegant solution to this problem. Instead of wasting memory by overallocating what you need, you can allocate the exact number of pages for a given block of data. (On average, the wasted memory will be one-half a page, or 2,048 bytes.) But that is the second half of the solution.

Before allocating any pages for an object that might grow, you need to reserve a range of addresses that can accommodate the maximum expected size. Once addresses have been reserved, you allocate memory by committing memory pages from the range of reserved addresses. At first, you only allocate for the initial memory needed. As memory needs increase, you commit incremental pages. This makes efficient use of memory by avoiding the wasteful practice of overallocating. In addition, new pages added to the existing set are accessible in a range of addresses that are contiguous with previously allocated pages.

An example will help clarify what we mean. Suppose you need to read a file into memory that occupies 100K, and you anticipate that this object will never grow larger than 500K. Using the Win32 virtual memory APIs, you first reserve a 500K range of memory addresses. Within the range of reserved addresses, you commit 100K to "real" memory so that you can read the file into memory. As needed, you extend the size of the committed pages to accommodate the growth in your object.

It's important to understand when memory actually gets consumed. In particular, no pages of physical memory are consumed by reserving addresses (aside from a small amount on the virtual memory manager's address list). As proof, try to access memory in a range of reserved (but not committed) addresses. You'll get an error — a general protection fault — which, if unhandled, causes your program to terminate.

Although reserving addresses doesn't give you access to physical memory, it's a necessary first step to plan for the object's growth. Otherwise, another part of your application — or a DLL used by your application — might use addresses just beyond the end of your allocated area. If that happens, you're back to the problem of having to move the entire data object when you need the object to grow.

To reserve a range of addresses, call VirtualAlloc( ) and pass the MEM_RESERVE flag. This is one of three flags defined for VirtualAlloc( )'s third parameter. The function itself is defined as follows:

```
LPVOID VirtualAlloc(LPVOID lpvAddress,
                    DWORD dwSize,
                    DWORD dwAction,
                    DWORD dwAccess);
```

Where:

- *lpvAddress* is a memory address. When reserving a range of addresses, set this to NULL for the system to pick a starting address, or to a non-NULL value if you have a desired starting address. When committing a previously reserved address to memory pages, this is rounded down to a page (4K) boundary. When reserving a range of addresses, this is rounded down to a region (64K) boundary.

- *dwSize* is the number of bytes to reserve or commit. This number is rounded up to the nearest page (4K) boundary when committing and to the nearest region (64K) boundary when reserving.

- *dwAction* is MEM_RESERVE to reserve a range of addresses, MEM_COMMIT to commit previously reserved addresses to memory pages, or a combination of MEM_RESERVE|MEM_COMMIT to reserve and commit the memory. (MEM_COMMIT by itself does the same thing.)

- *dwAccess* is a flag field for specifying the page access status. Among the defined flags are PAGE_READWRITE for full access and PAGE_NOACCESS to make pages off limits. (Windows 95 doesn't support PAGE_GUARD.) See the Win32 API documentation or the help database for a complete set of flags.

The return value to VirtualAlloc( ) is either the base address of the memory region, or NULL to indicate failure.

A set of reserved addresses is referred to as a *region*. The granularity of regions — for both Windows 95 and Windows NT — is 64K. In other words, if you reserve a one-byte range of addresses, at least 64K addresses are included in the region. To put it another way, the entire 4GB virtual address space could hold 64K regions if each were 64K.

As mentioned, reserving memory addresses is only half the story. The other half is connecting memory pages to addresses.

Allocating memory pages

You can allocate memory pages with VirtualAlloc( ) in either two steps or one step. The two-step approach involves first reserving the memory and then committing the memory to pages. Here's an example of the two-step approach:

```
// Reserve a 64K range of addresses.
LPVOID p = VirtualAlloc(0, 0x10000, MEM_RESERVE, PAGE_READWRITE);
if (!p)
{ /* Error. */ }
...
// Commit a 4K range of addresses.
LPVOID pTemp = VirtualAlloc(p, 0x1000, MEM_COMMIT, PAGE_READWRITE);
if (!pTemp)
{ /* Error. */ }
```

The first call to VirtualAlloc( ) reserves a 64K region of addresses, located at a site chosen by the operating system. The second call commits 4K of the reserved addresses to a memory page. Notice how this code fragment stores the return value from each call separately. Because of the different granularity of pages and regions, as well as the possibility of failure of either call, you need to think of each type of call as a separate, independent memory allocation action.

The one-step approach involves a call to VirtualAlloc( ) with the MEM_COMMIT flag. In other words, you don't reserve addresses before you get pages; instead, you combine a reserve and a commit request into a single call:

```
// Commit a 4K range of addresses.
LPVOID pTemp = VirtualAlloc(0, 0x1000, MEM_COMMIT, PAGE_READWRITE);
if (!pTemp)
{ /* Error. */ }
```

To decommit previously committed pages, or to unreserve a range of previously reserved addresses, you call VirtualFree( ). When called with the MEM_DECOMMIT flag, pages are decommitted (but the address range stays reserved). To release a range of reserved messages, you call VirtualFree( ) and specify MEM_RELEASE.

The complete set of Win32 virtual memory functions is summarized in Table 16-3. Most are straightforward and require no further explanation other than to direct your attention to the Win32 function name in the Win32 help database or documentation.

The final set of private pages that are directly allocated for a Win32 process are the pages for the stack. We'll look at these next.

Table 16-3

Functions That Control Process Page Allocation

Function	Description
VirtualAlloc()	Reserves a range of addresses and/or allocates pages of memory.
VirtualFree()	Decommits a reserved range of addresses and/or frees pages of allocated memory.
VirtualLock()	Adds a set of pages to the core working set of a process. Although the pages can be written to the page file, they will be read back into memory whenever threads in the process are scheduled to run.
VirtualProtect()	Changes the access protection on a set of committed pages in the current process.
VirtualProtectEx()	Changes the access protection on a set of committed pages in any process in the system for which the caller has sufficient access.
VirtualQuery()	Returns virtual memory details about a specific address in the current process.
VirtualQueryEx()	Returns virtual memory details about a specific address in any process in the system for which the caller has sufficient access.
VirtualUnlock()	Removes a set of pages from the core working set of a process so it doesn't have to be in memory when threads in the process are executing.

Allocating stack space

A stack is a temporary memory area used by the compiler for short-term memory needs. The stack holds four types of data: a function's local variables, parameters passed when a function is called, register values, and return addresses. Use of the stack is quite dynamic, rising and falling like the tides.

Perhaps the most important issue regarding stacks is the stack size. The default stack size for Win32 threads on both Windows 95 and Windows NT is 1MB. For Win32 programs running on Win32s, a slightly smaller stack is available: only 128K. If you write a Win32 program that either uses a lot of local variables or does a lot of recursion, you should test your application on Win32s to make sure that you don't overflow available stack space.

This concludes our look at raw pages used in a process. Our next topic is default memory allocation — via operator new and malloc( ) — from an MFC program.

COMPILER MEMORY ALLOCATION

Although understanding page allocation enhances your knowledge of the Win32 API, most MFC programmers will probably rely on the default Visual C++ allocator to get dynamically allocated memory. For that reason alone, the compiler memory allocator has earned the right to be described prior to the native Win32 and Win16 heap allocators.

An important characteristic of the compiler's allocator is that individual heaps are created on a per-module basis. (In Microsoft-speak, the term *module* doesn't refer to a program source file, but to an executable image such as a .EXE program or a .DLL dynamic link library.) This is an important factor when building dynamic link libraries, because an application can use any memory object that its dynamic link libraries create for it (because all exist in a single address space). However, if a DLL exits from memory, the C-runtime library destroys the heaps that the compiler created for that DLL.

When deciding which allocator to use, an important issue is cost in terms of memory consumed per allocated object. We didn't address this issue in our discussion of VirtualAlloc( ) because page allocation overhead is small relative to page size. But because heap allocators are often used to allocate relatively small chunks of memory, issues such as per-allocation overhead and granularity can become important.

MFC uses a custom allocator instead of using the native Win32 allocator. [By *native* allocator, we mean HeapAlloc( ) and associated API functions.] The reasons are mostly historical: The Win32 heap allocator on Windows NT 3.1 was inefficient. With a granularity of 32 bytes and an overhead of 16 bytes per object, it proved too costly when allocating large numbers of tiny objects. As we'll discuss, heap support is significantly improved in Windows NT 3.5, and even better on Windows 95. At some point, Microsoft may modify MFC to rely on the operating system allocator instead of its own. To give you an idea of what might motivate such a change, we are going to discuss the default Visual C++ heap allocator.

MFC's default memory allocator

The MFC default allocator is an old friend with a new face. The friend — familiar to C programmers — is malloc( ). Its new face is a Win32-specific implementation that relies on VirtualAlloc( ) to allocate pages for its heap. (Allocator source files are available on the Visual C++ 2.1 CD-ROM in

\msvc20\lib\crtsrc. They can also be downloaded in a packed file as VC20CRTL.EXE on CompuServe, over the Internet, or from the Microsoft Download Service. Be sure to expand using the -D switch.)

The cost of allocation for each heap object is 12 bytes. Those 12 bytes are consumed in the following way: each heap block has a 4-byte header plus an 8-byte node on a linked list of block descriptors. As a result, allocating a 24-byte buffer costs 36 bytes. Here's an example:

```
//   Data bytes:        24
// + Header bytes:       4
// + Block descriptor:   8
//                     ———————
//   Total Cost:       36 bytes
void * pData = malloc(24);
```

Another allocation issue involves allocation granularity. Allocation granularity is the rounding factor or multiple when a particular size is requested. The default allocator has a granularity of four bytes. The average waste due to rounding up in a large number of objects is approximately two bytes — a relatively small amount to waste.

The Visual C++ default allocator is a straightforward, general-purpose allocator. When searching through the heap to satisfy allocation requests, it uses a first-fit algorithm. As it searches, it coalesces adjacent free blocks. As needed, it adds more pages to its free store in 64K increments. Each region can grow to 1MB, and the allocator itself can accommodate 64 regions, for a total 64MB heap.

When building a Release version of an MFC program, calls to operator new( ) — for both CObject-derived and non-CObject-derived classes — cause calls to malloc( ). (To build a Release version of an MFC program, select Win32 Release as the build target in a project's make (.MAK) file.) The characteristic of Release programs that interests us here is that the _DEBUG preprocessor symbol is *not* defined. Also, half of MFC's link libraries are reserved for Release builds, which *don't* include the diagnostic assertions of the Debug version.

Memory allocation gets interesting with a Debug version of an MFC program. Debug builds cause the _DEBUG preprocessor symbol to become defined. Among other things, the definition of _DEBUG triggers the availability of the MFC diagnostic allocator. (It also triggers use of the Debug link libraries.) The source code to the diagnostic allocator appears in \MSVC20\MFC\SRC\AFXMEM.CPP. The diagnostic allocator is not a substitute for the Visual C++ allocator. Instead, it's a layer that does some extra work to help trap certain common memory problems. Ultimately, the debug allocator itself calls malloc( ). In the following section, we'll describe how the diagnostic allocator works and suggest some ways you can take advantage of it.

The MFC diagnostic allocator

Here's a loaded question that your manager may have already asked — or perhaps should ask: How do you find a bug that involves writing past the end of a memory buffer? Some developers rely on luck and hard work to avoid writing such code. Given the dynamic nature of code, however, managing that approach quickly becomes too complicated. Other developers use memory wrapper functions that are built to automatically detect such problems. When a problem is detected, a notification alerts the developer. MFC provides this type of memory wrapper function to make certain types of bug detection almost automatic.

The MFC diagnostic allocator defines its own global operator new( ) and its own CObject::operator new( ). Both eventually call malloc( ), but not before adding a few features to help catch common memory errors. Many of the techniques that MFC uses are described in greater detail in Steve Maguire's *Writing Solid Code* (Microsoft Press), a helpful resource for programmers and managers of programmers.

Among the types of problems that MFC's diagnostic allocator helps locate are memory leaks (allocated objects not freed), buffer underflow and overflow (writing prior to the start or after the end of a buffer), use of uninitialized buffers, and use of a buffer after it has been freed. Although the diagnostic allocator can't always diagnose the exact cause of these problems, it can get you started in the right direction. If there's a problem with a particular memory block, for example, the diagnostic allocator can identify the source file and the line of code that allocated that memory.

To do that, the diagnostic allocator has to store additional information, which it does by adding 36 bytes to every allocation using operator new( ). Every object so allocated has a 28-byte header that stores key values for allocated memory blocks. Eight extra bytes are also allocated as a no-man's land: four before and four after the object. These bytes help locate writes beyond the boundaries of an allocated memory block. (By the way, this is different from the address space no-man's land that a Win32 process sees when running on Windows 95 and Windows NT.) Here's the structure for the diagnostic allocator's memory block header, as defined in AFXMEM.CPP:

```
struct CBlockHeader
{
    struct CBlockHeader* pBlockHeaderNext;
    struct CBlockHeader* pBlockHeaderPrev;
    LPCSTR               lpszFileName;
    int                  nLine;
    size_t               nDataSize;
    enum CMemoryState::blockUsage use;
    LONG                 lRequest;
    BYTE                 gap[nNoMansLandSize];
    // followed by:
    // BYTE              data[nDataSize];
    // BYTE              anotherGap[nNoMansLandSize];
    BYTE* pbData()
        { return (BYTE*) (this + 1); }
};
```

Although 36 bytes are a lot to add to every object allocated, keep in mind that this is just development scaffolding. After you've found and removed all of your memory handling problems, you can create a *Release Build* of your program. As the name suggests, that's the build that gets released to the users of your software. Although the presence of some extra diagnostic bytes will consume more memory and cause your program to run slower, it's well worth the cost. After all, software developers often have the fastest, highest capacity systems. You may scarcely notice the performance hit caused by a Debug release.

In addition to allocating a memory block header, the diagnostic allocator fills memory with known, nonzero values. This helps detect various pointer problems, including buffer overflow, underflow, and access to objects that have already been freed. Figure 16-4 shows how the diagnostic allocator fills heap bytes. Even allocated areas are filled with a known value: 0xCD. Knowing this can help you determine whether a function has written any data to a buffer. If so, you see the data. If not, the debugger shows an array of 0xCD values instead of whatever you expected to be written to the buffer. (As an aside, the 32-bit OLE libraries fill empty memory with the value 0x0BADF00D, which a Microsoft developer suggests was prompted by a visit to a company cafeteria.)

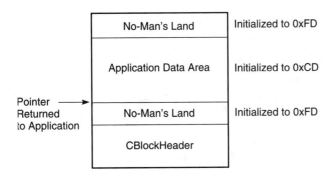

Figure 16-4

The diagnostic allocator fills free blocks and surrounds allocated blocks with known values.

In the diagnostic heap, *sentinels* — what MFC calls no-man's-land areas — are set up at the start and the end of allocated objects to catch buffer overflow and underflow problems. In production code, writing beyond either the beginning or the end of a buffer can cause program crashes, data loss, and endless user frustration. In a Debug build, however, overwritten objects are more easily identified, helping you find the source of a problem.

Incidentally, although the granularity of malloc( ) is 4 bytes, the granularity of the default allocator is only 1 byte. The location of the no-man's land is immediately after the end of the requested data area. If you overwrite by just 1 byte, you trigger an assertion. This makes the Debug version allocator much stricter than the allocator used for Release versions. Off-by-one overwrite errors that might not be detected in the Release version will set off alarms in the Debug version.

Here are the three values that the debug allocator uses to fill memory, as defined in AFXMEM.CPP:

```
#define bNoMansLandFill    0xFD   // fill no-man's land with this
#define bDeadLandFill      0xDD   // fill free objects with this
#define bCleanLandFill     0xCD   // fill new objects with this
```

A comment block that appears in the same source file just before these values explains why these particular values were chosen. These comments can be summarized as follows:

- The use of nonzero fill values makes memory overwrites more obvious, because the most common memory fill operation results in zero-filled data.

- Constant values make memory filling deterministic, which helps make bugs reproducible. Depending on how this data gets used, however, the use of a nonzero value can occasionally mask a bug.

- Mathematically odd numbers are helpful for finding bugs assuming a cleared lower bit, and for trapping on the Macintosh.

- Large numbers (byte values at least) are less typical, and are useful for finding bad addresses.

- Atypical values (that is, values that are not often used) are useful because they typically cause early detection in code.

- For the case of no-man's land and free blocks, if you store to any of these locations, the memory integrity checker will detect it.

In a Debug build of MFC, several global variables let you control the operation of the diagnostic allocator. One of these is a flag field that is stored in a global variable, *afxMemDF*. This integer variable is defined as follows in the MFC source file APPDATA.CPP:

```
int afxMemDF = allocMemDF;
```

This default setting turns on the debugging allocator. Other values for this flag, as defined in AFX.H, are shown in the following table:

Flag	*Value*	*Description*
n/a	0	Turn off the debugging allocator.
allocMemDF	0x01	Turn on the debugging allocator to add a header and no-man's land for each allocated object.
delayFreeMemDF	0x02	Delay freeing memory to test out-of-memory handling. This also helps make sure that freed pointers don't get referenced.
checkAlwaysMemDF	0x04	Check heap integrity on every call to allocator (both new and delete) as well as during idle-time processing. When this flag is set, AfxCheckMemory() gets called to validate heap. You can also call this function yourself at any time to verify heap validity.

You can also set a counter, _afxBreakAlloc, to break into the debugger after a certain number of allocations. When the debug allocator is enabled, it keeps count of the number of times it's been called and it tags each allocated object in sequence. When a leak is detected, the diagnostic allocator reports the lost block's sequence number. When you're using the IDE debugger, this feature lets you catch your program in the act of allocating a block that doesn't get freed, presumably to help you figure out the cause of a memory leak. The _afxBreakAlloc counter is defined in its disabled state as follows in AFXMEM.H:

```
static LONG _afxBreakAlloc = -1;     // for debugging memory leaks
```

But it's a simple matter to set this value to indicate how many allocations should pass before breaking into the debugger. Incidentally, you'll probably want to define this value within a conditionally compiled block of code such as the following, because this variable is not defined for the Release version:

```
#ifdef _DEBUG
_afxBreakAlloc = 1000;
#endif
```

Another feature that the diagnostic allocator provides to help you test your software is an allocation hook function. Right before it allocates an object, the allocator calls into the chain of hook functions to ask whether an artificial allocation failure should be created. By simulating a low-memory situation, this tests whether error handling is doing the right thing. For details, see the function AfxSetAllocHook( ) in AFXMEM.CPP.

To catch pointer errors that overwrite the heap, you can request heap validation. There are two ways to do this. You can simply call AfxCheckMemory( ), which validates the heap. Or, you can set the afxMemDF diagnostic flag to the value checkAlwaysMemDF. That causes AfxCheckMemory( ) to be called whenever memory is allocated or freed. It even causes the heap to get checked during idle time (from within CWinThread::-OnIdle( ), which is located in THRDCODE.CPP).

The diagnostic allocator also detects memory leaks, which are objects allocated but not freed. In a Debug build, the AfxDumpMemoryLeaks( ) function is automatically called when an MFC program terminates. Any objects still on the heap are displayed in the debugger's Output window. To get this output, you must run your program while the IDE debugger is running. That is, you can't just have the IDE running; you must have started your MFC program by selecting the Debug|Go command (or equivalent). The detection of memory leaks can be a great help in plugging those leaks so your program uses memory efficiently.

In the next section, we'll look at the set of Win32 API functions that provide subpage allocation. These functions also support the Win16 allocation functions, which are included as part of the Win32 API for backward compatibility.

WIN32 PRIVATE HEAPS

The Win32 API provides a set of functions for creating and allocating memory in multiple, private heaps. Although the Win32 page allocator should be used to allocate large objects — in multiples of 4K pages on Windows 95 — the private heap allocator provides memory allocation for subpage-sized data items.

We refer to Win32 heap support as a *private* heap allocator because Win32 doesn't provide any mechanism for sharing heaps between processes (although two threads in the same process can easily share a single heap). Because they are private to a process, heaps are created within the memory pages visible only to a single process. When sharing memory between Win32 processes, Win32 unfortunately doesn't organize the memory for you. You must do that yourself.

Win32 provides the capability to create multiple heaps, so you can separate your data any way that suits you. For example, a large application might create multiple heaps and put the data for different subsystems in different heaps. Problems created by memory leaks or bad pointers in one subsystem have a lower probability of harming the operation of other subsystems.

Another reason for creating multiple heaps is to segregate objects of different sizes. For general-purpose allocators, fragmentation occurs when many different objects of widely varying sizes get allocated and freed. For example, by creating a heap that is private to a particular class, you cut down on heap fragmentation and the resulting wasted memory.

Background on heap implementation

The following table summarizes some operating characteristics of the heap allocation routines in two Win32 implementations, Windows 95 and Windows NT 3.5:

Memory Allocation Issue	Windows 95	Windows NT 3.5
Minimum object size	12 bytes	8 bytes
Overhead per object	4 bytes	8 bytes
Allocation granularity	4 bytes	8 bytes

You might find it surprising that these two operating systems provide the same API so differently. But it's not terribly surprising when you consider that each was created by a different development group at Microsoft, with different goals and different constraints.

Perhaps a word or two on this table would be appropriate. The minimum object size should be self-explanatory. When allocating small objects, that value identifies the minimum amount of memory that's allocated. For both Windows 95 and Windows NT — if you add up the overhead per object — each allocation takes a minimum of 16 bytes.

The overhead-per-object value is the size of the header for each heap object. In both systems, the header is stored just below the address of the start of the allocated data area. Although you don't typically think about this overhead when allocating from a heap, it's a real cost which you may want to take into account when evaluating a program's memory use.

The granularity on the Windows 95 heap allocator is 4 bytes. For example, when the heap allocator is asked for 15 bytes, it supplies a 16-byte area. Add in the 4-byte header, and your 15-byte request actually ends up costing 20 bytes of actual memory space consumed.

As shown in this table, Windows 95 has lower allocation overhead and lower allocation granularity than Windows NT. The reason is that the target machine for Windows 95 is a lowly 80386-based system with 4MB of RAM. Windows NT, on the other hand, was built for systems with more RAM and more powerful processors. The "skinnier" heap allocator in Windows 95 helps that operating system run leaner overall.

When comparing memory allocators, you need some way to measure the differences. One way is to calculate the *memory tax* that the allocator charges for the size of objects that you allocate. In our example — in which a 15-byte request consumes a 20-byte area — the tax is 5/15 or 33%. Although 5 bytes doesn't seem very expensive, a 33% tax puts the relative cost into perspective. (In human terms, a 33% sales tax would be outrageous, yet a 33% marginal income tax somehow seems more reasonable.) On Windows NT, the same 15-byte object would consume 24 bytes — a 60% surcharge on the actual bytes you plan to store.

If some part of your Win32/MFC programs use the private heap functions, you'll want to make sure to test extensively on both platforms. Otherwise, you risk missing subtle bugs that appear on one platform but not the other. For example, a bug that overwrites 6 bytes past the end of an allocated object might not be noticed on Windows NT. But on Windows 95, such a bug would overwrite other objects.

On Windows 95, a heap always resides within the per-process, private memory ranges — that is, between 4MB and 2GB. Although the location of a heap in a Windows NT process won't tell you whether it's private or shared, heaps are, in fact, always private on Windows NT. To convince yourself that this is the case, you can call VirtualQuery( ) on a heap address. It reports that heap memory pages are private (MEM_PRIVATE) pages.

Although some of the operating characteristics differ, the allocation of private heaps from private pages is similar on Windows 95 and Windows NT. The Win32 API that creates a heap is HeapCreate( ), which in turn calls VirtualAlloc( ) twice. The first call to VirtualAlloc( ) reserves a range of memory addresses to anticipate heap growth. The second call commits memory pages at the start of this address range.

Let's take a look at the functions that make up Win32's private heap support.

The Win32 heap API

Table 16-4 summarizes Win32's heap management functions. Most are relatively straightforward. For details on calling these functions, refer to the Win32 documentation or the on-line help database.

Some basic design and implementation details are worth discussing. Chief among these is the fact that every Win32 process gets a heap. Most Win32 heap functions take a heap handle as a parameter. To get a handle to the system-provided heap, call GetProcessHeap( ). With the returned handle, you can allocate within a heap to your heart's content.

Table 16-4

The Win32 Private Heap Support Functions

Function	Description
GetProcessHeap()	Retrieves a handle to the default process heap.
GetProcessHeaps()	Retrieves a list of heap handles for all available heaps in the current process.
HeapAlloc()	Allocates memory from the heap identified by a heap handle. All objects are fixed, unlike Win16 objects which can be allocated as moveable or discardable. More on that later in this chapter.
HeapCompact()	Performs some cleaning of the heap by coalescing free areas and, when possible, releasing unneeded pages.
HeapCreate()	Creates a new heap in the process address space. Calls Virtual-Alloc() twice: first to reserve a range of addresses and then again to commit the requested minimum memory for the heap.
HeapDestroy()	Destroys a heap created with HeapCreate().
HeapFree()	Frees a heap object allocated with a call to HeapAlloc() or HeapReAlloc().
HeapLock()	Acquires the heap's critical section. This is only required when two or more threads will be accessing a heap. You should call HeapUnlock() as soon as possible.
HeapReAlloc()	Resizes an object allocated with a call to HeapAlloc() or a previous call to HeapReAlloc().
HeapSize()	Returns the size of an object. On Windows 95, this is the size of the allocated area (rounds to next 4-byte boundary) instead of the requested size. On Windows NT, HeapSize() returns the size requested in the call to HeapAlloc() or HeapReAlloc().
HeapUnlock()	Releases ownership of the heap's critical section. See HeapLock().
HeapValidate()	Checks the integrity of an entire heap or an object within the heap.
HeapWalk()	Enumerates all of the objects allocated in the heap.

Another important issue with Win32 heaps is serialization. Almost every heap function has a heap allocation flag parameter, and one possible flag is HEAP_NO_SERIALIZE. This flag disables the heap's default operation, which is to serialize — or synchronize — access to the heap by multiple threads. Please note that this use of the term *serialize* has nothing to do with C++ serialization. In other words, in this context serialization isn't related to moving data between memory and disk. When enabled, the heap serialization support forces two threads to wait in line if both want to modify the heap — that is, add or remove a data object — at the same time.

From our discussion in Chapter 2, you may recall that threads are a Win32 feature that allow for the creation of multiple, independently scheduled entities in a Win32 process. The Win32 heap functions allow multiple threads to access heaps at the same time. By default, the Win32 heap functions avoid having two threads modify the heap at the same time. The type of operating system object used to perform this task is a *critical section*.

Use the HEAP_NO_SERIALIZE flag when you have only one thread in your application. It helps the heap allocation functions run a little faster, because serialization does take a tiny bit of processor time. We don't mean to imply that it's sluggish or poorly implemented. But when allocating a very large number of objects, tiny savings such as this can add up.

The HeapValidate( ) function checks the integrity of a particular heap. This can be useful when you suspect a bad pointer or a buffer overflow is causing a problem. Even if you've coded defensively — as detailed in Steve Maguire's *Writing Solid Code* — you may find that memory sometimes gets overwritten. Strategic placement of calls to this function can help pinpoint the exact cause of such problems.

Another potentially useful function is HeapWalk( ). Win16 programmers may recall Microsoft's HeapWalker utility program. Called Luke HeapWalker (after Luke SkyWalker, the character in the Star Wars movies), the Win16 HeapWalker utility displays the contents of the various heaps. This function lets you programmatically examine all of the data objects that are allocated on a heap. To help you build your own memory testers and diagnostic routines, this function will let you know almost everything about a Win32 heap.

For backward compatibility with Win16 programs, Win32 provides support for the two Win16 allocation functions. In a Win32 program, both sets of allocators — GlobalAlloc( ) and LocalAlloc( ) — are implemented using the Win32 heap functions. Let's look at how Win16 allocation functions are supported.

Support for Win16 heap API

Tables 16-5 and 16-6 summarize the Win16 heap allocation functions. Microsoft provides these in the API mostly to help developers port Win16 code to Win32. But some interesting features — such as the capability to allocate moveable or discardable objects — are not supported by the Win32 heap functions. In particular, many of the Win16 allocation flags have no effect in Win32.

Table 16-5
Win16 Segment Allocation Functions

Function	Purpose
GlobalAlloc()	Allocate a segment, returning a handle.
GlobalReAlloc()	Resize a segment.
GlobalSize()	Query segment size.
GlobalLock()	Fetch a data pointer, while incrementing lock count.
GlobalUnlock()	Decrement lock count.
GlobalFree()	Deallocate a segment.

Table 16-6
Win16 Subsegment Allocation Functions

Function	Purpose
LocalAlloc()	Allocate a subsegment, returning a handle.
LocalReAlloc()	Resize a subsegment.
LocalSize()	Query subsegment size.
LocalLock()	Fetch a data pointer, while incrementing lock count.
LocalUnlock()	Decrement lock count.
LocalFree()	Deallocate a subsegment.

The Win16 allocators were introduced with the first version of Windows. As such, they have features that hearken back to the days when Windows ran on humble 8088 processors with only 1MB of RAM (or less!). Running in what Intel called Real mode, the 8088 CPU had little memory management support. Unlike today's processors, which provide protection and paging, Intel's 8088 had no memory protection. Because it gave programs direct access to real, physical addresses (hence the term *Real mode*), all memory management had to be done in software. In Windows, application software had to cooperate closely with the operating system.

One of the ways in which Win16 applications running in Real mode cooperated with the operating system was by picking memory attributes for allocated memory that was suitable for the type of data being stored. Three attributes — fixed, moveable, and discardable — played the most important roles. The fixed attribute was for objects that didn't change size. On the global heap, this attribute was reserved for device driver and operating system use. The moveable attribute was for resizeable objects, and was the most common type for read-write data. Discardable memory was for temporary and read-only objects that could be purged when the system ran short of memory.

On a 1MB system, the operating system continually had to contend with running out of memory. As a result, discardable objects — which typically included code segments and resources such as menus and dialogs — were continually being reread from disk. The resulting poor performance and disk thrashing was a primary reason that versions of Windows prior to 3.0 weren't very successful. Only with Windows 3.0 could Windows programs start to get the multimegabytes of memory that are required for acceptable performance of GUI applications.

In Win16, GlobalAlloc( ) is the global — or segment — allocator. To allocate memory but not store physical memory addresses, the allocator returns a memory *handle*. To access memory, a program locks a heap object which returns a pointer. But to allow the memory manager to reorganize memory, Win16 programs had to unlock an object immediately after accessing it. For example, here is a typical code fragment for creating an object, copying an initial value to the memory, and then unlocking it:

```
// Allocate global memory object.
HGLOBAL hmem = GlobalAlloc(GMEM_MOVEABLE, 1);

// Lock, use, then unlock.
LPVOID  pData = GlobalLock(hmem);
strcpy ((char *)pData, "AA");
GlobalUnlock(hmem);
...
// Sometime later...
GlobalFree(hmem);
```

Note that unlocking a memory object is not the same as freeing it. When a program again needs to access the allocated block, it's a simple — if somewhat tedious — matter to again lock the handle. The result is a pointer suitable for reading or writing.

The Win16 subsegment allocator is LocalAlloc( ). Just like the global allocator, it returns handles. A difference between the two types of allocators is that on native Win16 implementations, the granularity and overhead of local heaps was lower than for the global heap. For example, global objects on Windows 3.1 had an overhead of 16 to 32 bytes, and a granularity of 32 bytes. Local objects, on the other hand, had a 4- to 8-byte overhead and a 4-byte granularity. Like the example previously shown for the global allocator, code that uses the local allocator involves allocating first and then locking to get a pointer:

```
// Allocate local memory object.
HLOCAL hmem = LocalAlloc(LMEM_MOVEABLE, 1);

// Lock, use, then unlock.
LPVOID  pData = LocalLock(hmem);
strcpy ((char *)pData, "AA");
LocalUnlock(hmem);
...
// Sometime later...
LocalFree(hmem);
```

On Windows 95 (and Windows NT), both Win16 allocators are implemented by making calls to the Win32 heap allocator. So, what happens to these memory attributes? The simplest case involves fixed memory objects, because that's the basic type of object supported by the Win32 heap allocator. It's slightly more involved for the other two types, which we'll describe to help you port Win16 code to Win32. Or, you might decide that you're interested in these other two types of memory. We'll cover Windows NT first, because it's the simpler case.

The Win32 heap allocator on Windows NT supports the moveable attribute but not the discardable attribute. Hidden with the GlobalAlloc functions, calls are made to HeapAlloc( ) to allocate a handle table. As in Win16, calls to GlobalAlloc( ) return a memory handle for moveable objects. When unlocked, such objects can be moved around the heap to minimize heap fragmentation. To access such objects, you must lock the object — which increments the object reference count before returning a pointer. You can make multiple calls to lock a single object, and each call increments the reference count. For the object to move, then, the same number of calls to unlock the object — to GlobalUnlock( ) — must be made.

Our tests on the final beta of Windows 95 show that it also supports the moveable attribute but not the discardable attribute. However, we did get word from the Windows 95 development team that they were considering adding support for discardable objects. We have no way to verify it at this point. So, if the capability to create discardable objects is important to your ability to port Win16 code to a Win32 program, Microsoft might have good news for you. Stay tuned to see what shows up in the shipping version of Windows 95.

The final issues in comparing Win16 to Win32 heap allocation are granularity and overhead. The granularity of the two is the same, because both are implemented in terms of the Win32 heap functions. That is, the granularity is 4 bytes on Windows 95 and 8 bytes on Windows NT.

The overhead is also the same, with the exception of moveable objects. In addition to the 4 bytes per Win32 heap object, each Win16 moveable object — whether allocated by calling GlobalAlloc( ) or LocalAlloc( ) — consumes an 8-byte handle table entry. That brings the total overhead for moveable objects to 12 bytes. A small price to pay, perhaps, for an easy port from Win16 to Win32. For discardable objects, the overhead is probably similar. But finding that out will have to await the final shipment of Windows 95.

In summary, an MFC/Win32 program has five dynamic allocators to choose from: the compiler's default malloc( ), the VirtualAlloc( ) page allocator, the HeapAlloc( ) subpage allocator, and the two Win16 allocators: GlobalAlloc( ) and LocalAlloc( ). Because memory is the lifeblood of your program, you'll want to choose your allocators carefully. By now, you should have enough background on all of these to decide when it's appropriate to use each one.

Our next topic is one that few programmers will need to use very often. But because this chapter aims to cover all types of MFC/Win32 memory, we touch on it briefly. The following section describes two memory types — window extra bytes and thread local storage — that involve connecting data to operating system objects.

CONNECTING MEMORY TO OPERATING SYSTEM OBJECTS

The Win16 and Win32 APIs allow applications to connect memory to two types of operating system objects: windows and threads. To some extent, the need to connect data to windows has been supplanted with MFC's CWnd (and derived) class. But a basic understanding of this memory type may help in porting Windows code written in C to MFC and C++.

Your need to connect data to threads depends on the extent to which you use threads. As mentioned earlier, threads are the unit of scheduling in Windows 95 and Windows NT. These are multithreaded operating systems, because they support the creation of multiple threads of execution within system processes. Although thread-specific data will probably find the widest use in multithreaded dynamic link libraries (DLLs), it can also be reasonably used in application code.

Window memory

In an MFC program, there are scarcely any reasons to use Win32 window memory types, because you get the same result by creating class data members in CWnd-derived classes. MFC automatically makes the connection between a Windows window and your data. However, this may be useful in understanding the operation of Windows programs written in C that use these types of data. There are three ways to connect data to a Windows window: properties, class extra bytes, and window extra bytes.

A *window property* is a pair of values connected to a window: a name and a handle value. The name is a character string, such as "color" or "file." The handle value is a memory handle, which you may recall is how Win16 programs identify dynamically allocated memory. A given window can have many property values, which are linked together in a property list. The idea behind properties is that they provide a way to have runtime binding of data to windows. We have found that this data type is seldom useful, though Windows apparently uses it internally for its own purposes. (Windows SDK programmers writing in C often use window properties to store window procedure values when subclassing windows. Subclassing is the creation of a message filter for a particular window, and it is a topic not covered in this book.)

The second type of window memory is *class extra bytes*. In this context, a window class is not a C++ class. Instead, it's a way that Windows stores default window attributes. As represented by the Win16 and Win32 WNDCLASS data structure, a window class holds — among other attributes — the default icon and cursor for a group of windows. Although MFC automatically creates Windows window classes for you, you are seeing examples of window classes when you look at the various types of dialog box controls. For example, Windows defines the following dialog box control classes: button, edit, listbox, combobox, scrollbar, and static.

Window extra bytes are a set of bytes shared by every window in a given window class. Applications in C have to define their own window classes by filling in a WNDCLASS structure and passing a pointer to that structure to Windows' RegisterClass( ) function. Windows stores a copy of WNDCLASS in one of its heaps to be able to reference it as needed. Window extra bytes are application-defined bytes that are allocated at the end of a WNDCLASS structure.

Of the three window memory types, the last one — window extra bytes — is the most interesting. We say that because, of the three types, this is the one that Windows programs in C are more likely to use. And that, after all, is the real test of an API feature.

When a Windows window is created — in response to the CreateWindow( ) or CreateWindowEx( ) API functions — Windows allocates a block of memory for that window. In OOP terms, it allocates instance data. Window extra bytes are application-specific bytes that are stored at the end of the windowing system's window instance data. This instance data isn't stored where the application can see it, but in one of Windows' private heaps.

Because window extra bytes are stored in Windows' private data areas, the only way to access them is by making Windows API calls. The following table lists the four functions that can read and write window instance data:

Windows API	*Description*
GetWindowWord()	Fetch a 2-byte value from window instance data. Negative values are for predefined system values; zero and positive values are for application-specific values.
GetWindowLong()	Fetch a 4-byte value from window instance data. Negative values are for predefined system values; zero and positive values are for application-specific values.
SetWindowWord()	Write a 2-byte value into window instance data. Negative values are for predefined system values; zero and positive values are for application-specific values.
SetWindowLong()	Write a 4-byte value into window instance data. Negative values are for predefined system values; zero and positive values are for application-specific values.

Thread local storage

Thread local storage provides the capability to connect data to a thread. Win32 supports two types of thread local storage: dynamic and static. Although dynamic thread local storage is the most cumbersome to use, it also provides the greatest flexibility. (By this, we mean it can be used in a dynamically loaded dynamic link library — that is, a DLL loaded with a call to LoadLibrary( ).) Static thread local storage is much easier to use — so easy, in fact, that it is almost indistinguishable from regular global variables. Unfortunately, there is a limitation on when static thread local storage can be used. Operating system quirks disable this feature in dynamically loaded DLLs.

As mentioned earlier, threads are the unit of scheduling in a Win32 program. When a Win32 process on Windows 95 or Windows NT starts running, Windows starts a thread. (Threads are not supported in Win32s.) After that, the only way to get new threads is by calling a Win32 function, CreateThread( ). The C-runtime library provides a wrapper function, _beginthread( ), that calls CreateThread( ), which sets up the C-runtime library to be "thread-aware." MFC calls this function when it needs to create new threads [actually, it calls _beginthreadex( ), which is a slight variation on _beginthread( )].

To keep track of thread-specific data, operating systems such as Windows 95 and Windows NT allocate memory to hold thread instance data. On Windows NT, this memory area is called the *thread environment block* (TEB). And on Windows 95 — as reported by Andrew Schulman — it's the *thread control block* (THCB). Whatever the name, these memory blocks hold operating system instance data that Windows maintains on a per-thread basis. Among the types of data held as thread instance data are the state of processor registers when a thread is not running, a pointer to the thread's stack, and a pointer to the exception data that is stored on the stack.

Dynamic thread local storage — like window extra bytes — is nothing more than application data that's stored in an operating system's data structure. When a thread is created under Windows NT or Windows 95, a TEB or THCB structure gets allocated. In addition to the memory that each operating system allocates for its own use, an array of DWORD (unsigned long) values is set aside for application use. Any part of an application's code — whether it is EXE code or DLL code — can reserve an array entry by making an API call, which applies to every thread in a given process. For example, if a process has three threads, a successful call to reserve dynamic thread local storage provides access to three DWORD entries, with one for each thread. When a given block of code is running, it automatically reads thread local storage values for the current thread in which it is executing.

How might EXE code or DLL code use dynamic thread local storage? The 4 bytes in a DWORD easily accommodate any 32-bit pointer to, for example, dynamically allocated data. If a program created threads for background tasks (such as printing, data sorting, database integrity checks), thread-specific data could hold a queue of tasks to be accomplished.

The Win32 API functions that maintain dynamic thread local storage are described in the following table:

Function	*Description*
TlsAlloc()	For all threads in the current process, request an element into the arrays of application-specific storage set aside by Windows in the thread instance data structure of each thread.
TlsFree()	Relinquish an index in the current process to the thread instance data structures.
TlsGetValue()	For the current thread, query the contents of a specific element in thread instance data.
TlsSetValue()	For the current thread, set the contents of a specific element in thread instance data.

When a thread local storage area is allocated [with a call to TlsAlloc( )], an index into the arrays of thread data is returned. That index must be stored in a shared memory area, which probably means in a global variable. Per-thread data could then be allocated dynamically, and a pointer to that data stored as thread local storage.

The second type of per-thread data is static thread local storage. This is the easiest to use, because — once declared — it looks just like global variables. In reality, the compiler and loader work together to automatically allocate a new set for every thread that is created within a process. And if you examine the assembly language code that the compiler generates to access this data, you see that some additional instructions add an extra level of indirection to that normally used to access data. The beauty of static thread local storage is that it looks like a global variable, but acts like per-thread data.

The key to static thread local data is a pair of keywords specific to the Microsoft C compiler: __declspec and thread. Here is how to define an integer value on a per-thread basis:

```
__declspec (thread) int i = 0;
```

All compiler keywords that start with an underscore (_) represent non-ANSI-standard C/C++ keywords. In the past, Microsoft freely added new declarators to its compiler: _pascal, _cdecl, _near, _far, _stdcall, and so on. But a problem might arise if such declarators clash with new keywords that become part of standard C++.

To control the proliferation of new declarator specifications, Microsoft created one more general, all-purpose declarator: __declspec. This is supposed to be the master declarator. All new compiler extensions — like static thread local storage — will be accessed using modifiers to the master declarator. At present, we know of only three other declarator specifications: dllimport, dllexport, and naked. More will be created to extend the compiler as needed.

To make the declaration of static thread local storage somewhat more readable, create a preprocessor symbol:

```
#define THREADDATA __declspec (thread)
```

The previous per-thread integer can then be rewritten in a slightly more readable form:

```
THREADDATA int i = 0;
```

Per-thread data must be initialized. The preceding example sets the integer variable to zero. Although it's a tiny difference to the application programmer, it makes a big difference to the compiler, which treats initialized data differently from uninitialized data. The current compiler implementation does not support per-thread uninitialized data, but it does support initialized per-thread data. A small difference helps ensure that you get the data support you need. (In our discussion of shared data later in this chapter, you'll see that you must also initialize global data to be shared between processes.)

As we've mentioned, the chief advantage of this type of per-thread data is that it looks just like a regular global variable. Once it's defined, you don't need to fuss with API calls to access data: It just appears when you need it. If you look at the machine code that the compiler creates, you will notice that access to this type of per-thread data does involve some additional instructions. But when you need per-thread data, it's a small price to pay.

Another advantage to this type of per-thread data is that you can allocate as much of it as you need. Although this example shows the allocation of a single variable, it's no problem to allocate thousands or even tens of thousands of bytes. Variables allocated on a per-thread basis are placed in their own section in the executable file. So, like other code and data sections, such data can span multiple megabytes as needed.

However, there is one limitation to static thread local storage. It cannot be used in dynamic link libraries which are dynamically loaded into memory. If a program calls LoadLibrary( ) to explicitly load a DLL into memory, static thread local storage cannot be used. An example of DLLs loaded into memory this way are printer device drivers. For statically loaded DLLs, static thread local storage works fine. These are DLLs that are brought into memory when the calling executable file is started. Aside from this limitation, however, static thread local storage provides a great way to connect application data to system threads.

This concludes our look at the different types of private, per-process memory. We now turn our attention to all the types of memory that exist for sharing memory between processes.

Shared Memory

For the rest of this chapter, we'll focus on the part of the Win32 API used to allocate shared memory — that is, memory shareable between two or more processes. So far in this chapter, we have focused on private memory allocation. Private data is arguably more important than shared, because most process data is private data. Perhaps for this reason Win32 provides more private data routines than shared memory routines. An important benefit of private process memory is that it enhances system stability. Because it lessens the risk that one application will overwrite the memory areas of another application, this is the default type of memory allocated for a process. To share memory, an application must explicitly override this default.

To an application developer, the distinction between private and shared memory may seem arbitrary. After all, data that's private one moment can be shared the next. To an operating system, however, the difference between private and shared memory is fundamental and important. As mentioned earlier in this chapter, the Win32 API exposes this difference by providing two routines to create address space: VirtualAlloc( ) for private address space and MapViewOfFile( ) for shared. Before a process allocates pages — on either Windows 95 or Windows NT — it must decide whether sharing is to be allowed. Let's look at some of the subtle ways in which each operating system handles the distinction between shared and private memory.

Windows 95 puts private pages in one part of the address space and shared pages in another. Private pages reside between 4MB and 2GB. As described earlier in this chapter, when a context switch occurs from one Win32 process to another, one set of pages is mapped out and another set is mapped into this address range, which is done by updating the CPU's page tables. Shared pages, on the other hand, reside between 2GB and 3GB. During a context switch, the Windows 95 memory manager doesn't touch the page tables for pages mapped into this area. By leaving the shared pages alone, the Windows 95 memory manager makes it quick and easy to share memory between processes.

The way in which Windows 95 places the image of executable files in a process address space presents an apparent contradiction. Because executable files are shareable entities, you might think that Windows 95 would place them in the shared address range. Although one type of DLL — system DLLs — gets loaded to the shared address range, that's not where private executables reside. Windows 95 maps private executable (.EXE) files and private dynamic link libraries (.DLL) to the private address range. By placing them in the private range, Windows 95 can pick and choose how to handle private executables. For efficient use of private DLLs and private EXE files, for example, Windows 95 maps a single set of physical pages into the address space of several processes.

Windows NT also differentiates between shared and private pages, though in a way that's subtler than Windows 95's use of different address ranges. The difference has to do with how Windows NT sets up processor page tables. Private pages on Windows NT simply use the Intel-86 paged memory addressing scheme we described at the beginning of this chapter. Each process has its own page directory and page tables, and on a context switch the CPU's CR3 register is updated for a new address space.

Windows NT differentiates shared pages from private pages in a subtler manner than Windows 95. As described by Helen Custer in *Inside Windows NT* (Microsoft Press), and as verified in conversations with the Windows NT developers, access to a memory location in a shared page causes a page fault. In many operating systems, a page fault means either that a page resides in the page file or that a memory addressing error — such as a NULL pointer reference — has occurred. Windows NT recognizes these two traditional uses of a page fault, but adds some others as a way to reveal shared memory to a process. When a fault occurs on a range of shared pages, Windows NT responds to the page fault to cause shared pages to magically appear to a process. Such fault-on-access pages are specially coded in the page table in a format called a *prototype page table entry*. The prototype page table entry contains a reference to a set of system page tables — an additional level of page tables that's not required for private pages — that indicates the location of the shared page. Just as on Windows 95, the decision to share a page or make it private has a profound impact on how Windows NT shoehorns a page into the address space of a process.

Incidentally, we describe the differences between Windows 95 and Windows NT to promote a deeper understanding of how each operates. By no means should you write code that, for example, tests for shared memory by looking for pointer values between 2GB and 3GB on Windows 95. [This implementation-specific characteristic might change in a future version. To check for shared pages, call VirtualQuery( ).] Nor should you worry that Windows NT somehow runs slower because of the overhead required to handle page faults on shared memory access; the processor time required for handling these page faults is much less than the time taken to draw a single line in a window border!

A common element unites all shared pages. In one form or another, all memory sharing in Win32 relies on Win32's memory mapped file I/O support. A memory mapped file uses shared memory to provide a common image of file-based data to two or more processes. As Andrew Schulman so eloquently puts it, "memory-mapped file I/O ... in essence can make a data file into a Windows virtual-memory [page] file" (see pages 76–77 of *Unauthorized Windows 95*).

What's not so obvious about memory mapped file I/O is that it provides memory sharing. To turn Schulman's definition around, sharing memory in a Win32 process uses a portion of the operating system's virtual memory page file like a memory mapped file. Although the emphasis is on sharing memory, the data in the memory pages could end up on disk. But rather than ending up in a permanent, named file, shared pages reside in the system's page file.

In the following sections, we'll explore four ways to share memory between processes. The relationships among the various types of shared memory are illustrated in Figure 16-5. We'll start with memory mapped files, because they are the backbone for other types of sharing. We'll then look at sharing memory pages that are not in a specifically named memory mapped file. We'll look at both types of shared pages: dynamically allocated and statically allocated. The fourth and final type of memory sharing we'll discuss is custom resources — that is, data stored in an application-defined format that gets accessed on a read-only basis. Like other types of resources, custom resources are bound into an executable file — either a .EXE file or a .DLL file — at program build time. Custom resources provide a useful means for storing a large volume of look-up data that gets paged to memory from an executable file as needed.

Application Programming Interface				
Code	Shared Data	Resources	Memory Mapped File != System Page File	[Memory Mapped File = System Page File]
Executable Image Files (.EXE and .DLL files)				
Shared Pages – Allocated with Calls to MapViewOfFile()				
Hardware: Intel-86 Processor + RAM + Disk				

Figure 16-5
A layered view of every type of Win32 shared process memory.

MEMORY MAPPED FILE I/O

Memory mapped file I/O refers to a feature of the Win32 API that simplifies the movement of data between a disk-based file and a range of memory addresses. When a file is mapped into a region of memory, the reading of bytes in the mapped memory produces the same results as the reading of bytes from the file, except that the virtual memory manager handles data buffering. Writing to mapped memory produces the same results as writing to the disk file, except that, once again, the virtual memory manager handles data buffering.

Memory mapped file I/O is highly efficient. Using what we call *creative procrastination*, the virtual memory manager doesn't do any work that isn't needed. When a view into a memory mapped file is first created, a range of addresses is set aside, but no data is actually read. We first encountered the idea of reserving memory ranges in our discussion of reserving private address ranges with VirtualAlloc( ). With a memory mapped file, access to a memory location reserved for memory mapped pages causes a page fault, to which the virtual memory manager responds by reading pages from disk and restarting the faulting instruction. Modified pages are only written back to disk when the virtual memory manager needs more pages [or when an application wants to force a write by calling the Win32 FlushFileBuffers( ) API]. This lazy approach keeps memory and processor use to a minimum.

Memory mapped file I/O allows two (or more) processes to share file-based data. Each process involved in the sharing has direct access to a common set of pages. Because the sharing occurs with a minimum of overhead, sharing with memory-mapped file I/O can be quite useful when a large amount of data must be shared. And because each process has direct access to the data, high bandwidth sharing is handled very efficiently.

You don't have to share memory to take advantage of memory mapped file I/O. There is clearly a difference between memory that is shareable and memory actually shared between two or more processes. The pages that are set up as memory mapped file pages are *shareable* — that is, you *can* share them — but sharing isn't required if it doesn't suit your purposes. There's nothing wrong with using memory mapped file I/O to simplify access to disk-based data with no intent to share. The capability to share is just an added feature that can be used when you need it.

Three Windows KERNEL objects are required for memory mapped file support: a file object, a file mapping object, and a view object. (MFC provides no wrappers for these objects.) To map a file to memory, the file is first opened, which causes a file object to be created.

Next, a file object must be connected to a memory mapped file object, which provides a logical connection to a disk-based file for synchronizing data between different processes. However, the presence of a memory mapped file object doesn't provide a pointer to data. For that, a view object is required. A view object provides a pointer to some block of data from the file. Multiple views can be created from a single memory mapped file object, which allows a process to pick and choose the specific parts of a file to access. Figure 16-6 illustrates the relationship among these three objects, along with the Win32 API functions that create each type.

```
HANDLE
hfile = CreateFile("FILE.DAT", ...);


HANDLE
hfm = CreateFileMapping (hfile, ...);


LPVOID
pData1 = MapViewOfFile(hfm, ...);
LPVOID
pData2 = MapViewOfFile(hfm, ...);
LPVOID
pData3 = MapViewOfFile(hfm, ...);
```

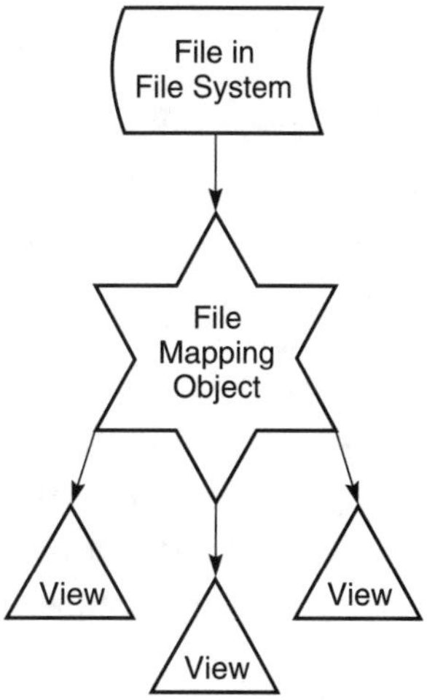

Figure 16-6
For memory mapped file I/O, you create three operating system objects using these three Win32 API functions.

Creating a file object

Two functions can be used to open files: one from the Win16 API and one from the Win32 API. We'll discuss the Win32 function first, though the Win16 function is easier to use. The Win32 function for opening files is CreateFile( ), which gets it name from the fact that it creates an operating system file object. This function can create files, open files, and open other operating system objects such as communications ports and named pipes. The Win16 function to open files is OpenFile( ). We prefer this function because it takes fewer parameters and has the added feature that it can be used to delete files. It isn't as capable as CreateFile( ), which can open other types of operating system objects as well as set file and security attributes. To open normal disk-based files, we prefer OpenFile( ) — which more or less simply wraps around a call to CreateFile( ). For details on an important difference in error handling between these functions and the rest of the Windows API, see the accompanying sidebar.

To open a file, we prefer the OpenFile( ) function, which is defined as follows:

```
HFILE WINAPI OpenFile(
    LPCSTR lpFileName,
    LPOFSTRUCT lpReOpenBuff,
    UINT uStyle);
```

Where:

- *lpFileName* is a text string which describes the path of the file to open.

- *lpReOpenBuff* is a pointer to a structure of type OFSTRUCT. This structure was created to support a style of file I/O required when accessing files on floppy disk, which requires that the files be kept closed most of the time. Otherwise, if a user changes disks, the entire file system of a floppy disk can be damaged. In fact, the only usable field in this structure is fFixedDisk, which indicates whether a floppy disk has been opened. (Despite its name, it doesn't detect CD-ROM drives, which appear as network drives.) The OFSTRUCT is defined in the Windows include files as follows:

```
typedef struct _OFSTRUCT {
    BYTE cBytes;
    BYTE fFixedDisk;
    WORD nErrCode;
    WORD Reserved1;
    WORD Reserved2;
    CHAR szPathName[OFS_MAXPATHNAME];
} OFSTRUCT, *LPOFSTRUCT, *POFSTRUCT;
```

- *uStyle* contains file-opening flags. Various flags indicate how the memory is to be accessed (OF_READ, OF_WRITE, OF_READWRITE); how the file is to be shared with other processes (OF_SHARE_EXCLUSIVE, OF_SHARE_DENY_WRITE, and so on); and the action to be taken

(OF_CREATE, OF_DELETE, OF_EXIST, and so on). For a complete set of flags, see the Win32 documentation.

Here is an example of calling this function to open a file:

```
HFILE hfile;
OFSTRUCT of;
hfile = OpenFile("FILE.DAT", &of, OF_READ | OF_SHARE_EXCLUSIVE);
if (hfile == (HFILE)-1)
{
    // Error opening file.
}
```

Windows File Handle Error Handling

While on the subject of files, we should mention an inconsistency between files and other types of Windows objects. The way you detect errors when opening files is different from the way you detect errors when creating other Win32 objects. For other types of objects, a handle value of NULL (zero) indicates failure. When a file-opening failure occurs, the file-opening functions return a handle value of –1. This value is represented by INVALID_HANDLE_VALUE, a long-winded but descriptive preprocessor symbol. Some developers prefer this symbol to hard-coding a test for a –1 return value.

For programmers new to Windows programming, the symbol INVALID_HANDLE_VALUE is twice confusing. First, its name suggests that it is generic to all types of handles when in fact it applies only to file handles. Second, there isn't a symbol for other types of invalid handles. Don't check for this value when testing for failure in the creation of windows, menus, dialog boxes, cursors, and icons; for GDI objects such as pens, brushes, fonts, DCs, bitmaps, and regions; or for KERNEL objects such as processes, threads, or semaphores. (As a form of protest against this inconsistency, one of the authors prefers to test for file-opening failure with a hard-coded –1.)

You might wonder why a failure to open a file in a Win32 program results in a handle value of –1 instead of 0. The reasons are historical. The Win32 API supports this feature to be backward compatible with the Win16 API. But you might wonder why Win16 works this way, given that NULL is also an invalid handle value in Win16? The answer is that Win16 programs (under Windows 3.x and earlier) rely on MS-DOS for file I/O, so Win16 programs must deal with what MS-DOS provides — which is a return value of –1 for file opening failure. The saga continues if you consider that MS-DOS itself was built as a CP/M clone by Tim Patterson at Seattle Computer, and CP/M itself uses –1 (actually 0xff) for an invalid handle value. The end result is that Win32 running on Windows 95 — and on Windows NT! — provides a file failure return value based on an operating system built in the mid-1970s.

Here's a comparable call to CreateFile( ):

```
HFILE hfile;
hfile = CreateFile (achFile,              // Filename.
                    GENERIC_READ,         // Access mode.
                    0,                     // Share Mode (0=None).
                    0,                     // Security.
                    OPEN_EXISTING,        // Create flags.
                    FILE_ATTRIBUTE_NORMAL, // File attribute flags.
                    0);                    // File to emulate.
if (hfile == (HFILE)-1)
{
    // Error opening file.
}
```

On success, the OpenFile( ) function — and its CreateFile( ) cousin — returns a valid HFILE file handle. To close the file, call CloseHandle( ). You'll use this same function to close several different types of KERNEL objects, including file mapping objects, which we discuss next. However, it cannot be used to close user-interface objects (such as windows, menus, cursors, and icons) or GDI drawing objects (such as DCs, pens, brushes, and fonts). It is unfortunate that the very generic name of this function suggests a widespread usability that does not exist for the Win32 API.

Creating a file mapping object

Once a file has been opened, the second step for memory mapped file support involves creating a file mapping object. This is done with a call to CreateFileMapping( ), a function which accepts a file handle as its first parameter. Although you might expect that this function would fail if you accidentally passed an invalid (–1) file handle, that's not what happens. As we'll discuss shortly, an invalid file handle for the first parameter creates shared memory instead of shared file access. The CreateFileMapping( ) function is defined as follows:

```
HANDLE WINAPI CreateFileMapping (
    HANDLE hFile,
    LPSECURITY_ATTRIBUTES lpsa,
    DWORD dwProtect,
    DWORD dwMaxSizeHigh,
    DWORD dwMaxSizeLow,
    LPCTSTR lpszMapName)
```

Where:

- *hFile* is a file handle returned from a call to OpenFile( ) or CreateFile( ).

- *lpsa* points to a SECURITY_ATTRIBUTES structure which defines the security attributes of the file mapping object on Windows NT. A value of NULL provides default security.

- *dwProtect* is a flag field for page protection flags, such as PAGE_READONLY, PAGE_READWRITE, and PAGE_WRITECOPY. These must be consistent with the access flags specified when opening the file.

- *dwMaxSizeHigh* is the high-order 32 bits for the maximum file size. (In anticipation of file systems that support files larger than 4GB, Win32 uses 64-bit file offsets.)

- *dwMaxSizeLow* is the low-order 32 bits for the maximum file size.

- *lpszMapName* is an optional string name that identifies the file mapping object. Provide NULL for none, or a character string that uniquely names the file mapping object.

Here's an example of calling this function to create an unnamed file mapping object:

```
// Create file mapping object.
HANDLE hfm
hfm = CreateFileMapping (hfile,        // File handle.
                         0,            // Ptr to Security.
                         PAGE_READONLY, // Page protection
                         0,            // File Size - Hi 32-bits
                         dwFileSize,   // File Size - Low 32-bits
                         0);           // Mapping Name.
```

When you create a file mapping object, you can give it a unique name if you'd like (in the lpszMapName field), such as "YAO_SHARED." Make sure that the name is unique, though, because an unexpected name collision with an unknown process will cause sharing in an unexpected and unwanted manner.

For two or more processes to share a single file, a single file mapping object must be created and shared between them. Once a file mapping object has been created with a call to CreateFileMapping( ), three different functions allow interprocess sharing: CreateFileMapping( ), OpenFileMapping( ), and DuplicateHandle( ). Let's take a moment to consider each function.

One way to share a single file mapping object is to give the file mapping object a name. Then, when two or more processes call Create-FileMapping( ) with the same name, a single file mapping object can be shared. The first process actually creates the file mapping object, and subsequent processes simply attach to the existing object. It might seem odd that only a single file mapping object is created even though several different processes might call this function, but the nature of sharing is that it isn't always easy to determine which process will get started first. To identify when a call to this function has not created a new and unique file mapping object, call GetLastError( ) and check for the ERROR_ALREADY_EXISTS return value.

A second function for interprocess sharing of a memory mapped file is OpenFileMapping( ), which takes as one of its parameters the name of the file mapping object. This function assumes that a file mapping object was already created with a call to CreateFileMapping( ). If the object named doesn't exist, this function returns a NULL file mapping handle. (Remember that a handle value of –1 only indicates file opening errors.)

A third function for connecting to an existing file mapping object is DuplicateHandle( ), which creates a KERNEL handle that another process can use. KERNEL handles are for the private use of a single process, but this function lets you freely create new handles from an existing handle for other processes. Notice that this function can only be used to map certain types of handles (a complete list is given in the Win32 documentation). In general, this function cannot duplicate user-interface object handles or GDI drawing object handles. It can, however, be used to duplicate KERNEL objects — which on Windows NT are more properly called Executive objects — including handles for files, file mapping objects, processes, threads, semaphores, mutexes, and events.

Creating a view object

Once a file object and a file mapping object have been created, the third step in accessing a memory mapped file is to create one or more views of the data file. When a view is created, address space is reserved to allow access to portions of the memory mapped file. On access to this range of addresses, memory pages are allocated and data is read from disk. Multiple views can be created into a single file, to allow selective access to different portions of the memory mapped file. For example, views might be created to the beginning of a file to access header information; to the end, where a duplicate header might be stored; and to areas in the middle, where various pieces of data reside.

To create a view into a memory mapped file, call MapViewOfFile( ). This function is defined as follows:

```
LPVOID
WINAPI
MapViewOfFile(
    HANDLE hFileMappingObject,
    DWORD dwDesiredAccess,
    DWORD dwFileOffsetHigh,
    DWORD dwFileOffsetLow,
    DWORD dwNumberOfBytesToMap);
```

Where:

- *hFileMappingObject* is a handle to a file mapping object.

- *dwDesiredAccess* is the access desired to the file mapping data. For example, it could be FILE_MAP_READ for read-only access, or FILE_MAP_READ | FILE_MAP_WRITE for read-write access.

- *dwFileOffsetHigh* is the high-order 32 bits of the offset in the file of the beginning of the area to map to memory.

- *dwFileOffsetLow* is the low-order 32 bits of the offset in the file of the beginning of the area to map to memory.

- *dwNumberOfBytesToMap* is the number of bytes to map. This will be rounded up to the nearest page boundary (4K on Intel). If zero, the entire file is mapped.

Here's an example of how this function might be called to create a view that references the first 4,096 bytes in a file:

```
// Create view of file mapping object.
LPVOID lpData;
lpData = MapViewOfFile (hFileMapping,
                FILE_MAP_READ,  // Page protection.
                0,              // File Offset - Hi 32-bits
                0,              // File Offset - Low 32-bits
                4096);          // Size of view
```

A slight variation on the routines that share access to a memory mapped file also allows sharing of pages between processes. Let's see what this involves.

DYNAMICALLY ALLOCATING SHARED PAGES

The second technique for memory sharing involves dynamically allocating shared pages. Although the Windows 95 and Windows NT implementations differ, when you use them, you want the same results: getting access to the same physical memory pages between two or more processes. For complete compatibility between Windows 95 and Windows NT, you should be aware of some of the implementation differences.

Windows 95 and Windows NT sharing differences

The key difference between the implementation of memory sharing on Windows 95 and Windows NT involves memory addresses. On Windows 95, a shared page is visible to all Win32 processes at the same address — guaranteed. That's because shared pages are mapped into the window of shared addresses between 2GB and 3GB. On Windows NT, on the other hand, the address of shared pages *can be* different within the address space of different processes. And they can be the same, depending on which objects are already mapped into a process address space. To properly share pages on both operating systems, a Win32 process must be prepared for the worst case — that is, for the way in which Windows NT shares pages.

Tempting shortcuts on Windows 95 will break in Windows NT. For example, if you merely share the address between two processes — which always works on Windows 95 — you are guaranteed to crash on Windows NT. This shortcut may be particularly attractive to developers who are porting Win16 programs from Windows 3.1 to the Win32 API for operation on Windows 95. Because Win16 programs on Windows 3.1 can share memory by just passing pointers, a quick fix to get running on Windows 95 would be to again share a pointer to a shared block. But don't do it; instead, make the calls to the necessary functions to ensure that you run on Windows NT and on future Win32 implementations.

There is an important difference between the way that Windows 95 and Windows 3.1 share data. To allocate a shared object in Windows 3.1, programmers called GlobalAlloc( ) and passed the GMEM_SHARE (or GMEM_DDESHARE) flag. That flag overrides some of the automatic memory cleanup that Windows 3.1 otherwise imposes on a dynamically allocated segment. In Win32, this flag has no effect. As described earlier in this chapter, all GlobalAlloc( )-allocated memory is placed within the range of addresses for process-private memory. This memory sharing mechanism that has no support under the Win32 API.

Win32 functions for sharing pages

The functions you call to share memory pages are the same ones you call to share memory mapped files. You first create a file mapping object by calling CreateFileMapping( ). When called with a file handle of (HFILE)–1, the file mapping object connects itself to a system page file. To access specific shared bytes, you call MapViewOfFile( ). We discussed both functions in the previous section.

The following code fragment creates a shared memory object with the name "YAO_DATA":

```
DWORD   dwSize; // Desired size of file mapping object.
HANDLE  hfm;    // Handle to file mapping object.
LPVOID  lpData; // Pointer to shared data.

// Create file mapping object.
hfm = CreateFileMapping ((HANDLE)0xffffffff, // File handle.
                          0,                  // Ptr to Security.
                          PAGE_READWRITE,     // Page protection
                          0,                  // File Size - Hi-bits
                          dwSize,             // File Size - Low-bits
                          "YAO_DATA");        // Mapping Name.

if (hfm == 0)
{
    MessageBox (hwnd, "Unable to Create File Mapping Object",
                achAppName, MB_OK);
    return FALSE;
}

// Exit if named object already exists.
if (GetLastError() == ERROR_ALREADY_EXISTS)
{
    MessageBox (hwnd, "File Mapping Object Already Exists.",
                achAppName, MB_OK);
    CloseHandle (hfm);
    return FALSE;
}
```

```
// Create view of file mapping object.
lpData = MapViewOfFile (hfm,
                        FILE_MAP_WRITE, // Protection.
                        0,              // File Offset - Hi 32-bits
                        0,              // File Offset - Low 32-bits
                        0);             // Size is whole object.

if (lpData == 0)
{
    MessageBox (hwnd, "Can't Create View of File Mapping Object",
                achAppName, MB_OK);
    CloseHandle (hfm);
    return FALSE;
}
```

Notice in this code fragment that the file handle provided in the call to CreateFileMapping( ) is 0xffffffff — or negative 1. We could as easily have provided INVALID_HANDLE_VALUE, which might make this code more understandable.

The size of the shared area is set in the call to CreateFileMapping( ) — dwSize in this example. The assumption here is that we are limiting ourselves to 4GB of shared data. The call to MapViewOfFile( ) in this example passes a view size of zero, which sets the view size equal to include all of the shared pages.

When creating shared memory areas, the protection attributes of the file mapping object limit what can be set in view objects. For example, a read-only (PAGE_READONLY) setting on a file mapping object can't be mapped by a writable (FILE_MAP_WRITE) view. The file mapping object sets the maximum allowable protection, which is enforced for individual views.

As mentioned earlier, a given shared page in Windows NT can be mapped to a different address in different processes. When designing a memory sharing strategy, you must be careful to avoid relying on the Windows 95 implementation, which guarantees that shared pages are at the same address for different processes. The Microsoft Visual C++ compiler supports the creation of based pointers — a feature that helps simplify access to shared data with a minimum of programming hassles.

Sharing pointers between processes using based pointers

Data containing absolute pointers cannot be easily shared between Win32 processes. By *absolute* pointers, we simply mean absolute memory addresses within the 4GB address space of a Win32 process. Because pointers are so useful and efficient in connecting data structures, the Visual C++ compiler supports a feature called *based pointers* which allows you to create relative pointers. At the cost of a tiny bit of hidden pointer arithmetic, based pointers provide all the advantages of pointers within the constraints of Win32 shared memory.

Absolute pointers are only a problem when sharing memory between Win32 processes on Windows NT. Under Win32s, in which all processes run in a common address space, absolute pointers create no problems. And on Windows 95, as we have discussed, a common shared memory area between 2GB and 3GB helps simplify memory sharing both for the operating system — which can run fast and lean — and for Win32 processes which all share a common view of objects in this address range. On Windows NT, all Win32 processes have a private address space between 0 and 2GB. Although it's possible for memory to be mapped to the same address in different address spaces, there's no guarantee. For that reason, if you want a Win32 program to share memory properly on Windows NT, you must assume that the shared memory will appear at a different address in each process that accesses the memory. Within the shared memory object, only relative pointers can be used.

A relative pointer is an offset — something familiar to programmers who have written Win16 programs, which rely on Intel's segmented addressing. Although you could do your own pointer arithmetic, the compiler's support for based pointers makes pointer arithmetic automatic. Microsoft first introduced support for based pointers for efficient access of segmented memory in a 16-bit program. Under Win32, this same feature is employed in the creation and use of relative pointers in shared memory.

To support based pointers, Microsoft added a new keyword to its compiler: __based, which takes as an operand a base address. Given a base address of pData — which is perhaps a char * — here is how to define a based pointer named pBasedPointer:

```
char __based(pData) * pBasedPointer;
```

Once declared, a based pointer can be used the same way as a regular pointer:

```
char * pData;
char __based(pData) * pBasedPointer;

pData = (char *)MapViewOfFile(...);
pBasedPointer = pData;
strcpy (pBasedPointer, "Relative (based) pointer");
strcpy (pData, "Absolute pointer");
```

To get an accurate idea of what the compiler does when using a based pointer, it helps to look at the assembly language generated for an access to an absolute pointer and a relative pointer. The following fragment was taken from the assembly language listing in the previous example:

```
; 30   :      strcpy (pBasedPointer, "Relative (based) pointer");

push   OFFSET FLAT:$SG17596
mov    eax, DWORD PTR _pBasedPointer$[ebp]
add    eax, DWORD PTR _pData$[ebp]
push   eax
call   _strcpy
add    esp, 8


; 31   :      strcpy (pData, "Absolute pointer");

push   OFFSET FLAT:$SG17597
mov    eax, DWORD PTR _pData$[ebp]
push   eax
call   strcpy
add    esp, 8
```

An extra machine instruction (add eax, DWORD PTR _pData) is generated for each use of the relative pointer. With a based pointer, you get the ease of using an absolute pointer, with the advantages of a relative pointer.

Based pointers are useful when you need to store a pointer within a shared memory block. You don't need to use relative pointers to access shared memory itself — for that, absolute pointers work quite nicely. If you're counting processor cycles — a practice which is becoming less important as processors get faster — absolute pointers are a bit faster than based pointers. But when you need to store an actual pointer inside the shared memory block, you should use a based pointer. This allows different processes to freely use the pointer without worrying about whether the shared block itself is at the same address in the address space of different processes.

In the following section, we'll discuss shared pages that are statically allocated by cooperation between the compiler, the linker, and the loader.

STATICALLY ALLOCATING SHARED PAGES

The Microsoft Visual C++ compiler provides the capability to share global variables between different processes. This feature relies on the compiler and the linker allocating shared pages within an executable file. At runtime, the loader allows such pages to get mapped into the address space of several processes at the same time. As with shared pages that are dynamically allocated, a single set of physical pages gets magically mapped into the address space of multiple processes.

Three requirements must be met for shared global variables to be available. First, the global variables must be initialized. Second, the shared global variables should be declared in their own section. And third, the shared attribute must be assigned to the executable file's section in which variables to be shared are contained. This is done by making an entry in the module definition (.DEF) file. Let's look at these requirements, one at a time.

Shared global variables must be initialized because the compiler, linker, and loader treat uninitialized data different from initialized data. A copy of the initialized data actually appears in the executable file. On the other hand, there isn't a need for uninitialized data to take up space on disk in executable files, so the loader can handle allocating memory for uninitialized data without reading data from the executable file. An added benefit of initializing the data is that it begins life in a known state without any process worrying about it.

The second requirement, that shared global variables should be declared in their own section, is not strictly necessary. For example, an executable file could share all of its global variables. After all, Win16 dynamic link libraries have a single data segment that is shared by all processes. But because this tends to cause more problems than it solves, you'll probably want both shared and private global variables.

To declare global variables in their own section, you sandwich the declaration between a pair of data_seg pragma statements. As you probably suspect, the *seg* part of this name is a holdover from the segmented addressing of 16-bit MS-DOS and Windows. Here's an example of a character array that is placed into a section named ".shared":

```
// Put shared data into section named ".shared".
#pragma data_seg (".shared")
char achPublic[BUFSIZE] = "";
// Set name of data section back to default _DATA
#pragma data_seg ()
```

The #pragma keyword looks like a preprocessor statement, but it's not. It's an instruction to the compiler to provide some special service. In this case, the data_seg keyword requests a change in the name of the segment in which data is stored. When no name is specified, as appears in the second #pragma data_seg statement, the default name of _DATA is used. Incidentally, the name we use for the shared memory section does not make it shared, so we could have provided it an arbitrary name such as "DanielBoone". Sharing only happens when a section is marked as shared in the module definition file, which happens in the third step.

The third step in sharing global variables between processes is to mark as shared the section which contains the variable(s) to be shared. To do this, you make an entry in the module definition file. This is a file that essentially contains a set of linker switches. When building dynamic link libraries, for example, a list of functions to make available to the outside world is listed under the EXPORTS keyword. To set the memory attributes for a section of an executable file, the SECTIONS keyword is required. The following example is the entire module definition file from a dynamic link library that contains shared global variables. The entry under the SECTIONS keyword allows the section named ".shared" to be shared between different processes:

```
LIBRARY DATASTOR

DESCRIPTION 'Sample Win32 DLL'

SECTIONS
    .shared READ WRITE SHARED

EXPORTS
    GetPrivateData
    SetPrivateData
    GetPublicData
    SetPublicData
```

The last type of shared memory that we'll discuss is custom resources.

CUSTOM RESOURCES

Custom resources hold look-up tables bound into Win32 executable files. We use the term *custom* to differentiate them from Windows' predefined resources. (Table 10-5 in Chapter 10 has a summary of types of predefined resources.) Any large set of data — say, more than 64K — that is read but not modified is a candidate for storing as a custom resource. Like other resource types, custom resources are listed in a program's resource (.RC) file and bound into an executable (either .EXE or .DLL) file by the linker.

Examples of custom resources

An example of data to store in a custom resource is sine and cosine tables in a program that needs fast access to such values. Although the sine and cosine can be calculated on-the-fly, that would slow down a program such as a game that needs to perform hundreds or thousands of complex calculations per second. Another example of custom resource use is tax tables in tax calculation software. Federal income tax in the United States can be calculated using several methods, including table lookup. A custom resource could be used by tax software for storing tax table data.

A custom resource has distinct advantages over other ways to store look-up data. For example, the placing of look-up data in separate data files creates the problem that such files can be misplaced or become corrupt. Because it is bound into an executable file, look-up data stays safe.

Another alternative is to store look-up tables in one or more global variables. But mixing read-only data with read-write data creates inefficiencies for the operating system's virtual memory manager. Memory pages with read-write data cannot be shared between processes. Also, when any change has been made to data in a read-write page, the page must be written to the page file before being purged from memory. If a read-write page contains any read-only data, it's a waste of memory to write that data to the page file and then read it back. On the other hand, read-only pages can be freely purged when a virtual memory manager needs to use a page for another purpose.

Storing look-up tables as global data creates practical problems when updating look-up data that has changed. (Sine and cosine data probably stays the same, but tax tables can change annually.) In particular, such updates require changes to program source code files. Although it's a simple task for a programmer, a person untrained in programming basics can easily create many problems when editing program source files. On the other hand, only minimal training is required to modify resource data.

Defining a custom resource

Creating a custom resource starts with the creation of a data file to hold the resource data. How you create the data file and what you put in it are up to you. You could use simple text files or a binary format of your own choosing. When you write the code to access the resource, you get a pointer to the resource data. Although it can be any format that you want, you will simplify coding issues if you design resource data formats that work well with the ways in which you plan to use the data.

Connecting a custom resource data file to an executable file requires an entry in the resource (.RC) file. In the Visual C++ IDE, you do this by first opening the .RC file. Next, select the Resource|Import... menu item, which prompts first for the name of the file to import and then for the resource type. The resource type is something you define for your own uses. When accessing the data from your source code, you must specify both the resource type and a unique ID for each resource block.

Accessing a custom resource

Accessing custom resource data from a Win16 or Win32 program requires a series of Win16 or Win32 function calls: FindResource( ), LoadResource( ), and LockResource( ). The reason why there are three rather than one is historical: In the Win16 API, each step performed a different function. In Win32, all three can be combined into a single step because the memory mapped file mechanism handles all low-level memory operations.

Here's an example of code to access a custom resource. Given a resource named "TAXTABLE" and a resource ID of IDR_HEADOF-HOUSHOLD, the following lines of code in an MFC program provide a pointer for accessing the tax data. This code assumes the existence of a mythical structure type named TAXBRACKET:

```
HINSTANCE hinstRes = AfxGetResourceHandle();
HRSRC hres1 = FindResource (hinstRes,
                        MAKEINTRESOURCE(IDR_HEADOFHOUSHOLD),
                        "TAXTABLE");
HGLOBAL hres2 = LoadResource (hinstRes, hres1);
TAXBRACKET * ptax = (TAXBRACKET *)LockResource(hres2);
```

This small fragment of code shows some Windows API programming quirks that are worth some additional comments. To access resources from an executable file, an instance handle identifies which executable file to use. This is the value passed to a program's WinMain( ) entry point. As shown in this example, an MFC program can access this value by calling AfxGetResourceHandle( ). Resources can be loaded from a DLL by substituting the DLL's resource instance handle [that is, the DLL's module handle, which is returned by calls to LoadLibrary( ) and Get-ModuleHandle( )].

The call to FindResource( ) contains two resource identifiers: the string "TAXTABLE" and IDR_HEADOFHOUSHOLD, an integer defined in resource.h. Because FindResource( ) expects two string (char *) resource identifiers, the Windows API provides the MAKEINTRESOURCE( ) macro around the resource integer value which packages the integer in a pointer and casts the pointer to char *. In general, integer resource identifiers are preferred to string identifiers because they occupy less space and a table of integers can be searched more quickly than a table of strings.

Summary

From the subjects covered in this chapter, you can see that the Win32 API provides many types of memory. Although the C-runtime malloc( ) function and the C++ new operator provide basic memory allocation, they are intended for general-purpose use. Specialized purposes may require more specialized allocation mechanisms that provide better control, better performance, or greater fine-tuning of memory operations.

How to Use the CD

*T*he accompanying CD contains the entire *Foundations of Visual C++ Programming for Windows 95* in easy-to-use hypertext form. It also contains copies of all the source code used in the book.

Installation Instructions

To install the CD, follow these steps:

1. Put the CD in your CD drive.
2. From Windows Program Manager (or File Manager) select File|Run.
3. Enter *d*:SETUP (where *d* is the drive letter of your CD drive).

This creates a program group "IDG Books" and the *Foundations of Visual C++ Programming* icon. Double-click on the icon to start the program.

Source Code

Source code is organized on the CD by chapter. For example, the BASE-MENU and CTRLBARS programs are in separate subdirectories under the directory CHAP11. You can load these programs into Visual C++ directly from the CD or you can copy them to your hard disk.

Viewer Documentation

The viewer used for this CD is the Microsoft Multimedia Viewer, which is used in many multimedia products, such as Microsoft Bookshelf. On the viewer's toolbar are the following buttons. To select an option, click on the appropriate button or press the underlined letter.

Contents	Move to the contents page.
Index	Display a list of key words and phrases.
Go Back	Return to the previously viewed page.
History	Display a list of the most recently viewed pages and select one to return to.
Search	Perform a full-text search for any word or phrase used in the text.
<<	View the previous page.
>>	View the next page.

Text References

Within the text, certain words and phrases are highlighted in red or blue.

A red highlight means there is a glossary definition for the term. When you click on the term, a pop-up window appears that contains the definition. When you click anywhere else or press Escape, the pop-up window disappears. (You may also use the tab keys to select a highlighted term and press Enter to display the reference.)

A blue highlight is a reference to another page in the document. When you click on a reference to a figure, table, or listing, a new window opens that contains the figure, table, or listing. When you click on a reference to a chapter or sidebar, the screen changes to the first page of the chapter or sidebar.

Search

When you select the Search button, a dialog box appears. Using this dialog box, you may search all of the book, or selected sections, for any word or phrase. To search the entire book, simply type the word or phrase in the Search by Word box and press Enter or click OK. To search only specific sections, select the parts to search in the Topic Groups box.

You can do more complex searches by using the keywords AND, OR, NEAR, and NOT to narrow the search; click the Hints button for some samples.

To limit the search to the topics selected on a previous search, select the Options button and check List of Previous Topics Found.

To limit the search to topic titles only, select the Options button and check Topic Titles Only.

Search Results

When a search has completed, the Search Results dialog box is displayed. You can use this dialog box to review all the "finds" of your search. All topics containing the searched text are listed. You can scroll through this list to look for likely areas to view.

Click the Go To button to display the topic. The Search Results dialog box stays open on top of the document so you can move easily from place to place within the list, reviewing all references to the searched text. In the document, the text found is highlighted wherever it appears.

The Previous Match and Next Match buttons move within a topic, stopping at each highlighted find.

The To Search button returns to the Search dialog box.

The Cancel button closes the Search Results box, leaving the current topic on display.

Index

The Index box provides a list of all indexed key words and phrases. Type the first character or characters of a word or phrase and the list will move to the first entry that matches the characters entered. Click OK to select a key word.

If only one topic contains a reference for the key word selected, that topic will be displayed immediately. If more than one topic is referenced, a dialog box listing all related topics is displayed. Select the topic desired and click OK. Click To Index to return to the index list, or click Cancel to close the dialog.

Glossary

absolute pointers: absolute memory addresses within the 4GB address space of a Win32 process.

access protection: the capability to designate members, both data and functions, as private to a class, as available only to a class, or inherited classes, or as available to all parts of the program.

anonymous union: a unnamed union that doesn't declare any members in the scope of the class in which it's defined.

bitmaps: arrays of pixels. A common way to create a bitmap is with dedicated scanner hardware that converts an image on paper into a digital bitmap.

class extra bytes: a way that Windows stores default window attributes. Among other attributes, a window class holds the default icon and cursor for a group of windows.

client area: the rectangular area that the system reserves for your use within the window. Your application is the client, so, as the developer, it's your job to manage the client area.

compound files: files that have a format that's often described as a "file system within a file," because the logical structure of the file mimics the hierarchical file system structure of operating systems such as MS-DOS and Unix.

constructor functions: member functions that give the programmer control over the actions at the creation of all objects of that class.

context menu: a menu displayed when the user selects an object and then clicks with the secondary (usually the right) mouse button. Sometimes called a pop-up menu.

critical section objects: high-performance synchronization objects used to coordinate the activities of two or more threads in the same process. Only one thread is allowed to access the protected data object. Typical use is to protect a critical section of code.

custom resources: resources that hold look-up tables bound into Win32 executable files.

data windows: windows that are contained by frames and dialogs to hold some piece of user data.

destructor functions: member functions that give the programmer control over the actions at the deletion of all objects of that class.

document templates: a type of object that creates frame windows and view windows as your application needs them.

events: interprocess synchronization objects used to start waiting threads. Events are like a starter's gun at a race. Two types are supported: manual-reset and auto-reset.

exceptions: events that don't usually happen.

friend functions: functions that aren't member functions of a class, but still have the same access privileges to members of the class as its member functions do.

friend: a data type that is granted limited access to hidden parts of another data type.

handles: integers that identify native WinAPI objects.

idle work: processing time that's not related to user input. For example, you might perform a sort, query a hardware device, or clean up leftover data. You tap into this processing time by overriding the OnIdle( ) function in your application class.

inheritance: the capability to define a new class that has all of the properties and procedures of an existing class, but with added elements. In object-oriented programming, one class can inherit all of the data and functions that are members of another class.

keyboard mnemonic: defines the keyboard interface to a menu item. It comes into play when the user activates a menu by holding the Alt key down while pressing the underlined letter, or mnemonic, for that menu. For example, because of keyboard mnemonics, File|Open can be selected with Alt-F-O, that is by holding down the Alt key and pressing F O.

member functions: functions associated with a class, that define how to use objects in that class.

memory leaks: an object that has been allocated but never de-allocated. Such problems are particularly insidious for programs that must run continuously, because all system memory is eventually consumed and a crash results.

memory wallets: extra bytes and thread local storage to tuck away data associated with operating system objects. They are "memory cubbyholes" which can help simplify the relationship between a program's data and operating system objects.

message loop: an "almost infinite" loop that runs for the life of a program to poll the system for user input to a program's window.

module: an executable image such as a .EXE program or a .DLL dynamic link library. In Microsoft "language" module doesn't refer to a program/ source file, but an executable image.

multiple inheritance: occurs when a class inherits from more than one parent class.

mutexes: interprocess synchronization objects used to prevent more than one thread at a time from accessing a protected data object.

naming mangling: mixing up a function name with the names of its argument types in a consistent way, so that when the program is linked the correction function calls and definitions are automatically put together.

nonclient area: everything outside the client area. The Windows system automatically manages this area for you. Among the components that can reside in the nonclient area are the caption bar, the system menu, the application menu, the sizeable border, and the scroll bars.

page tables: a special memory page that resides in a 4K memory page and can refer to 1,024 other pages that each hold application code or data.

persistence: the capability for a class to read and write its objects to and from a data stream such as a disk file.

prototype page table entry: a special table entry format that contains a reference to a set of system page tables that indicates the location of the shared page. System page tables are an additional level of page tables that are not required for private pages.

region: a set of reserved memory addresses.

scope resolution: the capability to resolve ambiguities in scope caused by inheritance problems, or by the natural protection that keeps a name from having a meaning outside of its scope.

segments: units of memory addressing. They can be as small as 1 byte or as large as 64K.

semaphores: interprocess synchronization objects used to limit the maximum number of threads that simultaneously access a particular resource.

signatures: function names plus argument types.

text keys: printable characters, that is, upper- and lowercase letters, numbers, punctuation marks, and other symbols.

threads: The unit of scheduling in Windows 95 and Windows NT. At start-up, a process is granted a single thread. A process can add threads by calling Win32 or C-runtime functions.

view windows: windows created from a CView-derived class. View windows provide a graphical representation of some piece of data.

virtual functions: the capability to declare special member functions in such a way that each inherited type has its own version, and so that the version of the member function defined for an object's declared type will be used, even if it's being used in an inherited procedure (and so is cast to its base type).

window property: a pair of values connected to a window — a name and a handle value. The name is the character string, such as "color" or "file." The handle value is a memory handle.

Window extra bytes: a set of bytes shared by every window in a given window class.

Recommended Reading

ANSI X3J16/ISO WG21 Joint Technical Committee. *Working Paper for Draft Proposed International Standard for Information Systems — Programming Language C++*. CBEMA, Washington, DC, 1994. (The 1995 *Draft Standard* is becoming available as this book goes to press.)

Object Oriented Design with Applications. The Benjamin/Cummings Publishing Company, Redwood City, CA, 1991.

Booch, Grady. *Object Oriented Design with Applications*. The Benjamin/Cummings Publishing Company, Redwood City, CA, 1991.

C/C++ Users Journal, R&D Publications Inc., Lawrence, KS.

C++ Report, SIGS Publications Inc., New York NY.

Cline, Marshall P., and Greg A. Lomow. *C++ FAQs: Frequently Asked Questions*. Addison-Wesley, Reading, MA, 1995.

Ellis, Margaret A. and Bjarne Stroustrup. *The Annotated C++ Reference Manual*. Addison-Wesley, Reading, MA, 1992.

Foley, J.D., and A. Van Damn. *Fundamentals of Interactive Computer Graphics*. Addison-Wesley, Reading, MA, 1984.

Gamma, Erich, Richard Helm, Ralph Johnson, and John Vlissides. *Design Patterns*. Addison-Wesley, Reading, MA, 1995.

Intel Corp. *i486 Microprocessor*. Intel Corp., Santa Clara, CA, 1989.

Intel Corp. *i486 Processor Programmer's Reference Manual*. Intel Corp., Santa Clara, CA, 1990.

Kernighan, Brian W., and Dennis M. Ritchie. *The C Programming Language, Second Edition.* Prentice Hall, Englewood Cliffs, NJ, 1988.

Maguire, Steve. *Writing Solid Code.* Microsoft Press, Redmond, WA, 1993.

Microsoft Corp. *Windows 95 User Interface Design Guide*, Microsoft Corp., Redmond, WA, 1995.

Microsoft Systems Journal, Miller Freeman Inc., San Mateo CA.

Pietrek, Matt. "Understanding Windows 95 Memory Management: Paging, Address Spaces, and Context" in *Microsoft Systems Journal*, volume 10, no. 4, April, 1995.

Schulman, Andrew. *Unauthorized Windows 95 Developers Resource Kit.* IDG Books Worldwide, Inc., San Mateo, CA, 1994.

Stroustrup, Bjarne. *The C++ Programming Language.* Addison-Wesley, Reading, MA, 1993.

Stroustrup, Bjarne. *The Design and Evolution of C++.* Addison-Wesley, Reading, MA, 1994.

IDG Books Worldwide License Agreement

3. **Other Restrictions.** You may not rent or lease the Software. You may transfer the Software and user documentation on a permanent basis provided you retain no copies and the recipient agrees to the terms of this Agreement. You may not reverse engineer, decompile, or disassemble the Software except to the extent that the foregoing restriction is expressly prohibited by applicable law. If the Software is an update or has been updated, any transfer must include the most recent update and all prior versions.

4. **Limited Warranty.** IDG Warrants that the Software and disc are free from defects in materials and workmanship for a period of sixty (60) days from the date of purchase of this Book. If IDG receives notification within the warranty period of defects in material or workmanship, IDG will replace the defective disc. IDG's entire liability and your exclusive remedy shall be limited to replacement of the Software, which is returned to IDG with a copy of your receipt. This Limited Warranty is void if failure of the Software has resulted from accident, abuse, or misapplication. Any replacement Software will be warranted for the remainder of the original warranty period or thirty (30) days, whichever is longer.

5. **No Other Warranties.** To the maximum extent permitted by applicable law, IDG and the authors disclaim all other warranties, express or implied, including but not limited to implied warranties of merchantability and fitness for a particular purpose, with respect to the Software, the programs, the source code contained therein and/or the techniques described in this Book. This limited warranty gives you specific legal rights. You may have others which vary from state/jurisdiction to state/jurisdiction.

6. **No Liability for Consequential Damages.** To the extent permitted by applicable law, in no event shall IDG or the authors be liable for any damages whatsoever (including without limitation, damages for loss of business profits, business interruption, loss of business information, or any other pecuniary loss) arising out of the use of or inability to use the Book or the Software, even if IDG has been advised of the possibility of such damages. Because some states/jurisdictions do not allow the exclusion or limitation of liability for consequential or incidental damages, the above limitation may not apply to you.

7. **U.S. Government Restricted Rights.** Use, duplication, or disclosure of the Software by the U.S. Government is subject to restrictions stated in paragraph (c) (1) (ii) of the Rights in Technical Data and Computer Software clause of DFARS 252.227-7013, and in subparagraphs (a) through (d) of the Commercial Computer—Restricted Rights clause at FAR 52.227-19, and in similar clauses in the NASA FAR supplement, when applicable.

Index

(continued)

SYSTEM MESSAGES

• M •

• **T** •

5/8/95

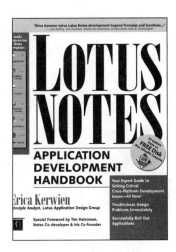

Lotus Notes Application Development Handbook
by Erica Kerwien

ISBN: 1-56884-308-9
$39.99 USA/$54.99 Canada

Covers versions 3.01 and 3.1.
Software included.

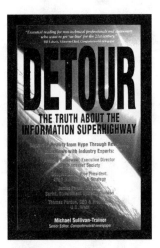

Detour: The Truth About the Information Superhighway
by Michael Sullivan-Trainor

ISBN: 1-56884-307-0
$22.99 USA/$32.99 Canada

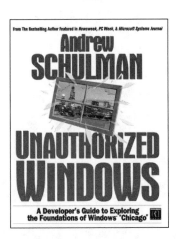

Unauthorized Windows 95: A Developer's Guide to Exploring the Foundations of Windows 95
by Andrew Schulman

ISBN: 1-56884-169-8
$29.99 USA/$39.99 Canada

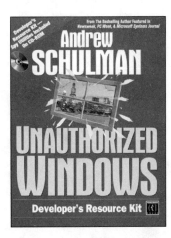

Unauthorized Windows 95: Developer's Resource Kit
by Andrew Schulman

ISBN: 1-56884-305-4
$39.99 USA/$54.99 Canada

Includes Software.

Order Center: **(800) 762-2974** *(8 a.m.–6 p.m., EST, weekdays)*

uantity	ISBN	Title	Price	Total

hipping & Handling Charges

	Description	First book	Each additional book	Total
Domestic	Normal	$4.50	$1.50	$
	Two Day Air	$8.50	$2.50	$
	Overnight	$18.00	$3.00	$
nternational	Surface	$8.00	$8.00	$
	Airmail	$16.00	$16.00	$
	DHL Air	$17.00	$17.00	$

* For large quantities call for shipping & handling charges.
* Prices are subject to change without notice.

ip to:

me _____

mpany _____

dress _____

ty/State/Zip _____

ytime Phone _____

yment: ☐ Check to IDG Books (US Funds Only)

☐ VISA   ☐ MasterCard   ☐ American Express

rd # _____ Expires _____

nature _____

Subtotal _____

CA residents add
applicable sales tax _____

IN, MA, and MD
residents add
5% sales tax _____

IL residents add
6.25% sales tax _____

RI residents add
7% sales tax _____

TX residents add
8.25% sales tax _____

Shipping _____

Total _____

Please send this order form to:

IDG Books Worldwide
7260 Shadeland Station, Suite 100
Indianapolis, IN 46256

Allow up to 3 weeks for delivery.
Thank you!

 **YES!**
Please keep me informed about IDG's World of Computer Knowledge
Send me the latest IDG Books catalog.

The Power Programming Workshops™ on Microsoft® Windows®.
Send in the card below for more information on any of these workshops.

- Introduction to Windows Programming
- Introduction to Windows Printer Device Drivers
- Introduction to C++ and MFC Programming for Windows
- Advanced Win16 Programming
- Advanced Win32 Programming for Windows 95 or Windows NT
- Windows OLE 2.0 Programming

Building DLLs for C/C++ Programmers
A multimedia technical brief on CD-ROM.

A practical introduction to building DLLs including tips and techniques for avoiding common pitfalls, errors, and traps. Covers building DLLs for Win16, Windows 95, and Windows NT. Includes sample source code to speed your own DLL development.

If you enjoyed this book and would like to get more information, or better yet, get expert instruction from the author, just fill out this card:

Shed some light on the following subjects...

Please let us know what you thought of the book:

I am also interested in the following technical topics:

Name

Company

City

State   Zip

e-mail address

I would like to know more about:

☐ Power Programming Workshops

☐ Building DLLs for C/C++ Programmers CD-ROM

Phone

Fax

The Paul Yao Company, based in Seattle, has been training

Windows programmers since 1986 when its founder and

president, Paul Yao, co-authored the first book ever published

on Windows programming. More recently, Paul initiated

"The Paul Yao Programming Series", a series of six books

on topics critical to Windows development. This focus on

MS-Windows training has allowed The Paul Yao Company

to take a leading role in the growth and development of

technical training opportunities and material. The Paul

Yao Company's Power Programming Workshops on Win 16,

Win32, OLE and MFC are five-day, on-site classes for

C and C++ programmers.

**Look for
Upcoming Books
in this Series**

**No Postage
Necessary if
Mailed in the
United States**

BUSINESS REPLY MAIL
FIRST CLASS MAIL   PERMIT NO. 813   BELLEVUE, WA

P O S T A G E   W I L L   B E   P A I D   B Y   A D D R E S S E E

THE PAUL YAO COMPANY
UNIT 300
1075 BELLEVUE WAY NE STE B5
BELLEVUE WA 98004-9872